THE FATHERS
OF THE CHURCH

A NEW TRANSLATION

VOLUME 136

THE FATHERS OF THE CHURCH

A NEW TRANSLATION

EDITORIAL BOARD

David G. Hunter
University of Kentucky
Editorial Director

Andrew Cain
University of Colorado

William E. Klingshirn
The Catholic University of America

Brian Daley, S.J.
University of Notre Dame

Joseph T. Lienhard, S.J.
Fordham University

Mark DelCogliano
University of St. Thomas

Rebecca Lyman
Church Divinity School of the Pacific

Susan Ashbrook Harvey
Brown University

Wendy Mayer
Australian Lutheran College

Robert A. Kitchen
Sankt Ignatios Theological Academy

Trevor Lipscombe
Director, The Catholic University of America Press

FORMER EDITORIAL DIRECTORS

Ludwig Schopp, Roy J. Deferrari, Bernard M. Peebles,
Hermigild Dressler, O.F.M., Thomas P. Halton

Carole Monica C. Burnett
Staff Editor

ST. MAXIMOS THE CONFESSOR

ON DIFFICULTIES IN SACRED SCRIPTURE: THE RESPONSES TO THALASSIOS

Translated by

FR. MAXIMOS CONSTAS

Holy Cross Greek Orthodox School of Theology

THE CATHOLIC UNIVERSITY OF AMERICA PRESS
Washington, D.C.

Copyright © 2018
THE CATHOLIC UNIVERSITY OF AMERICA PRESS
All rights reserved

Cataloging-in-Publication data is available
from the Library of Congress.
ISBN 978-0-8132-3571-4

CONTENTS

Acknowledgments	vii
Abbreviations, Sigla, and Note to the Reader	ix
Bibliography	xiii

INTRODUCTION 1

I. Maximos the Confessor and the *Quaestiones ad Thalassium*	3
II. Date and Literary Genre	5
III. Thalassios the Libyan	8
IV. The *Responses to Thalassios*	12
V. The Passions as Hermeneutical Crisis	21
VI. Stages of Spiritual Progress	25
VII. Scripture and Creation	29
VIII. The Transfiguration of Christ	32
IX. The Interpretation of Scripture	37
X. The Scholia	52
XI. A Note on the Text and Translation	57

ON DIFFICULTIES IN SACRED SCRIPTURE: THE RESPONSES TO THALASSIOS 63

Contents	63
Prologue Concerning the Scholia in the Margins	69
Introduction Addressed to the One who Commissioned This Work	73

Question 1	94	Question 7	111
Question 2	97	Question 8	113
Question 3	100	Question 9	114
Question 4	104	Question 10	116
Question 5	106	Question 11	120
Question 6	108	Question 12	122

CONTENTS

Question 13	123	Question 40	230
Question 14	126	Question 41	238
Question 15	127	Question 42	241
Question 16	130	Question 43	246
Question 17	134	Question 44	249
Question 18	137	Question 45	253
Question 19	138	Question 46	255
Question 20	140	Question 47	257
Question 21	143	Question 48	267
Question 22	150	Question 49	280
Question 23	157	Question 50	297
Question 24	161	Question 51	305
Question 25	163	Question 52	317
Question 26	172	Question 53	326
Question 27	182	Question 54	333
Question 28	190	Question 55	355
Question 29	196	Question 56	389
Question 30	200	Question 57	399
Question 31	202	Question 58	402
Question 32	204	Question 59	412
Question 33	207	Question 60	427
Question 34	210	Question 61	434
Question 35	212	Question 62	450
Question 36	215	Question 63	465
Question 37	218	Question 64	487
Question 38	223	Question 65	519
Question 39	226		

INDICES

General Index	561
Index of Holy Scripture	573
Index of Greek Words	581

ACKNOWLEDGMENTS

A project of this scope and duration amasses numerous debts of gratitude. First and foremost I must express my indebtedness to the work of Dumitru Stăniloae, Eleutherios Meretakis, Ignatios Sakalis, and Françoise Vinel, whose translations of the *Responses to Thalassios*—into Romanian, Modern Greek, and French—greatly helped my efforts. For collegial support, encouragement, and advice, I am grateful to Paul Blowers, Jean-Claude Larchet, Andrew Louth, Demetrios Bathrellos, Nikolaos Loudovikos, Alexander Alexakis, Sotiris Mitralexis, Dionysios Skliris, Jeremy Wallace, Sharon Gerstel, Veronica Della Dora, Gary Anderson, Eleanor Dickey, Stavros Lazaris, and Wendy Larson.

Christos Simelidis gave generously of his time and expertise, and assisted me in disentangling the complexities of the Confessor's prose. Tikhon Pino read and made helpful comments on Questions 1–20, and graciously translated the twenty Latin scholia into English. Calinic Berger read and made valuable comments on the Introduction, translated parts of Stăniloae's Romanian translation of the *Responses*, and was a vital conversation partner. Emanuel Sabau also assisted me in working through material in Romanian. Bishop Maxim Vasilijević invited me to give a series of lectures on the *Responses to Thalassios* (San Diego, February 2016), which enabled me to share my developing ideas with an informed and interested audience. My participation in the International Workshop on Dionysios the Areopagite (Oxford, July 2016) was an opportunity to explore some major themes in Dionysios and Maximos before a select group of scholars.

I am thankful to the students in my seminar on the *Responses to Thalassios* at Holy Cross School of Theology (fall 2015), especially to Peter Hasiakos and Antonios Papathanasiou, who prepared draft versions of Questions 58 and 63, respectively. I am likewise thankful to the students in my seminar on Byzantine Literature at Harvard University (spring 2016), who read through and translated portions of the Greek text.

The completion of this project would have been greatly delayed without the help of my research assistants, Peter Hasiakos (2015–2016), John Tsikalas (2017), and Lukas Buhler (2017). For prompt and amicable assistance with bibliography, I am grateful to Joachim Cotsonis, director of the Holy Cross library, and his staff.

I am grateful to Trevor Lipscombe, the Director of the Catholic University of America Press, and to David Hunter, the Director of the Fathers of the Church series. A special debt of gratitude is owed to the editor of this volume, Carole Monica Burnett, for the exemplary care she took in bringing this work to publication. As a graduate of CUA, I am delighted to offer the Fathers of the Church series its first-ever translation of a work by St. Maximos the Confessor.

V. Rev. Maximos Constas
June 2017

ABBREVIATIONS, SIGLA, AND NOTE TO THE READER

Periodicals and Series

ACO	Acta conciliorum oecumenicorum
CAG	*Commentaria in Aristotelem Graeca*
CCSG	Corpus Christianorum series graeca
CPG	Clavis Patrum Graecorum
DOML	Dumbarton Oaks Medieval Library
DOP	*Dumbarton Oaks Papers*
GCS	Die griechischen christlichen Schriftsteller
GNO	*Gregorii Nysennis Opera*
HTR	*Harvard Theological Review*
JECS	*Journal of Early Christian Studies*
JTS	*Journal of Theological Studies*
LCL	Loeb Classical Library
LSJ	Liddell, Scott, Jones
OCA	Orientalia Christiana Analecta
OCP	*Orientalia Christiana Periodica*
PG	Patrologia Graeca
PGL	Lampe, *Patristic Greek Lexicon*
PO	Patrologia Orientalis
PTS	Patristische Texte und Studien
SC	Sources chrétiennes
SP	*Studia Patristica*
TU	Texte und Untersuchungen
VC	*Vigiliae Christianae*

The Works of Maximos the Confessor

Amb.	Ambigua to John and Thomas
Ascet.	Dialogue on the Ascetic Life
Cap.	Diverse Chapters 1–15
Cap. theol.	Chapters on Theology and the Incarnate Dispensation
Carit.	Chapters on Love
Disp. Biz.	Dispute at Bizya
Ep., Epp.	Letter, Letters
Exp. Ps. 59	Commentary on Psalm 59
Myst.	Mystagogy
Opusc.	Opuscula
Or. Dom.	Commentary on the Lord's Prayer
Pyrr.	Disputation with Pyrrhos
QD.	Questions and Doubts
QThp.	Questions to Theopemptos
Rel. mot.	Record of the Trial

In the notes to the translation, the works of Maximos the Confessor are cited by their abbreviated titles, and are generally not preceded by "Maximos"; thus, for example, *Cap. theol.* 1.66 (PG 90:1108AB); *Amb.* 7.15 (DOML 1:95); *Carit.* 3.29 (ed. Ceresa-Gastaldo, 156–58), etc.

The Works of Dionysios the Areopagite

CH	On the Celestial Hierarchy
DN	On the Divine Names
EH	On the Ecclesiastical History
Ep., Epp.	Letter, Letters
MT	On Mystical Theology

The works of Dionysios the Areopagite are cited by abbreviated title, chapter, section, page and line number from the Berlin edition, followed by the corresponding PG reference. Thus, *DN* 2.9 (133, lines 8–9; 648A) is a reference to a passage from *On the Divine Names*, chapter 2, section 9,

ABBREVIATIONS, SIGLA, NOTE xi

which can be found on p. 133, lines 8–9, in the Berlin edition, as well as in PG volume 3, column 648, section A.

Other Abbreviations

fr. fragment
LXX Septuagint
Or. *Oration*
Qu. Question, Questions
schol. scholion

Sigla

[1] Superscript numbers in brackets in the text indicate a scholion; scholia appear at the end of the respective Response.

< > Angle brackets indicate words that have been supplied by the translator.

Note to the Reader

In order to avoid confusion regarding the antecedents of pronouns, in this volume the personal pronouns referring to God or to any of the Persons of the Trinity are capitalized. This practice is unconventional but deemed necessary for clarity in this translated text.

BIBLIOGRAPHY

Editions of the Works of Maximos the Confessor

Boudignon, Christian, ed. *Maximi Confessoris, Mystagogia.* CCSG 69. Turnhout: Brepols, 2011.
Ceresa-Gastaldo, Aldo, ed. *Massimo Confessore, Capitoli sulla carità.* Verba seniorum N.S. 3. Rome: Editrice Studium, 1963.
Constas, Nicholas [Maximos], ed. *Maximos the Confessor, On Difficulties in the Church Fathers. The Ambigua,* DOML, 2 vols. Cambridge, MA: Harvard University Press, 2014.
Combefis, François, ed. *S. Maximi Confessoris operum.* 2 vols. Paris: André Cramoisy, 1675.
Declerck, J. H., ed. *Maximi Confessoris, Quaestiones et Dubia.* CCSG 10. Turnhout, Brepols, 1982.
Laga, Carl, and Carlos Steel, eds. *Maximi Confessoris, Quaestiones ad Thalassium.* CCSG, vols. 7 and 22. Turnhout: Brepols, 1980, 1990.
———, eds. *Maxime le Confesseur, Questions à Thalassios.* Introduction and notes by Jean-Claude Larchet. French translation by Françoise Vinel. SC 529, 554, 569. Paris: Les Éditions du Cerf, 2010, 2012, 2015.
Migne, J.-P. *S.P.N. Maximi Confessoris, Opera Omnia.* PG 91–92. Paris, 1860.
Roosen, Bram, and Peter Van Deun, eds. "A Critical Edition of the *Quaestiones ad Theopemptum* of Maximus the Confessor (CPG 7696)." *Journal of Eastern Christian Studies* 55 (2003): 65–79.
Van Deun, Peter, ed. *Maximi Confessoris, Opuscula exegetica duo. Expositio in psalmum LIX, Expositio Orationis Dominicae.* CCSG 23. Turnhout: Brepols, 1991.
———, ed. *Maximi Confessoris, Liber Asceticus.* CCSG 40. Turnhout: Brepols, 2000.

Translations of the *Responses to Thalassios*

Blowers, Paul. *On the Cosmic Mystery of Jesus Christ. Selected Writings from St Maximus the Confessor.* Crestwood, NY: St Vladimir's Seminary Press, 2003. = Qu. 2, 6, 17, 21–22, 42, 60–61, 64.
Ćaković, Aleksandar. «Одговори Таласију I–VI. Са старогрчког

превео и напомене.» Луча/*Luca* 21-22 (2004-2005): 234-43 (= Questions 1-6).
Jevremović, Petar. «Свети Максим Исповедник. Три одговора Таласију,» *Источник* 14-16 (1995): 5-6, reprinted in *Луча/Luca* 21-22, (2004-2005): 243-45 (= Questions 8, 14, and 46).
Jevtić, Atanasije. «Одговори Таласију LIX, LX. Са старогрчког превео и напомене,» Луча/*Luca* 21-22 (2004-2005): 245-59 (= Questions 59-60).
Meretakis, Eleutherios, and Ignatios Sakalis. *Μαξίμου τοῦ Ὁμολογητοῦ, Πρὸς Θαλάσσιον περὶ ἀπόρων τῆς Ἁγίας Γραφῆς, Φιλοκαλία τῶν νηπτικῶν καὶ ἀσκητικῶν*, vols. 14Β-14Γ. Thessalonica: Byzantion/Gregorios o Palamas, 1992.
Stăniloae, Dumitru. *Filocalia. Sau culegere din scrierile Sfinților Părinții care arată cum se poate omul curăți, lumina și desăvârși*, vol. 3: *Maxim Mărturisitorul, Răspunsuri către Talasie*. Sibiu: Tipografia Arhidiecezană, 1947.
Vinel, Françoise. *Maxime le Confesseur, Questions à Thalassios*. SC 529, 554, 569. Paris: Les Éditions du Cerf, 2010, 2012, 2015.

Editions of the Works of Dionysios the Areopagite

Heil, Günter, and Adolf Martin Ritter, eds. *Corpus Dionysiacum II: Pseudo-Dionysius Areopagita, De coelesti hierarchia, De ecclesiastica hierarchia, De mystica theologia, Epistulae*. PTS 36. Berlin and New York: Walter de Gruyter, 1991.
Suchla, Beate Regina, ed. *Corpus Dionysiacum I: Pseudo-Dionysius Areopagita, De Divinis Nominibus*. PTS 33. Berlin and New York: Walter de Gruyter, 1990.
———, ed. *Corpus Dionysiacum IV/1: Ioannis Scythopolitani Prologus et scholia in Dionysii Areopagite librum de Divinis Nominibus*. PTS 62. Berlin and New York: Walter de Gruyter, 2011.

General

Allen, Pauline, and Bronwen Neil, eds. *Maximus the Confessor and His Companions: Documents from Exile*. Oxford: Oxford University Press, 2002.
Balthasar, Hans Urs von. *Cosmic Liturgy: The Universe According to Maximus the Confessor*. Translated by Brian E. Daley. San Francisco: Ignatius Press, 2003.
Bathrellos, Demetrios. *The Byzantine Christ: Person, Nature, and Will in the Christology of Saint Maximus the Confessor*. Oxford: Oxford University Press, 2005.
———. "The Temptations of Jesus Christ according to St Maximus the Confessor." *SP* 42 (2006): 45-49.
Berthold, George. "History and Exegesis in Evagrius and Maximos." In

Origeniana Quarta: Die Refarate des 4. internationalen Origeneskongresses (Innsbruck, 2–6. September 1985), edited by Lothar Lies, 390–404. Innsbruck and Vienna: Tyrolia-Verlag, 1987.

———. "Levels of Scriptural Meaning in Maximus the Confessor." *SP* 27 (1993): 129–43.

Blowers, Paul M. *Exegesis and Spiritual Pedagogy in Maximus the Confessor: An Investigation of the Quaestiones ad Thalassium*. Notre Dame: University of Notre Dame Press, 1991.

———. "Maximos the Confessor, Gregory of Nyssa and the concept of 'Perpetual Progress.'" *VC* 46 (1992): 151–71.

———. "The Anagogical Imagination: Maximus the Confessor and the Legacy of Origenian Hermeneutics." In *Origeniana Sexta: Origen and the Bible. Actes du Colloquium Origenianum Sextum, Chantilly, 30 août–3 septembre 1993*, edited by Gilles Dorival and Alain le Boullec, 639–54. Leuven: Leuven University Press, 1995.

———. "Gentiles of the Soul: Maximus the Confessor on the Substructure and Transformation of the Human Passions." *JECS* 4 (1996): 57–85.

———. "Realized Eschatology in Maximus the Confessor, Ad Thalassium 22." *SP* 33 (1997): 258–63.

———. "The World in the Mirror of Holy Scripture: Maximus the Confessor's Short Hermeneutical Treatise in *Ambiguum ad Joannem* 37." In *In Dominico Eloquio—In Lordly Eloquence: Essays on Patristic Exegesis in Honor of Robert Louis Wilken*, edited by Paul M. Blowers et al., 408–26. Grand Rapids, MI: Wm. B. Eerdmans Publishing Company, 2002.

———. *Maximus the Confessor: Jesus Christ and the Transfiguration of the World*. Oxford: Oxford University Press, 2016.

Bornert, Robert. "Explication de la liturgie et interpretation de l'écriture chez Maxime le Confesseur." *SP* 10 (1970): 323–27.

Boyarin, Daniel. "Origen as Theorist of Allegory: Alexandrian Contexts." In *The Cambridge Companion to Allegory*, edited by Rita Copeland and Peter T. Struck, 38–54. Cambridge: Cambridge University Press, 2011.

Boys-Stones, George R. *Metaphor, Allegory, and the Classical Tradition: Ancient Thought and Modern Revisions*. Oxford: Oxford University Press, 2003.

Bussières, Marie-Pierre, ed. *La littérature des questions et réponses dans l'Antiquité profane et chrétienne: De l'enseignement à l'exégèse*. Turnhout: Brepols, 2013.

Canévet, Marie. *Grégoire de Nysse et l'herméneutique biblique. Étude des rapports entre le langage et la connaissance de Dieu*. Paris: Études augustiniennes, 1983.

Cappuyns, Maïeul. "Jean Scot Erigène et les Scholiae de saint Maxime le Confesseur: Introduction, texte critique et traduction." *Byzantion* 24 (1964): 415–45.

Constas, Maximos [Nicholas]. "St. Maximus the Confessor: The Reception of his Thought in East and West." In *Knowing the Purpose of Creation through the Resurrection. Proceedings of the Symposium on St Maximus the Confessor, Belgrade, October 18–21, 2012*, edited by Maxim Vasilievć, 27–34. Belgrade and Alhambra: Sebastian Press, 2013.

———. "'Nothing is Greater than Divine Love': Evagrios of Pontos, St. Maximos the Confessor, and the *Philokalia*." In *Rightly Dividing the Word of Truth: Studies in Honour of Metropolitan Kallistos Ware*, edited by Graham Speake, 57–74. Oxford: Peter Lang, 2016.

———. "The Reception of Paul and Pauline Theology in Byzantium." In *The New Testament in Byzantium*, edited by Derek Kreuger and Robert S. Nelson, 147–76. Washington, DC: Dumbarton Oaks Research Library and Collection, 2016.

———. "A Greater and More Hidden Word: Maximos the Confessor and the Nature of Language." In *Maximus the Confessor as a European Philosopher*, edited by Sotiris Mitralexis, 95–109. Eugene, OR: Cascade Books, 2016.

———. "Maximus the Confessor, Dionysius the Areopagite, and the Transformation of Christian Neoplatonism." *Analogia* 1.2 (2017): 1–12.

Constas, Nicholas [Maximos]. *Proclus of Constantinople and the Cult of the Virgin in Late Antiquity*. Leiden: Brill, 2003.

Cooper, Adam G. "Maximus the Confessor on the Structural Dynamics of Revelation." *VC* 55 (2001): 161–86.

———. *The Body in St Maximus the Confessor: Holy Flesh, Wholly Deified*. Oxford: Oxford University Press, 2005.

Dalmais, Irénée-Henri. "La manifestation du Logos dans l'homme et dans l'Église: Typologie anthropologique et typologie ecclésiale d'après Qu. Thal. 60 et la Mystagogie." In *Maximus the Confessor. Actes du Symposium sur Maxime le Confesseur, Fribourg, 2–5 septembre 1980*, edited by Felix Heinzer and Christoph Schönborn, 13–25. Fribourg: Éditions Universitaires Fribourg, 1982.

Dawson, David. *Christian Figural Reading and the Fashioning of Identity*. Berkeley: University of California Press, 2002.

Dickey, Eleanor. *Ancient Greek Scholarship*. Oxford: Oxford University Press, 2007.

Dixon, Thomas. *From Passions to Emotions: The Creation of a Secular Psychological Category*. Cambridge: Cambridge University Press, 2003.

Ermilov, Pavel. "Towards a Classification of Sources in Byzantine Question-and-Answer Literature." In *Theologica Minora: The Minor Genres of Byzantine Theological Literature*, edited by Antonio Rigo, 110–25. Turnhout: Brepols, 2013.

Gallagher, E. L. *Hebrew Scripture in Patristic Biblical Theory: Canon, Language, Text*. Leiden and Boston: Brill, 2012.

Gavin, John. *They Are Like Angels in Heaven: Angelology and Anthropology*

in the Thought of Maximus the Confessor. Studia Ephemeridis Augustinianum 116. Rome: Institutum Patristicum Augustinianum, 2009.
Grabbe, Lester L. *Etymology in Early Jewish Interpretation: The Hebrew Names in Philo.* Atlanta: Scholar's Press, 1988.
Hadot, Pierre. *Philosophy as a Way of Life: Spiritual Exercises from Socrates to Foucault.* Translated by Michael Chase. Oxford: Blackwell, 1995.
Hanson, R. P. C. "Interpretation of Hebrew Names in Origen." *VC* 10 (1956): 103–23.
Hausherr, Irénée. *Philautie: De la tendresse pour soi à la charité selon saint Maxime le Confesseur.* OCA 137. Rome: Pontifical Oriental Institute, 1952.
Helmig, Christoph. *Forms and Concepts: Concept Formation in the Platonic Tradition.* Berlin and Boston: Walter de Gruyter, 2012.
Kattan, Assad Elias. *Verleiblichung und Synergie: Grundzüge der Bibelhermeneutik bei Maximus Confessor.* Leiden: Brill, 2003.
———. "The Christological Dimension of Maximus the Confessor's Biblical Hermeneutics." *SP* 42 (2006): 169–74.
Kugel, James. *In Potiphar's House: The Interpretive Life of Biblical Texts.* Cambridge, MA: Harvard University Press, 1994.
Laga, Carl. "Maximi Confessoris *ad Thalassium Quaestio* 64." In *After Chalcedon: Studies in Theology and Church History Offered to Professor Albert van Roey for His Seventieth Birthday,* edited by Carl Laga et al., 203–15. Orientalia Lovaniensia Analecta 18. Leuven: Departement Oriëntalistiek, 1985.
———. "Maximi Confessoris *ad Thalassium* Quaestio 64: Essai de lecture." *Orientalia Lovaniensia Analecta* 81 (1985): 203–15.
Lagarde, Paul. *Onomastica Sacra.* Göttingen: Adalbert Rente, 1870.
Lamberton, Robert D. *Homer the Theologian: Neoplatonist Allegorical Reading and the Growth of the Epic Tradition.* Berkeley: University of California Press, 1986.
Lampe, G. W. H., ed. *A Patristic Greek Lexicon.* Oxford: Oxford University Press, 1961.
Larchet, Jean-Claude. "La pensée de saint Maxime le Confesseur dans les Questions à Thalassius." *Messager Orthodoxe* 113 (1990): 3–41.
———. *La divinisation de l'homme selon saint Maxime le Confesseur.* Paris: Les Éditions du Cerf, 1996.
———. *Maxime le Confesseur, médiateur entre l'Orient et l'Occident.* Paris: Les Éditions du Cerf, 1998.
———. "L'Enseignement spirituel des *Questions à Thalassios.*" In *Maxime le Confesseur, Questions à Thalassios,* 26–81. SC 529. Paris: Les Éditions du Cerf, 2010.
———. "Le martyre, l'exil et la mort de saint Maxime le Confesseur et de ses deux disciples, Anastase le Moine et Anastase l'Apocrisiaire. Quelques précisions en rapport avec des découvertes archéologiques récentes," *Revue d'histoire ecclésiastique* 108 (2013): 65–97.

Liddell, Henry George, Robert Scott, Henry Jones, et al., eds. *A Greek-English Lexicon*. Oxford: Oxford University Press, 1996.

Lollar, Joshua. *To See into the Life of Things: The Contemplation of Nature in Maximus the Confessor and his Predecessors*. Turnhout: Brepols, 2013.

Madden, Nicholas. "The Commentary on the Pater Noster: An Example of the Structural Methodology of Maximus the Confessor." In *Maximus the Confessor. Actes du Symposium sur Maxime le Confesseur, Fribourg, 2–5 septembre 1980*, edited by Felix Heinzer and Christoph Schönborn, 147–55. Fribourg: Éditions Universitaires Fribourg, 1982.

Martens, Peter W. "Revisiting the Allegory/Typology Distinction: The Case of Origen." *JECS* 16 (2008): 283–317.

———. *Origen and Scripture: The Contours of the Exegetical Life*. Oxford: Oxford University Press, 2012.

Meyvaert, Paul. "Eriugena's Translation of the *Ad Thalassium* of Maximus: Preliminaries to an Edition of this Work." In *The Mind of Eriugena: Papers of a Colloquium, Dublin, 14–18 July 1970*, edited by John J. O'Meara and Ludwig Bieler, 78–88. Dublin: Royal Irish Academy, 1973.

Muller, Pascal. "La Question LX à Thalassios de Lybie. Lecture, questions, commentaire et thèmes connexes." License en sciences religieuses, Faculté de théologie Université de Fribourg, semester d'été 1997. Fribourg: Université de Fribourg, 1997.

Neil, Bronwen, and Pauline Allen, eds. *The Life of Maximus the Confessor: Recension 3*. Strathfield, New South Wales: St Paul's, 2003.

O'Meara, Dominic. *Pythagoras Revived: Mathematics and Philosophy in Late Antiquity*. Oxford: Clarendon Press, 1989.

Perl, Eric D. *Theophany: The Neoplatonic Philosophy of Dionysius the Areopagite*. Albany: State University of New York Press, 2007.

Φιλοκαλία τῶν ἱερῶν νηπτικῶν. (*The Philokalia of the Neptic Saints*.) 5 vols. Athens: Aster-Papademetriou, 1957.

The Philokalia: The Complete Text. Compiled by St Nikodimos of the Holy Mountain and St Makarios of Corinth. Translated from the Greek and edited by G. E. H. Palmer, Philip Sherrard, and Kallistos Ware. 4 vols. New York: Faber and Faber, Inc., 1979–1995.

Plass, Paul C. "Moving Rest in Maximus the Confessor." *Classica et Mediaevalia* 35 (1984): 177–90.

Rorem, Paul. *Biblical and Liturgical Symbols within the Pseudo-Dionysian Synthesis*. Toronto: Pontifical Institute of Medieval Studies, 1984.

Rorem, Paul, and John Lamoreaux. *John of Skythopolis and the Dionysian Corpus: Annotating the Areopagite*. Oxford: Clarendon Press, 1998.

Runia, David. *Philo and the Church Fathers*. Leiden: Brill, 1997.

———. "Etymology as an Allegorical Technique in Philo of Alexandria." *Studia Philonica Annual* 16 (2004): 101–21.

Schamp, Jacques. "Maxime le Confesseur et Photios: À propos d'une édition récente des *Questions à Thalassius*." *Revue belge de philosophie et d'histoire* 60 (1982): 173–76.

Schönborn, Christoph. "Plaisir et douleur dans l'analyse de S. Maxime, d'après les *Quaestiones ad Thalassium*." In *Maximus Confessor. Actes du Symposium sur Maxime le Confesseur, Fribourg, 2–5 septembre 1980*, edited by Felix Heinzer and Christoph Schönborn, 273–84. Fribourg: Éditions Universitaires Fribourg, 1982.

Schoors, Antoon. "Biblical Onomastics in Maximus Confessor's *Quaestiones ad Thalassium*." In *Philohistôr. Miscellanea in honorem Carlo Laga septuagenarii*, edited by Antoon Schoors and Peter Van Deun, 257–72. Orientalia Lovaniensia Analecta 69. Leuven: Peeters, 1994.

Sedley, David. "The Etymologies in Plato's *Cratylus*." *Journal of Hellenic Studies* 118 (1998): 150–54.

Sherwood, Polycarp. *The Earlier Ambigua of Saint Maximus the Confessor and His Refutation of Origenism*. Studia Anselmiana 36. Rome: Herder, 1955.

———. "Exposition and Use of Scripture in St Maximus as Manifest in the *Quaestiones ad Thalassium*." *OCP* 24 (1958): 202–7.

Stăniloae, Dumitru. *Filocalia. Sau culegere din scrierile Sfinților Părinții care arată cum se poate omul curăți, lumina și desăvârși*, vol. 4. Sibiu: Tipografia Arhidiecezană, 1948.

Stewart, Columba. "Evagrius Ponticus and the Eight Generic Logismoi." In *In the Garden of Evil: The Vices and Culture in the Middle Ages*, edited by Richard Newhauser, 3–34. Toronto: Pontifical Institute of Medieval Studies, 2005.

———. "Evagrius Ponticus and the Eastern Monastic Tradition on the Intellect and the Passions." *Modern Theology* 27 (2011): 263–75.

Stroumsa, Guy G. "The Christian Hermeneutical Revolution and its Double Helix." In *Barbarian Philosophy: The Religious Revolution of Early Christianity*, edited by Guy G. Stroumsa, 8–43. Tübingen: Mohr Siebeck, 1999.

Struck, Peter T. "Allegory and Ascent in Neoplatonism." In *The Cambridge Companion to Allegory*, edited by Rita Copeland and Peter T. Struck, 57–70. Cambridge: Cambridge University Press, 2010.

Thunberg, Lars. *Microcosm and Mediator: The Theological Anthropology of Maximus the Confessor*. Chicago: Open Court, 1995.

Tollefsen, Torstein Theodor. *The Christocentric Christology of St Maximus the Confessor*. Oxford: Oxford University Press, 2008.

Törönen, Melchisedec. *Union and Distinction in the Thought of Maximus the Confessor*. Oxford: Oxford University Press, 2008.

Van Bekkum, Wout Jac. "Jewish Messianic Expectations in the Age of Heraclius." In *The Reign of Heraclius (610–41): Crisis and Confrontation*, edited by Gerrit J. Reinink and Bernard H. Stolte, 96–112. Leuven: Peeters, 2002.

Van Deun, Peter. "Les extraits de Maxime le Confesseur contenus dans les chaînes sur le Nouveau Testament." *Orientalia Lovaniensia Periodica* 23 (1992): 205–17.

Völker, Walther. *Maximus Confessor als Meister des geistlichen Lebens.* Wiesbaden: Franz Steiner, 1965.

Wilken, Robert. "The Restoration of Israel in Biblical Prophecy: Christian and Jewish Responses in the Early Byzantine Period." In *To See Ourselves as Others See Us: Christians, Jews, "Others" in Late Antiquity,* edited by Jacob Neusner and Ernest S. Frerichs, 443–71. Chico, CA: Scholars Press, 1985.

Zirnheld, Claire-Agnès. "Le double visage de la passion: Malediction due au péché et au dynamisme de la vie: *Quaestiones ad Thalassium* de S. Maxime le Confesseur XXI, XXII et XLII." In *Philohistôr: Miscellanea in honorem Caroli Laga septuagenarii,* edited by Antoon Schoors and Peter Van Deun, 361–80. Leuven: Peeters, 1994.

INTRODUCTION

INTRODUCTION

I. Maximos the Confessor and the
Quaestiones ad Thalassium

Maximos the Confessor (ca. 580–662) is now widely recognized as one of the greatest theological thinkers, not simply in the entire canon of Greek patristic literature, but in the Christian tradition as a whole.[1] A peripatetic monk and prolific writer, his penetrating theological vision found expression in an unparalleled synthesis of biblical exegesis, ascetic spirituality, patristic theology, and Greek philosophy, which is as remarkable for its conceptual sophistication as for its labyrinthine style of composition.[2] Maximos's unrelenting defense of two natural wills and activities in Christ challenged the politically compromised theology of the imperial church and government, which responded by severing his right hand and cutting out his tongue.[3] Sent into exile, he died shortly afterwards in a military prison on the eastern coast of the Black Sea, receiving the title of "Confessor" for the torments inflicted on him by his persecutors.[4] Within twenty years of his death, his doctrine of Christ

1. For a detailed discussion of the life of Maximos the Confessor, including a survey of earlier bibliography, see Paul M. Blowers, *Maximus the Confessor: Jesus Christ and the Transfiguration of the World* (Oxford: Oxford University Press, 2016), 25–63.

2. Maximos's works are concisely cataloged in *CPG* 7688–7721, and more exhaustively in Peter van Deun and Pascal Mueller-Jourdan, "Maxime le Confesseur—Oeuvres," in *La théologie byzantine et sa tradition* I/1, ed. Carmelo Giuseppe Conticello (Turnhout: Brepols, 2015), 390–423.

3. On Maximos's Christology, see Demetrios Bathrellos, *The Byzantine Christ: Person, Nature, and Will in the Christology of Saint Maximus the Confessor* (Oxford: Oxford University Press, 2005); and Blowers, *Maximus the Confessor*, 135–65.

4. For a collection of primary sources documenting Maximos's arrest, trial, and final days, see Pauline Allen and Bronwen Neil, eds., *Maximus the*

was vindicated by the Sixth Ecumenical Council (680–81), and so thoroughly did his voice come to resound throughout the Byzantine theological and spiritual tradition that it is not possible to understand the true significance of Orthodox Christianity without knowledge of his work.

Modern scholarship has increasingly focused on the Confessor's use of Greek philosophical categories, often in isolation from his larger monastic and ecclesial commitments. A purely philosophical approach, however, can easily overlook the central role of Scripture in Maximos's theological vision and practice, which is already evident in his earliest writings.[5] The *Responses to Thalassios*,[6] presented here for the first time in a complete

---

Confessor and his Companions: Documents from Exile (Oxford: Oxford University Press, 2002). The last document in this collection, a *Commemoration* dated to ca. 668 (pp. 148–71), is among the first to identify Maximos as a "Confessor" (ὁμολογητής); cf. the *acta* of the Seventh Ecumenical Council (Nicaea, 787): "Maximos, full of divine wisdom and equal to the Fathers, was surely both a Confessor and defender of the truth" (ACO 3.2/2:342–44).

5. The *Dialogue on the Ascetic Life (Liber asceticus)* (CCSG 40), a work of around 30 pages, contains more than 150 biblical citations; cf. Paul M. Blowers, *Exegesis and Spiritual Pedagogy in Maximus the Confessor: An Investigation of the Quaestiones ad Thalassium* (Notre Dame: University of Notre Dame Press, 1991), 53: "Throughout the *Liber asceticus*, the responses place profuse scriptural citations in the mouth of the elder that are aimed at casting the monk's struggle in scriptural imagery and identifying it with the exemplary suffering of Christ and of the divine Apostle." See also the remarks of Pablo Argárate, "'Car mes iniquités dépassèrent ma tête': Les fonctions du text biblique dans la section katanyktique du *Logos Asketikos* de Maxime le Confesseur," in *The Reception and Interpretation of the Bible in Late Antiquity*, ed. Lorenzo DiTommaso and Lucian Turcescu (Leiden: Brill, 2008), 17–36, at 34: "Le *Logos Asketikos* est d'une certaine perspective une méditation biblique prolongée." In the *Questions and Doubts* (CCSG 10), the overwhelming majority of its 239 chapters are responses to questions concerning difficult passages of Scripture; both works are dated to before ca. 633/34.

6. The work's traditional title, the *Questions to Thalassios*, is inexact and misleading, since these are not Maximos's questions to Thalassios, but rather his responses to questions submitted to him by Thalassios. The title found in the manuscripts is: *To Thalassios, On Various Difficulties in Sacred Scripture* (πρὸς Θαλάσσιον περὶ διαφόρων ἀπόρων τῆς ἁγίας Γραφῆς) (CCSG 7:17); cf. *Opusc.* 1, dated to 645/46, where Maximos refers to a passage in the *Responses to Thalassios* as: πρὸς τὸν ... ἐν τοῖς περὶ τῶν ἀπόρων τῆς ἁγίας Γραφῆς ἐκτεθεῖσι Θαλασσίῳ (PG 91:29D). In what follows, I refer to the work as the *Responses to Thalassios* or simply *Responses*.

INTRODUCTION 5

English translation, contains Maximos's virtuosic theological interpretations of sixty-five difficult passages from the Old and New Testaments.[7] Because of its great length, along with its linguistic and conceptual difficulty, the work as a whole has been largely neglected. Yet alongside the *Ambigua to John*, the *Responses to Thalassios* deserves to be ranked as the Confessor's greatest work; it is one of the most important patristic treatises on the interpretation of Scripture, combining the interconnected traditions of "monastic devotion to the Bible, the biblical exegesis of Origen, the sophisticated symbolic theology of Dionysius the Areopagite, and the rich spiritual anthropology of Greek Christian asceticism inspired by the Cappadocian Fathers."[8]

II. Date and Literary Genre

Though any precise date can only be conjectural, the *Responses to Thalassios* was most likely written before 633/34, at a time when Maximos was living in a Greek-speaking monastic community in Carthage (modern Tunis) in North Africa.[9] Internal evidence, moreover, indicates that the work was written not long after Maximos had completed his other *magnum opus*, the *Ambi-*

---

7. With the exception of Qu. 1, which deals with the nature of the passions and their attribution to God in Scripture. In the 9th century, Photios, *Library*, cod. 192A, counted only 64 Questions, considering Qu. 1 to be part of the work's introduction (ed. René Henry, *Photius, Bibliothèque*, vol. 3 [Paris: Les Belles Lettres, 1962], 77–80); the 10th-century Greek *Life* counts the standard 65 Questions (Ed. Bronwen Neil and Pauline Allen, *The Life of Maximus the Confessor, Recension 3* [Strathfield, New South Wales: St. Pauls Publications, 2003], 74).

8. I borrow this apt formulation from Blowers, *Exegesis and Spiritual Pedagogy*, 15.

9. Carthage was the largest city in the western Mediterranean after Rome. Captured by the Vandals in 439, the city was retaken by Justinian's armies early in 533, and later became the seat of the Byzantine exarch; cf. Frank M. Clover, "Felix Carthago," *Dumbarton Oaks Papers* 40 (1986): 1–16; Averil Cameron, "Byzantine Africa: The Literary Evidence," in eadem, *Changing Cultures in Early Byzantium* (Aldershot: Variorum, 1996), 25–32; and Blowers, *Maximus the Confessor*, 29–31. Maximos's literary style, noted above, finds an intriguing parallel in contemporary North African floor mosaics; cf. Rebecca Molholt, "Roman Labyrinth Mosaics and the Experience of Motion," *Art Bulletin* 93 (2011): 287–303.

gua to John.¹⁰ Both works belong to a period of intense literary activity (from the late 620s to 635) during which Maximos wrote, among other things, the *Dialogue on the Ascetic Life, Questions and Doubts, Chapters on Love, Commentary on the Lord's Prayer, Chapters on Theology and the Incarnate Dispensation*, the *Mystagogy*, the *scholia on Dionysios the Areopagite*, and the *Ambigua to John*.

As its title suggests, the *Responses to Thalassios* was composed in the literary form of "Questions and Responses" (ἐρωταποκρίσεις), which was widely employed in the patristic period.¹¹ The form, or rather format, was inherently flexible. It could accommodate, for example, biblical exegesis either in a continuous exposition or as a series of discontinuous glosses.¹² At the same time, it allowed one to offer responses to a range of pastoral problems, as well as solutions to difficult, ambiguous, or disputed theological topics (ἀπορίαι, ἄπορα).¹³ As such it gave writers creative freedom to explore different subjects and themes without having to organize disparate material into a larger sequence, structure, or narrative. Maximos apparently found the format useful, and employed it to compose the *Questions and Doubts*, the *Responses to Theopemptos*, the *Ambigua to John*, and the *Ambigua to Thomas*.¹⁴ But whereas the two sets of *Ambigua* deal

10. In Qu. 39.5, Maximos refers Thalassios to the expanded discussion on the same topic found in *Amb*. 67.12–13 (DOML 2:299–301). The remarks about the division of being in Qu. 48.5 would likewise seem to presuppose the larger discussion in *Amb*. 41.2 (DOML 2:102–104).

11. See Heinrich Dörrie and Hermann Dörries, "Erotapokriseis," *Reallexikon für Antike und Christentum* 6 (1966): 342–70; Herbert Hunger, "Erotapokriseis," *Lexicon des Mittelalters* 3 (1986): 2183–84; Annelie Volgers and Claudio Zamagni, eds., *Erotapokriseis: Early Christian Question and Answer Literature in Context* (Leuven: Peeters, 2004); and Marie-Pierre Bussières, ed., *La littérature des questions et réponses dans l'Antiquité profane et chrétiennes: De l'enseignement à l'exégèse* (Turnhout: Brepols, 2013).

12. On which the classic study remains that by Gustave Bardy, "La littérature patristique des 'Quaestiones et responsiones' sur l'Écriture Sainte," *Revue Biblique* 41 (1932): 210–36; 341–69; 515–37; 42 (1933): 14–30; 211–29; 328–52 (on Maximos, cf. 332–39).

13. The study by Pavel Ermilov, "Towards a Classification of Sources in Byzantine Question-and-Answer Literature," in *Theologica Minora: The Minor Genres of Byzantine Theological Literature*, ed. Antonio Rigo (Turnhout: Brepols, 2013), 110–25, is helpful in sorting out some of the internal classifications within this disparate body of literature.

14. Cf. Peter van Deun, "Maximus the Confessor's Use of Literary Genres,"

INTRODUCTION 7

with difficult passages (ἄπορα) in patristic texts, the *Questions and Doubts* and the *Responses to Thalassios* deal with difficult passages in Scripture.[15] Thus, in composing the *Responses*, Maximos fused the exegetical tradition of biblical questions and responses, exemplified in works such as Eusebios's *Questions and Answers on the Gospels* and Theodoret's *Questions on the Octateuch*,[16] with the pedagogical tradition of monastic questions and responses, such as Basil's *Long Rules*, the *Questions and Responses on Baptism* by Mark the Monk, the *Questions and Responses* of Anastasios of Sinai, and the *Questions and Responses* of Barsanouphios and John.[17] Combining a primarily exegetical genre with the pedagogical format of a monastic conference was hardly accidental,

The Oxford Handbook of Maximus the Confessor, ed. Pauline Allen and Bronwen Neil (Oxford: Oxford University Press, 2015), 274–86; Blowers, *Exegesis and Spiritual Pedagogy*, 28–94; and Blowers, *Maximus the Confessor*, 90–96 (= "Genre and Style in Maximus' Literary Corpus").

15. More precisely, the *Ambigua* as a whole deals with 70 theological difficulties in the writings of Gregory Nazianzus, along with one passage from Dionysios the Areopagite (*Amb.* 5 [DOML 1:30–59]); the *Questions and Doubts* (see above, n. 5) deals primarily with difficult biblical passages, although a number of questions concern passages from the writings of Basil of Caesarea, Gregory Nazianzus, Gregory of Nyssa, Dionysios the Areopagite, and Diadochos of Photiki.

16. Both works have recently been made available in English translations: David J. Miller and Adam C. McCollum, trans., *Eusebius of Caesarea, Gospel Problems and Solutions* (Ipswich, UK: Chieftain Publishing, 2010); Robert C. Hill, *Theodoret of Cyrus, The Questions on the Octateuch*, 2 vols. (Washington, DC: The Catholic University of America Press, 2007). In addition to the *quaestio-responsio* format, one should also include biblical scholia (σχόλια, σημειώσεις), which are short, usually discontinuous, glosses on important or difficult passages of Scripture, such as those by Origen on Exodus; cf. Eric Junod, "Que savons-nous des 'scholies' d'Origène?" in *Origeniana Sexta*, ed. Gilles Dorival, et al. (Leuven: Peeters, 1995), 133–49.

17. On the *Long Rules*, which in its longer recension contains 376 questions and responses, see Anna M. Silvas, *The Asketikon of St Basil the Great* (Oxford: Oxford University Press, 2005). On the 17 questions answered by Mark the Monk; cf. SC 445:296–397. On the Anastasian collection of 127 questions and responses, see Joseph A. Munitiz, *Anastasios of Sinai, Questions and Answers* (Turnhout: Brepols, 2011), 18–25. The 800 questions answered by Barsanouphios and John were originally a collection of letters, re-edited by an anonymous monk in the form of *quaestio-responsio;* cf. François Nyet and Paula de Angelis-Noah, *Barsanuphe et Jean de Gaza, Correspondence*, vol. 1 (Paris: Les Éditions du Cerf, 1997), 21, 47–61.

and indeed rather aptly expressed the nature of Maximos's exegetical enterprise in the *Responses*. As we shall see, Maximos's aim—consistent with Thalassios's request—was to open the horizon of biblical exegesis to the major themes of the spiritual life, namely, the fall of Adam and the origin of the passions; the struggle against impassioned thoughts and impulses; the practice of bodily and spiritual purification; progress in the life of virtue; the pivotal role played by natural contemplation; and the experience of divinization through union with the incarnate Word.

III. Thalassios the Libyan

As indicated in the work's opening paragraphs, Maximos composed the *Responses* in answer to a letter he had received from a certain Thalassios, whom he addresses as "presbyter and abbot." The letter, which we shall consider in a moment, contained a lengthy series of questions concerning the origin and nature of the passions, along with a collection of difficult biblical passages, for which Thalassios requested written interpretations.[18] Though information about him is limited, Thalassios was a renowned spiritual teacher and the head of a monastic community probably in Carthage (hence his surname "the Libyan" or "the African"). In a contemporary *Spiritually Beneficial Tale*, he is hailed as the "great and divinely wise Thalassios, the adornment of all Africa."[19] Maximos most likely met Thalassios during his prolonged sojourn in the region (ca. 632–42), and the two men subsequently became close friends and colleagues.[20]

18. Intro. 1.2.3; 1.2.9–10.

19. Διήγησις ψυχωφελής, ed. François Combefis, *Bibliothecae Graecorum Patrum auctarium novissimum*, vol. 1 (Paris: Sumptibus Aegidii Hotot, 1672), 325; the text is also available in François Nau, "Le texte grec des récits utiles à l'âme du moine Anastase sur les saints pères du Sinaï," *Oriens Christianus* 2 (1908): 58–89; at p. 84, lines 12–14. "Libya" and "Africa" refer to the Byzantine Exarchate of Carthage (formerly the Prefecture of Africa), comprising the territory of Tunisia, parts of Algeria, and the coasts of Libya and Morocco.

20. Cf. Intro. 1.2.4, where Maximos (citing a phrase from Gregory Nazianzus, *Or.* 43.20) describes himself and Thalassios as "possessing a single soul residing in two bodies."

In addition to the *Responses*, Maximos wrote other works addressed to Thalassios: a Christological treatise, *On Energies and Wills*, and five letters (although no letters from Thalassios to Maximos have survived).[21] The treatise, which argues against the Christological errors of Severos and Nestorios, is not directly relevant to the *Responses* and need not detain us any further. The letters, on the other hand,[22] indicate that Maximos and Thalassios were in the habit of pondering difficult passages from Scripture and solving various problems using scriptural principles and concepts.[23] In these letters, as well as in the Introduction to the *Responses*, Maximos praises Thalassios in the highest possible terms and refers to himself as Thalassios's "servant" and "disciple." These statements, however, should not be taken to mean that Thalassios was Maximos's teacher or that Maximos was a monk in Thalassios's monastery, as has sometimes been maintained.[24] Instead, such statements were stan-

21. *On Energies and Wills* (mistakenly said to be addressed to Marinos) survives only in fragmentary form as *Opusc.* 2–3 (PG 91:40–45; 45–56); and *Additamentum* 24; cf. CPG Supplementum 7697 (nos. 2–3; 25). In the Φιλοκαλία τῶν Ἱερῶν Νηπτικῶν, vol. 2 (Athens: Aster-Papademetriou, 1957), 52, Maximos's *Chapters on Theology and the Incarnate Dispensation* is also addressed to Thalassios; cf. *The Philokalia: The Complete Text*, vol. 2 (London: Faber & Faber, 1981), 114, 306. The *editio princeps*, however, edited by François Combefis (*S. Maximi Confessoris operum*, vol. 1 [Paris: André Cramoisy, 1675], 461), and later reprinted by J.-P. Migne (PG 90 [Paris, 1860], 1084), does not include such a dedication.

22. I.e., *Epp.* 9, 26, 41–42, and *Ep.* A (cited below, n. 23).

23. See, for example, *Ep.* 9, which responds to a practical question with an exegesis of 1 Cor 2.14–3.1 (PG 91:445C–449A); *Ep.* 26 responds to a question about child sacrifice, referencing 4 Kgs 3.21–27 (PG 91:616A–617B); and *Ep.* 42, which allegorizes the building of Solomon's Temple, citing 2 Kgs 7.5 and Ps 44.5 (PG 91:636C–637B). *Ep.* A, as it is called, which survives in a Latin translation by Anastasius Bibliothecarius, notes the arrival of the representatives of Pope Severinus in Constantinople (PL 129:583–86). According to the manuscripts, *Ep.* 40 (PG 91:633C–636B) is addressed not to Thalassios but to the presbyter and abbot Stephanos, the recipient of *Ep.* 23 (PG 91:605D–608B; cf. CCSG 48, p. xxiv).

24. E.g., Marcel Viller, "Aux sources de la spiritualité de saint Maxime: Les œuvres d'Évagre le Pontique," *Revue d'Ascétique et de Mystique* 11 (1930): 262; Aimé Solignac, "Thalassius," *Dictionnaire de spiritualité*, vol. 15 (Paris: Beauchesne, 1991), 324; and Michel van Parys, "Un maître spirituel oublié: Thalassios de Libye," *Irenikon* 52 (1979): 218.

dard expressions of deference that a monk was expected to show toward an ecclesiastical superior, and all the evidence indicates that it was Thalassios who turned repeatedly to Maximos for help in answering his questions.

A revered monastic leader, Thalassios was also the author of a work called *Four Centuries on Love, Temperance, and the Spiritual Life*, a series of four hundred ascetic and spiritual aphorisms that was included in the *Philokalia* immediately after the works of Maximos.[25] In what was without precedent in late antique monastic prose writing, Thalassios prefaced each *Century* with an acrostic, three of which are addressed to a certain presbyter named Paul, to whom the work is dedicated.[26] Composing four acrostics (that is, one for each "Century") of one hundred words each requires no small degree of literary talent, and this, together with the often finely turned and at times poetical aphorisms themselves, attests to Thalassios's skill as a writer. Scholars have debated the extent to which the *Centuries* are indebted to the writings of Maximos, or if their similarities are simply the result of a common reading of Evagrios.[27] If, however, we accept the argument that the acrostic of the third *Century* is in fact a summary of Question 58 of the *Responses*, then Thalassios must have compiled his *Centuries* after he received the *Respons-*

---

25. Φιλοκαλία 2:206–29 (the text is also available in PG 91:1427–70). The pairing of the *Four Centuries* with Maximos's work goes back to the so-called "pre-Philokalic" anthologies of the late Byzantine period.

26. On which, see Paul Géhin, "Les Collections de *Kephalaia* monastiques: Naissance et succès d'un genre entre création originale, plagiat et florilège," in *Theologica Minora*, ed. Rigo, 1–50, esp. 13–14. Hesychios of Sinai's *Centuries on Watchfulness* is extant in an alphabetical acrostic recension of 24 chapters, but this seems to be a product of the later Byzantine period; cf. Jean Kirchmeyer, "Hésychius le Sinaïte et ses centuries," in *Le millénaire du Mont Athos, 963–1963. Études et Mélanges I* (Chevtogne: Éditions de Chevtogne, 1963), 319–29. Gregory Nazianzus made use of acrostics in his poetry (cf. II.1.14; PG 37:1244, lines 10–12), which Thalassios may quite possibly have known, but collections of gnomic utterances with acrostics became popular only in the middle Byzantine period, and typically in secular prose works; cf. Karl Krumbacher, *Geschichte der byzantinischen Literatur* (Munich: C. H. Beck, 1897), 717–20; and Ernst Vogt, "Das Akrostichon in der griechischen Literatur," *Antike und Abendland* 13 (1967): 80–95.

27. Blowers, *Exegesis and Spiritual Pedagogy*, 10.

es, and under its immediate influence.²⁸ Indeed, the thematic parallels indicate that Thalassios had studied not only the *Responses* but also the *Chapters on Love* and the *Ambigua to John* before composing the *Four Centuries*, which latter, in addition to their ascetic and spiritual doctrine, are fluent in the conceptual procedures of apophatic theology, and present nuanced formulations of Trinitarian theology and Chalcedonian Christology.

What Maximos recorded on the pages of the *Responses*, then, was part of a larger, ongoing conversation between two friends— both of whom were prominent spiritual leaders, writers, and theologians—situated within the living praxis of monastic culture. It is difficult, however, to reconstruct the process that led to the writing of the *Responses*, since, with the exception of the work's "cover letter" (that is, the Introduction), none of the other letters exchanged between Thalassios and Maximos on this subject have survived.²⁹ As mentioned a moment ago, Thalassios had presented Maximos with two sets of thematically different questions: on the nature of the passions and on difficult passages of Scripture. In response, Maximos asked that the "discussion of the passions be deferred until God grants me a more propitious opportunity to examine these matters and devote myself to them with greater industry."³⁰ This display of reluctance notwithstanding, Maximos proceeded to write what is essentially an entire essay on the nature of evil, the fall of Adam, and the origin of the passions, which is his most important and sustained analysis of these questions.³¹ When, moreover, he subsequently turned

28. The link between the acrostic and Qu. 58 was discovered by Dumitru Stăniloae, *Filocalia. Sau culegere din scrierile Sfinților Părinții care arată cum se poate omul curăți, lumina și desăvârși*, vol. 4 (Sibiu: Tipografia Arhidiecezană, 1948), 19, n. 1.

29. See Intro. 1.2.4, where Maximos alludes to these previous communications: "When I received and read your list of these passages, I was overwhelmed in mind, hearing, and thought, and subsequently implored you to permit me to decline your request ... I consequently renewed and indeed enlarged my request—more than once—to be released from such a task, but I saw that you were in no way disposed to my pleas."

30. Intro. 1.2.10.

31. I.e., Intro. 1.2.11–22. The importance of the essay can be gauged by the fact that it was excerpted and circulated (often with its partial counterpart,

his attention to the biblical difficulties, he did not leave the questions about the passions behind, but to the contrary made them central to his exegesis. If Thalassios submitted two sets of questions in the hope of receiving two separate sets of responses, Maximos effectively treated them as a single set of questions, and wove his responses to the questions about the passions into his interpretation of the biblical difficulties. Bringing the two sets of questions together in this way was not an arbitrary move or a confusion of categories. As we shall see below, the entry of the passions into human life precipitates a radical hermeneutical crisis, and as such is of fundamental importance for the interpretation of Scripture. Before pursuing this question any further, it will be helpful to undertake a brief survey of the general contents of the *Responses*.

IV. The *Responses to Thalassios*

As mentioned above, the *Responses to Thalassios* comprises a series of sixty-five Questions and Responses on difficult passages of Scripture. Because many of Thalassios's questions contain two or more scriptural passages, the actual number of passages treated in the work is eighty-one.[32] In terms of their content, twenty-eight of these passages are from the Old Testament, and fifty-three are from the New Testament, although thirteen of the Old Testament passages receive monograph-length treatment and together make up nearly half the entire work.[33] Despite Maximos's promise to "respond to each of the passages as briefly and concretely as is possible for me,"[34] the responses vary greatly in length from a few sentences to dozens of pages, becoming progressively longer as the work unfolds.

As is typical of the genre, the questions are prompted by

Qu. 43) in later Byzantine anthologies as an independent treatise; cf. CCSG 7, p. xi.

32. This number refers to scriptural verses cited in the actual Questions, not the additional scriptural verses that Maximos cites or alludes to in his responses, which run into the hundreds.

33. I.e., Qu. 48–53 on 2 Chronicles; Qu. 54–56 on 1 Esdras; Qu. 62–63 on Zechariah; Qu. 64 on Jonah; and Qu. 65 on 2 Kings.

34. Intro. 1.2.6.

INTRODUCTION 13

various difficulties in the sacred text, which range from basic philological problems to larger hermeneutical issues concerning the nature and meaning of the biblical narrative. Considerable attention is given to apparent or perceived contradictions in Scripture, although only two Questions (Qu. 2 and 10) deal directly with contradictions between the Old and New Testaments.[35] Contradictions in the New Testament, on the other hand, account for the largest number of questions in the entire work. These include contradictions between the Gospels (for example, Qu. 4); between Matthew and Acts (Qu. 27); between Paul and John (Qu. 9); or within a single biblical book or author, such as the Gospel of John, the Johannine letters, or the letters of Paul (Qu. 6, 8, 18, 19, 22, 58).[36] Scripture's superfluity of language constitutes another area of difficulty (Qu. 14, 30, 46, 51),[37] although its silence could be equally perplexing (Qu. 3).

The Hermeneutical Framework

The greatest area of concern, however, arises from narrative elements that have no edifying meaning on the historical or literal level. For such passages, Thalassios requests a spiritual interpretation, as is evident from the way he frames his questions: "What is the meaning of these things on the level of contemplation?" (Qu. 49.1); "What is the meaning of these words, and how might we contemplate them spiritually?" (Qu. 65.1); and: "What is the meaning of this passage, which appears to be so unworthy of the Spirit, preoccupied as it is with the exact numbering of

---

35. Qu. 15–17 deal with internal discrepancies in the Wisdom of Solomon and Exodus, respectively, while Qu. 43 deals with a contradiction between a passage in Proverbs and another in Wisdom.

36. Bringing together and seeking to reconcile seemingly contradictory passages of Scripture was a standard exegetical procedure, especially in the *Questions and Responses* literature. In the *Ambigua*, Maximos had likewise dealt with seeming contradictions in the writings of Gregory Nazianzus; cf. *Amb.* 1.2 (DOM 1:9–11); *Amb.* 42.2; and *Amb.* 63.1 (DOML 2:123–25; 271).

37. A problem also presented by the writings of Gregory Nazianzus; cf. *Amb.* 6.2 (DOML 1:69–71); *Amb.* 20.3 (DOML 1:411–13); *Amb.* 42.2–4 (DOML 2:123–29).

camels, horses, mules, and donkeys?" (Qu. 55.1).[38] Many of these difficulties—such as the "soiled tunic" (Qu. 12) or the "mountain cast into the sea" (Qu. 33)—are what modern readers might classify as "metaphors" and consequently disregard because they are *merely* metaphors. For readers like Thalassios, however, even seemingly minor problems in the surface texture of Scripture prevent one from adopting a simple, uncomplicated attitude to the passages in which they appear. Obscure and allusive language, marred by a lack of coherence or credibility on a literal level, was believed to conceal a deeper meaning, specifically (if obliquely) expressed through the particular "metaphor" in question. Whatever meaning was to be found, for example, in Zechariah's "flying sickle" (Qu. 62) could hardly be incidental to the specific features of its literal language and imagery. Far from being mere ornaments of language, such "metaphors" constitute one of the sacred text's controlling modes of thought and representation.

As Maximos had argued in the *Ambigua*, such difficulties cannot be resolved on the literal level of the text, but only on the level of "spiritual contemplation." When the literal account presents the reader with insurmountable difficulties, spiritual contemplation is "able to smooth out the apparent contradictions perceived among different elements on the literal level of things," because contemplation perceives the "truth present in all things, which is by nature simple and free of the thickness of words and bodies."[39] Maximos brings this same hermeneutical model to the *Responses*, where the shift in awareness from the perception of words on a page to the contemplation of their inner meaning is understood as a movement from the "letter" to the "spirit" (cf. 2 Cor 3.6). This perceptual shift, and the distinction it reveals between the surface of the text and its

38. Most of the Questions simply ask about the "meaning" of the passage in question (cf. Qu. 7, 9, 11–16, 19–21, 24–25, 29–30, 32–34, 38–39, 45, 47–48, 50, 52–54, 56–57, 61–63), which is to be understood as the "meaning on the level of anagogy or contemplation," consistent with Thalassios's original request that Maximos interpret all the passages "according to the principles of anagogical contemplation" (Intro. 1.2.3).

39. *Amb.* 20.3 (DOML 1:423); on the "thickness of words and bodies," see below, Qu. 31.2.

INTRODUCTION 15

depth, between the corporeal sign and that which transcends it, is the key to the Confessor's hermeneutics and the driving force behind the *Responses* as a whole. As we shall see in a moment, apprehending the depth of the sacred text does not come about simply through the mechanical application of exegetical techniques. Instead it is a spiritual practice deeply connected to cosmology and anthropology, embodying in a single hermeneutical moment the passage from letter to spirit, from surface appearance to ontological ground, and from sense perception to contemplative insight and understanding.[40]

Sequences of Thought

This hermeneutical framework is employed systematically throughout the *Responses*, giving the work as a whole a high degree of conceptual unity. It remains an open question, however, if the work's constitutive parts are organized according to an equally systematic plan or structure, since the sixty-five Questions do not appear to follow any kind of meaningful order. Efforts to uncover an organizing principle have not been entirely successful, and some scholars have characterized the *Responses* as a random miscellany of biblical questions and answers.[41] Apart from the irony that the Bible itself has been seen as a confused and miscellaneous jumble of disparate texts, such a characterization of the *Responses* is inadequate, not to say superficial, since the work contains significant structural features, including extended sequences of Questions dealing with particular biblical themes and books.

Questions 38–41, for example, are focused on the symbolism of biblical numbers, such as the seven brothers in the Gospel of Matthew (Qu. 38), the six jars of water at the wedding in Cana (Qu. 40), and the five husbands of the Samaritan woman (Qu. 41). These Neo-Pythagorean exercises in the theology of arithmetic—a mode of analysis in which the meaning of

40. A process Maximos summarizes in Qu. 32.3.
41. For discussion, see Jeremy Wallace, "Virtue and Knowledge as the Hermeneutical Key for Unlocking Maximus the Confessor's *Quaestiones ad Thalassium*" (Ph.D. diss., Princeton Theological Seminary, 2013), 38–50.

physical and literary phenomena is grasped on the level of numerical units and their combinations—rank among the most elaborate exegetical treatments of numbers in all of Greek patristic literature.[42] Another thematic sequence of Questions (Qu. 58–61) constitutes a sustained analysis of the nature and unity of human consciousness, addressing the tension between the intellect and the senses, different modes and objects of cognitive awareness, and the interaction of human reason and divine grace.[43] Two additional series of Questions (Qu. 48–53 and Qu. 54–56) are focused respectively on 2 Chronicles and 1 Esdras, and together comprise about 25 percent of the entire work.[44] In the first of these two series, which consists of six Questions, Maximos begins with an elaborate prayer to the Word, asking for divine assistance in the interpretation of the passages at hand (Qu. 48.2). Many pages later, he concludes his remarks with a short doxology (Qu 53.8). This is the only place in his writings where Maximos begins with a prayer to the Word, or concludes a response with a doxology, a framing device that gives the activity of scriptural interpretation a distinctly liturgical and indeed sacramental character.[45]

42. Qu. 55 also deals extensively with number symbolism; cf. *Amb.* 66–67 (DOML 2:283–303); and *QD.* 17, 36, 39, 49, 56, 80, 155, 176, 191, 193 (CCSG 10). For commentary, see Hans Urs von Balthasar, "Number and What is Beyond," in idem, *Cosmic Liturgy: The Universe According to Maximus the Confessor,* trans. Brian E. Daley (San Francisco: Ignatius Press, 2003), 109–14; Blowers, "Arithmology," in idem, *Exegesis and Spiritual Pedagogy,* 211–19; Kattan, *Verleiblichung und Synergie,* 246–48 (cited below, n. 47); and Peter Van Deun, "La symbolique des nombres dans l'oeuvre de Maxime le Confesseur," *Byzantinoslavica* 53 (1992): 237–42. See also Dominic O'Meara, *Pythagoras Revived: Mathematics and Philosophy in Late Antiquity* (Oxford: Clarendon Press, 1989), and Joel Kalvesmaki, *The Theology of Arithmetic: Number Symbolism in Platonism and Early Christianity* (Washington, DC: Center for Hellenic Studies, 2013), although these two studies do not consider the work of Maximos. The "theology of arithmetic" constitutes one of Maximos's more formidable hermeneutical tools and awaits detailed study by scholars.

43. These Questions constitute a "mixed" group, since the thematic focus unfolds in a series of questions on 1 Peter.

44. An additional thematic cluster, Qu. 62–63 (on Zechariah), also receives extensive treatment.

45. This liturgical framing suggests that these thematic and biblical clusters may have been assembled from pre-existing notes or partial commentaries that Maximos subsequently reworked for inclusion in the *Responses.* As

Finally, while the theological topics treated in the *Responses* are so rich as to defy simple summary, there are five Christological Questions that merit attention.[46] These Questions are critical for an integral understanding of Maximos's hermeneutics, and are his most important Christological statements prior to his involvement in the controversy over Christ's natural wills and energies.[47] For Maximos, the incarnate Word is at the center of the twofold purpose of the *Responses*, which is concerned to liberate the spirit from the constraints of the letter, and the mind from its enslavement to the passions. The relationship of letter and spirit, and the values associated with these terms, had long been understood as analogous to the human body and soul.[48] Maximos likewise uses this analogy,[49] but he also sees it as being grounded in the dual natures of the incarnate

---

such they would reflect sustained study of the biblical books in question (and not simply glosses on random, isolated passages), and may perhaps also be written echoes of Maximos's exegetically based teaching, offered to his immediate disciples and fellow monks.

46. I.e., Qu. 21; Qu. 42; and Qu. 60–62. See also Qu. 18–19; and Qu. 22, which also make important Christological points.

47. Paul Blowers, *On the Cosmic Mystery of Jesus Christ: Selected Writings from St Maximus the Confessor* (Crestwood: St Vladimir's Seminary Press, 2003), 33, describes Qu. 60 as an "uncontested *locus classicus* in the Confessor's writings." On the relationship between Maximos's Christology and biblical exegesis, see the detailed study by Assad Elias Kattan, *Verleiblichung und Synergie: Grundzüge der Bibelhermeneutik bei Maximus Confessor* (Leiden: Brill, 2003), esp. 125–272; and idem, "The Christological Dimension of Maximus Confessor's Biblical Hermeneutics," *SP* 42 (2006): 169–74.

48. See, for example, Origen, *On First Principles* 4.2.4, where the "threefold" division of meaning in Scripture (literal, moral, and spiritual) is analogous to human "flesh, soul, and spirit" (SC 268:310).

49. Cf. *Cap. theol.* 1.91: "We say that the whole holy Scripture is divided into flesh and spirit, as if it were a spiritual human being. For he who says that the literal word is flesh, but that its inner meaning is spirit, or soul, will not miss the mark of truth" (PG 91:1120D–1121A); ibid., 1.97, where the incarnate Word in Scripture is said to have "two forms: one that is visible and one that is hidden" (PG 91:1121D); and *Myst.* 6, where Maximos, reporting on the teaching of the anonymous elder, notes: "Holy Scripture may be understood as a spiritual human being, with the Old Testament as the body, and the New Testament as soul, spirit, and intellect. Moreover, the entire historical letter of Scripture is a body, while the meaning of the letter is the soul" (CCSG 69:31–33).

Word, who is at once visible and invisible, human and divine.[50] These two natures, moreover, being hypostatically united in the person of the Word, mutually permeate each other without confusion, so that the invisible divinity is revealed to human eyes only insofar as it is concealed in the veil of the flesh.[51] To perceive the spirit in the letter is analogous to perceiving the divinity concealed within the flesh of the Word. To fail to perceive the depth of the spirit, on the other hand, and to be fixated on surface appearances, were the principal effects of the passions, which obstruct spiritual vision on every level of human awareness. By assuming the natural, blameless human passions and restoring them to their proper use,[52] the incarnate Word offers those who become members of his mystical body the possibility of freedom from the passions. Through the Incarnation, human passibility, which is essentially creaturely passivity, becomes the condition for the possibility of divinization.[53]

50. Cf. Intro. 1.2.8; Qu. 35; Qu. 50.2; *QD.* 142 (CCSG 10:101, lines 13–14); *Amb.* 10.28–34 (DOML 1:191–203); *Amb.* 47–48 (DOML 2:207–23).

51. Cf. *Cap.* 1.9: "This is because in Himself, according to His essence, God always remains a mystery. He expresses His natural hiddenness to the same degree that He makes it the more hidden through the revelation" (PG 90:1181C); *Amb.* 5.5 (DOML 1:37), *Amb.* 10.32–33 (DOML 1:197–201); and *Amb.* 33.2 (DOML 2:63–65). On the notion of revelation as concealment, see Nicholas [Maximos] Constas, "Symeon of Thessaloniki and the Theology of the Icon Screen," in *Thresholds of the Sacred: Architectural, Art Historical, Liturgical, and Theological Perspectives on Religious Screens, East and West,* ed. Sharon Gerstel (Washington, DC: Dumbarton Oaks, 2006), 163–83.

52. The Word's assumption of these passions is discussed in Qu. 21 and 42; cf. Qu. 61.10; Qu. 55.7; and *Amb.* 4 (DOML 1:21–31). The natural, blameless passions, which human beings have no choice but to endure patiently, become in the incarnate Word freely chosen acts of will, as Maximos explains in *Pyrr.*: "These natural things of the will are present in Christ, but not exactly in the same way as they are in us. He truly experienced hunger and thirst, not in a mode similar to ours, but in a mode that surpasses us, in other words, voluntarily" (PG 91:297D); cf. John of Damascus, *On the Orthodox Faith* 64.3.20: "Nothing is perceived in Christ as taking place by necessity, but rather all things are voluntary, for He willed to be hungry, He willed to be thirsty, He willed to fear death, and He willed to die" (ed. Boniface Kotter, *Die Schriften des Johannes von Damaskos,* vol. 2 [Berlin: De Gruyter, 1973], 163, lines 25–27).

53. Cf. *Amb.* 7.6–12 (DOML 1:81–93); and *Amb.* 20.2–3 (DOML 1:409–13). For discussion, see Paul M. Blowers, "The Passion of Jesus Christ in Maximus

Text and Context

These sequences of Questions provide some of the major structural supports for the edifice of the *Responses*. They cannot, however, be said to constitute an overarching plan or organizing principle, but are rather more like archipelagos in a seemingly amorphous ocean. To search the *Responses* for a hidden structural key seems to be in any case the wrong question to ask, partly because it does not correspond to the way the writer wishes the reader to gain insight. In the *Responses*, writing does not express a closed proposition, but performs an act of thinking, which is heuristic and digressive, requiring the reader to circle back to find the lost thread, so that the experience of reading has to be constantly re-enacted and re-created. A shorter road would miss the beauties of the landscape that are only discovered by meandering through open, unstructured space. Sequential reading is merely a prelude to multiple readings, through which the work's extravagant fractal divisions come into focus in a rich and multilayered network of words, images, and concepts. Such textured improvisations account for the "symphonic" metaphor that scholars have used to describe the Confessor's literary style, although perhaps a more fitting metaphor would be a double or triple fugue, in which two or more slightly different versions of a melody are played at the same time.[54]

---

the Confessor: A Reconsideration," *SP* 37 (2001): 370–74; and Adam Cooper, *The Body in St Maximus the Confessor: Holy Flesh, Wholly Deified* (Oxford: Oxford University Press, 2005), 144–50; 241–50.

54. Cf. Georges Florovsky, "St Maximus the Confessor," in idem, *The Byzantine Fathers of the Sixth to Eighth Century* (Vaduz: Büchervertriebsanstalt, 1987), 213: "It is the rhythm of the spiritual life rather than a logical connection of ideas which defines his vision of the world, and one could say that his system has more of a musical structure than an architectural one. It is more like a symphony—a symphony of spiritual experience, than a system"; and Balthasar, *Cosmic Liturgy*, 283–84: "The texture of his spiritual syntheses is so manifold, so changeable, that it would be impossible and also pointless to try to present all their interconnections. Here, as everywhere, Maximos plays with traditional patterns of thought, as if they were established cadences and themes; his originality is in the rhythm that constantly recurs in his richly orchestrated symphonies."

To expect a work like the *Responses to Thalassios* to construct a system, and to exhibit its structure on the surface, is to ignore the practical and discursive context in which and for which the work was written. Addressing the false assumptions at the basis of such expectations, Pierre Hadot noted: "We often have the impression that ancient authors wrote badly, that the sequence of their ideas lacks coherence and connection. But it is precisely because the true figure escapes us that we do not perceive the form that renders all the details necessary: once discovered, the hidden form will make necessary all of the details that seemed arbitrary or without importance."[55] According to Hadot, the "hidden form" is the living praxis in which the work was produced, the knowledge of which transforms a seemingly disconnected series of texts into a rigorously structured work. The organizing form, in other words, is not to be found immediately in the work's content, but in the surrounding armature of lived experience. An essential element of this experience was the oral transmission of doctrine from master to disciple, for which written texts were but material supports for the spoken word, comprising intermediary moments between two dialogical events. The written *logos* as such was neither the focus nor the goal of such a life, but rather the living *logos*, for which written texts were but preparations and complements: mnemonic devices ancillary to the concrete and practical experience of dialogue.[56] A work such as the *Responses*, then, is a written echo or icon of its dialogical archetype, which is why it is addressed to a friend. The dimension of the interlocutor is always present within it, and it resonates with the halting reticence and vagrant wanderings of its originary context. The writer is in re-

---

55. Pierre Hadot, "Patristique latine," in *Problèmes et méthodes d'histoire des religions. Mélanges publiés par la Section des sciences religieuses à l'occasion du centenaire de l'École pratique des hautes études* (Paris: Presses universitaires de France, 1968), 216–17, cited in Arnold L. Davidson, "Introduction: Pierre Hadot and the Spiritual Phenomenon of Ancient Philosophy," in Pierre Hadot, *Philosophy as a Way of Life: Spiritual Exercises from Socrates to Foucault*, trans. Michael Chase (Oxford: Blackwell, 1995), 8.

56. Davidson, "Introduction," 19–20; cf. John Sallis, *Being and Logos: Reading the Platonic Dialogues* (Bloomington and Indianapolis: Indiana University Press, 1996), 1–22.

ality a speaker. This same context also explains why so many of the responses end with a protreptic or exhortation to moral action, which is the application of theory to practice.

Though dynamic and open-ended, this living praxis is itself the instantiation of a complex repertoire of theological commitments and beliefs, a set of canonical first principles mapping a range of territory extending from creation to redemption. These first principles constitute the Confessor's spiritual worldview and the "hidden form" (to use Hadot's phrase) of the *Responses*. There is no reason to doubt that Thalassios, the recipient of the work, embraced these same first principles, and while each response presupposes detailed knowledge of them, they are never fully or systematically articulated. At this juncture, then, it will be helpful to sketch out, however briefly, the principal features of this doctrinal framework or worldview as it relates directly to the *Responses*, namely, Maximos's understanding of the causes and effects of the passions, their transformation through successive stages of spiritual ascent, and the manner in which these and related principles inform his biblical hermeneutics.[57]

V. The Passions as Hermeneutical Crisis

Human life derives its origin and meaning from the Word (*Logos*), who fills the mind (*logos*) and the senses with rationality and purpose. The fall was a complex event brought about by a combination of demonic suggestion, an error in human judgment, and the misuse of free will. The result was a shift of spiritual energy to a lower, biological plane of animal life: a fallen mode of existence that introduced the passions into human consciousness.[58] The corruption of rationality (*logos*) in turn

57. For an excellent survey of these doctrinal themes, see Jean-Claude Larchet, "La pensée de saint Maxime le Confesseur dans les 'Questions à Thalassios,'" *Le Messager Orthodoxe* 113 (1990): 3–41; reprinted with minor modifications in idem, "L'Enseignement spirituel des *Questions à Thalassios*," in *Maxime le Confesseur, Questions à Thalassios*, SC 529 (Paris: Les Éditions du Cerf, 2010), 26–81.

58. Qu.1.2: "The passions were introduced on account of the fall from perfection, emerging in the more irrational part of human nature, and it was

corrupted the whole of human nature.[59] It further introduced a radical inversion of the natural order, of which the disproportionate power of the senses, their domination of the mind, and the mind's attachment to sensory phenomena are the primary symptoms.[60] The role of the demonic in this human tragedy would be difficult to exaggerate. From the initial deception in the garden (Gn 3.1–6) to the subsequent enslavement of the human will to passions under the influence of malevolent powers, the shadow of the demonic looms large in the *Responses*, but is a subject that has yet to be studied fully by scholars.[61]

The disordered movements of the passions, to the extent that they impel the mind to attach itself to the material surface of the world, create the conditions for a profound hermeneutical crisis. Fixated on surfaces now rendered opaque to the divine presence, the passions impede insight into the intelligible structure of phenomena and their inner unity.[62] The passions

---

through them that, at the very moment of the transgression, the likeness to irrational animals appeared in man instead of the divine image [Gn 1.26]." See also Intro. 1.2.13; and *Amb.* 10.60 (DOML 1:247).

59. Qu. 42.2: "Adam's natural power of free choice was corrupted first, and corrupted nature together with itself.... Thus the fall of free choice from the good toward evil became the first and blameworthy sin. The second sin, which came about as a result of the first, was the blameless alteration of nature from incorruptibility to corruption."

60. These are the major themes of Intro. 1.2.11–22, which recur in various forms throughout the *Responses*.

61. Cf. 1.2.9–10; and Questions 4.2–3; 14.2; 21.4; 25.8; 26.10, 12; 38.3–4; 49.6, 9–10; 50.11; 52.9, 13; 54.11, 25; 56.5–8; 64.23; and 65.32. Origen, *On First Principles*, 3.2.1–2, argues that the whole of Scripture testifies to the unrelenting assault of demons against humanity, beginning with the devil's deception of Eve (Gn 3.1–6), through Judas's possession by Satan (Jn 13.2), to Christ's crucifixion by the "princes of this world" (1 Cor 2.6–8), and Paul's declaration that "our struggle is not against flesh and blood, but against the rulers of this world's darkness, against the spiritual armies of wickedness in the heavenly places [Eph 6.12]" (SC 268:152–63); cf. Lars Thunberg, *Microcosm and Mediator: The Theological Anthropology of Maximus the Confessor* (Chicago: Open Court, 1995), 154–56; John Gavin, *They Are Like Angels in Heaven: Angelology and Anthropology in the Thought of Maximus the Confessor* (Rome: Institutum Patristicum Augustinianum, 2009), 127–31; and Sotirios Kollias, "The Devil, Demons, and their Work According to St. Maximus the Confessor" (Ph.D. diss., University of Athens, 2003).

62. Cf. Qu. 49.4: "The passions are of a nature to be created around the

are interested in pleasure, not truth, and a mind dominated by the passions perceives neither the metaphysical ground of creation nor the spiritual meaning of Scripture.[63] With respect to creation, the presence of the passions limits human awareness to the outward appearances of visible objects. With respect to Scripture, the same passions limit the mind to the literal level of the text, concealing the deeper meaning inherent in the letter.[64] Both result in a hermeneutical failure to understand the meaning of what is given in creation and revelation, a failure that inevitably leads to the abuse of both nature and Scripture.[65]

The mind's fixation on surface appearances and its enslavement to irrational sensations lock the human person in a relentless, inescapable cycle of pleasure and pain.[66] Whereas some aspects of the sensible world are pleasing to the body, others are not, yet the two experiences are inseparable.[67] Seeking the pleasures of the body, moreover, while fleeing from whatever causes pain, only further entraps the person within an endless series of empty and isolated sensations. Reduced to the finite strictures of hankering, irrational wants, human desire for the infinite can never be satisfied, but causes only endless frustration, pain, and psychological fragmentation. At

---

surface appearances of visible things, and the activity of reason within us is made to cease"; Qu. 58.9: "If the intellect becomes ensnared by the surface appearances of visible realities ... it falls away from realities that by nature are intelligible and seizes corporeal realities contrary to nature"; Qu. 59.2: "All those with a share in human nature had their power of intellect and reason narrowed to the surface appearances of sensible objects, and had no conception of any reality beyond what could be perceived by the senses."

63. *Cap. theol.* 2.75: "Understandings of Scripture that are limited solely to the literal meaning, and impassioned contemplations of the sensible world that rely exclusively on sense-perception, are indeed scales blinding the soul's visionary faculty and preventing passage to the pure Word of truth" (PG 91:1160C).

64. Forcefully argued in Qu. 65.

65. Cf. Qu. 55.7; Qu. 61.10; Qu. 64.11; and *Amb.* 10.32 (DOML 1:197–99). Both Origen (SC 375:82–85) and Gregory of Nyssa (GNO 6:14–15) emphasize that the Song of Songs cannot be understood by a person under the influence of the passions, because its spiritual meanings are available only to those who have been purified in mind and spirit.

66. Intro. 1.2.14–19; cf. Qu. 58.

67. Ibid., 1.2.17–19; cf. Qu. 43.

the center of this tragic situation stands love of the self and love of the body (φιλαυτία), which the impassioned mind seeks to satisfy through selfish exploitation and abuse of the material surface of the world.[68]

The orientation to sensory phenomena likewise distorts the dominant passions of desire and anger, whose energies are squandered in the pursuit of bodily satisfaction, awakening a whole new set of bodily needs and desires along with the instinct for self-preservation.[69] As long as they are under the control of reason, such passions are "blameless," their use being limited to what is natural and necessary for the body.[70] When, however, they function independently of reason and are preoccupied solely with sensible objects, they become sinful, "blameworthy" passions.[71] The solution to this psychic conflict is to transform the passions and return them to their proper uses, not to suppress or uproot them (which is in any case impossible). The passions have their place and function not simply in bodily life but in the return of the self to God through the motivating force of desire.[72]

The possibility for fallen human beings to be delivered from bondage to irrational sensations and the vicious cycle of pleasure and pain is offered by the Word made flesh, who is the new Adam. The incarnate Word freely offers his own victory over the passions to believers,[73] who must nonetheless under-

68. Intro. 1.2.14.
69. Cf. Intro. 1.2.16; Qu. 16.2; Qu. 51.20; Qu. 53.2; Qu. 55.18–19; Qu. 65.29; Amb. 6.3 (DOML 1:7173); Amb. 10.60 (DOML 1:247–49); Amb. 107, 111, 114–15, 118 (DOML 1:323, 327, 333–35, 339–43); Amb. 21.9 (DOML 1: 433–35); Amb. 45.3 (DOML 2:195–97).
70. Prol. 1.1.3, to cite only the first of many examples.
71. Cf. Intro. 1.2.9; Qu. 21.2; Qu. 55.7; Qu. 61.10; Amb. 4.4, 6 (DOML 1:23–25, 27).
72. Qu. 1.3, the first of many examples.
73. Cf. Qu. 21.4: "Christ clearly won victory over them (i.e., the demons) not for His sake but for ours, because it was for our sake that He became man and, in His goodness, offered to us the whole of what He accomplished"; Qu. 21.6: "Christ considered what He accomplished for us as something that He, in His love for humanity, was accountable for—or rather, in His goodness, He reckoned to us the glory of the accomplishment"; Qu. 49.10; Qu. 52.6; and Qu. 54.6.

take the struggle of asceticism in order to break the hold of sensation over reason and contemplation.[74] When this occurs, it is through the same material world that the person discovers—or rediscovers—the inner depth of creation, and rises toward God.[75] This transformation is initiated by the incarnate Word in those who freely collaborate with him, having been incorporated into his mystical body through the grace of baptism.[76] All that is required is that one's power of choice, the disposition of one's natural will, remain faithful to the Word, who is present in each believer, assisting him in his struggles, freeing him from the passions, and restoring his spiritual capacities as the means of union with God.[77]

VI. Stages of Spiritual Progress

This is not the place to present a detailed account of progress in the spiritual life, but it will be important to outline its three principal stages,[78] forms and figures of which Maximos finds on

---

74. The rationale is given in *Pyrr.*: "Asceticism and all the toils that go with it were established in order to ward off deception, which intruded itself through sensory perception. Virtues are not placed within us from outside, but inhere within us from creation. Thus when deception is completely expelled, the soul immediately exhibits the splendor of its natural virtue ... just as when rust is removed, the natural clarity and sheen of iron is manifest" (PG 91:309C).

75. This was the divine intention for Adam before the fall; cf. Intro. 1.2.18: "Having already become God through divinization, he might have been able without fear of harm to examine with God the creations of God, and to acquire knowledge of them, not as man but as God, having by grace the very same wise and informed knowledge of beings that God has, on account of the divinizing transformation of his intellect and powers of perception"; and *Amb.* 10.60: "The fallen Adam was unable, by means of sense perception, to make his own (as one must not) the things of God without God, and before God, and not according to God, which is impossible" (DOML 1:247–49).

76. Qu. 6; *Amb.* 42 (DOML 2:123–87); cf. Jean-Claude Larchet, "Le Baptême selon Maxime le Confesseur," *Revue des sciences religieuses* 65 (1991): 51–70; and Cooper, *The Body in St Maximus*, 218–27; 243–44.

77. Cf. Qu. 6.2: "What is lacking, therefore, in each of us who is still able to sin, is the unequivocal desire to surrender our whole selves, in the disposition of our will, to the Spirit."

78. The classic three stages of spiritual progress were established by Origen, *Commentary on the Song of Songs* 3.1–16 (SC 375:128–39); subsequently

virtually every page of sacred Scripture.[79] The first stage, which the Confessor typically calls "ascetic practice" or "practical philosophy," encompasses the keeping of the commandments, the purification of the passions, and the acquisition of the virtues. The aim of this stage is not the suppression of physical sensations or sense perception, but rather the purification and restoration of their proper activities, removing from them the distorting lenses of pleasure and pain. The life of virtue does not place one in opposition to creation. Instead it is a return to a way of life according to nature, freeing the mind from its passionate attachment to the world, which it had exploited and abused for selfish gratification.[80] Through the practice of asceticism, human beings learn to use the world solely for their natural needs and for the restoration through love of ties with their neighbors—which is the restoration and reunification of

---

expanded and systematized by Evagrios (cf. Jeremy Driscoll, *Steps to Spiritual Perfection: Studies on Spiritual Progress in Evagrius Ponticus* [Mahwah, NJ: Newman Press, 2005], 11–37); and later modified by the Confessor; cf. Maximos Constas, "Nothing is Greater than Divine Love: Evagrios of Pontos, Maximos the Confessor, and the *Philokalia,*" in *Rightly Dividing the Word of Truth: A Volume in Honour of Metropolitan Kallistos Ware,* ed. Graham Speake (Oxford: Peter Lang, 2016), 57–74. For a superb modern account of these three stages, see Dumitru Staniloae, *Orthodox Spirituality,* trans. Jerome Newville and Otilia Kloos (South Canaan, PA: St Tikhon's Seminary Press, 2002).

79. Cf. Evagrios, *Gnostikos* 18: "It is necessary to search for allegorical and literal passages relevant to ascetic practice, natural contemplation, or theology. If the passage is relevant to ascetic practice, it is necessary to determine whether it concerns anger, desire, or the intellect and its movements. If it is relevant to natural contemplation, it is necessary to know which doctrine of nature it concerns. And if theology, it is necessary to determine if it concerns the Trinity or the Monad" (SC 356:116–18).

80. Cf. Qu. 51.18: "We have not been commanded to fight against the sense-perceptible creations that are outside of us, but rather to wage perpetual war within ourselves against the 'dishonorable passions' [Rom 1.26]"; Qu. 58.2: "A passion of a natural power ... is the mode according to which natural activity is misused, and such misuse of natural activity is the movement of our natural power toward that which is unnatural and does not exist according to nature"; and *Cap. theol.* 2.41: "Those who animal-like live solely according to the senses make the Word flesh for themselves in a dangerous way: they misuse God's creation in order to indulge their passions. They do not understand the principle of that wisdom which is revealed to all: that we should know and praise God through His creation" (PG 91:1144B).

human nature itself.[81] In this way, the human person is raised from a state contrary to nature to one according to nature—which means according to Christ, who is the essence of the virtues—and thus the first manifestation of divine grace is the restoration of nature.[82] The new life according to nature does not arise solely from capacities inherent within nature, but through the synergy of embodied human rationality (*logos*) with the embodied Word (*Logos*).

From this first stage—which is human nature's initial liberation from the benighted prison of sensation to the light of reason and the Word—the person rises to the second level, which is the vision of divine principles (*logoi*) embedded within creation and Scripture. Maximos distinguishes this activity into two categories or moments: the contemplation of visible and of intelligible realities, applied to both nature and Scripture as its two proper fields of vision.[83] At this stage the Word no longer works merely inwardly or invisibly through the virtues, but reveals himself through the increasing transparency of the natural world and the world of the sacred text. As one enters more deeply into these fields, the bond between human reason and the Word becomes more pronounced and thus stronger. This level of spiritual vision is called "natural contemplation," not because it takes place exclusively through the natural power of human knowledge, but because its object is typically the *logoi* of beings, and because it presupposes a human nature freed from the passions and capable of exercising its contemplative faculty.[84] This is not knowledge arrived at through a process of

81. Qu. 29.3; Qu. 62.6; Qu. 64.32; and *Ep.* 2 (PG 91:392–408).

82. Cf. *Amb.* 7.21: "The essence of all the virtues is our Lord, Jesus Christ ... and anyone who participates in virtue participates in God" (DOML 1:103); and *Pyrr.* (PG 91:309B–311A).

83. Cf. Qu. 10.7, where Maximos distinguishes those who through natural contemplation "attained understanding of God's judgments," from those who "received immaterial knowledge of intelligible realities free of any sensory image." Maximos can also speak of a distinct "scriptural contemplation" (γραφικὴ θεωρία) or "scriptural mystagogy" (γραφικὴ μυσταγωγία), although only very rarely, and not in the *Responses;* cf. *Amb.* 37.5 (DOML 2:79); and the lemma (no. 30) at *Amb.*10.63 (DOML 1:253–54), which is probably the work of a later scribe or editor.

84. This is why Maximos almost always qualifies the term as "natural con-

deductive reasoning, but a simple, direct insight, representing a new elevation of the mind from the level of discursive reasoning (which is characteristic of the first stage) to simple, intuitive insight and true understanding.[85]

Finally, at the third and highest stage of spiritual progress, the human person is raised beyond its own proper limits—beyond all sensory, cognitive, and rational abilities—being completely filled by divine and uncreated energy, becoming God by grace.[86] This stage is differentiated into two moments, the first called "theology" and the second called "mystical theology" or "theological mystagogy." In the former, through analogies and concepts the mind comes to know God as the cause of beings.[87] In the latter, the mind knows God without the mediation of created beings or concepts.[88] This takes place after all the effort and activity of human nature ceases, having reached the limit of its natural potential. This is a kind of mystical death, the "Sabbath" of the self, in which the mind no longer moves

---

templation *in the spirit*" (e.g., Qu. 27.5; 55.27; 65.21, etc.). Qu. 49 is one of Maximos's most important and sustained treatments of natural contemplation, emphasizing in particular the inherent dangers of the practice; cf. Qu. 55.27, where similar warnings are issued. Qu. 51 offers a more positive assessment; see also Questions 27.5; 47.2; 65.9–10, 16–17, and 19–21. See also the discussions in Walther Völker, *Maximus Confessor als Meister des geistlichen Lebens* (Wiesbaden: F. Steiner, 1965), 296–318; and Michael Harrington, "Creation and Natural Contemplation in Maximus the Confessor's *Ambiguum* 10.19," in *Divine Creation in Ancient, Medieval, and Early Modern Thought: Essays Presented to the Rev. Dr. Robert D. Crouse*, ed. Michael Treschow et al. (Leiden: Brill, 2007), 191–212.

85. Cf. *Amb.* 45.5: "Adam possessed the untainted principles of the virtues, and had no need to rely on ideas drawn discursively from sensible objects in order to understand divine realities, but had solely the simple putting forth (προβολή) of the unitary, simple, all-embracing virtue and knowledge of things sequent to God, which needs only to actualize its own movement in order to be voluntarily manifested. Thus those who wish to raise themselves up from the forefather's fall begin by completely negating the passions ... and, peering beyond natural contemplation, they catch a glimpse of immaterial knowledge, which has absolutely no form susceptible to sense perception or any meaning that can be contained by spoken words" (DOML 2:199–201).

86. Qu. 59.8–11; *Amb.* 20 (DOML 1:409–19).

87. Qu. 13.2–3; 60.5.

88. Qu. 3.3; 25.5–6; 40.3; 55.28; 64.35; 65.28.

toward finite objects or concepts, but has been taken up into the reality of the infinite God, in whose presence it can only renounce, indeed has no need for, any attempt to grasp at God.[89] In mystical theology, the mind united to God no longer knows God by analogy or in any kind of cataphatic way, but apophatically, in the silence that is beyond all speech and affirmation, through an "unknowing" superior to understanding.[90]

Even at the highest stage of divinization, the Word does not cease to possess a human nature, but rather makes human nature the transparent field and environment of the divine energies. It is through the human nature of the Word, through the mediating veil of his flesh, and in his gracious communion with human nature (which through the human person extends to all creation and matter itself) that created human beings are filled with divine grace and life.[91]

VII. Scripture and Creation

In the classical philosophical tradition, the contemplation of nature was based on the belief that to everything that is manifest, outward, and material, there corresponds something hidden, inward, and spiritual. That the visible world was the reflection of an invisible world implied that visible objects were physical signs or symbols pointing beyond themselves to intelligible realities. No element or aspect of the cosmos, no matter how seemingly insignificant, was without a corresponding counterpart in the realm of the spirit. Because physical objects contained intelligible meanings that were "legible," as it were, by human beings, it seemed self-evident that such objects were constituted by a kind of code or script, so that the structure of the material world was

---

89. Qu. 65.20; *Cap. theol.* 1.36–41; 2.64–65 (PG 90:1097AD; 1152D–1153A); *Amb.* 65.2 (DOML 2:277–79); and *QD.* 10; 113 (CCSG 10:9; 83–84).

90. Cf. Prol. 1.1.1; and Intro. 1.2.22.

91. Cf. *Amb.* 10.52: "On that summit ... [the spiritual Moses] will be made worthy to see and hear in his intellect the ineffable and supernatural divine fire that exists, as if in a burning bush, within the essence of things, that is, God the Word, who shone forth in these latter days from the holy Virgin and spoke to us through the flesh" (DOML 1:233); and Staniloae, *Orthodox Spirituality*, 374.

closely correlated with the structure of language and speech. This analogy was partly encouraged by the Greek language itself, in which the word for the "elements" of matter and for the "letters" of the alphabet is one and the same (that is, στοιχεῖα). It followed that the universe had an alphabet and was organized like a language with combinations of elements producing the physical equivalents of letters, syllables, and words.[92]

The Book of Nature

That idea that the universe was a cosmic "book" arose naturally in such a context and was adopted by late-antique Christian writers, especially those in the Alexandrian tradition. Evagrios, for example, reports an event from the life of St. Antony, in which the saint invokes the "book of nature" in a debate with Greek philosophers: "My book, O philosophers, is the nature of things that have come into being, and it is always at hand whenever I wish to read the words (*logoi*) of God."[93] Authorization for the idea of a cosmic book was also found in various passages of Scripture.[94] But the analogy was not typically extended to

---

92. See, for example, L. G. Westerink, ed., *Anonymous Prolegomenon to Platonic Philosophy* 2 (Amsterdam: North-Holland, 1962), 16: "Formless matter is analogous to the 24 letters of the alphabet, bodies without qualities to syllables, and the four elements to words"; Robert Lamberton, *Homer the Theologian: Neoplatonist Allegorical Reading and the Growth of the Epic Tradition* (Berkeley: University of California Press, 1989), 76–77; Timothy Crowley, "On the Use of Stoicheion in the Sense of 'Element,'" *Oxford Studies in Ancient Philosophy* 29 (2005): 367–94; and the bibliography cited below, at Qu. 55.13.

93. Evagrios, *Praktikos* 92 (SC 171:694); cf. Athanasios, *Life of Antony* 73 (SC 400:322). See also Evagrios, *Letter to Melania*, trans. A. M. Casiday, *Evagrius Ponticus* (London: Routledge, 2006), 64–77 ("The Great Letter"), for an extended discussion of creation as composed of symbolic "letters."

94. Cf. Origen, *Philokalia* 23.15: "Like a volume of prophecy, the heavens as a whole, being one of God's books [cf. Is 34.4], may contain the future, and this is how the words of Jacob may be understood: 'For I read in the pages of the sky what shall befall you and your sons'"; ibid., 23.20: "For just as in our books things are written so that we might know them, it is possible that the writings of the heavens are read by angels so that they might rejoice in their knowledge" (SC 400:180–82; 200–202); and Evagrios, *On the Psalms:* "The 'book' of God (Ps 138.16) is the contemplation of corporeal and incorporeal beings. In this book are written the principles of providence and judgment,

writings or texts, sacred or otherwise, which were not said to constitute a "world" or "cosmos," perhaps due to the mistrust of written language characteristic of the Platonic tradition.[95]

Maximos, however, had no such reservations, and took the analogy to its logical conclusions, indeed much further than any of his predecessors and in a wholly new direction.[96] For the Confessor, it is not merely the cosmos that is fully a sacred text, but the text of Scripture is fully "another cosmos" in such a way that the two are equal and interconnected manifestations of the divine Word's self-disclosure.[97] The presence of the Word in these complementary "texts" embodies the divine act of speech, a palpable (and legible) objectification of the transcendent Word under the conditions of multiplicity, place, and time. These objectifications are analogous to the stabilization of spoken language in the form of written script, since each is a "spelling out" of the Word, who makes himself "legible" by "inscribing" himself in the multi-layered parchments of creation, Scripture, and the human nature he assumed when he became flesh.[98] It was thus that the "Word became thick," according to Gregory Nazianzus, a phrase that Maximos understood as re-

---

and through this book God is known as creator, wise, provider, and judge ... as wise on account of the words (λόγοι) stored up in this book" (PG 12:1661CD).

95. Notably Plato, *Phaedrus* 275d–278a, to which the *Anonymous Prolegomenon to Platonic Philosophy* offers a notable exception: "Plato used the literary form because the dialogue is a kind of cosmos. For in the same way as the dialogue has different personages each speaking in character, so does the universe comprise existences of various natures expressing themselves in various ways ... and thus the dialogue is a cosmos and the cosmos a dialogue" (ed. Westerink, 28, 30).

96. The idea, if not the specific analogy, is found in Dionysios, for whom the "intelligible names" of Scripture and the "sensible forms" of nature are two continuous sets of symbols that cannot be sharply differentiated; cf. Eric D. Perl, *Theophany: The Neoplatonic Philosophy of Dionysius the Areopagite* (Albany: State University of New York Press, 2007), 101–3.

97. *Amb.* 10.30–31 (DOML 1:195–97).

98. *Amb.* 10.31 (DOML 1:195); cf. Origen, *Scholia on Matthew*: "In the same way that the spoken word is by nature impalpable and invisible, but when it is written in a book, and acquires a body, as it were, then it is both seen and touched, so too the fleshless and incorporeal Word of God, who according to His divinity is neither seen nor written, but because He was incarnate, can be both seen and written" (PG 17:289).

ferring to three distinct but related manifestations (or "densifications") of the immaterial divinity, namely, the "Word's manifestation in the flesh; His concealment in the principles (*logoi*) of creation; and His consent to be embodied and expressed through the letters, syllables, and sounds (of Scripture), so that from all these he might gradually raise us up to the simple and unconditioned idea of Him."[99]

VIII. The Transfiguration of Christ

These unified manifestations of the Word—in creation, Scripture, and the Incarnation—converge in Maximos's interpretation of the Transfiguration of Christ, which receives detailed treatment in *Ambiguum* 10.[100] This interpretation constitutes the symbolic center of the entire *Ambiguum*—which is by far the longest in the collection—and is the culmination of a series of thirteen biblical passages illustrating aspects of the mind's "passage" (*diabasis*) to God through the material world, and of God's manifestation to the mind through the flesh.[101]

According to the Gospel of Matthew, Christ was "transfigured" in the presence of Peter, James, and John, so that his face "shone like the sun," and his "garments became white like light."[102] Such a vision was possible because the disciples had "crossed over from flesh to the spirit," having their power of "sense perception purified and supplanted by the activity of the

---

99. *Amb.* 33.1–2 (DOML 2:63–65), citing Gregory Nazianzus, *Or.* 38.2 (SC 358:106, lines 16–17); cf. idem, *Letter* 101.49 (SC 208:56, lines 15–18); and below, Qu. 31.2.

100. *Amb.* 10.28–34 (DOML 1:191–203). Maximos also comments on the Transfiguration in *QD*. 191–92 (CCSG 10:132–35); and *Cap. theol.* 2.13–16 (PG 90:1129D–1132C).

101. Blowers, *Exegesis and Spiritual Pedagogy*, 102–12; idem, *Maximus the Confessor*, 79–86 ("Transfiguration as Paradigm"); and idem, "The Transfiguration of Jesus Christ as 'Saturated Phenomenon' and as a Key to the Dynamics of Biblical Revelation in Saint Maximus the Confessor," in *What is the Bible? The Patristic Doctrine of Scripture* (Minneapolis: Fortress Press, 2016), 83–101.

102. In general, Maximos follows the account in Mt 17.2. Mk 9.3 notes only that Jesus was "transfigured" and that his garments became "glistening, intensely white," while Lk 9.29 states that Jesus's "countenance was altered," and his "raiment shone like lightning."

Holy Spirit," who "removed the veils of the passions" that had obscured the light of Christ.[103] Maximos maps this movement by means of four biblical passages, as the disciples progress from seeing Christ as "one who had no form or beauty" (Is 53.2) and as the "Word who had become flesh" (Jn 1.14), to a vision of him as "one more beautiful than the sons of men" (Ps 45.2) and who "in the beginning was with God and was God" (Jn 1.1). The shift from one mode of awareness to another is the result of a "theological negation" that raised the disciples beyond the level of ordinary knowledge to the "glory of the only-begotten Son" (Jn 1.14).[104]

With their minds cleansed of the passions by the Holy Spirit, and having been raised up beyond the human aspect of Christ to the glory of his divinity, the three disciples recognize that the "dazzling white garments" are "symbols of both Scripture and creation."[105] As symbols of the words of Scripture, the garments have now become "clear and transparent," no longer obscured by any "dark riddles or symbolic shadows," as the disciples apprehend the presence of the incarnate Word throughout the whole of Scripture.[106] In the light of the Transfiguration, they see that the true content and meaning of Scripture is the presence of the Word, and that the words of Scripture in turn

---

103. *Amb.* 10.28 (DOML 1:191); cf. *Amb.* 10.64 (DOML 1:255–57). Maximos suggests that this was a special dispensation granted to the disciples, who had not yet completed the work of spiritual growth and progress. See Blowers, *Maximus the Confessor*, 82: "Christ's garments are rendered translucent not by human perception but by the underlying divinity of the Logos ... the focus is less on the unique visionary experience of Peter, James, and John than on the factitive nature of the Transfiguration."

104. *Amb.* 10.29 (DOML 1:193); cf. *Cap. theol.* 2.39 (PG 91:1141D–1144A).

105. That the shining garments of Christ at the Transfiguration were a symbol of the words of Scripture is an idea found in Origen, *Commentary on Matthew* 17.1–9 (GCS 10:150–70), a passage that was excerpted in the Cappadocian *Philokalia* (SC 302:436–39); cf. Origen, *Against Celsus* 6.75–77 (SC 147:366–74). Note that Maximos understands "symbol" in the strong, Dionysian sense; on which, see Perl, *Theophany*, 101–9 ("Symbolism").

106. Cf. *Amb.* 10.65, where the identification of the incarnate Word with Scripture is highlighted by the presence of Moses and Elijah, symbolizing the "teaching of the law and the prophets, which must always be present together with God the Word, for they are from Him and speak of Him, and have been established and built around Him" (DOML 1:257).

reveal and illumine that presence. As symbols of the outward forms of creation, the disciples understand these same garments to be "creation itself," freed from the distorting lens of a "mind bound to superficial sense perception." Rendered transparent, the surface of creation discloses the "variety of its different forms," the wise ordering of which reveals that its creator is the Word, just as a "garment reveals the dignity of the one who wears it."[107] This dual interpretation of the "garments" is fitting, Maximos argues, because Christ is both Word and Creator, and thus he is the ultimate referent of the words of Scripture and the forms of creation. Maximos therefore concludes that both the "natural law" and the "written law," as he calls them, "are of equal value and dignity: they both reciprocally teach the same things, and neither is superior or inferior to the other."[108] Both laws are fulfilled in the "law of grace," which is Christ.[109]

Maximos, continuing his interpretation of the Transfiguration, enters into greater detail regarding the two books of nature and Scripture. He states that creation is a "book, whose letters and syllables are individual physical phenomena," and in "whose words the Word has ineffably inscribed Himself, making Himself legible through the combination of multiple impressions

---

107. *Amb.* 10.29 (DOML 1:193); cf. Qu. 4.3, where the demons are said to divide Christ's garments into four parts (cf. Jn 19.23), symbolizing the four elements of creation, "contriving that we, being ignorant of creation's divine principles, should see the world according to sense perception and surrender to the passions."

108. *Amb.* 10.30 (DOML 1:193–95). In *Amb.* 10.31 (DOML 1:197), Maximos states that the written law is "identical" (ταὐτόν) to the natural law "according to potential," while the natural is identical to the written "according to ἕξις," a word that can mean "permanent state or condition" as well as "outward appearance" (cf. Dn 1.15). When Maximos returns to this question in *Amb.* 10.54, he distinguishes the two laws in a way suggestive of the soul's "linear" and "circular" motions described by Dionysios, *DN* 1.9 (705AB; 153–54). Thus nature is said to be the field of "practice," while Scripture is the field of "reason and contemplation," since the simplicity of nature requires differentiation into a symbolic order, while the complexity of Scripture requires reduction to a "uniform simplicity," at the end of which the saints "will possess the law of nature spiritually" (DOML 1:239).

109. On which, see Questions 19.2; 39.3–4; and Blowers, *Exegesis and Spiritual Pedagogy*, 117–22.

INTRODUCTION

gathered from nature."[110] At the same time, Scripture is an "intelligible cosmos," the gracious unfolding of the divine into a world of language, images, and stories. It is a world teeming with peoples and places, moving through history on a narrative stage possessing its own "heaven, earth, and all that comes between them, namely, ethical, natural, and theological philosophy."[111] That the world of Scripture is internally structured by the three stages of spiritual progress, outlined above, indicates the central importance of these stages to Maximos's understanding of Scripture, and why he finds them in virtually all of the difficult passages submitted to him by Thalassios. For the Confessor, the narrative of the Transfiguration epitomizes the spiritual passage (*diabasis*) through the symbols of creation and Scripture that is the hidden meaning and purpose of Scripture as a whole.

The Confessor subsequently draws our attention to a paradox: these symbols both conceal and reveal the Word, and they do so at the same time. Symbols conceal precisely to the extent they reveal, and reveal precisely to the extent they conceal. Any symbolic manifestation or representation of God, whether literary or physical, can never be absolutely identified with God himself, who is thus concealed in his very manifestation.[112] The

---

110. *Amb.* 10.31: ὁ διαχαράξας καὶ ἀρρήτως αὐτοῖς ἐγκεχαραγμένος Λόγος ἀναγινωσκώμενος ἀπαρτίζεται (DOML 1:194). Because *logos* denotes not simply "word" but also "reason," the forms of creation are not reducible to "words" in the sense of metaphorical lexical units, but are intelligible realities, and thus the Word who is revealed through them is the intelligible, causal principle that determines their identities, structures, and forms.

111. *Amb.* 10.31 (DOML 1:195–97); cf. *Amb.* 37.5–10 (DOML 2:79–89); and Paul M. Blowers, "The World in the Mirror of Holy Scripture: Maximus the Confessor's Short Hermeneutical Treatise in *Ambiguum ad Joannem* 37," in Paul Blowers, Angela Russel Christman, David Hunter, and Robin Darling Young, eds., *In Dominico Eloquio/In Lordly Eloquence: Essays on Patristic Exegesis in Honor of Robert Louis Wilken* (Grand Rapids: Eerdmans, 2002), 408–26.

112. Cf. Dionysios, *Ep.* 3: "The Word of God remains hidden after His manifestation, or to speak more divinely, even in His manifestation" (1069B; 159, lines 6–7); and Qu. 28.1: "Scripture calls God a lion, a bear, a leopard, a panther, a man, an ox, a sheep, the sun, a star, fire, wind, and a thousand other things—and whereas He Himself is none of these things, He is nonetheless contemplated according to the meaning of each term." For Dionysios, *CH* 2.1–5, all such symbols are "similar" to God and at the same time infinitely "dissimilar" to him (9–17; 136D–145C).

same symbols also serve to conceal the Word from those who approach him unworthily, and reveal him to those whose spiritual vision is not obscured by the passions.

Like human clothing, symbolic "garments" are measured to the body or form of the one who wears them, simultaneously concealing that form and revealing it. But insofar as these garments are words and objects that can be spoken and seen by human beings, they are "measured" to human beings, to whose capacities God has kindly adapted himself, without departing from himself and from the infinity of all that cannot be expressed in words or concepts.[113] Maximos therefore exhorts his readers to "make manifest what is hidden by means of an apophatic negation," in order to be "lifted up from written words and visible things to the Word Himself." To refuse the process of ascent, to cling instead to surface phenomena, is to become a "murderer of the Word," either like Greeks who adhere to the surface of the material world, or like Jews who adhere to the literal level of the text, "for both fail to discern the Word, who became like us through the body, and grew thick in syllables and letters."[114]

For the person who has ascended the mountain of contemplation, Scripture and creation do not vanish or disappear, but are transfigured. No longer obscure and impenetrable, the literal level of Scripture and the physical phenomena of creation become transparent "garments" through which the Word is made visible, and through which he communicates with human beings. Nature and Scripture assume a depth of meaning far beyond their literal, visible content, because ordinary sense perception is penetrated by the very power and activity that created the world and continues to give meaning to the sacred text. If, on the other hand, a person does not make the passage from letter to spirit, then he is bound by an idolatry of surfaces, enacting a false worship, mistaking the image for the imageless, and the figure for what is beyond figuration.[115] The way beyond the world is through the world, and the way beyond language is

---

113. See Perl, *Theophany*, 104–5.
114. *Amb.* 10.32 (DOML 1:197–99).
115. Intro. 1.2.16.

through language. If one fails to make the passage, he remains a stranger to the Word and outside the mystery of salvation in the Church, a mystery ordained by the Holy Trinity from all eternity.

IX. The Interpretation of Scripture

An integrative and innovative thinker, Maximos the Confessor's interpretation of Scripture is in many ways the summation of the entire patristic exegetical tradition.[116] While the Confessor's hermeneutical principles are closely tied to the work of Alexandrian writers, especially Philo and Origen, they were substantially modified by his reading of the Cappadocians and Dionysios the Areopagite. The monastic and contemplative exegesis exemplified by Evagrios of Pontus (and Gregory of Nyssa) was another important influence. To be sure, whatever Maximos received from the Origenist tradition was recontextualized within a radically revised cosmology (partly expressed through the language of late Neoplatonism) and a highly developed Christology, neither of which was available to a third-century writer like Origen. What Maximos nonetheless shares with all his predecessors is a dynamic vision of the Word's presence and activity in Scripture.

The Intention of Scripture

In agreement with virtually all ancient Christian exegetes, Maximos understands the language of Scripture as a divine accommodation to human limitations.[117] The purpose of this accommodation is to communicate God's providential concern for his fallen creatures and to provide them with the remedy

---

116. For outstanding studies of Maximos's biblical hermeneutics, see Blowers, *Exegesis and Spiritual Pedagogy;* and Kattan, *Verleiblichung und Synergie.* My remarks in this section are not meant to be exhaustive, but simply to gesture toward some of the major hermeneutical themes of the *Responses.*

117. Qu. 44.2: "Scripture fashions God speaking in terms relative to the underlying disposition of the souls under His providence"; cf. Qu. 62.2: "God presented to the prophet's sight, as it were, an object enabling him to understand the power of His imminent manifestation in the flesh."

for their existential dilemma. This claim was supported by the witness of Scripture itself,[118] not least in 2 Timothy 3.16–17: "All Scripture is inspired and useful for teaching, rebuking, correcting, and training in righteousness, so that the man of God may be complete, equipped for every good work," implying that the aim of Scripture is to inculcate virtue in its readers and guide them in their progress toward salvation.[119] For Maximos, the principal dilemma afflicting humanity is the problem of the passions, a pathology he finds diagnosed and remedied throughout the whole of Scripture, and he interprets the sacred text accordingly.

That the meaning of Scripture as a whole can be reduced to a particular intention or purpose might seem to limit the range of interpretive possibilities available to the reader or exegete. Surprisingly, this is not the case, and Maximos affirms that the sacred text is inexhaustible in its capacity to generate meaning. It is a "boundless ocean," the depths of whose "hidden mysteries" can be fathomed only with the help of the Holy Spirit.[120] As the Confessor explains: "The divine word can never be circumscribed by a single individual interpretation, nor does it suffer confinement in a single meaning, on account of its natural infinity."[121] Returning to this theme later in the *Re-*

---

118. E.g., Rom 15.4; and 1 Cor 10.11, which state that Scripture is not merely a record of past events but directly addresses the concerns of contemporary readers; cf. Qu. 52.12 and 54.13.

119. Cf. Origen, *On First Principles* 3.2–3, where Scripture's inspired aim is the correction of evil (SC 268:152–69); ibid., 4.2.8, where God is said to have two aims in inspiring Scripture: to reveal the mysteries of salvation and to conceal them from the unworthy (SC 268:332–34); Basil, *On the Psalms,* states that the whole of Scripture was written by the Spirit so that each person might, as in a "public hospital, find the remedy for his own particular passion, which Scripture can completely cure" (PG 29:209C); idem, *Ep.* 2: "Scripture is like a public hospital, where one will find the cure for his sickness" (LCL 1:15); and Gregory of Nyssa, *On the Lord's Prayer:* "Of the true saints, inspired by the Holy Spirit, whose sayings have been recorded by divine dispensation for the instruction of later generations, their words aim solely at the correction of the evil that holds sway over human nature ... for our struggle is 'against the spirits of wickedness in high places' (Eph 6.12)" (*GNO* 3/4:15, lines 6–10, 27–29).

120. Intro. 1.2.3; cf. Qu. 55.2.

121. Intro. 1.2.8.

sponses, Maximos notes that the natural infinity of Scripture is an attribute the sacred text shares with God: "The God who spoke through Scripture is unlimited according to nature … and we should believe that the word spoken by God resembles God Himself. For if God is the one who spoke, and if God is by nature unlimited, it is obvious that the word spoken by Him is also unlimited."[122]

The Limits of Meaning

The infinity of the sacred text, however, should not be taken in the postmodern sense of an endless deferral of meaning or radical absence of meaning, since Maximos would not consider as admissible any interpretation that would, for example, contradict the teachings of the Church or the salvific purpose of Scripture. As noted above, biblical interpretation unfolds within a framework of ethical, doctrinal, and ecclesial commitments, which are constraints on any potential infinity of interpretation.[123] One must therefore understand this as a potential infinity of *viable* interpretations.[124] This infinity of meaning, moreover, is not directionless, but has a decided eschatological orientation. In its diachronic dimension, the relation of the Old Testament to the New Testament is not a closed, binary opposition of "prophecy and fulfillment" or "figure and reality." Instead, Maximos argues for an open-ended, threefold pattern of "shadow, image, and reality," based on Hebrews 10.1: "The law possessed but a shadow of the good things to come; it was not the image of the realities themselves." In Maximos's understanding of this verse, the "shadow" of the Old Testament

---

122. Qu. 50.2.

123. This is why Maximos always stresses that interpretations of Scripture have to be "consistent with piety," or "worthy of God," or "not unworthy of the Spirit"; cf. Intro. 1.7.5; Questions 17.5; 54.13; 55.1; 63.4; 65.21; see also *Amb.* 14.2; 21.14; 67.15. That the biblical exegete must tailor his exegesis to the spiritual capacities of his audience (Qu. 43.2), and must not commit the "deeper secrets" of Scripture to writing (Qu. 21.8), are additional limiting factors.

124. In his actual exegesis, Maximos in some cases provides up to eight or ten interpretations of a particular phrase or passage, all of them within the bounds of orthodox doctrine.

is cast backwards in time by the "image" of the New Testament, which in turn points forward to a future reality that has not yet been fully revealed. The incarnate Word, in his historical manifestation, is himself the living embodiment and model of this dynamic structure, being a "symbol, figure, and forerunner" both of himself and of his future manifestation in glory.[125]

Because the whole of Scripture expresses the divine plan for human salvation, "every syllable, even the most trifling" is filled with meaning.[126] This meaning, however, is not limited to the significance of the historical events described in Scripture, because Scripture as a whole embodies the living voice of the Word of God and thus is always contemporary: its unity, significance, and impact emerge directly in the life and experience of the reader. To the extent that the letter crosses over into spirit, the words of Scripture function as thresholds between two worlds: the bounded, finite realm of history, and the unlimited freedom of the spirit: "Even though the word of holy Scripture is limited according to the letter—because it is delimited chronologically according to the times of the events that were written down—it nevertheless always remains unlimited according to the spirit through the contemplation of spiritual realities."[127] The literal or historical sense does not vanish, but remains the irreducible medium or means for conducting the mind from the contingency of sensible appearances to a more abiding truth: "Strictly speaking, the force of the literal sense continues to exist. For that which in the literal account took place in the past is always standing before us being mystically present in contemplation."[128]

---

125. In the sense that, by assuming human nature, the Word becomes, like all human beings, an "image" of God, but by virtue of his divine nature he is the archetype of that image, and so becomes an image and symbol of himself; cf. *Amb.* 21.13–16 (DOML 1:439–47); *Amb.* 10.77 (DOML 1:269); *Cap. theol.* 1.97; 2.29 (PG 91:1121D–1124A; 1137D); and Maximos Constas, "A Greater and More Hidden Word: Maximos the Confessor and the Nature of Language," in *Maximus the Confessor as a European Philosopher*, ed. Sotiris Mitralexis et al. (Eugene, OR: Cascade, 2017), 95–109, esp. 102–7.

126. Qu. 47.3.

127. Qu. 50.2.

128. Qu. 49.4; cf. Qu. 50.3: "Having examined the things that took place

Words become Flesh

Maximos further argues that the meaning contained in the literal account, which is "always standing before us," is not something static, but rather is augmented by its reception and internalization by the reader: "Let us leave aside the written account of what has already occurred corporeally in Moses's time, and consider, with the eyes of the intellect, its spiritual power, which is constantly occurring and becoming ever greater by its very occurrence."[129] Elsewhere, Maximos notes that the participation of the faithful in liturgical worship has the same effect: "Every sacred feast becomes—in us and through us—more sublime than itself, because through our faithful celebration the mystery signified through the feast acquires its proper power to lead us to perfection ... always attaining greater sublimity among us, and thus surpassing itself."[130]

The actualization of Scripture's spiritual power in the lives of believers is nothing less than the mimetic possibility to as-

---

figuratively during the times of Hezekiah, which reached their historical end, and having contemplated spiritually the matters issuing from the written record of the events, we must surely marvel at the wisdom of the Holy Spirit who wrote them, and how He arranged the meaning of whatever was written so that it would accord and fit with each and every one of us who share in human nature." See also Origen, *Homilies on Luke* 7.7: "Everything with respect to Jesus: His birth, growth, maturity, passion, and resurrection, took place not only at a given time (*non solum illo tempore*), but continues to act in us even today (*sed etiam nunc operentur in nobis*)" (SC 87:160); and Evagrios, *Scholia on Psalms*: "The text does not say, 'He *turned* (μεταστρέψας) the sea into dry land' but that 'He *turns* (μεταστρέφων) the sea into dry land' [Ps 65.6], for according to history, this happened once (ἅπαξ) in Judea, but on the level of the mind (κατὰ τὴν διάνοιαν) this event is always taking place (ἀεὶ τοῦτο συμβαίνει), inasmuch as God, by means of virtue and knowledge, rescues lost and troubled souls from the bitter waves of life" (PG 12:1500B).

129. Qu. 17.2.
130. *Amb.* 63.2 (DOML 2:271–73); cf. Rom 6.4, and Col 2.12, where through baptism believers are put to death, buried, and raised from the dead in solidarity with Christ. On the intersection of biblical and liturgical interpretation, see René Bornert, "Explication de la liturgie et interprétation de l'Écriture chez Maxime le Confesseur," SP 10 (1970): 323–27; idem, *Les Commentaires byzantins de la divine liturgie* (Paris: Institut Français d'Études Byzantines, 1966), 83–124; and below, n. 148.

similate the virtues and spiritual qualities of biblical saints, and ultimately those of Christ himself. If figures such as Abraham, Melchizedek, Moses, David, and Hezekiah were themselves embodiments of divine virtues, then the possibility exists that the faithful reader can also become "another Abraham" or "another Moses," not by imitating the external features of their lives, but by imitating their virtues, which is participation in the very attributes of God himself.[131] By imitating the imitators of Christ (cf. 1 Cor 11.1), the faithful extend the body of the incarnate Word through time and into the present moment toward its completion, "for the Word of God wills always and in all things to bring about the mystery of His embodiment."[132] Far from being limited to the events of the past, the narratives of Scripture contain and hold forth the possibility of divine and transformative grace far beyond their original context, as the sacred drama of biblical history continues to unfold in endless variations on the stage of human existence.[133]

Aporia: The Benefits of Obstacles

If it is true that every word of sacred Scripture is "divinely inspired" (2 Tm 3.16), and that its every "syllable" is able to yield a

---

131. The idea was already implicit in the words of Christ: "If you are Abraham's children, do the deeds of Abraham!" (Jn 8.39); cf. Questions 23.2 (Abraham); 65.15 (David); 50.3; 51.20 (Hezekiah); 47, scholion 2 (Enosh); *Amb.* 10.46; 10.50; 10.112 (Abraham); *Amb.* 10.46–47 (Melchizedek); *Amb.* 10.46; 10.51; 10.53 (Moses); and *Amb.* 21.14: "All the saints can stand in the place of each other: all can stand in place of all, and each in place of each ... and the Lord Himself demonstrates this when he calls John the Baptist 'Elijah,' either because the two were equal in the habit of virtue, in their purity of intellect, in the austerity of their way of life, or because of their identical power of grace" (DOML 1:441); ibid. 21.15: "... and so they become living images of Christ, or rather become one with Him through grace, or even, perhaps, become the Lord Himself, if such an idea is not too onerous for some to bear" (ibid., 445).

132. *Amb.* 7.22 (DOML 1:107).

133. Intro. 1.2.7: "This is because the divine word is like water, for just as water operates in different species of plants and vegetation in different kinds of living things—by which I mean in human beings who drink the Word Himself—the Word is manifested in them through the virtues, in proportion to their level of knowledge and ascetic practice ... so that the Word becomes known to others through other qualities and characteristics."

INTRODUCTION   43

sense useful for salvation, it is not equally true that every word and syllable can be comprehended by the common modalities of sense perception and understanding. This is because the object of the sacred text, its deeper meaning, is not an "object" at all, but God, who is universally present in Scripture just as he is in creation. And just as one can be ignorant of the providential workings of God in creation—or blinded to them because of the passions—one can be equally ignorant of the deeper meaning of difficult and obscure passages in Scripture.[134]

Such passages, which contain seemingly irreconcilable contradictions, or verbal and conceptual material that is illogical or offensive, were believed to have been placed throughout Scripture by the Holy Spirit as a form of divine pedagogy.[135] The purpose of these passages, which interrupt the continuity of the narrative, is to confront the reader with an unresolvable paradox and so spur the mind to the spiritual level on which such passages have their proper resolution and meaning.[136] Biblical obscurities, notable for their *failure* to signify, are in fact sites of hidden meaning accessible only through the transformation of

134. Origen, *On First Principles* 4.1.7 (SC 268:284–92), was among the first to make this comparison, in a passage that was excerpted in the Cappadocian *Philokalia* (SC 302:60–64).

135. Argued by Origen, *On First Principles* 4.2.9 (SC 268:334–40), in a passage that was excerpted and placed at the very beginning of the Cappadocian *Philokalia* (SC 302:182). For Dionysios, *CH* 2 (9–17; 136D–145C), following the hermeneutics of Proclus, incongruities in the sacred text were construed as non-mimetic symbols of transcendent realities that were related to their referents, not by resemblance or direct representation, but only by analogy; cf. Radek Chlup, *Proclus: An Introduction* (Cambridge: Cambridge University Press, 2012), 188–93.

136. Cf. Qu. 48.11: "I am astonished and amazed at how Uzziah, though he was king of Judah, according to the literal account, had 'vine-dressers on Mount Carmel,' which did not belong to the kingdom of Judah ... apparently the text has mixed into the literal account something that has no existence (τὸ μηδαμῶς ὑπάρχον), thereby rousing our sluggish minds to an investigation of the truth"; Qu. 65.19: "Here, as it seems, something illogical (τὸ παράλογον) has been mixed in with the literal account in order for us to search for the true meaning of what has been written"; and Qu. 54.20: "According to the literal account, Zerubbabel nowhere appears to hold in his hand a stone having 'seven eyes' ... thus, since it is completely impossible to sustain (ἀμήχανον στῆναι) such an interpretation on the level of the literal words, let us proceed to the inner meaning of what has been written."

both the text and the reader that takes place in spiritual contemplation.[137] Like a detour made necessary by an insurmountable obstacle, difficult passages in Scripture mark the point of entry to the mysterious path of ascent, since they are the site of irruption into the world by something beyond the world.

These "obstacles" are called ἄπορα, a word that appears in the work's title, where it is rendered as "difficulties."[138] The Greek word, which is the source of the English word "aporia," literally means something that prevents one's progress, and by extension designates a metaphorical place that is "impassable" by thought and thus causes perplexity. Coupled with the desire to understand, such "places" were the point of departure for philosophy in the Aristotelian tradition.[139] The human person has a natural capacity not simply to know but to be puzzled and perplexed. The mind is not content simply observing phenomena, but by nature wants to know why they occur and what they mean. When this natural desire is frustrated, it troubles the mind and propels it toward exploration, investigation,

---

137. Cf. Qu. 32.3, where Maximos describes this process as requiring a series of interrelated distinctions the exegete must make between the letter and spirit in Scripture; between outward manifestation and inner *logos* in nature; and between sensation and intellect in his own awareness.

138. Origen, *On First Principles* 4.2.9, refers to obstacles in the text of Scripture variously as "stumbling blocks, hindrances, and impossibilities" (σκάνδαλα, προσκόμματα, ἀδύνατα) (SC 268:336, line 267).

139. Aristotle, *Metaphysics* III 1 995a27–b4. For Aristotle, an *aporia* is a particular state of mind in which one does not simply "wonder" at the sight of an unknown thing (as in Plato, *Theaetetus* 155d; but cf. *Metaphysics* 982b), but in response formulates questions based on actual states of knowledge. Aristotle calls this process διαπορία or διαπόρησις—an exploration of various routes—which is reminiscent of Maximos's διάβασις, both of which are ordered to εὐπορία, which is the proper resolution of the difficulty. Aristotle's own philosophical obscurity ironically proved perplexing to his later commentators; cf. Ammonios, *Commentary on Aristotle's Categories*: "Let us ask why Aristotle was so fond of obscure (ἀσαφή) teaching. We reply that it is just as in the temples, when curtains are used to prevent people, especially the impure, from encountering things of which they are unworthy. So too Aristotle uses the obscurity of philosophy as a veil, so that the zealous may for that very reason stretch their minds even more, whereas empty minds that are lost through carelessness will be put to flight when they encounter obscure sentences like these" (*CAG* 4/4:7, lines 10–14).

and the formulation of conjectures and explanations. It is only by working through such obstacles that knowledge and insight can grow.[140] This is exactly the challenge Maximos faced in responding to the questions of Thalassios. In the sixty-five biblical passages sent to him by his friend, exegetical challenges rise up like sheer cliff faces, and we have ample opportunity to observe the Confessor's ingenious efforts to scale them, along with the breathtaking vistas obtained from the heights. As sense perception deepens into spiritual contemplation, vision is flooded with clarifying light, and the mind is opened to the Word's presence in the natural and written law, being guided in an upward metamorphosis to places beyond the mind, passing into the "innermost place of divine silence in a manner beyond cognition," and "suffering union with God Himself."[141]

Anagogy: The Upward Path

Climbing the upward path, however, is not easy. When understood in its relation to the life of virtue and knowledge, and as an initiatory ascent to the very reality of God, the work of transforming the "letter into spirit" is the highest calling—and supreme challenge—of human existence. It is the "earth" that Adam must "eat in the sweat of his face," painfully removing all its "thorns and thistles" before he can partake of the "bread of theology."[142] One thus understands Maximos's repeated refusals to undertake such a task as more than a rhetorical modesty topos.[143] Yet because no text can capture or reproduce the experience of life, our sources cannot fully convey the physical, psychological, and spiritual experiences—the exertions of the ascetic life, the agony of repentance, the experience of grace, the joy of reconciliation with God and neighbor—that inform the exegetical practices operative in Maximos's interpretation

140. Cf. Qu. 59; and 55.2.
141. Intro. 1.2.6, 9.
142. Qu. 5.3.
143. Intro. 1.2.4; cf. Alexander Alexakis, "The Modesty Topos and John of Damascus as a Not-So-Modest Author," *Byzantinische Zeitschrift* 97 (2004): 521–30.

of Scripture, and which his interpretations express.[144] What follows, then, is an overview of the principles and practices that give outward form to the experience of biblical contemplation in the *Responses*.

To resolve the difficulties in the biblical passages submitted to him by Thalassios, Maximos employed a traditional exegetical practice known as "anagogy" or "anagogical exegesis."[145] The word itself (ἀναγωγή) denotes a "lifting" or "leading upwards," which for Maximos signifies both a lifting up of spiritual meaning from the letter, and the mind's ascent from material attachments to intelligible realities.[146] In this way, the anagogical process is closely interwoven with *diabasis*, which is the mind's passage through the material symbols of creation and Scripture. Both express the dynamic condition of humanity in motion from its beginning to the culmination of its quest for complete assimilation to God.

Anagogy was already a technical term for Origen, who was the first to apply it systematically to the interpretation of Scripture.[147] Maximos's anagogical exegesis, however, is more directly indebted to Dionysios, who developed the notion extensively and extended it to include the interpretation of liturgical symbols.[148] For Dionysios, anagogy is the upward movement from

144. In Qu. 56.7, Maximos mentions the following ascetic practices: "... temperance, fasting, the distribution of wealth, hospitality, chanting, reading, sleeping on the ground, keeping vigil," which he says are "among the things characteristic of a life lived according to God."

145. Cf. Intro. 1.2.3; and *QD*. 44; and 77 (CCSG 10:37–38; 58). For detailed discussions of Maximos's anagogical exegesis, see Blowers, *Exegesis and Spiritual Pedagogy*, 184–248; and Kattan, *Verleiblichung und Synergie*, 225–43.

146. Cf. *QD*. 122: "Moses is a type of the pious and their final goal ... for he receives the impression (ἐκτύπωσιν) of the divine commandments ... and because Egypt is the lowest lying land on the earth, Scripture says that he is not only 'led out' (ἐξήγαγεν) but also 'led up' (ἀνήγαγεν), indicating both a leading out (ἐξαγωγήν) from passionate attachments of the flesh to the spirit, and a leading up (ἀναγωγήν) from material to intelligible realities" (CCSG 10:90).

147. Cf. Blowers, *Exegesis and Spiritual Pedagogy*, 185; Wolfgang Bienert, *Allegoria und Anagoge bei Didymos dem Blinden von Alexandria*, PTS 13 (Berlin and New York: Walter de Gruyter, 1972); and Richard A. Layton, *Didymus the Blind and his Circle in Late-Antique Alexandria: Virtue and Narrative in Biblical Scholarship* (Urbana and Chicago: University of Illinois Press, 2004).

148. Paul Rorem, *Biblical and Liturgical Symbols Within the Pseudo-Dionysian*

effects to their causes, a movement from multiplicity to unity, in the way that one might move, for example, from the biblical image of an angel to angelic simplicity. The symbols of Scripture, as we have seen, have an inherently uplifting function, partly through the power of their outward forms to engage the mind, and partly because the motive force of the divine is operative within them.[149] Moreover, it is precisely the act of interpretation—the perception of the spirit in the letter—that constitutes the epistemological aspect of the anagogical ascent, the "theological negation" that raised up the disciples to the glory of Christ at the Transfiguration.

For Maximos, anagogy is thus a comprehensive term or process, under which other exegetical techniques and practices—such as typology, tropology, and allegory—are effectively subsumed.[150] This is partly why he does not make sharp distinctions between typology, tropology, and allegory, which are simply tools to draw out the nonliteral meanings of a word or passage in the larger anagogical process.[151] The goal of the process, on the other hand, is "contemplation" (θεωρία), which is spiritual insight of the highest order, transcending "every mental image arising from sense perception, and able to behold the principles of sensible realities naked of their outward forms, grasping the figures of intelligible realities."[152]

Synthesis (Toronto: Pontifical Institute of Medieval Studies, 1984), 99–116 (= "The Anagogical Movement").

149. Ibid., 102–3.

150. Blowers, *Exegesis and Spiritual Pedagogy*, 191.

151. Recent scholarship has demonstrated that rigid distinctions between typology and allegory do not accurately represent the practice of early Christian exegetes, and that the distinction itself is largely a modern scholarly construction that can no longer be maintained; cf. Peter W. Martens, "Revisiting the Allegory/Typology Distinction: The Case of Origen," *JECS* 16 (2008): 283–317.

152. Qu. 27.4; cf. Qu. 25.6: "Every intellect that becomes a lover of mystical theology ... without eyes sees the true God the Word naked of every concept and knowledge."

The Literal Sense

Though often a functional equivalent for allegory, anagogy does not suppress or negate the literal level of the text, but completes the literal by finding within it a higher ideal or level of meaning. Whereas letter and spirit—analogous to sense and intellect—are in tension because of the fallen and disordered state of the human mind, it would be a mistake to see this tension as expressing an ontological or metaphysical dualism. Maximos understands letter and spirit as the expressions of two distinct but intertwined realities that are wholly present and interior to each other. For those with "eyes to see," the entire spiritual world is "mystically imprinted" in the sensible world, while the entire sensible world "subsists cognitively" in the intelligible world through the activity of the mind.[153] The two worlds are related in a dynamic continuity, the one being an intensification of the other on a unified spectrum of experience and consciousness.[154] As a tree extending from the earth and reaching into the sky is supported and nourished by roots sunk deeply in the earth, so too the intensifying of consciousness through spiritual ascent is unintelligible without its literal and historical foundations.

The world of Scripture is densely populated with characters who provide the reader with colorful examples of the struggle for virtue and knowledge. The men and women described in these narratives are accepted as real people, and the narratives

---

153. Cf. *Myst.* 2: "The whole intelligible world is mystically imprinted (τυπούμενος) in the whole sensible world in symbolic forms (for those who are capable of seeing this); and the whole sensible world subsists cognitively within the whole intelligible world by means of its inner principles. In the intelligible world it is in principles, in the sensible world it is in figures (τύποι), and their activity and function is one, like 'a wheel within a wheel' [Ezek 1.16]" (CCSG 69:16–17, lines 241–47); and Qu. 27.4, where "through the invisible world," God reveals to Peter "the visible world conceived on the level of its inner principles—or the invisible world made visible by means of its sensible figurations."

154. Cf. Plotinus, *Ennead* 6.7.7, 30–31: "Sensations here [i.e., in the sensible realm] are dim intellections; intellections there [i.e., in the intelligible realm] are vivid sensations" (LCL 7:108).

INTRODUCTION   49

as real, historical events.¹⁵⁵ History is not reduced to myth or otherwise rejected, but it is simply a point of expansion, since the meaning of the historical narratives is always in excess of what can be grasped from the letter alone. The *Chapters on Love* provides a striking example of how historical and spiritual realities are located on a single continuum: "The human intellect is a holy place and temple of God, in which the demons, having desolated the soul by means of impassioned thoughts, set up the idol of sin (cf. Mt 24.15). That these things have already happened in history no one, I think, who has read Josephus will doubt, though some say that these things will also come to pass when the Antichrist comes."¹⁵⁶ In this passage, a particular event from the historical past serves to express the present experience of the human soul, and at the same time generates a warning about the future, all within a single moment of contemplation. History makes particular statements, but anagogy expresses what is universal in the particular, the aspect of it that is "always occurring." The symbolic "temple" of God is not confined to history, but extends over past, present, and future. Thus any interpretation of history that is reductively literal is essentially an indifference to God's sacred presence in history, a flight from the potentially unbearable radiance of that presence, and a way of canceling and finally denying that presence altogether.

The Mystery of Christ

It follows, then, that the purpose of the entire interpretive project is oriented toward, and finds its unity in, what Maximos calls the "mystery of Christ," a phrase that denotes the Incarnation of the Word in all its many dimensions.¹⁵⁷ It is the real-

---

155. Maximos only rarely claims that the literal narrative contains elements that are historically impossible or irrational; cf. above, n. 136.
156. *Carit.* 2.31 (ed. Ceresa-Gastaldo, 106), referring to Josephus, *Jewish War* 6.4.3–5; and 5.1.3.
157. On the "mystery of Christ," see *Amb.* 2.2; 4.10; 5.5; 5.11; 5.16; 5.24–25; 7.22; 7.30; 7.35; 7.37–39; 21.14–15; 41.2; 42.17; 42.29; 71.2–3; Questions 22.3; 22.5; 50.4; 54.15; 55.13; 59.6; 60.2–4; 60.7; 62.3–4; 63.18–19; *Cap. theol.* 2.23 (PG 90:1136A); *Cap.* 12–13 (PG 90:1184BD); *Epp.* 13; 15; 16; 17; 19 (PG 91:528D–529B; 572B; 577B; 581AB; 593B); and Kattan, *Verleiblichung und Synergie*, 170–77.

ity of Christ, and not any exegetical technique or model, that governs all of Maximos's exegesis, which is simply a method for contemplating the presence of the Word in Scripture and creation: "The mystery of the Word's embodiment contains all the power of the riddles and figures of Scripture, as well as the true understanding of both visible and intelligible realities."[158] Biblical interpretation is an attempt to explore the hidden facets of this mystery. It aims to discover the larger meanings of narratives, symbols, and their organic interconnection, engaging cosmology, anthropology, salvation history, ethics, and ecclesiology in light of the mystery of the incarnate Word.[159] All the various interpretations put forward in the *Responses* are ultimately expressions of the mystery of Christ and of the recapitulation of all creation in his person.

This freedom of approach allows Maximos to make use of a wide range of interpretive techniques and strategies, including typology, allegory, tropology, and etymology, in which latter the Confessor finds particular value: "Anyone who wishes to receive, with knowledge according to Christ, the holy Scripture within his soul, must labor diligently over the interpretation of names, which by themselves are able to elucidate the whole meaning of what has been written."[160] Consistent with this assessment, the *Responses to Thalassios* analyzes over fifty personal and geographic names, some of which receive elaborate etymological interpretations. Though many of these etymologies have been adopted from the commentaries of Philo and Origen, others are of unknown origin, and may have originated with Maximos himself, although he may have acquired them through contact with Jewish scholars, or from Jewish converts to Christianity.[161]

---

158. *Cap. theol.* 1.66 (PG 91:1108A). This process is also necessary given the dual character of the human person; cf. Qu. 55, scholion 2; and *Myst.* 6, where "anagogical contemplation" differentiates Scripture into "body" and "soul" (CCSG 69:31–32).

159. Blowers, *Exegesis and Spiritual Pedagogy*, 191.

160. Qu. 50.3.

161. Cf. Antoon Schoors, "Biblical Onomastics in Maximus Confessor's *Quaestiones ad Thalassium*," in *Philohistôr: Miscellanea in Honorem Caroli Laga Septuagenarii*, ed. Antoon Schoors and Peter Van Deun (Leuven: Peeters, 1994),

Etymology attains the level of a complex discourse in the *Responses*, since any particular name can generate more than one meaning, "because the names of each of the things signified in Scripture, according to the possibilities inherent in the Hebrew language, in fact have multiple meanings."[162] In Maximos's discussion of the name of Jonah, for example, the prophet's name is said to have four typological senses (for example, Adam, Christ, and so forth), expressed in eight different meanings, unfolding within five different narrative moments or contexts (for example, in Joppa, in Nineveh, and so forth).[163] The result is an exegetical *tour de force* in which multiple story lines are played out simultaneously on various historical and spiritual levels integrating history, anthropology, spirituality, Christology, and ecclesiology.[164]

For Maximos the Confessor, the natural and written laws are parallel symbolic orders for conducting the mind from sensible appearances to intelligible realities, that is, to the Word Himself, who is the origin and goal of rational creatures. The true interpreter, then, is someone who mediates between the sensible and the intelligible, between surface and depth—between the "letter" and the "spirit" broadly understood—in an ongoing process of uncovering and unfolding the symbolic structure of the Word's presence in creation and Scripture.

257–72; Blowers, *Exegesis and Spiritual Pedagogy*, 203–11; R. P. C. Hanson, "Interpretations of Hebrew Names in Origen," *VC* 9 (1955): 103–23; and Lester L. Grabbe, *Etymology in Early Jewish Interpretation: The Hebrew Names in Philo* (Atlanta: Scholar's Press, 1988).

162. Qu. 64.2; cf. Qu. 54.2.
163. Qu. 64.2–4.
164. This passage has received a fair amount of commentary; cf. Carl Laga, "Maximi Confessoris ad Thalassium Quaestio 64: Essai de lecture," in *After Chalcedon: Studies in Theology and Church History Offered to Professor Albert van Roey for his Seventieth Birthday*, Orientalia Lovaniensia Analecta 18, ed. Carl Laga et al. (Leuven: Departement Oriëntalistiek, 1985), 203–15; Blowers, *Exegesis and Spiritual Pedagogy*, 205–11; and idem, "Exegesis of Scripture," in *The Oxford Handbook of Maximus the Confessor*, 259–61.

X. The Scholia

After completing the *Responses to Thalassios*, Maximos reviewed the entire work and subsequently published a "second edition," for which he wrote a new Prologue and added a series of annotations, known as scholia.[165] As Maximos explains in the Prologue, he considered the scholia to be an integral part of the work, and expressly urged his readers and copyists not to neglect them, but to utilize them and reproduce them in any copies made of the *Responses*, respecting their proper position on the page in relation to the main text:

> I considered it necessary to include in this present work some additional support in the form of the written scholia that appear in the margins. They complete the beauty of the work. They make the conceptual nourishment offered to its readers all the more delectable, and in general serve to clarify the meaning of the argument. For after the publication of this work, I had the opportunity to read through the whole of it, and found certain places that were in need of clarification, along with other places that seemed to require further reflection, as well as still others that stood in need of a brief supplementary note or comment, which this present edition has enabled me to include. Thus it was, as I said, that I wrote these scholia, inserting each one in its proper place.
>
> I therefore ask all readers of this book, as well as those who may wish to copy it, to read the scholia and copy them in their proper place as indicated by the special marks that I have given them, so that the work will be complete in every way, being in no way truncated by any negligence.[166]

Altogether, the *Responses to Thalassios* contains about 465 scholia.[167] The majority of the initial responses have only a

---

165. On these scholia, see CCSG 7:xcix–ci. The Greek word "scholion" (σχόλιον) is the diminutive of σχολή, and means a brief explanation or concise annotation; cf. Eleanor Dickey, *Ancient Greek Scholarship* (Oxford: Oxford University Press, 2007), 11–16, 18–71. I am thankful to Eleanor Dickey for her generosity in discussing this material with me, and for her invaluable suggestions.

166. *Responses*, Prologue 1.1.4–5. The word *scholion* itself does not imply anything about the *mise en page* or *mise en texte*, which is why Maximos was obliged to give precise instructions regarding their placement. The format of this present volume does not allow for the scholia to appear in this manner, and instead they are printed at the end of each Response.

167. John Eriugena's Latin translation (ca. 850) contains an additional 20

small number of scholia, but as the responses become progressively longer, the number of scholia increases proportionately. Thus, while Questions 1–15 collectively have a total of only ten scholia, Question 47 alone has fifteen, a number which continues to increase: Qu. 48 has eighteen scholia; Qu. 49 has twenty-one scholia; Qu. 54 has twenty-eight scholia; and so on through Qu. 65, which has forty-seven scholia. Some of the scholia are quite lengthy—Qu. 65, scholion 32, for example, is thirty-nine lines long—and thus the amount of material in question is considerable.

Several other works attributed to Maximos also have scholia appended to them, but these do not appear to be authentic, and in most cases are of only minor interest.[168] This circumstance underlines the singular importance of the scholia added to the *Responses to Thalassios*, in terms of both their large number and the accompanying explanatory Prologue. It is worth emphasizing that scholia appended to Greek patristic texts are relatively rare and limited to major authors, such as Basil of Caesarea, Gregory Nazianzus, Dionysios the Areopagite, or to certain texts like the *Ladder of Divine Ascent* by John Klimakos.[169] It is even more unusual to find a writer annotating his

---

scholia that are not found in the Greek text, many of which were written by Eriugena himself. There are, moreover, four Greek scholia that are not found in Eriugena. Photios, *Bibliotheca* cod. 192(A) (ed. Henry, 3:74–81), a Byzantine intellectual who read and commented on the *Responses* at a moment contemporary with Eriugena, seems to have had access only to the "first edition," without the Prologue or scholia, neither of which he mentions; cf. Jacques Schamp, "Maxime le Confesseur et Photios: À propos d'une édition récente des *Questions à Thalassius*," *Revue belge de philosophie et d'histoire* 60 (1982): 173–76.

168. The *Commentary on the Lord's Prayer* has 8 scholia (PG 90:909AD); the *Chapters on Love* has 50 "anonymous" (ἀνεπιγράφου) scholia (PG 90:1073B–1080D); the second *Century on Theology and the Incarnate Dispensation* has 12 scholia, again by an "anonymous" scholiast (PG 90:1173–76), which, if they were all written by the same hand, are no earlier than the 8th century, since scholion 3 says: "These words are opposed to the Iconoclasts" (PG 90:1173B); the various *Opuscula* and Letters have a total of 15 and 19 scholia, respectively, which may be found at the end of these works in PG 91:37B–576C.

169. On the scholia to Basil's *Long Rules*, see Silva, *Asketikon*, 4–8; for those on the *Orations* of Gregory Nazianzus, see CPG 3011–31; for the *corpus Dionysiacum*, see Paul Rorem and John Lamoreaux, *John of Skythopolis and the Dionysian Corpus: Annotating the Areopagite* (Oxford: Clarendon Press, 1998). The

own work. To my knowledge, there are no examples of this in Greek antiquity, and only one among Greek patristic writers, namely, Anastasios of Sinai, who in this regard may have been influenced by Maximos the Confessor.[170]

Scholars in general tend to ignore the scholia, neglect to translate them when translating select *Responses*, and without argument typically question or simply reject their authenticity.[171] Yet it is well known that Maximos wrote a series of scholia for the *corpus Dionysiacum*, and thus there are no grounds for rejecting summarily the possibility that he likewise composed scholia for the *Responses to Thalassios*. In addition, the Prologue to the "second edition" is found in all the extant manuscripts, which would tend to confirm its authenticity. Moreover, the scholia were an integral part of the *Responses* already by the mid-ninth century, and as such were available in the Greek manuscript containing the *Responses* translated into Latin by John Eriugena. This manuscript was undoubtedly an early uncial, and likely reached the Carolingian court from North Africa via Rome or Southern Italy, indicating, again, that the scholia had become part of the work at a very early stage.[172]

---

text of the *Ladder* has never been critically edited, and the mass of scholia remains largely unknown, although many are available in PG 88:632–1248; cf. Nonna Papademetriou, *Ἡ θεορρήμων Κλίμαξ τῶν βυζαντινῶν* (Athens: Melissa, 2014), 198–240, who provides a detailed survey of Byzantine scholiasts and anonymous scholia through the 10th century.

170. Anastasios of Sinai, *Hodegos*, contains 60 scholia written by the author, ranging in length from a single line to an entire page (cf. CCSG 8, pp. ccxvi–ccxviii). Many are introduced by the formula σημειωτέον or ἰστέον (which Maximos uses only in his scholia on Dionysios). Like Maximos, Anastasios understands his scholia to be an integral part of the work (CCSG 8:76, lines 1–8); cf. Fausto Montana, "Anything but a Marginal Question: On the Meaning of παρακείμενον σχόλιον and παραγράφεσθαι," *Trends in Classics* 6 (2013): 24–38, esp. 29–30; and Karl-Heinz Uthemann, "Anastasios Sinaites," in *La théologie byzantine*, 557–59.

171. Some scholars reject the scholia on the basis of the mistaken belief that *all* of them were written during the later Byzantine period, but this is to confuse the scholia with various marginalia that were later added to the work; on which, see CCSG 22:327–45; and Jacques Noret, "Une allusion à Léon de Chalcédoine et non à un Ps.-saint Cédonius. Datation de scholies de l'Angelicus Gr. 120," *Analecta Bollandiana* 108 (1990): 320–23.

172. On this question, see Maïeul Cappuyns, "Jean Scot Erigène et les

INTRODUCTION   55

There are, then, compelling reasons to accept in principle the authenticity of the Prologue and the scholia. At the same time, it is clear that not all of the scholia were written by Maximos, for the simple reason that many of them are written in the third person, using phrases such as: "Here he says," or "Here he means," or "Here, when he says God, he means the Word of God," and so on. Scholia containing these formulaic phrases[173] are hardly likely to have been written by Maximos, since no scholiast in antiquity ever refers to himself in the third person. Moreover, these are the same third-person phrases that Maximos used when referring to Dionysios in his scholia on the *corpus Dionysiacum*.[174] In addition, the *Responses* contain scholia using first-person formulae, such as "I say," which, when not manifestly the voice of a later scholiast, should be accepted as a genuine scholion by Maximos, along with instances of "they say," which in some cases may also be genuine, since Maximos often uses this phrase to refer, for example, to secular authors.[175]

The fourth scholion of Qu. 59 is a good case in point. It does not include the third-person formula "he says" or any such equivalent, and contains two of Maximos's signature doctrines: the triad of "being, well-being, and eternal well-being," and the notion of divinized saints as being "without beginning or end."[176] Yet, precisely because these are signature items, it would not have been difficult for a scholiast to reproduce them. Turning, however, to the scholion's linguistic features, we find support for the scholion's authenticity in the use of the slightly

---

Scholiae de saint Maxime le Confesseur: Introduction, texte critique et traduction," *Byzantion* 24 (1964): 415–45; and Maximos Constas, "St. Maximus the Confessor: The Reception of his Thought in East and West," in *Knowing the Purpose of Creation through the Resurrection*, ed. Maxim Vasilievič (Belgrade and Alhambra: Sebastian Press, 2013), 27–34, esp. 30, n. 15.

173. I.e., φησί, λέγει, καλεῖ, ἐθεώρησεν, ἀνήγαγε, ἀποφαίνεται, etc.

174. See, for example, Beate R. Suchla, ed., *Corpus Dionysiacum IV/1: Ioannis Scythopolitani Prologus et scholia in Dionysii Areopagite librum de Divinis Nominibus* (Berlin: De Gruyter, 2011), 177, line 13 (apparatus).

175. E.g., *Amb.* 10.101 (DOML 1:315).

176. For the triad, see *Amb.* 10.12 (DOML 1:167); and *Amb.* 10.48, where divinization endows Melchizedek with the quality of being "without beginning or end" (DOML 1:225).

rare word γλιχόμενος, which appears as γλίχεται in a similar context in *Amb.* 32.6; and again as γλιχόμενοι in *Amb.* 48.2, also in a similar context. Taken together, the theological content and language argue strongly for Maximian authorship, and at the same time for the authenticity of the Prologue to the second edition. Many other such examples could be brought forward.

The identity of the scholiast(s) responsible for the other annotations remains an open question. It seems clear, however, that the highly learned character of many of these scholia, uttered in impeccable Maximian diction, attests to, or at least strongly suggests, a school of disciples devoted both to the writings of the Confessor and to questions of Christian philosophy more generally.[177] The elaborate series of scholia appended to Qu. 55, for example, many of which use the third-person formulae, discusses at length the nature of the monad, motion, knowledge, divinization, the nature of substrates and accidents, potency and actuality, and the symbolism and qualities of letters, numbers, and their various mathematical combinations.

Finally, it is worth noting that, in the history of the work's reception, the scholia were understood as a direct and integral part of the work. For example, the Maximian anthology known as the *Diverse Chapters*, compiled in the middle Byzantine period, is a collection of five hundred excerpts, more than four hundred of which are taken from the *Responses to Thalassios*. Many of these excerpts are simply isolated scholia presented as an individual "chapter." The *Diverse Chapters* were included in the *Philokalia* and insured for both the *Responses* and the scholia a popular reception they might not have otherwise enjoyed.[178] One should also note the importance of scholion 14 of

---

177. Including Maximos's disciple Anastasios, who may have been the compiler of the Christological florilegium known as the *Doctrina patrum*, which is closely tied to the works of Maximos; cf. Joseph Stiglmayr, "Der Verfasser der *Doctrina Patrum de Incarnatione Verbi*," *Byzantinische Zeitschrift* 18 (1919): 14–40; and Rudolf Riedinger, "Griechische Konzilakten auf dem Wege ins lateinische Mittelalter," *Annuarium Historiae Conciliorum* 9 (1977): 253–301, at p. 257, n. 14.

178. The text is available in the Φιλοκαλία 2:91–186; and PG 90:1177–1392. For a concordance of the *Diverse Chapters* with the *Responses*, see CCSG 7, pp. lxxvi–lxxxii; Disidier (cited below), 167–78; and *Philokalia*, vol. 2 (London: Faber & Faber, 1981), 391–95. See also Wilhelm Soppa, "Die *Diversa Capita*

INTRODUCTION 57

Qu. 61 in the late Byzantine Hesychast controversy. In the body of the text, at Qu. 61.12, Maximos had spoken of "divinization without origin" (ἀγένητος θέωσις), which can also be translated as "ingenerate divinization," in the sense of "uncreated divinization." The phrase prompted the scholion, which, in light of the criteria presented above, was not written by the Confessor. The scholion speaks of an "enhypostatic illumination of the divinity," and Hesychast theologians cited both the passage and the scholion, typically taking the two as forming a single, unified statement.[179] The reception of the scholia in the later tradition indicates that they were understood as integral parts of the work, just as the Confessor had intended, and their value in clarifying the overall argument of the *Responses* should not be minimized.

XI. A Note on the Text and Translation

In addition to consulting a number of manuscripts, my translation is based primarily on the critical edition of the Greek text published by Carl Laga and Carlos Steel in *Corpus Christianorum, series graeca*, vols. 7 and 22, which appeared in 1980 and 1990, respectively. The critical apparatus reveals a surprisingly small number of (mostly insignificant) variant readings, which indicates a remarkably stable manuscript tradition. Like the *Ambigua to John*, the *Responses to Thalassios* was translated into Latin in the ninth century by John Eriugena—an Irish scholar resident in the Carolingian court—and the Laga-Steel edition helpfully includes a critical edition of the Latin translation printed in a

---

unter den Schriften des heiligen Maximus Confessor in deutscher Bearbeitung und quellenkritischer Beleuchtung" (diss., Breslau-Dresden, 1922), who was the first modern scholar to discover the connection between the two works; and M.-Th. Disidier, "Une oeuvre douteuse de saint Maxime le Confesseur," *Échos d'Orient* 30 (1931): 160–78. While Soppa (pp. 129–31) argued that the compiler of the *Capita* was Antonios Melissa, Peter van Deun, "Les *Diversa Capita* de Pseudo-Maxime et la chaîne de Nicétas d'Héraclée sur l'évangile de Matthieu," *Jahrbuch der Österreichischen Byzantinistik* 45 (1995): 24, has more recently made a persuasive case that the compiler was Niketas of Heracleia.

179. See below, Qu. 61.12, and the note at schol. 14.

facing-page format with the Greek.[180] In general, and with only a very small number of exceptions, I have followed the paragraph divisions of the Greek text established by Laga and Steel.

Having had no compelling reasons to alter them, I have adhered to the principles of translation outlined in my introduction to the *Ambigua*, which interested readers may consult.[181] In the only significant departure from that translation, the word ἐπιστήμη, which in the *Ambigua* was rendered as "science," is in the present translation rendered as "true understanding" (and in a small number of instances, determined by context, as "consummate skill," "expert knowledge," or "specialized knowledge"). Maximos himself often qualifies the word as "*spiritual* understanding" or "*contemplative* understanding."[182]

The word αἴσθησις presents particular problems for the translator. The Greek terminology of perception is often ambiguous and can mean a "capacity for perception," the "activity of perception," and a "sensory organ of perception." These usages are further complicated by the common confusion in English between "sensation" and "sense perception." When Maximos emphasizes the irrational aspect of αἴσθησις, I generally render this as "sensation," whereas sensation that is informed by reason and/or subject to the judgment of intellect is generally rendered as "sense perception."[183] The word ἀρχή is difficult to trans-

---

180. Thanks to the vagaries of history, Eriugena's translation (ca. 862–864), based on a now lost Greek manuscript, is the oldest surviving witness to the text of the *Responses:* the oldest surviving Greek manuscripts containing the *Responses* are from the 11th century. Eriugena was, moreover, an extremely literal translator, and his work is of the highest importance for establishing the text of the *Responses;* see above, n. 167.

181. Constas, *Maximos the Confessor, On Difficulties in the Church Fathers,* DOML 1:xxiv–xxvi.

182. Qu. 55, schol. 30 (which may have been written by Maximos), identifies ἐπιστήμη with *infallible* knowledge: "... it remains for the perfected intellect to receive the infallible knowledge (ἄπταιστον γνῶσιν) of ages and intelligibles, that is, true understanding (ἤγουν ἐπιστήμην) of these things, for true understanding is defined as infallible knowledge of the substrate."

183. Maximos's distinction between *aisthetos* and *aisthetikos* is paralleled in Meletios, *On the Nature of Man,* where the *aistheton* is the perceptible object (i.e., that which is subject to sense perception), whereas the *aisthetikos* is the perceiver (i.e., the perceiving subject), illustrated by the difference between

late consistently: "beginning," "origin," and "principle" are the three primary meanings it can have, depending on the context. In this translation, however, "principle" serves as the primary translation of (lower-case) λόγος, and "origin" as the primary translation of γένεσις (that is, "coming into being," "coming to be," "generation," or "creation"). I therefore adopt the word "beginning" but alert the reader in a note when another rendering has been adopted. I do not render the word γνωστικός as "gnostic." An argument has been made, noted at the word's initial appearance in the translation, that for Maximos the word "gnostic" signifies a person who knows and can explicate the mysteries of Scripture, although in other contexts it indicates a person who can discern the inner principles of creation.[184] The word ἕξις has various shades of meaning, among which are "habit," "state" (or "state of mind"), "condition," and "disposition," despite the latter being the standard translation of διάθεσις.[185] The noun κακία, which occurs frequently in the *Responses*, means both "evil" and "vice," the latter especially when paired with "virtue" (ἀρετή). I translate (upper- case) Λόγος as "Word," even though this does not do justice to the Greek. Renderings such as "principle" (for lower-case λόγος) may be more accurate but tend to displace the root meaning. The technical term πρακτική does not mean "practice" (or "activity") in contrast to "contemplation," but denotes the stage of "practical life" in the Evagrian stages of spiritual progress.[186] The present translation generally renders this word as "ascetic practice." Another difficult word is σχέσις, normally translated as "relation," which I adopt, along with "condition" and "attachment" (based on its root sense of

the stone (*aistheton*) and St. Stephen (*aisthetikos*), who was struck by it (PG 64:1144D–1145B).

184. See the note below, at Intro. 1.2.6.

185. See John of Scythopolis, scholion on Dionysios *CH* 7.1 (205B; 27, line 13): "A habit is an abiding quality" (ἕξις δέ ἐστι ποιότης ἔμμονος) (PG 4:65C); and the multiple definitions in Franz Diekamp, ed., *Doctrina patrum de incarnatione Verbi: Ein Griechisches Florilegium aus der Wende des Siebenten und Achten Jahrhunderts* (Münster in Westfalen: Aschendorff, 1907), 258–59; cf. above, n. 177.

186. See Robert E. Sinkewicz, *Evagrius of Pontus: The Greek Ascetic Corpus* (Oxford: Oxford University Press, 2003), xxiv; cf. Constas, "Nothing is Greater than Divine Love," for a discussion of Maximos's modification of the Evagrian practical life.

having, holding, and possessing), depending on the context.[187] Maximos's use of the word φύσις ("nature") in many contexts, not all of which are obvious, means "*human* nature," although I have been reserved in adding the qualifying adjective.[188] Throughout the translation, I have added footnotes providing the original Greek word whenever my English rendering of that word is unconventional or might lead to confusion.

Passages from the Old Testament are cited from the Septuagint version, following the chapter and verse divisions established in *A New English Translation of the Septuagint*.[189] The Psalm numbering is that of the Septuagint. The names of Old Testament persons and places are adopted from the Revised Standard Version of the Hebrew Bible. Thus: "Eliakim the son of Hilkiah," not "Heliakim the son of Chelcias"; "Nebuchadnezzar," not "Nabuchodonosor"; "Carmel," not "Karmelos"; and so forth.

---

187. For alternative renderings, see Ilaria Vigorelli, "Desiderio e beatitudine: *Schesis* nell'*In Canticum Canticorum* di Gregorio di Nissa," *Annales Theologici* 28 (2014): 277–300.

188. Cf. Pascal Mueller-Jourdan, "À propos d'une définition de la nature chez Maxime le Confesseur. Ambiguïté d'un appel à l'autorité patristique," *Freiburger Zeitschrift für Philosophie und Theologie* 54 (2007): 224–29; and Andreas Lammer, "Defining Nature: From Aristotle to Philoponus to Avicenna," in *Aristotle and the Arabic Tradition*, ed. Ahmed Alwishah and Josh Hayes (Cambridge: Cambridge University Press, 2015), 121–42.

189. Albert Pietersma and Benjamin G. Wright, eds., *A New English Translation of the Septuagint* (Oxford: Oxford University Press, 2007).

ON DIFFICULTIES IN SACRED SCRIPTURE: THE RESPONSES TO THALASSIOS

CONTENTS

Contents of the First Book of Difficulties
in Sacred Scripture[1]

1. Prologue Concerning the Scholia in the Margins

2. Introduction Addressed to the One who Commissioned This Work

Question 1. On grief, pleasure, desire, and fear

Question 2. On the words, "My Father is still working" (Jn 5.17)

Question 3. On the man in the Gospels carrying a jar of water (Lk 22.7–13)

Question 4. On the words, "One should not have two tunics" (Mt 10.10)

Question 5. On the "earth that was cursed in the works of Adam" (Gn 3.17)

---

1. Eriugena's translation of this heading does not include mention of a "first book" (CCSG 7:2) and consequently does not include the second heading, below, concerning a "second book" (cf. CCSG 7:6), indicating that he had a single codex containing the entire work. Later Greek scribes copied the work as a single item, often in a large codex containing other works by Maximos, but retained the headings regarding the original division of the *Responses* into two books; cf. Jacques Schamp, "Maxime le Confesseur et Photios: À propos d'une édition récente des *Questions à Thalassius*," *Revue belge de philologie et d'histoire* 60 (1982): 163–76, esp. 173–76.

Question 6. On the words, "He who is born of God does not sin" (1 Jn 3.9)

Question 7. On the words, "This is why the Gospel was preached even to the dead" (1 Pt 4.6)

Question 8. On the words, "God is light" (1 Jn 1.5)

Question 9. On the words, "Brethren, now we are the children of God, but what we shall be has not yet been made manifest" (1 Jn 3.2)

Question 10. On the words, "He who fears has not been perfected in love" (1 Jn 4.18)

Question 11. On what is the "principle that was not kept by the angels" (Jude 6)

Question 12. On what is the "tunic soiled by the flesh" (Jude 23)

Question 13. On the words, "Ever since the creation of the world, the invisible things of God have been clearly visible in the things made" (Rom 1.20)

Question 14. On the words, "They worshiped and served creation instead of the Creator" (Rom 1.25)

Question 15. On the words, "Your incorruptible Spirit is present in all things" (Wis 12.1)

Question 16. On the molten calf in the wilderness (Ex 32.4)

Question 17. On the angel sent to kill Moses on the road to Egypt (Ex 19.26)

Question 18. On the words, "It is the doers of the law who will be justified" (Rom 2.13)

Question 19. On the words, "All who have sinned without the law will also perish without the law" (Rom 2.12)

Question 20. On the withered fig tree in the Gospel (Mt 21.18–21)

Question 21. On the words, "He stripped off the principalities and authorities" (Col 2.15)

Question 22. On the question if God "in the coming ages will show His riches" (Eph 2.7), how is it that "the ends of the ages have come upon us" (1 Cor 10.11)?

Question 23. On the words, "God will give him the throne of his father David" (Lk 1.32)

Question 24. On the words, "When they passed the first and second guard" (Acts 12.10)

Question 25. On the words, "The head of every man is Christ," and what follows (1 Cor 11.3–5)

Question 26. On the king of Babylon, the king of Judah, and the nations (Jer 34.1–11)

Question 27. On the revelation to Peter, which took place with respect to Cornelius (Acts 10.1–29)

Question 28. On the words, "Come, let us descend and confound their tongues" (Gn 11.7)

Question 29. On the words, "Certain men, inspired by the Spirit, told Paul not to go up to Jerusalem" (Acts 21.4)

Question 30. On the difference between the "cup" and "baptism" (Mk 10.38)

Question 31. On the words, "God does not dwell in temples made by human hands" (Acts 17.24)

Question 32. On the words, "Perhaps they might grope after and find God" (Acts 17.27)

Question 33. On the words, "Truly I say to you, whoever says to this mountain …" (Mk 11.23)

Question 34. On the words, "Therefore I say unto you, all things you ask for, when you are praying, believe that you have received them" (Mk 11.24)

Question 35. On how we are commanded to "eat the flesh of the Word and drink His blood," but "not to crush his bones" (Jn 6.53, 19.31–36)

Question 36. On what are the bodies of sacrificial animals (Dt 12.27)

Question 37. On the viper that bit St. Paul (Acts 28.3–5)

Question 38. On the question the Sadducees put to the Lord (Mt 22.23–28)

Question 39. On the three days during which the crowds remained with the Lord (Mt 15.32)

Question 40. On the six jars at the wedding in Cana (Jn 2.6)

Question 41. On the five husbands of the Samaritan woman (Jn 4.16–18)

Question 42. On how we are said to commit sin while the Lord is said to have "become sin" without knowing sin (2 Cor 5.21)

Question 43. On the Tree of Life and the Tree of Disobedience (Prv 3.18; Gn 2.9)

Question 44. On the words, "Behold, Adam has become like one of us" (Gn 3.22)

Question 45. On the "breast and the shoulder that is removed" (Lv 7.24)

Question 46. On the "mirror" and the "enigma" (1 Cor 13.12)

Question 47. On the "voice crying out in the wilderness" (Lk 3.4)

Question 48. On the cisterns and towers of Uzziah the king of Judah (2 Chr 26.4–10)

Question 49. On the words, "And Hezekiah saw that Sennacherib had come" (2 Chr 32.2–4)

Question 50. On the prayer of Hezekiah and Isaiah (2 Chr 32.20–21)

Question 51. On the words, "And many brought offerings for the Lord, and gifts to the king" (2 Chr 32.23)

Question 52. On the words, "Hezekiah did not make recompense to God according to the benefit that God gave to him" (2 Chr 32.25)

Question 53. On the words, "And they buried him on a high place among the tombs of the sons of David" (2 Chr 32.33)

Question 54. On Zerubbabel and his prayer (1 Esd 4.58–60)

Question 55. On the number of men and animals that came out of Babylon (1 Esd 5.41–42)

Contents of the Second Book

Question 56. On the arrival of the enemies of Judah and Benjamin (1 Esd 5.63–66)

Question 57. On the words, "The supplication of a righteous man accomplishes much when it is rendered effective" (Jas 5.16)

Question 58. On the words, "In this you rejoice, even though now for a little while it may be necessary for you to experience grief" (1 Pt 1.6)

Question 59. On the salvation that was "researched and investigated by the prophets" (1 Pt 1.10–11)

Question 60. On Christ, the "pure and spotless lamb" (1 Pt 1.20)

Question 61. On the words, "The time has come for judgment to begin from the house of God" (1 Pt 4.17–18)

Question 62. On the sickle that Zechariah the prophet saw (Zec 5.1–4)

Question 63. On the lampstand that the prophet Zechariah saw (Zec 4.2–3)

Question 64. On Jonah and his prophecy (Jon 4.11)

Question 65. On the offspring of Saul killed by the Gibeonites during the time of David (2 Kgs 21.1–14)

MAXIMOS THE MONK
TO THE MOST RIGHTEOUS PRESBYTER
AND ABBOT THALASSIOS
*CONCERNING VARIOUS DIFFICULTIES
IN HOLY SCRIPTURE*

Prologue[1] Concerning the Scholia in the Margins

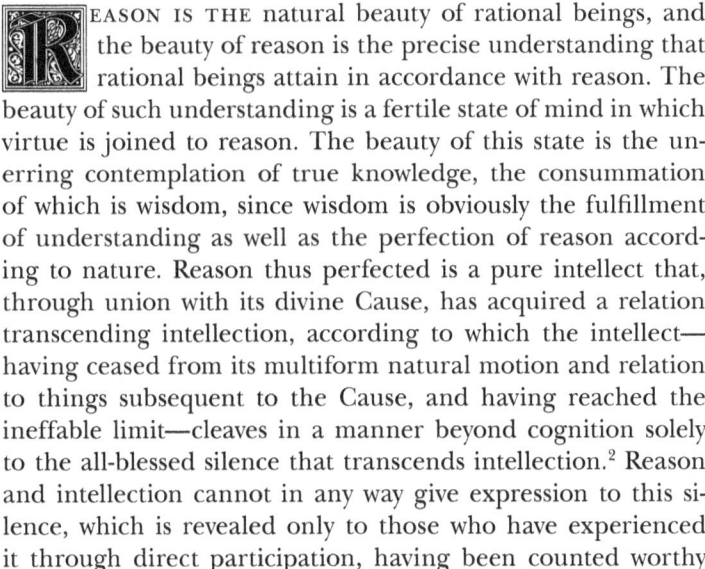EASON IS THE natural beauty of rational beings, and the beauty of reason is the precise understanding that rational beings attain in accordance with reason. The beauty of such understanding is a fertile state of mind in which virtue is joined to reason. The beauty of this state is the unerring contemplation of true knowledge, the consummation of which is wisdom, since wisdom is obviously the fulfillment of understanding as well as the perfection of reason according to nature. Reason thus perfected is a pure intellect that, through union with its divine Cause, has acquired a relation transcending intellection, according to which the intellect—having ceased from its multiform natural motion and relation to things subsequent to the Cause, and having reached the ineffable limit—cleaves in a manner beyond cognition solely to the all-blessed silence that transcends intellection.[2] Reason and intellection cannot in any way give expression to this silence, which is revealed only to those who have experienced it through direct participation, having been counted worthy

---

1. I.e., to the Second Edition; see above, p. 52.
2. Paraphrasing Dionysios the Areopagite, *DN* 1.1 (108, lines 2–5; 585B); cf. idem, *MT* 1.1 (142, line 2; 997B). For the explanation of these citations, see the note in the list of abbreviations in the front matter of the present volume.

of spiritual joy transcending all intellection.[3] The sign of this joy, which is readily discernible and distinctly clear to all, is the soul's disposition of absolute imperturbability[4] and detachment with regard to this age.

1.1.2. Knowing, then, that nothing is more proper to rational beings than reason, and that nothing is more fitting for the spiritual nobility of those who love God than the understanding and exercise of reason—and when I speak of "reason" I am not referring to a reasoned discourse,[5] fashioned through mere rhetorical artifice and cleverly concocted to please the ear through lovely speech, which even immoral men are capable of producing.[6] Rather, I am speaking of the hidden reason that nature—essentially and independently of any learning—possesses by its inner character, which it has received for the unerring examination of beings and for the true comprehension of their inner principles. Once this reason has been well formed by means of the virtues, the Holy Spirit of God naturally becomes its intimate companion, and fashions it into a divine image, according to the likeness of the Spirit's own beauty,[7] so that by grace it lacks nothing of the attributes that belong to the Divinity by nature. For reason is the instrument that with consummate skill gathers together the whole manifestation

---

3. For a parallel formulation, see *Amb.* 6.3 (DOML 1:71).

4. Literally, "insensitivity" (ἀναισθησία), for which Lampe, *PGL*, s.v., suggests "freedom from feeling" and "detachment"; cf. Evagrios, *On Prayer* 1.120: "Blessed is the intellect which during the time of prayer has acquired perfect *anaisthesia* with respect to the senses" (PG 79:1193B).

5. I.e., λόγος, which means both "reason" and "speech" (or "discourse").

6. Compare Maximos's Prologue to the *Mystagogy*: "I have remained quite ignorant of the art of discourse, which finds favor through mere eloquence, in which many people especially delight while limiting their enjoyment to the sense of hearing" (CCSG 69:5, lines 33–35); and the Prologue to the *Ambigua to John:* "[Do] not look to me for any literary refinement, since I have not that power over words to make them ring winningly in the ears of the audience" (DOML 1:67). Opposition to and suspicion of rhetoric had deep roots in the Greek philosophical tradition, and was shared by many Christian writers; see Seth Benardete, *The Rhetoric of Morality and Philosophy: Plato's Gorgias and Phaedrus* (Chicago: University of Chicago Press, 1991); and George A. Kennedy, *Classical Rhetoric and its Christian and Secular Tradition from Ancient to Modern Times* (Chapel Hill: University of North Carolina Press, 1999), 137–82.

7. Cf. Gn 1.26.

of the divine goodness, which like lightning intelligibly flashes forth in beings. Through this manifestation, reason enters into the magnificently wrought realm of beings, and bears to the generative Cause of beings (to which reason itself is borne) those who have fully transformed the whole impulse of their innate natural desire, no longer held captive by any of the things sequent to the Cause.

1.1.3. When we take care to honor reason and live according to it, we become expert tamers of all the evil passions. And when we are no longer enslaved by anything contrary to nature, we are shown forth as practitioners of all the divine virtues, stripping away, by means of all that is beautiful, the ugliness arising from the soul's attachment to matter, so that the soul appears in spiritual beauty. For where reason predominates, it naturally prevails over the domination of sensation, in which the power of sin has somehow been mixed, and which through pleasure moves the soul to pity for its kindred flesh, to which the soul is related in a union according to hypostasis.[8] It follows that the power of sin—having made the impassioned and pleasure-seeking indulgence of the flesh the soul's natural instrument—diverts the soul from a life according to nature, and induces it to become the creator of evil, which has no substantive existence.[9] For it is evil when a soul endowed with intellect, through an impassioned attachment to the flesh and the world, becomes oblivious of realities that are beautiful by nature. But this condition is removed when reason is in command and with spiritual understanding investigates the origin and nature of the world and the flesh, directing the soul to its kindred realm of intelligible realities. Into this realm the "law of sin"[10] cannot enter in any way at all, for it no longer has sensation as a kind of bridge conducting it to the intellect, for sensation's hold over

---

8. The language used here is distinctively Christological, the relation of body and soul being a traditional analogy for the union of divinity and humanity in Christ; cf. Cyril of Alexandria, *Scholia on the Incarnation* 2 (*ACO* 1.5, 220); Leontios of Byzantium, *Against Nestorios and Eutyches* 5.28 (PG 86:1289C); and Aloys Grillmeier, *Christ in Christian Tradition*, vol. 2, pt. 2, trans. Pauline Allen and John Cawte (London and Louisville: Mowbray and Westminster, 1995), 201–12.

9. Cf. below, Intro. 1.2.11.

10. Rom 7.25.

the soul has been dissolved and dispersed among the objects of sense perception; and the intellect, having passed beyond its relation to such objects and their nature, no longer so much as even perceives them.

1.1.4. Knowing this, I say, I considered it necessary to include in this present work some additional support in the form of the written scholia that appear in the margins.[11] They complete the beauty of the work. They make the conceptual nourishment offered to its readers all the more delectable, and in general serve to clarify the meaning of the argument. For after the publication of this work, I had the opportunity to read through the whole of it, and found certain places that were in need of clarification, along with other places that seemed to require further reflection, as well as still others that stood in need of a brief supplementary note or comment, which this present edition has enabled me to include. Thus it was, as I said, that I wrote these scholia, inserting each one in its proper place.

1.1.5. I therefore ask all readers of this book, as well as those who may wish to copy it, to read the scholia and copy them in their proper place as indicated by the special marks that I have given them, so that the work will be complete in every way, being in no way truncated by any negligence.

---

11. On the scholia, see the Introduction to this volume, above, pp. 52–57.

INTRODUCTION ADDRESSED TO THE ONE WHO COMMISSIONED THIS WORK

REETINGS from Maximos, the humble monk, to the most righteous servant of God, lord Thalassios, presbyter and abbot.[1]

1.2.2. Having separated your soul from its attachment to the flesh by the right use of reason, and having wholly withdrawn your intellect from sense perception through the power of the Spirit, O man of God, you made your soul a prolific mother of virtues, and rendered your intellect an ever-flowing fountain of divine knowledge. Moreover, in using the soul's bond to the flesh solely for the ordering of superior things, and in possessing sense perception as an instrument for the comprehension of the magnificence of visible realities,[2] your flesh,[[1]] through ascetic practice and proper conduct, is receiving the glory of your virtuous soul,[3] a glory given distinct form and displayed outwardly, so that we might have your life as an image of virtue put forward for imitation.[4] Your power of sense perception,[[2]] on the other hand, is symbolically inscribing the principles of intelligible realities onto the outward forms of visible realities, and through them is lifting up your intellect to the simplicity of intelligible visions, being entirely released from all that is complex and compounded in visible realities, so that we might

---

1. On Thalassios, see the Introduction to this volume, above, pp. 8–12.

2. Cf. Rom 1.19–20.

3. Cf. *Amb.* 7.26: "God will be to the soul what the soul is to the body, and through the soul He will likewise be present to the body, so that the soul will receive immutability and the body immortality" (DOML 1:113).

4. Cf. 1 Cor 11.1.

have your knowledge of the passage[5] to intelligible realities as an unerring way of truth.

1.2.3. When you had completely set aside the passionate attachment to sensation and the flesh, you thereupon, with true understanding and a vigorous intellect, took to swimming in the boundless sea of the words of the Spirit, searching out, together with the Spirit, the depths of the Spirit,[6] from whom you received the revelation of hidden mysteries, thanks, no doubt, to your great humility of mind.[7] You subsequently sent me a letter containing many difficult passages from holy Scripture, seeking even from me—though I am bereft of all virtue and knowledge—a written interpretation of each passage according to the principles of anagogical contemplation.[8]

1.2.4. When, however, I received and read your list of these passages, I was overwhelmed in mind, hearing, and thought, and subsequently implored you to permit me to decline your request, saying that the questions you had put to me were such as could scarcely be approached even by those who are greatly advanced in contemplation, and who have drawn near to the highest knowledge far beyond the reach of most men—to say nothing of myself, who slithers upon the ground like another serpent, in accordance with the ancient curse,[9] feeding only on the earth of the passions, and wriggling about like a worm in the rot of bodily pleasures.[10] I consequently renewed and indeed enlarged my request—more than once—to be released

---

5. "Passage" renders the Greek word διάβασις, which is Maximos's signature term for the mind's passage to divine realities *through* and *by means of* the forms of the material world; cf. Paul Blowers, *Exegesis and Spiritual Pedagogy in Maximus the Confessor: An Investigation of the* Quaestiones ad Thalassium (Notre Dame: University of Notre Dame Press, 1991), 95–117.

6. Cf. Jn 5.39; 1 Cor 2.10.

7. Here Maximos discloses the central theme of the entire work, namely, that the spiritual study of Scripture presupposes freedom from the passions, a virtue he sees embodied in the person of Thalassios.

8. On "anagogy" and "anagogical contemplation," see the Introduction to this volume, above, pp. 45–47; and Blowers, *Exegesis and Spiritual Pedagogy*, 184–228.

9. Cf. Gn 3.14.

10. Cf. *QThp.* (75, lines 32–33); below, Qu. 5; and *Amb.* 71.11 (DOML 1:331).

from such a task, but I saw that you were in no way disposed to accept my pleas, and I began to fear that our mutual love might be harmed, a love according to which we possess a single soul residing in two bodies.[11] I considered that my refusal to comply with your request would be taken as an act of disobedience, and thus I took the bold step—though I had no wish to do so—of undertaking to wrestle with matters far beyond my powers, deeming it better to be condemned for rashness and to become a universal object of ridicule, than to disturb or diminish in any way the love compared to which, as anyone with any intelligence knows, there is nothing more precious except God—or, better, that there exists nothing more beloved to God than this love, which gathers into unity those who are divided,[3] and which is able to create among many—indeed among all—an identity of the will's inclination, free of any contradiction.

1.2.5. Be therefore the first, honorable father, to forgive me for this undertaking, and ask the others to overlook my rashness. Above all, pray to God that He will be propitious to me and be my helper in what I have undertaken to write; or rather pray that He will provide me with the complete and correct response to each of your questions, for "every good giving and every perfect gift"[12] is from God, since He is the Fount and Father of all enlightening knowledge and all spiritual gifts granted in proportion to the worthiness of their recipients.[13] It was, then, having confidence in you, that I accepted your charge, receiving through you divine favor as the payment of my obedience.

1.2.6. In what follows, I have listed each of the passages in the order and sequence in which you arranged them, and will respond to each in turn, as briefly and concretely as is possible for me—and to the extent that God gives me the grace and power to think and express my thoughts piously—for I have no wish to burden the ears of my readers with a profusion of words, especially since I am addressing myself to individuals[14]

---

11. Following Gregory Nazianzus, *Or.* 43.20: "We seemed to have a single soul animating two bodies" (SC 384:164, lines 9–10).

12. Jas 1.17.

13. Alluding to Dionysios, *CH* 1.1 (7; 120B).

14. The shift from the singular to the plural occurs frequently in Maximos's writings. Though the work is addressed to Thalassios, Maximos under-

who truly possess knowledge[15] and accurate insight into divine things; who have passed beyond the disturbance of the passions, outstripped the hold of nature, acquired reason as a guide and a most just judge of your duties; and who, through a superior ignorance,[16] have established the intellect[4] in the innermost place of divine silence,[17] where one apprehends only the divine gladness in a manner beyond cognition—a gladness whose proper greatness[18] is taught only to those who have been made worthy to experience it. And this is the reason why your questions require me to do little more than adumbrate the wholly luminous beauty of the mystical visions hidden in the divine words, offering only cursory indications of their spiritually elevated meanings—if, that is, it is even proper for me to speak to you in this way, since you have already become, according to the word of the Lord, the "salt of the earth" and the "light of the world,"[19] thanks to your wealth of virtue and the great outpouring of your knowledge, as well as your ability to cleanse even the putrefaction of the passions of others by means of your virtues, shining the light of knowledge on ignorance, which is the blindness of the soul.

---

stands that it will be shared with other members of the monastic community and ultimately the reading public; cf. *Amb.* 5.27 (DOML 1:59, n. 23); and below, Qu. 65.2.

15. The phrase "individuals who possess knowledge" renders the Greek word γνωστικοί ("gnostics"), which according to Walther Völker, *Maximus Confessor als Meister des geistlichen Lebens* (Wiesbaden: Franz Steiner Verlag, 1965), 271–86, signifies a person who knows and can unveil the mysteries of Scripture; cf. idem, "Der Gnostiker als Deuter des geheimen Schriftsinnes," in *Gregor von Nyssa als Mystiker* (Wiesbaden: Steiner Verlag, 1955), 167–74. See below, Intro. 1.2.10; Qu. 26.9; 40.4; 54.25; 56.4; and 63.18, where γνωστικός and its cognates have this same sense, although in other contexts it indicates a person who can discern, not the inner *logoi* of Scripture, but the *logoi* of creation.

16. "Ignorance" renders the Greek word ἀνοησία, although according to Larchet (SC 529:122, n.1) the "negation of the intellect" here does not correspond to a moment of negative or apophatic theology, which consists in affirming or denying divine qualities in relation to created beings, but refers instead to the intellect's cessation from all forms of knowing and understanding, insofar as it has renounced its own proper activity altogether.

17. Cf. Dionysios, *MT* 1.1 (141–42; 997AB).
18. Cf. Eph 1.19.
19. Mt 5.13–14.

1.2.7. I beseech you, who are most holy—along with all those who, as is likely, will read what I have written—not to take what I say as a definitive spiritual interpretation of the passages in question, for I am very far from the mind and meaning of the divine words, with respect to which I need to be taught by others. If it should happen that you—on your own or with others—are able to provide a better interpretation or perchance to learn something from the following, this is for you to determine and produce a more elevated and true understanding, the fruit of which is the heart's fulfillment[20] for those who long for spiritual insight into the things that puzzle and perplex them.

1.2.8. This is because the divine word is like water,[5] for just as water operates in different species of plants and vegetation and in different kinds of living things—by which I mean in human beings who drink the Word Himself[21]—the Word is manifested in them through the virtues, in proportion to their level of knowledge and ascetic practice, like burgeoning fruit produced according to the quality of virtue and knowledge in each, so that the Word becomes known to others through other qualities and characteristics. For the divine word[22] could never be circumscribed by a single individual interpretation, nor does it suffer confinement in a single meaning, on account of its natural infinity.[23]

1.2.9. You had asked me first to say something about the passions that trouble us, namely, how many and what kinds there are. What is their origin and to what sort of end does each one

---

20. Cf. Heb 10.22; Col 2.2.
21. Cf. Jn 4.14.
22. Or "Word," according to Dumitru Stăniloae, *Filocalia. Sau culegere din scrierile Sfinților Părinții care arată cum se poate omul curăți, lumina și desăvârși*, vol. 3: *Maxim Mărturisitorul, Răspunsuri către Talasie* (Sibiu: Tipografia Arhidiecezană, 1947), 25.
23. Cf. Dionysios, *Ep.* 9.4, where Scripture is said to provide readers with both "solid" and "liquid" forms of nourishment, the latter being the "abundant outflowing which reaches out eagerly to all beings ... and which is compared to water, milk, wine, and honey, for like water it has the power to produce life, like milk to give growth, like wine to revive, and like honey to purify and preserve" (203–204; 1112B).

tend through its proper means? In what faculty of the soul or member of the body are they rooted, so that they are able invisibly to shape the intellect and influence the body, coloring, as if with a dye, the whole of the wretched soul with thoughts leading to sin? What is the meaning of each of their names, and what are their respective powers and activities? At what times and in what forms are they manifested, and how do the unclean demons use them in their cunning schemes against us?[24] What are their unseen machinations and subterfuges? How do some of them imperceptibly project themselves through others, while others persuasively beguile us by means of still others? How are they subtle and small, and vast and imposing? What makes them either slacken or increase their hostilities against us? What prompts their invasions and attacks, as well as their retreats, retrenchments, and delays—whether of shorter or longer duration? What, you asked, are the accusations they bring against the soul, as if in a courtroom? What are the verdicts they pronounce in the mind, and their seeming defeats and victories? What is the particular propensity of each, and why are they permitted to assault the soul through one or many passions, either through themselves or through others? How do they instantly usher in with themselves their own appropriate matter, by means of which they secretly mount their bitter war against us, so that we pursue things having no existence as if they were present,[6] and either act impulsively because of these material fantasies or avoid them altogether,[7] suffering[25] the former action through our love of pleasure, and the latter through our fear of pain? What is the mode of their existence

---

24. Thalassios's questions concerning the passions quickly extend to include questions concerning the reality of the demonic. Disturbances of the mind were believed to have at least two sources: an internal source consisting of one's character and habits, and an external source in the provocations of demons. The two sources overlapped, as can be seen in the equivocation of demons with the "eight principal sins (or vices)," and thus were difficult to distinguish, a psychological ambiguity compounded by the fact that both "the passions" (τὰ πάθη) and "the demons" (τὰ δαιμόνια) are neuter plural nouns, sharing the same pronoun, and thus difficult and at times impossible to differentiate in writing; cf. below, Qu. 38.3.

25. "suffering": see n. 4 on Qu. 65.2.

within us, and of the diverse and convoluted fantasies they stir up in our dreams when we are sleeping?[26] Are they confined to only one part of the soul or body, or do they pervade the whole soul and the whole body? And if, on the one hand, they are interior to us, do they use the natural passions[27] to persuade the soul to take into itself exterior realities through the intermediary of the body, deceiving the soul so that it might be completely subjected to sensation and abandon what is proper to itself? Or if, on the other hand, they are exterior to us, do they use the body's contact with external realities to configure the invisible soul according to material objects, giving it a composite shape by imposing on it the form of the matter received through the imagination? Does there exist among them an order and a sequence, wickedly contrived so that certain demons first test the soul after which others wage war on it? And which ones precede the others, and by which ones are they accompanied and followed? Or are they utterly confused and disordered, troubling the soul through random passions? Is it, moreover, apart from Providence that the soul is permitted to suffer such things by them, or does this happen according to Providence?[28] If the latter, what is the reason for which Providence abandons the soul to a particular passion? And in what manner can each of the passions we have enumerated be removed from the soul? And by means of what works or words or thoughts is the soul freed from them and able to shake off the defilement of its conscience? What specific virtue does the soul need to oppose each passion in order to triumph over it, putting the wicked demon to flight and making it completely vanish along with the movements of the passion? Having been freed from the passions, how is the soul able rightly to examine the things that are proper to it? And once the soul, through its

26. Maximos touches on the nature of dreams in *Amb.* 19.3 (DOML 1:407).

27. John of Damascus, *On the Orthodox Faith* 64.3.20, defines the "natural blameless passions" as natural conditions or processes that are not subject to voluntary control, such as hunger, thirst, growing tired, experiencing pain, etc. (ed. Boniface Kotter, *Die Schriften des Johannes von Damaskos* [Berlin and New York: De Gruyter, 1973, 162], lines 9–10); cf. below, Qu. 55.7.

28. For an extended discussion on this question, see Origen, *On First Principles* 3.2 (SC 268:184–89).

power of reason exercised according to nature, has appropriated the dispassionate relation of sensible objects to the senses,[8] through what principles or modes does it conform itself to virtue, just as it had formerly conformed itself to sin through the passions? And how will the soul fittingly bring about its beautiful conversion, using the passions—through which it had formerly committed errors—to give birth and subsistence to the virtues?[29] And how, being freed from its former impassioned attachments, will it reexamine with true understanding the principles of created beings, released from their sensible symbols by means of natural contemplation in the spirit? Moreover, having applied these principles to intelligible realities—by virtue of an intellect purified from forms of discursive thinking prompted by sensations—you asked how the soul will be able to receive simple intellections, and lay hold of simple, unqualified knowledge, which binds all things together reciprocally according to the primary, original principle of wisdom. After this, having passed beyond all beings, including the mental representations that naturally accompany them, and being entirely set free even from its own proper capacity of intellection, the soul in a manner beyond all intellection suffers union with God Himself. Through this union,[9] the soul will ineffably receive from God the knowledge of real truth, as if it were a seed, and will no longer change and turn to sin, since the devil will no longer have a way to beguile it persuasively toward evil through ignorance of that which is beautiful by nature and which beautifies everything that has the capacity to participate in it.[30]

1.2.10. Though you asked about the principles, modes, and causes of these and other such things, and charged me to submit my responses to you in writing, I ask that, your instructions notwithstanding, a discussion of these matters be deferred until God grants me, among other things, a more propitious opportunity to examine these matters and devote myself to them with greater industry—if indeed it should happen that I feel

---

29. Cf. below, Qu. 1.
30. Over the course of the *Responses,* Maximos will effectively answer these questions, treating them as they arise in the difficult passages of Scripture sent to him by Thalassios.

the intellectual capacity to be so bold as to dive into and swim across this great and deep sea. For I am not ashamed to say that I have never understood the labyrinthine wiles and devices of the unclean demons,[31] surely because the dust of matter darkens the eyes of my soul and allows me neither to see clearly the nature of created things nor, using my power of reason, to distinguish beings from things that only seem to exist[10] and which deceive irrational sensation.[32] Indeed, to inquire into such things and to speak of them is truly the work only of those who have an exceptionally contemplative and lofty mind, and who through long experience have acquired the ability to discriminate between good things and their opposites, and—what is greater than everything else, and far more precious—who have received from God the grace and power to understand correctly and express clearly all that has been grasped by the intellect. Nonetheless, so that my discourse on these matters will not remain completely lacking in support of evidence with respect to this topic, I will offer a few thoughts about the origin of the passions, just enough to point out—to those among you who are men of true knowledge—the end from the beginning, after which I will proceed to an interpretation of the aforementioned passages from holy Scripture.

[Definition of Evil][33]

1.2.11. Evil neither was, nor is, nor ever will be an existing entity having its own proper nature,[34] for the simple reason

31. Cf. Eph 6.11.
32. For a similar qualification, see *Amb.* 45.2 (DOML 2:192–193).
33. Here begins what is essentially a short treatise on evil, the fall of Adam, and the origin of the passions, which J.-P. Migne prefaced with a subtitle, "Definition of Evil (ὅρος κακίας)" (PG 90:253A), similar to the one provided by François Combefis, *Sancti Maximi Opera*, vol. 1 (Paris: Cramoisy, 1675), 9: "Another Definition of Evil" (ὅρος ἄλλος κακίας), both of which are attested in the manuscripts; cf. CCSG 7:29, apparatus; and CCSG 22:330. This section circulated independently of the *Responses*, and is found in many patristic florilegia; cf. CCSG 7, p. xi.
34. Cf. below, Qu. 55, schol. 14; and *Carit.* 3.29 (ed. Ceresa-Gastaldo, 156–58). Maximos's argument is indebted to Dionysios, *DN* 4.18–35 (162–80; 716A–736B), a passage on which he also wrote a scholion (ed. Beate Regina

that it has absolutely no substance, nature, subsistence, power, or activity of any kind whatsoever in beings. It is neither a quality, nor a quantity, nor a relation, nor place, nor time, nor position, nor activity, nor motion, nor state, nor passivity[35] that can be observed naturally in beings—indeed, it subsists in no way whatsoever in any beings according to their proper nature—for it is neither a beginning, nor a middle, nor an end. But so that I might speak as if encompassing it in a definition, evil is nothing other than a deficiency of the activity of innate natural powers with respect to their proper goal.[36]

1.2.12. Or, again, evil is the irrational movement of natural powers toward something other than their proper goal, based on an erroneous judgment. By "goal" I mean the Cause of beings, which all things naturally desire,[37] even if the evil one—by concealing his envy behind a counterfeit kindness, and by us-

---

Suchla, *Corpus Dionysiacum IV/1. Ioannis Scythopolitani Prologus et scholia in Dionysii Areopagitae librum de Divinis Nominibus cum additamentis interpretum aliorum* [Berlin and Boston: De Gruyter, 2011], 262). See also Basil, *Hexaemeron* 2.4: "Evil is not a substance but a disposition in the soul opposed to virtue" (SC 26bis:158); Gregory Nazianzus, *Or.* 40.45: "Believe that evil has neither substance nor sovereignty, nor is it without beginning, nor does it have its own subsistence, nor does it come from God. Rather, it is our work and that of the Evil One, and it was introduced by our inattention, not by that of the Creator" (SC 358:304, lines 16–20); Diadochos of Photike, *Gnostic Chapters* 3: "Evil is not in nature, nor is anyone evil by nature, for God made nothing that was evil. But when in the desire of his heart someone brings to form that which does not exist in substance, then that which he wishes begins to be" (SC 5:86); and Eric D. Perl, *Theophany: The Neoplatonic Philosophy of Dionysius the Areopagite* (Albany: State University of New York Press, 2007), 53–64.

35. With the exception of "motion," these terms correspond to Aristotle's celebrated rules for predication (Aristotle, *Categories* 1b25–2a4), which later Neoplatonist commentators transformed into a universal ontology; cf. A. C. Lloyd, "Neoplatonic Logic and Aristotelian Logic," *Phronesis* 1 (1955): 58–72; and John Dillon, "Iamblichus' *Noera Theoria* of Aristotle's *Categories*," *Syllecta Classica* 8 (1997): 65–77.

36. Evil is not the substance or hypostasis of any being or reality; rather, as Maximos will explain below, it is an erroneous (and ultimately abusive) mode of relation to reality, in which the person fails to understand his own nature and goal and consequently misapprehends the created order.

37. I.e., φυσικῶς ἐφίεται πάντα; cf. Aristotle, *Metaphysics* 1.1980a; and Jonathon Lear, *Aristotle: The Desire to Understand* (Cambridge: Cambridge University Press, 2010).

ing a ruse to persuade man to redirect his desire to something in creation instead of its Cause—has brought about ignorance of the Cause.[11]

1.2.13. The first man, consequently, being deficient in the actual movement of his natural powers toward their goal, fell sick with ignorance of his own Cause, and, following the counsel of the serpent,[38] thought that God was the very thing of which the divine commandment had forbidden him to partake.[39] Becoming thus a transgressor and falling into ignorance of God, he completely mixed the whole of his intellective power with the whole of sensation, and drew into himself the composite,[12] destructive, passion-forming knowledge of sensible things.[40] It was thus that he was "ranked among the irrational beasts and came to resemble them,"[41] in every possible way acting for, seeking after, and wishing for the very same things as they, and indeed surpassing them in their lack of reason by exchanging natural reason for something contrary to nature.[42]

1.2.14. Thus the more that man was preoccupied with knowledge of visible things solely according to the senses, the more he bound himself to the ignorance of God; and the more he tightened the bond of this ignorance, the more he attached himself to the experience of the sensual enjoyment of the material objects of knowledge in which he was indulging; and the more he took his fill of this enjoyment, the more he inflamed the passionate desire of self-love[43] that comes from it; and the

---

38. Gn 3.2–6.

39. Gn 2.16–17. In the case of Adam, the evil that is "deficiency" arose from entering into a relationship with created reality before developing the proper cognitive and moral capacity for such a relationship.

40. The fall, in addition to being a shift of human energy from a spiritual to a biological plane, also brought about the mixture and confusion of intellect and sensation (cf. below, Intro., 1.2.16; Qu. 16.2–4; Qu. 32.3; Qu. 44.5; Qu. 54.3; Qu. 55.16; Qu. 65.11), which mirrors the Christological concern for an "unconfused union" of the divine and human natures in Christ; see n. 8 on Prologue 1.1.3.

41. Ps 48.12, 20.

42. Cf. Rom 1.23–25. See below, Qu. 1.

43. Cf. 2 Tm 3.2. In *Carit.* 2.8, 2.59; 3.8, 3.57, Maximos defines self-love as "the passion of attachment to the body" and "mindless love for the body" (ed. Ceresa-Gastaldo, 92, 122; 146, 170; cf. the study by Irénée Hausherr,

more he deliberately pursued the passionate desire of self-love, the more he contrived multiple ways to sustain his pleasure, which is the offspring and goal of self-love. And because it is the nature of every evil to be destroyed together with the activities that brought it into being, he discovered by experience that every pleasure is inevitably succeeded by pain, and subsequently directed his whole effort toward pleasure, while doing all he could to avoid pain, fighting for the former with all his might and contending against the latter with all his zeal. He did this believing in something that was impossible, namely, that by such a strategy he could separate the one from the other, possessing self-love solely in conjunction with pleasure, without in any way experiencing pain. It seems that, being under the influence of the passions, he was ignorant of the fact that it is impossible for pleasure to exist without pain. For the sensation of pain has been mixed with pleasure even if this fact escapes the notice of those who experience it, due to the passionate domination of pleasure, since whatever dominates is of a nature always to be prominent, overshadowing the perception of what is next to it.[44]

1.2.15. Thus the great and innumerable mob of passions was introduced into human life and corrupted it. Thus our life became filled with much groaning—a life that honors the occasions of its own destruction and which, out of ignorance, invents and cherishes excuses for corruption. Thus the one human nature was cut up into myriad parts, and we who are of one and

---

Philautie: De la tendresse pour soi à la charité selon saint Maxime le Confesseur, OCA 137 (Rome: Pontifical Oriental Institute, 1952).

44. Maximos's dialectic of pleasure and pain has distant roots in Stoic psychology, but is more immediately related to Gregory of Nyssa, *On Virginity* 3 (GNO 8/1:258–59), although Lars Thunberg, *Microcosm and Mediator: The Theological Anthropology of Maximus the Confessor* (Chicago: Open Court, 1995), 157, argues that Maximos "puts forward the dialectic of pleasure and pain more energetically than his predecessors," and that "the word play of ἡδονή-ὀδύνη is particularly original." See also, Christoph Schönborn, "Plaisir et douleur dans l'analyse de S. Maxime, d'après les *Quaestiones ad Thalassium*," in *Maximus Confessor. Actes du Symposium sur Maxime le Confesseur, Fribourg, 2–5 septembre 1980*, ed. Felix Heinzer and Christoph Schönborn (Fribourg: Éditions Universitaires Fribourg, 1982), 273–84; and below, Qu. 61.6–7.

the same nature devour each other like wild animals.⁴⁵ Pursuing pleasure out of self-love, and for the same reason being anxious to avoid pain, we contrive the birth of untold numbers of destructive passions. For example, if through pleasure we give heed to self-love, we give birth to gluttony, pride, vainglory, grandiosity, avarice, greediness, tyranny, haughtiness, arrogance, folly, rage, conceit, pomposity, contempt, insolence, effeminate behavior, frivolous speech, profligacy, licentiousness, ostentation, distraction, stupidity, indifference, derision, excessive speech, untimely speech, and everything else that belongs to their offspring. If, on the other hand, our condition⁴⁶ of self-love is distressed by pain, then we give birth to anger, envy, hate, enmity, remembrance of past injuries, reproach, slander, oppression, sorrow, hopelessness, despair, the denial of providence, torpor, negligence, despondency, discouragement, faint-heartedness, grief out of season, weeping and wailing, dejection, lamentation, envy, jealousy, spite, and whatever else is produced by our inner disposition when it is deprived of occasions for pleasure. When, as the result of certain other factors, pleasure and pain are mixed together resulting in depravity—for this is what some call the combination of the opposite elements of vice—we give birth to hypocrisy, sarcasm, deception, dissimulation, flattery, favoritism, and all the other inventions of this mixed deceitfulness.⁴⁷ But you should know that here I cannot possibly enumerate and explain all of these things in terms of their proper forms, modes, causes, and occasions. When God grants me the strength, however, I shall take up the examination of each of these in a separate discussion.

1.2.16. Evil, then, as I said a moment ago, is ignorance of the benevolent Cause of beings. This ignorance, which blinds the human intellect and opens wide the doors of sensation, utterly

---

45. On the division and fragmentation of human nature, see *Ep.* 2 (PG 91:396D).

46. I.e., *tropos*.

47. Larchet (SC:529:138, n. 2) states that here Maximos points to three sources of the passions arising from self-love: the search for pleasure, the avoidance of pain, and the combination of these two tendencies, resulting in three categories of passions. He notes that such a theory is original to Maximos and finds no equivalent in earlier patristic literature.

estranged the human intellect from divine knowledge and filled it with the impassioned knowledge of objects of sense. Partaking unreservedly in the latter solely to indulge his sensations—and discovering through experience, after the manner of irrational beasts, that participation in sensible realities is what sustains the physical nature of the body,[48] and having by this time gone far astray from intelligible beauty and the splendor of divine perfection—man unsurprisingly mistook the visible creation for God[49] and consequently made a god out of creation, since the created order had become necessary for the sustenance and survival of his body. Thus he became enamored of his own body, which was of the same nature as the creation he deemed to be God, and with all his zeal he "worshiped creation rather than the Creator,"[50] by cherishing and pampering the body alone. For it is not possible for someone otherwise to worship creation if he does not lavish care on the body, just as one cannot worship God if he does not purify his soul by means of the virtues. It was thus with his body that man conducted his corrupting worship of creation, and it was according to the body that he became a lover of his own self, ceaselessly engendering pleasure and pain, always eating from the Tree of Disobedience, which through experience offered to his perception the knowledge of good and evil thoroughly mixed into one.[51]

1.2.17. If perhaps someone were to say that the Tree of the Knowledge of Good and Evil[52] is the visible creation, he would not fail to hit the mark of truth, for to partake of it naturally produces pleasure and pain.[53]

48. See *Amb.* 10.60 (DOML 1:247–249).
49. Cf. Rom 1.20–21.
50. Rom 1.25.
51. Gn 2.17. That love of the body is a rival form of worship resonates with Maximos's criticism of Greek and Jewish religion, both of which he sees as fixated on surface appearances and concerned solely with corporeal observances; cf. *Amb.* 10.32 (DOML 1:199). In the *Responses,* these criticisms converge in the forceful rejection of reductively literal readings of the biblical text; cf. below, Qu. 65.
52. Cf. Gn 2.17.
53. Maximos's interpretation follows Gregory of Nyssa, *On Virginity* 13 (GNO 8/1:303–304); idem, *On the Making of Man* 19, 20 (PG 44:197B; 197CD, 200B); idem, *Catechetical Oration* 8 (GNO 3/4:18, lines 11–16); idem, *Commentary on the*

1.2.18. Or again, one could say that, insofar as the visible creation contains spiritual principles[13] that nourish the intellect, and, at the same time, possesses the natural potential both to delight the senses and distort the intellect, it was called the Tree of the Knowledge of Good and Evil. That is, when spiritually contemplated it possesses the knowledge of the good, but when it is received in a corporeal manner it possesses the knowledge of evil, and to those who partake of it corporeally it becomes the teacher of passions, making them oblivious to divine realities.[54] It was perhaps for this reason that God temporarily forbade man to partake of it, rightly delaying for a while his participation in it, so that, through participation in grace, man might first know the Cause of his own being, and afterwards, by partaking of grace, add impassibility and immutability to the immortality given to him by grace. Having in this way already become God through divinization, man might have been able without fear of harm to examine with God the creations of God, and to acquire knowledge of them, not as man but as God,[55] having by grace the very same wise and informed knowledge of beings that God has, on account of the divinizing transformation of his intellect and powers of perception.[56]

Song of Songs 12 (GNO 6:348–352); and Makarios/Symeon, *Or.* 3.1 (ed. Heinz Berthold, *Makarios/Symeon Reden und Brief. Die Sammlung I des Vaticanus graecus* 694[b], vol. 1 [Berlin: Akademie-Verlag, 1973], 5–6). See also Thunberg, *Microcosm and Mediator*, 162; and Richard A. Norris, "Two Trees in the Midst of the Garden (Genesis 2:9b): Gregory of Nyssa and the Puzzle of Human Evil," in Paul Blowers, et al., eds., *In Dominico Eloquio-In Lordly Eloquence. Essays on Patristic Exegesis in Honor of Robert Louis Wilken* (Grand Rapids and Cambridge: Eerdmans, 2002), 218–41; and Dumitru Stăniloae, "The Tree of the Knowledge of Good and Evil," in idem, *The Experience of God: Orthodox Dogmatic Theology*, vol. 2, *The World: Creation and Deification*, trans. Ioan Ionita and Robert Barringer (Brookline: Holy Cross Press, 2000), 163–78.

54. Through the contemplation of the *logoi*, which refer the intellect to God, creation can be seen to "possess knowledge of the good," but when, on the other hand, through the passions, the mind attends only to creation's superficial, sensible forms, it "possesses knowledge of evil."

55. Cf. *Amb.* 10.60: "Adam, by means of sense perception, sought to make his own (as one must not) the things of God without God, and before God, and not according to God, which is in any case impossible" (DOML 1:247–49).

56. Divinization does not exclude knowledge of creation, but through God it is known dispassionately, and indeed in the very manner that God knows it,

1.2.19. Whereas this anagogical interpretation concerning the tree is suitable for everyone, it should be understood that the more mystical and superior sense is reserved for the understanding of mystics, and is honored by us through silence.[57] As for the Tree of Disobedience, I have referred to it now only in passing, wishing to show that ignorance of God made a god out of creation, the worship of which is the self-love that human beings have for their own bodies. It is with respect to this self-love that the experience of pleasure and pain is a kind of mixed knowledge, through which all the impurity of evil was introduced into human life in many different ways and in manifold forms, which no discourse could encompass, since all who share in human nature possess, according to varying degrees of quantity and quality, a vital and active affection for the visible part of that nature, by which I mean the body. Moreover, this affection forces man, as if he were a slave, to contrive all kinds of passions in his desire for pleasure and fear of pain—relative to the times and circumstances, and as his manner of life allows—with the aim of enjoying pleasure in every aspect of his life while avoiding all possible contact with pain.[58] This

---

which is to say from the perspective of the *logoi*, which are God's eternal intentions for created beings; cf. *Amb.* 7.24: "God neither knows sensory things by sensation, nor intelligible things by intellection ... but <knows them> as His own wills" (DOML 1:109).

57. Cf. *Amb.* 17.6 (DOML 1:386–87); and below, Qu. 43.2. The phrase διὰ τῆς σιωπῆς τιμωμένου, in the standard form of σιωπῇ τιμάσθω, occurs frequently among the Cappadocians, where it is linked to "honoring in silence" the divine nature which is beyond speech; cf. Gregory Nazianzus, *Or.* 28.20 (SC 250:140, line 5); idem, *Or.* 29.8: (SC 250:192, line 25); and Basil, *On the Holy Spirit* 18:44 (SC 17bis:404, line 18). In *Or.* 2.62 (SC 247:174, line 62), Gregory uses the phrase to conceal the words of the angel to Joshua (Jos 5.14–15). In the later Christological debates, the formula was extended to include the Incarnation; cf. Nicholas [Maximos] Constas, *Proclus of Constantinople and the Cult of the Virgin in Late Antiquity* (Leiden: Brill, 2003), 281. See also Brian Daley, "Apokatastasis and 'Honorable Silence' in the Eschatology of St. Maximus the Confessor," *Maximos Confessor. Actes du Symposium*, ed. Heinzer and Schönborn, 309–39.

58. The perceived good for the body is the sensation of pleasure, while its perceived opposite, pain, is taken to be evil. This reductive and distorted scale of values is sustained by the sensible world, apprehended in separation from God, without whom it becomes like a tree bearing false good and evil. The

affection for the body teaches us to undertake something that can never be accomplished or ever reach the limit it has set for itself. Insofar as the entire nature of physical bodies is corruptible and subject to dissolution, whatever a person does to keep it in a condition of stability, he succeeds only in hastening the body's corruptibility, for out of fear he does not always wish for the object of his desire, but instead, contrary to all sense and his own free will, he pursues what is not desirable through what is desirable, having become dependent on things that by nature can never be stable. He is consequently subject to change together with those things[59] that break up and scatter the disposition of his soul, which is ceaselessly tossed about like a ship on a sea of perpetual flux and change, while he himself fails to perceive his own destruction, for the simple reason that his soul is completely blind to the truth.

1.2.20. Deliverance from all these evils, and the shortest way to salvation, is the true and conscious love of God, along with the total denial of the soul's affection for the body and this world. Through this denial, we cast off the desire for pleasure and the fear of pain, and being freed from evil self-love we are raised up to knowledge of the Creator. In place of evil self-love, we receive good, intellective self-love, which is utterly separated from affection for the body, and through it we never cease to worship God, ever seeking from Him the sustenance of our soul, because true worship that is pleasing to God is the care of the soul by means of the virtues.[60]

1.2.21. Thus whoever does not desire bodily pleasure and has absolutely no fear at all of pain has become dispassionate with respect to them, and with one accord has put to death all the passions, the self-love that gives birth to pleasure and pain, and all the passions that result from them, as well as ignorance, which is their primary cause. Such a person comes to be wholly under the rule of what is naturally good and beautiful, which

---

mind can either know creation on the level of its *logoi*, or through sensation can attach itself passionately to the outward appearances of things for the purposes of sensory pleasure.

59. Cf. *Amb.* 10.6 (DOML 1:156–58).
60. Cf. Jn 4.23.

is stable, permanent, and always the same, so that he remains uninterruptedly with the good in a state of motionlessness,[61] and "with unveiled face reflects the glory of God,"[62] beholding the divine and unapproachable glory from the radiant splendor shining within himself.

1.2.22. Since reason has shown us the right and easy way,[63] which is followed by those who are being saved, let us deny, as much as we can, the pleasures and pains of this present life, and, with much supplication, let us teach those in our care to do the same, and thus we will be freed, and will free them, from every idea of the passions and from every demonic wickedness. Let our sole aspiration be divine love, and nothing will be able "to separate us from God: neither tribulation, nor distress, nor famine, nor peril, nor sword," nor anything else mentioned by the holy Apostle in that passage,[64] for through knowledge realized in action, this love will remain within us immutably, and God will grant us eternal, ineffable joy and sustenance of soul. And when we are deemed worthy of this love, we shall acquire an ignorance that preserves us from this world, no longer seeing the world with a carnal mind, as we once did, when the "face" of our senses was "uncovered,"[65] and we mistook the superficial manifestation of sensible things as "glory," when in reality it was the source of the passions.[66] Instead, with the "uncovered face"

---

61. "Motionlessness" simultaneously denotes fixity in the good and the cessation of motion on the part of the creature that has reached its end in God; cf. below, Qu. 65; and *Amb.* 7.9–14 (DOML 1:85–95).

62. 2 Cor 3.18.

63. Cf. Jn 14.6.

64. Cf. Rom 8.35.

65. Cf. 2 Cor 3.18. The "uncovered face of the senses" is the impassioned fascination with the sensible aspect of the world and its surface phenomena. This "uncovering" of sense perception is simultaneously the "covering" or "veiling" of the intellect. Conversely, the more the "face" of the senses is veiled, the more the sensory veils are lifted from creation, enabling the intellect to grasp its inner meaning and purpose.

66. This "preserving" or "saving" (σώζουσαν) ignorance is not the "knowing beyond knowing" that pertains to God, but is rather that mode of the intellect that no longer misapprehends creation through the passions, no longer being fixated on isolated sensations and surface phenomena, thereby allowing creation to become fully transparent to the divine glory; cf. *Amb.* 10.52,

of the mind, freed from every covering of sensation, we will "reflect," through our virtues and spiritual knowledge, the "glory of God,"[67] through which naturally comes about our union with God by grace, raising the intellect far beyond all ignorance and stumbling. For in the same way that, being ignorant of God, we deified creation (which we came to know through the sensory enjoyment of sustaining the body from it), so too, having received the knowledge of God that is actually accessible to thought—since it is from Him that our soul derives its sustenance to exist, to exist well, and to exist eternally[68]—let us be ignorant of every experience of all sensation.[14]

Scholia

[1] He says that the flesh, through its external conduct, is the instrument indicating the soul's disposition toward virtue, and that it has been bound to the soul for the manifestation of virtue.

[2] Sense perception, he says, conveys to the intellect the images of visible realities so that it might comprehend the inner principles in beings, because sense perception is an instrument for the intellect's passage to intelligible realities.

[3] He says that the characteristic property of love is to show that all who seek for it possess the same inclination of will.[69]

[4] When the intellect has passed beyond the substance of intelligible realities, it becomes ignorant, for it is drawing near to God who according to essence is beyond both knowledge and intellection.[70]

---

where, like Moses, the purified consciousness "will be made worthy to see and hear the ineffable and supernatural divine fire that exists, as if in a burning bush, within the essence of things" (DOML 1:233).

67. 2 Cor 3.18.

68. The triad of "being, well-being, and eternal well-being," which structures the nature of human existence and experience, is an essential feature of Maximos's thought, and receives its fullest expression in *Amb.* 65.2–3 (DOML 2:277–81).

69. To this scholion Eriugena added a concluding gloss: "... so that all who participate in it may taste of one and the same thing" (CCSG 7:42, lines 8–9).

70. To this scholion Eriugena added a concluding gloss: "Concerning this

[5] The Word of God grants different gifts in a manner consistent with the dispositions of the souls of those who receive Him.[71]

[6] It is in the mind that the demons wage their invisible wars against us, as if the material realities were actually present.

[7] Because of pleasure, he says, we love the passions, and because of pain we run from the virtues.

[8] Just as when reason, prevailing over the passions, makes the senses the instruments of virtue, so too, when the passions prevail over reason, they shape the senses to be suitable for sin.

[9] Once it is released from its natural relation to beings, the soul is united to God according to a settled habit of mind, and acquires immovable permanence with respect to the good.

[10] By "existing things" he means the substances of existing things. By things that "seem to exist" he is referring to the flux and efflux of qualities and quantities,[72] which deceive the senses and give rise to sin.[73]

[11] Since man, finding himself between God and matter, did not move toward God as the cause and goal of his existence, but instead moved toward matter, he consequently became ignorant of God, and by means of his inclination to matter, he turned his intellect to the earth.

'unknowing' the Apostle says: 'The foolishness of God is wiser than men' [1 Cor 1.25]" (CCSG 7:42, lines 12–13).

71. To this scholion Eriugena added a concluding gloss: "For just as water is poured out for the multiplication of bodies, through the hidden courses of nature, on all bodies, both those that produce and those that are produced, so the Word of God, though it is indivisible by nature, is invisibly and incomprehensibly meted out to rational creatures for the multiplication of virtues and the reasons of things" (CCSG 7:42, lines 15–20); cf. Paul Meyvaert, "Eriugena's Translation of the *Ad Thalassium* of Maximus: Preliminaries to an Edition of this Work," in *The Mind of Eriugena: Papers of a Colloquium, Dublin, 14–18 July 1970*, ed. J. J. O'Meara and L. Bieler (Dublin: Royal Irish Academy, 1973), 78–88, at 81, who cites this scholion as an example of Eriugena's shift from more literal translation to "a more fluent and literary vein," and states that the "Latinity" of the addition is a clear sign of Eriugenian scholarship.

72. On these terms, cf. *Amb.* 45.3 (DOML 2:195, n. 5).

73. To this scholion Eriugena added a concluding gloss: "For a substance is not subject to growth or diminution. Rather, its accidents, that is, quantity, quality, and other such things, are ever subject to change" (CCSG 7:44, lines 33–36).

[12] He called the sensory experience of sensible realities "composite knowledge" since by nature it generates pleasure when it comes into being, and pain when it is destroyed.

[13] The visible creation, he says, contains spiritual principles, intellective understanding, and a natural capacity for sensation. The mental representations of visible realities subsist like trees in the midst of the heart, which is understood as a figure of paradise.[74]

[14] A person becomes ignorant of the experience of the pleasure and pain that arise from sensation when, freeing his intellect from its attachment to the body, he attaches his intellect to God.

*

1.2.23. Since God deemed it good for you to command me to write down and send to you what I had noted concerning those headings I found difficult, I placed first those that seemed to me to be the more indispensable.[75]

---

74. Cf. Gn 2.8–9.
75. This paragraph—which is not found in Eriugena's Latin translation—is difficult to reconcile with Maximos's earlier promise to "list each of the passages in the order and sequence in which you [i.e., Thalassios] arranged them" (Intro, 1.2.6). Prior to the writing of the *Responses*, Maximos and Thalassios exchanged several letters (cf. Intro, 1.2.4) that have not survived, and these may have clarified how the work took shape. This paragraph suggests that Maximos may have only written responses to those questions that were of particular difficulty or interest to him, while retaining, despite the omissions, Thalassios's original ordering. Moreover, the mention of certain passages that Maximos had "noted" (or "commented on," i.e., σεσημειωμένα) may perhaps be taken to mean that not all the biblical passages under consideration were selected solely by Thalassios.

QUESTION 1

RE THE PASSIONS evil in and of themselves or only when they are used in an evil way? By passions I mean pleasure, grief, desire, fear, and what follows from them.[1]

Response

1.2. These passions, as well as the rest of them, were not originally created together with human nature; otherwise, they would constitute part of the definition of human nature. Based on what I have learned from the great Gregory of Nyssa,[2] I believe that the passions were introduced on account of the fall from perfection, emerging in the more irrational part of human nature, and it was through them that, at the very moment

---

1. Here, "pleasure" (which takes the place of "anger" in the Stoic enumeration of the four vices) translates ἡδονή, which is often rendered as "concupiscence" (ἐπιθυμία). The Greek word λύπη is translated as "grief" and not "pain," for which Maximos uses ὀδύνη, on which see above, Intro. 1.2.14; and the treatment of these passions in *Amb.* 10.108–11 (DOML 1:324–29). That the passions were evil *per se* was a traditional Stoic notion.

2. A reference to Gregory of Nyssa, *On Virginity* 12.2 (GNO 8/1:297–300); ibid., 18.25 (317); and idem, *On the Soul and the Resurrection* 3 (GNO 3/3:31–46). Thunberg, *Microcosm and Mediator*, 153–59, notes that Maximos avoids Gregory's notion of the "garments of skin," since it could suggest that a physical body was subsequently added to an originally incorporeal spiritual being (i.e., the doctrine of a "double creation"). Thunberg cites Maximos, *Amb.* 45.3, where Adam's original nakedness is understood literally, and which after the fall requires the manufacture of actual clothing (DOML 2:194–97); cf. Maximos, *Amb.* 8.2 (DOML 1:144–45), which alludes to the "girding of dead skins," and the commentary by Polycarp Sherwood, "Maximus and Origenism: ΑΡΧΗ ΚΑΙ ΤΕΛΟΣ," *Berichte zum XI. Internationalen Byzantinisten-Kongress* III.1 (Munich: C. H. Beck, 1958), 16–21.

of the transgression, the distinct and definite likeness to irrational animals appeared in man instead of the divine and blessed image.[3] For it was only fitting that, since the dignity of reason had been covered over, human nature should be justly punished with the characteristic marks of irrationality that man had intentionally taken to himself. Thus did God arrange things so that man might be brought wisely to the conscious perception of the magnificence of his reason.

1.3. Nonetheless, even the passions become good among the diligent,[4] when they wisely separate them from corporeal objects and use them to acquire the things of heaven.[5] This happens, for example, when they refashion desire into an appetitive movement of intellective yearning for divine realities; or pleasure into the untroubled joy of the intellect's active enticement to divine gifts; or fear into a concern to preserve themselves from future punishment for their failings; or grief into corrective repentance of a present evil.[6] To speak succinctly, the diligent—like

---

3. Gn 1.26. The passions are irrational impulses that permeated human life at the moment of the primal transgression. As a transfer of spiritual energy to a lower, biological plane, the passions assimilated human beings to animals, who are moved solely by instinctual impulses. In a slightly different context, Gregory of Nyssa, *Contra Eunomium* 3.2, evokes the Homeric image of Circe transforming Odysseus's men into beasts (GNO 2:77–79).

4. "Diligent" (σπουδαῖοι) is a technical term designating those who practice asceticism with the aim of acquiring virtue; cf. E. Wipscyck, "Les confréries dans la vie religieuse de l'Egypte chrétienne," in the *Proceedings of the XII International Congress of Papyrology: Ann Arbor, 13–17 August, 1968*, ed. Deborah H. Samuel (Toronto: Hakkert, 1970), 511–25.

5. That the passions could be "educated" and transformed was a doctrine initially promulgated by the Stoics, and subsequently taken up by Christian ascetic writers, who describe their proper use and transformation; cf. Basil, *Against Anger:* "The passions become good or evil for their possessor according to the use made of them" (PG 31:365CD); Evagrios, *Praktikos* 86 (SC 171:676–77); Maximos, *Carit.* 2.48 (ed. Ceresa-Gastaldo, 116–17); *Amb.* 6.3 (DOML 1:70–71); *Amb.* 10.108 (DOML 1:325); and below, Qu. 55. See also the study by Paul Blowers, "Gentiles of the Soul: Maximus the Confessor on the Substructure and Transformation of the Human Passions," *JECS* 4 (1996): 57–85.

6. Because the passions have the power to set the body in motion in terms of either attraction or repulsion, they can be harnessed for the life of virtue. The momentum they provide is a greater force than reason or rational concepts alone, and thus they are instrumental in the process of human transfor-

wise physicians, who use the venom of deadly vipers as a remedy against present or expected harm resulting from the bite[7]—will use these passions for the removal of a vice that is either present or incipient, as well as for the acquisition and safeguarding of virtue and knowledge. Thus, as I have said, these passions become good through their use by those who "take every thought captive to the obedience of Christ."[8]

1.4. If, however, Scripture should ascribe any of these passions either to God[1] or the saints, we should know that, in the case of God, this is done for our benefit, so that through the language of our own passions Scripture might reveal to us the saving and beneficent processions of providence.[9] In the case of the saints,[2] it is because, in using corporeal speech, there is no other way for them to convey the relations and dispositions of their intellect to God apart from the passions that are familiar to us.

Scholia

[1] By means of the passions associated with human nature, Scripture gives shape to the different modes of God's providence for human beings.

[2] By these names Scripture signifies the kind of relation that the saints have with God.

---

mation, propelling the person toward a final union with God, when they will no longer be needed; cf. below, Qu. 55.7.

7. On the notion of extracting useful medicines from the venom of serpents; cf. Gregory Nazianzus, *Or.* 43.11, who uses it as an image for the Christian handling of pagan literature, citing 2 Cor 10.5 (SC 384:138, lines 18–20).

8. 2 Cor 10.5. Cf. Gregory Nazianzus, *Or.* 43.64: "For certain people have not badly philosophized about this, namely, that the vices are closely rooted beside the virtues, and, in a certain sense, are next-door neighbors" (SC 384:266, lines 20–22).

9. Cf. Dionysios, *CH* 2.1 (10–11; 137C–140B).

QUESTION 2

F IN SIX DAYS the Creator fashioned all the species[1] that completely fill up the world,[2] how is the Father subsequently said to be "working"? For the Savior says: "My Father is still working, just as I am working."[3] Is He speaking of the ongoing preservation of the species that, once and for all, had been brought into being?[4]

Response

2.2. God, as He alone knew how, brought to completion the primary principles and the universal essences of the things that were brought into being. He nonetheless continues to work, not only to preserve the existence of these beings and essences, but also for the actual creation, growth, and sustenance of the individual parts that exist potentially within them.[1] At the same time, He works providentially to bring about the assimilation[5] of particulars to universals,[2] until such time as He—having united the voluntary impulse of the particulars with the naturally more general principle of rational being[6] through the move-

---

1. Or "forms" (εἴδη).
2. Cf. Gn 1.31–2.2.
3. Jn 5.17.
4. For a discussion of this question, linking Maximos's argument with the cosmology of Basil and Gregory of Nyssa, see Paul Blowers, *Drama of the Divine Economy: Creator and Creation in Early Christian Theology and Piety* (Oxford: Oxford University Press, 2012), 159–66.
5. Cf. Gn 1.26.
6. The reciprocal union of particulars and universals is a process in which the will voluntarily subordinates itself to ever higher or "more general" rational principles (*logoi*), the highest of which is the Divine Principle (*Logos*) itself, which uniformly contains all particulars. In this process of rising toward

ment of the particulars toward well-being—will unite them reciprocally to each other and to the whole universe in an identity of movement.[7] And He will do this in such a way that the particulars will not differ in inclination from the universal, but that one and the same principle will be seen in all things, admitting of no division because of the modes predicated of each.[8] In this way, the grace that divinizes all things will manifestly appear to have been realized—the grace of which God the Word, becoming man, says: "My father is still working, just as I am working."[9] That is, the Father bestows His good pleasure on the work, the Son carries it out, and the Holy Spirit essentially completes in all things the good will of the former and the work of the latter, so that the one God in Trinity might be "through all things and in all things,"[10] being wholly contemplated in proportion to each of those made worthy by grace, and wholly complete throughout the whole of them, in the same way that, in each and every member of the body, the soul exists naturally and without diminution.

Scholia

[1] It is in matter, that is, in the universal substance of beings, that particulars (which take their origin from matter) exist in potential, and it is for their creation that God is obviously still working.

---

greater accord with nature and its divine Cause, Maximos underlines the cooperation of grace (i.e., divine providence) and human freedom; cf. Balthasar, *Cosmic Liturgy*, 156–57; and Torstein Theodor Tollefsen, *The Christocentric Christology of St Maximus the Confessor* (Oxford: Oxford University Press, 2008), 97–101.

7. On universals and particulars, cf. *Amb.* 10.83; 10.101 (DOML 1:275–77; 313–15); and *Amb.* 17.4 (DOML 1:385).

8. The universe is a dynamic field in which the fixed identity of beings depends on their mutual unfolding and relation in a web of universal interdependence; cf. *Amb.* 10.36–37; 10.100 (DOML 1:205–207; 309–13); *Amb.* 41.10–11 (DOML 2:115–17). As scholion 2 makes clear, the fulfillment of God's creative design requires the cooperation of rational beings, working together in harmony with each other and the divine Cause of their existence.

9. Jn 5.17.
10. Eph 4.6.

[2] By the "assimilation of particulars to universals," he is referring to the union of all men according to a single movement of the will's inclination toward the principle of nature, a union that is the work of God through His providence, so that, just as all human beings have one nature, they might also have one voluntary inclination, and thus all shall be united to God and to each other through the Spirit.

QUESTION 3

IN THE GOSPEL, who is the man in the city carrying a jar of water (and why water?), to whom Christ sent the disciples, commanding them to find and follow him? And who is the master of the house? And why do the Evangelists keep silent regarding his name? And what is the great upper room furnished and prepared, in which the fearsome mystery of the divine supper is accomplished?[1]

Response

3.2. Not only did Scripture keep silent regarding the name of the man to whom the Savior sent the two disciples for the preparation of the Passover, but it also kept silent regarding the name of the city to which they were sent. According to my initial understanding, I take this to mean that the city signifies the sensible world, whereas the man signifies universal human nature, to which were sent—like disciples and forerunners of God the Word, preparing His mystical feast with human nature—the law of the First Testament and the law of the New Testament. Through practical philosophy, the former[2] cleanses nature from every defilement, while the latter, through initiation into the mysteries of contemplation, cognitively elevates the intellect to kindred visions of intelligible realities. This is proven by the fact that the two disciples were Peter and John,[3] for Peter is a symbol of ascetic practice, and John is a symbol of contemplation.[4]

---

1. Lk 22.7–13; cf. Mk 14.12–16.
2. I.e., the Old Testament.
3. Lk 22.8.
4. Maximos discusses the symbolism of Peter and John in *Amb.* 57 (DOML 29:252–55).

QUESTION 3

3.3. This is why it is fitting that the first man to meet them was the one carrying the jar of water,[5] for this man in himself signifies all those who, through practical philosophy, carry the grace of the Spirit on the shoulders of the virtues,[6] a grace that they preserve, as if in an earthenware jar, by means of the "mortification of the members of their body that are on the earth,"[7] and which through faith purifies them of defilement. After him there is the second man, the "master of the house,"[8] who showed the disciples the furnished upper room. In himself he is an example of all those who in contemplation have furnished the height of their pure and noble minds with cognitive thoughts and doctrines, as if the mind were an upper room, furnished in a divinely fitting manner for the reception of the Great Word.[9] The house signifies the settled state of piety, toward which the practical intellect progresses, striving after virtue. The master of the house, who dwells in it as if it were his by nature, is the intellect illumined by the divine light of mystical knowledge, which is why, together with the practical intellect,[10] it is made worthy of the supernatural presence and feast of the Word and Savior.

5. According to Lk 22.10: "And He said to them, 'As you enter the city, a man carrying an earthenware vessel of water will meet you.'"
6. Cf. *Amb.* 32.4: "Those who possess scientific knowledge of symbols say that the 'shoulder' is a token of ascetic practice" (DOML 2:59); *Exp. Ps.* 59: "They say that the shoulder is the symbol of ascetic practice" (CCSG 23:13, lines 181–82); *Cap. theol.* 1.80: "The Word commands him to raise his intellect up from the love of pleasure which dominates him, and to shoulder the body of virtues, for it is better that the higher should raise the lower up on the shoulders of ascetic practice" (PG 91:1116A); Evagrios, *Scholia on Ecclesiastes* 26: "The hands are a symbol of practical activity" (SC 397:102); idem, *Scholia on Proverbs* 203: "The practical virtues correspond to the hands" (SC 340:298); and Dionysios, *CH* 15.3: "The shoulders and elbows, as well as the hands and arms, signify the power of making, operating, and accomplishing" (352C; 54, lines 4–5).
7. Cf. Col 3.5.
8. Lk 22.11.
9. Cf. Gregory Nazianzus, *Or.* 41.12: "And this (i.e., the descent of the Holy Spirit on the day of Pentecost) took place in an upper room ... because of the ascent of those who receive the gift and their lifting up from the earth, since also certain upper chambers are covered with divine waters through which God is praised in song" (SC 358:342, lines 15–18).
10. I.e., the intellect oriented toward or engaged in ascetic practice.

3.4. Thus we are speaking of one man here but also of two, if, that is, the one who is described as carrying the jar of water is different from the one who is called the master of the house. Perhaps they are one, as I said, on account of the unity of human nature, but also two, on account of the division of this nature in terms of piety, that is, into those living the practical life and those living the contemplative life, who, once they are joined together by the Spirit, are called and made one by the Word.

3.5. If, however, someone wishes to take all that has been said and apply it to each and every particular man, he will not have gone outside the truth. From this point of view, the city is each particular soul, to which the principles of virtue and knowledge, like disciples of God the Word, are always being sent. The one who carries the jar of water signifies the way of life and thinking that patiently carries on the shoulders of self-control, without ever putting it down, the gift of faith received in baptism. The house is the condition and habit of the virtues, built up, as if from stones, from many different solid and virile manners of life and thought.[11] The upper room is the broad and spacious mind with its suitability for knowledge, adorned with divine visions of mystical and ineffable doctrines.[12] The master of the house is the intellect that has been widened[13] in light of the splendor of the virtuous house and by the sublimity, beauty, and grandeur of knowledge. It is in such an intellect that the Word wishes to indwell and to offer Himself for communion, together with his disciples—that is, with the primary spiritual notions of nature and time. For the true Passover is the pas-

---

11. Cf. 2 Cor 5.1: "For we know that if the earthly house (οἰκία) we live in is destroyed, we have a building (οἰκοδομή) from God, a house not made with hands, eternal in the heavens"; and the architectural symbolism studied by Carmel Brendon Davis, *Mysticism and Space: Space and Spirituality in the Works of Richard Rolle, the Cloud of Unknowing, and Julian of Norwich* (Washington, DC: The Catholic University of America Press, 2008). Note that some manuscripts subtitle this section as "A contemplation of the house (οἰκία)" (CCSG 7:57, line 36, apparatus).

12. For a similar interpretation of the upper room, see Origen, *Homilies on Jeremiah* 19.13.4 (SC 238:226).

13. Cf. 2 Cor 6.11.

sage of the Word to the human intellect, a passage in which the Word of God is mystically present and grants His fullness to all those who are worthy, by making them share in the good things that are proper to Him.[14]

14. See *Amb.* 50.3–4 (DOML 2:227–31), for a discussion of three different types of the Passover/Pasch.

QUESTION 4

WHY DID the Lord command His disciples not to have two tunics[1] when, according to Saint John the Evangelist, He had five, which is evident from the number of those among whom they were divided? And what are the "mantles"?[2]

Response

4.2. The Savior did not have five tunics, but one, which he wore on his body, along with another as an outer garment. The former they call a "tunic," while the latter they call a "mantle." To be sure, the great Evangelist John, through the Spirit, mystically gave the literal word of the narrative the wordless character of a contemplation, so that through it he might guide our intellect to the truth of its intelligible meaning.[3] Thus the Savior's tunic, "woven seamlessly from above"—which those who crucified Him did not tear apart, even though they were permitted to strip it off Him[4]—is the inseparable cohesion and intertwining of the virtues one with another, and which, for our part, serves as an appropriate and fitting covering for the Word; or it is the grace of the new man, "woven from above" by the Spirit according to the Word.[5] The outer garment, on the other hand, is the sensible world,[6] divided into four elements,

---

1. Mt 10.10.

2. Jn 19.23. Part of the biblical difficulty is that the Gospel of John refers to Jesus's (singular) outer mantle in the plural (τὰ ἱμάτια).

3. For an extended discussion of the symbolic character of the Gospel of John, see *Amb.* 21 (DOML 1:420–47). On the patristic exegesis of Christ's tunic "woven from above," see Constas, *Proclus of Constantinople*, 321–25.

4. Jn 19.23.

5. Cf. Lk 24.49; see also below, Qu. 12.3.

6. In Maximos's celebrated exegesis of the Transfiguration, the "garments"

QUESTION 4

which, as if it were four mantles, is allotted to those who crucify the Lord in their minds. Thus do the demons divide the visible creation, which is composed of four elements, contriving that we, being ignorant of creation's divine principles, should see the world according to sense perception and surrender to the passions. As for the tunic of virtues, even if the demons are able to remove it from us through our failure to do what is morally right, they are not able to convince us that virtue is evil.

4.3. Let us not, therefore, use the Savior's five mantles as an excuse to accumulate possessions, but rather let us know both the intention[7] of Scripture and how the Lord is crucified in us whenever we are neglectful of what is good; how He is stripped naked through our idleness in performing good works; and how it is through us that the demons divide the Lord's creation, like mantles, in the service of the passions.[8] Let us therefore become unfailing guardians of the good things that God has given us; let us rightly look upon creation with a view to His glory alone; and let us, through zeal in good works, preserve intact the tunic of the knowledge of the Word, by which I mean the virtues.

4.4. If, in addition to what has been said, you wish to understand the "tunic woven from above" as signifying the incorporeal world of intelligible essences, and the outer garment (which Scripture divides into four parts, like the four elements) as signifying corporeal nature, you will not miss the mark of truth. When we transgressed the commandment, strength was given to those[9] who frayed the body through corruption, yet they were not able to tear the soul into pieces, since it takes its subsistence from above.[10]

(ἱμάτια) of Christ are understood as a "symbol of creation itself," *Amb.* 10.29 (DOML 1:193); see the Introduction to this volume, above, pp. 32–37.

7. I.e., βούλημα.

8. Those who neglect the commandments crucify Christ within themselves, having first stripped away His tunic of virtues. For those in whom Christ is so crucified, creation is no longer seen as an integral fabric clothing the body of the *logoi*, but as disconnected and isolated fragments apprehended by sense perception in order to satisfy the passions.

9. I.e., the demons.

10. The soul is the "tunic" that cannot be divided; the body is the "mantle" that sin sunders and dissolves into its constituent four elements.

QUESTION 5

WHAT, ACCORDING to the anagogical sense, is the "earth" that is "cursed in the works" of Adam?[1] And what is the meaning of the phrase: "In pain you will eat it"?[2] And what is the meaning of the phrase that follows, namely: "It will bring forth thorns and thistles, and you will eat the grass of the field"?[3] And what is the meaning of the last part, which says: "In the sweat of your face you will eat your bread"?[4] For men do not eat earth or grass, and neither when they eat bread do they do so according to the punishment recorded in the text, that is, in the sweat of their face.

Response

5.2. The "earth" that is "cursed in the works" of Adam is the flesh of Adam, which perpetually comes into being through his works[1]—by "works" I mean the passions of the intellect, which has become earthly—and this flesh is "cursed" because it is barren of the virtues, which are the works of God. This is the "earth" that Adam eats with great pain and sorrow, deriving from it but meager pleasure. This flesh, moreover, in recompense for such corruptible pleasure, brings forth cares and concerns, like thorns, along with great temptations and trials, like so many thistles, which painfully pierce him on all sides of his mind, spirit, and desire, so that he is scarcely able to maintain its health and good condition, for it is a thing that withers

---

1. Gn 3.17.
2. Ibid.
3. Cf. Gn 3.18.
4. Gn 3.19.

like grass.⁵ And after many turns on this dreadful cycle and in the sweat of his face, that is, in the sensory toil and weariness of his endless meddling into sensible things, he "eats"—which is to say he obtains, as if it were bread—the means to sustain his present life, either through artifice or through some other contrivance for living.⁶

5.3. Or, rather, the earth of Adam is the heart, which through the fall was cursed by the loss of the good things of heaven. He "eats" this earth through practical philosophy and by means of "many afflictions"⁷ once it has been purged of the curse of the works of shame that burden the conscience. And, again, having removed from this earth the thorns concerning the generation of bodies, and uprooted by the power of reason the arid thistles of his speculations concerning the providence and judgment of bodiless realities,⁸ he will spiritually gather up, like grass, natural contemplation. Thus, in the sweat of his face, that is, through true understanding of mind, he will eat the incorruptible bread of theology, which alone truly gives life and preserves existence in incorruptibility for those who partake of it.⁹ The "earth," accordingly, which is deservedly eaten, is the purification of the heart through ascetic practice; the "grass" is the true understanding of beings according to natural contemplation; and the "bread" is true initiation into the mystery of theology.¹⁰

Scholion

[1] Here he calls the dishonorable passions¹¹ the "works of Adam," since it is God alone who works the virtues in those who are willing, using their good disposition alone as an instrument for the manifestation of the virtues.

5. Cf. 1 Pt 1.24; Is 40.7; Ps 102.15.
6. Maximos discusses Adam's original freedom from "artifice" (τέχνη) in *Amb.* 45 (DOML 2:192–201).
7. Acts 14.22.
8. On "providence and judgment," see below, Qu. 63.18.
9. Cf. Evagrios, *Gnostic Chapters* 5.35, where the contemplation of beings is described as "eating bread in the sweat of our brows" (Gn 3.19) (PO 28:190–91).
10. I.e., the three stages of spiritual ascent: purification, natural contemplation, and theology; cf. the Introduction to this volume, above, pp. 25–29.
11. Cf. Rom 1.26.

QUESTION 6

IF, ACCORDING to Saint John, "he who is born of God does not sin, because God's seed is in him, and he cannot sin,"[1] and if he who is "born of water and Spirit" is himself born of God,[2] then how are we who are born of God through baptism still able to sin?[3]

Response

6.2. The mode of our spiritual birth from God is twofold.[1] The first bestows on those born in God the entire grace of adoption, which is entirely present in potential;[4] the second ushers in this grace as entirely present in actuality, transforming voluntarily the entire free choice[5] of the one being born so that it conforms to the God who gives birth. The first possesses this grace in potential according to faith alone;[2] the second, in addition to faith, realizes on the level of knowledge the active, most divine likeness of the God who is known in the one who knows Him.[6] In those whom the first mode of birth is ob-

---

1. 1 Jn 3.9.
2. Cf. Jn 3.5–6.
3. Maximos's response is indebted to Mark the Monk, *On Baptism*, which is a series of Questions and Answers on the problem of sin after baptism (SC 445:297–397); and Diadochos of Photike, *Gnostic Chapters* 89 (SC 5:149–50); cf. Jean-Claude Larchet, "Le baptême selon Maxime le Confesseur," *Revue des sciences religieuses* 65 (1991): 51–70.
4. Cf. Rom 8.15.
5. In this response, Maximos shows a decided preference for the words "free choice" (προαίρεσις) and "voluntary intention" (γνώμη), and not "will" (θέλησις), the former terms expressing actual choices and decisions of the will, and not volition as an abstract possibility.
6. Here "knowledge" renders the Greek word ἐπίγνωσις, which in this con-

served, it happens that—because the disposition of their will has not yet been fully extracted from its passionate fixation on the flesh, and because they have not been completely imbued by the Spirit with active participation in the divine mysteries that have taken place—it happens, I say, that their inclination to sin is never very far away for the simple reason that they continue to will it. For the Spirit does not give birth to a disposition of the will without the consent of that will, but to the extent that the will is willing, He transforms and divinizes it. Whoever has shared in this divinization through experience and knowledge is incapable of reverting from what he, once and for all, truly and precisely became cognizant of in actual deed, to something else besides this, which merely pretends to be the same thing—no more than the eye, once it has seen the sun, could ever mistake it for the moon or any of the other stars in the heavens. In those, on the other hand, undergoing the second mode of birth, the Holy Spirit takes the whole of their free choice and transposes it completely from earth to heaven, and, through true knowledge realized in actual deed, refashions the intellect with the blessed beams of light of God the Father, so that it is deemed another God, experiencing, through a permanent state obtained by grace, that which God does not experience but simply *is* according to His essence. In them, their free choice clearly becomes sinless in conformity with their state of virtue and knowledge, since they are unable to negate what they have become cognizant of through actual experience. So even if we should possess the Spirit of adoption—which is a life-giving seed that bestows the likeness of the Sower upon those who are born of it—but do not offer Him a disposition of the will pure of any propensity or inclination toward something else, we will, as a result, willingly sin even after "being born through water and the Spirit."[7] But if, to the contrary, we were to prepare the disposition of our will to receive cognitively the operations of the water and the Spirit, then, through our ascetic practice, the mystical water would

---

text also means "recognition," in the sense that those born through baptism come to resemble the one who gave them birth (i.e., God) by receiving His characteristics, on which see *Amb.* 10.43 (DOML 1:215–17).

7. Jn 3.5.

cleanse our conscience, and the life-creating Spirit would actualize in us the unchanging perfection of the good through knowledge acquired in experience. What is lacking, therefore, in each of us who is still able to sin, is the unequivocal desire to surrender our whole selves, in the disposition of our will, to the Spirit.

Scholia

[1] In the first mode, we are given the grace of adoption only in potential, since the possibility to become sons of God is given generally to all the baptized, for Scripture says: "Unless a man has been born again of water and the Spirit, he does not have the potential to enter the kingdom of heaven,"[8] and: "To whoever received Him, He gave them the power to become children of God."[9] But in the second mode, through the keeping of the commandments and the knowledge of the truth, we are given the perfection of adoption itself, that is, the inability to sin brought about by divinization, which we do not yet have in the first mode. For in this mode the power to sin has not yet been removed by our free will, since all of our love has yet to be united to God by grace.[10]

[2] Faith that is inactive, he says, possesses the grace of adoption only in potential, insofar as those who possess it do not move in accordance with the commandments.

8. Ibid.
9. Jn 1.12.
10. This scholion is extant only in Eriugena's Latin translation (CCSG 7:70, lines 1–10); Steel and Laga believe it was written by Eriugena (CCSG 7:ci).

QUESTION 7

HAT IS meant by: "For this is why the Gospel was preached even to the dead, so that they might be judged according to man in the flesh, but live according to God in the spirit"?[1] How are the dead "judged in the flesh"?

Response

7.2. It is the custom of Scripture[2] to alter times, exchanging one for another, speaking of the future as past, of the past as the future, and of the present in terms of the time that both precedes and succeeds it—which is obvious to those who are experienced in the study of Scripture. Thus, some say that by "the dead," Scripture is speaking here of those men who died before the coming of Christ, such as during the time of the flood,[3] or when the tower was built,[4] or in Sodom,[5] or in Egypt,[6] and of others who, at different times and in various ways, received the manifold justice and the fearsome manifestations of the divine judgments. These men were punished not so much for their ignorance of God as for their hateful conduct to each other. It was these men, Scripture says, who were already "judged according to man in the flesh," to whom the great proclamation of salvation was preached. In other words, since they had already been duly judged for their crimes in the flesh in the form of their mutual reproaches and accusations, the Gospel was

1. 1 Pt 4.6.
2. Cf. below, Qu. 28.4.
3. Gn 7.21–23.
4. Gn 11.8.
5. Gn 19.24–26.
6. Ex 12.29, 14.27–29.

preached to them so that "they might live according to God in the spirit," that is, receiving in their souls (for they were in Hades) the message of the knowledge of God, having found faith through the Savior who descended into Hades to save the dead.[7] In order, therefore, to grasp the meaning of this passage, we understand it thus: "For this is why the Gospel was preached even to the dead, *who were* judged according to man in the flesh, *so that they might* live according to God in the spirit."[8]

7.3. Or, again, perhaps Scripture uses the word "dead" in a hidden way to refer to those who "bear in their body the dying of Jesus,"[9] those, I mean, to whom the holy Gospel was given in truth, on account of their actual works. For the Gospel teaches the rejection of carnal life and the acceptance of spiritual life to those who are always dying "according to man"—by which I mean to human life in the flesh according to this present age—but who live according to God in the Spirit alone,[10] after the example of Saint Paul and his followers, for they do not in any way live their own life but have Christ alone living in their souls.[11] This is how, for the sake of God, the "dead" in this age are "judged in the flesh," that is, by suffering many tribulations, torments, and difficulties, and by bearing with joy persecutions and innumerable forms of temptations.[12]

---

7. Cf. 1 Pt 4.6.
8. 1 Pt 4.6. The italics indicate the changes that Maximos has introduced to the tense of the biblical verbs, as explained in his interpretation of this passage.
9. 2 Cor 4.10.
10. Cf. Gal 5.25.
11. Cf. Gal 2.20. Cf. the Prologue to the *Ambigua to Thomas* (DOML 1:5).
12. This entire Response was included in the *Catena on 1 Peter,* ed. John Antony Cramer, *Catena in Epistolas Catholicas,* vol. 8 (Oxford: Oxford University Press, 1849; repr. Hildesheim: Olms, 1967), 74–76.

QUESTION 8

SINCE SAINT John again says that: "God is light,"[1] and, again, after a few lines: "If we walk in the light, as He is in the light,"[2] how is it that one and the same God is said to be both "light" and "in the light," as if He were one reality existing in another?

Response

8.2. God, who is truly light according to His essence, is present to those who "walk in Him" through the virtues, so that they too truly become light. Just as all the saints, who on account of their love for God become light by participation in that which is light by essence, so too that which is light by essence, on account of its love for man, becomes light in those who are light by participation.[3] If, therefore, through virtue and knowledge we are in God as in light, God Himself, as light, is in us who are light. For God who is light by nature is in that which is light by imitation, just as the archetype is in the image.[4] Or, rather, God the Father is light in light; that is, He is in the Son and the Holy Spirit, not that He exists as three separate lights, but He is one and the same light according to essence, which, according to its mode of existence is threefold light.[5]

1. 1 Jn 1.5.
2. 1 Jn 1.7.
3. Cf. *Amb.* 10.9 (DOML 1:162–65); and Dionysios, *DN* 4.10 (154, lines 7–22; 705C), for parallel formulations.
4. "Imitation" here does not designate mere external correspondence or superficial conformity, but is a metaphor for the ontological participation of effects in their causes.
5. On the interpenetration of multiple lights as an image of the Trinity, see Dionysios, *DN* 2.4 (127–28; 641BC); and Gregory of Nyssa, *On Virginity* 23 (GNO 8/1:338, lines 19–22). This entire Response was included in the *Catena on 1 John*, ed. John Antony Cramer, *Catena in Epistolas Catholica*, vol. 8, 121–22.

QUESTION 9

WHAT DOES Saint John mean when he says: "Brethren, now we are the children of God, but what we shall be has not yet been made manifest"?[1] Because if this is true, how can Saint Paul say: "To us, however, God has revealed <our future state> through the Spirit, for the Spirit searches everything, even the depths of God"?[2] How, then, can Saint John profess not to know "what we shall be"?

Response

9.2. The holy evangelist John is saying that he is ignorant of the *manner* of the future divinization of those who, through the virtues established by faith, became children of God, because the self-subsisting visible form[3] of the good things to come has not yet been made manifest. For "we walk by faith, not by sight."[4] And whereas Saint Paul says that it was through a revelation[5] that he grasped the divine goal concerning the good things of the future age, he does not say that he knows the *manner* of divinization in relation to the divine goal. This is why he says quite clearly, interpreting his own thought: "I press on toward the goal for the prize of the heavenly call."[6] With these words he expresses his desire to know by experience the manner of the actual fulfillment of the divine goal, which he learned

---

1. 1 Jn 3.2.
2. 1 Cor 2.10. Here I have inserted the words "our future state," consistent with Paul's argument in 1 Cor 2.9.
3. I.e., εἶδος.
4. 2 Cor 5.7. (οὐ διὰ εἴδους).
5. Cf. 2 Cor 12.1; Gal 1.12.
6. Phil 3.14.

through revelation, namely, the power that divinizes those who are worthy of it. Thus the two apostles are in accord with each other, expressing the same truth through a seemingly contradictory teaching, being moved by one and the same Spirit. The one acknowledges his ignorance of the manner of the future divinization according to grace, while the other magnanimously shares what he has learned about the goal. That this is the view of the great Apostle himself is evident from all his divine utterances, for in one place he says: "All knowledge and prophecy will pass away";[7] and elsewhere that: "I do not consider myself yet to have taken hold of it";[8] and elsewhere that: "As if in a mirror and in enigmas"[9] he sees the future, when we will enjoy the great gift, beyond understanding, of the "face-to-face" vision[10] of the things hoped for. Elsewhere he acknowledges that: "Now we know in part and we prophecy in part";[11] and elsewhere he states expressly that he desires: "To know even as I have been known,"[12] obviously because he does not yet know that which will be known. Simply put, the words of the Apostle: "When the perfect comes, the partial will pass away,"[13] seem to me to be the same as those of the Theologian, when he says: "What we shall be has not yet been made manifest."[14]

7. Cf. 1 Cor 13.8.
8. Phil 3.13.
9. 1 Cor 13.12. See below, Qu. 46.
10. 1 Cor 13.12.
11. 1 Cor 13.9.
12. 1 Cor 13.12.
13. 1 Cor 13.10.
14. 1 Jn 3.2.

QUESTION 10

IF IT IS TRUE that: "He who fears has not been perfected in love,"[1] how then can "nothing be lacking to those who fear Him"?[2] If there is nothing lacking, then it is obvious that they have been perfected. How is it, then, that the one who fears God has not been perfected?

Response

10.2. The good arrangement of holy Scripture, according to the salvific law of the Spirit, distinguishes different degrees among those who are moving from the external multiplicity of the passions toward divine unity. Thus by "those who fear God," Scripture designates those who are beginners and who stand at the outer gate of the divine court of the virtues.[3] It describes as "advancing" those who have acquired a permanent habit of mind encompassing equally the principles as well as the modes of the virtues. It designates as "perfect" those who cognitively have already attained the summit of that truth which reveals the virtues.[4] Thus "he who fears the Lord," having abandoned his former life of corrupt passions, and who out of fear has submitted his entire disposition to the divine commandments, will lack none of the good things that are appropriate to beginners, even though he has not yet acquired the habit of the virtues

---

1. 1 Jn 4.18.
2. Ps 33.9.
3. Cf. Ex 27.9–19.
4. This is another division of spiritual ascent into three stages or levels (i.e., beginners, advanced, perfect), which will subsequently be presented in two stages (active and contemplative), and finally in four (fulfillment of commandments, contemplation of nature, contemplation of the intelligible, vision of God).

or come to share in the "wisdom spoken among those who are perfect."[5] Likewise the one who is advancing will lack none of the good things that belong to his degree, even though he has not yet acquired the preeminent knowledge of divine realities possessed by the perfect.

10.2. Again, we also understand those who manfully pursue practical philosophy, but who have not yet released their souls from the fear and remembrance of the divine judgments, as "those who fear God." For they "lack nothing," according to the blessed David, when compared to those who on behalf of the truth struggle against the opposing power, even though they still lack the pure communication of mystical visions granted to the intellect of the perfect. But those who have already been made worthy of mystical initiation into contemplative theology, and who have purified their intellect of every material fantasy, so that it has become an image wholly imitating the divine beauty without any lack, should be understood as "those who love God."

10.3. Thus there is "nothing lacking" among those who fear the Lord, according to the blessed David, inasmuch as they fear Him, even if the one who fears does not have the fullness and perfection of immediate union with the Word equal to that enjoyed by those who love Him. For "each one is in his proper rank,"[6] and possesses the perfection of the "mansion"[7] appointed to him, even if one person is higher than another according to the quality or measure of his spiritual maturity.[8]

10.4. And since fear is twofold—on the one hand, according to the words: "Do not fear those who kill the body but cannot kill the soul; rather fear him who can destroy both in hell";[9] and, on the other hand: "The fear of the Lord is pure, endur-

---

5. Cf. 1 Cor 2.6.
6. 1 Cor 15.23.
7. Jn 14.2, 23.
8. Cf. 1 Cor 15.23. The Johannine word "mansion" (μονή) is the same word for the Neoplatonic state of "remaining" or "abiding" in the Good and Beautiful, referring to the way that effects "remain" in their causes; cf. *Amb.* 7.2 (DOML 1:76–77).
9. Mt 10.28.

ing unto ages of ages";[10] and: "He is great and fearsome to all those who are round about Him"[11]—we must inquire how "love casts out fear"[12] if fear "endures forever," and how, throughout infinite ages, God will remain "fearsome" to "those who are round about Him."

10.5. Or rather, because fear, as I said, is twofold—one kind being pure and the other impure—it happens that fear that is born from the expectation of punishment for offenses, and which has sin as its cause, is not pure, and does not exist forever, for when the sin is obliterated through repentance such fear will disappear. Fear that is pure, on the other hand, is always present even without remembrance of offenses committed. Such fear will never cease to exist, because it is somehow rooted essentially by God in creation and makes clear to everyone His awe-inspiring nature, which transcends all kingship and power. Thus he who does not fear God as judge but holds Him in awe because of the surpassing excellence of His infinite power will justly not lack anything; for being perfect in love, he loves God with awe and fitting reverence, and it is he who has acquired the fear that endures for ages and ages, and he will lack for absolutely nothing.[13]

10.6. It follows, then, that the prophet and the evangelist are in accord. The one says that nothing will be lacking to those who fear the Lord with pure fear,[14] while the other says that he who fears the Lord as a judge, on account of his soiled conscience, has not been perfected in love.[15] Consistent with this interpretation, perhaps God is "fearsome to all those who are round about Him"[16] insofar as he mixes fear with the love of those who love Him and who will love Him. For when love is

10. Ps 18.9.
11. Ps 88.7.
12. 1 Jn 4.18.
13. Cf. *Carit.* 1.81: "Fear is twofold. The first is generated in us by fear of punishment ... the second is linked with love and constantly produces reverence in the soul, so that it does not grow indifferent to God because of the intimate communion of its love" (ed. Ceresa-Gastaldo, 80).
14. Cf. Ps 33.10.
15. Cf. 1 Jn 4.18.
16. Ps 88.7.

separated from fear, it often turns into contempt because it no longer has fear to place a limit on the license of speech that it naturally produces.

10.7. If it seems good to you, let us try to understand what is meant by: "Those who are round about Him."[17] Whoever is encircled round about has others who are round about him, both in front and behind, and on the left and right. Since the Lord has attendants encircling Him, let us understand the ones behind Him as those who followed our Lord and God blamelessly through the commandments according to practical virtue. On His left are those who attained natural contemplation in the spirit along with the pious understanding of God's judgments—for the book of Proverbs, speaking of Wisdom, says: "On her left is wealth and glory."[18] On His right are those who received immaterial knowledge of intelligible realities free of any sensory image—"For on her right are years of life."[19] In front of Him are those who through the extreme loving warmth of their intellective desire for divine beauty have been made worthy to enjoy this beauty face to face.

10.8. If beyond this there is another greater and loftier meaning, it will be apprehended by you and the holy fathers with you.

17. Ibid.
18. Prv 3.16.
19. Ibid. The spiritual stages on the "left" and the "right" correspond roughly to Evagrios's "second" and "first" natural contemplations: the former ("natural contemplation in the spirit") requires that a sensible object be present to the mind, while the latter ("immaterial knowledge free of any sensory image") directly contemplates noetic realities without the mediation or imaginal imprinting of a sensible object; cf. below, Qu. 49, schol. 1; *Carit.* 1.94, 98–99 (ed. Ceresa-Gastaldo, 87–89); *Amb.* 45.5 (DOML 2:201); Evagrios, *Gnostic Chapters* 1.74; 2.20; 2.47; 3.61; 3.67; 4.10; 5.12; 5.57; idem, *Letter on Faith*, which distinguishes between the ἔνυλον γνῶσιν of Christ's kingdom and the ἄϋλον γνῶσιν of God the Father (LCL 1:71 = *Letters of Basil, Ep.* 8); and Thunberg, "Maximus and the Evagrian Understanding of Contemplation," in *Microcosm and Mediator,* 347–52. These two Evagrian contemplations appear only rarely in Maximos, and in general are not sharply differentiated.

QUESTION 11

HAT IS THE "PRINCIPLE"[1] that was "not kept by the angels," and what is the "dwelling place" that they "left"? What are the "everlasting chains," and what is the "gloom in which they are kept," and what will happen to them "on the judgment of the great day"?[2]

Response

11.2. The exact account[3] of these matters is known[4] only to those who have the mind of the apostles, to whom the Word directly taught the true knowledge of beings and their good and just administration by wise Providence. Between the minds of such men and the Word[5] there stands no obstructing wall of partition.

11.3. To one such as myself, on the other hand, who is earthbound and possesses many obstacles hindering the Word's passage to his mind, the "principle" that was "not kept by the angels" is perhaps the reason[6] according to which they were created;[7] or the natural lordship given to them by grace with a view

---

1. "Principle" renders the Greek word ἀρχή. According to Dionysios, *DN* 4.23, demons are said to be evil "not by nature" but by "being weak, as Scripture says, in preserving their ἀρχή," citing Jude 6 (170, lines 12–14; 171, lines 5–6; 724C–735C); cf. Perl, *Theophany*, 58–59.
2. Jude 6.
3. I.e., *logos*.
4. Literally, "being kept" (τετηρημένος), picking up on the "not kept" (μὴ τηρησάντων) of the preceding paragraph (Qu. 11.1).
5. Here I render *logos* as "Word," although it may perhaps also be understood as a reference to the "account" (*logos*) in the previous sentence.
6. I.e., *logos*.
7. Cf. *Amb.* 7.16 (DOML 1:94–97).

toward their divinization; or the place assigned to them in the orders of the angelic ranks corresponding to their worthiness of grace. The "dwelling place" is heaven, or the permanent state of wisdom concerning the good things that transcend thought, a state in which they were created to dwell, for Scripture calls it the "house of wisdom";[8] or it signifies the vigilant oversight of their natural and acquired gifts received from the immaculate Divinity, which they lost after their tyrannical abuse of it.[9] The "everlasting chains" signify the total and continuous immobility of their free will to do good, as a result of which they will never in any way enjoy divine rest;[10] or they signify the providential power of God, which for the sake of our salvation restrains their fury against us, preventing the advance of their wicked contrivances against us.[11] The "gloom" is their complete and total blindness to divine grace, a gloom that wholly pervaded the disposition of their will and separated them from the blessed and all-radiant outpouring of divine light. This was how they squandered all the natural intellective power given to them when they were brought into being out of nothing. What will happen to them on the terrible Day of Judgment is something known only to the Just Judge. He will determine the just and deserved recompense for everyone, assigning a form of punishment equal to the degree of wickedness, and, consistent with His good decrees, will render with justice the eternal sentence.

8. Cf. Prv 9.1.
9. On the "tyranny" of the angels, see Origen, *Homilies on Luke* 35.5–6 (SC 87:418–22).
10. Which would seem to rule out any possibility of their repentance and restoration to their previous state.
11. See above, Intro., 1.2.9.

QUESTION 12

HAT IS THE "tunic soiled by the flesh"?[1]

Response

12.2. A "soiled tunic" is a life stained with many faults because of the passions of the flesh. For each man's manner of life, as if it were a kind of tunic, reveals whether he is righteous or unrighteous, and thus the righteous man is clothed in a life of virtue like a clean tunic, whereas the unrighteous man has a life soiled by evil deeds.[2]

12.3. Or, rather, a "tunic soiled by the flesh" is the habit and disposition which through the conscience forms the soul through the recollection of the evil impulses and deeds of the flesh. When the soul constantly sees that it is wrapped in this condition as if in a kind of tunic, it is filled with the stench of passions. For through the Spirit the virtues are woven together in accordance with reason and become a tunic of incorruptibility for the soul, which, when clothed in it, becomes beautiful and resplendent—so too, because of the flesh, the passions are woven together under the sway of irrationality, and become a filthy and soiled tunic, which reveals the character of the soul, imposing on it a form and image other than that which it received from God.

1. Jude 23. See above, Qu. 4.
2. Cf. Origen, *Homilies on Luke* 14.3-4, who deals with the "stained garments of humanity" in an exegesis of Zec 3.3, arguing that "every soul that has been clothed with a human body has its own stain" (SC 87:218–22).

QUESTION 13

HAT IS THE meaning of: "Ever since the creation of the world, the invisible things of God, namely, His eternal power and divinity, have been clearly visible, being understood by the things that are made"?[1] What are the "invisible things of God"? And what is His "eternal power and divinity"?

Response

13.2. The principles of beings—which were prepared before the ages in God, in a manner known only to Him, and which divine men customarily call "good wills"[2]—are invisible in themselves, yet are "clearly visible in the things that are made," when, that is, they are seen with the eyes of the intellect.[3] For when with true understanding we contemplate cognitively all of God's creatures according to their nature, they secretly announce to us the principles by which they were created, disclosing in themselves the divine intention for each one, consistent with the words: "The heavens declare the glory of God, and the firmament proclaims the work of His hands."[4] As for God's "eternal power and divinity," this is His providence that holds beings together, and His providential activity that divinizes those under its care.

13.2. Or perhaps the "invisible things of God" are nothing other than His "eternal power and divinity" themselves, whose thunderous heralds are the supernatural splendors of the

---

1. Rom 1.20.
2. A reference to Dionysios, *DN* 5.8 (188, lines 8–9; 824C), a passage that Maximos cites in *Amb.* 7.24 (DOML 1:106–109).
3. That is, the *logoi* are visible in creation through natural contemplation.
4. Ps 18.1. Maximos comments on this verse in *Amb.* 10.20 (DOML 1:179–81).

things that have come into being.[5] For just as from created beings[1] we believe in the existence (in the truly proper sense) of God, so too, from the essential differences of beings according to their specific forms, we learn of His Wisdom, which is naturally inherent in His essence, and which holds beings together. And, again, from the essential motion of beings according to their specific forms, we learn of His Life, which is naturally inherent in His essence, and which brings completion to beings. And from the wise contemplation of creation, we apprehend the principle concerning the Holy Trinity, I mean of the Father and of the Son and of the Holy Spirit, because the "eternal power" of God is the Word, since He is consubstantial, and the "everlasting divinity" is the consubstantial Spirit.[6]

13.3. Accordingly, those who do not apprehend the Divine Cause of beings from the contemplation of beings, together with the properties that belong to this Cause[2] by nature—I mean its power and divinity—stand condemned.[7] But through the things that God has made, creation cries out and, as it were, proclaims—to those who are intellectively capable of hearing it—the same Divine Cause being hymned in a threefold manner, by which I mean God the Father and His ineffable "power" and "divinity," that is, the only-begotten Word and the Holy Spirit. For these are the invisible things of God, which ever since the creation of the world are clearly visible to the intellect.[8]

   5. Larchet (SC 529:212, n. 1) suggests that here Maximos is referring to the divine energies as manifested in creation, which can be contemplated through their inner principles; cf. *Amb.* 22 (DOML 2:448–51).
   6. In this adumbration of the Trinity in creation, the existence of creatures is understood as an image or reflection of God the Father; their organization into unity and diversity as an image of the Son (as Wisdom); and their movement and life as an image of the Holy Spirit; cf. *Amb.* 10.39, where the contemplation of nature reveals to the saints that "the <divine> cause exists, is wise, and is something living, from which they learned the divinizing and salvific principle of the Father, the Son, and the Holy Spirit ... into which they were piously initiated with respect to the mode of God's existence" (DOML 1:209); and the discussion in Polycarp Sherwood, "The Triune God," in idem, *St. Maximus the Confessor: The Ascetic Life, The Four Centuries on Charity* (New York: Newman Press, 1955), 37–45.
   7. Cf. Rom 1.20: "Therefore they are without excuse."
   8. On this question, cf. Blowers, *Exegesis and Spiritual Pedagogy,* 177, n. 188;

Scholia

[1] From beings, he says, we know the Divine Cause of beings; from the differences between beings we learn about the enhypostatic Wisdom of being; and from the natural movement of beings we discern the enhypostatic Life of being, which is the Life-creating Power of beings, that is, the Holy Spirit.

[2] By "Cause" he means the Father. That which is proper to Him are power and divinity, that is, the Son and the Holy Spirit.[9]

Thunberg, *Man and the Cosmos,* 32, 45–46; and Maximos Constas, "The Reception of Paul and Pauline Theology in the Byzantine Period," in *Byzantium and the New Testament,* ed. Derek Krueger and Robert Nelson (Washington, DC: Dumbarton Oaks, 2017), 147–76, at 167–69.

9. This scholion is extant only in Eriugena's Latin translation (CCSG 7:96, lines 6–7); Steel and Laga tentatively ascribe it to Eriugena (CCSG 7:ci).

QUESTION 14

HAT DOES IT mean that: "They worshiped and served creation instead of the Creator"?[1] What is "worship"[2] and what is "service"?[3]

Response

14.2. "Worship" is the veneration of God in faith, while "service" is reverence given to God through works. Having transferred their worship, that is, their faith, to creation, human beings venerated creation instead of the Creator, believing in demons, which they served and venerated through their evil works.[4] Let us, however, worshiping God through faith in Him, be eager to offer Him pure service through a manner of life made perfect by the virtues.

1. Rom 1.25.
2. I.e., σέβας.
3. I.e., λατρεία.
4. Cf. above, Intro., 1.2.16.

QUESTION 15

HAT DOES Scripture mean when it says: "Your incorruptible Spirit is present in all things, and for this reason You progressively correct those who trespass"?[1] And if it says this about the Holy Spirit, how can this be reconciled with: "Wisdom will not enter into a heart lacking understanding, and will not dwell in a body enslaved by sins"?[2] I have noted this because the first passage says the Spirit is unconditionally "present in all things."

Response

15.2. The Holy Spirit is absent from no being, and especially not from those that in any way partake of reason. For the Spirit contains the knowledge of each being,[1] inasmuch as He is God and the Spirit of God, providentially permeating all things with His power. The Spirit stirs into motion[3] the natural inner principle of each, through which He leads a man of sense to consciousness of whatever he has done contrary to the law of nature, a man who at the same time also keeps his free choice pliant to the reception of right thoughts arising from nature. And thus we find even some of the most barbarous and uncivilized men exhibiting nobility of conduct and rejecting the savage laws that had prevailed among them from time immemorial.

1. Wis 12.1.
2. Wis 1.4.
3. "Stirs into motion" renders the Greek ἀνακινεῖν, which in the Platonic tradition describes the awakening or arousing required for the soul to grasp or recollect innate knowledge. The word is employed extensively by Proclus and Dionysios the Areopagite; cf. Christoph Helmig, *Forms and Concepts: Concept Formation in the Platonic Tradition* (Berlin and Boston: De Gruyter, 2012), 276–78.

15.3. This, then, is how the Spirit is unconditionally "present in all things." But He is present more specifically and according to another sense in all those who live according to the law. To these He gives laws[2] and proclaims in advance mysteries to come, imbuing them with the awareness of where they have broken the commandments, as well as with true understanding of the proclaimed perfection in Christ. Consequently, and for the same reasons, we find that many abandon the old religion of shadows and types[4] in order eagerly to embrace the new and mystical worship.

15.4. In addition to these modes of the Spirit's presence, there is another,[3] which is found in all those who through faith have inherited[5] the divine and truly divinizing name of Christ. In this mode, the Spirit is not present simply as one guarding and providentially setting in motion the principle of nature, nor as one pointing out the keeping and breaking of the commandments and announcing the coming of Christ, but rather as one creating the adoption given by grace through faith. For the Spirit is productive of wisdom only in those who have been purified in soul and body through the strict keeping of the commandments. With them He communicates intimately through simple and immaterial knowledge, and, by means of pure thoughts of ineffable mysteries, He configures their intellect for divinization.

15.5. Consequently, the Spirit is present unconditionally in all things, insofar as He contains all things, providentially cares for all things, and stirs into motion their natural seeds. He is present more specifically in all who are under the law, for He shows them where they have failed to keep this law, and enlightens them regarding the promise of Christ. In all Christians, however, He is present in another way, namely, as the power of their adoption as children of God.[6] But as the author of wisdom He is unconditionally present only in those who have understanding, and who by their godly way of life have made them-

---

4. Cf. Heb 10.1.
5. I.e., through baptism.
6. Cf. Rom 8.14–15.

selves fit to receive His divinizing indwelling.[7] For everyone who does not carry out the divine will, even though he is a believer, has a "heart lacking in understanding," because it has become a workshop of evil thoughts, and a body deeply in debt to sin, because it perpetually subjects itself to the defilements of the passions.

Scholia

[1] The Holy Spirit, as productive of all and providential for all, is present in all.

[2] The Holy Spirit, as establishing laws and declaring things in advance, is present in all who are under the law.

[3] The Holy Spirit is present *par excellence* in Christians as the creator of divine adoption.

---

7. Cf. Rom 8.9. I.e., θεωτικῆς ἐνοικήσεως: cf. below, Qu. 47.9 (θεωτικὴ ἕξις, translated there as "divinizing condition"). The adjective θεωτική was coined by Dionysios, *CH* 2.2 (18, line 8; 165B), but appears in Proclus, *Elements of Theology* 165, as ἐκθεωτική (ed. E. R. Dodds [Oxford: Clarendon Press, 1963], 144, line 2); cf. *QThp.* (73, line 10); and Norman Russel, *The Doctrine of Deification in the Greek Patristic Tradition* (Oxford: Oxford University Press, 2004), 264, n. 32.

QUESTION 16

WHAT IS THE "molten calf,"[1] and why is it spoken of in the singular, when afterwards it says, in the plural: "These are your gods, O Israel"?[2] And what does it mean that this calf was "ground into powder and scattered under the water"?[3] And what is the meaning of the "earrings" and the other pieces of jewelry?[4]

Response

16.2. When, after the manner of Israel, the intellect comes out of the Egypt of sin, it bears within itself the accompanying mental image[5] of sin's delusional wanderings, just like an impression of evil in the mind. Through even a little negligence, such an intellect will be deprived of its power of rational discernment, just as the Israelites of old were deprived of Moses,[6] and will establish within itself an irrational state of mind—like that of a calf—which is the mother of all the passions. To build this calf, the mind hands over its "earrings," that is, the principles of theology acquired naturally through the pious understanding of beings. It offers its "necklaces," which are its divinely fitting notions concerning beings, strung together through

---

1. Ex 32.4.
2. Ex 32.4, 9.
3. Ex 32.20.
4. Ex 32.2–3, 24.
5. "Mental image" renders the Greek word φαντασία, the verbal form of which Lampe, *PGL*, s.v., defines as "to form a conception of, picture to oneself, imagine." It denotes the active "impression" (here, ἐκτύπωμα) of evil and impassioned thoughts in the mind as well as the production of new, impassioned thoughts based on accumulated impressions and deeds.
6. On Moses as a symbol of reason, see *Amb.* 10.14 (DOML 1:171).

natural contemplation. Into the furnace, so to speak, it throws the natural activities associated with the practice of the virtues, as if they were so many "bracelets." All of these it melts down in the red-hot fires of its impassioned disposition for anger and desire, and, following the form and image of evil that it has stored up[7] in its mind, it produces sin by actualizing the image. Whenever this happens, sin invariably fragments and disperses the intellect (which has brought this about) along with itself, dividing it from its singular identity with the truth, splintering it into many unstable fantasies and notions about things that do not exist, all of which constitute its habituated irrational state. But when divine reason[8] arrives, it grinds this irrational state into powder and scatters it under the water. With the subtlety of contemplation, it breaks down the density of the mind oriented to sensation plainly manifested in the passions, and distinctly separates the mutual variation and confusion of its natural faculties brought about by the passions, and elevates them once again to their proper principle of knowledge. This, according to my understanding, is the meaning of "scattered under the water."

16.3. With the above remarks, my discourse has briefly provided you with a complete contemplation of the events described in this passage of Scripture. For the meaning of this passage to become even clearer, let us consider, if it seems good to you, each element in terms of definitions.

16.4. The "molten calf" is the mutual mixing and confusion of our natural powers, or rather the impassioned and irrational concurrence of these powers producing the irrational energy of unnatural passions.[9] The calf is "one," because there is one habitual state of evil, dispersed into multiple forms of evil. And it is a "calf," the ruminations of which represent what is persistent, assiduous, earth-bound, as well as the chewings and

---

7. "Stored up" translates the word προαποκειμένη; cf. Helmig, *Forms and Concepts*, 181, on the cognate Porphyrian term ἀποτίθεσθαι, which describes the mental "storing away" of forms and concepts within the soul.

8. Stăniloae, *Filocalia*, vol. 3, 75, suggests "Divine Word" instead of "divine reason."

9. On the "mixing and confusion of natural powers," see above, Intro. 1.2.13–16.

regurgitations of an evil propensity for the passions. It is "molten" because the habitual state of the passions and their activity is constituted according to the form of the evil imaginings stored up in the mind. The word "gods" in the phrase, "These are your gods, O Israel," is in the plural, because evil by nature is fragmented, unstable, multiform, and divisive. If the good by its nature unifies and gathers together things that are divided, it is obvious that evil divides and destroys what is united.[10]

16.5. The "earrings" are the principles of theology that exist naturally in the intellect through the pious understanding of beings. The "necklaces" are right judgments concerning beings acquired through natural contemplation. The "bracelets" signify the actualization of virtues through the practice of asceticism. Or, again, the "earrings" represent the power of reason implanted in our nature[11]—for the ear is a symbol of reason—while the "necklace" signifies the irascible faculty—for the neck typifies what is high up and despotic.[12] The "bracelet" is desire, which is revealed through the active pursuit of pleasure. The intellect takes all of these things, according to the meaning given to each, and throws them into the fire of the passions, where it forges the irrational and mindless state of ignorance, which is the mother of all evils. This state, however, can be broken down whenever the intellect—observing in thought the density of the passion as it is manifested externally to the senses—breaks apart the combination of elements producing the passion and brings each one back to its proper principle of origin. This is how it "scatters them under the water," which is to say "under the knowledge of truth," clearly distinguishing and decoupling them from their mutually evil coalescence and combination.

16.6. What I mean is something like this: every passion always consists of a combination of some sensible object, sensa-

---

10. In the Introduction (1.2.11), Maximos had initially defined evil as a "deficiency," and subsequently described the ways in which it leads to the division and fragmentation of human consciousness (ibid., 1.2.15).
11. Cf. Jas 1.21.
12. On the sense of hearing as symbolic of reason, cf. *Amb.* 21.7 (DOML 1:431).

tion, and a natural power, by which I mean anger, desire, or reason as turned aside from their natural functions.[13] Thus if the intellect considers the final result of this combination—of the sensible object, sensation, and the natural power involved with sensation—it can distinguish each from the other two, and lead them back to their proper natural principle. It can, in other words, consider the sensible object in itself, apart from its relation to sensation; and sensation apart from the sensible object's connection to it; and the natural power—desire, for example, or any other natural power—apart from its impassioned disposition toward sensation and the sensible object.[14] In this way, and to the extent that the movement of the passion in question makes these observations possible, the intellect "grinds the molten calf into powder."[15] That is, it breaks down the combination of whatever passion arises and "scatters" its constituent elements "under the water"[16] of knowledge, and utterly obliterates even the mere, residual image of the passions, by restoring each of its elements to its natural state. May we also be granted to "grind the molten calf" of the soul "into powder," utterly obliterating it, so that the soul possesses the divine image of God[17] alone and unadulterated, absolutely undefiled by the things of the world.[18]

16.7. The subjoining verse: "And Moses gave the water to the sons of Israel to drink,"[19] indicates the manner by which one teaches the purification of passions, which is given to those who are learning from those who are teaching.

13. See the discussion in *Amb.* 10.8 (DOML 1:161).
14. Maximos describes a similar process in *Carit.* 3.43 (ed. Ceresa-Gastaldo, 162), as does Evagrios, *On Thoughts* 8 (SC 438:178, lines 14–21); cf. Maximos Constas, "'Nothing is Greater than Divine Love': Evagrios of Pontos, St. Maximos the Confessor, and the *Philokalia*," in *Rightly Dividing the Word of Truth: Studies in Honour of Metropolitan Kallistos Ware* (Oxford: Peter Lang, 2016), 57–74, esp. 66–67.
15. Ex 32.20.
16. Ibid.
17. Cf. Gn 1.26.
18. Cf. Blowers, *Exegesis and Spiritual Pedagogy*, 176, n. 185; and Thunberg, *Microcosm and Mediator*, 219.
19. Ex 32.20.

QUESTION 17

IF GOD SENT Moses into Egypt, why was the angel of God seeking to kill him? And the angel would have killed him, had Moses's wife not hastened to circumcise their young son and thereby halted the angel's attack.[1] And if the circumcision of the child was necessary, why did God not gently direct Moses to circumcise him before sending him into Egypt? And why, moreover, even if Moses was in error, did the good angel of God not kindly advise him of this, seeing that he was being sent to serve God in Egypt?[2]

Response

17.2. Anyone who examines the inner meaning of Scripture's enigmas[3] with the fear of God and for the sake of the divine glory alone, and who removes the letter from around the spirit as though it were a veil,[4] "shall find all things in front of him," according to the word of Wisdom,[5] with no impediment hindering the mind's blameless motion toward divine things. Let us therefore leave aside the written account of what has already occurred corporeally in Moses's time, and consider, with the eyes of the intellect, its spiritual power, which is constantly occurring and becoming ever greater by its very occurrence.

17.3. The desert, from which Moses was sent to Egypt to lead out the sons of Israel, is either human nature, this world, or the

---

1. Cf. Ex 4.19–26.
2. For an analysis of this Question, see Blowers, *Exegesis and Spiritual Pedagogy*, 63–65.
3. Cf. 1 Cor 13.12.
4. Cf. 2 Cor 3.6, 13–16.
5. Cf. Prv 8.9.

settled state of the soul free of the passions. In accordance with this state and in this world, the intellect acquires the knowledge of beings through contemplation. At the same time, it receives, in the unseen recesses of the heart, a hidden and mystical power from God to lead the Israelites out of Egypt, that is, to lead out the divine thoughts of beings from the flesh and from sense perception, where they toil and suffer mindlessly in the clay, that is, in the passions of the flesh. Being entrusted with this divine task, the intellect—in the company of wisdom, which is joined to it through knowledge like a wife, along with the noble manner and way of thinking to which she gives birth—will without exception travel on the road of a reverent way of life in the virtues, a road that in no way admits of any standing still on the part of those who walk in it, but only their ever-moving and swift race toward "the goal of the upward call."[6] This is because the halting of virtue is the beginning of vice, which comes about whenever the intellect becomes passionately absorbed in something material found on either side of the road, and thereby makes the pure and wholly circumcised manner and way of thinking of life's pious journey into something uncircumcised and profane.[7]

17.4. This is why the intellect immediately sees the reproving reason as an angel threatening death, and testifying that the threat was caused by standing still on the way of virtue, a lapse that places a carnal covering over the intellect's way of thinking. In response, the wisdom that dwells with the intellect importunes it, and, like Zipporah, uses the "small stone"[8] of the word of faith to cut away the mental image that arises in its way of thinking, which is its child, and to drain any thought within it of sensual life. For Zipporah says: "The blood of the boy's circumcision has ceased to flow,"[9] which is to say that the impassioned life and its imagination and motion have abated, because the defiled way of thinking has been purified with the wisdom of faith. After this purification, the reason, like

---

6. Phil 3.14.
7. Here Maximos is following Gregory of Nyssa, *On the Life of Moses* 5 (SC 1bis:48); cf. Paul Blowers, "Maximos the Confessor, Gregory of Nyssa and the concept of 'Perpetual Progress,'" *Vigiliae Christianae* 46 (1992): 151–71.
8. Ex 4.25.
9. Ibid.

an angelic messenger, ceases from smiting the sinful intellect through the conscience and opposes every thought that moves beyond what is proper. For the way of the virtues is in truth filled with many holy angels who can actuate every virtue according to its kind, by which I mean both the principles and modes of the virtues and the angels who invisibly cooperate with us and who stir these kinds of principles into motion.

17.5. This passage of Holy Scripture, then, is beautifully and brilliantly set forth. It always makes present—to those who possess healthy spiritual eyes—the objects of contemplation prior to their written forms, and contains nothing to discredit God or His holy angels. For when Moses was sent by God, he did not have, in terms of Scripture's spiritual meaning, an "uncircumcised son," that is, a carnal covering over his way of thinking; otherwise, God would have enjoined him to circumcise the child before sending him on his way. Neither was the divine angel harsh when he warned Moses of the death that would befall him by his stopping and staggering on the way of the virtues, a death that was perhaps provoked by Moses's weakness on the road of the virtues.

17.6. When you examine more precisely the literal meaning of the story, you will clearly notice that the angel who threatened Moses with death because of the passion that imperceptibly arose in his mind did not meet him at the beginning or middle or end of the road, but at the inn.[10] Because if Moses had not stopped on the road and brought his journey to an end, he would not have been accused, and would not have received, through the angelic messenger, the message of divine indignation over the child's foreskin.

17.7. If indeed we are walking in the way of the divine commandments, let us entreat God not to stop sending, to our every transgression, like an angel, the word that announces death in our conscience, so that, by coming to our senses we will learn through our natural prudence to circumcise, like a foreskin, the impurity of the passions that imperceptibly arises within us on the road of life.

---

10. Cf. Ex 4.24.

QUESTION 18

F, ACCORDING to Saint Paul: "It is the doers of the law who will be justified,"¹ how is it that he later says: "Whoever has been justified by the law has fallen away from grace"?²

Response

18.2. It is not simply the doers of the law who will be justified, but rather those who in spirit practice the spiritual law³ understood spiritually according to the inner man.⁴ Those who so practice do not fall away from grace insofar as the Word has passed into the depth of their souls through their purification. Those, on the other hand, who corporeally serve the outer aspects of the law completely fall away from divine grace, for they are ignorant of the perfection of the spiritual law, which through grace purifies the intellect from every stain, and whose perfection is Christ.⁵

1. Rom 2.13.
2. Gal 5.4.
3. Cf. Rom 7.14.
4. Cf. Rom 7.22; 2 Cor 4.16.
5. Cf. Rom 10.4.

QUESTION 19

HAT IS the meaning of the words: "All who have sinned without the law will also perish without the law, and all who have sinned under the law will be judged through the law"?[1] And how is the same apostle able elsewhere to say: "When God will judge the secret things of men, according to my gospel, through Jesus Christ"?[2] If they are to be judged "through the law," how will they be judged "through Jesus Christ"?

Response

19.2. The Word of God, Jesus Christ, as the creator of all things, is also the maker of the natural law. As provider and lawgiver, He clearly is also the giver of both the written law and the spiritual law, which latter is the law of grace, for when it says: "Christ is the end of the law,"[3] this means the written law understood spiritually. If, then, the natural law, the written law, and the law of grace are all gathered together in Christ, insofar as He is creator, provider, lawgiver, and atonement, the divine apostle speaks the truth when he says that "God will judge the secrets of men according to his gospel,"[4] that is, according to the gospel proclaimed through Jesus Christ, who is God's own only-begotten and essential Word, present in all things, reproving some, agreeably receiving others. To those who live according to nature, the law, and grace, God renders whatever they are worthy of through His ineffable, only-begotten Word, who is united to Him according to essence. For the Word of

1. Rom 2.12.
2. Rom 2.16.
3. Rom 10.4.
4. Cf. Rom 2.12–16.

QUESTION 19

God is the author of every nature, and of every divine law, regulation, and order, from which it follows that He is the judge of those who live under nature, law, regulation, and order, for apart from the Word who promulgates it, there is no law. So if someone is "judged by the law,"[5] he will be judged as being in Christ, and if he is judged apart from the law, it is absolutely in the same Christ that he will be judged, for the Word, as creator, is the beginning, middle, and end of all beings, words, and thoughts.

5. Rom 2.12.

QUESTION 20

WHAT IS THE meaning in the Gospel of the fig tree that to all appearances withered contrary to reason? And what is the inordinate hunger of Christ that sought for figs out of season? And what is the meaning of a curse placed upon something that is devoid of sense?[1]

Response

20.2. The Divine Word, who governs everything with wisdom for the sake of human salvation, first trained human nature with a law requiring a more corporeal observance, because humanity's ignorance of, and estrangement from, the archetype of divine realities was preventing it from receiving the truth free of figurative veils. Afterwards, manifestly becoming man[2] by taking on flesh possessing an intellective and rational soul, He redirected the course of human nature—insofar as He is the Word—toward immaterial and cognitive worship in the Spirit.[3] Once the truth was made manifest to human life, the Word did not want a shadow to hold sway over that life, a shadow whose very type and figure is the fig tree. This is why Scripture says that He encountered the fig tree "while *returning* from Bethany to Jerusalem."[4] In other words, after His figurative, shadowy, and hidden presence in the law, He becomes present anew to human nature through the flesh (for this is how one must understand "returning"), for it was then that "He saw a fig tree on the way having

---

1. Mt 21.18–21; Mk 11.12–14; cf. Lk 13.6–9.
2. Cf. Jn 1.14.
3. Cf. Jn 4.23–24.
4. Mt 21.18; Mk 11.11.

nothing but leaves."[5] It is evident that the tree is the corporeal observance of the law, existing in shadows and figures, having an unstable and transient tradition, which is why it is found "on the way," being a sign of passing figures and precepts. Seeing that, like a fig tree, it was ostentatiously and extravagantly adorned by the outward leaves of the corporeal observances of the law, but finding no fruit on it—clearly no fruit of righteousness—He cursed it, since it did not provide nourishment for the Word. Or rather He commanded that the figures of the law should no longer hold sway over and conceal the truth. And this was subsequently proven to be the case through actual deeds, when the beauty of the law,[1] which exists merely in external forms, was completely withered, and the pride that the Jews took in it was extinguished.[6] For insofar as the truth of the fruits of righteousness was now visibly displayed, it was neither reasonable nor seasonable that the appetites of those who travel on the road of life should be beguiled and deceived by mere "leaves," and in the process neglect the edible fruitfulness of the Word. This is why it says: "It was not the season for figs."[7] In other words, the time when the law prevailed over human nature was not the time for the fruits of righteousness, but was rather a prefiguration of those fruits and in some way indicative of the future divine and ineffable grace that is able to save all. Since the ancient people did not arrive at this grace, they were lost through unbelief. For the divine Apostle says that: "Israel, which pursued righteousness based on the law"—referring, of course, to the law in shadows and figures—"did not arrive at the righteousness of the law,"[8] that is, the law fulfilled in the Spirit through Christ.

20.3. Or, again, because the majority of priests, scribes, lawyers, and Pharisees were sick with vainglory—manifested in their outward display of false piety and customs—and because they only appeared to practice righteousness when in fact they

---

5. Mt 21.19; Mk 11.13.
6. Here the word τύφος ("pride" or "vanity") would seem to pun on the verb τύφω, which means "to smoke," alluding to the "extinguishing" of the fires of the Jewish sacrificial cult.
7. Mk 11.13.
8. Rom 9.31.

were nourishing their pride, the Word says that their pride is like an unfruitful fig tree,[9] rich only in leaves, which He, who desires the salvation of all human beings and hungers for their divinization, curses and causes to wither away. He does this so that they might prefer to be righteous in reality rather than in appearance, removing the tunic of hypocrisy so that they might be clothed in a tunic of virtue, as the Divine Word wishes them to be. They will then pass the rest of their life in piety, presenting to God the disposition of their souls rather than display their counterfeit piety to men.

20.4. If it happens that some of us who are Christians are also like this, feigning piety through outward displays while having no works of righteousness, we have only to accept the Word, who in His love for humanity hungers for our salvation, and He will wither the seed of evil in our souls, that is, the evil of pride, so that we may no longer seek to please men, which is the fruit of corruption.

20.5. Here you have, according to the measure of my impoverished abilities, the meaning of this passage, in which my explanation showed the Lord rightly to be hungry, and usefully to have cursed the fig tree and to make it wither at the right time, for it was an impediment to the truth, either as the ancient tradition of the law's corporeal figures, or as the empty religious pride of the Pharisees and ourselves.

Scholion

[1] The beauty of the law and the pride of the Jews had nothing real or substantial apart from its outward forms, the law which was made void by the advent of the Lord.[10]

---

9. Mt 21.19–21.
10. This scholion is extant only in Eriugena's Latin translation (CCSG 7:124, lines 65–67).

QUESTION 21

HAT IS THE meaning of: "He stripped off the principalities and authorities," along with the rest of this verse?[1] And how in general was He able to "put them on" when He was begotten without sin?[2]

Response

21.2. When the Divine[3] Word clothed Himself in human nature without undergoing any change,[4] and became perfect man like us in every way but without sin,[5] He manifested the first Adam in both the mode of His creaturely origin[1] and the mode of His birth.[6] I mean this in the sense that the first man, hav-

1. Col 2.15.
2. On this Question, see the study by Claire-Agnès Zirnheld, "Le double visage de la passion: Malediction due au péché et/ou dynamisme de la vie: *Quaestiones ad Thalassium* de S. Maxime le Confesseur XXI, XII et XLII," in *Philohistôr: Miscellanea in honorem Caroli Laga septuagenarii* (Leuven: Peeters Press, 1994), 361–80. See also Demetrios Bathrellos, "The Temptations of Jesus Christ according to St. Maximos the Confessor," *SP* 42 (2006): 45–49; and idem, "The Sinlessness of Jesus: A Theological Exploration in the Light of Trinitarian Theology," in *Trinitarian Soundings in Systematic Theology*, ed. Paul Louis Metzger (London and New York: T&T Clark, 2006), 113–26.
3. Literally: θεαρχικός ("thearchic"), which is of Dionysian coinage; cf. *EH* 3.3.12 (92, line 22; 444A).
4. I.e., the Chalcedonian ἀτρέπτως.
5. Heb 4.15.
6. "Creaturely origin" (γένεσις) refers to Adam's direct origin from God through an act of creation, while "birth" (γέννησις) refers to subsequent human origin through sexual intercourse and biological reproduction; on this distinction, see *Amb.* 42 (DOML 2:122–87). As Maximos will explain below, the incarnate Word assumed the sinlessness that Adam had originally received through creation, and the blameless passions received through birth, but not the passions that are contrary to nature, which would nullify sinlessness.

ing received his being from God and coming to be by the very genesis of his being,[7] was, according to his creaturely origin, free from corruption and sin—for neither corruption nor sin was created together with him. But when by sinning he transgressed God's commandment, he was condemned to birth propagated through passion and sin, so that henceforth sin originates in the passible part of our nature, associated with birth, as if by a kind of law, under which no one is sinless, for all are subject by nature to the law of birth, introduced after man's creaturely origin in consequence of his sin.

21.3. Since, therefore, sin appeared through the transgression, and because of sin the passibility associated with birth entered human nature,[8] so that through sin the original transgression continued to thrive together with the passibility associated with birth, there was no hope of freedom, since human nature was bound in the disposition of its will by an indissoluble bond of evil. The more human nature hastened to propagate itself through the process of birth, the more tightly it bound itself to the law of sin, insofar as nature's very passibility reactivated the transgression within it. For in possessing, by virtue of its natural, contingent condition, the increase of sin within its very passibility, human nature came to possess the activities of all the opposing powers, principalities, and authorities—on account of the universal sin inherent in human passibility—operating through unnatural passions[2] concealed under the guise of the natural passions.[3] Through the unnatural passions, and by exploiting nature's passibility, every evil power is actively at work, driving

7. That is, without birth.
8. Cf. Rom 5.12. The notion of "passibility" (πάθος) in its most basic sense denotes what happens to a substance, body, quality, or soul that undergoes, suffers, or experiences any kind of change, often in the sense of harmful changes or alterations. As the internal accusative of πάσχειν, "passibility" carries strong connotations of passivity. Bodily passions that are not subject to voluntary control (e.g., hunger, thirst, experiencing pain) constitute a kind of second-order passivity, linked to the passive entry of beings into existence from nothing, both of which conditions, as Maximos will explain in a moment, the Word voluntarily assumed in the Incarnation, consistent with the "passivity" of Adam's (involuntary and passive) "creaturely origin"; cf. below, Qu. 42, where these themes are further developed; and Qu. 22.7, for the role of passivity in divinization.

the inclination of the will by means of the natural passions into the corruption of unnatural passions.

21.4. In order to rescue human nature from this evil state of helplessness, the only-begotten Son and Word of God, becoming perfect man out of His love for mankind, assumed the sinlessness—without the incorruption—of Adam's original constitution according to his creaturely origin. He also assumed the passibility—without the sin—from the birth that was subsequently[4] introduced[5] into human nature. As I said a moment ago, it was in the passibility of Adam, on account of sin, that the wicked demons conducted their invisible operations concealed under the law of contingent human nature. Thus it was only to be expected that, on account of the flesh, they beheld Adam's passible nature in God the Savior, and thought that, in this contingent state, He was necessarily a mere man subject to the law of nature, but not moved by the inclination of his will.[9] They therefore assailed Him, hoping that they might prevail even upon Him, through His natural passibility, to form an image in His mind[6] of an unnatural passion and act on it as they would. But in His first experience of temptations by pleasures,[10] He allowed the demons to be "mocked" by their own tricks,[11] and He "stripped off" their powers by expelling them from human nature. At the same time, He remained inaccessible[12] and beyond their grasp, clearly winning victory over them not for His sake but for ours, because it was for us that He became man and, in His goodness, offered to us the whole of what He accomplished. For He himself had no need to be tested by experience, since He is God and Master and by nature free from all passions. Instead, He provoked, by means of our temptations,[7] the wicked power, thwarting it by His own attack, and putting to death the very power that expected to thwart Him just as it had thwarted Adam in the beginning.[13]

9. On this theme, see Nicholas Constas, "The Last Temptation of Satan: Divine Deception in Greek Patristic Interpretations of the Passion Narrative," *HTR* 97 (2004): 139–63.
10. Cf. Mt 4.1–11; Mk 1.12–13; Lk 4.1–13.
11. Cf. Ps 103.26.
12. Cf. 1 Tm 6.16.
13. For Maximos, Christ's proper use of his natural human passions is the

21.5. This, then, is how, in His initial experience of temptation, He "put off the principalities and authorities"[14] that assailed Him, removing them from human nature, healing the passibility associated with pleasure, and in Himself "canceling the bond of indebtedness"[15] of Adam's voluntary assent to the passions arising from pleasure.[16] For it is by this bond that man's power of choice inclines toward wicked pleasure to his own disadvantage—for by his actions he tacitly proclaims his condition of domination, which, on account of his fear of death, prevents him from freeing himself from his subjugation to pleasure.

21.6. Having overcome and vanquished the powers, principalities, and authorities through this initial[8] experience of pleasure, the Lord allowed them to launch a second[9] attack against Him, and to place before Him the one remaining experience of temptations, namely, those which arise through pain and sufferings. His aim was to pour out completely, through Himself, the corrupting poison of their wickedness, consuming it like fire, and to obliterate it totally from human nature. And He did this by utterly "stripping off the principalities and

---

basic paradigm of all spiritual practice; cf. below, Qu. 61; *Ascet.* 3–5, where the ascetic life mirrors and continues the incarnate Word's battle against evil; and *Ascet.* 10, where Christ's temptations in the desert are paradigmatic for mankind's struggle against temptation (CCSG 40:9–15; 23–25). See also Gregory Nazianzus, *Or.* 40.10, where Christ's victory over the devil in the wilderness becomes the source and model of the Christian's triumph over temptations (SC 358:216–18); and Hesychios of Sinai, *On Watchfulness* 12: "Through His incarnation, God gave us the model for a holy life and recalled us from our ancient fall. In addition to many other things, He taught us, feeble as we are, that we should fight against the demons with humility, fasting, prayer, and watchfulness. For when, after His baptism, He went into the desert and the devil came up to Him as though He were merely a man, He began His spiritual warfare by fasting and won the battle by this means—though, being God, and God of Gods, He had no need of any such means at all" (*Philokalia* 1:164).

14. Col 2.15.
15. Col 2.14.
16. The "bond of indebtedness" or "contract" is a metaphor for the human will, driven by the desire for pleasure, and habitually placing itself in bondage to the passions and the devil. In refusing the pleasure offered by Satan, Christ abrogated this long-standing "contract"; cf. Michael Stone, *Adam's Contract with Satan: The Legend of the Cheirograph* (Bloomington: University of Indiana Press, 2002).

QUESTION 21   147

authorities" at the time of His death on the cross, remaining unconquerable in His sufferings, and appearing formidable in the face of death, thereby extracting from our nature the passibility associated with pain. It was to this trial that man, on account of his cowardice, was ill-inclined, and was constantly being tyrannized against his will by the fear of death, and through his desire to live had embraced the chains of pleasure that slavery had thrown around him.[17]

21.7. So the Lord "stripped off the principalities and authorities"[18] at the time of His first experience of temptations in the desert, thereby healing the whole of human nature of the passibility associated with pleasure.[10] He "stripped them off" yet again at the time of His death, likewise removing from our nature the passibility associated with pain, considering what he accomplished for us as something that He, in His love of humanity, was accountable for—or rather, in His goodness, He reckoned to us the glory of the accomplishment. Because He assumed the passible condition of our nature—like ours but without sin[19]—a condition through which every evil power and destructive force carried out its particular wickedness, it came about that, at the moment of his death, he "stripped them off" and "triumphed over them and made a spectacle of them" while on His cross,[20] that is, at the departure of His soul, insofar as the evil powers could find nothing at all in the natural passibility of His human nature[21] that was properly His own.[11] To be sure, at that moment they were certainly expecting to find something utterly human in Him, in view of the natural passibility of the flesh. But, as was to be expected, by His own power He freed—as if through the "first fruits" of His own holy flesh (which He took from us)—

17. As described above, Intro. 1.2.14. On Christ's natural human fear of death at the time of his Passion, cf. *Or. Dom.* (CCSG 23:34–35); *Opusc.* 6 (PG 91:65–69); *Opusc.* 15 (PG 91:160C–169C); *Pyrr.* (PG 91:297B); François-Marie Léthel, *Théologie de l'agonie du Christ: La liberté humaine du Fils de Dieu et son importance sotériologique mises en lumière par saint Maxime le Confesseur* (Paris: Beauchesne, 1979); and Paul M. Blowers, "The Passion of Jesus Christ in Maximus the Confessor: A Reconsideration," *SP* 37 (2001): 361–77.

18. Col 2.15.
19. Heb 4.10.
20. Cf. Col 2.15.
21. Cf. Jn 14.30.

the whole of human nature from the wicked power that had been mixed into its condition of passibility, subjugating to this very same passibility of nature the evil power that had formerly ruled within it, I mean in the possibility of nature.

21.8. It would have also been possible to give this theme a more mystical and sublime interpretation. But because, as you know, the deeper secrets of the divine doctrines must not be committed to writing,[12] let the above be enough to satisfy those who seek a more detailed understanding of this question. When God grants us to be together again, we shall inquire assiduously into the apostolic mind regarding this question.

Scholia[22]

[1] By "creaturely origin" he is speaking of God's original formation of man; "birth" refers to the succession of human beings one from another, which was the condemnation that followed the transgression.

[2] He means the vices, in which the unclean spirits are operative. There are two kinds of passions: those that are contrary to nature, as are the vices that always oppose the virtues and can never be changed into virtue; and those that, though they were not placed in human nature by God, but rather cleaved to nature shortly after the primal sin (and are therefore evil in themselves), can nevertheless be converted to good in those who use them well. Such are pleasure and grief, desire and fear; and in these vices are hidden, whereby the iniquitous powers are wont to perform the works of unrighteousness.

[3] That is, motions of the soul, namely pleasure and grief, desire and fear, which occur in both good and evil, and in which the vices are accustomed to lurk.

[4] By "the birth subsequently introduced into nature" he

---

22. Of the following scholia, only nos. 1, 7, and 11 are found in the Greek text; the remaining nine scholia (2–6, 8–10, 12) were written by Eriugena; cf. Meyvaert, "Eriugena's Translation," 81: "Here once again the Latinity of the additional scholia seems to confirm that we are dealing, not with translation, but with original comments by Eriugena.... It would seem that this *Quaestio* held special interest for Eriugena and one must hope that further study will throw more light on the reasons for his particular preoccupations at this point."

means the succession of human beings one from another through bodily union after the likeness of beasts. For if human nature, in the first man, had not sinned, the multiplication of the human race would have proceeded not through the union of bodies, which is the penalty of sin, but in a miraculous and divine manner, without the contamination of any seed.

[5] That is, the succession of human procreation through seminal union, which is not natural but is the penalty of sin subsequently introduced into nature.

[6] The unclean spirits are accustomed to lead men astray by deceitfully exciting passions that are contrary to nature under the appearance of those that are natural.

[7] He who by His nature and as man is not subject to the passion of pleasure, appropriated our temptation to pleasure in order to provoke the one who was tempting Him. As mortal man He was by nature passible in the flesh, but insofar as He was sinless, He was without passion in the inclination of His will.

[8] He means the temptations that the devil leveled against the Lord in the desert, in the temple, and on the high mountain.

[9] That is, His passion on the cross, whereby the devil was altogether vanquished and human nature freed from death and sin.

[10] The passibility of pleasure is one thing, and the passibility of the flesh is another. The passibility of pleasure, that is, sin, did not exist in Christ. But He did possess the passibility of the flesh, that is, the potential to die.

[11] By "what is proper to nature" he means that very perdition that came about voluntarily, out of weakness, after the deviation towards sin. This the Lord did not naturally have according to the flesh while He subsisted according to substance in the flesh, without sin.

[12] No one who interprets Holy Scripture piously ought to dogmatize as if it were not able to be understood any other way.[23]

---

23. Though Eriugena here seems to misinterpret Maximos's point, he has once again applied a lesson from elsewhere in the *Responses*; cf. above, Intro., 1.2.8.

QUESTION 22

F GOD "in the coming ages will show His riches,"[1] how is it that "the ends of the ages have come upon us"?[2]

Response

22.2. He who brought all visible and invisible creation into being solely through the momentum of His will, had in His good counsel[3] determined—before all the ages and even before the very genesis of created beings—an ineffably good plan for His creations. And this plan[1] was for Him to be mingled,[4] without change, with human nature through a true union according to hypostasis, uniting human nature, without alteration,[5] to Himself, so that He would become man—in a manner known to Him—and at the same time make man God through union with Himself, and thus He wisely divided the ages, determining that some would be for the activity of His becoming man, and others for the activity of making man God.

22.3. Thus, inasmuch as the actual "ends of the ages"[2] predetermined for Him to become man "have come upon us"[6]—since the divine purpose of the Incarnation has been fulfilled through the events themselves—the divine Apostle, having care-

---

1. Eph 2.7.
2. 1 Cor 10.11. On this Question, see the study by Paul Blowers, "Realized Eschatology in Maximus the Confessor, *Ad Thalassium* 22," *SP* 33 (1997): 258–63.
3. Cf. Eph 1.11.
4. I.e., ἐγκραθῆναι, from κρᾶσις (mixture), which denotes a close union preserving the identity of each of the participating elements, without the implication of "confusion."
5. I.e., the Chalcedonian ἀναλλοιώτως.
6. 1 Cor 10.11.

fully examined this <...>⁷ and seeing that the end of the ages intended for God to become man had come about through the very Incarnation of the Word of God, says: "The ends of the ages have come upon us"⁸—not simply "the ages" as we ordinarily understand them, but clearly those which, intended for the actualization of the mystery of embodiment, have reached their proper limit⁹ according to the purpose of God.

22.4. Since, then, the "end of the ages," predetermined¹⁰ according to God's purpose to become man, "has come upon us"—inasmuch as God has in truth actualized and brought to completion His own perfect Incarnation—we must henceforth await those other ages that are to come for the actualization of the mystical and ineffable divinization of human beings, in which "God will show the overflowing riches of His goodness to us,"¹¹ completely and actively effecting divinization in those who are worthy. For if He Himself reached the limit of his mystical activity of becoming man,[3]—becoming like us in every way but without sin,¹² and having descended into the lowermost parts of the earth¹³ to where the tyranny of sin had driven man—then there will certainly also be a limit of God's mystical activity for the divinization of man in every way (with the obvious sole exception of any identification of man with God's essence), making man like Himself and raising him beyond all the heavens¹⁴ to where the natural grandeur of grace dwells and calls fallen man through the infinity of goodness. And this is what the great Apostle mystically teaches when he says: "In the ages to come, the overflowing riches of God's goodness will be shown to us."¹⁵

22.5. Let us, then, also separate the ages in thought, setting aside some for the mystery of the divine Incarnation, and oth-

---

7. There is a small lacuna in the Greek text at this point.
8. 1 Cor 10.11.
9. I.e., πέρας.
10. Cf. Eph 1.11.
11. Eph 2.7.
12. Heb 4.15.
13. Cf. Eph 4.9.
14. Cf. Eph 4.10; Phil 2.9.
15. Eph 2.7.

ers for the grace of human divinization, and we shall find that the former have already reached their proper end, while the latter have not yet arrived. To state the matter briefly, of these ages, the former belong to God's descent to man, while the latter belong to man's ascent to God. If we understand them in this way, we will not stumble over the obscurity of the divine words, nor think that the divine Apostle had made the same mistake.[16]

22.6. Or rather,[4] since as our Lord Jesus Christ is the beginning, middle, and end of all the ages past, present, and future,[17] one could say that through the power of faith, "the end of the ages"—I mean that end which will be actualized by grace according to its proper form in the divinization of the worthy—"has already come upon us."[18]

22.7. Or, again,[5] since the principle of activity is different from the principle of passivity, the divine Apostle at once mystically and wisely separated the active and the passive principles respectively into past and future ages.[19] For example, the ages

---

16. Cf. below, Qu. 28.4.
17. Cf. below, Qu. 19.2.
18. 1 Cor 10.11. Cf. *Myst.* 24, where Maximos speaks of a movement from "grace that is in faith" to "grace according to specific form" (CCSG 69:59, line 943). George Berthold, *Maximus Confessor: Selected Writings* (Mahwah, NJ: Paulist Press, 1985), 207, renders this phrase as: "Then we shall pass from the grace which is in faith to the grace *of vision*," which does not seem correct. In his translation of this Question, Paul Blowers, *The Cosmic Mystery of Jesus Christ: Selected Writings from St Maximus the Confessor* (Crestwood, NY: St Vladimir's Seminary Press, 2003), 117, renders this phrase as a simple adverb (i.e., "specifically") modifying the "end," which is grammatically sound, although it would seem that, in light of the passage from the *Mystagogy*, the text intends something more than just this. Eriugena renders the phrase as: *per speciem secundum gratiam* (CCSG 7:138, line 54).
19. On the opposition of "activity" (ποιεῖν) and "passivity" (πάσχειν), see Aristotle, *Categories* 2a3; *On Generation and Corruption* 322b11; and *Physics* 225b13. See also Polycarp Sherwood, *The Earlier Ambigua of Saint Maximus the Confessor and His Refutation of Origenism* (Rome: Herder, 1955), 133–35, who studies this passage in his excursus on ecstasy, and cites a parallel in Philo, *On the Cherubim* 77: "For it belongs to God to act (ποιεῖν), and this we may not ascribe to any created being; what belongs to the created is to suffer (πάσχειν)" (LCL 2:54–55); cf. Proclus, *The Elements of Theology* 80: "The proper nature of all bodies is to be acted upon, and of all incorporeals to be agents" (ed. E. R. Dodds [Oxford: Clarendon, 1963], 75).

of the flesh, in which we now live—for the Scripture also knows temporal ages, as when it says that "man toiled in this age and shall live unto its end"[20]—have the characteristic property of activity, but the future ages of the Spirit, which will come about after this present life, are characterized by the transformation of man through passivity. Existing here and now, we will reach the ends of the ages in a state of activity, at which point our power and ability to act will reach its limit.[21] In the ages that will follow, we shall passively experience by grace the transformation of divinization, no longer being active but passive, and for this reason we will not cease being divinized.[6] For then passivity will transcend nature, having no principle limiting the infinite divinization of those who passively experience it. For we act to the extent that our power of reason, which by nature is productive of the virtues, is active within us,[7] and the power of the intellect, which by potential is unconditionally receptive of all knowledge, passes through the whole nature of beings and whatever can be known, and leaves behind itself all the ages. And we are passive when, having completely traversed the inner principles of the beings created out of nothing, we will have come, in a manner beyond knowledge, to the Cause of beings, and, since all things will have reached their natural limits, our potentials for activity appropriate to them will come to rest. And we will become the very thing that is not in any way the outcome of our natural capacity, since nature does not possess the capacity to grasp what is beyond nature. For nothing created is by its nature capable of actualizing divinization, since it cannot grasp God. For this is the property of divine grace alone, that is, to grant the gift of divinization proportionately to created beings, brightly illumining nature by a light that transcends nature, actively elevating nature beyond its own proper limits through the excess of divine glory.[22]

20. Ps 48.10.
21. Cf. *Amb.* 7.13 (DOML 1:93); *Amb.* 15.7 (DOML 1:369–71); *Amb.* 20.4 (DOML 1:413–15); and *Cap. theol.* 1.47 (PG 90:1100BC).
22. Cf. *Amb.* 20.2 (DOML 1:408–11). The human capacity for reason can grasp the different principles of created beings, but having reached the limit of such knowledge, the same capacity cannot go further and know God, whose infinity cannot be contained within finite human reason. It is then that God

22.8. Thus in truth "the ends of the ages have come upon us,"[23] though we have not yet received through the grace that is in Christ the gift of the good things that transcend the ages and nature. Of these good things, the modes of the virtues and the inner principles of what can be known by nature have been established as figures[8] and foreshadowings, through which[24] God always willingly becomes man in those who are worthy.[25] Blessed therefore is the one who through wisdom has actively made God man in himself, who has brought to fullness the inception of this mystery, and who passively experiences becoming God by grace, for this experience will never come to an end. For He who grants this to the worthy is infinite in His essence and possesses the infinite power to divinize, a power which in fact transcends all infinity, and which never comes to an end in the things it has brought into being—unlike our own power—but rather by itself sustains those that received being from it, apart from which they are not capable of existing. This is why Scripture speaks of the "riches[9] of His goodness,"[26] since the divine and luminous disposition for our transformation unto divinization never ceases in its goodness toward us.

Scholia

[1] The union according to hypostasis of the Word with the flesh revealed the ineffable purpose of the divine counsel in that it did not mix the divine essence with the flesh, but rather showed forth one hypostasis of the Word even in His becoming flesh, so that the flesh might both remain flesh according to its essence and become divine according to the hypostasis.

[2] Some ages, he says, are revelatory of the divine Incarnation, "the end of which has come upon us,"[27] while others

---

Himself enables human beings to transcend the limits of nature, so that they experience ("suffer") a divinizing knowledge that does not have its source in created nature.

23. 1 Cor 10.11.
24. I.e., through the modes of the virtues and the inner principles of knowledge.
25. Cf. *Amb.* 7.22 (DOML 1:107); and *Amb.* 10.9 (DOML 1:164–65).
26. Eph 2.7.
27. 1 Cor 10.11.

demonstrate our divinization, of the latter of which the "riches"[28] of glory have not yet been revealed.

[3] A firm assurance, he says, for looking forward with hope to the divinization of human nature is provided by the Incarnation of God, which makes man God to the same degree that God Himself became man. For it is clear that He who became man without sin[29] will divinize human nature without changing it into the divine nature, and will raise it up for His own sake to the same degree that He lowered Himself for man's sake.[30]

[4] This is a contemplation indicating that in Christ the beginning, middle, and end of the ages are circumscribed without intervals. For it was through the Incarnation that He "came to us" as the "end of the ages,"[31] possessing the fullness of the Father's goodness, of which He made us in Himself partakers by grace, establishing hope for us as an assurance of faith.[32]

[5] The principle of activity is the natural capacity for actualizing the virtues. The principle of passivity is the grace of things beyond nature or the occurrence of what is contrary to nature. For just as we do not have a natural capacity for what is above being, neither do we have by nature a capacity for what lacks being. Thus we passively experience divinization by grace as something that is above nature, but we do not actively accomplish it; for by nature we do not have the capacity to attain divinization. Again, we passively experience evil as something contrary to nature that occurs in the will; for we do not have a natural capacity for generating evil. Thus while we are in our present state we can actively accomplish the virtues, since we have a natural capacity for accomplishing them. But in the age to come we experience divinization passively, receiving as a gift the grace to experience it.

[6] We cease to accomplish the virtues, he says, after this present life. But, on a level higher than that of the virtues, we

28. Eph 2.7.
29. Cf. Heb 4.15.
30. Cf. *Amb.* 10.9 (DOML 1:165).
31. Cf. 1 Cor 10.11.
32. Cf. Cor 1.3–7.

never cease passively to experience divinization by grace. For this experience, which transcends nature, is infinite, and so is always active and effective, whereas a passive experience contrary to nature is without real existence, and so is inefficacious.

[7] When, he says, reason is in control of anger and desire, it actively accomplishes the virtues. When the intellect devotes its attention to the principles of created things, it reaps true knowledge. Thus reason, after rejecting everything that is contrary, discovers what is worthy of love according to nature; and when the intellect, after passing through the things that are known, apprehends the divine cause of beings that transcends being and knowledge, it experiences divinization by grace. Here, reason's power of natural discrimination is suspended, for there is no longer anything to discriminate; while the intellect's natural intellection is brought to a halt, for there is no longer anything to be known; and the one found worthy to participate in the divine is made God by an identity grounded in stability.

[8] The modes of the virtues, he says, and the principles of beings are figures of divine good things, and in them God continually becomes man. As His body He has the modes of the virtues, and as His soul the spiritual principles of knowledge. In this way He divinizes those found worthy, giving them the enhypostatic stamp of virtue and bestowing on them the essential subsistence of true knowledge.

[9] The "riches"[33] are understood to be the goodness of God's disposition toward us.

33. Eph 2.7.

QUESTION 23

F DAVID ruled only over the "Israel that is according to the flesh,"[1] and if this Israel spurned the kingdom of Christ, which is why it passed to the Gentiles,[2] how then can the words of the archangel stand, which say: "And the Lord God will give to Him the throne of His father David, and He will reign over the house of Jacob unto the ages"?[3]

Response

23.2. It seems to me that this difficulty has a clear and obvious explanation. Insofar as "not all who are descended from Israel are Israel, and not all are children of Abraham because they are his seed, but only the children of the promise who are reckoned" by God "as his seed,"[4] and if "the number of the sons of Israel will be like the stars of heaven and like the sands of the sea, but only a remnant will be saved,"[5] then it is clear that "Israel" is the faithful people who "sees God"[6] through its

---

1. Cf. 1 Cor 10.18.
2. Cf. Gal 3.4.
3. Lk 1.32–33.
4. Rom 9.6–7.
5. Rom 9.27; Heb 11.12.
6. Cf. *Amb.* 10.17 (DOML 1:175); *QD.* 25; 80 (CCSG 10:21, lines 4–5; 61, lines 8–9); *Exp. Ps.* 59 (CCSG 23:4, line 30; 15, lines 223–34); *Ep.* 8 (PG 91:444C); Philo, *On the Change of Names* 81: "We shall also find that the change of Jacob's name to 'Israel' is much to the purpose. Why so? Because Jacob is the supplanter, and Israel is he who sees God" (LCL 5:183; cf. 10:334); Clement, *Paedagogus* 1.9.77.2: "Understanding is the sight of the soul, which is why Israel means 'he who sees God,' that is, he who understands God" (SC 70:248); Cyril of Alexandria, *Glaphyra (on the Pentateuch):* "The name 'Israel' means an intellect that sees God" (PG 69:85); and C. T. R. Haywood, *Interpretations of the Name Israel in Ancient Judaism and Some Early Christian Writings* (Oxford: Oxford University Press, 2005), 156–93.

works of righteousness and true knowledge according to faith, whether such a people is the bearer of Israel according to the flesh, or comes from the portion of the Gentiles. For the one who bears in himself the clear and undefiled character of the faith of Abraham, Isaac, and Jacob, will not be estranged from the calling and grace of the true Israel.[7]

23.3. The blessed David himself ruled over the faithful in Israel; but at the very moment when Israel extinguished the light of its faith, it immediately fell away from the rule of David.[1] Thus when God spoke prophetically to Moses, he told him that He would establish the spiritual throne of David, the intelligible rule of rational souls, the faithful house of Jacob, and the holy and great nation—not the corporeal Israel that had embittered Him. In other words, He would establish the Israel that was figuratively understood in the promise He made to Moses, when he said: "Let me destroy this nation once and for all, and I will establish you as a nation far greater and stronger than this one."[8] Here He was not referring to the faithless house of Jacob, which had embittered Him; not to the sinful nation; not to the wicked seed nor the lawless sons; not to the rulers of Sodom and the people of Gomorrah; not to those who turned away through a wicked turning,[9] those, I mean, who forsook the Lord, and who provoked the Holy One of Israel, who neither recognized God nor understood Him, and who were wounded by the incurable wound of faithlessness, which in no way admits of any rational treatment capable of curing the soul's lack of faith. This is why Scripture says: "Woe, sinful nation, an evil seed, and lawless sons: you have forsaken the Lord, and provoked the Holy One of Israel. Why do you continue to wound yourself, adding lawlessness to lawlessness? It is not possible to apply a healing balm, or oil, or bandages."[10] Neither was He

---

7. See *Amb.* 10.50, where Maximos contends that anyone can become a "spiritual Abraham" by adopting the patriarch's "same marks of virtue and knowledge" (DOML 1:229–31); cf. *Amb.* 10.46, 54, 112 (DOML 1:223, 237, 329–31).

8. Cf. Dt 9.14.

9. Cf. Jer 8.5. The same allusion to Jeremiah is found in Gregory Nazianzus, *Or.* 16.15 (PG 35:956A).

10. Is 1.4–6.

referring to those who "limp along on both of their feet,"[11] who turned away from the truth and who were cast out of the divine inheritance,[2] after the manner of Cain, Ishmael, Esau, Ruben, Er, Onan, Manasseh, Eliaph, and Amnon, who were the first-born sons of the patriarchs and prophets and who were cast out and rejected as unworthy. This is why Scripture says: "Israel, my *first*-born son,"[12] for he was not the *only*-begotten son. Instead, there was the hope for the introduction of another people, godly and pious, created according to God, and led to adoption by grace through the casting out of the faithless Israel, which like Cain rises up[3] in envy against the intelligible Abel and murders him;[13] which like Ishmael mocks the divine way of life of the intelligible Isaac;[14] which like Esau rages against the intelligible Jacob;[15] which like Er and Onan spills the seed of faith and of faith's righteousness on the ground of delusion and passions;[16] which denied the church of God, like those who denied Tamar;[17] which like Manasseh became oblivious of the virtues,[18] and which through pride was troubled when the kingdom was taken by the intelligible David, and which for this reason was set at naught like Eliaph; and which became the creator of strange transgression like Amnon.[19] Indeed, the "great and strong nation" does not consist of these "strange sons who fell away from their paths through lameness,"[20] "breathing forth rage and murder,"[21] who are fleshly, and sons of the flesh only, and thus strangers to grace, "whose God is the stomach, and whose shame is their glory,"[22] whose "memorial" of faithlessness "will be destroyed with a loud noise."[23] No, not these,

11. 3 Kgs 18.21.
12. Ex 4.22.
13. Gn 4.8.
14. Cf. Gn 21.
15. Gn 27.41.
16. Cf. Gn 38.9.
17. Gn 38.11.
18. Cf. 4 Kgs 21.
19. 2 Kgs 13.
20. Ps 17.45.
21. Acts 9.1.
22. Phil 3.19.
23. Ps 9.6.

but rather, as I have said, it consists of the faithful and spiritual Israel, who by faith sees God, an Israel gathered together from all the gentile nations "according to the election of grace,"[24] a "people for God's own possession, a holy nation, and a royal priesthood."[25] A people that, through the words uttered by the angel to the Virgin,[26] God promised to give to the Savior of all, who would be born from her. And the proof of these promises was demonstrated by subsequent events, for the Lord fulfilled the promises to the fathers,[27] blessing and adopting all the Gentiles in the spiritual Abraham, through faith establishing Abraham as the spiritual father of all the nations, so that now Christ sits upon the spiritual throne of David, and rules over the faithful house of Jacob unto the ages, in a kingdom having no end.

Scholia

[1] During the reign of Jeroboam, Israel was separated from the house of David, having lost its faith in God.

[2] This is a recounting of the firstborn who were cast out through the ages, to whom the people of Israel are also likened. If we grant that Israel suitably received the title of "my firstborn son,"[28] he was nonetheless cast out as "firstborn" owing to the call of the Gentiles, who after him were adopted through faith.

[3] Here he says that the brothers against whom the firstborn sons conspired are a type of the Lord and of the new people of faith.

24. Rom 11.5.
25. 1 Pt 2.9.
26. Lk 1.25–28.
27. Cf. Rom 15.8; Lk 1.55.
28. Ex 4.22.

QUESTION 24

HAT IS THE meaning of the passage in Acts concerning Peter, which says: "When we had passed the first and second guard, we came to the iron gate"?[1]

Response

24.2. An intellect that is faithful and practical, like Saint Peter when he was taken prisoner by Herod—that is, by the law of skin, since Herod means "made of skin,"[2] which is the "mind of the flesh"[3]—such an intellect, I say, is closed in by two "guards"[1] and one "iron gate," being besieged by the activity of the passions and by the mind's assent to that activity. When, with the help of the principle of practical philosophy, as though with the help of an angel, the intellect passes through these, as if they were guards—that is to say, prisons—it "comes to the iron gate, which leads to the city,"[4] by which I mean the obdurate and stubborn attachment of the senses to sensible objects, which is hard to overcome. This attachment, being opened by the principle of natural contemplation in the spirit, spontaneously impels the intellect, now free from the wrath of Herod, fearlessly toward intelligible realities that are kindred to it.

---

1. Acts 12.10.
2. Maximos introduced this etymology in *QD*. 71 (CCSG 10:54), and offered an expanded treatment of it in *Amb*. 38.2 (DOML 2:89). Note the connection here between the "law of skin" and the "garments of skin," which God made for Adam and Eve after the fall (Gn 3:21). On "Herod," cf. *Cap. theol.* 1.72, 75–76 (PG 90:1109B; 1112AB).
3. Rom 8.6–7.
4. Acts 12.10.

Scholion

[1] He calls the fixed habit of vice and its activity "guards," for the characteristic mark of habit is assent, and it is through such a fixed habit and activity that the evil one endeavors to place the saints under subjection. The "iron gate" is the natural attachment of sense perception to objects of sense, from which, like an angel, the principle of knowledge that comes from ascetic practice frees the one who is truly faithful.

QUESTION 25

HAT IS THE meaning of the words: "But I want you to understand that the head of every man is Christ, the head of a woman is her husband, and the head of Christ is God."[1] Any man who prays or prophesies with his head covered dishonors his head, but any woman who prays or prophesies with her head unveiled dishonors her head—it is the same as if her head were shaven"?[2] And what, moreover, is the meaning of: "This is why a woman ought to have a veil on her head, because of the angels"?[3]

Response

25.2. One should know that when the divine Apostle said that Christ is the head of every "man," he obviously means of every believing[4] man who is engaged in the practice of the divine commandments, and who contemplates pious doctrines, because the inclusive sense of the word does not include men who are not believers. For how could Christ be the head of those who do not believe in Him?

25.3. Thus, according to one interpretation, employing the principle of anagogy, we say[1] that "man" here signifies the in-

---

1. The Greek words ἀνήρ and γυνή mean both man/husband and woman/wife, although the context and argument do not allow for consistent translation; on this problem, see William Orr and James Arthur Walther, *I Corinthians: A New Translation. Introduction with a Study of the Life of Paul, Notes and Commentary*, The Anchor Bible (New York: Doubleday, 1976), 259.

2. 1 Cor 11.3–5.

3. 1 Cor 11.10.

4. The Greek word πιστός means both "believing" and "faithful," and both senses are operative throughout this entire Question.

tellect[5] engaged in practice, having as its head the rationale[6] of faith. Looking to this head as if it were Christ, the intellect establishes its own proper life, being built up through ascetic practice by the graces of the commandments, and does not dishonor its head[2]—that is, its faith—by any external, material veil or covering, placing nothing transitory and fleeting above the faith. The "wife" of such an intellect is, we say, the very habit of ascetic practice, richly adorned and veiled with many diverse ascetical thoughts and practices. Or rather she has as her veil the intellect itself, which is her proper head according to the abundance and beauty of these thoughts and manners. And we say that Christ is substantive[7] faith,[3] whose head is clearly God, to whom the rationale of faith leads, showing to those being led the God in whom He exists by nature.[8]

25.4. And, again, "man"[4] is the intellect diligently engaged in natural contemplation in the spirit, having as its "head" the creator Word who is revealed by faith through the beautiful order of visible realities.[9] Such an intellect does not dishonor the Word by covering it and placing it, as it were, beneath anything visible; neither does it make anything else whatsoever higher than the Word. The "wife" of this intellect is the power of sensation that dwells with it, through which the intellect ranges over the nature of sensible realities. From these latter the intellect gathers together[10] the more divine principles, but it does not allow sensation to be stripped of its rational coverings, lest it become the servant of irrationality and sin (by rejecting the covers of the more divine principles), and exchange its head, the intellect, for the passion of irrationality. But the head[5] of Christ, that is, the Creator Word—who through faith appears proportionately in beings by means of the natural contempla-

---

5. In Greek the word "intellect" (ὁ νοῦς) is a masculine noun, and thus presents itself as an anagogical equivalent of "man" (or "husband").

6. Or "principle" or simply "word" (*logos*).

7. I.e., *enhypostatos*.

8. In this first moment of spiritual ascent, the intellect cultivates the habit of ascetic practice under the rationale of faith.

9. Cf. Rom 1.20.

10. "Gathers together" renders the Greek ἀναλέγεται, which can also have the sense of "to read through" something; cf. *Amb.* 21.7 (DOML 1:431).

tion of creatures—is the ineffable Intellect[11] that begets Him according to essence, in relation to whom the Word, through Himself, firmly establishes the human intellect that is elevated to Him through the pious contemplation of beings, providing it with intelligible reflections of divine realities in proportion to its knowledge of visible ones.[12]

25.5. From still another perspective, "man"[6] is the intellect that has entered into mystical theology, having Christ as its uncovered head, who, by means of initiations beyond demonstration,[13] is understood in a manner beyond knowledge, or, to speak strictly, whose uncovered head is the Word of faith known in a manner beyond intellection.[7] Above this, such an intellect places nothing from beings: neither sensation, nor reason, nor intellect, nor intellection, nor knowledge, nor anything known, thought, or capable of being spoken, nor what is sensible or sensed, inasmuch as it cooperates with the praiseworthy and transcendent[14] privation,[8] which transcends both itself and beings, and which is preeminently divinizing. The "wife" of this intellect[9] is the mind which purifies itself of every sensory image,[15] inasmuch as it has the intellect as its head, thickly covered with intuitions—without origin and beyond understanding—of ineffable and unknowable doctrines. But the head of Christ,[10] that is, of the Word that is mystically manifested according to its preeminence, is the Intellect, absolutely and in all ways in-

11. I.e., God the Father.
12. In the second moment of ascent, the intellect contemplates the *logoi* of nature, not simply under the rationale of faith, but under the headship of the Logos Himself. In this the intellect is necessarily assisted by sense perception, informed by the structures of reason. Not simply a human project, intellection and sensation are both aided by grace, without which it cannot comprehend the mystery of creation.
13. Cf. *Amb.* 45.5: "The head [i.e., of Christ the Lamb] shall be partaken of by whosoever possesses, from first principles beyond demonstration, a faith whose rational principles are entirely free" (DOML 2:219).
14. I.e., ὑπερέχουσαν (στέρησιν), a Dionysian technical term, usually rendered as καθ' ὑπεροχήν, and often used in conjunction with "negation" (ἀφαίρεσις). It signifies not absolute privation but rather superabundance (e.g., *DN* 1.5; 7.3; *CH* 13.4; *MT* 5; *Ep.* 4.1) as a way to remove all finite connotation in a union of both affirmation and negation; cf. *Amb.* 71.3 (DOML 2:315–17).
15. I.e., φαντασία.

finitely separated from all things, which Christ makes known to those who are worthy, since He is the natural Word of this Intellect, "for he who has seen me," He says, "has seen the Father."[16] For truly the intellect's understanding of the Word becomes the clear knowledge of the Intellect that begot Him, since He shows that the Intellect subsists in Himself essentially, and it is to this Intellect that He leads the intellect that desires identity with God by grace,[11] insofar as it has been released from the diversity and quantity it apprehended intellectually in the multiplicity of beings, and is now gathered together into deiform unity by means of the identity and simplicity of its perpetual and intensive motion around God.[17]

25.6. Thus, every intellect engaged in ascetic practice, when it "prays or prophesies,"[12]—that is, when it seeks, as if in petition, the inner principles of the virtues (for thus one must understand "prays"), or when it manifests their modes by its deeds (for thus one must take "prophecies")—ought to see nothing but the naked principle of faith, neither understanding nor thinking nor doing anything[13] to cover its head, as it has been summoned to, by placing something else above it. And every wife, that is, the habitual state of the intellect engaged in ascetic practice, when it "prays or prophesies"—that is, when it is secretly moved according to its disposition, or when it gives form to its virtue through its external behavior without the discernment of reason—dishonors its head, pursuing the good in a passionate manner, since it is deprived of the beautifying presence of reason that covers it like a veil. And every intellect, engaged in the exercise of natural contemplation, when it either "prays or prophesies" with its head covered—that is, when it cognitively seeks after the principles of beings, or imparts them to others through teaching, along with any kind of inclination, in any manner whatsoever, toward anything but the goal consistent

16. Jn 14.9.
17. In the third moment of ascent, the Logos is known directly, but in a manner beyond ordinary understanding. In negating all knowledge of created beings, the intellect is assisted by a mind purified of sensory images. Here the *via negativa* does not result in total ignorance but rather opens a space for participation in divine knowledge.

with piety—dishonors its head, for it has placed something transient above right knowledge consistent with piety. And every wife, that is, sensation, which is naturally oriented towards objects of sense, when it does not have its head covered all around with the intellective principles of visible realities, dishonors its head, passionately approaching contemplation through its natural relation to visible realities. And every intellect that has become a lover of mystical theology, when it "prays or prophesies" with its head covered—that is, if, when seeking without cognition to enter into the innermost contemplations, or when teaching and initiating others into theology, it should introduce some intelligible form in the course of being initiated or initiating others into the Word beyond intellection—dishonors its head, placing the One who is simple and who transcends every intellection beneath a created being or object of knowledge, whereas without eyes[18] it must see the true God the Word naked of every concept and knowledge, knowing clearly that, in the case of God, it is rather the preeminent privations that hold true,[14] and to a certain extent affirm something positive of the divine[19] through the complete negation of beings.[15] And every wife, being the discursive faculty of such an intellect, when it "prays or prophesies" with its head uncovered, that is, untethered from its intellective power, which is thickly covered with mystical contemplations, dishonors its head, casting aside the divine and ineffable knowledge which covers the intellect like a head.

25.7. Every man, then, by which I mean every intellect engaged in ascetic practice, natural contemplation, or theology, when it "prays or prophesies"—that is, when it is teaching or being taught—should have Christ, who is its head, uncovered. Thus, the intellect engaged in ascetic practice should prefer nothing over faith and virtue; the intellect engaged in natural contemplation should hold no other principle higher than the first principle; and the theological intellect should give no outward shape, based on intellections derived from created beings, to the One who is beyond intellection and knowledge.

18. Borrowing an image from Dionysios, *DN* 4.11 (156, line 18; 708D); and *MT* 1.1 (142, line 4; 997B).
19. Literally: "... to a certain extent disclose the divine affirmation ..."

And let every woman—that is, the habitual state of the practical intellect, or the sensation of the natural intellect, or the wise mind of the theological intellect—keep her head covered. Let the first be covered by the discernment of reason concerning what must and must not be done; let the second be covered by reason's capacity for the highest degree of understanding when examining visible realities; and let the third have the completely indemonstrable knowledge of realities beyond intellection. For every habit, perception, or mind not covered in the manner mentioned above, in no way differs from a head that is shaved, that is, which possesses no principle of virtue, reverence for God, mystical knowledge, or divine love.

25.8. Every such woman, therefore, is always obliged—as is only natural—to have the authority of reason on her head, by which I mean rational oversight, and certainly on account of the angels, who behold our visible and invisible movements, and who keep a record of our every thought and action, unto our praise or censure, for the dread day of examination. And also on account of the thoughts of the conscience, these also being understood figuratively as angels, either accusing us for our deeds, or defending us both now and later on the Day of Judgment. And, finally, on account of the wicked angels, who observe our habitual disposition, perception, and mind, so that when they see us stripped naked of both rational and intellective discernment as well as piety and knowledge, they will put in place what gives rise to their contraries, I mean the lack of discernment, impiety, and ignorance, through which the wicked demons are of a nature to actualize evil, delusion, and godlessness within us.[20]

25.9. But God is called the head of Christ, since the Intellect by nature is the principle (according to cause) of the Word.

Scholia

[1] "Man" also signifies the intellect that pursues practical philosophy.

---

20. See above, Intro. 1.2.9, where these are among the questions raised by Thalassios.

[2] He called Christ the "head" as the substance of the good things to come, because "faith," according to the divine Apostle, is the "substance" of things to come and the "evidence of things not seen,"[21] which very thing is Christ Himself, "in whom are the hidden treasures of wisdom and knowledge."[22]

[3] "Substantive faith" is faith that is actual and active, so that, in those engaged in ascetic practice, the Word of God is shown to be embodied by means of the commandments, through which the Word raises up the practitioners toward the Father, in whom He subsists by nature.

[4] "Man" is also the intellect piously engaged in natural contemplation, having as its head the Word of God, whom it contemplates in its mind according to faith as the cause of the coming into being of visible realities.

[5] Inasmuch as the Intellect, he says, is conceived of simultaneously with the Word that created beings (to which the Word refers all beings as their cause), he called God the Father the "head" of Christ, like an intellect naturally bringing forth a word.

[6] "Man" is also the one who is taught mystical theology.

[7] Understand the phrase, "in a manner beyond intellection," according to preeminence, for our faith, by which I mean God, is a reality beyond intellection.

[8] Here he is saying that if a person, in a manner beyond cognition by means of the preeminent negation of created beings, has received the immediate vision[23] of the Word that transcends every word, then that same person has the Word as his head, that is, the absolutely unique Word, beyond, or with whom, or after whom, no other word[24] wholly alien to it in nature has ever existed. For the begetter of this Word is the Intellect, which is single in nature, and to whom, as to the head, the Word through the Spirit (with whom He is consubstantial) elevates the intellect that follows Him.

---

21. Heb 11.1.
22. Col 2.3.
23. I.e., αὐτοψία, a word heavily attested in Greek medical and philosophical writers, but rather infrequent among Christian authors.
24. Or "principle."

[9] The wife of the practical intellect is, he says, its habitual state of mind, since it gives birth to the modes of virtue. The wife of the natural intellect is sensation, made noble by the principles of the spirit, inasmuch as it gives birth to dispassionate images[25] of beings. The wife of the theological intellect is the pure mind, since the latter is receptive of the One, thrice-radiant Light in a single manner.

[10] He calls the super-essential and super-essentially incarnate Word "Christ," for by means of natural reason the intellect cannot comprehend even His Incarnation. The "head" of the Word, he says, is the Intellect that is Cause by nature, which is causally understood together with the Word from the point of view of both nature and causation. For the one who by faith has timelessly seen the Word has also mystically seen, simultaneously with the Word, the Intellect that begot Him, for the latter is in the former according to essence. Some people say that "Christ" refers to the humanity of Christ, since He is the head of all, that is, the whole of nature, and it is clear that the head of Christ's human aspect is His divinity, for by naming the parts with the name of the whole, they set forth the correct understanding of the matter.

[11] The perfected intellect's identity with God by grace is the simple and indivisible motion around that which is identical by nature, with respect to which[26] there is no acquisition of intelligible realities that differ according to the quantity of their substance or the quality of their potency, but rather ineffable enjoyment possessing a sensation that transcends intellection.

[12] He calls the "prayer" of the practical intellect its petition for the virtues, while he calls "prophecy" the true teaching concerning the principles contained in the virtues. He says that the "prayer" of the natural intellect is its petition for the true knowledge of beings, while its "prophecy" is the transmission of this knowledge to others through true teaching. The "prayer" of the theological intellect is ineffable silence, according to which the intellect, preeminently through the privation of beings, becomes worthy of the union that is beyond under-

---

25. I.e., φαντασίαι.
26. I.e., motion.

standing and knowledge, while its "prophecy" is its initiation of others into this union. For prayer to God brings about the union of the one praying with God, while prophecy, for the sake of God, persuades the one prophesying to share with others the good things that have been given to him.

[13] Not to understand anything is to understand that the Word of God is not anything that can be understood; not to think or do anything is to believe that the Word is not anything that can be thought—that is, brought into the mind—or that can enter into generation and corruption (for these are properly called "things made").[27]

[14] When, he says, we speak affirmatively about the Divine, together with it we simultaneously think of beings, but only insofar as the Divine is the cause of their creation.[28] When, on the other hand, we completely negate the Divine from beings, we do not think of the Divine even as their cause, for to speak truly it has no relation to beings, for it is according to relation that we naturally speak of two related items together.[29] It follows that the good theologian will make preeminent unknowing the affirmation of the true knowledge of God, who is absolutely beyond intellection.

[15] He says that the preeminent privations give us a small amount of positive knowledge. For they only show that God exists, but they deny that he is any of those things that exist or are able to be understood, thought, or spoken.[30]

---

27. This scholion appears only in Eriugena's Latin translation (CCSG 7:170, lines 61–66); Steel and Laga tentatively ascribe it to Eriugena (CCSG 7:ci).

28. Cf. *Amb.* 5.2 (DOML 1:33).

29. God has "no relation to beings" in the sense of not being bound in a relation to anything contrary to his will, that is, by a necessity of his nature that would require fulfillment from or dependence on something else; cf. *Cap. theol.* 1.7: "No origin, intermediary state or consummation can ever be altogether free from the category of relationship. God, being infinitely beyond every kind of relationship, is by nature neither an origin, nor an intermediary state, nor a consummation, nor any of those things to which it is possible to apply the category of relationship" (PG 90:1085B); and *Or. Dom.*: "The divinity has within it no mediating relationship of cause and effect, since it is altogether identical with itself and free from relationships" (CCSG 23:54, lines 457–59).

30. This scholion appears only in Eriugena's Latin translation (CCSG 7:170, lines 75–78); Steel and Laga inadvertently omitted it from their list (CCSG 7:ci).

QUESTION 26

IF THE KING of Babylon allegorically[1] represents the devil, why does God, through the prophet Jeremiah, threaten the kings of the nations and the king of Judah, with chains, bonds, famine, death, the sword, and captivity if they refuse to serve Him,[2] while those who serve Him willingly, it says, will live freely in their land? And why does God call the devil his "servant," saying: "I have given the whole earth to Nebuchadnezzar, king of Babylon, my servant, and I have given him the wild beasts to serve him"?[3] What is this "servitude" of the devil, and what are these beasts? What are the six kinds of threats? And who are the kings of the nations? And who is the king of Judah?[4]

Response

26.2. The devil[1] is both God's enemy and God's avenger.[5] He is God's enemy when he appears, in his hatred for God, somehow to have acquired a love for us human beings that is destructive, persuading our power of free choice, through pleasure and modes of voluntary passions, to value what is transitory more than eternal good things. In this way, stealing the whole of the soul's appetite for God, he utterly separates us

---

1. This is the first appearance of the word "allegory" in this work, which is attested only three other times; cf. below, Qu. 38.2; Qu. 52.6; and Qu. 54.17.
2. Cf. Jer 34.1, 8, 11.
3. Jer 34.6.
4. Cf. Origen, *Homilies on Jeremiah* 1.3.2 (SC 232:200, lines 22–29); idem, *Homilies on Ezekiel* 1.1–2 (SC 352:36–47); and Theodoret, *Commentary on Ezekiel* 34:27–28 (PG 81:1164D–1165), which offer a similar interpretation of the Babylonian captivity.
5. Cf. Ps 8.2.

from divine love, making us willing enemies of the One who created us. He is an avenger, on the other hand, when—inasmuch as we have become subject to him on account of our sins—he lays bare his hatred for us and demands our chastisement. For nothing pleases the devil so much as a man being chastised. This being granted to him, he devises one assault of involuntary suffering after another, like a raging storm, and, with God's permission, cruelly attacks those over whom he has received authority, not because he wishes to carry out God's command, but because he desires to satisfy the passion of his hatred for us, so that, when the weakened soul stumbles under the great weight of its painful misfortunes, it might lose its capacity to hope in God, reckoning the onslaught of all the things it has so grievously suffered, not as a divine admonishment,[2] but as a reason to deny the existence of God altogether.[6]

26.3. For inasmuch as God is good, and wishes completely to uproot from us the seed of evil[7]—that is, the pleasure that robs the intellect of God's love—He allows the devil to inflict sufferings and chastisements on us, using the soul's pains to scrape away the poison[3] of past pleasure, and instilling within us hatred and utter revulsion for the things of this present life, which pander to the senses alone, for when we have acquired these things we gain nothing from their use save chastisement.[4] For God wishes to make the devil's power of chastisement and hatred for human beings the contingent cause of the return to virtue in those who by their own free choice fell away from it.

26.4. Thus, insofar as the devil has permission to chastise sinners, he is called the "servant" of God, even though he is an apostate and a malicious thief. He possesses, moreover, very much the same inclination of mind as those who have willingly distanced themselves from God through sensual pleasure—for it is fitting and just that those who have gladly accepted his evil suggestions to commit sins through their own volition should also be punished by him. For through our voluntary passions the devil is the sower of pleasure, and through our involuntary passions he is the inflictor of pain.[8]

6. For a similar argument, cf. *Amb.* 11.2 (DOML 1:345).
7. Suggesting a contrast to the divine "seed" mentioned above, Qu. 6.
8. Cf. above, Intro. 1.2.14–21.

26.5. When the inhabitants of Judea and Jerusalem, that is, those who, seeking the "glory of men,"[9] abandon the habitual state of mind acquired through ascetic practice or contemplative understanding, and adopt instead a superficial manner of virtuous behavior—uttering words of wisdom and knowledge without the corresponding works of righteousness—and when, in addition, they display to others their vanity because of their supposed virtue and knowledge, then they are rightly handed over to suitable hardships, thereby learning through suffering the humility that was previously unknown to them because of their vain conceit.[10] Having this in mind, the admirable apostle Paul handed over to Satan the Corinthian who had transgressed the law, "unto the destruction of the flesh, so that his spirit might be saved on the day of the Lord Jesus."[11] By the same logic, the kings of Judea and Jerusalem are handed over to the king of the Assyrians; that is, the contemplative and cognitive intellect is given to the devil for chastisement, and he justly inflicts on it sufferings and misfortunes, so that through suffering it might learn to philosophize about endurance and patience in sufferings, instead of boasting vainly and arrogantly about things that do not exist.

26.6. It follows, then, that anyone who is aware of his actions, and who willingly[5] endures to accept with due thankfulness the painful inflictions of involuntary trials, is not exiled from his state of grace according to virtue and knowledge—as happened to the men of Judea and Jerusalem—because he has submitted willingly to the yoke of the king of Babylon,[12] and pays his debt, as it were, by accepting the inflictions of torments.[13] In

---

9. Jn 12.43; cf. 1 Thes 2.6.
10. See above, Intro. 1.2.15, where these are among the vices listed among the consequences of "pursuing pleasure for the sake of self-love"; cf. *Amb*. 10.120 (DOML 1:343).
11. 1 Cor 5.5.
12. Cf. Jer 27.17.
13. True to his teaching, Maximos, at his first trial in 655, was willing to accept the punishments threatened by the imperial government, provided his accusers could bring forward actual evidence of his guilt, which they could not; see the eyewitness *Rel. mot.* 1–2: "Maximos: If you are speaking the truth, let the evidence be produced, and I will submit to the punishments decreed

this way, while remaining in a state of grace according to virtue and knowledge, he pays tribute to the king of Babylon not only with his compulsory sufferings, which have arisen within the passible side of his nature, but also with his mental assent to these sufferings, accepting them as his due on account of his former offenses—and through his true worship, by which I mean through his humble disposition, he offers to God the correction of his errors.

26.7. But anyone who does not accept with due thankfulness the misfortune that, by God's permission, comes upon him through involuntary trials for his own correction, and who does not repent and rid himself of the conceited pretense that he is righteous, and who resists the just judgments decreed by God—as did the Judeans of old—and who does not willingly submit to the yoke of the king of Babylon according to the divine command, such a person, I say, is given over to the captivity of the king of Babylon, and to chains, and bonds, and death, and famine, and the sword, and will be completely exiled from his own native land, that is, from the habitual state that appears to conform to that of virtue and knowledge. For his apostasy from divine things, he is condemned to captivity; for his erroneous opinion about beings, he is bound in chains; for his utter inactivity with respect to good works, he is placed in bonds; for being barren of divine teachings, he is subjected to famine; for his abject hardness of heart and insensitivity to good things, he suffers death; and for his impassioned and licentious thoughts, which destroy the memory of God, he is given over to the sword.

26.8. All these things and more are suffered by whoever is exiled from his habitual state of mind according to virtue and knowledge, as if from his own native land, because in his pride

---

by the law." Subsequently threatened with being burned at the stake, Maximos said: "I give thanks to God who cleanses me of my voluntary sins by means of involuntary chastisement" (ed. Pauline Allen and Bronwen Neil, *Maximus the Confessor and His Companions: Documents from Exile* [Oxford: Oxford University Press, 2002], 51). The Greek *Life of Maximos* likewise emphasizes the Confessor's "superior endurance and his utmost distinction in suffering" (ibid., 76–77; cf. 85–86). In *Amb.* 53.3, Maximos explores the same theme in an allegorical exegesis of the "good thief" (DOML 2:237).

and empty conceit he willingly pays the penalty incurred by his transgressions, and accepts "afflictions, hardships, and calamities,"[14] as the divine Apostle would have it, even though he himself was exempt from any such debt on account of his righteousness. For the great Apostle knew that humility produced from external bodily toils safeguards the divine treasures of the soul, and for this reason he acquiesced to endure these things patiently, both for his own sake and for the sake of those to whom he was an example of faith and virtue, so that, even if they were to suffer as being guilty for their sins—like the Corinthian who was penanced[15]—they might have him who suffered innocently as consolation and a model of patience.

26.9. In the passage of Scripture that you have cited, I think that the "kings of the nations" are those people who preside over the rest of the "dishonorable passions,"[16] who will justly be subjected to chastisement for the debts they have accumulated, which is why they are handed over to the king of Babylon, who is a chastising power and rejoices in tormenting human nature. Thus the king of Egypt is the intellect infatuated with sensual pleasure and licentiousness; the Moabite king is the voluptuary and effeminate intellect; the Ammonite king is the greedy intellect; the Syrian king is the intellect that is superstitious and contentious—for the Syrian is the only one, according to Scripture, who was opposed to Solomon,[17] that is, to peace and wisdom[6]—the king of Tyre is the intellect that loves the world and this present life. And there are all the other kings, whose proper meaning the man of knowledge will know by interpreting the meaning of their names, the location of their kingdoms, their hereditary transmission of power, their mutual alliances, and their particular animosity to Israel <...>.[18] For it is not the case that they all receive one and the same interpretation, but rather an interpretation based on the underlying purpose and the sense of the prophecy. To be sure, Scripture is accustomed to

---

14. 2 Cor 6.4.
15. Cf. 1 Cor 5.1–5.
16. Cf. Rom 1.26.
17. 3 Kgs 11.23–25.
18. There is a small lacuna in the text at this point.

identify Pharaoh with the devil, to the extent that he destroys Israel, but it also identifies him with the law of nature, when, through divine dispensation, Joseph is subjected to him[19] and thus signifies, prophetically through his own person, God the Word, who willingly placed Himself in slavery to our nature and passions, but of course without sin.[20] Likewise, the king of Tyre is also understood to represent the devil when through Sisera he wages war on Israel.[21] Yet the king of Tyre may also be taken as a figure of the natural law, when he makes a treaty with David and contributes lavishly to the construction of Solomon's temple.[22] It follows that each one of the kings mentioned in Scripture is to be understood by means of many other different significations, according to the underlying sense of the prophecy.

26.10. The "wild beasts," moreover, which God gives to the king of Babylon, are the demons, each of whom operates according to its own innate propensity, provoking this or that temptation, for each one generates a different evil, and each one is clearly more vile than the other, being more skilled at its own form of evil. But even the demons themselves cannot assist the devil, the originator of evil, in any way at all, without divine permission, for it is God Himself who knows, with His fitting, philanthropic, and good providence, to permit the devil to inflict various chastisements through his assistants because of our sins. The book of Job shows this plainly, describing how the devil was utterly unable to approach Job without God's permission.[23]

26.11. As for Nebuchadnezzar, the king of Babylon, even he is very often understood to be the natural law.[24] And this is made clear by those who were not able to cherish the spiritu-

---

19. Gn 39.1–3.
20. Cf. Heb 4.15.
21. Cf. Jgs 4–5. Sisera was the commander of the Canaanite army of King Jabin of Hazor.
22. Cf. 1 Kgs 5.1–12.
23. Cf. Jb 1.11–12; and *Amb.* 11, which touches on the question of Job's sufferings (DOML 1:344–45).
24. Here, "natural law" does not designate the "law" inscribed in the *logoi* of creation, but the law of the flesh and sin, that is, the fallen condition of human nature.

al law, and thus were dragged away to the land of Babylon, by which I mean to a habitual state of mind confused with matter. And this is why they wrote to those in Jerusalem: "Pray for the life of Nebuchadnezzar,[25] the king of Babylon, and for the life of Balthasar, his son"—that is, for the natural law[7] and for the state of mind consistent with its motion, to whose authority they had then become subject—"so that their days might be like the days of heaven."[26] Through these words, they asked those who had remained in the dispassion of virtue and the truth of knowledge to pray that the thoughts[27] of the natural law and its habitual state according to its motion (a law under which they found themselves after they had abandoned the spiritual law) might be like the divine thoughts of the law of the Spirit, calling these thoughts "days," and the spiritual law "heaven." It is clear that these words expressed their search and aspiration[8] that the natural and toilsome law, under which they were living, would not be at variance with the spiritual law.

26.12. In harmony with these things is what the great Daniel mystically uttered concerning the divine threat to him, when he interpreted the dream he saw, saying: "And they will banish you from men, and your dwelling will be with wild beasts, and they will feed you with grass as an ox, and you will have your lodging under the dew of heaven, and seven seasons will pass over you, until you know that the Most High is Lord of the kingdom of men, and will give it to whom He shall please. And whereas they said, 'Leave the stumps of the roots of the tree in the earth,' your kingdom abides to you from the time that you shall know the kingdom of heaven."[28] Here the word "banish" may perhaps refer to the expulsion from paradise into this world subsequent to the transgression,[29] as well as the estrangement from the way

---

25. This verse finds a similar interpretation in Dorotheos of Gaza, *On the Grateful Endurance of Temptations* (= *Doctrinae Diversae* 13.143) (SC 92:410–12).

26. Bar 1.11. The setting of the Book of Baruch is indeed Babylon, where Baruch reads his scroll to King Jeconiah and the exiles, who respond by sending the scroll to Jerusalem (Bar 1.1–14).

27. Or, "mental representations."

28. Dn 4.22–23; 4.25–26. Hippolytus, *Commentary on Daniel* 3.10 (GCS 1:142), states that the "seven times" that will pass over Nebuchadnezzar were interpreted by some as seven years, and by others as seven seasons.

29. Cf. Gn 3.24.

of life of the holy angels, that is, from a relation to intelligible visions to the sensory perception of the law of nature. The "dwelling with wild beasts," moreover, signifies continued persistence in a state between the passions and the demons who set them in motion, that is, their dwelling and cohabiting with them. The "grass" with which "they fed him"—"they" meaning human beings, obviously, and not the wild beasts with whom he was dwelling, inasmuch as wild beasts do not feed anyone with food by hand but rather tear it to pieces—this "grass," I say, signifies the natural apprehension of visible realities based on sense perception, as well as the laborious practice of virtue, both of which the angels provide to human beings like grass. To have one's lodging "under the dew of heaven"[30] signifies persevering in such a state of existence with the help of divine providence, for Scripture has called providence the "dew of heaven,"[31] through which man, in this present age—along with all that we have recounted—has been sustained in his existence, in other words, the natural law, which in no way is subject to destruction. Or perhaps it is the analogical knowledge of intelligible realities, which, by the grace of God, comes about through the perception of visible realities, and which supports man in this life with hope in the things to come. As for the words, "seven seasons will pass over you," they indicate the seven-fold extension of time in this present age,[32] according to which extension the natural law has come about, having relinquished its proper habitual state and activity, and with which, when it will have reached its consummation in the hoped-for resurrection through the setting aside of its irrational properties, will return to itself once more, enjoying the good inheritance of the kingdom promised to it from the beginning, having realized—through the dispensation of providence for this present age—the dominion of the true kingdom. For the words, "leave the stump of the roots of the tree to grow in the earth," make it clear that the transgression did not utterly destroy the seed of nature nor its potentials

---

30. Gn 27.28.
31. Cf. Jgs 6.37–40; Is 26.19; Hos 6.4, 14.6.
32. On the extension of the age into periods of time, see *Amb.* 46 (DOML 2:200–207).

for goodness, according to which, by resuming its growth, it will be led back through the resurrection to its former natural stature and beauty.

26.13. But for us, it is better to conform ourselves to the law of the commandments, educating ourselves ascetically, through voluntary sufferings, to eradicate the "mind of the flesh."[33] And this is not simply better, but exceedingly philosophical and appropriate for those who have re-established their innate reason as the master of the passions. And if not this, then let us do what is second to it; namely, when we are involuntarily disciplined, let us accept gladly, with the proper gratitude, the intention of the one who chastises us, humbly accepting, as if it were the yoke of the king of Babylon, the punishment for our sins.[9] In this way, we will never be exiled from our land; that is, the noetic king of Babylon will never dislodge our intellect from faith and hope, or from the habitual state of virtue.

26.14. In the manner described above, the devil is called a servant of God, and to him are handed over the kings of the nations, the king of Judah, and the wild beasts of the field.

Scholia

[1] He speaks of the mode according to which the devil is God's servant and avenger.

[2] The soul, led astray by the devil, either disregards or spurns the divine admonition that comes in the form of trials, that is, his castigation. He thereby makes such admonition an occasion for impiety, inasmuch as he abandons God and finds refuge in the devil, confusing his enemy with his liberator.

[3] Suffering, he says, cleanses the soul infected with the filth of sensual pleasure and detaches it completely from its relation to material things by showing it the penalty incurred as a result of its affection for them. This is why God, by His just judgment, allows the devil to afflict men with torments.

[4] He says that we gain nothing but punishment from loving the things of this present life that we lustfully acquired, and which pander to the senses alone.

33. Rom 8.6.

QUESTION 26   181

[5] Whoever suffers, he says, for having transgressed the grace of God, and recognizes the principle of divine providence that is healing him, accepts the affliction with joy and gratitude, and corrects the fault for which he is being disciplined. But if he is insensitive to this treatment, he is justly deprived of the grace that was once given him and is handed over to the confusion of the passions;[34] and he is abandoned so that he may acquire by ascetic labor those things for which he inwardly longs.

[6] In other words, Solomon possessed peace consistent with the meaning of his name, but his wisdom was a gift from God, being the fruit of prayer.[35]

[7] Here he takes Nebuchadnezzar as the natural law, and his son Balthasar as the habitual state of the same natural law.

[8] From this prayer it is clear, he says, that Nebuchadnezzar and Balthasar signify the natural law and the habitual state to which it gives birth, and not the devil. For no one ever requests a prayer to be made for the benefit of the devil.[36] For inasmuch as the word of the prophecy did not condemn this prayer, we must not think that it is directed to God for the benefit of the devil.

[9] If we cannot make inborn, natural reason the guide of our passions, which is the first thing, let us at least embrace what is second to it; namely, let us embrace divine chastisements with thanksgiving.

34. Cf. below, Qu. 54.2–3.
35. 1 Kgs 3.4–9.
36. While Maximos is not the author of this particular scholion, Larchet (SC 529:318, n. 1) sees the scholiast as confirming Maximos's rejection of a universal restoration in which the devil would be redeemed.

QUESTION 27

SINCE THE Lord, after the resurrection, clearly commanded the apostles to "make disciples of all the nations,"[1] why did Peter need a revelation concerning the nations from Cornelius?[2] And why did the other apostles, upon hearing of what took place with Cornelius, criticize Peter?[3]

Response

27.2. The leader of the apostles, the all-holy Peter, had great need of a divine revelation concerning the nations, since he did not realize that, with respect to the faith, there is no distinction to be made between circumcision and non-circumcision. Neither was he certain that the Lord said to "make disciples of the nations" without the external cultic service prescribed by the law.[4] He did not clearly understand any of these things until the mystery of the ineffable counsel was manifested to him through a revelation, persuading him through the example of the sheet,[5] as well as through the grace of the Holy Spirit[6]—which was given equally to him and to the nations according to faith alone—that in the worship of Christ "there is no distinction between Jew and Greek."[7] The other apostles in Jerusalem were likewise ignorant of this and criticized him, until they too learned the hidden treasure of divine goodness that had been

---

1. Mt 28.19.
2. Acts 10.1–29; 11.3–18.
3. Acts 11.2.
4. Cf. above, Qu. 14.
5. Acts 10.11.
6. Acts 10.19, 28, 44–45; 11.12.
7. Rom 10.12.

lavished on all mankind.[1] For the grace transmitted by the preaching of the Gospel was at once the introduction of divine life and new service (in contrast to the service of the law); instruction for the soul willingly inclined to detach itself from the body; and the adumbration of the beginning of a new and more divine source of birth. For this reason, all those entrusted with this ministry required, for their every word, the instruction of Him who commanded them to preach.

27.3. Though I may appear to be inquiring into these matters beyond what is proper,[8] permit me to say that every word of a divine commandment[2] stands in absolute need of instruction and revelation for the realization of its determinate manner of application. For nowhere does there exist anyone who can know the manner in which a word is to be applied without a revelation from the one who uttered the word. The all-praiseworthy Peter knew this, and though he had already received the word of the Lord to preach the Gospel to the nations, he did not undertake this task, but was waiting to be instructed in the manner of the word's application by the one who gave the word.

27.4. But perhaps there were other things, in addition to these, that the great Peter was taught by the sheet which descended from heaven, as well as by the different animals contained within it[9]—or I should say the whole human race, and not just Peter, who through faith had attained the divine summit, having expressly learned to extinguish completely his entire power of sensation. Because for as long as his perception of visible realities was dominated by sensation, he understood that, in and of itself, God's creation contained its own destruction, for by itself it was not able to be free of corruption and confusion. Thus, by means of the sheet and the animals con-

---

8. A phrase borrowed from Gregory Nazianzus, *Or.* 41.12 (SC 358:342, lines 15–16), which was delivered on the feast of Pentecost, commemorating the descent of the Holy Spirit (Acts 2.1–4), and as such may have been within Maximos's frame of reference in responding to this difficulty. In the *Ambigua to John*, Maximos had commented at length on four excerpts from *Or.* 41; cf. *Amb.* 65–68 (DOML 2:274–307).

9. Cf. Acts 10.11–12.

tained within it, the one who spoke to him[10] revealed to him, through the invisible world, the visible world conceived on the level of its inner principles—or the invisible world made visible by means of its sensible figurations, which[11] is suitable for spiritual food.[12] This is why He told him: "Rise, Peter, kill and eat."[13] And from where is he commanded to rise? From where else if not from the habitual state of mind and relation bound to sensation, and from the earth-bound opinion concerning beings, or from the supposed righteousness given by the law. God's purpose was that Peter,[3] by his intellect alone—having rid himself of every mental image arising from sense perception, and being able to behold the principles of sensible realities naked of their outward forms, grasping the figures of intelligible realities—might learn that none of the things brought into existence by God is unclean. For anyone who has contemplated the visible creation manifested through the inner principles of the intelligible world, or who has seen the figures of intelligible realities through the beautiful order of visible things—like a sheet descending from heaven—would never believe that any visible reality is unclean, for he beholds no opposition in the inner principles of beings. This is because the corruption of the things that have come into existence, and the war between them, takes place on the level of sensation, while in their inner principles there is absolutely nothing contrary or in opposition.

27.5. The sheet[14] signifies the sensible world, composed of four principles, as if from four elements, by which it is also governed.[15] The reptiles, wild animals, and birds of the air[16] repre-

---

10. Acts 10.13–15.
11. I.e., the invisible world made visible.
12. Cf. *Myst.* 2: "The whole intelligible world is mystically imprinted in the whole sensible world through symbolic forms (for those who are capable of seeing this); and the whole sensible world subsists cognitively within the whole intelligible world by means of its inner principles. In the intelligible world it is in principles, in the sensible world it is in figures, and their activity and function is one, like 'a wheel within a wheel' (Ezek 1.16)" (CCSG 69:16–17).
13. Acts 10.13.
14. Acts 10.11.
15. The composition of the physical and spiritual world from four elements is a major theme in *Amb.* 21.5–12 (DOML 1:425–39).
16. Acts 10.12.

sent the different inner principles of the things that have been brought into being, principles that are unclean as regards sense perception, but in themselves are clean and nutritious and sustain intelligible life. The voice heard three times[17] respectively teaches practical, natural, and theological philosophy. For one must "rise," not once but twice and a third time, to "kill"[4] the creation made of visible realities in order to eat it cognitively,[18] obeying God wholly and sincerely. First, he who "rises" from a disposition passionately attached to visible things "kills" their motion and by ascetic practice "eats" virtue. Second, he who "rises" from false opinions about beings "kills" the outward forms of visible realities and, "eating" their invisible principles, achieves natural contemplation in the spirit. Third, he who "rises" from the error of polytheism "kills" the very essence of created beings and by faith "eats" the Cause of those beings and is filled with a power to theologize. Therefore, every intellect engaged in contemplation, having in hand "the sword of the Spirit, which is the word of God,"[19] and having put to death within itself the motion of the visible creation, has achieved virtue and, having cut off its mental images of outward, sensible forms, has discovered truth in the inner principles of created beings, the very truth that is constitutive of natural contemplation. Moreover, by transcending the essence of created beings, the intellect is enlightened by the divine and invincible Monad, the very enlightenment that is constitutive for the mystery of true theology.[20]

27.6. Or perhaps the all-glorious Peter, the summit of the apostles, having risen from a power commensurate with nature to the good inheritance according to divine grace, was com-

---

17. Acts 10.16.
18. I.e., for the mind to know and absorb the spiritual substance of phenomenal realities.
19. Eph 6.17.
20. Larchet (SC 529:326, n. 1) notes that, to practice the virtues, one must move solely in accordance with spiritual motion and not the movements of sensible realities. Subsequently, through natural contemplation, the soul separates itself from the mental images of sensible realities and attaches itself to the spiritual representations of their *logoi*. On a still higher level, that of theology, the saint renounces all relation even to the essence of beings and thus is able to receive the knowledge of God, who is beyond nature and essence.

manded by God and with God's help to slay with the sword of reason the depraved passions within man, and to prepare good food—suitable for the Word and susceptible of being given over to spiritual digestion—by setting aside the former impassioned and animal way of life.[21] For they say that blood is a symbol of life,[22] and is naturally spilled out when an animal is killed. And perhaps the diversity of the animals manifested in the sheet points to the variety of passions within human beings. The creeping reptiles, for example, signify those whose entire faculty of desire is dragged around among earthly things. The wild beasts are those who are aroused in their spirited faculty to frenzied, mutual destruction. The birds of the air are those whose entire faculty of reason soars upwards into pride and arrogance, from which "they uttered" haughtiness and "unrighteousness to the heights, and set their mouth against heaven."[23] These are the things that the great Peter, the coworker of God, "killed" with the word of the spirit, and so he made the first group desire heavenly realities; the second he made gentle, loving, and attached to one another; and the third, lovers of God and humble in their thoughts.[24]

27.7. Let us now consider what the city of Joppa[25] signifies, based on the interpretation of its name, for it was there that the great Foundation of the Church, the all-holy Peter, saw the vi-

---

21. On the spiritual consumption of the Word, cf. *Amb.* 48 (DOML 2:212–23).

22. Cf. Lv 17.14; a question famously discussed by Origen, *Dialogue with Heraclides* (SC 67:76–80).

23. Ps 72.8–9. Larchet (SC 529:327, n. 3) contends that here Maximos puts forward a theory of the origin of the passions different from the one he presented in the Introduction, by associating the passions with the evil use of the soul's essential powers. Such a theory is closer to the view of Evagrios (e.g., *Gnostic Chapters* 3.59), which Maximos had already adopted in *Carit.* 3.3: "It is through the misuse (παράχρησις) of the soul's powers that the vices come upon us, that is, the vices of desire, anger, and the rational element. Misuse of the rational element is found in ignorance and folly; of anger and desire in hatred and licentiousness. Their proper use is in knowledge, prudence, and love" (ed. Ceresa-Gastaldo, 144).

24. Cf. *QD.* 116 (CCSG 10:85), a short text in which Maximos had adumbrated the essential lines of the foregoing exegesis and argument.

25. Acts 10.8.

sion. The word "Joppa" means "observation"[26] and signifies the guarding of the mind appropriate to those engaged in the practice of asceticism.[27] Located near the shore of the sea, such a city, were it not located on a height, would be struck by many waves. From this it seems to me that it points to the one who builds virtue, as if it were a city, upon the height of knowledge. Such a person is not far from involuntary trials, and—having nearby and next to him, just like the sea, an attachment to sense perception that he has not yet completely beaten back—he is in need of "observation." Otherwise, the unclean demons, slipping in undetected through involuntary trials, will launch a sudden attack of voluntary passions against him. But insofar as Joppa belongs to the portion of the tribe of Issachar—and Issachar means "hire" and "work"[28]—we are further given to understand that Joppa is the mind's habitual state of being on guard with respect to its ascetic practice, keeping watch for the invisible attacks of the spirits of wickedness.[29] Perhaps it was from this state that the great Apostle was ordered to rise up and to relocate his intellect to the knowledge of all things that are high and lofty.

27.8. We can say, therefore, that whoever dwells on the height of observation of practical philosophy lives in Joppa,[5] while he who dwells in Zion of Jerusalem, that is, in the watchtower oriented with a view toward peace—for this is what Jerusalem means—is far from every relation according to the senses, as far as the actual city of Zion's position was from the sea. And, while living on the height of knowledge, he observes solely the intelligible visions of beings—insofar as his intellect has negated their visible forms—and he receives the impressions of divine realities, to the extent that God allows them to be manifested, configuring his governing faculty according to

---

26. "Observation" translates the Greek word κατασκοπή, which has the strong sense of reconnaissance, spying, looking out, and keeping watch in order to observe and consider things from on high, and thus to "contemplate"; cf. Clement, *Paid.* 1.5.21 (SC 70:148); and Paul Lagarde, *Onomastica Sacra* (Göttingen: Adalbert Rente, 1870), 1:169: "Joppa means 'observation.'"

27. This interpretation is found in Gregory Nazianzus, *Or.* 2.109 (SC 247:228–30), and Maximos had already deployed it in *QD.* 184 (CCSG 10:125).

28. Cf. Gn 30.18.

29. Cf. Eph 6.12.

a more divine model. It follows that anyone dwelling in Joppa is devoted to the practical life of asceticism, carefully observing the traps of the opposing powers, while the one who makes his home in Zion is a man of knowledge, contemplating in his intellect solely the beauty of divine visions.

27.9. But if the vessel of the sheet was taken back up into heaven,[30] let us understand that, after the great Peter was shown that the spiritual principles of sensible realities coexist with intelligible realities, God would again raise these spiritual principles back up to Himself, teaching that nothing to which these principles lie near can ever be considered unclean. Thus, knowing the meaning of the things he saw, the great Apostle learned to say that no man is unclean,[31] and that there is no partiality with God,[32] a view that would render unjust the distinctions between beings.[33] Subsequently, and without taking any further thought for anything, he fulfilled the divine commandment and "sacrificed" unto spiritual life those who had willingly circumcised their heart by means of the word of grace, and who had cut away, like a foreskin, every impurity of faithlessness and ignorance. And he did this without mutilating any of the natural properties of the flesh, the constitution of which did not come about from an impassioned will, but which has its creation and origin from God. For none of the things of nature are impure, since they have God as the cause of their existence.

Scholia

[1] He says that the mystery proclaimed by the New Testament is a change of life, angelic worship, the willing estrangement of the soul from the body, and the beginning of divine renewal in the spirit.

[2] The word of a commandment, he says, is one thing, and the application by means of which the commandment is real-

---

30. Cf. Acts 11.10.
31. Cf. Acts 10.28.
32. Cf. Acts 10.34.
33. Origen believed that diversity among human beings was a punishment from God for sins committed in a former, disembodied existence; cf. *On First Principles* 2.9 (SC 252:352–73).

ized is another. The great Peter, having received the command to preach to the nations, was ignorant of the manner of the commandment's application, which he was taught through the vision of the sheet, namely, that the calling of the nations must not include circumcision or any of the other corporeal rites of the law. For there is a spiritual circumcision, which is the cutting away of the soul's impassioned relation to the body.

[3] Whoever does not stop short at the outward forms that visible realities present to the senses, but seeks with his intellect to contemplate their inner principles, seeing them as figures of intelligible realities or the inner principles of sensible creations, will be taught that nothing belonging to the visible world is unclean. For by nature all things were created exceedingly good.[34]

[4] He who is not changed, he says, together with the motion of sensible things, practices the virtues in a manner that is truly pure. He who does not permit the outward forms of sensible things to imprint themselves on his intellect has received the true understanding of beings. He whose mind has outstripped the very essence of beings has, as an excellent theologian, come close to the Monad through unknowing. It follows that the one who has thrice killed within himself the creation made of visible realities has become worthy of the rank of the perfect.

[5] Joppa, he says, is the habitual state of virtue that is protected[35] from the harm of sensible realities that are lying alongside it. Zion is a stable, cognitive habit of mind whose aim is to receive intelligible graces.

34. Cf. Gn 1.31; Acts 10.15.
35. I.e., "watched over."

QUESTION 28

o whom was God speaking when He said: "Come, let us descend and confound their tongues"?[1]

Response

28.2. We find that holy Scripture fashions[2] God in terms relative to the underlying disposition[3] of those under His providential care.[4] Thus He is called a lion, a bear, a leopard, a panther, a man, an ox, a sheep, the sun, a star, fire, wind, and a thousand other things—and whereas He Himself is none of these things, He is nonetheless contemplated according to the meaning[5] of each term. When, therefore, God appeared to Abraham—who was perfect in knowledge and who already possessed an intel-

---

1. Gn 11.7. Maximos had already commented briefly on this verse in *QD*. 2 (CCSG 10:3–4); cf. Origen's remarks on Gn 11.7 in *Against Celsus* 5.29–32 (SC 147:84–96).

2. "Fashions," which has the sense of "molding" and "shaping" as in the plastic arts, renders the Greek διαπλάττειν, which is a term Dionysios uses to describe the manner in which biblical authors gave shape and form to divine realities and revelations; cf. *CH* 15.2: "Knowing that the divinity is like fire, those who are divinely wise fashion (διαπλάττουσιν) the celestial beings out of fire, emphasizing how closely deiform they are" (53, lines 4–5; 329C); and *EH* 4.1 (95–96; 473B–476A).

3. The phrase "underlying disposition" (ὑποκειμένη διάθεσις) occurs only rarely in late-antique ecclesiastical literature, although it is heavily attested among Greek medical writers.

4. Cf. Origen, *Homilies on Genesis* 15.1: "Divine Scripture was not composed in illiterate and uncultivated language, but was adapted in accordance with the discipline of divine instruction" (SC 7bis:237).

5. I.e., ἐπίνοια, which also has the sense of "concept" or "signification." Blowers, *Exegesis and Spiritual Pedagogy*, 110, renders the word as "designation."

lect completely beyond matter and its figurations[6]—He taught him that the immaterial principle of the Trinity inheres in the principle of its Unity, and for this reason God appeared to him as three and spoke to him as one.[7] [1] When, on the other hand, God appeared to Lot—who had not yet purged his intellect of the composite forms of corporeal things, insofar as he was still conditioned by the generation of corporeal things from matter and form, and still believed that God was the Creator solely of the visible creation—He appeared as a duality and not as a trinity,[8] indicating through the outward form in which He fashioned Himself that Lot's intellect had not yet gone beyond matter and form.[9] Thus, if you examine with true understanding the words in each passage of Scripture when it fashions God in a variety of ways,[10] you will find that the reason for the many variations in the forms of the divine realities is, as we said, the disposition of those who are subject to the activity of providence.

28.3. Now—to take up the question—those who built the tower had previously "departed from the east,"[11] the place of light, by which I mean the unique and true knowledge of God, and went to Shinar, which means "blasphemous teeth."[12] There they

---

6. An "intellect beyond matter" is not a disembodied intellect, but one that does not function as receptive "matter" to be shaped and formed by sensory impressions; cf. *Amb.* 10.42–45 (DOML 1:212–21).

7. Gn 18.1–15. In Scripture, Abraham addresses the three visitors in both the singular and the plural, while they respond to him speaking in the voice of a single individual (Gn 18.5).

8. Cf. Gn 19.1.

9. Maximos had already touched on this question in *QD.* 39 (III.10) (CCSG 10.32–33), following the exegesis of Philo, *On Abraham* 119–32 (LCL 6:62–69), and idem, *Questions on Genesis* 4.2, 4.30 (LCL Supplement 1:270–74, 305–6), on which see the summary by Blowers, *Exegesis and Spiritual Pedagogy*, 160, n. 62; see also Lars Thunberg, "Early Christian Interpretations of the Three Angels in Genesis 18," *SP* 7 (1966): 560–70, esp. 568–69.

10. Cf. Heb 1.1.

11. Gn 11.2.

12. Cf. *QD.* 2 (III.10), where Shinar is etymologized as the "wakefulness (γρηγόρησις) of teeth" (CCSG 10:3, lines 5–6). Origen, *Against Celsus* 5.30 (SC 147:88, line 8), says it means ὀδόντων ἐκτιναγμός ("shaking of teeth"), following Philo, *On the Confusion of Tongues* 68 (LCL 4:46), where the "shaking" is a fragmentation signaling a fall from unity into multiplicity; cf. Athanasios,

fell into a multiplicity of opinions about the divinity, and, compounding the rationale of each opinion, like so many bricks made of clay, they constructed the tower of their godless belief in multiple gods.[13] It was therefore only reasonable that God, bringing to naught the compact of the evil concord[14] of those deluded men,[15] should have named Himself in the plural, on account of the disposition of those under His providence, insofar as their disposition was itself brought to naught and scattered in an infinity of erroneous opinions.[16] By this He showed that, though He is one, among them He is divided into many, which also seems to be the case with Adam, of whom God said: "Behold, Adam has become like one of us."[17] It is, then, on account of our presuppositions that God is either multiplied by the words of Scripture or contracted into unity.

28.4. With whom, then, is God conversing? It is the custom of Scripture to fashion the ineffable and secret counsels of God in corporeal figures, so that by means of words and sounds that are familiar to us, we might be able to understand divine realities. For God is Intellect unknowable, Word unutterable, and Life incomprehensible; and He neither speaks nor can be spoken, for in essence He is Word itself[18] and Counsel itself. And if

---

On the Psalms, who discusses the symbolic connections between "teeth" and "sinners" (PG 27:69).

13. I.e., πολύθεον ἀθεΐαν, an assonant phrase borrowed from Gregory Nazianzus, *Or.* 25.15 (SC 284:192). Cf. Gn 11.2–4.

14. "Compact" and "concord" render ὁμολογία and συμφωνία, both of which play on words for speech and language.

15. Cf. Wis 10.5.

16. Cf. Origen, *Against Celsus* 5.29–32 (SC 147:84–96), for whom the biblical narrative concerning the confusion of tongues and the subsequent dispersal of the nations alludes to the "way in which souls became bound to a body," a doctrine which in Genesis is "concealed under the guise of a story" (ibid., 5.29). Concerning the dispersion of the nations, Marguerite Harl (SC 302:195, n. 3) suggests a slightly expanded reference, i.e., *Against Celsus* 5.25–33 and 35. This expanded cluster of nine passages comprises chapter 22 of the Cappadocian *Philokalia,* a chapter singled out by its Byzantine editor for particular criticism, since it alludes to the fall of souls into bodies (SC 302:166, lines 58–60).

17. Gn 3.22.

18. I.e., Αὐτολόγος, which Lampe, *PGL,* s.v., renders as "very Word," or "very Reason"; cf. Origen, *Contra Celsum* 3.41: "He is Word itself, and Wisdom

QUESTION 28 193

we understand the words of the divine Scriptures[19] in this way, we will not stumble over the obscurity of any of the things that have been written.

28.5. If someone, however, were to say that the plural designations of God found in Scripture are not in every case grounds for censure, and if he were to support this argument by citing the words: "And God said, 'Let us make man after our own image and likeness,'"[20] pointing out that we certainly do not understand anything in these words to be suggesting any kind of polytheism, we would respond by saying that, whenever sacred Scripture uses the plural in speaking piously about God to the pious, it is referring to the three All-Holy Hypostases, mystically signifying the mode of subsistence of the all-holy Unity that is without beginning,[21] for the all-venerable and all-worshipful and all-praised Trinity of hypostases is a Unity according to its essence (for our God is a Unity in Trinity and a Trinity in Unity). But when, on the other hand, Scripture uses the plural when speaking about God to the impious, it is exposing, it seems to me, their blameworthy opinion concerning the divinity, since they think that the difference in properties belongs to nature[2] and not hypostasis, and this is clearly how the error of polytheism arises among those who hold this view of divinity.

28.6. Should even this, however, fail to persuade—and insofar as the Spirit and the friends of the Spirit do not love to quarrel—let us accept, in mutual accord, the holy Scripture as introducing the all-holy Trinity in unity, sometimes as creator,

---

itself, and Truth itself" (SC 136:96, line 3); repeated at ibid., 6.63 (SC 147:336, line 4); see also idem, *Commentary on John* 2.3.20: "The *logos* which is in each rational being has the same principle of relation to the Logos which is in the beginning with God, which is God the Logos. For as the Father is very God (αὐτόθεος) and true God in relation to the image and images of the image ... so is the very Word (αὐτολόγος) in relation to the *logos* in each one" (SC 120:220); and Athanasios, *Contra gentes* 46, where a string of seven such *auto*-epithets is used (SC 18bis:208, lines 6–7); and idem, *On the Incarnation* 54 (SC 199:458, line 18).

19. Or, the "sounds of the divine words"; cf. *Amb.* 21.13 (DOML 1:439–40, n. 11).
20. Gn 1.26.
21. I.e., the Monad.

as when it says: "Let us create man,"[22] since the existence of beings is clearly the work of the Father, the Son, and the Holy Spirit. Let us likewise accept that at other times Scripture introduces the Trinity as receptive of those who live piously according to its laws—since it exercises providence for those who received the origin of their being from it, just as it appeared as a Trinity yet spoke as a Unity to Abraham[23]—and at still other times as chastising, that is, as judging those who have perversely corrupted the laws of nature, and correcting those who deviated from the proper law of nature, as when it says: "Let us descend and confound their tongues."[24] For the holy and consubstantial Trinity not only created beings, but also maintains them in existence and dispenses to each one whatever corresponds to its worth, for God, who is one by nature, is creator, provider, and judge of the things He has created. For the activity of judging and wisely providing for creatures, just like the work of creation, is common to the Father, the Son, and the Holy Spirit.

Scholia

[1] God, he says, appears to each one according to the underlying opinion he has concerning God. To those who by their desire have passed beyond material composition, and whose powers of soul are in a state of equilibrium in one and the same ceaseless movement around God, God appears as a Unity and a Trinity, in order to show forth His own proper existence, and mystically teach the mode of that existence. To those, on the other hand, whose desire moves solely around material composition, and whose powers of soul are disconnected from each other, God appears not as He is, but as they are. In this way He shows that both their hands are bound to the material dyad,

---

22. Gn 1.26. A traditional interpretation of Genesis 1.26; cf. Irenaeos, *Against Heresies* 4.20.1 (SC 100:626); Basil, *Hexaemeron* 9 (SC 26bis:514–18); Gregory of Nyssa, *On the Making of Man* 6 (PG 44:140BC); and idem, *Sermon on the Creation of Man* 1 (GNO Supplementum, 5–10).
23. Gn 18.1–2.
24. Gn 11.7.

QUESTION 28

through which the material world is compounded out of matter and form.²⁵

[2] Whoever, he says, asserts with respect to God that the difference of properties is natural rather than hypostatic, is not inspired by God but is a polytheist, since he subscribes to the notion that the Divine admits of being numbered in terms of the properties of essences, not in hypostases.

25. On the "material dyad," see *Amb.* 10.96–107 (DOML 1:303–23).

QUESTION 29

HAT IS THE meaning of the passage found in the Acts of the Apostles: "Certain men, inspired by the Spirit, told Paul not to go up to Jerusalem"?[1] And why, moreover, did Paul disobey the Spirit and ascend?[2]

Response

29.2. The holy prophet Isaiah says in his prophecy that, upon the Savior, who sprouted forth from the root of Jesse, there rested "seven spirits."[3] This does not mean, of course, that the prophet recognizes the existence of seven spirits of God, or teaches others to adopt such a view, but rather he used the word "spirits" to name the activities of the one and the same Holy Spirit,[4] because the actuating Holy Spirit exists proportionately in all of its activities whole and without diminishment.[[1]] The divine apostle Paul, on the other hand, calls the different activities of the same one and Holy Spirit different "gifts,"[5] since it is clear that these gifts are activated by one and the same Holy Spirit.[6] If, then, the manifestation of the Spirit is given accord-

---

1. Acts 21.4.
2. Cf. Acts 21.5.
3. Cf. Is 11.1–3; and below, Qu. 54.22 and Qu. 63.6.
4. An interpretation inspired by Gregory Nazianzus, *Or.* 41.3 (SC 358:31).
5. Cf. 1 Cor 12.4.
6. Here the focus is on God's activities in and for the world, that is, on the level of the divine economy. From this point of view, divine "activity" (or "energy") corresponds to the uncreated grace imparted by the Holy Spirit, which is one in its nature and origin, but multiple in its manifestations, each one taking the form of various "gifts" (*charismata*), presented here, following Isaiah, as a group of seven (cf. below, Qu. 63.1). According to Maximos, the Holy Spirit is both entirely present in his activity and at the same time present

ing to the measure of each person's faith, it follows that each of the faithful, through participation in such a gift, receives a measure of grace "according to the proportion of his faith"[7] and to the underlying disposition of his soul, a grace which endows him with[2] a fitting state of mind adapted to the activity required to realize this or that commandment.

29.3. Thus, just as one person receives the principle of wisdom, another of knowledge, another of faith, and another some other gift of the Spirit enumerated by the great Apostle,[8] so too does another person receive, through the Spirit, the gift of perfect and immediate love for God, containing nothing material, according to the due proportion of his faith. Another person, through the same Spirit, receives the gift of perfect love for his neighbor, because, as I said, while each one possesses a gift that is proper to him, it is activated by the same Spirit. Now if someone, following the holy Isaiah, were to call these gifts "spirits," he would not miss the mark of truth, for the Holy Spirit exists in every gift, be it great or small, being actively present in proportion to it.

29.4. Thus when the truly great Paul, being the servant of mysteries transcending the human mind, directly received in proportion to his faith the spirit of perfect grace in the love[3] of God, he disobeyed those who had received the gift of perfect love for him. For those men, being "inspired by the Spirit"— that is, by the spiritual gift of love for Paul, which was actualized within them, for their sake, by the Spirit (for "spirit" is the same as "gift," as I said a moment ago, in reference to the passage by the prophet Isaiah)—"told him not to go up to Jerusalem."[9] But Paul disobeyed them because he regarded the love which is divine and beyond understanding as incomparably su-

---

in each and all of his activities. The difference and multiplicity of activities does not divide the unique action, from which proceed all the others, which are manifestations of it (cf. *Amb.* 22 [DOML 1:448–51]). Likewise, it is this diversity of activities that permits the faithful—who receive them in diverse "proportions" according to their different degrees of "worthiness"—to share in the very life of God and to be divinized; cf. Larchet (SC 529:344, n. 1).

7. Rom 12.6.
8. Cf. 1 Cor 12.8–11.
9. Where there was a plot against Paul's life; cf. Acts 21.11, 27–32.

perior to the spiritual love which the others had for him. And indeed he did not go up "disobeying" them at all, but rather by his own example he drew them—who prophesied through the activity of the Spirit measured out in due proportion to them according to the gift of grace—towards that yearning desire for the One who is beyond all. In this way, the great Paul did not disobey the Spirit, but rather he taught those who were prophesying about him, according to their gift of love, to ascend from the lower to the higher spirit, that is, from the lower to the higher gift.

29.5. And, again, inasmuch as the prophetic gift is greatly inferior to the apostolic gift, it was not appropriate to the Word—who governs the universe and assigns each one his due rank—that the superior should submit to the inferior, but rather that the inferior follow after the superior. For those who prophesied through the prophetic spirit in them—which was not the apostolic spirit—revealed the way in which Saint Paul would suffer for the Lord. But he, looking only towards the divine purpose, regarded the intervening things[4] as nothing at all.[10] His concern was not simply to survive the things that would befall him, but to become another Christ through the imitation of Christ,[11] and thereby to accomplish all those things for the sake of which Christ, in His love and dispensation for us, chose life in the flesh.

29.6. To conclude, the seeming disobedience of the great Apostle preserves the good order that arranges and governs all sacred matters, and which keeps each person from falling away from his proper place of remaining and abode.[12] It also clearly teaches that the particular ranks within the Church, which the Spirit has fittingly arranged and assigned, are not to be confused with one another.

---

10. Cf. Phil 3.8; Rom 8.39.
11. Cf. 1 Cor 11.1.
12. On "remaining and abode," see *Amb.* 7.2 (DOML 1:76–77).

Scholia

[1] The Spirit, whose activity is manifested differently in each of the things in which it is active, exists wholly in whole things and at the same time without division. For, he says, the Holy Spirit is manifested through the whole of beings without being confused with them, and exercises its activity in particular beings indivisibly with one and the same power, because the Spirit is that which fills all beings, for the Spirit is God, and transcends the ability of all beings to contain it, for the Spirit is beyond being.

[2] Here he says that every stable habit activated to bring about a commandment is a gift of the Spirit.

[3] The one "who loves God from all his heart, and soul, and power" is superior, he says, to the "one who loves his neighbor."[13] Thus it is not logical that the superior should be subjected to the law of the inferior, but rather that the inferior should be led by the superior. This is why the divine Apostle rightly did not permit the apostolic dignity and rank to be ruled over by those who are ranked below its authority, lest the beauteous arrangement of all beings, and especially the order of divine realities, be dissolved.

[4] By "intervening things" he means the different kinds of trials that were seen in advance through the Spirit by those who prophesied concerning Saint Paul's struggles on behalf of the truth—trials to which he gave absolutely no thought, hastening instead to be united to Christ[14] in a union according to the substance, in the form of good things, awaiting him after his passage through created realities in faith.[15]

---

13. Mt 22.37–39; cf. Dt 6.5.
14. Cf. Acts 21.13.
15. Cf. Heb 11.1; 2 Cor 5.7. Cf. *Amb.* 20 (DOML 1:408–19).

QUESTION 30

HAT IS THE meaning of the words: "Are you able to drink the cup that I drink, or to be baptized with the baptism with which I am baptized?"[1] And what is the difference between the "cup" and "baptism"?

Response

30.2. The "baptism" of the Lord[1] is a figure of our voluntary labors undertaken deliberately for the sake of virtue. Through these labors, we purify our conscience of its stains and accept the voluntary death of our free choice in relation to visible realities.[2] The "cup," on the other hand, is a figure of involuntary trials suffered for the sake of truth, which through various circumstances rise up against us contrary to our free choice. Through these trials, we come to learn that longing for God is to be preferred over nature itself, and we voluntarily embrace the death of nature brought upon us by circumstances.[3]

30.3. This, then, is the difference between "baptism" and

---

1. Mk 10.38.
2. The "voluntary death of free choice" is not a question of renouncing one's freedom, but rather the renunciation of a false freedom based on choices that are uncertain, variable, and seemingly somewhere between good and evil, but which in the end are most often evil. For Maximos, human liberty arises neither from choice (προαίρεσις) nor from the inclination of the will (γνώμη), but from the natural will (θέλημα, θέλησις), which spontaneously inclines toward the good and which accords with the will of God; cf. John Meyendorff, "Free Will (*proairesis*) in Saint Maximos the Confessor," in *The Ecumenical World of Orthodox Civilization. Essays in Honour of G. Florovsky*, ed. A. Blaine and T. E. Bird (The Hague: Mouton, 1974), 71–75; and Thunberg, *Microcosm and Mediator*, 213–18.
3. Cf. *Carit.* 1.1–10 (ed. Ceresa-Gastaldo, 51–52).

QUESTION 30

the "cup": baptism, for the sake of virtue, puts to death our free choice with respect to the delights of this life, while the cup persuades the pious to prefer the truth over nature itself. Christ placed the cup before baptism, because virtue exists for the sake of truth,[2] but truth does not exist for the sake of virtue. It follows that the one who practices virtue for the sake of truth is not wounded by the arrows of vainglory, but the one who pursues truth for the sake of virtue dwells with the conceited thought of vainglory.

Scholia

[1] The "baptism" of the Lord, he says, is the complete mortification of our free will in relation to the sensible world. The "cup," on the other hand, is the denial of this life itself for the sake of truth.

[2] "Truth," he says, is divine knowledge, and "virtue" is the struggle undertaken for the sake of truth by those who desire it. The man who endures the labors of virtue for the sake of such knowledge is not vainglorious, because he knows that truth cannot be grasped naturally through human efforts—for it is not in the nature of what is first to be circumscribed by things that are second. But the man who expects to attain knowledge by means of the struggles he undertakes for the sake of knowledge is invariably vainglorious, because he imagines that he has obtained crowns even before he has broken a sweat, not knowing that the labors are for the sake of the crowns, and that such crowns do not exist for the sake of the labors. For by nature every pursuit ceases to be practiced when it has accomplished or when it seems to have accomplished that which it set out to pursue.

QUESTION 31

F "GOD DOES not dwell in temples made by human hands,"[1] how did God dwell in the temple of the Jews?

Response

31.2. God, who wisely and in due proportion takes thought for those under His providence, in the past used figures naturally suited to those ruled by sense perception in order to lead them to the truth, invisibly mingling Himself in all of the figures given to the ancient people, actively bringing about the spiritual elevation of those being instructed. Thus God dwelled in the temple of the Jews figuratively,[2] but not truly,[3] marking out, by dwelling in the temple in this manner, the ineffable design of the whole pedagogical initiation for those under His providential care. For the only suitable dwelling place for God is the purified intellect, for whose sake God permitted the figurative temple to be built, using rather coarse symbols, for no other reason than to tear the intellect of the Jews away from matter—for their intellect was far more coarse than those senseless figures—hoping that they might realize that it was not suitable for God to dwell in an ill-fitting material structure,[[1]] and from this to become conscious of His natural attributes.[4]

---

1. Acts 17.24.
2. Cf. 1 Cor 10.11.
3. I.e., τυπικῶς ἀλλ' οὐκ ἀληθῶς.
4. The word "coarse," which appears twice in this sentence, renders the Greek παχυτέρων and παχυνθέντα, respectively, and describes the occlusion of spiritual vision in the "thickening" or "densification" of the soul's powers of perception; cf. Mt 13.15 and Acts 28.27, both citing Is 6.10 ("The heart of this people has become thick" [ἐπαχύνθη]); and Evagrios, *Gnostic Chapters* 4.36: "The intelligible fat is the thickness (πάχος) that arises in the intellect as a

31.3. But the Jews did not understand this knowledge, because their piety became nothing but a source of pride and arrogance to them,[2] and thus they were deprived of the figure and wickedly estranged themselves from the truth.

Scholia

[1] It is not fitting, he says, to construct a temple for God out of corporeal matter and carnal intellects. For these are coarser symbols and are not like God, and therefore it is necessary to build Him a temple out of things that are fitting for and naturally like Him.[5]

[2] Whoever is concerned with only the outward form of knowledge, which is mere rationality, and whoever pursues the semblance of virtue, which is a mere morality, is, he says, "Jewish," being puffed up with figures of the truth.

---

result of evil" (PO 28:151; cf. PG 12:1220CD); idem, *Letter on Faith:* "But since our intellect has become thick (παχυνθείς), bound to earth and mixed with clay, it is unable to fix its gaze in simple contemplation" (LCL 1:72 = *Letters of Basil, Ep.* 8); idem, *Gnostic Chapters* 2.62: "When the minds have received the contemplation that concerns them, then the thickness of bodies shall also be removed" (PO 28:85); and Maximos, *Cap. theol.* 2.61: "As we gradually get nearer to the spirit, we scrape off the coarseness (πάχος) of the words of Scripture by means of more subtle contemplations" (PG 91:1152B). In *Amb.* 33, Maximos responds to a question abut Gregory Nazianzus's use of this difficult word (i.e., "the Logos becomes thick [παχύνεται]"), to which he gives a positive interpretation (DOML 2:63–65); cf. *Cap. theol.* 2.37: "Through the modes of the virtues, the Logos becomes thick in those living the practical life" (PG 91:1141D).

5. This scholion is found only in Eriugena's Latin translation (CCSG 7:222, lines 1–4); Laga and Steel suggest that it may have been translated from a now lost Greek scholion (CCSG 7:ci).

QUESTION 32

HAT DOES IT mean that, "perhaps they might grope after and find God"?[1] How can a person find God by "groping after Him"?

Response

32.2. Whoever does not look upon all the visible and corporeal worship of the law through sense perception alone, but carefully examines with his intellect each of the visible symbols, thoroughly apprehending the divinely perfect *logos* hidden in each, finds God in that *logos*. In this way he rightly uses the power of his intellect to "grope" through the material ordinances of the law, as if groping through a heap of rubbish,[2] hoping to find buried somewhere "in the flesh of the law"[3] the pearl of the *logos*, which utterly escapes sense perception.[4] To be sure, the one who does not limit his perception of the nature of visible things to what his senses alone can observe, but who in his intellect wisely searches after the *logos* in every crea-

---

1. Acts 17.27.

2. I.e., ὡς ἐν φορυτῷ τῇ ὕλῃ; cf. below, Qu. 59.1; *Disp. Biz.*: "With the letter alone blocking their minds like rubbish" (μόνῳ τῷ γράμματι ὥσπέρ τινι φορυτῷ ἐγχώσαντες τὸν νοῦν) (ed. Allen and Neil, *Documents from Exile*, 92); *Amb.* 45.2: "[I am] like a blind man with outstretched hands, who, groping his way through the rubbish of the material world [φορυτὸν ὕλης], often stumbles upon something of value" (DOML 2:193); *QThp.*: τῷ φορυτῷ συμφυρομένῳ (75, lines 31–32); and Clement of Alexandria, *Protreptikos* 10.92.4, citing Democritus, fr. 147 (SC 2:160).

3. Origen, *Commentary on Romans* 6.12.8, the Greek text of which is extant in the catenae; cf. A. Ramsbotham, "Documents: The Commentary of Origen on the Epistle to the Romans," *JTS* 14 (1913): 10–22 (= fr. 46, p. 18, line 16).

4. Cf. Mt 13.45–46.

ture, likewise finds God, for from the manifest grandeur of beings he learns who is the Cause of their being.

32.3. Inasmuch as the ability to make distinctions is the characteristic mark of the one who "gropes after God," it follows that the one who examines the symbols of the law with knowledge,[1] and who contemplates the visible nature of beings with true understanding of its cause, makes distinctions within Scripture, nature, and himself. In Scripture, he distinguishes between the letter and the spirit;[5] in nature, between its inner *logos* and its outward manifestation; and in himself, between intellect and sensation. And by having chosen the spirit of Scripture, the *logos* of nature, and his intellect, and by uniting them indissolubly to each other, he found God—in the sense that he came to know God, as much as this was necessary and possible—in the intellect, in the *logos*, and in the spirit, for he is utterly removed from all that deceives and seduces the mind into countless erroneous opinions, by which I mean the letter, the outward appearance, and sensation, in which there exist differences of quantity, which is the antithesis of the Monad.[6] But if someone mixes up the letter of the law with the superficial manifestation of visible things and his own power of sensation, and so confuses them all together, he is "blind and short sighted,"[7] being sick through ignorance of the Cause of beings.[8]

Scholion

[1] Anyone, he says, who has seen the spirit of Scripture separated from figures, and the *logoi* of creation separated from their outward forms by means of his intellect alone, freed from the activity of sensation, has found God. That is, he has found Him in the spirit of Scripture as the Cause[9] of goodness; in the *logoi* of beings as the Cause of power; and in himself as the Cause of wisdom. For the *logoi* of beings created *ex nihilo* de-

---

5. Cf. 2 Cor 3.6.
6. I.e., the absolutely simple divine unity.
7. 2 Pt 1.9.
8. Cf. above, Intro. 1.2.13; Qu. 16.2; and Maximos's discussion of Scripture in *Myst.* 7 (CCSG 69:35–36).
9. I.e., αἴτιον, which can also mean "author" and "source."

clare the power of the Creator; and the spirit of Scripture, leading those who are in error back to divinization, proclaims the goodness of its Author;[10] while our own intellective capacity, inseparably containing the *logoi* of all that has come into being, clearly proclaims the wisdom of the divine Artisan.[11]

10. I.e., τοῦ γράψαντος.
11. Wisdom is the unitary content of all the *logoi*, and the primal and perfect Wisdom is the Logos, to which each human mind (*logos*) is assimilated according to the degree that it has gathered the *logoi* within itself.

QUESTION 33

HAT IS THE meaning of: "Truly, I say to you, whoever says to this mountain, 'Be taken up and cast in the sea,' and does not doubt[1] in his heart, but believes that what he says will come to pass, it will be done for him"?[2] And how are we to understand the words: "and does not doubt"?

Response

33.2. The divine and great Apostle, defining the meaning of faith, says "faith is the substance of things hoped for, the conviction of things not seen."[3] But if someone should define faith as an innate good, or as true knowledge demonstrative of ineffable good things, he would not miss the mark of truth. The Lord, moreover, when teaching about these ineffable good things, and about the things hoped for but not seen, said: "The kingdom of heaven is within you."[4] Thus faith in God is identical with the kingdom of God, the two being separated only on the level of thought.[5] For faith is the kingdom of God without visible form,[1] while the kingdom is faith given a form in a manner befitting God.[6] For this reason, faith is not outside of us, and when it is actualized through the keeping of the divine

---

1. "Doubt" is the standard translation of the Greek word διακριθῇ in Mk 11.23, although the sense of the word here is "to distinguish, to make a distinction, to divide," and "to separate"; cf. Acts 11.12: μὴ διακρίναντα ("making no distinction").
2. Mk 11.23.
3. Heb 11.1.
4. Lk 17.21.
5. See Maximos's remarks on the meaning of God's "kingdom" in *Or. Dom.* (CCSG 23:40–57).
6. Cf. above, Qu. 25.3.

commandments it becomes the kingdom of God, known only to those who possess it. If, then, the kingdom of God is actualized faith, and if the kingdom of God brings about an unmediated union of God and those in His kingdom, faith is clearly demonstrated[2] to be a relational power, or a relationship that effectively realizes in a manner beyond nature the unmediated union of the faithful with the God in whom they have faith.

33.3. Since the human person is composed of soul and body, he wavers between two laws, by which I mean the law of the flesh and that of the spirit.[7] On the one hand, the law of the flesh operates by virtue of the senses, but that of the spirit by virtue of the intellect. Now the law of the flesh, operating by means of the senses, is of a nature to bind one closely to matter, but the law of the spirit, operating by means of the intellect, brings about an unmediated union with God.[3] Thus it is only reasonable that "he who does not doubt in his heart,"[8] that is, who does not distinguish in his intellect—which is to say, who does not sever the unmediated union with God, which has come about through faith, inasmuch as he is dispassionate, or rather because he has already become God through union with Him by faith—is able to "say to this mountain, move, and it will be moved,"[9] indicating, through the demonstrative pronoun "*this* mountain," the mind and law of the flesh,[10] which truly is heavy and difficult to move, and as far as our natural powers are concerned, is absolutely immovable and unshakeable.

33.4. This is because the capacity for irrationality is rooted so deeply in human nature that the majority of people think that a human being is nothing more than flesh possessing the power of sensation for no other purpose than to enjoy this present life. But "all things are possible[4] to the one who has

---

7. Cf. Rom 7.23.
8. Mk 11.23.
9. Cf. Mt 17.20. Note that here Maximos is citing the biblical verse not from Mark but from Matthew, although this is not due to Maximos's emphasis on the demonstrative pronoun (τῷ ὄρει τούτῳ), which is used in both Gospels; cf. *QThp.* (77, lines 92–97), for one of Maximos's rare excursions into grammar and the accentuation of verbs.
10. Cf. Rom 8.6.

faith"[11] and does not doubt, that is, who does not separate himself from union with God—which faith has brought about in him through the intellect—on account of the soul's relation to the body through the senses. Whatever estranges the intellect from the world and the flesh, brings it, perfected by its spiritual achievements, into close intimacy with God.

Scholia

[1] He calls mere faith the "kingdom without visible form," since it lacks the divine likeness that arises from the practice of the virtues. By "faith" he means the kingdom possessing the divine form and goodness through works.

[2] Faith, he says, is knowledge that cannot be rationally demonstrated. And if such knowledge cannot be rationally demonstrated, then faith is a relationship that transcends nature, through which, in a manner beyond knowledge and demonstration, we are united to God in a union beyond intellection.

[3] In taking hold of unmediated union with God, the intellect is completely at rest from the natural power of knowing and being known. The moment, however, it ceases from this rest by thinking about something sequent to God, it "doubts" by dividing the union that is beyond intellect—and it is according to this union, inasmuch as the intellect is united to God, being beyond nature and becoming God by participation, that, like an immovable mountain, it will remove from itself the law of nature.

[4] One must understand, he says, the words: "All things are possible to the one who has faith,"[12] in the sense of one who estranges his intellect from the things of the world and the flesh, for these are the things that are possible.

11. Mk 9.23.
12. Ibid.

QUESTION 34

WHAT, AGAIN, is the meaning of: "Therefore I say unto you, all things you ask for, when you are praying, believe[1] that you have received them, and they will be yours"?[2] How is it possible for someone to believe that he will receive absolutely whatever he asks for, when only God knows if what he is asking for is helpful or not?[3] And if in ignorance he asks for something that is not helpful for him, how can God grant it to him? And if God does not grant him what is not helpful for him, and which he asked for in ignorance, how is it possible for someone to believe that he will receive whatever he asks for and that it shall be so unto him?[4]

Response

34.2. All the difficulties in this heading have been resolved in summary fashion in the one that precedes it. Simply put, only those who have understood how they should believe know how they should pray, and in what manner, and what kinds of things to ask for. For not all have knowledge, just as "not all have faith."[5] But the Lord, in saying: "Seek first the kingdom of God and His righteousness"[6]—that is, *before* all things seek first "the knowledge[7] of truth,"[8] and then act in ways consistent with it—clearly

---

1. In this Question, the words "belief" and "faith" (and their cognates) are both used to render the Greek word πίστις/πιστεύειν.
2. Mk 11.24; cf. Mt 21.22.
3. Cf. 1 Cor 6.12.
4. Cf. Evagrios, *On Prayer* 31–32 (PG 79:1173BC).
5. 2 Thes 3.2.
6. Mt 6.33.
7. I.e., ἐπίγνωσις.
8. Heb 10.26.

showed that those who believe should seek divine knowledge[9] alone, together with the virtue that adorns such knowledge through corresponding works. And because there are many things that believers must seek in order to acquire the knowledge of God—such as the deliverance from passions, patient acceptance of trials, the inner principles of the virtues, suitable modes of activities, the uprooting of the soul's proclivity for the flesh, the estrangement of sense perception from its condition of relation to objects of sense, the utter withdrawal of the intellect from all created beings, and in general everything that is required for the rejection of evil and ignorance and the acquisition of knowledge and virtue—it was only natural that the Lord said: "All things that you ask for in faith, you will receive."[10] By "all things" he was telling the pious that, with true understanding and faith, they should seek only those things that tend toward the knowledge[11] of God[12] and the life of virtue.[13]

34.3. For it is assuredly these things that are beneficial,[14] and the Lord assuredly gives them to those who ask for them. Whoever, then, on account of his faith alone, that is, for the sake of unmediated union with God, asks for all the things that tend toward this union, will assuredly receive them. But whoever asks either for these things or for other things, being motivated by some other reason or cause, will not receive them, for he does not believe, and lacking faith he is concerned with divine things for the sake of his own glory.

9. I.e., γνῶσις, which occurs three more times in this paragraph.
10. Cf. Mt 21.22.
11. I.e., ἐπίγνωσις.
12. Cf. Heb 10.26; Rom 10.2.
13. Note the distinction here between the two kinds of "knowledge," i.e., γνῶσις and ἐπίγνωσις (from Heb 10.26, cited above), the latter referring to a higher form of divine knowledge; cf. Qu. 64.15, where ἐπίγνωσις is defined as "active knowledge of the cause of the virtues," with knowledge having the sense of experientially based recognition. The scholion (no. 15) attached to this definition notes that the "cause" of the virtues is God, and that the "actualized knowledge (γνῶσις) of God occurs when the habitual state of the one who knows (ἐπεγνωκότος) God is transformed in the direction of the spirit." Ἐπίγνωσις is thus knowledge that transforms the knowing subject.
14. Cf. 1 Cor 6.12.

QUESTION 35

SINCE "THE Logos became flesh"[1]—and not simply flesh, but blood and bones—and we are commanded to "eat His flesh and drink His blood,"[2] but "not to crush His bones,"[3] I would like to learn what is this threefold power of the Logos made man.[4]

Response

35.2. When the Logos, who transcends being and who is the Creator of all beings, determined to enter into being in a manner known to Himself alone, He bore within Himself the natural *logoi* of all visible and intelligible beings together with the incomprehensible forms of thought[5] proper to His divinity. Of the former, the *logoi* of intelligible beings would be the "blood" of the Logos, while those of sensible beings can be understood as the visible "flesh" of the Logos. Moreover, insofar as the Logos is the teacher of the spiritual *logoi* that exist in both visible and intelligible realities, He gives those who are worthy—as if it were flesh to eat—the true understanding of the *logoi* found in visible realities, in a manner that is appropriate to the recipients and consistent with reason.[6] He likewise gives them—as

---

1. Jn 1.14.
2. Jn 6.53.
3. Cf. Jn 19.31–36; Ex 12.46.
4. The "threefold power" refers to the "flesh, blood, and bones."
5. "Forms of thought" renders the Greek word νοήματα.
6. In addition to the sacrament of the Eucharist, Maximos recognizes other forms of communion with the Word made flesh, including the practice of the virtues, natural contemplation, and the experience of theology; cf. *Amb.* 48 (DOML 2:212–23); and Larchet, *La Divinisation*, 424–46 ("Non-Eucharistic forms of communion").

QUESTION 35   213

if it were blood to drink—the knowledge of the *logoi* found in intelligible realities, which God's Wisdom mystically prepared long ago in the bowl for mixing wine and in the sacrificial animals described in Proverbs.[7] But He does not give us His bones, that is, the *logoi* of His divinity, which transcend intellection, since they are equally and infinitely remote from every created nature, because the nature of beings possesses no state or condition on the basis of which it might be able to receive them.

35.3. Again, the "flesh" of the Logos is true virtue, His "blood" is true knowledge, and His "bones" are ineffable theology.[1] This is because, consistent with the manner of blood, which in its appearance[8] is changed into flesh, knowledge is transformed by ascetic practice into virtue; and after the manner of bones, which are constitutive of blood and flesh, the *logoi* of His divinity, which transcend all intellection, exist within beings and create—in a manner beyond our cognition—the essences of those beings, and preserve them in existence, and are constitutive for all knowledge and all virtue.

35.4. But if someone were to say that the "flesh" and the "blood" are the *logoi* of judgment and providence—since at some point they will be entirely consumed and drunk—and that the "bones" are the ineffable *logoi* of divinity hidden within them, then it seems to me that he would not fall outside of what is likely to be true.[9]

35.5. But perhaps the "flesh" of the Logos is the perfect return and restoration of nature to itself through virtue and knowledge; and the "blood"[2] is the future divinization, which by grace will maintain nature in eternal well-being; while the "bones" are the unknowable power itself that sustains human nature, through the process of divinization, in eternal well- being.

35.6. If, however, someone were to say what is more readily grasped,[10] namely, that the "flesh" is voluntary mortification

7. Cf. Prv 9.1–2. Cf. Dionysios, *Ep.* 9.2–5 (198–206; 1108B–113C), for an extensive discussion of this passage from Proverbs.
8. I.e., κατ' εἶδος.
9. On providence and judgment, see below, Qu. 63.18.
10. Reading ληπτότερον with the CCSG text; the SC translation retains the Greek but renders it as "plus de subtilité" (p. 377), seemingly following Eriugena (*subtilius*), CCSG 7:240, l. 40.

through the virtues, and "blood" is the perfection through death resulting from tribulations for the sake of truth; and that the "bones" are the primary *logoi* concerning the divinity, which are inaccessible to us, he too would have spoken well, and in no way have fallen outside the proper meaning of things.

Scholia

[1] "Ineffable theology" is absolute unknowing according to preeminence,[11] which is unknown to us to the same extent that things naturally known to us fall within our knowledge.

[2] "Blood" is here used to indicate divinization, since it is the future life of those who will be made worthy of it, for blood is the symbol of life.[12]

---

11. On this term, see above, Qu. 25.5.
12. Lv 17.14; cf. above Qu. 27.6.

QUESTION 36

HAT ARE THE bodies and the blood of the irrational animals that the Jews used in their worship? And why did they eat only the bodies but not the blood, which latter they poured out in a circle around the altar of sacrifice?[1]

Response

36.2. Those who of old worshiped God according to the shadow of the law were a figure of those being initiated into piety, although they themselves were barely able to understand the external ordinances of the symbolic figures. But inasmuch as the law was not principally given to them, but to us, in whom it was spiritually perfected according to Christ,[2] let us examine with piety the inner logic of those sacrifices.

36.3. The beginner who is being initiated into piety, being instructed in the works of righteousness, engages solely in practical activity in all obedience and faith, nourishing himself on the outward appearances of the virtues as if they were flesh.[1] But the inner principles of the commandments, in which is found the knowledge[3] of perfect things, he surrenders to God in faith, being unable to extend himself to the magnitude of knowledge.[4] This is because the altar of sacrifice is a symbol

---

1. Cf. Dt 12.27.
2. Cf. 1 Cor 10.11; Rom 4.23–24; Rom 7.14.
3. I.e., εἴδησις.
4. On the phrase, "extend himself (συνεπεκταθῆναι) to the magnitude," cf. *QThp.* (74, line 19); Gregory of Nyssa, *Commentary on the Song of Songs* 3: "All our thinking is inferior to the divine understanding, and every explanatory word of speech seems to be an abbreviated trace unable to extend itself (συνεπεκτείνεσθαι) to the breadth of understanding" (GNO 6:87, lines 2–5); idem, *On the Life of Moses* 2.225, 238 (συνεπεκτείνεται) (SC 1bis: 262, 270); and Elias,

of God, to whom we all make spiritual sacrifices, surrendering our knowledge of things beyond our powers, so that we might live. The altar's pedestal, on the other hand, is a figure of faith in God, for faith is the foundation supporting the entire edifice of divine things, works, and forms of thought. And it is to this foundation that every one turns who is not able to enjoy the strong drink of the chalice of God's Wisdom[5] with temperance and the cognition of the knowledge of things beyond his reach—and such a person does well in pouring out the inner principles before the altar, that is, in surrendering to faith the knowledge of those inner principles that are beyond his powers to grasp.

36.4. Thus, inasmuch as the ancient people were a figure of those being initiated into piety, they ate the flesh of the sacrifices, but the blood they poured out around the pedestal of the sacrificial altar,[2] being unable, on account of their infantile way of thinking,[6] to grasp the mystical knowledge of what was taking place. "But when Christ appeared as a high priest of the good things to come,"[7] sacrificing an ineffable sacrifice, He offers Himself and His blood together with His flesh to those whose "faculties of soul have been trained to distinguish good from evil."[8] For the one who is perfect, having worked his way not simply to the rank of those being initiated, but to the rank of those who are advancing, is not ignorant of the inner principles of his actions undertaken according to the commandments. On the contrary, having first spiritually consumed these principles by means of his actions, he eats the entire flesh of the virtues, raising up the motion of his perceptible actions to the level of spiritual knowledge.

36.5. There are many other interpretations[9] of these things, which are especially appropriate to you, who love God supreme-

---

Commentary on Aristotle's Categories, where the term is used to describe the ability of universals to extend to particulars, or the point of a circle to its perimeter (CAG 18.1:154, lines 19–24); and below, Qu. 56, schol. 7.

5. I.e., the "bowl for mixing wine" of Qu. 35.2, above. Cf. Prv 9.2.
6. Cf. Heb 5.13; 1 Cor 13.11.
7. Heb 9.11.
8. Heb 5.14.
9. I.e., *logoi*.

ly, but on account of their great number let us for now leave them aside.[10]

Scholia

[1] By "outward appearances of the virtues" he means instruction in morals.[11]

[2] Here, according to contemplation, he understands "blood" to mean "knowledge," since knowledge nourishes the body of the virtues.

10. Cf. above, Qu. 21.8.
11. This scholion is not found in Eriugena's Latin translation.

QUESTION 37

ONCERNING Saint Paul, the book of Acts says that "handkerchiefs and semicinctia[1] were carried away from his body[2] to those who were sick, and they were cured of their diseases."[3] Did this take place for the sake of his ministry and for those without faith, or did these things happen insofar as the skin of Paul's body was sanctified? And if this is why he suffered no harm when he was bitten by the viper,[4] what was the reason why the body of the saint suffered no harm from the venom of the serpent, and yet was killed by a sword? I have the same question concerning the body of Elisha.[5] And what, finally, are "semicinctia"?

Response

37.2. It was neither solely because of Saint Paul's holiness, nor solely because of the faith of those receiving the miracle,[1] that the shadow of his body worked cures through the handkerchiefs and the semicinctia. Instead it was whatever divine grace, out of love for mankind, distributed both to him and to them, rendering Saint Paul's holiness active and effective in them through their faith. Thus, again, when grace wished, Paul's body was not susceptible to suffering, not being destroyed by the venom

---

1. I.e., σημικίνθια, a rare word transliterated from Latin; *LSJ*, s.v., cites only Acts 19.12. This was probably a leather belt, a thinner version of the *cinctium* or "girdle" (ζώνη) commonly worn by men and women. I have chosen not to translate it, since calling it a "leather belt" or some other such word would obviate the nature of the difficulty.
2. I.e., χρώς, literally "skin" or "flesh."
3. Acts 19.12.
4. Cf. Acts 28.3–5.
5. Cf. 4 Kgs 13.21.

of the snake,[2] either because the lethal quality of the snake's venom was neutralized, or because the body of Paul neutralized the venom, or because of some other dispensation, known by God, who is the creator and transformer of these things. And when Paul fell by the sword, this was also the determination of grace. For Saint Paul was not immortal by nature, even if, by grace, he was able to work miracles. If, on the one hand, he was by nature immortal, then we would be justified in seeking the reason why, contrary to nature, he fell to the sword. But since he remained mortal by nature even after his sanctification, it is not necessary to seek the reason why the divine Apostle passed from life not in this manner but in some other. For in whatever way He wishes, God—who before the ages determined the limit of each man's life in the manner most expedient for each—leads every man, whether just or unjust, toward the final end he deserves.[6]

37.3. If, then, the principle of nature and grace were both one and the same,[3] it would be cause for wonder and astonishment that what came about was according to nature but contrary to grace, or according to grace but contrary to nature. If, however, the principle of nature is one thing, and the principle of grace is something else, then it is clear and obvious that, as saints, they worked miracles on account of grace, but as men they suffered on account of nature. For grace does not destroy the passible part of nature, neither are the principles of nature and grace in any way ever confused with each other. Let us therefore accept that the grace of God, according to the dispensation of providence, works all things through the saints both while they are alive and after their deaths, as if through its own proper instruments for the salvation of others—but it is not according to nature that the saints by grace work these miracles for others. The same holds true for the body of Elisha.[7]

6. The question of whether or not God predetermined the day, hour, and manner of one's death was taken up by Maximos's contemporary, Anastasios of Sinai, who rejected the idea, which remained a controversial topic among subsequent Byzantine theologians; cf. Joseph A. Munitiz, "The Predetermination of Death: The Contribution of Anastasios of Sinai and Nikephoros Blemmydes to a Perennial Byzantine Problem," *DOP* 55 (2001): 9–20.

7. Cf. 4 Kgs 4.32–35.

37.4. But since it is rather the spiritual meanings of the literal accounts that make glad the souls of those who love God, we say that the "body" is the piety of the great Apostle, according to which he was "to some the odor of life unto life,[4] but to others the smell of death."[8] The "handkerchiefs" are the manifest principles of his cognitive contemplation, while the "semicinctia" are the honorable modes of practical philosophy concerned with virtue, for they say that semicinctia are things covering the hands.[9] These principles and modes, which permeate and emanate from the body like a fragrance (being the great piety of the blessed Apostle), became, to those who received it, the cure for the sickness that was oppressing them. Some of them, through the principles of contemplation—as if they were handkerchiefs—wiped away the disease of ignorance; others, through the virtuous modes of ascetic practice, completely removed the sickness of vice. Further, it would seem that the dark storm that beset him[10] is the weight of involuntary trials,[11] while the island[12] is the firm and unshakeable state of divine hope. The fire is the state of knowledge; the firewood[13] is the nature of visible realities, which he gathered by hand, I mean by the intellect's power to grope for things during contemplation,[14] a power that nourishes the state of knowledge by means of the thoughts that arise from it—a state that allayed the dejection which the storm of trials inflicted on the mind. The viper[15] is the wicked and deadly power hidden secretly in the nature of sensible things, which bites the hand, that is, the activity of the intellect as it gropes for things during contemplation, but which does not injure the intellect's

8. 2 Cor 2.16.
9. Cf. above, Qu. 3.3.
10. Acts 27.13–20.
11. Cf. *Record of the Trial* 13: "'Pray that God might perfect His mercy with our lowliness, and that He might teach us that those who sail along with Him experience a savage sea, like a ship which is driven about by winds and waves but stands firm and unshakeable.' For He allowed them to be tried by a great storm, testing their disposition toward Him so that they might cry aloud, 'Lord, save us, we are perishing' (Mt 8.25)" (ed. Allen and Neil, 73).
12. Acts 27.26.
13. Acts 28.2–3.
14. Cf. above, Qu. 32.
15. Acts 28.3.

clear-sighted vision, which, with the light of knowledge, as if with fire, immediately burns up the destructive power that had fastened itself to the practical movement of the intellect through its contemplation of sensible realities.

37.5. I understand what took place in the case of Elisha in the same way: any person who is dead on account of his trespasses, when placed upon the tomb of the prophet[16] containing his body, that is, upon the memory[5] containing a trace of the prophetic life,[17] in which the body of the virtues is securely guarded—such a person, I say, is restored to life by the imitation of the prophet's way of life, being transposed from the deadness of the evil passions to a life of virtue.

Scholia

[1] The faith of those who were in need of healing, he says, called forth the power of the Spirit in the saints, so that through faith the hitherto secret power might be revealed, and that the faith which had been hidden might be made manifest to all. For the true manner of healing is of a nature to be shown forth when the power of those who act in the Spirit coincides with the faith of those who are being acted on.

[2] The one, he says, who by the inclination of his will purifies himself of the corruption of sin, destroys the corrupting activity of things that naturally cause corruption. For the incorruptibility of free will maintains nature's corruptibility in a state of incorruption, because through the grace of the Spirit that is in it,[18] it providentially does not permit nature to be dominated by the opposing qualities.

[3] Because the principle of nature and grace is not, he says, one and the same thing, there is no difficulty in understanding that some of the saints were sometimes immune to sufferings, and at other times were subject to sufferings, since we know that the miracle was because of grace, while the suffering was from nature.

---

16. Cf. 2 Kgs 13.21.
17. Playing on the words for "tomb" (μνῆμα) and "memory" (μνήμη).
18. I.e., in free will.

[4] The Apostle was an "odor of life unto life"[19] because by his example and practice he prepared the faithful to move toward the good fragrance of the virtues, or because he was a preacher leading those who obeyed the word of grace from the life of the senses to life in the Spirit. But he was an "odor of death unto death" for those who passed from the death of ignorance to the death of unbelief, giving them a sense of the condemnation that awaits them. Or, again, he is the "odor of life unto life" for those who rise up from ascetic practice to contemplation, and the "odor of death unto death" for those who, through the cessation of sin, advance from the "death of their members that are upon the earth"[20] to the praiseworthy death of their impassioned thoughts and fantasies.

[5] Whoever, he says, preserves the memory of the saints by imitating their way of life not only sets aside the deadness of the passions but also receives the life of the virtues.

19. 2 Cor 2.16.
20. Cf. Col 3.5.

QUESTION 38

AS IT BY chance¹ that the Sadducees used the number seven when they spoke of the seven brothers who were married to one woman,² or is there a deeper meaning? And if there is, who are these seven, and who is this one?

Response

38.2. Some people say that the words of blameworthy persons in Scripture should not be given an allegorical interpretation.³ Because, however, it is a greater thing by far to devote oneself to labor, and ceaselessly to entreat God to provide wisdom and strength so that we might understand the whole of Scripture spiritually, I take courage from your prayers and offer the following concerning this present difficulty.

38.3. According to the principle of anagogy, the Sadducees are the demons who introduce the idea of chance⁴ or evil

---

1. I.e., ὡς ἔτυχεν.
2. Mt 22.23–28.
3. An allusion to Evagrios, *Gnostikos* 21: "You must not allegorize the words of blameworthy persons, neither must you seek for anything spiritual in them, except in those instances when God was acting by way of dispensation, as in the case of Barlaam (Nm 24.17–19) and Caiaphas (Jn 11.49–51), so that the one might predict the birth, and the other the death, of our Savior" (SC 356:122); cf. below, Qu. 49.9; Qu. 55.27; and Qu. 64.11 and 18; and the parallel formulations in Philo, *On the Cherubim* 24: "When God is with us, all we do is worthy of praise (ἐπαινετόν); but all that is done without Him merits blame (ψεκτόν)" (LCL 2:22–23); and Didymos, *On Genesis* 1.61 (SC 233:154–56). See also the *Physiologus*, which likewise understands various biblical animals to have both praise- and blameworthy characteristics, allowing them to be predicated of both Christ and the devil; cf. Francesco Sbordone, ed., *Physiologus* (Milan: Dante Alighieri, 1936), 15.
4. I.e., αὐτοματισμός, "that which happens by itself," or "by chance." This

thoughts. The wife is the nature of human beings. The seven brothers are the laws that, at different times from the beginning of the age, have been given by God to human nature for its education and the generation of the fruits of righteousness.[5] Having intercourse with these laws as if they were men, she bore a son from none of them, and for this reason she was barren of the fruit of righteousness. The first law was given to Adam in paradise.[6] The second law was given to Adam after the fall, in the order of punishment.[7] The third was given to Noah in the ark.[8] The fourth was the law of circumcision given to Abraham.[9] The fifth was also given to Abraham, when he received Isaac.[10] The sixth was the law of Moses.[11] The seventh law was the grace of prophetic inspiration.[12] For nature had not yet been betrothed to the Gospel through faith so that it might live together with a man who would remain with her forever.

38.4. It is these laws that the demons continually present to our inner reason through the thoughts, contending against the faith by subjecting the Scriptures to superficial logic, posing

---

somewhat rare word appears frequently in Theophilos of Antioch, *To Autolycus* 2.4; 3.3, 26, etc., where it refers to pagan notions that the world is either eternal or came into being by chance (SC 20:102; 210, 260). Porphyry, *On the Cave of the Nymphs* 32, likewise uses the word in rejecting the notion that the world is irrational and the product of fate (ed. Seminar Classics, Arethusa Monographs 1 [Buffalo: Arethusa, 1969], 609). Didymos, *Commentary on Ecclesiastes* (ed. Michael Gronewald, *Didymos der Blinde, Kommentar zum Ecclesiastes* [Tura-Papyrus], Teil II, PTA 22 [Bonn: Rudolf Habelt, 1977], 116, lines 17–18 = fol. 88); Evagrios, *Scholia on Ecclesiastes* 36 (SC 397:122, line 19); and Cyril of Alexandria, *Against Julian* 2.16 (SC 322:236, line 10), all use the word in the course of criticizing pagan cosmology. Maximos, however, uses the word not to describe the random generation of the cosmos, but the demonic suggestion that there is no providence and that human existence is subject to necessity; cf. *Amb.* 7.4 (DOML 1:78–79).

5. In Greek, the word "nature" (φύσις) is a feminine noun, whereas "law" (νόμος) is masculine.
6. Cf. Gn 2.16–17.
7. Cf. Gn 3.17–19.
8. Cf. Gn 9.1–7.
9. Cf. Gn 17.9–14.
10. Cf. Gn 22.1–2.
11. Cf. Ex 20.1–17.
12. Cf. Dt 18.15.

difficulties such as: "If there is a resurrection of the dead, and we must await another form of life after the present one, then of all the laws that have been given through the ages, by which one will human nature be governed?" And if we respond by naming one of the aforementioned laws, they will conclude that "human life once again will be futile and unprofitable, since it will not be released from its former evils, if nature will again be troubled by the very same things"—a line of thinking that clearly introduces chance and expels God's providential care of beings. But the Lord and saving Word silences these demons as well as these thoughts when He gestures toward the incorruptibility of nature, which, according to the Gospel, will be made manifest in the future, and when He shows that human nature will not be governed according to any of the former laws,[13] since it will already have been divinized and united, being betrothed through the Spirit to the Word Himself and God, from whom and unto whom nature has received and will receive the beginning of its existence as well as its end.

38.5. If someone should subscribe to the notion that the seven men are seven thousand years, that is, the seven thousand ages with which human nature has conducted its intercourse, he will have grasped, not without reason or a fitting contemplation, the meaning of this passage, for in the future life, nature will be the wife of none of those ages, inasmuch as temporal nature will have reached its end, and she will have been wedded by the eighth man, who is the age without end or limit.

13. Cf. Mt 22.29–30.

QUESTION 39

HAT ARE THE three days during which the crowds remained with the Lord in the wilderness?[1]

Response

39.2. The wilderness is the nature of human beings, or this world, in which those who suffer hardships in faith and in the hope of the good things to come remain with the principle[2] of virtue and knowledge. The three days, according to one mode of contemplation,[3] are the three powers[1] of the soul, by means of which they remain close to the divine principle of virtue and knowledge: with the one they seek, with the other they yearn, and with the third they strive to receive incorruptible nourishment, enriching their intellect with the knowledge of created beings.

39.3. According to another mode of interpretation, the three days signify the three more universal laws,[2] by which I mean the written law, the natural law, and the spiritual law, which latter is the law of grace.[4] Each one of these laws, in a manner proper to itself, illumines human nature, because the source[5] of each law's light is the "Sun of righteousness."[6] For just as it is absolutely impossible for there to be daylight without the sun,

---

1. Mt 15.32.
2. I.e., *logos*, which here should be taken as inclusive of the divine Logos, who is Himself the substance of virtue and knowledge; cf. *Amb.* 7.21 (DOML 1: 103).
3. Cf. Gn 40.12.
4. Cf. Gal 6.2.
5. Literally, "creator."
6. Mal 3.20.

neither can the law of righteousness exist without the essential and "hypostatic Wisdom,"[7] which makes its own proper light arise in each law, and fills the intellective eyes of souls with intelligible light. Knowing this, the blessed David said: "Your law is a lamp unto my feet and a light on my paths."[8] He called the written law a "lamp,"[3] because through its various combinations of corporeal symbols, riddles, and figures it skillfully sets fire to and consumes the depravity of the passions among those who, through ascetic practice undertaken against the opposing powers, broaden the steps of their soul's progress. But the spiritual law of grace he called "light,"[4] for without any artifice and without the use of sensible symbols it reveals the eternal "paths." Making its way along these paths, the contemplative intellect is led to the highest summit[9] of good things, which is God, without the motion of the mind being limited by any created beings. For the light of the law of grace is unwaning, there being no horizon of knowledge able to limit its wholly brilliant beams. Or perhaps the prophet used the word "feet" to describe the entire course of life according to God, or the movements of good thoughts in the soul, which like a lamp guide one with the light of the written law. By "paths" he speaks of the modes of virtue in accordance with the natural law, and the principles of knowledge in accordance with the spiritual law, which are revealed by the presence of God the Word, and which, through virtue and knowledge, lead nature back to itself[5] and to its Cause.

39.4. Having remained with God the Word during these three days, which are three laws, and having readily endured the labors associated with each law, those whose desire is turned toward salvation are not sent away hungry but receive nourishment which is rich as well as divine. For the written law[6] they receive

---

7. This phrase occurs in the *Exposition of Faith* of Gregory Thaumaturgus, found in Gregory of Nyssa, *Life of Gregory Thaumaturgus* (GNO 10:17, line 25), a passage which figures as the first excerpt in the 6th-century anti-Origenist *Collectio Sabbaitica* (ACO 3, p. 3), and again in the florilegium *Doctrina patrum de incarnatione Verbi* (ed. Franz Diekamp [Münster in Westfalen: Aschendorff, 1907], 284, lines 4–5).
8. Ps 118.105.
9. Or, "most extreme limit."

the total deliverance from passions contrary to nature. For the natural law they receive the true activity of things according to nature—an activity through which a relation of mutuality is constituted, which drives out from nature every fragmenting otherness and division. For the spiritual law they receive union with God Himself. Through this union, they stand outside of all that has come into being, and they receive the glory that transcends nature, through which God alone is known among them, shining forth like lightning.

39.5. You have an expanded interpretation of this passage in the *Ambigua*, on the oration on Holy Pentecost by Saint Gregory.[10]

Scholia

[1] He is speaking of reason, irascibility, and desire, for it is by means of reason that we seek; it is by means of desire that we long for the good that we seek; and it is by means of irascibility that we strive for it.

[2] He called the powers of the soul both "days," since they are receptive of the light of the divine commandments, and "three more universal laws," since they illumine the souls that receive them. For just as Genesis called the light "day," saying: "And God saw that the light was good, and God called the light 'day,'"[11] as well as "air illumined by light," saying: "And there was evening, and there was morning, one day,"[12] so too did he not only call the powers of the soul "days," but also the laws that illumine them. For their full and mutual interpenetration creates the composite day of the virtues, which in no way separates the powers that continually produce it from the divine light of the Word.

[3] The Word of God is Himself both a "lamp" and a "light"[13]

---

10. A reference to *Amb.* 67.12–13 (DOML 2:299–301), indicating not only that the *Ambigua to John* was written before the *Responses to Thalassios*, but that the former work was already in circulation in North Africa, if only among Maximos's closest colleagues.
11. Gn 1.4.
12. Gn 1.5.
13. Ps 118.105; Prv 6.23.

inasmuch as He illumines the thoughts of the faithful that are in accordance with nature, but also burns those that are contrary to nature. He dispels, moreover, the darkness of life according to the senses among those who, through the commandments, hasten to the life that is hoped for, but He punishes, by the burning heat of judgment, those who by their own inclination to carnal pleasure are attached to the dark night of this existence.

[4] The law, he says, when understood in its symbolic form, is a lamp, which through ascetic practice destroys the depravity of the passions, but when it is clearly understood without symbols, it is light, which through contemplation elevates to divine kinship those who are being led by grace.

[5] He is saying that anyone who has not first been reintegrated with himself by casting off the passions that are contrary to nature will not be reintegrated with the Cause of his being, which is God. With God's grace, this is accomplished by the fresh acquisition of good things beyond nature, because the one who is truly gathered up in God must have a mind separated from created things.

[6] The function of the written law, he says, is deliverance from the passions; that of the natural law is the equal distribution of goods to all men according to equality of honor; and the fulfillment of the spiritual law is likeness to God,[14] as much as this is possible for man.

---

14. Cf. Gn 1.27.

QUESTION 40

HAT IS signified by the number of the six jars at the wedding in Cana of Galilee?[1]

Response

40.2. God, who created human nature, simultaneously gave it being and the power of intention,[2] and thus joined to this nature the creative power[1] to realize what is proper to it. The six jars signify this natural creative power to perform the divine commandments. Human beings, however, poured out the knowledge of this power in their vain preoccupation with material things, and came to possess this power as something empty and waterless.[3] This is why they did not know how to cleanse themselves from the stain of evil, because someone who has no share in knowledge is completely ignorant of the way in which virtue cleanses vice. This was the situation that prevailed until the arrival of the Word, the creator of nature, who filled[2] the power of natural knowledge (which is able to perform the things proper to it) and changed[4] it into wine, by which I mean

---

1. Jn 2.6. For a parallel interpretation of the "mysteries" of the Wedding at Cana, cf. QD. 35 (CCSG 10:28–29).
2. "Power of intention" here renders the Greek word βούλησις, a technical term designating the starting point of an actual act of willing. Strictly speaking, the προαίρεσις, the faculty of free choice, is related to the means by which one's wished-for goals may be attained; βούλησις is not unlike γνώμη, since it manifests the intention of a freely acting human being; cf. Thunberg, *Microcosm and Mediator*, 219–20.
3. Cf. Ps. 62.1.
4. "Changed" translates μετέβαλεν, which is the word used to describe the transformation of the Eucharistic gifts from bread and wine into the Body and Blood of Christ in the Divine Liturgy of St. John Chrysostom.

the principle of knowledge, which is beyond nature and the law, and the principle of nature itself. Thus those who drink of it stand outside the nature of all beings, and fly off to the hidden place of divine interiority, where they receive the joy and delight that transcend all multiform knowledge—and they drink the "good wine,"[5] that is, the ineffable Word who brings about divinization, which they drink last, after all the dispensations given by Providence on behalf of mankind.[3]

40.3. With respect to the number six, we understand it to signify the creative power of nature, not simply because God created heaven and earth in six days,[6] but also because the number six alone is the most perfect number contained in the decad of numbers, and as a number is constituted from its own parts.[7] Further, Scripture says that the "jars held two or three measures,"[8] since they contain, according to natural contemplation, as if it were two measures, the natural potential of practice, which is the entire knowledge[4] of created beings (by which I mean they contain the knowledge of corporeal natures composed of matter and form), and the intelligible essenc-

---

5. Jn 2.10.
6. Gn 1.1–25; Ex 20.11.
7. On the symbolism of the number six, cf. Philo, *On the Creation of the World* 3.13–14 (LCL 1:12–15); idem, *On the Allegorical Interpretation of Genesis* 1.3 (LCL 1:148–50); idem, *On the Decalogue* 8.6 (LCL 7:18–19); Nicomachus of Gerasa, *Introduction to Arithmetic* 1.16.3 (trans. Martin Luther D'Ooge [London: Mac-Millan, 1926], 209–10); David, *Prolegomenon to Philosophy* (CAG 18/2:22, line 22; 51, line 18); Pseudo-Iamblichos, *Theology of Arithmetic* (ed. De Falco and Klein [Leipzig: Teubner, 1975]; trans. Robin Waterfield [Grand Rapids: Phanes Press, 1988], 75–85 = "On the Hexad"); and Constas, DOML 2:359, n. 6. See also below, Qu. 49.9–10; Qu. 55.15; *Amb.* 66.2 (DOML 2:282–85); *QD.* 29; 35; 49; 176; 191 (CCSG 10:24–25; 29; 42; 121; 132–33); and Peter van Deun, "La symbolique des nombres dans l'oeuvre de Maxime le Confesseur," *Byzantinoslavica* 53 (1992): 237–42. The Johannine jars are cited by Origen, *On First Principles* 4.2.5 (SC 268:316–18, a passage excerpted in the Cappadocian *Philokalia* [SC 302:182–83]), who sees in them the basic principles of his biblical exegesis, so that the two measures of water allude to the psychological and spiritual levels of Scripture, while the third points to the corporeal level, which he says this particular passage lacks. That there are six jars refers to "those being purified in this world, which was created in six days, a perfect number."
8. Jn 2.6. Two to three Greek "measures" are approximately twenty to thirty gallons, or 75 to 115 liters.

es composed of substance and accidents, which is to say comprehensive knowledge of corporeal and incorporeal realities. According to the mystagogical initiation into theology that is accessible to our nature,[9] they contain, as if it were three measures, the knowledge and illumination of the Holy Trinity, that is, of the Father and the Son and the Holy Spirit.

40.4. I leave it to you, then, as men of knowledge, to consider that which remains, namely, how the general power of nature that is creative of superior things is divided into the six[5] general modes of the virtues. And what, in relation to the universal power of nature, which is productive of the virtues, is the universal virtue that is more general than the others, and which is divided into six kinds—these also being general—so that, being adapted to the power of nature, it might be contained by the modes of this virtue distinguished into six forms. In addition to these, you may consider who are the "servants filling the jars with water";[10] and who is the bridegroom, and who is the bride; who is the "master of the banquet";[11] and who is the mother, announcing with boldness of speech: "They have no wine."[12] All of these things remain to be examined by the initiate and initiator of divine principles and concepts, if, that is, his intellect takes pleasure in the anagogical mode of interpretation. Nonetheless, so that the discussion of these things not be passed over at present in utter silence by us and be lost, and we fail to offer even a small portion of the spiritual banquet to those whose hunger is noble, I will speak to the extent that I am able, though I cannot promise to reveal the entire meaning contained in the things mentioned above—my intellect is far too weak to comprehend such intelligible visions—but only as much as the capacity of my mind is naturally able to grasp.

40.5. They say that love is the most general of the virtues,[13]

---

9. "Theological mystagogy" is the supernatural revelation of divine mysteries, which nature may receive by divine grace, but which it cannot produce through its own power.
10. Jn 2.7.
11. Jn 2.8.
12. Jn 2.3.
13. Cf. *Ascet.* 6 (CCSG 40:15); *Ep.* 2 (PG 91:393B–96D); *Carit.* 4.74 (ed. Caresa-Gastaldo, 226); and *Amb.* 21.9 (DOML 1:432–35).

and that the most general power of nature productive of love is reason, which, holding on tightly to its own Cause,[6] is parted through its activity into six more general modes, encompassing the various forms by which the principle of love is distinguished,[7] namely, attending physically and spiritually to the hungry and the thirsty, to strangers, to the naked, the sick, and to those in prisons.[14] This is because the principle of virtue is not limited to bodies alone, neither is the power of nature concerned solely with sensation.[15] Thus the most general power of nature gives form to the most general virtue, and it does this by dividing virtue into six forms that are analogous to nature's own six modes. Through these forms, nature is unified in the unity of the will's inclination,[8] showing that the principle of creation is indivisible and of equal honor in all, and is gathered into itself by giving and receiving benefits. When the intellect, through the requisite labors, takes hold of this principle in all its force, it cuts off all the extremes and deficiencies of nature, which were contrived by self-love through the voluntary inclination of each person, transforming our incomparably gentle nature into a savage beast, and dividing the one essence of human nature into multiple and opposing parts, which—and there is nothing worse that one could say—are mutually destructive. By removing these extremes, the intellect bears and brings to light an unwavering mean,[9] in accordance with which the natural laws of the virtues were written in the beginning by God. Perhaps this is the mystery that Scripture is hinting at when it introduces six jars empty and without water,[16] alluding to the inactivity of our nature's most general power with respect to the good. In this way, then, the most general power of our nature, divided in practice into six modes, fashions the most general virtue into the same number of forms, in such a way that the whole of nature encompasses the whole of virtue. Being conformed to virtue, nature receives its own most general law as the infallible judge of the truth,[10] a law which Scripture called the "master of the banquet,"[17] who clearly discerned the "good

14. Cf. Mt 25.35–36.
15. Cf. *Amb.* 10.2 (DOML 1:150–53).
16. Cf. Jn 2.7.
17. Jn 2.8.

wine,"[18] which the Word, through His own proper manifestation, subsequently mixed, for it was necessary that human nature should first drink this wine and become inebriated by it—I mean the superior and more sublime principle[19] concerning God—and afterwards, as happens with wines, to be initiated into principles of beings, inferior as they may be in comparison to the first principle. For it was truly most just and most proper for nature to be initiated concerning the reason[20] for which it came into being, and afterwards to seek out the reasons of the things that came into being for it.

40.6. Those who "filled the jars with water" are the "servants"[21] of both the Old and the New Testament; I mean the holy patriarchs, the lawgivers, the generals, the judges and the kings, the prophets, the evangelists, and the apostles, through whom the water of knowledge was replenished and given again to human nature, the very water that the Word—who in His goodness created nature, and out of His love for mankind divinized it by His grace—changed into the grace of divinization. If, however, someone should say that the "servants" signify true understanding and pious sequences of thought consistent with nature, which, at the command of the Word, draw out the water of knowledge from the orderly arrangement of the world, he would not, I think, miss the mark of truth.

40.7. The bridegroom is quite clearly the human intellect, which takes virtue to itself like a bride for marriage. Honoring their companionship, the Word responds eagerly to their wedding invitation, binding tightly the conjuncture of their spiritual marriage, and with His own wine warms their desire for spiritual fertility.

40.8. The mother of the Word is the true and unsullied faith. Just as the Word, who, as God, is by nature the creator of His mother who gave birth to Him according to the flesh, and made her His mother out of love for mankind, and accepted to be born from her as man, so too the Word first creates faith within

---

18. Jn 2.10.
19. I.e., *logos,* followed by *logoi* ("principles").
20. I.e., *logos,* followed by *logoi* ("reasons").
21. Jn 2.9.

us, and then becomes the son of that faith, from which He is embodied through the practice of the virtues. And it is through faith that we accomplish all things, receiving from the Word the graces necessary for salvation. For without faith, through which the Word is God by nature and a son by grace, we have no boldness of speech to address our petitions to Him.[22]

40.9. May we always be celebrating a wedding such as this, with Jesus present with His own mother, so that He might restore to us the knowledge that flowed away from us on account of sin, and change it unto our divinization, which separates the intellect from the genesis of beings, and fortifies the knowledge of nature, giving it the strength to be immutable, just as water is fortified by the quality of wine.

Scholia

[1] When he says "power," he is speaking of the motion that is implanted throughout the essence of nature for the actualization of the virtues, and which is made manifest through the inclination of the will, when it is used intentionally by the one who possesses it.

[2] When the Word of God became man, He filled human nature anew with the knowledge it had formerly received but did not retain, and, fortifying this knowledge so that it might be immutable, He divinized it, not in terms of its nature, but in terms of its quality, fully giving it the characteristic properties of His own Spirit, mingling them together, so that nature might be strengthened, just as water is mingled with the quality of wine. For this is why in truth He became man, so that He might by grace establish us as Gods.[23]

---

22. Cf. *QD*. 35: "But when the Lord came, he elevated even nature into what is beyond nature through faith. And this holds true in the person of the Theotokos. For just as the Theotokos, who exists because she was created by her Lord and Son, herself gave birth to Him according to the flesh, so too faith, which exists from the Word, through actual practice actualizes the Word" (CCSG 10:29, lines 23–30).

23. The water became wine not from its own substance or power, but through a divine power imbuing it with a new quality, which points to the divinization of human nature, which is transformed not through its own natural power or capacity, but through divine grace.

[3] He calls the Word, who makes the human person stand outside of nature in the process of divinization, the "good wine," which Adam was not formerly able to drink because of his transgression, but which He Himself—by grace emptying Himself[24] as God on account of His love for mankind, through His Incarnation, and in a manner known only to Him—made potable. For He Himself is also Providence, insofar as He maintains beings in existence; so too is He the Principle of Providence, insofar as He is the method of healing for those under His providential care; and He is Provident, insofar as He contains all things by means of their own principles of being.

[4] He is saying that, according to its nature, the power of the intellect is receptive of the knowledge of corporeal and incorporeal realities, but it is only by grace that it receives the manifestations of the Holy Trinity, for it simply believes, and does not arrogantly seek to know, what the Trinity is in its essence.

[5] The universal power of nature is divided into six modes and activities, while universal love is parted into six forms of virtue. Whoever assuages—either physically or spiritually—the hunger, thirst, nakedness, exile, sickness, or imprisonment[25] of those who have been overtaken by such things, has realized the love of God and neighbor,[26] which is constituted from the six virtues—and he did this while maintaining the desire of his soul imbued with the quality of God alone.

[6] God, he says, is the cause of reason, and man has received the power of reason in order to seek Him.

[7] The substance of love is divided into the things of which it consists.

[8] He is saying that whoever, through virtue and the voluntary inclination of his will, has become equal to all human beings manifests within himself God's equal treatment of all, for just as God has created one nature according to one and the same principle, so too has He established a single movement for the voluntary inclination of our will, with respect to which

24. Cf. Phil 2.7.
25. Cf. Mt 25.35–36.
26. Cf. Rom 13.8–9.

it is natural that the principle of nature be gathered into one, even though it seems to be scattered.

[9] The "mean" is what he calls the state delivered from passions that are contrary to nature, but which has not yet acquired the good things that transcend nature. Such a state shows that the inclination of the will is equally distributed throughout nature, possessing nothing that might incline it away from the principle of nature, and for this reason it recognizes all human beings as one, for it possesses the law of nature as a book written by God.

[10] We have the law of nature as a natural criterion for judgment, teaching us that before we can acquire the wisdom that is in all things, our desire must be in motion toward the mystagogy of the creator of all things.

QUESTION 41

HAT IS THE meaning of the five husbands of the Samaritan woman, and the sixth, who was not truly her husband?[1]

Response

41.2. The Samaritan woman, as well as the woman who, according to the Sadducees, had married the seven brothers, and the woman with the flow of blood, and the woman who was bent down toward the earth, and the daughter of Jairus, and the Syro-Phoenician woman, symbolize both universal human nature and the particular soul of each human being, each one signifying—in terms of the underlying disposition of the passion in question—both nature and the soul.[2] For example, the woman mentioned by the Sadducees is nature or the soul, which, while cohabiting in ignorance with all the divine laws that had been given throughout the ages, does not receive the expectation of the good things of the future.[3] The woman with the flow of blood is likewise nature and the soul, which, on account of the passions, allows the power that had been given to it for the generation of works and words of righteousness to flow outward toward matter. The Syro-Phoenician woman is the same nature and particular soul of each, whose daughter is the mind that, in its weakness, is grievously torn apart by epilepsy on account of its love of matter. The daughter of Jairus is likewise nature and the soul under the law, which has com-

---

1. Jn 4.16–18.
2. Mt 22.25–28; Mt 9.20; Lk 13.11; Mk 5.22–35; Mk 7.25–30.
3. In Greek, the word "law" (νόμος) is masculine, while the words "nature" (φύσις) and "soul" (ψυχή) are feminine.

pletely died by not practicing the commandments of the law, and by failing to act on the divine ordinances. The woman who was bent down is nature or the soul, which, through the devil's deceit, has bent toward matter the whole of its intellective power, which was intended for the practice of the virtues. The Samaritan woman, like the previous women, signifies nature or the particular soul, which, without the gift of prophecy, lived with the laws that had been given to nature, as if cohabiting with men, of which she already had five, while the sixth, even though he was present, was the husband of neither nature nor the soul, in that he does not father from it the righteousness that is eternal salvation.

41.3. It follows, then, that nature's first husband was the law given in paradise.[4] The second was the law given after the expulsion from paradise.[5] The third was during the flood in the time of Noah.[6] The fourth was the law of circumcision given to Abraham.[7] The fifth was the offering of Isaac.[8] Nature received all these laws, and all of them she rejected, since they were dead and fruitless to her with respect to works of virtue. The sixth was the law of Moses,[9] which she had but in a way did not have, either because she did not perform the righteousness prescribed by it, or because she was going to take another law as her husband, namely, the Gospel, inasmuch as the law of Moses was not given to the nature of human beings for all eternity, but rather as a dispensation leading them by the hand to a greater and more mystical law—and I think this is what the Lord meant when He said to the Samaritan woman: "And the one you now have is not your husband."[10] Because He knew that human nature would be given to the Gospel. This is why He conversed with her around the sixth hour,[11] when, to be sure, the soul is shining with the rays of knowledge owing to

4. Cf. Gn 2.15–17.
5. Cf. Gn 3.16–19.
6. Cf. Gn 9.8–17.
7. Cf. Gn 17.1–14. See above, Qu. 38.3.
8. Cf. Gn 22.15–18.
9. Cf. Ex 20–21.
10. Jn 4.18.
11. I.e., around noon.

the Word's presence to it, dispelling the shadow of the law—and this is also why the conversation took place at the well of Jacob,[12] that is, where the soul could stand, together with the Word, close to the source of the divine visions of Scripture.[1]

41.4. For now, let these things suffice for this question.

Scholion

[1] Jacob's well[13] is Scripture. The water is the knowledge that Scripture contains. The depth of the well is the meaning[14] of the biblical enigmas, which are all but beyond one's reach.[15] The "bucket"[16] used for drawing out the water is learning about the Divine Word acquired through written letters, which the Lord did not require, since he is the Word Himself,[17] and He does not give this knowledge to the faithful through learning and study, but to those who are worthy He grants a measure of the ever-flowing wisdom of spiritual grace. For like the bucket, that is, ordinary learning, the soul receives but the smallest part of knowledge, letting go of the whole, which no mind can grasp; whereas the knowledge that comes from grace possesses, without study, the whole of wisdom that man can possibly contain, which bubbles forth in a variety of ways with a view towards his needs.[18]

12. Jn 4.5–6.
13. Cf. Jn 4.5–15.
14. I.e., θέσις.
15. See Origen, *Homilies on Genesis* 13.1–2 (SC 7bis:312–20), for an extended allegorical interpretation of the wells of the patriarchs.
16. Jn 4.11.
17. I.e., Αὐτολόγος, on which, see above, Qu. 28.4.
18. Cf. below, Qu. 65.5.

QUESTION 42

ow is it that we are said to commit sin and to know that we have sinned, while the Lord is said to have "become sin" without knowing sin? And how is sinning, and knowing that one has sinned, not a graver offense than sinning and not knowing it? For it says: "He who did not know sin, was made sin for us."[1]

Response

42.2. Because Adam's natural power of free choice was corrupted first, it corrupted nature together with itself, losing the grace of impassibility. And thus the fall of free choice from the good toward evil became the first and blameworthy sin. The second sin, which came about as a result of the first, was the blameless alteration of nature from incorruptibility to corruption. Thus two sins came about in the forefather through his transgression of the divine commandment: the first was blameworthy, but the second was blameless, having been caused by the first. The first was a sin of free choice, which voluntarily abandoned the good, but the second was of nature,[1] which involuntarily and as a consequence of free choice lost its immortality. Our Lord and Savior corrected this mutual corruption and alteration of nature when He assumed the whole of our nature,[2] and by virtue of the assumed nature He too possessed passibility as something adorning the incorruptibility of His free choice.[2] And

---

1. 2 Cor 5.21.
2. I.e., προαίρεσις, a term that became problematic in the later Christological controversy, and to which Maximos returned in *Opusc.* 1: "Having thought about this carefully, I said, in what I wrote to Thalassios in the work concerning difficult passages of Holy Scripture, that Christ had 'free choice,' knowing

for our sakes, through the passibility of nature, He became sin, but He did not commit voluntary sin,[3] thanks to the immutability of His free choice—to the contrary, He corrected the passibility of nature through the incorruptibility of His faculty of free choice, making the end of nature's passibility, by which I mean death,[3] into the beginning of the transformation of our nature into incorruptibility. In this way, just as the alteration of nature from incorruptibility to corruption came to all men through one man, who voluntarily turned his free choice away from the good, so too, through one man, Jesus Christ,[4] who did not turn His faculty of free choice away from the good, the restoration of nature from corruption to incorruptibility came to all men.[5]

42.3. The Lord, then, did not know my sin, that is, the turning away of my free will: He did not assume my sin, neither did He become my sin, but [He became][6] sin because of me; that is, He assumed the corruption of nature which came about through the turning away of my free choice, and He became, for our sake,

---

that the creator of human beings for our sakes also created immutability of free choice, assuming within Himself the dishonorable passions, which for us He made the cause of the free will's dispassion, granting us the incorruptibility of nature. This is because Christ's human nature does not, like us, move according to free choice ... but having received its being by virtue of its union with God the Word, it possesses an unwavering movement, or better, it possesses the natural appetitive movement of its free choice in a condition of absolute stability; or, to speak strictly, it possesses an immovable stability perfectly divinized by virtue of its unalloyed substantification (οὐσίωσις) in God the Word" (paraphrased) (PG 91:29D–32B); cf. Bathrellos, *Byzantine Christ*, 148–53.

3. I.e., γνωμικὴν ἁμαρτίαν.

4. Cf. Rom 5.12, 15–20.

5. 1 Cor 15.53–54. Larchet (SC 554:23, n. 2) notes that there are two senses of "sin" operative in this passage (cf. Qu. 42.5), the "sin of nature," which properly speaking is not "sin" but rather the state of nature resulting from the sin of Adam, marked by passibility, corruption, and death. It is called "sin," Larchet suggests, by metonymy. The descendants of Adam, including Christ in His human nature, inherit this "sin" without in any way being responsible or culpable for it. This distinction explains Maximos's subsequent differentiation between Adam's sin and "my sin" (below, Qu. 42.3), the latter designating sin in its proper sense, i.e., personal and voluntary, the choice to turn away from or reject the will of God. This sin was absent from Christ, the disposition of whose human will and free choice were always in accordance with the will of God.

6. There is a minor textual problem with the verb placed in brackets, i.e., γέγονεν, although it seems to be the better reading; cf. CCSG 22:347.

man passible by nature, abolishing my sin through the sin that came about because of me.[4] And just as in Adam, the individual free choice for evil rescinded the common glory of nature's incorruptibility—since God judged that it was not good for man, who had used his free choice for evil to have an immortal nature—so too, in Christ, the individual free choice for good took away the common disgrace of corruption, with the whole of nature being recreated incorruptible through the resurrection on account of the immutability of the faculty of free will, since God judged that it was good for man again to receive an immortal nature, in that he did not turn away his free will. By "man" I am referring to the incarnate God the Word, on account of the flesh endowed with a rational soul that He united to Himself according to hypostasis. For if the turning away of the faculty of free will in Adam brought about passibility, corruption, and mortality in nature, it follows quite naturally that the immutability of the same <capacity> in Christ brought about, through the resurrection, a return of impassibility, incorruptibility, and immortality.

42.4. The condemnation of Adam's freely chosen sin was thus the alteration of nature toward passibility, corruption, and death. Man did not receive this alteration from God from the beginning, but it was rather man who made it and knew it, creating the freely chosen sin through his disobedience, making his free will into something sinful, the offspring of which is clearly his condemnation to death. The condemnation of my freely chosen sin—I mean, of human nature's passible, corruptible, and mortal elements—was assumed by the Lord, who for my sake became "sin" in terms of passibility, corruption, and mortality, voluntarily by nature assuming my condemnation—though He is without condemnation in His free choice—so that He might condemn the sin of my free choice and nature as well as my condemnation, simultaneously expelling sin, passibility, corruption, and death from nature, bringing about a new mystery concerning me, who had fallen through disobedience: the dispensation of Him, who for my sake and out of His love for mankind, voluntarily appropriated my condemnation through His death, through which He granted that I be called back and restored to immortality.

42.5. In many ways, I think, it has been succinctly demonstrated how the Lord "became sin" without "knowing sin," and how man did not become sin, but rather committed and knew sin, both in his free choice, which he himself initiated, and on the level of his nature, which latter for his sake the Lord accepted, while being completely free of the former.[5] Consistent, then, with the understood aim of my argument, and with the proper distinction between the two senses of the word "sin," we can say that committing and knowing sin is in no way superior to "becoming" sin.[7] For the one brings about separation from God, inasmuch as the faculty of free will voluntarily drives away from itself divine things, while the second quite often hinders evil, not permitting the evil intention of our free choice to proceed to the level of action.

Scholia

[1] The sin of nature, he says, is death, according to which we withdraw from existence even against our will. The sin of free choice, on the other hand, is the choosing of things that are contrary to nature, according to which we willingly fall away from well-being.

[2] He says that even though the Lord, when he became incarnate, was corruptible (insofar as He was man, according to which He is also said to have "become sin"), He nonetheless is naturally incorruptible according to His free choice, inasmuch as He is without sin.

[3] The death of the Lord, he says, became the beginning of the incorruptibility for the whole of nature.

[4] The sin of which we are the cause is the corruption of nature, while our own sin is the constitutive turning away of our free choice. This is why man became mortal, being subjected to

---

7. Origen offers similar examples, such as the words "regret" and "wrath," which mean one thing when said of human beings and another when said of God, for which he cites Aristotle's definition of homonyms (*Categories* 1a1–2), in his *Homilies on Jeremiah* 20.2: "A homonym is where the name alone is common, but its meaning, according to the name of its substance, is other" (SC 238:252–54), cited in Larchet, SC 554:26, n. 3.

the just judgment of natural death, unto the destruction of the death of his free will.

[5] The first sin, he says, is the turning away of free will, which the Lord did not possess, even if He indeed assumed the passibility of human nature, which was the punishment for the turning away of Adam's faculty of free will. This is why He alone was "free among the dead,"[8] for He was without sin, through which death came into being.

8. Ps 87.5; cf. Athanasios, *On Psalm* 88: "Only Christ is 'free among the dead,' for He alone is without sin" (PG 27:380); Epiphanios, *Ancoratus:* "Christ is 'free among the dead,' for Hades had no power over Him" (GCS 25:34); and Ps.-Gregory of Nyssa, *Biblical Testimonies:* "Who is 'free among the dead' if not God? For it was He who became man, and 'humbled his flesh to death, even death on a cross' [cf. Phil 2.8]" (PG 46:216).

QUESTION 43

F WISDOM is said by Scripture to be a "Tree of Life,"[1] and if the work of wisdom is to discern and know "the Tree of Knowledge of Good and Evil,"[2] how then does it differ from the Tree of Life?[3]

Response

43.2. Even though the teachers of the Church, through the grace that is in them, are able to say many things about the question that is now before us, they considered it far better to honor this passage by silence,[4] for seeing that the minds of most people are not able to reach the depth of the written words, they refrained from saying anything deeper. If, however, some of them spoke about this question, it was only after they had first discerned the capacity of their listeners, and having thus said something for the benefit of those they were teaching, they left the greater part of the matter unexamined. This is why I too would have passed over this passage in silence, had I not considered that to do so would bring sorrow to your God-loving soul. Thus, for your sake, I will say what is suitable for all, and meaningful for both beginners and the more advanced.

43.3. There is a great and unutterable difference between the Tree of Life and the one that is not the Tree of Life. This is clear from the simple fact that one is called the Tree of Life, whereas the other is not called the Tree of "Life" but solely the Tree of the "knowledge of good and evil."[5] For while the Tree

---

1. Prv 3.18.
2. Gn 2.9.
3. Maximos discusses the Trees in the Garden above, at Intro. 1.2.17–19.
4. See the note on this phrase above, at Intro. 1.2.19.
5. Gn 2.9.

of Life unquestionably produces life, the tree that is not called the Tree of Life obviously produces death—since that which does not produce life, in that it was not named the Tree of Life, must clearly produce death, for nothing else is so categorically distinguished in its opposition to life.

43.4. As wisdom, moreover, the Tree of Life exhibits the greatest difference from the Tree of Knowledge of Good and Evil, which latter neither is nor is called wisdom. To be sure, the characteristic mark of wisdom is intellect and reason, while the characteristic mark of the state that is opposed to wisdom is irrationality and sensation. Since, then, man was brought into existence composed of intellective soul and sensible body, let us grant that, according to one interpretation, the Tree of Life is the soul's intellect, in which the reality of wisdom resides, while the Tree of the Knowledge of Good and Evil is the body's sensation, in which irrational motion clearly resides, and, though man received the divine commandment not to touch it or have actual experience of it, he failed to keep the commandment.

43.5. According to Scripture, both of these trees, that is, intellect and sensation, have respective powers of discrimination. For example, the intellect has the power to discriminate between intelligible and sensible things, between the temporary and the eternal—or rather, insofar as the intellect is a discriminating power of the soul, it persuades the soul to adhere to the former while passing beyond the latter. Sensation, on the other hand, has the power to discriminate between bodily pleasure and pain—or rather, insofar as sensation is a power of animate and sense-perceptive bodies, it persuades sensation to embrace pleasure while rejecting pain. If man, then, having transgressed the divine commandment, confines himself solely to discriminating between pleasure and pain, then he "eats" from the Tree of the Knowledge of Good and Evil, that is, <he succumbs to> the irrationality of sensation, having the ability only to discriminate with respect to what sustains bodies, which embraces pleasure as something good, and rejects what is painful as evil. But if, on the other hand, man, having kept the divine commandment, adheres exclusively to the intellective discrimination that discriminates the eternal from the temporary, "eats" from the Tree of Life, by which I mean to say <he partakes of> the wisdom that is constituted on the level of the intellect, which embraces the glory of eternal realities as good, and rejects the corruption of temporary things as evil.

43.6. It follows, then, that there is a great difference between the two trees, and between their natural powers of discrimination, along with the respective significance of each, so that the words "good" and "evil" are uttered equivocally and without distinction, which can create great spiritual deception among the learned who do not approach the text with wisdom and circumspection. But you, being truly wise through grace, should know that what is simply said to be evil is not absolutely evil, but is evil in relation to something else,[1] just as what is simply said to be good is not absolutely good, but is good in relation to something else,[6] and if you know this you will be kept safe from any harm arising from the equivocation.

Scholion

[1] The good of the intellect is the dispassionate disposition oriented to the spirit, while its evil is the impassioned relation to sensation. The good of sensation is the impassioned motion of pleasure oriented to the body, while its evil is the disposition that comes about through the deprivation of this pleasure.

---

6. "In relation to something else" renders the Greek phrase πρός τι, which is the Aristotelian "relative" or "reciprocal relation" and one of the ten predicates defined in *Categories* 6a36–8b26. Aristotelian "relatives" are things that stand in relation to each other in such a way that the relation is constitutive of their identity. Such correlatives are "reciprocal" and "simultaneous" since the loss of either one will lead to the destruction of the other; consequently, according to Aristotle, "there are relatives for which being is the same as being somehow related to something."

QUESTION 44

O WHOM did God say: "Behold, Adam has become like one of us"?[1] If, on the one hand, these words are addressed to the Son, how can Adam be compared to God, not being of His nature? If, on the other hand, these words are addressed to the angels, how can God compare an angel with Himself, as if He were speaking to one who was equal to Him in essence, saying: "like one of us"?[2]

Response

44.2. I have already said, in the chapter concerning the Tower of Babel,[3] that Scripture fashions God speaking in terms relative to the underlying disposition of the souls that are under His providence, hinting at the divine counsel through modes that are inherently united to our nature. In this instance, therefore, Scripture is not simply portraying God as saying in any absolute sense: "Behold, Adam has become like one of us," but instead it is quite clear that this was spoken *after* the transgression, adding the reason for the statement, which you neglected to include in the citation, which clarifies the entire meaning of this passage. For having said: "Behold, Adam has become like one of us," the text adds: "knowing good and evil—and now, lest he put forth his hand and partake of the Tree of Life and live forever," and so on.[4] Inasmuch as the devil had, together

---

1. Gn 3.22.
2. The Greek is much stronger: "Like one *from (ἐκ) among us*," which suggests organic or ontological derivation, like the procession of the Spirit "from (ἐκ) the Father" in the Nicene Creed.
3. See above, Qu. 28.
4. Gn 3.22.

with his counsel, taught Adam polytheism, saying: "On the day you shall eat of the tree, your eyes will be opened, and you will be as gods, knowing good and evil,"[5] it is with some dissimulation,[1] and, we could say, with a measure of irony and reproach in order to censure man who had obeyed the devil, that God uses the plural in the phrase, "he has become like one of us," corresponding to the notion of divinity that the serpent slipped in and used to deceive Adam.

44.3. And let no one think that ironic forms of speech are foreign to the custom of Scripture.[6] Whoever thinks this way should listen to Scripture saying, in[7] the person of God: "If you come to me crookedly, I too will come to you crookedly,"[8] and he should know that the ironic and the crooked in no way differ from each other. Again, let him find the passage describing the deception of Ahab, to whom a lie was proffered as the truth,[2] through which God brought upon him the just punishment for his sins.[9] In other words, if Scripture did not introduce God as saying, "as one of us" with the aim of deceiving Adam, why did it add: "knowing good and evil"? For this would suggest that God's knowledge is composite and built up from contrary principles, which is impossible even to think of in the case of God, to say nothing of daring even to utter such a thing, for He alone[3] is simple in essence, power, and knowledge, and possesses only the knowledge of good—or rather He is essence itself, and power, and knowledge. But none of the rational beings[4] created by God and sequent to God possesses, as one and the same thing in the simple motion of its mind, any kind of knowledge constituted by a composition of contrary principles. For the knowledge of one of two principles brings about ignorance of the knowledge of the other, since the knowledge

---

5. Gn 3.5.
6. Epiphanios, *Panarion* 64.65.16 (GCS 31:506, lines 21–25), endorses the same view, arguing that God's words to Adam were not uttered ἀποφαντικῶς but ἐλεγκτικῶς, which was opposed by Didymos, *On Genesis* 3.22 (SC 233:254–56), who rejected the idea that irony or sarcasm could be attributed to the deity, although Maximos's view of the matter is more nuanced than this.
7. Literally, "from" (ἐκ).
8. Lv 26.23–24.
9. 3 Kgs 22.15–23.

of contraries is incapable of being mixed together or coexisting,[5] because the knowledge of the one constitutes the ignorance of the other of the contraries, in the same way that the eye cannot apprehend together both above and below, or simultaneously what is from both the one and the other, without independently shifting its gaze to each, in a manner completely unrelated to the one and utterly separated from the other.[10]

44.4. Thus Scripture represents God as making Adam's misfortune His own, or censuring Adam for the serpent's counsel, with the aim of leading him to consciousness of the polytheistic nonsense through which he was deceived. If these things are as I have said, then all is well and our inquiries are at an end. If you, however, on your own, should discover something greater, convey to me as well the gift that is given to you from God concerning beings.

44.5. The phrase: "And now, lest he put forth his hand[6] and take from the Tree of Life and live forever,"[11] providentially produces, I think, the separation of things that cannot be mixed together, so that evil might not be immortal, being maintained in existence by participation in the good. For the creator of man wishes man's knowledge to be unmixed with respect to the relation of contraries.

Scholia

[1] God speaks to Adam using the notion of divinity that Adam had been taught by the devil.

[2] Whoever loves falsehood is handed over to it for his destruction, so that he might know involuntarily through suffering what he had voluntarily sought to cultivate, and might learn by experience that he mistakenly preferred death instead of life.

---

10. Cf. Gregory of Nyssa, *On Virginity* 20: "There are two marriages, the one effected in the flesh, the other in the Spirit, and preoccupation in the one necessarily causes the alienation of the other, just as the eye is not able to look at two objects at once, but must concentrate its attention on one thing at a time" (GNO 8/1:325, lines 16–18); and below, Qu. 58, on the mutual exclusivity of intellective and sensory pleasure.

11. Gn 3.22.

[3] God possesses only knowledge of the good, because He is in essence the nature and the knowledge of the good. He is ignorant of evil, because He possesses no capacity for evil, for whatever things one has the capacity for by nature, of the same things he possesses essential knowledge.

[4] Evil is observed in rational beings according to passion that comes about contrary to nature, not by natural potential.

[5] The existence, he says, of contraries in those who receive them is of a nature to be observed separately according to their parts.

[6] Whoever has forced his conscience to take hold of what is utterly evil as if it were something good achieved by nature, has, like a hand, stretched forth the practical part of his soul and taken, in a false manner, from the Tree of Life, for he thinks that what is utterly evil is something immortal by nature. This is the reason why God, naturally placing within man's conscience the accusatory censure of evil, separated him from life, for he had become evil through the faculty of his free will, so that, in doing what was evil, he would not be able to persuade his own conscience that what is utterly evil is good by nature.

QUESTION 45

HAT IS THE MEANING OF the phrase in Leviticus: "The breast that is offered and the shoulder that is removed,"[1] which is consecrated by the priests as an honor to God?[2]

Response

45.2. I think the "breast" indicates contemplation that is superior and lofty,[1] and the "shoulder" indicates ascetic practice,[3] that is, the stable habit and activity of the mind. Or they signify knowledge and virtue, since knowledge leads the intellect immediately to God, while virtuous practice separates it from the generation of beings, which are the very activities that Scripture has ordained for priests, who from all things have God alone as their inheritance, and who have acquired absolutely nothing earthly.

45.3. Or, again, those who through knowledge and virtue have been thoroughly imbued with the Spirit, and who through the word of their teaching make the hearts[2] of others receptive of piety and knowledge, and who, by removing their practical habitual state and power from its preoccupation with corruptible nature, transfer it to the actualization of good things that are beyond nature, can reasonably be understood as the ones who bring forward "the breast that is offered" as a sacrifice to God, that is, who bring forward the heart, and the

---

1. I.e., the "wave offering" of the breast, and the "heave offering" of the right thigh.
2. Lv 7.24.
3. Cf. above, Qu. 3.3.

"shoulder," which is their ascetic practice, which is what Scripture has ordered them to consecrate to God.[4]

Scholia

[1] The breast is a symbol of contemplation; the shoulder of ascetic practice, for contemplation is of a nature to be the habitual state of the mind, and its activity is practice, and true priesthood is characterized by both of these things.

[2] The one who through his pious word offers to God the hearts of others (which correspond to the chest) and their power for ascetic practice (which corresponds to the shoulder), consecrating them for the doing of the commandments, has become a priest, receiving from others the sacrifice of their chest and shoulder that they have offered to God.

---

4. Cf. Origen, *Homilies on Leviticus* 5.12 (SC 286:260–62).

QUESTION 46

ow does the "mirror" differ with respect to the "enigma"?[1]

Response

46.2. The mirror, to speak in terms of a definition, is a state of consciousness possessing the total form of all the good things that have been wrought in practice, and it is through this form that a man with a pure mind is able to see God.[2] Or it is the stable habit of mind committed to ascetic practice, encompassing all the virtues uniformly combined together like a single divine face.[3] The enigma, on the other hand, is knowledge that—through the highest contemplative grasp of the divine principles attainable by human nature—has received the impression of realities beyond intellection. More simply,[1] a mirror is a stable habit of mind indicative of the archetypal form of the virtue that will be revealed in the future to the worthy; for to those who possess it the mirror reveals the future consummation of practical philosophy, whereas the enigma is an indication of the archetype of things understood on the level of knowledge.

46.3. Every righteous action in this life, when compared with the future righteousness, is like a mirror containing the image

---

1. 1 Cor 13.12. The *Novum Testamentum Graece* reads: "βλέπομεν γὰρ ἄρτι δι' ἐσόπτρου ἐν αἰνίγματι" (1 Cor 13.12), and all English translations take the dative construction as an adverb, e.g., darkly, dimly, obscurely, indistinctly, indirectly, in an allegory, blurred, in darkness, etc. With the exception of Chrysostom, however, the text of 1 Corinthians cited by virtually all patristic exegetes read: δι' ἐσόπτρου καὶ ἐν αἰνίγματι, or δι' ἐσόπτρου καὶ δι' αἰνίγματος, which did not allow for a simple adverbial sense of ἐν αἰνίγματι.
2. Cf. Mt 5.8.
3. Cf. 1 Cor 13.2.

of archetypal realities—not the realities themselves as they subsist according to their own form.[4] And in this life all knowledge of lofty things, when compared with the future knowledge, is an enigma, possessing the reflection of the truth—but not the self-subsisting truth itself that will be revealed in the future. Inasmuch as divine things are apprehended through virtue and knowledge, the mirror displays the prototypes of things wrought through virtue, while the enigma reveals the archetypes grasped by knowledge. And this is the difference between the mirror and the enigma, inasmuch as the mirror announces the future consummation of practice, while the enigma reveals the mystery of contemplation.

Scholion

[1] The mirror is revelatory of the good things that are most suitable to practical philosophy, while the enigma is indicative of future mysteries relative to knowledge.

---

4. Cf. *Amb.* 21.15 (DOML 1:442–45); *Amb.* 37.8 (DOML 2:84–85).

QUESTION 47

HAT IS THE "voice of one who cries out in the wilderness,"[1] and what are the other things mentioned in this passage? What is the "wilderness"? What is meant here by the "way of the Lord," and what are its "preparations"? What are the "paths," and what does it mean to "make them straight"? What are the "valleys," and what does it mean that "every valley will be filled"? What, also, are the "mountains" and the "hills," and what is their "humiliation"? What are the "crooked things" that will be "made straight"? What are the "rough roads" that will be made "smooth"? And what is the meaning of what is said after all of this, namely, that: "all flesh will see the salvation of God"?[2]

Response

47.2. The "voice of the one who" from the beginning "cries out in the wilderness"—by which I mean in human nature or in this world—is quite clearly every saint of God the Word, who, like Abel, rightly and sincerely offers the first movements of his soul's contemplation, fattened by the virtues.[3] [1] Or like Enosh, who by means of the steadfast hope of faith, took hold of the good things to come, for which he had hoped, and vigorously called out to God.[4] [2] Or like Enoch, who, having pleased God by all his virtues, and having completely removed his intellect from its relation to and knowledge of beings, was completely and unconditionally translated to the Cause that is beyond

---

1. Lk 3.4; cf. Is 40.3–5.
2. Lk 3.4–6.
3. Cf. Gn 4.4; Ezek 39.18.
4. Cf. Gn 4.26.

intellection.⁵ **[3]** Or like Noah, who, having contemplated by faith the future forms of the divine judgment, built for himself, after the manner of an ark, an ascetic way of life, covering him "from the coming wrath"⁶ **[4]** and secured on all sides by the fear of God.⁷ Or like Abraham, who, having seen with the pure eye of faith the beauty of the good things to come,⁸ readily obeyed the command to depart from his country, and his kindred, and his father's house,⁹ **[5]** and, leaving behind relation and attachment to flesh, sensation, and sensory things, and being above nature in the time of testing and struggles, he preferred the Cause of nature over nature, just as he, the great Abraham, preferred God over Isaac.¹⁰ Or like Isaac, who, through extreme dispassion and the beautiful greediness of his soul for contemplation, possessed a habit of virtue and knowledge that was immovable**[6]** from the truth, even when he was under attack by wicked spirits. Or like Jacob, who purified his intellect of the hairiness of material things and the tangled confusion that surrounds them, making it smooth; and who, by covering himself with the skins of goats—by which I mean the rough treatment of the flesh through a godly life—acquired power from God to rule over the mind of the flesh.¹¹ Fearing, however, the insurrection of the passions, and yearning for loftier instruction according to experience, he relocated to Harran,¹² by which I mean he advanced to natural contemplation, from which he received, through many practical labors, the whole spiritual understanding of the visible world, a knowledge gathered up from various thoughts and concepts, after which he returned to his father's land and home, that is, the knowledge of intelligible realities, bringing with him, as if they were women and servants, the fixed habits of mind and activities that were born to him equally from ascetic practice and contemplation, along with the

5. Cf. Gn 5.19–24.
6. Lk 3.7.
7. Cf. Mt 3.7; Lk 3.7.
8. Cf. Heb 11.1.
9. Gn 12.1.
10. Cf. Gn 22.1–8.
11. Cf. Rom 8.6.
12. Cf. Gn 27.11–16, 23–28.

sons who were born to him from these, whoever they might happen to be.[13] [7] And to put it simply—so that my response is not unduly prolonged by going through every life in detail—every saint, through his own way of life, possessing a word that cries out his intentions to other men, is clearly the voice and forerunner of the Word in proportion to the righteousness and faith that is in him.[14] More than all the others, however, the voice and forerunner of the Word is the great John the Baptist, the messenger and herald of God's real presence—devoid of figures and symbols—which he revealed to those who were ignorant of it, pointing visibly to "the one who takes away the sin of the world,"[15] and joining his ministry of baptism to the dispensation of the fulfillment of the mystery.

47.3. Because the wealth of grace enables those who desire virtue and knowledge to understand with profit every syllable of the divine Scripture, even the most trifling, let us henceforth contemplate, as much as we are able, the questions before us from another point of view.

47.4. To begin, then, the "wilderness," as I said a moment ago, is human nature, as well as this world, and each particular soul, which because of the ancient transgression is barren of good things. The "voice of the Word that cries out" is each person's conscious awareness of his offenses, crying out, as it were, from the hidden place of the heart: "Prepare the way of the Lord."[16] To be sure, a clear and obvious "preparation" of the divine way is the transformation and correction of one's manner of life and thought to what is better, along with the purification of former defilements. The good and glorious "way" is the life of virtue, on which, as if on a way, the Word unfolds the course of salvation in each person through faith, indwelling and walking about by means of the various ordinances and doctrines consistent with virtue and knowledge. The "paths" of the Word are the different modes of the virtues and the differ-

---

13. Cf. Gn 31.17–21.
14. Cf. *Amb.* 21.14 (DOML 1:440–41), where Maximos discusses this notion at length.
15. Jn 1.29.
16. Lk 3.4.

ent modes of living according to God, that is, behaviors consistent with God. These paths are made straight by those who give no thought to pursuing the ascetic life or the study of the divine words for the sake of glory or as a cloak for personal advantage,[17] or from love of flattery and popularity, or to engage in self-display—but all that they do and say and think is for the sake of God. For the divine Word is not of a nature to enjoy frequenting roads that are not straight, even if among some men He should find the way prepared. I mean something like this. If someone fasts and avoids a mode of life that excites the passions, and does all the other things that are able to contribute to his deliverance from evil, he has "prepared" what is called "the way." But if someone else undertakes these practices out of self-esteem, love of flattery, the desire to please men, or for another reason other than to please God, he did not "make straight the paths" of God, and whereas he endured the labor of preparing the way, he did not have God walking on his paths. This is to say that the "way" of the Lord is virtue, and the "straight path" is the upright and guileless manner of virtue.

47.5. "Every valley will be filled," that is, of those who well "prepared the way of the Lord," and who "made straight his paths." In other words, not every valley in general, and not of everyone, and certainly not of those who did not prepare the way of the Lord and who did not make straight His paths. A "valley" is the flesh of each man, which has been completely eroded by the torrential force of the passions, so that its spiritual continuity and conjunction with the soul—to which it was bound by the law of God—have been severed. One may also, however, understand the soul as a valley, which has been hollowed out by the long winter of ignorance, and which through evil has lost the beauty of its fine spiritual evenness.[8] Every valley, then—that is, the flesh and the soul—of those who prepared the way of the Lord and made straight His ways, will be filled by the removal of the passions, which create, like a valley, an evenness of flesh and spirit, and with the restoration of the virtues they once again enjoy their natural appearance, smoothed out by the Spirit.

17. Cf. 1 Thes 2.5.

47.6. "And every mountain and hill will be humbled." It stands to reason that mountains and hills are of a nature to be bound in some way to valleys. A "mountain" is "every height that exalts itself against the knowledge of God,"[18] while a "hill" is every vice that rises up and revolts against virtue. If, then, "mountains" are the spirits that bring about ignorance, and "hills" are those spirits that produce evil, it clearly follows that every "valley"—that is, the flesh and soul of those who, as I said, prepared the way of the Lord and made straight His paths by the presence of God the Word walking within them through the commandments—will, when filled with knowledge as well as virtue, "humble" all the spirits of false knowledge and evil,[19] because the Word will be treading on them and placing them under submission, and He will cast down the wicked power that had raised itself against human nature, razing to the ground, as it were, the height of the mountains and the hills, thereby filling up the valleys.[9]

47.7. The "humiliation," then, of the intelligible and wicked mountains and hills is the restoration of the natural powers of the flesh and the soul to themselves. Thanks to this restoration, the God-loving intellect, being guided evenly by the wealth of virtue and knowledge, passes through this age and is borne with headlong speed toward the ageless and incorruptible world of intelligible and holy powers. In so doing, it is neither deceived by the voluntary passions of the flesh arising from various forms of crooked pleasure, nor hardened by the involuntary trials of pain,[20] and abandoning, out of care for the flesh, the path of the commandments as being difficult to tread owing to the sufferings of the flesh.

47.8. "Crooked things" will be "made straight"[10] when the intellect, having freed the members of the body (that is, the faculties of sense perception) from the passions, and having cut off the rest of its activities linked to pleasure, will teach them to move according to their simple principle of nature, guiding them in a straight line to the Cause by which they came into be-

---

18. 2 Cor 10.5.
19. Or "vice" (κακία).
20. See above, Qu. 26.3–4; and below, Qu. 58.2, 10–12.

ing. The "rough ways," that is, the attacks of involuntary trials,[11] will become "smooth" when the intellect rejoices and accepts infirmities, tribulations, and distress,[21] removing, by means of involuntary sufferings, all the power of the voluntary passions. For whoever desires true life, and who recognizes that every pain, whether voluntary or involuntary, is the death of pleasure, which is the mother of death,[12] will accept with gladness all the "rough" attacks of involuntary passions. And he finds joy in his patient endurance, and makes his troubles into "ways that are broad and smooth," and, piously making his course along them, they convey him undeviatingly toward the "reward of his calling from on high."[22] Anyone, then, who through chaste self-control has unraveled the twisted and tangled threads of pleasure, which in many different ways have been interwoven equally with all the faculties of sense perception, has "made the crooked ways straight." And anyone who with patience has trampled down the impassable and "rough" attacks of sufferings, has "made the rough ways smooth." Thus, as the prize of virtue[13] and of labors undertaken for virtue—since he contended nobly and "according to the rules of the contest,"[23] and defeated pleasure by his longing for virtue, and trampled down pain by his ardent love of knowledge, and through both nobly passed through the divine contests—he will see the salvation of God. For it says that: "All flesh will see the salvation of God,"[24] in accordance with the promise: "I will pour out my Spirit upon all flesh."[25] That is, all flesh that is *faithful* will see the salvation of God, not all flesh in general—and certainly not the flesh of the impious, if the word is true which said: "Let the impious be taken away, so that he may not see the glory of the Lord"[26]— but specifically all flesh that is faithful. To be sure, the word of Scripture customarily uses a part to refer to the whole, and in this case the "flesh" refers to the whole human being, as if

---

21. 2 Cor 6.4, 12.10.
22. Phil 3.14.
23. 2 Tm 2.5.
24. Cf. Lk 3.6; Is 40.5.
25. Acts 2.17; Jl 3.1.
26. Is 26.10.

Scripture were proclaiming: "Every human being will see the salvation of God." That is, every human being who has heard the "voice crying out in the wilderness," and who has "prepared the way of the Lord" according to the principle of the interpretation given above. Every human being, in other words, who has "made straight His paths," and who, by throwing down the intelligible and wicked "mountains and hills," has "filled the valley" of his soul, which through his own "hollowness," brought about by his transgression of the divine commandment,[14] consequently gave "height"[27] and elevation to those wicked "mountains and hills," in a "filling up" that was also the "humiliation" of the wicked powers. This is every human being who, through his temperance, "made straight" the "crooked" and voluntary passions, by which I mean the movements of pleasure, and who through his patience "made even" and transformed into ways that are "smooth" the "rough" misfortunes of involuntary trials, by which I mean his pain and sufferings. Such a person, I say, will see the salvation of God, having become pure in heart, by means of which, through the virtues and through pious contemplations, he sees God at the end of his struggles, according to the words: "Blessed are the pure in heart, for they shall see God,"[28] receiving for his labors undertaken for virtue the grace of dispassion, which more greatly than anything else manifests God among those who possess it.

47.9. Consistent with this, it is possible for those who seek the loftier contemplations perhaps to view this passage differently, understanding the soul—as if "in a wilderness" barren of the passions—as the "voice" of divine wisdom and knowledge invisibly crying out through the virtues.[15] For in proportion to each, the one and the same Word becomes "all things in all,"[29] entering into each, and, like a precursory voice, gives in advance the grace that prepares each one for His coming.[30] In some, this grace is repentance as a precursor to the coming righteousness; in others, it is virtue as preparation for the

---

27. 2 Cor 10.5.
28. Mt 5.8.
29. 1 Cor 9.22.
30. Cf. *Amb.* 21.14–16 (DOML 1:440–47).

hoped-for knowledge; and in still others, it is knowledge as the distinctive mark of the divinizing condition that is to come.[31] Simply put, time will fail[32] the contemplative intellect in its cognitive efforts to grasp the divine ascents of the Word,[33] and to adapt His transcendent and loving manifestations[34] to each, according to which He becomes "all things in all,"[35] so that He might "save all through the riches of His goodness."[36]

Scholia

[1] The one who offers knowledge "fattened" by the virtues,[37] that is, knowledge informed by practice, has become Abel, having God upon him and beholding his gifts.[38]

[2] The one who has recognized and truly hoped for[39] the things of the future never ceases to call out, through his practice, for that which he hopes, and becomes another Enosh, calling upon God.[40]

31. Cf. above, Qu. 15.5.
32. Cf. Heb. 11.32.
33. Cf. Ps 83.5.
34. "Manifestations" renders the Greek word *epinoias* (ἐπινοίας) which Maximos uses in this same sense in *Amb.* 31.9; *Amb.* 32.4; *Amb.* 62.2 (DOML 2:50; 56; DOML 2:268); and below, Qu. 63.7. Normally translated as "notion" or "concept" (in the sense of a rational or mental construct), *epinoia* here means something like "idea" or "aspect" in the sense of "principle" (*LSJ*, s.v., lists "purpose" as well as "design"). The relation of these usages to Origen's use of the term is not immediately clear, since Origen distinguished between *epinoiai* belonging to the Logos in Himself (and in His relation to God), and those He possessed in His relation to creation. God the Father had no such *epinoiai* because of His absolute simplicity. The Logos, on the other hand, was multiform from a soteriological point of view, as well as in respect of His ontological constitution. When this latter concept was radicalized by the Neo-Arians, for whom multiplicity signaled the inferior ontological status of the Logos, the Cappadocians were forced to reduce the term to human notions about Christ, in order to avoid positing multiplicity in the divine essence; cf. Aloys Grillmeier, *Christ in Christian Tradition*, vol. 1, trans. John Bowden (Westminster: John Knox, 1975), 141–43.
35. 1 Cor 9.22.
36. Rom 2.4.
37. Cf. Ezek 39.18.
38. Gn 4.4.
39. Cf. Gn 4.26.
40. Cf. ibid.

[3] The one who has been "well-pleasing to God" through his practice, has, through contemplation, "translated" his intellect to the realm of intelligible realities, in order that he not behold, through any kind of mental image, the death that the passions introduce through the senses, for he is absolutely "not found" by any of those things that seek to entrap him.[41]

[4] The one, he says, who on account of "the wrath to come"[42] pursues a life of hardships has become Noah, for by slightly constraining the flesh he has escaped the coming condemnation of the impious.

[5] Here he calls the flesh "earth," the senses "kindred," and the sensible world the "father's house," from which the patriarch departed, setting aside his soul's relation to them.

[6] Of Isaac alone it is written that he did not move from the land of promise, whereas his father Abraham came out from Mesopotamia and went into Egypt, and his son Jacob was driven into Mesopotamia and afterwards dwelt in Egypt, where he also died.[43]

[7] The "women" signify the states of virtue and knowledge; the "servants" signify the activities of these states, from which are generated, like sons, the principles found in nature and time.

[8] In the same way that the flesh, worn away by the force of the passions, becomes a "valley," so too, he says, the soul also becomes a "valley" hollowed out by the currents of evil thoughts.

[9] The casting aside of passions contrary to nature, and the taking up of virtues according to nature, fill up the soul that had been hollowed out like a valley, and humble the power of wicked spirits that had been raised up like a mountain range.

[10] The movements of the senses contrary to nature he called "crooked," and they can be straightened out when the intellect teaches them to move according to nature and in the direction of their proper Cause, by which I mean God.

[11] He called the occurrences of involuntary trials "rough ways," which can be transformed into "ways that are smooth" through patient endurance and gratitude.

---

41. Gn 5.24 (all quotations in this sentence).
42. Cf. Lk 3.7.
43. Cf. Gn 26.2–6; 47.28; 50.1–3.

[12] The mother of death is pleasure, and the death of pleasure is pain, whether it is freely chosen or not.

[13] The person who loves virtue voluntarily extinguishes the furnace of pleasures; and he who conditions his intellect by the knowledge of the truth is not overcome by involuntary sufferings, because his ever-moving desire bears him to God.

[14] The soul, being hollowed out because of transgression, gives the demons "height" as if it were a mountain, that is, domination over its own self.

[15] Virtue that is actualized in practice becomes the "voice" of knowledge "crying out," as it were, "in the wilderness," which is the condition of the soul when barren of the virtues. This is because virtue is the precursor of true wisdom, announcing the truth that will come after it according to dispensation, even though it exists prior to it and as its cause.

QUESTION 48

HE[1] SECOND book of Chronicles says that Uzziah "did that which was right in the sight of the Lord, and he sought the Lord in the days of Zechariah, who understood the fear of the Lord, and the Lord made him prosper.... And Uzziah built towers in Jerusalem, both at the gate at the corner, and at the corner of the valley, and at the corners,[2] and he fortified them. And he built towers in the wilderness and hewed many cisterns out of the rock, for he had many flocks in Shephela and in the low country, and vinedressers in the hill country and on Mount Carmel, for he was a husbandman."[3] What are the "towers," and what is the "gate of the corner"? What is the "valley," and what is its "corner"? And what, again, are the "corners" and the "towers in the wilderness"? What are "Shephela" and the "low country," and who are the "vinedressers"? And what are the "hill country" and "Mount Carmel," and the meaning of the fact that he was a "husbandman"?

---

1. Questions 48–53 form a closely integrated unit devoted to 2 Chronicles. That this Question marks the beginning of a unit is signaled by the fact that Maximos begins with a prayer (below, Qu. 48.2), which is without parallel in this work and largely without precedent in his entire corpus. The unit ends with a closing doxology at Qu. 53.8. Note, too, that Maximos adopts a different exegetical style, citing the biblical passage line by line and commenting on each word and verse.

2. Cf. the Masoretic version: "Uzziah built towers at the Corner Gate and at the Valley Gate, and at the Angle, and fortified them" (2 Chr 26.9).

3. Cf. 2 Chr 26.4–5; 9–10. This is a heavily excerpted rendering of the cited biblical passages, and is exceptional among all the quotations cited in the *Responses to Thalassios* in omitting multiple verses and in some instances presenting a different version of the text.

Response

48.2. Come, O all-hymned Word of God, and give us, in the degree commensurate to us, the revelation of your own words! Remove the thickness of the veils that cover them, and show us, O Christ, the beauty of their inner meanings! Take us by our "right hand," that is, the intellective power within us, and, "guiding us in the way of your commandments,"[4] "lead us to the place of your wondrous tabernacle,[1] unto the very house of God with a voice of rejoicing and confession,"[5] so that, through confession manifested in practice, and through joy realized in contemplation, we too may be counted worthy to come to the ineffable place of your feasting, and join our voices of praise to those who spiritually keep festival, singing, with the silent voices of the intellect, the praises of the knowledge of the unutterable mysteries. And forgive me, O Christ, and have mercy on me, for at the command of your worthy servants, I have recklessly dared to attempt things beyond my power, and enlighten my unenlightened mind for the contemplation of the questions now before me, so that you may be glorified even more, for giving light to eyes that were blind, and articulate speech to a tongue that was mute.[6]

---

4. Ps 118.35.
5. Ps 41.4.
6. Mk 7.32; Is 35.5–6; cf. *Amb. to Thomas* Prologue 4 (DOML 1:5). Apart from the prayer offered by the anonymous elder to God the Father in *Ascet.* 37–39 (CCSG 40:766–851), this is the only place in his writings where Maximos addresses a prayer directly to the Word, which bears comparison with the various prayers and invocations at the beginnings and conclusions of Origen's works; see, for example, *Against Celsus* 8.1 (SC 150:180); *Homilies on Genesis* 15.7 (SC 7:247); and *Commentary on John* 20.1.1 (SC 290:150). For both Origen and Maximos, the divine sense of Scripture is available only through prayer and the gift of grace. Origen's subordination of the Word, however, led him to reject prayer to Christ (*On Prayer* 15.1; GCS 2:333–34), which he calls a "sin of ignorance" (ibid., 16.1; 336), a rule that he himself later came to break, e.g., *Against Celsus* 8.26 (SC 150:232), and *Homilies on Exodus* 13.3 (SC:321:385); but even here, Christ is simply the mediator of human prayer, and not, as in the prayer of Maximos, the one who uncovers and reveals the inner meaning of Scripture. For a thorough discussion of prayer and biblical exegesis in Origen, see Peter Martens, *Origen and Scripture: The Contours of the Exegetical Life* (Oxford: Oxford University Press, 2012), 186–91.

48.3. I think that, just as Solomon, up to a certain point, was a figure of Christ, so too Uzziah, up to a certain point, is also a figure of Christ. For the name of Uzziah, translated into Greek, means the "might of God,"[7] and the natural might and enhypostatic power of God the Father is our Lord Jesus Christ, "the stone who became the head of the corner,"[8] by which I mean the Church. For in the same way that a corner constitutes through itself the mutual conjunction of two walls, so too the Church of God is the union of two peoples, the one coming from the Gentiles and the other from the Jews, whose common bond[9] is Christ. [2] And it is Christ who builds the towers "in Jerusalem"—by which I mean He builds them "in the vision of peace"—and these "towers" are the divine and inviolable primary principles of the doctrines concerning divinity, that is, the fortresses, built "at the gate of the corner,"[3] which are the principles of the doctrines concerning the Incarnation. For the Gate and the Door of the Church is the same one who said: "I am the Door."[10] This gate is surmounted by towers, that is, the fortresses of the divine doctrines of the Incarnation, through which those who wish to believe rightly must make their entrance, finding protection in the "corner," by which I mean the Church. For the one who is fully armed with the towers of the divine doctrines, as fortresses of the truth, does not fear insolent arguments or demons who might threaten them.

48.4. "And at the corner of the valley."[4] The "valley" is the flesh, and its "corner" is its union with the soul according to their conjunction in the spirit. At this conjunction, the "towers," that is, the fortresses of the commandments, are built along with the doctrines that are upon them with discernment in order to safeguard, as if in a corner, the indissoluble union of the flesh to the soul.

48.5. "And at the corners he built towers." Perhaps Scripture used the word "corners"[5] to describe the way separated creatures are variously united through Christ. For Christ unified

---

7. 1 Cor 1.24.
8. Ps 117.22; Acts 4.11; cf. 1 Pt 2.7.
9. Cf. Eph 4.3; Col 2.19.
10. Jn 10.9.

the human being,[11] mystically removing, by means of the Spirit, the difference of male and female,[12] freeing the principle of nature in both from the properties characteristic of the passions.[13] He also united the earth, driving away the variation between the sense-perceptible paradise and the rest of the world. He united earth and heaven, demonstrating that the nature of sensible things is one and inclines toward itself. He also united sensibles and intelligibles, and demonstrated that the nature of the things that have come into being is one, being conjoined according to a certain mystical principle. According to a principle and mode beyond nature, He united created nature to the uncreated. And at each unity,[6] that is, at each corner, He built and fortified the supportive and connective towers of the divine doctrines.[14]

48.6. "And he built towers in the wilderness."[7] The "wilderness" is the nature of visible realities and signifies this world, in which the Word naturally builds towers, granting pious notions about beings to those who ask, that is, correct spiritual principles of the doctrines concerning natural contemplation.

11. I.e., τὸν ἄνθρωπον.
12. Cf. Gal 3.28.
13. The terms used here, "male" (ἄρρεν) and "female" (θῆλυ)—and not "man" (ἀνήρ) and "woman" (γυνή)—do not refer to biological or physiological realities but are symbolic expressions of the passionate parts of the soul, namely, the sinful misuse of "anger" and "desire," as is clear from Maximos's remarks in *Or. Dom.*, where Paul's statement that "there is neither male nor female in Christ" (Gal 3:28) is understood to mean that "in the image of God there is neither anger nor desire" (CCSG 23:47, 51); cf. *Amb.* 41.2–3, 7, 9 (DOML 2:105–107; 111; 115); Clement of Alexandria, *Stromateis* 3.13.93: "They [i.e., heretics] are not aware that 'male' and 'female' refer to 'wrath' and 'desire' ... of which one may repent becoming 'neither male nor female'" (Gal 3.28) (GCS 2:238–39); and Philo, *On Husbandry* 73, alluding to the Platonic "chariot" (*Phaedrus* 246): "Anger and desire are horses, the one male, the other female" (LCL 3:145). For Maximos, the passions (including anger and desire) are not to be uprooted but rather transformed; cf. above, Qu. 1; and Thunberg, *Microcosm and Mediator*, 379: "The mediation [i.e., of 'male' and 'female'] is not effected by the elimination of anything that is human and which therefore pertains to man and woman, nor by the elimination of the passible faculties themselves."
14. On these five unities mediated in Christ, see *Amb.* 41.2 (DOML 2:102–105); and Thunberg, *Microcosm and Mediator*, 331–32.

48.7. "And he hewed many cisterns out of the rock, for he had many flocks in Shephela and in the low country, and vinedressers in the hill country and on Mount Carmel, for he was a husbandman." The Lord "hews wells out of rock"[8] in the wilderness, by which I mean in the world and in the nature of human beings, where He removes the earth from the hearts of the worthy, purges its material weight and way of thinking, and thus makes them deep and wide so that they might receive the divine rains of wisdom and knowledge, and He waters the "flocks" of Christ, by which I mean those in need of moral teaching on account of the immaturity of their souls.

48.8. "The flocks in Shephela."[9] Shephela means "narrow basin," and denotes those who through trials are purified and whitened from their defilements of soul and body, and who need to drink, as if it were water, the principle of perseverance and patient endurance.

48.9. "And those in the low country."[10] Those, in other words, who prosper by means of the breadth[15] of their right actions, which come to them like a flow of water; or those who make haste on the road of virtues, and who are broadened dispassionately by keeping the law of the commandments, who likewise need to drink of the principles of humility, sharing, and compassion for those who are weaker, along with the principle of gratitude for the things they have been given.

48.10. "And vinedressers in the mountains and on Mount Carmel." "Vinedressers in the mountains"[11] are those who, on the height of contemplation, work diligently on the divine principle that stands outside of knowledge and "makes glad the heart."[16] The "vinedressers on Mount Carmel"[12] are those who, according to heightened contemplation, labor over the principle concerning perfect purification and the total negation of beings. For "Carmel" means "expert knowledge of circumcision,"[17] and whoever cultivates a vineyard upon it culti-

---

15. Cf. 3 Kgs 2.35.
16. Ps 103.15.
17. The same etymology is given by Origen, *Scholia on the Song of Songs* (PG 17:281); Eusebius, *Commentary on Isaiah* 2.9 (GCS 9:87); Procopius, *Catena on Isaiah* (PG 87:2285); and Cyril of Alexandria, *Commentary on Micah* 2 (ed. P. E.

vates the mystical principle of circumcision, for he expertly circumcises matter and material things from the intellect,[18] but not in a Jewish manner, "considering his shame to be his glory."[19] Scripture says that these individuals also need the divine stream of Wisdom's flowing water, streaming forth from the cisterns hewn in the wilderness, so that each of them, "according to the proportion of his faith,"[20] might be able to accept the suitable word from those who have been entrusted with the grace of teaching the saving word, through which the soul of each person is magnanimously cared for by our Lord Jesus Christ, who is the good and expert "husbandman," who is and who always will be bringing about everything mentioned above for the sake of our salvation.

48.11. This is how you should contemplate these passages, according to one mode of interpretation, albeit in summary fashion,[21] so that they lead you to our Lord Jesus Christ. If, according to another mode of interpretation, we contemplate each particular item in light of its own meaning, we will see that each one possesses great power for the completion of the perfection of those who are protected by the fear and the love of the Lord. Before touching on the contemplation of these matters, however, I am astonished and amazed at how Uzziah, though he was king of Judah, according to the literal account, had "vine-dressers on Mount Carmel," which did not belong to the kingdom of Judah, but rather to the kingdom of Israel, during whose reign the city of the kingdom of Israel was built. But apparently the text has mixed into the web of the literal

---

Pusey, S.P.N. Cyrilli archiepiscopi Alexandrini in XII prophetas, vol. 1 [Oxford: Clarendon Press, 1868; repr. Brussels: Culture et civilisation, 1965], 735, line 1).

18. The activity of contemplation involves the vision of the *logoi* that are in beings, having moved beyond the surface appearances and outward forms of beings, which are the objects of passionate attachments. It is the activity of *praxis* or *praktikê* that allows the intellect to be free of such attachments and exercise its proper contemplative function; cf. Larchet, SC 554:80, n. 1.

19. Phil 3.19.

20. Rom 12.6.

21. I.e., ἐπιτόμως, which underlines Maximos's exegetical style throughout much of this Question, which tends toward the format of writing short scholia for each verse; cf. *QThp.* (77, line 73); and *Or. Dom.* (CCSG 23, line 755).

account something that has no existence whatsoever, thereby rousing our sluggish minds to an investigation of the truth.

48.12. To begin, then, Uzziah is the intellect that has acquired divine might with respect to practice and contemplation, for as I said a moment ago, his name means the "might of God." "And Uzziah," it says, "had sought the Lord in the days of Zechariah, who understood the fear of the Lord." Zechariah means "recollection of God."[22] The intellect, then, to the extent that it holds within itself the living recollection of God, seeks for the Lord through contemplation, and it does not do this simply[23] but in the fear of the Lord,[13] that is, by practicing the commandments. For the one who seeks the Lord through contemplation without such practice does not find Him, since he did not seek the Lord in the fear of the Lord.

48.13. "And the Lord made him prosper." The Lord grants prosperity to all who practice the commandments with knowledge, teaching them the modes of the commandments as well as revealing to them the true principles of being.

48.14. "And Uzziah built towers in Jerusalem." Whoever richly prospers in seeking the Lord through contemplation with the appropriate fear (that is, with the practice of the commandments), "builds towers in Jerusalem,"[14] which means to raise aloft the principles of divinity to the simple, peaceful condition of the soul.

48.15. "And at the gate of the corner." The "gate of the corner," which is the faith of the Church, is the pious way of life through which we are introduced into the inheritance of good things. At this gate, as if upon mighty and noble towers, the intellect engaged with knowledge builds the fortresses of the divine doctrines concerning the Incarnation, composed of different concepts like so many precious stones, and of the modes of the virtues put in place for the safeguarding of the work of the commandments.

48.16. "And at the corner of the valley." The "valley" is the flesh, and its "corner" is its union with the soul through the law

---

22. The same etymology is given by Origen, *Commentary on Luke* (SC 87:484 = fr. 31).
23. I.e., without qualification.

of the commandments. Upon this union the intellect builds up, like a tower, the understanding[24] that subordinates the flesh to the soul according to the "law of the Spirit."[25]

48.17. "And at the corners." This means that there are many "corners" at which the intellect, supremely mighty in God, is said to build its towers. Here, a "corner" is the union of particulars with respect to universals according to the same nature and principle of being, as happens, for example, in the case of individuals with respect to their species, and of species to genera, and of genera to substance.[26] In each instance, all are uniquely conjoined to the limit of their extremes, at which extremes, as if they were "corners," the aforementioned universal principles of the particulars[15] produce the multiple and diverse unions of things that are divided.[27] In addition, a "corner" is also the union of the intellect with respect to sensation, and of heaven to earth, and of sensible realities[16] to intelligible realities, and of nature to the intelligible principle of nature.[28] At these corners the contemplative intellect—using its own understanding, and having firmly established true opinions concerning each reality—builds intelligible towers; that is, at each of the unions it establishes the doctrines that conjoin the unions.

48.18. "And he fortified them, and he built towers in the wilderness and hewed many cisterns out of the rock." Whoever has proved capable of detaching his senses from the passions, and separating his soul from its attachment to the senses, has "fortified" the wall preventing the devil from gaining entrance to the intellect by means of the senses. This is the reason why it is "in the wilderness" (by which I mean natural contemplation) that he builds pious notions concerning beings, like so many

---

24. I.e., διάγνωσις, which is not simple or general knowledge (γνῶσις), but an insight enabling the person to see both the unity of soul and body and the need for the body to be subordinate to the soul, consistent with the spiritual law.

25. Cf. Rom 8.2.

26. On this system of classification, associated with the philosopher Porphyry, see *Amb.* 10.89 (DOML 1:489, n. 62).

27. Suggesting that in every individual the particular is joined to the universal in a unique, unrepeatable way.

28. Cf. *Amb.* 41.1 (DOML 2:102–105).

secure towers. Seeking refuge in such notions, one has nothing to fear[17] from what lurks in this wilderness; that is, in the nature of visible things, by which I mean those thieving demons who through the senses deceive the intellect and drag it away to the gloomy darkness of ignorance.

48.19. "And he hewed out of the rock many cisterns." These are the different permanent states of mind with respect to superior things, which are receptive of lessons concerning knowledge sent to them from God.

48.20. "For he had many flocks in Shephela and in the low country, and vinedressers in the hill country and on Mount Carmel, for he was a husbandman." The one who, with the weapons of the right and the left,[29] lawfully contends for the sake of the truth,[30] teaches patience to the "flocks in Shephela," that is, to the movements of the soul in relation to the body, which are trained by suffering involuntary trials. He does this by giving them to drink, as if from "cisterns hewed out of the rock," the principles of patient endurance. "The flocks in the low country," on the other hand, which are the movements of the soul that are directed and broadened through the virtues on the right, are given to drink the principles of humility and moderation, so that they may never fall because of things on the left nor grow high-minded because of things on the right.[31]

48.21. "And vinedressers in the hill country and on Mount Carmel." The "vinedressers in the hill country" are those pi-

29. Cf. Dt 28.14.
30. 2 Cor 6.7; 2 Tm 2.5.
31. Cf. below, Qu. 49.6; Qu. 63, schol. 11; and Qu. 64.14–18. "Right" and "left" designate two extremes of behavior and thought, with the "left" designating bad thoughts, actions, passions, and demons, and the "right" designating good deeds and impulses that may make one prideful and conceited, along with the possibility that demons may present destructive behaviors under the guise of the good. This structure is further linked to the idea of virtue as a "mean" between "extremes," often described as the "middle" or "royal" way, which inclines neither to the right nor left; cf. Philo, *On the Immutability of God* 164 (LCL 3:91); idem, *On the Posterity of Cain* 102 (LCL 2:385–87); John of Damascus, *On the Faith (Against the Nestorians)* 1: "Our teachers led us to walk in the royal way, which is the middle way, so that we incline neither to things on the right that appear good, nor to things on the left which we know are obviously bad" (ed. Kotter 4:238).

ous thoughts that remain on the height of contemplation and which lovingly tend to knowledge that is ecstatic[18] and cannot be uttered. And the "vinedressers on Mount Carmel" are those thoughts that cultivate the principle of perfect dispassion and purification through the negation of all things, which latter are like a fleshly covering impeding the soul's generative power, and in a certain way these thoughts cognitively perform a complete circumcision of the intellect's relation to material things. For "Carmel" means the "expert knowledge of circumcision."

48.22. Uzziah is said to be a "husbandman" because every intellect possessing the might of God for contemplation is also a true husbandman, keeping the divine seeds of good things free from weeds by means of his personal zeal and attention, until such time as he has the remembrance of God preserving him. For it says: "He had sought the Lord in the days of Zechariah in the fear of the Lord." The name Zechariah translated into Greek means "remembrance of God." For this reason let us always beseech the Lord to safeguard within us the saving remembrance of Him, lest what we have achieved corrupt our soul, so that being exalted we may never recklessly dare, as did Uzziah, to grasp at things beyond nature.[32]

Scholia

[1] He calls the holy flesh that God assumed from us a "wondrous tabernacle," since without seed it received its existence in Him. He calls the intellective soul a "house," because in becoming man the Word ineffably united to Himself flesh intellectively ensouled, "purifying like by means of like."[33] By "place" he means the Word Himself, who according to hypostasis and without change firmly established human nature within Himself. It is thus toward this flesh that we make our way, sanctifying our own flesh through the virtues, through which we are

---

32. Cf. 2 Chr 26.16–21.

33. A commonplace philosophical notion (cf. Aristotle, *On the Soul* 404b16a: "like is known by like") adopted and transformed by Christian thinkers; in this instance the scholiast is citing directly from Gregory Nazianzus, *Or.* 38.13 (SC 358:130, line 21); cf. idem, *Ep.* 101.51 (SC 208:58).

QUESTION 48 277

of a nature to be "conformed" to the "body of His glory"[34] according to the grace of the Spirit, reaching the house of God through unmixed contemplation according to simple and indivisible knowledge, and arriving at the very intellective soul of the Lord, so that we too might have, according to the Apostle, "the intellect of Christ,"[35] through participation in the Spirit, by grace becoming for Him all that He is by nature and that according to dispensation He became for us.

[2] He called the "cornerstone" the "bond of the corner," that is, of the Church.

[3] He calls the Incarnation the "gate of the corner," since this is the entrance gate of the Church; the correct doctrines concerning the Incarnation he calls "towers."

[4] He called both the natural union of the flesh with the soul and the spiritual conjunction of the soul with the flesh the "corner of the valley," insofar as the flesh is in the service of virtue.

[5] He says in a general sense that "corners" are the different unions of being, that is, the unions of different and more general natures united to one another in a single inclination.

[6] Every unity of the aforementioned creations possesses a principle of wisdom, according to which the unity in question comes to exist. Scripture calls these principles the "towers of the corners," for they are the fortresses and towers of each and every being, comprising the essential principle of the knowledge they support along with the principle that joins all of them together in a unity of inclination.[36]

[7] He calls the principles of nature "towers in the wilderness."

[8] Hearts capable of receiving the heavenly gifts of holy knowledge he called "cisterns," which have been carved out by the firm principle of the commandments, and which have been cleared, as if of stony accumulations, of the affection for the passions as well as of the natural attachment to objects of sense. Such cisterns are filled with the spiritual knowledge that flows

34. Phil 3.21.
35. 1 Cor 2.16.
36. I.e., συνένευσις.

from above, which both purges the passions and in a certain manner gives life to and nourishes the virtues.

[9] He is saying that the flocks of Shephela are those who are instructed in ethical philosophy "through many afflictions,"[37] since they are in need of the principles that teach patience.

[10] The "flocks in the low country" are what he calls those who prosper in virtues and who are unmoved in relation to what is worse, although they are still in need of the principles and teachings concerning gratitude.

[11] By "hill country" he is referring in a general sense to the higher form of the spiritual contemplation of nature, which is cultivated by those who have rejected the mental images that arise from objects perceived by the senses, and who, by means of the virtues, have passed through to their very principles.

[12] "Mount Carmel" is the height of the "expert knowledge of circumcision," and "circumcision" means either the negation of the natural disposition toward generation or the degeneration of the intellect's disposition toward beings. The "vineyard" of this condition is obviously the principle of Providence, cultivated by human beings, which grants one chaste ecstasy and thoughts that are moved only around the simple Monad that is without beginning. For whoever is moved toward this alone, has cut off from himself, as if it were a fleshly covering, the disposition that covers the Cause of the generation of beings.

[13] He called the whole of practical philosophy the "fear of the Lord," from its beginning to its end, "for the beginning of wisdom is the fear of the Lord."[38]

[14] The higher principle concerning the divinity is a "tower" in the soul, which is fortified by the keeping of the commandments.

[15] The principles of particulars, he says, inasmuch as they approach universals, produce the unions of things that are divided, because the principles that are more universal contain in unity the principles of things that are more particular, to which the particulars are naturally related.[39]

---

37. Cf. Acts 14.22.
38. Prv 1.7.
39. Cf. *Amb.* 10.83 (DOML 1:274–77).

QUESTION 48

[16] Of these there exists a relative spiritual principle, giving them their mutual union.

[17] Whoever has acquired a pious notion about each particular thing does not fear the demons who deceive men by the external appearance of visible phenomena.

[18] The vineyard produces wine, wine produces drunkenness, and drunkenness produces ecstasy. It follows that the active principle, which is the vineyard, when it is cultivated by means of the virtues, gives birth to knowledge, while knowledge gives birth to beauteous ecstasy, which latter makes the intellect stand outside of its relation to sense perception.

QUESTION 49

AGAIN, IN the same book, what is the meaning of: "And Hezekiah saw that Sennacherib had come, and that his face was set to wage war on Jerusalem; and he took counsel with his elders and his mighty men to seal off the waters of the springs that were outside the city; and they joined and supported him. And he gathered a great many people and sealed off the waters of the springs and the brook that marked the boundary across the city"?[1] What is the meaning of these things on the level of contemplation?

Response

49.2. The intellect that pursues practical philosophy with knowledge, and is girded round about with every divine discernment against the opposing power, is a Hezekiah, whose name means "divine sovereignty,"[2] which is why he rules Jerusalem, which signifies the soul,[1] or the "vision of peace," which is cognitive contemplation freed from the passions. When such an intellect sees the opposing power already moving against it, it "takes counsel"—as it ought to—"with its elders and rulers in order to seal off the waters of the springs that are outside the city." The "rulers" belonging to such an intellect are the principles of faith, hope, and love,[3] which, like elders, exercise power over all the divine concepts and thoughts of the soul, and wisely counsel the intellect. At the same time, they also "join and support" the intellect against the opposing power, suggesting ways in which it might be destroyed. For without faith, hope,

---

1. 2 Chr 32.2–4.
2. Cf. Lagarde, *Onomastica Sacra*, 190: "Hezekiah means 'sovereignty.'"
3. Cf. 1 Cor 13.13.

and love, no evil thing can be completely abolished, nor can any good thing be completely established. This is because, on the one hand, faith persuades the intellect to align itself with God when it is under attack,[2] exhorting it to take courage and prepare the full range of its incorporeal[4] weapons.[5] Hope, on the other hand, becomes for it the most truthful pledge of divine assistance, promising the overthrow of the opposing powers. Love, finally, makes the intellect difficult to move, or rather entirely impossible to move, from the tender affection of God, and when the intellect is under attack, love impels it to concentrate the whole of its natural desire into longing for the divine.

49.3. The meaning of the names of the rulers is in agreement with this. At that time, the rulers under Hezekiah were "Eliakim the son of Hilkiah, who was the steward; Shebnah the secretary; and Joah, the son of Asaph, the recorder."[6] Eliakim means "resurrection of God,"[3] and the name of his father, Hilkiah, means "portion of God." Thus the first and only-begotten son of the "divine portion," that is, of true knowledge, is the principle of divine resurrection that takes place within us according to faith, together with the requisite oversight according to knowledge, by which I mean discernment, properly differentiating the uprisings of voluntary and involuntary trials. The name of Shebnah the secretary means "return,"[4] clearly signifying through itself the most complete principle of divine hope, without which there is absolutely no return to God of any kind whatsoever, since the characteristic property of hope is symbolized by scribal activity, that is, to give signs of, and to bring before the eyes, realities to come as if they were present, and to persuade us that God, who defends us, is never absent from those who are under attack by the opposing power, since it is for God's sake and on His account that

---

4. Following the suggestion of L. G. Westerink, *Byzantinische Zeitschrift* 76 (1983): 48, the CCSG editors have corrected this word to "corporeal" (cf. CCSG 22:348). I have, however, adopted the reading provided by Eriugena, i.e., *incorporalium*.

5. Cf. 2 Cor 10.4.

6. 4 Kgs 18.18. The manuscripts indicate confusion in the spelling of the names at this point. Further, while the LXX gives: Ἰωὰς ὁ υἱὸς Σαφὰτ ὁ ἀναμιμνήσκων (4 Kgs 18.18), Maximos has Ἰωὰχ ὁ τοῦ Ἀσάφ ὁ ὑπομνηματογράφος.

the saints are under attack.[7] Joah, the son of Asaph, the recorder, means "brotherhood of God," and the name of Asaph, his father, means "assembly."[5] Thus love is the offspring of the assembling and unification of the soul's powers around God, that is, the rational, irascible, and desiring powers, for it is by means of love that those who by grace have acquired equality to God inscribe within their memory the beauty of divine comeliness—since "brotherhood" obviously signifies the grace of equality—and they possess the indelible desire that records and imprints the inviolate beauty of divine love within the ruling part of the soul.

49.4. Since these things are so according to the foregoing mode of interpretation, my argument, which has proceeded through an examination of names, has in some measure aimed at the truth. Every intellect, after the manner of Hezekiah—girded about with divine sovereignty[8]—possesses the power of reason[6] as if it were certain elders and rulers, and reason naturally gives birth to faith grounded in knowledge. It is through faith, moreover, that the intellect is taught by God in a manner beyond words, and because God is always present, the things of the future are present, through hope, together with Him. The same intellect also possesses the power of desire, according to which divine love is constituted, and it is through such love that the intellect, attaching itself voluntarily to longing for the inviolate divinity, possesses the indissoluble desire for that for which it longs. Not least it possesses the power of spiritedness—by which it is tightly held by divine peace—and the intellect draws the movement of this spirited desire toward divine love. Every intellect possesses these powers collaborating with it in its efforts to overthrow evil and for the constitution and maintenance of virtue.[9] On the one hand, they collaborate like "elders," inasmuch as they are the most senior of the

---

7. Cf. above, Qu. 26.2, 10.
8. Cf. 1 Pt 1.13.
9. Cf. Gregory of Nyssa, *On Virginity* 12, where, in an allegorical exegesis of Lk 15.9, the "friends and neighbors" of the woman (who found the lost coin) symbolize the intellect's reasoning and appetitive powers (GNO 8/1:301); and *Amb.* 31.4–5 (DOML 2:43–47).

soul's powers and complete its very essence. On the other hand, they collaborate as "rulers," inasmuch as they rule over the initial[7] movements that proceed from the powers of the soul, and they jointly hold the ruling authority over their activities, in company with the will of the intellect that moves them. Altogether these powers counsel and support the intellect so that it might "seal off the waters of the springs that were outside the city," which, strictly speaking, even now continue to exist. For that which in the literal account took place in the past, is always standing before us being mystically present in contemplation. The intellect, then, having these aforementioned powers healthy and undeceived, gathers together "a great many people," which obviously signifies the natural pious movements and thoughts that arise from these powers. The "waters outside the city,"[8] that is, outside the soul, which cause the brook to flow through the middle of the city, are the mental representations that arise from natural contemplation. These representations stream forth from each sensation, welling up from objects of sense and flowing into the soul. Emerging from these representations, and coursing through the soul as if it were a city, the rational principle of the knowledge of sensible things is formed like a rising river. As long as the soul has this river rushing through it, it will not cast away from itself the mental images and fantasies flooding into it from the senses, through which the wicked and destructive power of the evil one naturally wages war on the soul.[10] And this is why Hezekiah says: "Let not King Ashur come and find much water and prevail

---

10. Cf. Evagrios, *On Prayer* 56: "Even when the intellect does not linger in the mere mental representations of objects ... through contemplation their inner principles leave their impress and form on the intellect and lead it far away from God"; ibid., 57: "Even if the mind has transcended the contemplation of corporeal nature ... it can be occupied with the knowledge of intelligible objects and so be involved with their multiplicity" (PG 79:1177D–1180B); and idem, *Ep.* 58: "The Holy Spirit wants the contemplative state to be without images and free of all impassioned thoughts ... the contemplation of created beings provides a multiplicity of information, but that of the Holy Trinity is a uniform knowledge, for it is substantial knowledge which is manifest to a mind divested of passions and bodies" (ed. Paul Géhin, "Nouveaux fragments grecs des Lettres d'Évagre," *Revue d'histoire des textes* 24 [1994]: 117–47, at 143).

over us."[11] It is as if the discerning intellect, faced with an uprising of the passions, were saying to its own powers: "Let us cease from natural contemplation[9] and let us devote ourselves to prayer alone and to the bodily hardship of practical philosophy." Of these, the king's ascent into the temple is the figure of prayer, and the clothing with sackcloth the figure of bodily hardship[12]—"lest through the thoughts arising from sense perception, the evil one with wicked stealth bring in the forms and outward shapes of sensible things, through which the passions are of a nature to be created[10] around the surface appearances of visible things, and the activity of reason within us is made to cease, and succeed in plundering the city, that is, the soul, and drag it off to Babylon, that is, to the confusion of the passions."[13]

49.5. Whoever, then, at the moment when he is faced with the uprising of the passions, courageously seals off his senses, and who completely repulses the images and memories of sensible things, and who restricts on all sides the natural tendency to examine things in the external world, has, after the manner of Hezekiah, "sealed off the waters of the springs that are outside of the city," and "cut off the brook that runs through the middle of the city," being "assisted" by the aforementioned powers and by the "great people that were gathered together," by which I mean the pious thoughts of each of the soul's powers. Through the hand of God he triumphed over and put to shame the wicked and tyrannical power that had risen up against him. And through the divine commandment, as if through an "angel"—I mean through the principle that naturally destroys the passions—he slew a "hundred and eighty-five thousand,"[14] that is, the habit of mind productive of evil, which irrationally[11] springs up on the three powers of the soul through sensible ob-

---

11. 2 Chr 32.4.
12. Cf. 4 Kgs 19.1.
13. The mind can contemplate the spiritual dimension of visible realities, either in their inner principles or as mental representations, or in a more "carnal" manner through sensation, imagination, and memory, through which faculties it can envision the outward forms and appearances of visible realities to which the soul can become passionately attached.
14. 4 Kgs 19.35.

QUESTION 49 285

jects, as well as on the activity of the senses pertaining to them.

49.6. It is necessary, therefore, that the intellect, which cognitively understands how to escape invisible entanglements, not engage in natural contemplation, nor do anything else during the moment when it is under attack by wicked demons. What it should do is pray, subdue the body through hardship, and work with all zeal to bring about the downfall of the earthly mind.[15] And of course it should guard the walls of the city—by which I mean those virtues which safeguard the virtues of the soul, or those qualities which safeguard the virtues, namely, self-control and patient endurance—by means of innate good thoughts,[12] but in none of its thoughts should it talk back to or contradict any of the invisible combatants ranged outside.[16] Otherwise, the intellect runs the risk of being deceived by things on the right,[17] of being distanced from God, and having its desire stolen by the one who gives the soul to "drink from the cup of dark ruin."[18] The one, I mean, who through superficial goods deceptively drags down the mind seeking goods to things that are worse; who "speaks in the language of Judah," namely, Rhapsaces, the general of Sennacherib the king of Ashpur.[19] The name "Rhapsaces" means "he who waters with many kisses," or "who possesses many kisses."[20] That is, the evil demon who, being accustomed to use weapons on the right to fight the intellect, "speaks in the language of Judah" through what appears to be virtue

15. Cf. 1 Cor 9.27; 15.47–48.
16. Cf. 4 Kgs 18.36. "Talking back" (ἀντιρρητική) was a monastic practice in which one responded to demonic suggestions by reciting relevant passages of Scripture. Inspired by the example of Christ's responses to the devil when he was tempted in the wilderness (Mt 4.1–11), the practice is attested across a wide range of late-antique monastic literature and was the subject of a special treatise by Evagrios, trans. David Brakke, *Evagrius of Pontus, Talking Back* (Collegeville: Liturgical Press, 2009). Arguing with demons, however, was considered dangerous for all but the most advanced ascetics, and monks were generally taught to pay no attention whatsoever to demonic thoughts and images.
17. Cf. above, Qu. 48.20.
18. Hab 2.15.
19. 4 Kgs 18.26.
20. The Greek translation of Kings understood the Hebrew word *Rab-Shakeh* to be the name of the Assyrian general, but the word is an Assyrian term for a military commander.

but is not, and offers the soul to "drink from the cup of ruin," revealing his deceptive and deadly affection—in comparison to which the wounds inflicted on us by a real friend are better, for it says: "The wounds of a friend are more to be trusted than the kisses of an enemy."[21][13] The name Sennacherib means "trial of desiccation" or "sharpened teeth," which is the devil, whose thoughts, which are truly sharpened for evil (for this is how I understand the meaning of "sharpened teeth"), evaporate within us the flow of the knowledge of the divine streams, a natural effect in those who receive him, from which he obtains an appropriate name, truly called and being a "trial of desiccation," for by means of his cunning he renders those under his control a wasteland barren of every spiritual and life-giving gift.

49.7. Or perhaps Sennacherib, that is, the devil, is called "trial of desiccation"[14] inasmuch as he is impoverished, destitute, and deprived of any personal power in his uprisings against us, for without sensible things—through which he is accustomed to wage war on the soul—he is not able to harm us in any way, and this is why his cunningly contrived tyranny against us has need of "sources of water outside the city," that is, the mental images of material things, by means of which he introduces into the soul the outward appearances and the forms of sensible things. It is through these that sense perception, naturally shaped by its relation to sensory objects, often becomes an evil and deadly weapon in the hands of the devil for the destruction of the soul's divine beauty, persuading it, through the inducements of pleasure, to surrender to the enemy the whole power of reason that is within us.

49.8. But whoever has courageously closed his senses by rational self-control, and through the powers of his soul has blocked the entrances of the intellect to the outward appearances of sensory things, easily destroys the wicked machinations of the devil, making him retreat in shame down the very road he came on, a road made up of material things considered vital for the constitution of the body.[15] And while the devil is retreating in shame to his world of confusion, he slays him by

---

21. Prv 27.6.

means of the very evil thoughts generated by the devil, transferring them to the "proximity of rest." For whoever is capable of subduing the devil by means of the very thoughts generated by him, by using them collectively for the good, has "slain Sennacherib by the hand of his own sons and banished them to the land of Armenia,"[22] obviously transferring his thoughts to the proximity of rest,[16] for through sensation they confused his soul. And Armenia means precisely "proximity of rest."[23] To be sure, the "proximity of rest" is the projection of the divine virtues, and when the intellect transfers to it the thoughts that had formerly dragged it down to the dishonorable passions of the senses, it slays the devil who gave birth to them in order to ruin human nature.

49.9. Hezekiah therefore, on the level of the text's spiritual meaning, acted well and very wisely when, on account of Sennacherib the king of Assyria, he "sealed off the waters of the springs that were outside of Jerusalem." The "springs outside the city," that is, outside the soul, are all the senses, while their "waters" are the mental images of sensible things. The brook that flows through the middle of the city is the knowledge gathered together in natural contemplation from these mental images.[17] This knowledge passes through the middle of the soul because it is a kind of borderland between the intellect and sensation.[24] For the knowledge of sensible realities is not

---

22. 4 Kgs 19.36.
23. The etymology of the name Armenia is disputed by historians and philologists. "Armenia" and "Ararat" are often used interchangeably or simply identified in classical and patristic literature, and the notion of "rest" may be related to Ararat, although Cyril of Alexandria provides μαρτυρία καταβάσεως for the latter (*Glaphyra in Pentateuchum* [PG 69:72]). The name *Arām* is ultimately derived from the Proto-Indo-European word *h,rem*, which means "to rest, become quiet, calm."
24. The soul was believed to stand midway between intellect and sensation, where it was productive of images and concepts; cf. Plato, *Timaeus* 35a; Origen, *On First Principles* 2.6.3: "The soul of Christ acted as a medium between God and the flesh, for it was not possible for the nature of God to mingle with a body apart from some medium" (SC 252:314); Maximos, *Amb.* 3.2 (DOML 1:18–19); Dionysius, *Ep.* 9.1: "The impassible part of the soul borders upon the simple and most deeply interiorized visions of deiform images ... this is evident in those who, having beheld the things of God beyond the veils,

wholly disconnected from the intellective power, but neither is it allocated solely to the activity of sensation. To the contrary, it is found in the middle, as it were, at the convergence of the intellect toward sensation, and of sensation toward the intellect, and itself brings about the mutual conjunction of the one with the other. With respect to sensation, it impresses on it the specific outward forms of sensible realities; with respect to intellect, it transmutes these impressions into principles. This is why the knowledge of visible realities is not unreasonably called a brook running through the middle of the city, for it is the middle ground between two extremes, that is, of the intellect and sensation. Whoever seals off this knowledge when the passions initiate their disturbances, so that the intellect is not disturbed by the offensive onslaught of the outward forms of material things, and with knowledge severs the invisible entanglements of the wicked demons, slays the "one hundred and eighty-five thousand."[25] By this I mean the state that produces evil, which irrationally springs up, as I said, by means of sensible things, on the three powers of the soul, as well as on the activity of the senses concerned with them, that is, the irrational activity of the soul's natural powers with regard to the senses. This is because numbers consisting of six or multiples of six—whether they are composed of units of one, ten, one hundred,[26] or some other number—signify the state which is productive of either virtue or vice, depending on the final sum of its multiplication, and which makes present to the mind the disposition that yields the sum producing one state or the other—at least to the minds of those who apply themselves with specialized knowledge to the science of numbers. When to any number consisting of six or a multiple of six the number five is joined, added, or combined, it points obliquely to the senses, that is, to the potential, state, or activity of sense perception that is adjacent to,[18] or supervenes upon, or is compounded with, the nat-

---

subsequently shape within themselves a certain figure" (198, lines 8–14); and H. J. Blumenthal, *Plotinus' Psychology* (The Hague: Martin Nijhoff, 1971), 88–95.

25. 4 Kgs 19.35.

26. Or "monads, decads, and centuries"; cf. Ps.-Iamblichus, *Theology of Arithmetic*, ed. Victor De Falco (Leipzig: Teubner, 1975), 42–54.

ural powers of the soul. For example, when, by units of one, as a simple number to another simple number, the number five is conjoined[19] with the number six, it makes present to the mind the productive aptitude[27] of the senses solely in terms of their power. If, on the other hand, the number five, understood to be simple in terms of its constitutive units, is added to a number composed of multiples of six, it signifies the productive state of sense perception according to power. And if a multiple of the number five is combined with a multiple of the number six, it signifies the actual production of sense perception according to power, state, and activity, that is, the realization of virtue or vice, depending on whether or not the number yields a blameworthy or praiseworthy sum, according to the particular passage of Scripture being contemplated or at any rate carefully examined.[28]

49.10. The number six, therefore, when added to or combined with units of ten, produces the number sixty. The number sixty, when multiplied by the three general powers of the soul, with the addition of the five innate senses, produces the number one hundred eighty-five. This number manifests the state which, supervening upon the natural powers of sense perception, is productive of evil—which is why in this particular passage of

---

27. I.e., ἐπιτηδειότης, which means aptitude, habitual fitness, and suitability to receive something. This is a technical term related to the Aristotelian doctrine of potentiality and actuality, hinging on the notion that potentiality is a necessary condition for actuality, but not a sufficient one. "Wood" is a necessary condition for fire, but it is not necessarily sufficient, if, for example, it is soaked with water. Among Neoplatonists, the term denotes the "sufficiency" or "suitability" of the *paschon* to receive the influence of the divine cause (and thus denotes a "capacity" for divine influence). Maximos explains the concept in *Pyrr*: "Aptitude produces, through discipline, a stable habit and an execution of intention in accordance with that disposition" (PG 91:313AB). In the sense of denoting "fitness" or "suitability" characteristic of the patient in relation to the potencies of the causal agent, the term first appears in Iamblichus as applied to certain psychic states which are "suitable for receiving the influence of the gods" (*On the Mysteries of the Egyptians* 105.1); Proclus speaks of a substrate as "fit for the participation of the Forms" (*Commentary on Parmenides* 903, 36–39); cf. Gersh, *Iamblichus to Eriugena*, 37–38, 211.

28. On "blameworthy" and "praiseworthy" interpretations, see above, Qu. 38.2.

Scripture the number is presented as blameworthy—and it is this evil state that the intellect slays, through the divine principle of knowledge, as if it were a mighty angel, by its own proper power being bolstered by prayer, and it ascribes to God its every accomplishment and every victory against the demons. Whoever, then, when faced with the onslaught of trials, refrains from natural contemplation, and at the same time holds fast to prayer, and, withdrawing from all things, focuses his intellect on itself and God, puts to death the state of natural powers moving contrary to nature which produces evil through the senses. And by overthrowing this state he routs the devil and casts him out in shame, for arrogantly seeing an opportunity in this state, he had arrogantly approached the soul through its prideful thoughts and through them exalted himself against the truth.

49.11. This is perhaps what the great David recognized, experienced, and put into practice, for he, more than anyone else, had experience on the front line of battle against armies of invisible invaders. For "when," he says, "the sinner arrayed himself before me, I was dumb, and humbled myself, and refrained from uttering even good words."[29] And after him, in the same spirit, the divine Jeremiah warned the people "to go not forth from the city, because the sword of the enemy lay round about it."[30] And there is this: if the blessed Abel[20] had guarded himself and had not gone "out into the plain" together with Cain,[31] that is, into the broad place of natural contemplation prior to attaining a state of dispassion, the "law of the flesh"[32] would not have "risen up and killed him," springing upon him cleverly[33] and deceiving him through things on the right during the contemplation of beings, before he had attained a perfect state of mind—for this is what "Cain" means, and was, and was called, namely, the "law of the flesh," and consistent with the meaning of his name, he was what the first man Adam acquired as the first fruit of his transgression, giving birth to the law of sin,

29. Ps 38.2.
30. Cf. Jer 6.25.
31. Gn 4.8.
32. Cf. Rom 7.25; 8.7.
33. Cf. Gn 4.8.

which God did not create in paradise, which is why Cain also means "creation."[34] Similarly, if Dinah, the child of the great Jacob, had not "gone forth in the company of her daughters to the people of the land," that is, with her mental images derived from sensations, then Shechem, the son of Hamor, would not have risen up against her and defiled her.[35] Shechem means "the back," and Hamor means "donkey," that is, the "body." Thus the "back" (in other words, Shechem), who is the son of Hamor (in other words, the body), is the law which is "behind" the body, and not in front of it, which is to say it is the law that came later,[21] and not first. For in the beginning—that is, with respect to what is first and foremost—before the transgression of the divine commandment, this human body (which is Hamor), did not possess the law of sin (by which I mean Shechem), but rather it was only afterwards that the law of sin attached itself to the body through disobedience. And it was this law that, after careful examination, true reason called "Shechem" on account of its belated birth, for his name, as I said, means the "back," which is that which comes afterwards, for the "back" by nature signifies belatedness. Thus, before we have acquired perfect stability, it is good for us to abstain from natural contemplation, lest while seeking the spiritual principles in visible creations, we unwittingly find ourselves harvesting a crop of passions. For among imperfect men, the outward appearances of visible things have greater power over the senses than the principles hidden in the forms of created things have over the soul.

Scholia

[1] The unerring contemplation of beings requires that one be free of passions. This is why it is called "Jerusalem," on account of its perfect virtue and immaterial knowledge,[36] which is attained not simply by the privation of the passions but also by the privation of mental images derived from objects of sense, which the biblical text calls the "waters outside the city."[37]

---

34. Cf. Maximos's interpretation of Cain and Abel in *QD.* 77 (CCSG 10:58).
35. Gn 34.2.
36. I.e., knowledge free of material-based forms.
37. Cf. above, Qu. 10.7.

[2] Faith encourages the intellect under attack, strengthening it with the hope of assistance. Hope, in turn, brings before our eyes the promised assistance, and repels the attack of the opposing powers. Love, finally, puts to death the assault by attackers taking place in the God-loving intellect, and utterly extinguishes it by means of the desire for God.

[3] The first resurrection that takes place within us, he says, is faith in the God whom we have slain through our ignorance, and such faith is rightly dispensed through the fulfillment of the commandments.

[4] The realities, he says, agree with their names, for without at least some expectation, whether it is a faint hope or something within reach, the return of anyone to the good is impossible.

[5] He says that nothing more effectively gathers together those who are scattered than love, for it creates a single inclination of will held together by mutual agreement and inspiration, the mark of which is the beauty of the equality of honor.

[6] Without the power of reason, he says, there can be no true knowledge, and without such knowledge there can be no faith, the good offspring of which is hope, according to which believers experience future things as though they were present; and without the power of desire there is no longing, the goal of which is love—for to love something is the characteristic sign of desire; and without the spirited power intensifying the desire for union with its object, there is no possibility for peace to be born, for peace is the complete and undisturbed possession of what is desired.

[7] Reason, he says, rules over cognitive thoughts, just as irascibility and desire rule over desires and objects of desire.

[8] According to the anagogical sense, he understood Hezekiah as the philosophical mind engaged in practice, and also as the soul; and he understood the different forms of the senses as "sources," and their mental images or representations as "waters"; and the opinion or supposition deduced from them a "brook," with respect to which one must completely seal off one's senses when the passions rise up in rebellion against reason.

[9] He says that the one who has not been purified of pas-

sions should not engage in natural contemplation inasmuch as the mental images of sensory objects are able to shape an impure intellect so that it conforms to the very shape of the passions.

[10] The intellect, which in a moment of imagination remains on the surfaces of sensible objects through the power of sensation, becomes the creator of impure passions, for it has not advanced to intelligible realities through contemplation.

[11] When reason functions without the intellect, and irascibility becomes rash, and desire irrational, the soul becomes dominated by ignorance, tyranny, and licentiousness. When these rule over the soul, the disposition for evil will naturally be realized in practice, being compounded by the pleasure of the senses. This is the state indicated by the number one hundred and eighty-five thousand, for if you multiply sixty three times for the completed movement in evil of each of the powers of the soul, and then add five for the pleasure that is actualized by the five senses, you will obviously obtain the number that signifies the state productive of evil. For as long as the devil is in possession of this state, he will rule over the soul tyrannically—but God, through the power of reason equipped with knowledge and wisdom, as if it were an angel, destroys this state and saves the soul, which is the true Jerusalem, and makes the intellect within the soul free of all evil.

[12] Here he calls the people on the walls "innate thoughts."

[13] Here the "friend" is the Lord, and the "wounds" he inflicts are the forms of chastisement that come upon each person for the punishment of his flesh and his salvation, that is, for the punishment of the "mind of the flesh,"[38] "so that his spirit may be saved in the day of the Lord."[39] The "enemy" is the devil, and his "kisses" are different kinds of sensual pleasures, by means of which he deceives the soul and persuades it to separate itself from the love of its Creator.

[14] Sennacherib means "trial of desiccation." One reason for this is because he dries the hearts of those who are opposed to him, separating their holy thoughts from the source

---

38. Rom 8.6.
39. 1 Cor 5.5.

of grace. Another reason is because he himself is dry, and poor, and impoverished, having nothing of his own, and thus like a robber he deceptively conceals himself beneath the surfaces of material things and from there launches his attacks on us.

[15] He says that anything which is superfluous and goes beyond natural need is intemperance, which is the road on which the devil approaches the soul, and it is on this same road that he returns in disgrace to his own region, whenever self-control chastens nature. Or the road is the natural passions, the use of which beyond what is natural leads the devil to the soul, but when their use is limited to what is necessary, they naturally make the devil return to his region. The region of the devil is the permanent state of evil and confusion, toward which he is always moving, and toward which he leads those who have been defeated by their life of material things.

[16] Whoever has transposed his thoughts to virtue has given them rest, distancing them from the troubled confusion of the passions.

[17] The intellect that has naturally united sensation to itself through the medium of reason reaps true understanding from natural contemplation, and this knowledge is called a "brook," which runs through the soul whose thoughts are preoccupied with sensation.

[18] Adjacent to the inclination of the will is the natural capacity for aptitude, while supervening upon it is a fixed state, for fixed states follow aptitudes. Compounded with this state is always activity, even if many times it is not immediately manifest due to obstacles created by matter.

[19] "Numerical conjunction" is what he calls the pronunciation of simple numbers within the decad, which is distinguished by the conjunction "and," such as six and five, and, depending on either a good or a bad meaning, in Scripture it indicates the potential, productive aptitude of virtue or vice.

"Numerical addition" is what he calls the addition, distinguished by the conjunction "and," of a simple number made up of single units that is obtained through multiplication by a single number. For example, sixty and five, or one hundred twenty and five, or one hundred eighty and five, as is the case with the number given in the text, indicate not simply three productive aptitudes in relation to the senses, but also the productive state of virtue or vice in relation to the senses.

"Numerical synthesis" is what he calls the aggregation, resulting from the multiplication of the same numbers with themselves, which is distinguished by the conjunction "and," as in the case of sixty and fifty, or six hundred and five hundred, and other numbers of this sort, which indicates not simply the potential aptitude for production and a fixed state, but also the actuality of virtue or vice arising from a fixed state in relation to the senses.

Whoever knows the value of each number within the decad—namely, that the monad signifies what is unmixed, the dyad difference, that three is equal and intelligible, four is sensible, five is perceptible and circular, six is active and perfect, seven is revolving[40] and unmixed, eight is fixed and unmoving, nine borders on matter and form, that is, objects of sense and sense perception, while ten is the most perfect number—will understand the meaning of every number according to Scripture, according to either conjunction, addition, or synthesis.

[20] Cain is the law of the flesh, whom Adam first begot when he had transgressed the commandment. Abel is the "mind of the Spirit,"[41] who was born afterwards, when Adam repented. Before Abel attained to a perfect state, however, and while he was still preoccupied with natural phenomena, he was killed by Cain. "But whoever kills Cain," God says, "vengeance will be taken on him sevenfold."[42] In the Gospels, this same one is called a "wicked spirit," which brings along with it seven even more wicked spirits.[43] This spirit is perhaps the thought of self-love, that is, the spirit of gluttony, which is inevitably followed by the thought of fornication, greed, sorrow, wrath, listlessness, vainglory, and pride. He, then, who according to the divine sentence kills Cain, by which I mean gluttony, will at the same time kill all those passions that arise from it, according to the

---

40. Or "rounded" (περιφερής).
41. Cf. Rom 8.27.
42. Gn 4.15.
43. Mt 12.45.

words: "Whoever kills Cain, vengeance will be taken on him sevenfold."[44]

[21] The law, he says, of the generation and corruption of the body was only afterwards imposed on the nature of human beings, and it is according to this law that we are born and give birth, because we did not keep but rather trampled on the divinizing law of the Spirit, which was the first commandment given to us.

44. Gn 4.15.

QUESTION 50

HAT, AGAIN in the same book, is the meaning of the words: "And King Hezekiah and Isaiah the prophet, the son of Amoz, prayed concerning these things, and they cried to heaven. And the Lord sent an angel, and he destroyed every mighty man and warrior and leader and captain in the camp of King Ashur, and he returned with shame of face to his own land"?[1]

Response

50.2. Even though the word of holy Scripture is limited according to the letter—because it is delimited[2] chronologically according to the times of the events that were written down—it nevertheless always remains unlimited according to the spirit through the contemplation of spiritual realities.[3] And let no one who is troubled by this have any doubts, for he should know that the God who spoke through Scripture is unlimited according to nature, and those whose genuine intention is to hear and give heed to the intention of God should believe that the word spoken by God resembles God Himself. For if God[1] is the one who spoke, and if God is by nature unlimited, it is obvious that the word spoken by Him is also unlimited.[4]

50.3. Having examined the things that took place figuratively during the times of Hezekiah, which reached their historical

---

1. 2 Chr 32.20–21.
2. I.e., συναπολήγων, having the sense of being completed or exhausted with or in something else.
3. I.e., Scripture is limited in its literal and historical sense, but is unlimited in its spiritual, symbolic, and anagogical senses.
4. See above, Intro., 1.2.8.

end, and having contemplated spiritually those matters issuing from the written record of the events, we must surely marvel at the wisdom of the Holy Spirit who wrote them—how, that is, He arranged the meaning of whatever was written so that it would accord and fit with each and every one of us who share in human nature, so that anyone who wishes to become a pupil of the divine word, and who is not burdened by the things of this world that weaken virtue, can become equal to and another Hezekiah in spirit, and another Isaiah, without being hindered by anyone or having to pray and cry out to the heaven to be heard and receive from God an angel to come and destroy those who are spiritually attacking him. Moreover, anyone who wishes to receive, with knowledge according to Christ, the holy Scripture within his soul, must labor diligently over the interpretation of names, which by themselves are able to elucidate the whole meaning of what has been written. He must, however, be concerned with the exact understanding of what has been written, and not strive in a Jewish manner simply to drag down the sublimity of the Spirit to the level of the body and the earth, limiting the divine and pure promises of spiritual good things to the corruption of what is fleeting and transitory. For this is what some so-called Christians among us mistakenly think,[2] revealing that in their case the name of "Christian" is in reality a pseudonym, for the facts prove that they have completely denied the power of this name, and walk on a path contrary to Christ, as my discourse will briefly demonstrate.[5]

50.4. Together with the other mysteries—to which no words can draw near—God became man and came to us to fulfill the law spiritually by abolishing the letter.[6] He came to establish His life-giving principle, by which I mean the law, and to make it manifest by removing that aspect of it which killed, and, ac-

---

5. Maximos elsewhere characterizes literalist readings of Scripture as "Jewish," and makes strong theological arguments against such readings (e.g., *Amb.* 10.32 [DOML 1:199]). Here, however, he is clearly referring to a group within the Christian community, perhaps including a general reference to Antiochene writers. His criticisms are reminiscent of Origen's frustrations with the *simpliciores* (οἱ ἁπλούστεροι); cf. Gunner Hällström, *Fides Simpliciorum according to Origen of Alexandria* (Helsinki: Societas Scientiarum Fennica, 1984).

6. Cf. Mt 5.17.

cording to the divine Apostle, that aspect is the "letter," just as the life-giving principle of the law according to him is the "spirit," for he says: "The letter kills, but the spirit gives life."[7] From this it is clear that they chose the portion opposed to Christ, and are ignorant of the entire mystery of the Incarnation—those, I mean, who bury the power of their minds solely in the letter, not wishing to be the "image and likeness of God."[8] Instead, they prefer "to be earth,"[3] according to the curse: "to earth you shall return,"[9] on account of their relation to the letter, as if it were earth, rather than to the spirit "in the air," that is, spiritual illumination, and "in the clouds," by which I mean lofty contemplations, and through spiritual knowledge "being caught up and meeting the Lord in the air, and thus we shall always be with the Lord."[10] For such as these, it is right for one to grieve—because through ignorance they suffer the unbearable loss of falling away from the truth—and to feel pain as well, for they provide the Jews with many occasions to confirm their disbelief. But let us leave them aside, inasmuch as they have what they want, and let us turn to the task at hand and embark upon a spiritual examination of the text before us, beginning with an interpretation of the names.

50.5. The name Hezekiah means the "sovereignty of God," while the name of his father[4] Ahaz means "might." Isaiah means the "uplifting of God," that is, the "height of God." The name of his father, Amoz, means "toil of the people." The "sovereignty of God" is virtue that overthrows the passions and safeguards pious thoughts. It is born from the practice of the commandments, which is understood figuratively as "sovereignty," and it is by this that we utterly destroy, with the help of God—or rather solely by the power of God—the wicked powers opposed to the good. The "height of God" is the knowledge[5] of the truth, which is born from the toil expended on the contemplation of beings and the sweat required for the practice of the virtues, by which we become fathers of toil, and

---

7. 2 Cor 3.6.
8. Gn 1.26.
9. Gn 3.19.
10. 1 Thes 4.17.

by this knowledge we completely obliterate the opposing power of falsehood which is opposed to the truth, putting to shame and casting down "every height and obstacle set up against the knowledge of God"[11] by the wicked spirits.

50.6. "Prayer" is the request for things that God is naturally disposed to give to human beings for their salvation. And this of course is very reasonable. For if a vow is the promise of good things offered by human beings to God, then it may be inferred that prayer is petition for good things provided from God to human beings for their salvation, being an exchange for the good disposition of those who offer the prayer.[12]

50.7. A "cry" is the progress and increase[13] of virtuous modes of practice and cognitive objects of contemplation when the wicked demons are rising up to attack. God naturally hears this cry no less than others, accepting instead of a loud voice the inner disposition of those who give heed to virtue and knowledge.

50.8. "Heaven" in holy Scripture often means God himself, just as the great preacher of truth John the Forerunner says: "No one can receive anything except what is given him from heaven,"[14] by which he means "from God," since "every good endowment and every perfect gift is from above, coming down from the Father of lights."[15] It is in this sense that we should understand the passage of Scripture cited in the heading of this chapter. At the same time, Scripture is also in the habit of calling the celestial powers "heaven," as in the passage: "Heaven is my throne,"[16] insofar as God rests among holy and incorporeal natures. And if someone should say that the human intellect, purged of every material image and adorned with the divine principles of intelligible realities, is "heaven," he would not, as it seems to me, place himself outside the truth. And again if someone were to call the height of intellective knowledge that can be reached by human beings "heaven," he would not miss

11. 2 Cor 10.5.
12. Part of this definition of prayer is cited in the *Doctrina patrum*, 257, lines 17–20.
13. On these two terms, cf. *Amb.* 70 (DOML 2:308–13).
14. Jn 3.27.
15. Jas 1.17.
16. Is 66.1.

the mark of what is proper. For true knowledge becomes like a heavenly throne for God,[6] receiving Him enthroned according to the immovable stability of its firm and lofty desire for the good. In the same way, the pure practice of the virtues is said to be God's "footstool," inasmuch as it receives upon itself the divine feet, in no way allowing them to be dirtied, as if from the earth, by the stains of the body.

50.9. Thus the name of King Hezekiah bears the outline of virtue, for in Greek his name means "sovereignty of God," and the sovereignty of God over the opposing powers is nothing other than virtue. The name of Ahaz, the father of Hezekiah, means "might," which a moment ago we said was the driving force of practice, which gives birth to the divine sovereignty of virtue; and the prophet Isaiah signifies the knowledge of lofty things (for Isaiah means the "height of God") since he himself manifests the height of divine knowledge, which is born from the toil required for the various contemplations of beings (for Amoz means "toil of the people," as was stated above). Insofar, then, that the significance of the names has such force of meaning, it is obvious that every philosophical and pious person, guarded about by virtue and knowledge, or by practice and contemplation, when he sees the wicked power rising up against him through the passions, like the king of Assyria rising up against Hezekiah, should realize that only with God's help can he repel such evils. And he propitiates God by crying out silently through his heightened pitch of virtue and knowledge; and he receives for an ally, or rather for his salvation, an "angel," which is obviously the higher principle of wisdom and knowledge, "destroying every mighty man and warrior and leader and captain in the camp[7] of King Ashur, and returning him with shame of face to his own land."[17]

50.10. The wicked and destructive kingdom of the devil—typified by the kingdom of the Assyrians—in waging war against those who pursue virtue and knowledge, endeavors to ruin the soul through its own natural power. It does this first by stimulating a desire and appetite for things contrary to nature, persuading the soul to prefer sensory objects over intelligible real-

---

17. 2 Chr 32.20–21.

ities. It subsequently excites the irascible element to fight with all its might to attain the sensory object of its desire. Finally it instructs reason to contrive ways of indulging in sensual pleasures, so that the powers of the soul come under the rule of sensory objects, that is, for the devil to appoint the law of the earth as the master of the soul's powers.

50.11. This is why Scripture gave the name of "mighty man" to the wicked demon who presides over desire, and who inflames it toward the unseemly appetites of shameful passions—and nothing is more powerful or violent than natural appetite. Scripture called the demon that presides over anger, and who causes it to fight unceasingly for pleasures, the "warrior." It gave the name of "leader" to the demon who dwells invisibly upon the surfaces of the senses, and who with every sensation deviously entices the appetite to himself. The text called this demon a "leader," because in every passion it naturally rules and leads the corresponding organ of sense perception, for without a <material> substrate[8] to attract the powers of the soul toward him by means of a sensation, no passion could ever come into existence. And it called a "captain" the demon that abuses the power of the rational part of the soul for the contrivance of evils and the invention of all the pursuits of evil.

50.12. The smoothness of pleasure is the "face" of the devil, through which he naturally rules over every soul that is drawn to him, and which prefers sensory objects that beguile the senses more than the contemplation of intelligible realities that enrich the intellect. This face is "shamed" by the person who through prayer has acquired from God the principle of wisdom that destroys every wicked power, that is, the principle that utterly obliterates the oppressive wicked tyranny harassing the soul. For Scripture says that it "destroyed" them—it does not say that they were merely incapacitated.[9] For the latter only brings to a halt the activity of impassioned actions, while the former utterly obliterates even the wicked movements of thought.

50.13. The "land" of King Ashur, by which I mean the place of the devil, the wicked originator of evil, is the firm and implacable state of evil and ignorance,[10] which is deprived of all the vital warmth of virtue and devoid of all the intellective light of knowledge. Only the devil "returns" to such a state, having tried and failed to move Jerusalem to his own state. Of course by "Jerusalem" I mean the soul that loves God and is free of all passion, which possesses in itself both the perfect principle of practice, which is Hezekiah, and an intellect illumined by knowledge, which is Isaiah, which propitiates God and through an angel obliterates the wicked power.

50.14. This at least is how I understand the passage, according to the best of my abilities. Whoever is able to understand these words in a loftier manner would bring joy both to himself and to me, setting forth the meaning of what has been written more richly than I have done. For I had said that the word of the divine Scripture is always unlimited, and whereas it limits all those who speak, it itself is not limited by the speakers in any way whatsoever, and thus even if I have said something that has hit the mark of truth, and even if such a thing were reckless on my part, I have nonetheless not encompassed all the meaning of the things that have been written, for this is infinitely beyond my capacity.[18]

Scholia

[1] That is, just as God in His essence cannot be the object of human knowledge, so too neither can His word be fully comprehended by us.

[2] Those who in a Jewish manner bind their minds solely to the letter, he says, interpret the promises of pure, good things in a worldly manner, being ignorant of what are the natural, good things of the soul.

[3] Whoever, he says, "wears the image of Him who is from heaven,"[19] hastens in all things to follow the spirit of holy Scripture, for it is in the spirit, through virtue and knowledge, that the soul finds the means to preserve itself. On the other hand, whoever "wears the image of him who is from earth" is preocccupied solely with the letter, in which one finds the sensory worship of the body, which produces the passions.

18. Cf. above, Intro. 1.2.8.
19. 1 Cor 15.49.

[4] Ascetic practice, he says, begets virtue, as Ahaz begot Hezekiah.

[5] Contemplation, he says, begets knowledge, as Amoz begot Isaiah.

[6] The person who combines knowledge with practice, he says, and conducts his practice with knowledge, is a throne and footstool of God:[20] a throne because of knowledge, and a footstool because of practice.

[7] The "camp" of King Ashur is the gathering of wicked thoughts, which gives strength to the one who moves the natural appetites to pleasure. A "warrior" is the thought that excites the irascible part of the soul to be protective of pleasures; a "leader" is the thought that arouses the senses through the surface appearances of visible phenomena; and a "captain" is a thought that gives forms to the passions and contrives the matter and modes for their activity.

[8] In the absence of a material object, he says, a passion cannot be constituted. For example, in the absence of a woman, there can be no unchastity; and if there is no food, there can be no gluttony; and if there is no gold, there can be no love of money. It follows that every impassioned stimulation of our natural powers is ruled by a sensible object, that is, by the demon who through the object incites the soul to sin.[21]

[9] To "incapacitate," he says, is to suppress the actualization of evil, while "destruction" obliterates even the very thought of it.

[10] Just as the north wind, he says, does not have the sun passing through it, neither does a wicked state of mind, in which the devil dwells, admit of the light of knowledge.

---

20. Cf. Is 66.1.
21. Cf. *Amb.* 10.8 (DOML 1:161).

QUESTION 51

"AND MANY brought offerings to Jerusalem for the Lord, and gifts to Hezekiah the king of Judah; and he was exalted in the eyes of all the nations."[1] What are these offerings, and what are these gifts? And why does God receive "offerings" while the king receives "gifts"? And what does it mean that "he was exalted in the eyes of all the nations"?

Response

51.2. Having granted existence to the entire visible creation, God did not leave it to be moved about solely by means of sense perception, but implanted, within each of the species comprising creation, spiritual principles of wisdom and modes of graceful conduct. His aim was not only that mute creations should loudly herald Him as their Creator, proclaimed by means of the principles of the things that came into being, but also that the human person, being tutored by the natural laws and ways of visible realities, should easily find the road of righteousness, which leads to Him.[2]

51.3. And this in fact was the sign of God's extreme goodness, namely, that He did not simply establish the divine and incorporeal essences of the intelligible hosts as images of divine glory—each one proportionately receiving, as much as is permitted, the inconceivable splendor of the unapproachable beauty—but He also intermingled even among sensory creatures, who are greatly inferior to the intelligible essences, resonances[3] of His own magnificence. These have the power to

---

1. 2 Chr 32.23.
2. Cf. above, Qu. 39, and below, Qu. 64 and 65.
3. ἀπήχημα (pl. ἀπηχήματα) is a term well attested in later Neoplatonism,

bear and convey the human intellect unerringly to God, so that it comes to reside beyond the whole of visible reality, planting its foot on the extremity of blessedness and on all the intermediaries[1] it left behind when it passed through them and so completed its journey. And not only this, but also so that none of those who "worship creation rather than the Creator"[4] would have ignorance as a ground for justifying himself,[2] hearing creation heralding its own Creator more clearly and distinctly than any other voice.

51.4. Clearly, then, the nature of visible realities naturally has spiritual principles of wisdom and modes of graceful conduct implanted within it by the Creator. When, like the great king Hezekiah, every intellect naturally crowned with virtue and knowledge attains to rule over Jerusalem,[5] that is, over the state in which one beholds only peace, which is a condition free of every passion—for Jerusalem means "vision of peace"— such an intellect, I say, has all creation at its command, by means of all the species of which it is comprised. Through the mediation of the intellect, creation brings to God, like offerings,[6] the spiritual principles of knowledge.[3] To the intellect, creation brings, like gifts, modes for the realization of virtue, which exist within creation, according to the natural

---

where it is a sonic or auditory metaphor for the doctrine of emanation and participation (normally described as a diffusion of light), and usually designates a faint or distant echo of its source; cf. Proclus, *Platonic Theology* (ed. Henri Dominique Saffrey and Leendert Gerritt Westerink [Paris: Belles Lettres, 1968], 1:124, line 18); idem, *Commentary on Plato's Timaeus* (ed. Ernst Diehl [Teubner, 1906; repr. 1965], 3:158). The term appears among Christian writers, such as Eusebios of Caesarea, *Commentary on the Psalms* (PG 23:1288A); but especially in Dionysios, who is undoubtedly the bridge from Proclus to Maximos; e.g., *DN* 4.4 (147, line 12; 697D); *DN* 4.20 (166, line 1; 720A); *DN* 4.20 (167, lines 4–5; 720C); *DN* 7.2 (195, lines 16–17; 868C); and *CH* 2.4 (15, line 4; 144C). For a related use of ἀπηχήματα, see Maximos, *QD*. 119 (CCSG 10:87, lines 18–21).

4. Rom 1.25.

5. Cf. 4 Kgs 18.1–2.

6. The role of the human person in the cosmic order has a strong liturgical and indeed Eucharistic character, highlighted by the language of "offering," which bears comparison with Byzantine liturgical texts. In the theology of St Maximos, this was the "priestly" role that Adam was called to perform, returning creation to God, but which he failed to do; cf. *Amb.* 41.2–10 (DOML 2:103–15).

law. Through both,[7] creation welcomes and receives the one who is able mightily to esteem both, I mean the philosophical mind perfected in the principle of contemplation and in a life of practice. Thus the word of Scripture establishes a distinction when it says that whereas "offerings" are brought to the Lord, "gifts" are brought to the king. According to the experts on these matters, this is because "offerings" are distinctively said to be things brought to those who have no need of them, while "gifts" are given to those in need. And this is perhaps also why it is the general custom that things brought to kings are called "offerings," with the idea that they do not stand in need of anything.

51.5. Now someone ambitious for distinction might say that this is why the things the Magi brought to the Lord (who out of His love for us had become like us) were called "offerings,"[8] and in saying this he would not at all miss the mark of truth.

51.6. It follows, then, that when we bring to the Lord the spiritual principles we have discerned in creation, we bring him "offerings," for by nature He has no need of any of these things.[9] For we do not bring the principles of beings to Him as if He were in need of them as others would be, but rather so that we might, on behalf of all His creatures, praise Him in song for all that He has given us. "Gifts," on the other hand, are received by the one who eagerly pursues divine philosophy, for by his nature he stands in need of modes for virtue and principles for knowledge.

51.7. We can also understand the "offerings" in another way. Insofar as an "offering" is also something given to those who have previously brought forward nothing, the intellect engaged with knowledge receives "offerings"[4] from the contemplation of beings, and brings them to the Lord. These offerings, which the intellect both receives and gives, are the sustaining principles of faith beyond rational demonstration; a faith to which no one has ever brought anything,[5] insofar as a person naturally beholds his own Creator, proclaimed to him by creation, with-

7. I.e., the offerings and the gifts.
8. Mt 2.11.
9. Cf. Ps 15.2.

out any of the technical contrivances of various arguments[10]— for what could one possibly bring forward that would be equal to faith,[6] as if his faith were due to his own efforts, and not an offering to him from God? The same intellect also receives the "gifts" of the natural laws of beings, to the extent that it imitates their modes of existence. In other words, before the intellect can receive such gifts, it must have first offered the labors of repentance, through which it first strips off the clothing of the "old man,"[11] after which it can go forth and gather the fruits of righteousness,[12] selecting from within beings those modes of existence created for the life of virtue, which the intellect would never be able even to approach without first producing much labor and sweat, and without forcing itself to strip itself of the old man, like a snake sloughing off its skin.[13] Thus it is only natural that the intellect engaged with knowledge receives from God the "offerings" of the principles of beings that sustain faith,[7] without previously bringing forward absolutely anything at all, for "who," it says, "has ever first given anything to God, so that recompense should be given to him?"[14] The intellect also receives "gifts" by imitating the natural modes of beings.[15]

51.8. What I mean is something like this: when the intellect engaged with knowledge[16] imitates the natural law[8] of heaven, it receives gifts, preserving within itself the perfectly even

---

10. See above, Qu. 5.2, where sustaining life "through artifice or through some other contrivance" is said to be characteristic of human life after the fall of Adam.

11. Eph 4.22.

12. Cf. Mt 3.8; Phil 1.11.

13. Cf. Ps.-Basil, *Commentary on Isaiah* 1.1: "'Be as wise as serpents' (Mt 10.6), inasmuch as they wisely and intelligently slough off the skin of old age. Whenever the serpent needs to do this, it puts itself into a tight place that closely binds its body and so drawing itself through, it casts off the skin of old age. And perhaps Scripture wishes us also to 'pass through a narrow and afflicted way' (Mt 7.14), so that we might 'put off the old man and put on the new one' (Col 3.9–10)" (PG 30:120B).

14. Rom 11.35.

15. "Imitation" in the deeper ontological sense of "participation."

16. I.e., νοῦς διαγνωστικός, which denotes the intellect's activity of observing and making distinctions in nature; cf. above, Qu. 48.16.

and unchanging movement of virtue and knowledge, a movement which holds in fixity, like so many stars, the bright and shining principles of created beings. Imitating, on the other hand, the natural law of the sun[9]—which changes its position in the sky from one place to another, relative to the needs of the world—the intellect receives, as another gift, the understanding of how to adapt itself wisely, as it should, to all that happens to it, without ever losing anything of its illuminating identity in virtue and knowledge.

51.9. From the eagle[10] it receives eyes to gaze directly at the vision of the divine brilliance of the eternal light, without the pupil of its intellective eye ever being damaged by the exceedingly shining ray.[17]

51.10. Imitating the deer,[11] the intellect climbs the mountains toward the heights of divine visions, and by means of the principle of discretion it destroys the passions nesting like venomous serpents in the nature of beings; and the venom of evil, which perchance had haunted the memory, it extinguishes by drinking from many and different sources of knowledge.[18]

51.11. It also imitates the sharp-sightedness of the gazelle,[12] and the caution of the bird, when like a gazelle it leaps over and escapes the snares of the demons who war against virtue;

17. This and the following five paragraphs find parallels in the popular late-antique Christian bestiary known as the *Physiologus;* cf. Dimitris Kaimakis, ed., *Der Physiologus nach der ersten Redaktion,* Beiträge zur klassichen Philologie 63 (Meisenheim am Glan: Anton Hein, 1974), 84–86 (deer); and 36 (serpent); cf. 116 (gazelle); and Francesco Sbordone, *Physiologus* (Milan: Dante Alighieri, 1936), 97–101, 170–74 (deer); 43–44, 251 (serpent); 115, 218–21, 284 (dove); 92–94, 215–18 (turtledove). Maximos's description of the eagle has a number of precise verbal parallels to a passage in Philo, *On Husbandry* 58 (LCL 3:243); see also the *scholion* to Dionysios, *CH* 15.8: "The eagle is a creature of penetrating vision, able to distinguish its legitimate offspring from the illegitimate. If its young are able to look into the sun without closing their eyes, they are legitimate; if not, they are cast out from the nest. So too anyone who is not able to look directly at the Sun of Righteousness is illegitimate in his knowledge of God" (PG 4:112D–113A).

18. Origen, *Commentary on the Song of Songs* 3.12, reports that deer attack snakes (GCS 8:201; the Greek fragment of which has been preserved by Procopius; cf. PG 87:1596C). One of Origen's contemporaries, Aelian, *On the Characteristics of Animals* 2.9 (LCL 1:99–101), reports that deer kill snakes by exhaling on them through their nostrils.

and when like a bird it flies over the traps of the spirits who battle against knowledge.[19]

51.12. Some say that when the bones of the lion[13] are struck together they produce fire. The intellect that loves God and is engaged with knowledge also imitates this natural quality of the lion. It does this when, in its search for the truth, it strikes together its pious thoughts, as if they were bones, thereby igniting the fire of knowledge.[20]

51.13. "Be wise like the serpent[14] and gentle as a dove,"[21] in all things guarding the unbruised faith, as the serpent guards its head; and wisely remove all the bitterness from the incensive part of the soul, after the example of the dove, which bears no resentment against those who endeavor to afflict and harm it.[22]

51.14. From the turtledove[15] the intellect receives as a gift the imitation of chastity, transforming all the natural instincts of the body into acts freely chosen and intended.

51.15. In this way, then, according to each principle and mode of nature, the philosophically advanced intellect approaches the unfolding of created beings with knowledge. Insofar as it is engaged with knowledge, it receives as gifts the spiritual principles of beings offered to it by creation; insofar as it is engaged with practice, it receives as offerings the natural laws[16] of beings by imitating their manner of existence, revealing in itself, and through its whole life, the magnificence of the divine wisdom invisibly contained in created beings.[23]

51.16. And if someone should say that this line of argument implies that "offerings" should be given to God in order to manifest the infinite nature of divine goodness, since it brings

---

19. Cf. Prv 6.4–5; and Gregory of Nyssa, *Homilies on the Song of Songs* 5: "The gazelle signifies sharp-sightedness" (GNO 6:141).

20. The legend of the lion's bones appears in Aelian, *On the Characteristics of Animals* 4.34 (LCL 4:249); in a fragment from a contemporary work by Clement of Alexandria, *On Pascha,* preserved in the *Sacra Parallela* (GNO 17:217, fr. 32); and in a fragment from Origen, *Homilies on Jeremiah,* fr. 3 (GCS 6:200, lines 5–6).

21. Mt 10.16.

22. Cf. *Amb.* 56.2 (DOML 2:251); and Origen, *Homilies on Luke* 27.5, who describes the "meekness" of the dove (SC 87:348, lines 18–21).

23. Wis 13.7–8; cf. Rom 1.20.

nothing in advance yet accepts our offerings as gifts, reckoning the whole of what is given to be ours, such a person would not be outside of what is proper, for he has shown that God's goodness to us is great and ineffable, accepting the things that we offer to Him as ours when in fact they are His, and acknowledging His indebtedness to those things as if they were not His own, but rather the offerings of others.

51.17. "And Hezekiah was exalted," it says, "in the eyes of all the nations." Anyone who through ascetic practice and contemplation has attained the highest summit of virtue and knowledge after the manner of Hezekiah is, by his practice, naturally "exalted in the eyes of all the nations," by which I mean the carnal and blameworthy passions, being exalted over them as well as what are called natural bodies.[17] More generally, to express myself briefly, the same person, by means of knowledge and contemplation, will have passed through all the principles that exist within sensory forms, which themselves are figuratively called "nations" by Scripture, since they are, we might say, by their very nature of a different race and tribe than the soul and the intellect. And insofar as they do not fight against the intellect, God has commanded us never to fight against them.[18]

51.18. For we have not been commanded to fight against the sense-perceptible creations that are outside of us, but rather to wage perpetual war within ourselves against the "dishonorable passions"[24] that are contrary to nature, which reside in the earth of our hearts, until such time as we eradicate them and take possession of our own earth, which will remain unshakeable after the overthrow of the passions, which are foreign and hostile to us.[25] This is the reason why Scripture is very careful in the way it describes the bringing of the offerings to God and the gifts to the king, for it did not simply say that "everyone" brought offerings to God and gifts to the king, but "many," which means not all the nations, but many nations. From this it is clear that there are nations from which nothing is offered to God or given to the king. It stands to reason that only those creatures which complete the nature of beings bring as offerings to God their

24. Rom 1.26.
25. Cf. *Carit.* 3.40 (ed. Ceresa-Gastaldo, 162).

more divine inner principles, and as gifts to the king their own proper natural laws, because it was for Him that they were given existence, and it is in accordance with them that the human intellect is ordered and arranged and constitutes the modes of virtue. These nations indeed give something to God and the king, but not the nations that exist within us—which were not created by God—by which I mean the passions, which have only a dependent, parasitical subsistence,[26] and offer nothing either to God or human beings, because the dishonorable passions did not have their genesis from God.[27] To the contrary, the dishonorable passions arose within us when we transgressed the divine commandment, and from them no one is able to offer anything to God, for they are utterly devoid of the principle of wisdom or knowledge, having appeared parasitically alongside our lives after the loss of wisdom and knowledge.

51.19. With respect to the words: "Hezekiah the king was exalted in the eyes of all the nations," Scripture specifically stated: "all the nations," making clear that, whoever chooses to live in the condition of dispassion, as if it were Jerusalem, by means of his labors in the practical life—and who is free of all the disturbances of sin in all that he does and says and hears and thinks—is filled with peace, having received through natural contemplation the nature of visible realities. Through him nature will bring forward to the Lord, as if they were offerings, nature's own divine principles. And nature will bring like gifts to the king the laws that exist within itself, and the king will be exalted in the eyes of all the nations;[19] that is, he will rise above all the passions of the flesh through practice, and through contemplation will pass through and beyond all the spiritual principles and modes contained within natural bodies and all sense-perceptible forms. This is how I understand the meaning of "many brought," but not all, that is, the nations that

26. I.e., παρυπόστασις.
27. Cf. Dionysios the Areopagite, *DN* 4.31: "Thus evil has no subsistence (*hypostasis*), but a parasitical subsistence (*parhypostasis*), since it comes into being not of itself but in relation to the Good" (176–77; 732C); above, Intro., 1.2.11; and A. C. Lloyd, "Parhypostasis in Proclus," in *Proclus et son influence. Actes du colloque de Neuchâtel*, ed. Gilbert Boss and Gerhard Seel (Zurich: Grand Midi, 1987), 145–57.

are outside of us, by which I mean creatures, but not the ones within us, by which I mean the passions. For all the creations that fill the world sing hymns of praise to God and glorify Him in words of eloquent silence.[28] And their hymn becomes ours, "since it is from them that I take my hymn of praise," says Gregory, who bears the name of Theologian.[29]

51.20. It should be clear, then, that holy Scripture, as has been demonstrated, has shown forth its intention to all who desire salvation, and has not in any way restricted its message to one person alone. For each and every person can become another Hezekiah by imitating Hezekiah according to the spirit. Through prayer he can cry out to God and be heard, and receive an angel, I mean the principle of greater wisdom and knowledge, when he is under attack from wicked demons. And he will "destroy every mighty man and warrior and leader and captain,"[30] that is, the impassioned movements of anger and desire, and the passionate attachment to sensation, and the evil thought that, like a captain, devises strategies for sinning. Then to enter into a state of peace through freedom from the passions, and to find rest in the contemplation of beings, and receive the principles that preserve knowledge, as if they were offerings, and the modes constitutive of virtue, as if they were gifts, which will be brought to him from all creation, as much for the glory of God as for his own spiritual progress. And after all of this, he will be exalted, as is only right, in the eyes of all the nations; that is, he will find himself above all the passions because of his virtue, and above all creation because of his knowledge, and by means of his humility of mind he will guard the grace of salvation, and nothing of what Scripture subsequently recounts shall befall him.[31]

---

28. Cf. Ps 18.1–5.
29. Gregory Nazianzus, *Or.* 44: "All creation sings the glory of God in wordless strain, for it is through me that God is thanked for all his works. In this way their hymn becomes our own, since it is from them that I take my song" (PG 36:620B); trans. Martha Vinson, *St. Gregory of Nazianzus, Select Orations,* The Fathers of the Church 107 (Washington, DC: The Catholic University of America Press, 2003), 238. Maximos had earlier commented on this oration in *Amb.* 61–64 (DOML 2:267–75).
30. 2 Chr 32.21.
31. Cf. below, Qu. 52.1.

Scholia

[1] Sensible and intelligible realities are the intermediaries between God and human beings. In its progress toward God, the human intellect comes to find itself far above these realities, for ascetic practice frees it from subservience to the former, while contemplation frees it from any hindrance by the latter.

[2] Creation, he says, is the accuser of the impious, for through its inner principles it proclaims its own Creator, and through the natural laws, manifested in each individual species, it tutors us in the life of virtue. On the one hand, the principles are recognized by the cohesion and abiding stability manifested in species, while the laws are made visible through the identity of natural activity in each species. If we do not approach the principles and laws of nature through the intellective power that is within us, we remain ignorant of the Cause of created beings, and come under the control of all the passions that are contrary to nature.

[3] The person who understands the spiritual principles of visible realities is taught that such realities have a creator, but he leaves unexamined the concept of who or what God is, for this is beyond his ability to comprehend. For when creation is looked at with wisdom, it provides us with the understanding that there *is* a creator, but not who or what He is. This is why Scripture gave the name of "offerings" to the inner principles of visible realities, for they herald God's rule over all things; and to the natural laws of these realities it gave the name of "gifts," by means of which the particular species of each being is recognized, thereby teaching man not to corrupt the natural law by a law that is foreign to it.

[4] It was as an offering, he says, that we received faith in God, and such faith is unmediated knowledge firmly established around God, the true knowledge that is not susceptible of rational demonstration, for faith is "the substance of things hoped for,"[32] and none of these things has yet to be comprehended by knowledge.[33]

32. Heb 11.1.
33. Cf. 1 Cor 2.9.

[5] Faith is brought forward before virtue, he says, and virtue before knowledge, but before faith absolutely nothing can be brought forward. For faith is the beginning of good things among human beings, before which we have nothing to offer.

[6] Nothing, he says, is equal to faith.

[7] The intellect engaged with knowledge receives, he says, the principles of beings as advocates for its faith in God, but not as the producers of that faith. This is because the principles of beings are not the origin of faith, for in that case the object of one's faith would be something circumscribed. For if the origin of a thing can be demonstrated by means of knowledge, then the thing itself is by nature limited and subject to mental comprehension.

[8] To be borne about perpetually in a circle is the law of heaven, from which the person of knowledge deduces the principle for his fixed movement in the good, imitating the ever-moving motion of heaven in his movement around the identity of virtue.

[9] The natural law of the sun is to bring about the changes of seasons through its movement from place to place, from which the person of knowledge learns the principle of adapting to different circumstances, using reason to preserve the brightness of virtue pure from anything that takes place against our will.

[10] The natural law of the eagle is to receive the ray of the sun projected directly into its eyes, from which the person of knowledge allows his intellect to be illumined freely and unceasingly by the divine light.

[11] What does the person of knowledge learn from the natural law of the deer, examining the nature of beings?

[12] What does the person who through practice is advancing on the way of knowledge learn by imitating the gazelle and the bird, keeping its virtue unassailable?

[13] What good thing is learned by the philosopher of divine things, freely and with reason transposing to himself the natural contemplation of the lion?

[14] How one must become a philosopher by imitating the serpent and the dove.

[15] How one is able to derive benefit even from the dove.

[16] Whoever conforms the law of beings to his own law by imitating them becomes virtuous, for he endows with reason the movement of beings devoid of reason. But whoever conforms his own law to other laws by imitating them becomes impassioned, misdirecting the power of reason to irrationality.

[17] He calls "natural bodies" all things that are subject to generation and corruption.

[18] It is an excellent observation that we are not to fight against creation, which has been created by God, but to the contrary we must fight against the disordered and unnatural movements and activities of the powers within us that are part of our essence.

[19] Practical philosophy, he says, places the practitioner above the passions, but contemplation establishes the person of knowledge above visible realities, elevating the intellect to kindred intelligible realities.

QUESTION 52

"EZEKIAH did not make recompense to God according to the benefit that God gave to him, but he was exalted in his heart; and wrath came upon him and upon Judah and Jerusalem. And Hezekiah humbled himself after the exaltation of his heart, as did the dwellers in Jerusalem; and the wrath of the Lord did not come upon them in the days of Hezekiah."[1] What is this "recompense," and what is the meaning of the things that follow?

Response

52.2. After all the many and various benefits that God granted to Hezekiah, through which He saved him and delivered him from every constraint and difficulty, Hezekiah did not ascribe—as he should have—all the grace of his salvation to God. Instead, a certain human fault came upon him, like a kind of blemish, and he ascribed all the power of his accomplishments to himself.[2] This, it seems to me, is how Hezekiah "did not make recompense to God according to the benefit that God gave to him."[3] That is, he did not express his gratitude and thanksgiving in proportion to the magnitude of the divine accomplishments wrought on his behalf, but to the contrary became "exalted in his heart," falling sick with "swollen conceit"[4] on account of his virtue and knowledge.[5]

---

1. 2 Chr 32.25–26.
2. Larchet suggests that the "blemish" in question is original sin (SC 554:164, n. 1).
3. 2 Chr 32.25.
4. I.e., τῆς φυσιούσης οἰήσεως, an assonant, onomatopoetic phrase borrowed from Gregory Nazianzus, *Or.* 32 (SC 318:112, lines 21–22).
5. Cf. 1 Cor 8.1.

52.3. "And the wrath of God came upon him and upon Judah and Jerusalem." According to one interpretation, the "wrath of God" is the painful sensation experienced by those being chastised and corrected.[6] To be sure, the onslaught of involuntary sufferings is certainly a painful sensation, and it is through such sufferings that God curbs and humbles the intellect that has become conceited about its virtue and knowledge, providing it with the opportunity to become conscious of itself and aware of its weakness, in the hope that it will set aside the vain conceit of the heart. This is why it says that, after the "wrath came upon him," Hezekiah "humbled himself after the exaltation of his heart, as did the dwellers in Jerusalem; and the wrath of the Lord did not come upon them in the days of Hezekiah."

52.4. Or, again, the "wrath" of the Lord is the suspension[7] of the provision of divine gifts, which comes about for the benefit of every intellect that is exalted and lofty and which boasts of the good things it has received from God as if they were its own achievements. And it is worth pausing here to consider why the wrath of God did not come only upon Hezekiah, who was exalted in his heart, but also upon Judah and Jerusalem. Moreover, this same passage should also convince those preoccupied solely with the letter of Scripture that lovers of divine things must zealously expend all their efforts on the spiritual contemplation of the text—if indeed the word of truth is more precious to them than all things. For if we follow only the letter, we will naturally condemn God's judgment as being exceedingly unjust, inasmuch as it unjustly punishes together with the sinner those who did not sin at all. And how then would the word be true, which says: "A father shall not be put to death on account of his son, nor shall a son be put to death on account of his father, but each one shall die on account of his own sin";[8] and: "The soul that sins shall die, but the son shall not bear the iniquity of the father";[9] and: "You will recompense everyone

---

6. Cf. Basil, *That God is Not the Author of Evil* (PG 31:333A); and John of Damascus, *Against the Manicheans* 15 (ed. Kotter, 4:360, line 13).
7. I.e., divine "abandonment," as will become clear below, in Qu. 52.6.
8. Cf. Dt 24.16.
9. Ezek 18.20.

according to his works,"[10] words which David spoke to God?

52.5. For while the text says that Hezekiah was "exalted in his heart," it does not say that the hearts of those who dwelt in Jerusalem and Judea were likewise exalted. I am therefore at a loss to understand how those who adhere solely to the letter are able to explain why the innocent were punished with the guilty. For while it says: "Hezekiah was exalted in his heart; and wrath came upon him and upon Judah and Jerusalem," Scripture does not say that the latter were similarly "exalted." Since, then, those who adhere to the letter, and who prefer letters and words over their meanings, are completely incapable of resolving these difficulties, let us proceed to the spiritual understanding of what has been written, and we will easily discover the truth, concealed by the letter, already shining forth like light upon those who love the truth.

52.6. Accordingly, every intellect engaged with knowledge and philosophy possesses both a Judah and a Jerusalem. It possesses Judah understood spiritually as the mode of confession, that is, the state of repentance—together with the thoughts that maintain this state, which increases through ascetic practice and advances the ascent of the intellect—for Judah means "confession."[11] It possesses Jerusalem understood allegorically as the peaceful state of dispassion together with the divine contemplations that complete it. To state the matter concisely, the intellect engaged with knowledge possesses Judea as practical philosophy, and Jerusalem as contemplative mystagogy. From this it follows that, by means of divine grace and through practical and contemplative philosophy, the God-loving intellect drives away from itself every power opposed to virtue and knowledge. When it does this, it receives the crown of sovereign power for its perfect victory over the spirits of wickedness. If, however, it does not recompense God with the necessary gratitude (for God is the author of its victory), but to the contrary is exalted in its heart (believing itself to be the author of all its

10. Ps 61.12.
11. Cf. Lagarde, *Onomastica Sacra*, 193: "Judah means 'what has been confessed.'" Maximos offers an additional interpretation of Judah in his *Exp. Ps. 59* (CCSG 23:15, line 220).

accomplishments), then, insofar as it did not recompense God according to what God returned to him, not only does the intellect itself experience the wrath of God's abandonment, but so do Judah and Jerusalem, that is, the states of practice and contemplation. For with God's permission, the "dishonorable passions"[12] rise up in revolt against its life of ascetic practice,[1] defiling the conscience which until then had been pure, while false thoughts insinuate themselves into its contemplation of beings, distorting the opinion of knowledge which until then had been correct.

52.7. This happens because God in His providence has implanted a divine rule and law within created beings.[2] This law disciplines and educates the soul by means of contrary events and circumstances, aiming to introduce a feeling of gratitude in those who are manifestly ungrateful for the blessings they have received, inasmuch as the experience of reversals and adversities enlightens us with the knowledge of the divine power that is the source of all that is good in our lives. Otherwise, if divine Providence allowed us to hold an unrelievedly conceited opinion about our supposed achievements, we would slip and fall into a prideful disposition opposed to God, thinking that the virtue and knowledge we acquired by grace were ours by nature. Moreover, we would be found to be misusing the good for the creation of evil, and, by means of the very things that should have established divine knowledge all the more securely[13] and immovably within us, we would fall, as we should not, into the disease of ignorance.

52.8. For whoever is so conceited as to think that he has reached[3] the height of virtue by his own efforts will in no way be moved to seek the primal Cause of good things, for he has ascribed the power of desire to himself alone, and thereby undermined, by his own hands, the very premise of his salvation, by which I mean God. On the other hand, whosoever is

---

12. Rom 1.26.

13. I.e., διασφιγχθεῖσαν, which is rare in this form; cf. Gregory of Nyssa, *Homilies on the Song of Songs* 15: "They would all become one as the Apostle says, having been securely bound (διασφιγχθέντας) in the 'bond of peace' (Eph 4.3)" (GNO 6:466).

conscious of his natural deficiency concerning all that is good, does not cease to run with headlong speed to the one who is able to give him the fulfillment of what he lacks.

52.9. Wrath therefore comes justly upon the arrogant intellect, and this wrath is abandonment by God, that is, divine permission for the intellect to be troubled by demons, both on the level of its practice (as Judea) and contemplation (as Jerusalem), so that from the former it might become conscious of its own natural weakness, and from the latter acquire knowledge of divine power and grace, which shields it and accomplishes every good thing. But this happens also so that the intellect might be humbled, utterly discarding its alien and unnatural "exaltation," so that the other form of wrath does not come upon it, namely, the privation of the gifts of grace previously given.[14] This second wrath did not come upon Hezekiah, because immediately after the first wrath that came upon him, that is, his abandonment by God, he was humbled and recognized who it was that had granted him good things. For this is the meaning of the words: "And wrath came upon him and upon Judah and Jerusalem. And Hezekiah humbled himself after the exaltation of his heart, he and the dwellers in Jerusalem; and the wrath of the Lord did not come upon them in the days of Hezekiah." In other words, the second wrath did not come upon them, which is the privation of the gifts of grace, because the first wrath of abandonment had taught them gratitude. For whoever is not chastened by the first form of wrath, namely, abandonment, and is not humbled, inevitably brings upon himself the second wrath, which deprives him of the operation of God's grace and leaves him destitute of the power that until then had protected him. This is why God says of ungrateful Israel: "I will take away the hedge that is around it, and it shall be devoured; and

---

14. Cf. Evagrios, *Gnostikos* 28: "Remember the five causes of abandonment so that you can raise up again the weak souls brought down by this affliction. In fact, abandonment reveals hidden virtue. When virtue has been neglected, it is reestablished through chastisement.... Indeed, the one who has had an experience of evil, hates it; for experience is the fruit of abandonment, and such abandonment is the offspring of dispassion" (SC 356:134–35); and Jeremy Driscoll, "Evagrius and Paphnutius on the Causes for Abandonment by God," *Studia Monastica* 39 (1997): 259–86.

I will pull down its wall, and it will be trampled upon; and I will forsake my vineyard, and it shall not be pruned or hoed, and thorns shall come up upon it as on barren land; and I will command the clouds to rain no rain upon it,"[15] just as it is said to have befallen Saul, the first king of Israel. For by means of the unction he received at once his kingship and the grace of prophecy, but because he did not keep them, he was subjected to the first wrath, which came in the form of the attack by the wicked spirit.[16] And because he came to awareness of this, the second wrath[4] was kept in store for him, for shortly before his death he fell into ignorance and was stripped naked of all piety in God. And he reveals this by all the things he suffered, first when the demon made him his instrument, and afterwards when through the ventriloquist he willingly defiled himself with demons, and because through the godless demons themselves he conducted the rite of divination.[17]

52.10. Since we understand Hezekiah to be the intellect engaged in philosophy, Judea as ascetic practice, and Jerusalem as contemplation, it follows that when we perceive that the intellect has suffered a change of any kind, we must surely believe that its capacities for ascetic practice and contemplation have also suffered a change along with it, in particular on the level of their respective constitutive principles, because it is not possible for a substrate to suffer something without the qualities in the substrate suffering along with it.[5]

52.11. As you can see, the principle of contemplation accords rather well with the literal meaning of Scripture, laying no blame on the divine judgment and sentence, nor contradicting or overturning any other commandment. For on the level of contemplation it is only Hezekiah, that is, the intellect, which is arrogant and exalted because of its accomplishments, whereas Judea and Jerusalem, that is, ascetic practice and contemplation, are not said to be exalted together with him, for they are not of a nature to suffer such a change, since in themselves they are not understood to have independent self-subsistence. Yet

---

15. Is 5.5–6.
16. Cf. 1 Kgs 16.14.
17. 1 Kgs 16.14, 18; 28.1–19.

the wrath does not come solely upon Hezekiah, that is, the intellect, but also upon Judah and Jerusalem, for when the intellect is defiled with respect to something, its ascetic practice and contemplation are unavoidably sullied together with it, even if they were not responsible for the cause of the wrath.

52.12. Let us, then, also accept the inner meaning of what has been written. For even if "these things took place among them in figures," according to the literal account, they were nonetheless "written down for our spiritual instruction,"[18] since it is among us that the written words of Scripture are forever taking place; it is among us that the opposing power invisibly launches his attacks. As much as we can, then, let us transpose the entire Scripture to the level of the intellect, so that we might illumine the intellect through divine meanings, while making the body bright with the modes of the more divine principles that we have understood, making it a "rational workshop of virtue"[19] by rejecting those passions that are inherent within us by nature.[6]

52.13. From this it follows that, if any virtuous and God-pleasing person, having his mind girded with sovereign power against the demons, should come under attack by wicked spirits—who seek to wage invisible war against the intellect—and if through prayer he should receive the angel whom God sends to him (by which I mean the higher principle of wisdom), and should scatter and destroy the whole army of the devil, but does not ascribe the cause of his victory and salvation to God, but entirely to himself, such a person has not "made recompense to God for the benefit that God gave him." For he has not measured his gratitude in proportion to the magnitude of his salvation, nor matched his disposition to the benefaction of his savior—because a "recompense" is the proportional response and disposition, measured out in actual deeds, of the one who was saved to his savior. And not only this, but he becomes "exalted in his heart" and boasts about the gifts he received as if he had not received them from God.[20] Such a person, I say, finds wrath just-

---

18. 1 Cor 10.11.
19. A phrase from Gregory Nazianzus, *Or.* 43.12 (SC 384:140, line 8).
20. Cf. 1 Cor 4.7.

ly coming upon him,[7] inasmuch as God permits the devil to engage him in invisible combat, to shake to its foundations the virtuous quality of his ascetic practice, and to obscure the luminous principles of knowledge at the time of his contemplation. This is to make him recognize his weakness and become conscious of the only power that can overthrow the passions that are within us. If this happens, he may repent and be brought to a state of humility, discarding the load of his conceit, and propitiate God to avert the wrath that comes upon those who do not repent, and which deprives the soul of the grace that protects it, and leaves the ungrateful intellect destitute and barren.

52.14. By "the days of Hezekiah," Scripture is perhaps referring to the different illuminations received by every intellect that is pious and loves God, as it applies itself to the contemplation of created beings in order to understand the wisdom they proclaim through all things and in various ways. To the extent that ascetic practice and contemplation unfold in accordance with these witnesses,[8] they will not be deprived of virtue and knowledge, because within such an intellect the "sun of righteousness,"[21] through its own proper appearance, brings such days into being.[9]

Scholia

[1] Dishonorable passions will overtake any person who becomes conceited because of his works, while divine judgment will permit the one who becomes puffed up because of his knowledge to err with respect to true contemplation.

[2] Here he calls the Providence that holds beings together a "rule" and "law" existing within beings. With just judgment, Providence withholds good things as a way to teach gratitude to those who, having an abundance of good things, are manifestly ungrateful to God, who provides them and who by means of opposite things leads them to awareness and knowledge of the giver of these good things. This is because conceit based on virtue, if it remains uneducated, is of a nature to spawn the disease of pride, which brings with it a disposition opposed to God.

21. Mal 3.20.

[3] Anyone, he says, who has recognized his ignorance and insufficiency with respect to virtue, never ceases to direct his course toward virtue, so that he might not be deprived of virtue's beginning and end, which is God, by confining the movement of desire to himself. For by wrongly supposing that he had achieved perfection, he forfeits true being, toward which every diligent person strives.

[4] The way that leads headlong to impiety, he says, is insensitivity regarding the loss of the virtues. For whoever has accustomed himself to disobey God for the sake of indulging his carnal pleasures will, when the occasion arises, deny God, and he will choose carnal life over God Himself, for he places greater value on sensual pleasures than on the will of God.

[5] Here he calls the intellect a "substrate," insofar as it has the ability to receive virtue and knowledge, although practice and contemplation are also found in the substrate, to which they have the relation of accidents. Thus in every way they suffer change together with any change in the substrate, for any movement in the substrate is the principle and beginning of their alteration.

[6] If the naturally innate passions are governed by reason, they are not subject to condemnation. If, however, they operate apart from reason, they are subject to condemnation. It is these latter, he says, that we must reject, since while their movement itself is certainly something inherent within nature, the uses to which this movement is put are often contrary to nature, because they are not governed by reason.

[7] When God allows the arrogant intellect to be embattled by demons through its passions, it is intended as a means of salvation. By suffering the attacks of the dishonorable passions for having boasted of its virtues, it can learn who is the true giver of these virtues. Otherwise, it will be stripped of those things that are not its own, even though it regarded them as such, forgetting that it had received them as a gift.

[8] According to the principle of anagogy he calls Judea and Jerusalem ascetic practice and contemplation.

[9] The "sun of righteousness" is Jesus Christ, who is the Lord and God and Savior of all.

QUESTION 53

AGAIN concerning Hezekiah, Scripture says: "And they buried him on a high place of the tombs of the sons of David, and all Judah and the dwellers in Jerusalem gave him glory and honor at his death."[1] What is the meaning of "on a high place of the tombs of the sons of David," and of the things said after this?

Response

53.2. The spiritual David is our Lord Jesus Christ, for he is the "stone" that set at naught the "builders who rejected it"—the "builders" being the priests and rulers of the Jews—yet He "became the head of the corner," which is the Church.[2] According to Scripture, the Church is a "corner," because just as a corner is the union of two walls, binding the two tightly together in an indissoluble cohesion, so too is the holy Church the union of two peoples, binding together Gentiles and Jews according to a single principle of faith, joining them in a vital unanimity, the "chief and head cornerstone" of which is Christ, the "head of the whole body."[3] For David's name means "setting at naught," and "being held in contempt," which signifies the Word of God, who for my sake clothed Himself in the "form of a slave,"[4] and became a "reproach among men" who do not believe in the truth, and a "scorn among a people" filled with sins.[5] Yet He is the "good shepherd who laid down

---

1. 2 Chr 32.33.
2. Mt 21.42; cf. Ps 117.22.
3. Cf. Col 1.18. On the notion of the "corner," see above, Qu. 48.3.
4. Phil 2.7.
5. Cf. Ps 21.6.

his life for the sheep,"[6] and slew the "lion and the bear,"[7] by which I mean He separated anger and desire from our nature, for like wild animals they were tearing to pieces the rational form of the divine likeness. And He is "ruddy in appearance," suffering death "with the beauty of His eyes,"[8] that is, with the glory of the loftier principles of providence and judgment, for the "eyes" of the Word are judgment and providence, through which, even in His suffering for us, He conducts His universal oversight.[9] It was He who slew the invisible and arrogant Goliath, by which I mean the devil, who "stands at a height of five cubits,"[10] owing to the impassioned condition of our five senses,[1] for the devil's magnitude of evil extends to the same degree that our power of sensation passionately extends itself to sensory objects. It is He who is the king of the true Israel, which sees God,[11] even if Saul, who signifies the people of the old law, rages with envy and wastes away in disbelief, for he cannot endure being deprived of his fleeting glory. And it is David, my king, even though He is being pursued by Saul, who "removes from him[12] the spear and pitcher of water,"[13] that is, the power of practical virtue and the grace of cognitive contemplation[2] (even if He later "lends and gives them"[14] to those who approach Him in faith, for the sake of those Jews who will inherit salvation by embracing the proclamation of the kingdom). And it is this same Saul, "sitting in the cave and dropping his excrements," from whom the spiritual David "removes the extremity of his double garment,"[15] that is, the height of the refinement of ethical philosophy, or the higher concepts from

6. Jn 10.11.
7. 1 Kgs 17.36.
8. 1 Kgs 16.12.
9. On "providence and judgment," see below, Qu. 63.17. For an iconographic reading of the "eyes of the Word," see Maximos Constas, *The Art of Seeing: Paradox and Perception in Orthodox Iconography* (Alhambra, CA: Sebastian Press, 2014), 37–86.
10. Cf. 1 Kgs 17.4.
11. Cf. above, Qu. 23.2.
12. I.e., Saul.
13. 1 Kgs 26.12.
14. Cf. 1 Kgs 26.22.
15. 1 Kgs 24.4–5.

the symbolic and riddling veils of the law. For the Word did not deem it worthy or just that the Jewish people—sitting in the cave of the present age, in the darkness of the letter of the law,[3] which is "bound for corruption through its use,"[16] and who cling to the earth and love the body, and who reduced the divine promises of incorruptible realities to the corruption of transient things—should have, as if it were a "double garment," the intelligible beauty of the mystical veils that covered the prescriptions of the law.

53.3. Thus it is Christ who is the spiritual David, the true shepherd and king,[4] and the destroyer of the opposing powers. He is the shepherd of those who are still engaged with practical philosophy, and who feed on the herbage of natural contemplation. He is the king of those who by means of spiritual laws and principles have restored the beauty of the image they had received[17] by reorienting it toward the archetype, and who in their intellect stand immediately in the presence of the very King of the ages, and they reflect, as if in a mirror—if one may be permitted to put it this way—His unapproachable beauty.[18]

53.4. The "sons" of this David are all the saints who have existed from the beginning of time, having been born from Him in spirit. Their "tombs" are the memorials of their godly conduct on this earth. The "high place" of such tombs is the height of their knowledge and love of God, where "all Judah and the dwellers of Jerusalem" bury them with honors. In other words, the modes of ascetic practice[5] and the principles of knowledge, which "dwell" in true contemplation, establish[19] the

---

16. Col 2.22.
17. Cf. Gn 1.27.
18. Cf. 2 Cor 3.18. See above, Qu. 46; and *Amb.* 10.41: "Having been wholly united with the whole Word ... they [i.e., the saints] were imbued with His own qualities, so that, like the clearest of mirrors, they are now visible only as reflections of the undiminished form of God the Word, who gazes out from within them" (DOML 1:213). On the "purified intellect" as a "mirror" reflecting God, cf. Philo, *Rules of Allegory* 3.101 (LCL 1:368); idem, *On the Migration of Abraham* 190 (LCL 4:242); Athanasios, *Against the Pagan Greeks* 34 (SC 18bis:164, lines 19–24); and Gregory of Nyssa, *On the Beatitudes* 6 (GNO 3/4:143–44).
19. I.e., ἐνιδρύοντες.

intellect in a place of blessed abiding[20] according to its worthiness, for in a praiseworthy manner it has died to all beings: to sensory beings by the setting aside of its sensory activity, and to intelligible beings by the cessation of its intellective motion.

53.5. Hezekiah's name is interpreted as "sovereignty of God," and he signifies the intellect strong in ascetic practice and brilliant with respect to knowledge. When such an intellect "dies,"[6] that is, when it distances the inclination of its will from all beings, and draws near to realities that transcend beings, it is buried by "all Judah and the dwellers in Jerusalem," which are obviously the intellect's virtuous practice and its true contemplation in knowledge. And they bury it "on a high place of the tombs of the sons of David," namely, on the height of the memory of all the saints who have ever lived, giving it glory and honor. They give it glory,[7] inasmuch as it rose above all things in its intellective knowledge of the principles contained in beings, and honor inasmuch as it was purified of all the passions, and kept its sensory activity guiltless in relation to the natural laws in beings.

53.6. Now perhaps a great lover of beauty, impelled by no small love of honor, might say that "glory"[8] is the utmost degree of beauty of the "divine image" within man, while "honor" is the unvarying imitation of the "divine likeness."[21] The former is naturally produced by the contemplation of spiritual principles, while the latter is produced by the exact and unadulterated practice of the commandments. Because the great Hezekiah possessed both of these, he was "buried on a high place of the tombs of the sons of David"—as if someone, wishing to state the matter more clearly, were to say, instead of, "they buried him on a high place of the tombs of the sons of David," they "established the memory of Hezekiah on the height of the memory of all the saints who have ever lived."

53.7. But let us consider why Scripture did not say "in the tombs of David," or "on the high place of the tombs of David." This is because the Word cannot be compared to beings, and not simply to human beings, but to angels. For if even the human words spoken by the Lord as man, as well as His mode of

---

20. I.e., μονή, on which, cf. *Amb.* 7.1 (DOML 1:77).
21. Cf. Gn 1.27.

life on earth, are absolutely beyond comprehension, how much more so, then, the inaccessible idea of his infinite divinity? Indeed anyone conscious of the grandeur of it would desire to be buried even in the tombs of the sons of David, but Scripture says nothing about anyone being buried in the tombs of David, to say nothing of "on a high place" of the tombs of David.[9] This is because the life of our Lord, God, and Savior, which He lived according to the flesh, was in all ways, and with respect to His every word and deed, as I said, beyond comparison. Scripture says, for example, that "His virtue covered the heavens,"[22] which is to say that even the human righteousness of the incarnate Lord covered even the higher powers of heaven, through the excess of His preeminent righteousness in all things. For he was not a mere man, but rather God who became man, in order to renew human nature through and in Himself, since it had grown old at its own hands, and to make it a "partaker of divine nature,"[23] that is, having put away all corruption and alteration, through which human nature was "assimilated to beasts,"[24] inasmuch as sensation had the advantage over reason.

53.8. To Him be glory unto the ages. Amen.

Scholia

[1] The devil, he says, is five cubits tall,[25] owing to the senses, for without the senses the irrational impulse toward evil, which is around the soul, does not admit of progress in its growth and expansion toward evil.

[2] The spear, he says, is a symbol of the sovereign rule of virtue; the pitcher of water is the token sign of the mystery of knowledge.

[3] He calls this world and the letter of the law a "cave," and says that Saul represents the Jewish people, whose intellect turned away from the divine light of intelligible realities, and

---

22. Hab 3.3.
23. 2 Pt 1.4.
24. Ps 48.12, 22. See above, Intro., 1.2.13; and Qu. 1.2.
25. I.e., somewhere between seven and eight feet.

who now sit in the darkness of the senses and the shadow of the law, corrupting both the creation of God and His law. For whoever reduces the immortal promises of God solely to the letter of Scripture and to the superficial appearances of sensible realities, reduces them in the manner that food is reduced to corruption and excrement, so that the end of the process reveals the mistaken starting point in one's notion of God. The "double garment" is the enigmatic veil of the law, while its "extremity" is the conceptual height of spiritual contemplation, which is cut away from those who think that holy Scripture points to sense-perceptible realities alone.

[4] The Lord is called "shepherd" with respect to those who through natural contemplation are guided to the higher sheepfold; but He is the "king" of those who obey the law of the Spirit, and who, through the simple projection of the intellect's undivided knowledge, stand around the throne of God's grace.[26]

[5] He calls the modes of ascetic practice leading to virtue the "dwellers in Judah," and the principles of knowledge arising during contemplation the "dwellers in Jerusalem."

[6] The praiseworthy death of the intellect is its voluntary movement away from all beings, after which by grace it receives divine life, and, in a manner beyond discursive thought, receives instead of beings the very Cause of beings.

[7] "Glory" is what he calls knowledge that is unlimited, and which no word or principle can contain; "honor" is the unrestrained, virtuous movement of the will's inclination in relation to nature.

[8] He says knowledge that endures, inasmuch as it possesses an unlimited intellective movement beyond intellection concerning the divine infinity, resembles, through its absence of any limits, the glory of truth, which transcends every infinity. The voluntary imitation of Providence's wise goodness, on the other hand, bestows on the intellect's disposition the honor of the manifest likeness to God, as much as this is possible.

[9] He says that according to the principle of anagogy, David is Christ, whose "tomb" is the memorial of His righteousness, which cannot be compared to anything in the whole of

---

26. Cf. Heb 4.16.

rational nature. Because when He became man He did not measure righteousness by the natural law of the flesh, but rather through the flesh He actualized the righteousness that naturally belonged to Him as God, without the flesh ever losing its own natural activity.

QUESTION 54

N THE FIRST book of Esdras, it is written of Zerubbabel that: "When the young man had gone forth, he lifted up his face to heaven toward Jerusalem, and blessed the king of heaven, saying: 'From Thee is victory, from Thee is wisdom, and Thine is the glory, and I am Thy servant. Blessed art Thou, who hast given me wisdom; and to Thee I give thanks, O Lord of our fathers.'"[1] What is the meaning of the phrase: "he lifted up his face to heaven toward Jerusalem," and the other things in this passage?[2]

Response

54.2. The name Zerubbabel, according to the precise rules of the Hebrew language, admits of both rough and smooth pronunciations, along with synthesis, division, and sequence. With the rough, it means "seed of confusion."[3] With the smooth,

---

1. 1 Esd 4.58–60.

2. The figure of Zerubbabel was prominent in contemporary Jewish thought, primarily through the *Book of Zerubbabel* (*Sefer Zerubavel*), a Jewish apocalypse written in the first half of the 7th century (ca. 604–30). The work was written against the background of wars between the Byzantine Empire and Persia, which encouraged messianic hopes among some Jews, reflected in the *Book of Zerubbabel,* in which the wars were seen as eschatological events heralding the appearance of the Messiah; see W. J. van Bekkum, "Jewish Messianic Expectations in the Age of Heraclius," in *The Reign of Heraclius (610–641): Crisis and Confrontation,* ed. Gerrit J. Reinink and Bernard H. Stolte (Leuven: Peeters, 2002), 95–112; Robert L. Wilken, "The Restoration of Israel in Biblical Prophecy: Christian and Jewish Responses in the Early Byzantine Period," in *To See Ourselves as Others See Us: Christians, Jews, "Others" in Late Antiquity,* ed. Jacob Neusner and Ernest S. Frerichs (Chico, CA: Scholars Press, 1985), 443–71, esp. 453–61; and below, the note at Qu. 64.18.

3. Cf. Lagarde, *Onomastica Sacra,* 191: "Zerubbabel means 'rest from confusion.'"

"rising out of confusion."[4] When read as a synthesis, it means "rising in confusion." When divided, it means "rising from dispersion," and when read in sequence, it means "rest itself."[5]

54.3. It follows that Zerubbabel is the philosophical intellect, first in the sense that through repentance it sows righteousness in the confusion of the mind's captivity to the passions. Second, in the sense of "rising out of confusion," insofar as it reveals the shamefulness of the confusion of the passions. Third, in the sense of "rising in confusion," for through knowledge it illumines sense perception's confused relation to objects of sense, not permitting it to exercise itself on such objects apart from reason. Fourth, in the sense of "rising from dispersion," since it provides the powers of the soul, dispersed among objects of sense, with the rising of works of righteousness, from which rational practice is constituted—not without a share of contemplation in knowledge—and it leads the dispersed powers back to intelligible realities. And fifth, in the sense of being "rest itself," since it creates total peace, conjoining ascetic practice to what is naturally good, and contemplation to what is naturally true. For every ascetic practice[1] is naturally undertaken for the sake of the good, and every contemplation seeks after knowledge solely for the sake of the truth. When ascetic practice and contemplation have completed their course, there is absolutely nothing that can disrupt the soul's practical activity, and neither will its contemplative activity be disturbed by any strange speculations. For it will have gone beyond every being and concept, and entered into God Himself, who alone

---

4. "Rising" renders the Greek word ἀνατολή, which also means "dawn," or "Orient," which is a name of Christ; cf. Nm 24.17; Zec 6.12; Lk 1.78; 2 Pt 1.19; and Rv 2.28, 22.16.

5. For commentary on this passage, see Blowers, *Exegesis and Spiritual Pedagogy*, 204. Maximos's etymology is generally correct, even though he seems to be using the notion of Greek accent marks to distinguish word roots and gutturals. Professor Gary Anderson suggests a more narrative interpretation, so that "synthesis" understands the name of Zerubbabel in terms of an Israelite who is still living in Babylon during the exile ("rising amid the confusion of Babylon"); "division" as a reference to the first return under Ezra/Nehemiah ("rising away from the diaspora community in Babylon"); and "sequence" to the narrative end itself, i.e., the ingathering of all the Jewish people as a sign of the end of the exile ("rest") (personal communication, 8 Sept., 2015).

is goodness and truth, and who transcends every being and intellection.

54.4. Such an intellect, actualized in this manner by various progressions in virtue, "comes forth" after its victory over King Darius, that is, the natural law.[6] By contrasting the virtues with the passions, the intellect shows to this law the power of love and truth.[2] And when this intellect is legitimately appointed to rule (an appointment that also signals the rejection of its rivals), it knows the source of the gift of victory it received, and this is when it "lifts up its face to heaven toward Jerusalem, and blesses the king of heaven."

54.5. The "face"[3] of such an intellect is the intelligible disposition in the hidden part of the soul, which displays all the characteristic features of the virtues. It is this disposition which it "lifts to heaven," that is, to the height of contemplation, "toward Jerusalem," which is the state of dispassion. Or again, "it lifts up its face to heaven toward Jerusalem,"[4] seeking its "dwelling place in heaven,"[7] in the city of those "who are enrolled in the heavens,"[8] a city of which David says "glorious things are spoken."[9] For it is not possible to bless God[5] other than by raising the face of the soul's disposition toward the height of contemplation and knowledge in a state of dispassion, which latter is a condition of peace and freedom from cares, composed of many and various virtues, like the features of a face.

54.6. And as he lifts up his face, what does he say? "From Thee is victory,"[6] indicating that victory over the passions is the goal of ascetic practice, as if it were a prize won in divine contests against sin. And he also says: "From Thee is wisdom," indicating the goal of contemplation with respect to knowledge, which negates the whole of the soul's ignorance. And: "Thine is the glory," giving the name of "glory" to the divine beauty that shines forth, as much as is possible, from victory

---

6. In this instance, the "natural law" does not designate the original law of nature, which is a manifestation of its inner *logos*, but rather the condition of nature after the fall, which Maximos elsewhere calls the "law of the flesh"; cf. above, Qu. 26.
7. 2 Cor 5.2.
8. Heb 12.23.
9. Ps 86.3.

and wisdom—a glory which indeed constitutes the union of victory and wisdom, practice and contemplation, virtue and knowledge, and goodness and truth. When these are mutually united, they flash forth the single glory and daybreak of God. This is why he fittingly says: "and I am Thy servant," knowing that God, operating in us as His instruments, brings to completion all ascetic practice and contemplation, all virtue and knowledge, and all victory, wisdom, goodness, and truth. And he knows that, to all this, we contribute nothing at all, except an inner disposition desirous of good things. The great Zerubbabel, possessing precisely such a disposition, said, in addition to the foregoing, and while addressing himself to God: "Blessed art Thou who hast given me wisdom; and to Thee I give thanks, O Lord of our fathers." As a grateful servant, he ascribes all things to God, who had given him all things, and from whom he received wisdom, acknowledging and thanking the "Lord of his fathers" as the source of the good things he had received. He calls God "blessed" inasmuch as He possesses infinite wisdom, or rather that He is Wisdom itself,[10] from whom he received wisdom and now offers thanks for the gift. And he names Him "Lord of the fathers," wishing to declare that all the achievements of the saints are clearly gifts of grace from God, because the saints possessed nothing beyond the good things given to them by God, who measured them out in proportion to the gratitude and good will of each recipient, and thus all that can properly be said to belong to the saints are the things given to them by God. He calls "fathers"[7] all the saints from the beginning of time whose faith he received, and whose way of life he imitated, and from whom he desired and attained birth in the Spirit. In this way he became the voluntary son of voluntary parents, which, when compared to the involuntary birth of fathers and sons from the flesh, is more precious in the eyes of God to the same degree that the soul by nature transcends the flesh.

54.7. This Zerubbabel was one of the three young men who addressed Darius the king[11]—who I said was the natural law—

---

10. I.e., Αὐτοσοφία; cf. above, Qu. 28.4.
11. Cf. 1 Esd 4.13.

QUESTION 54   337

and in his address he defined the entire human capacity for divine good things in two words,[12] and thus overthrew the arguments of the other two speakers. This was how he attracted to himself the kingly law of nature, which decreed the release of the powers of the soul held captive by the deviations of the passions. For the evil spirits that preside over the passions are two—a number whose very property discloses their impassioned and ephemeral nature, given that bodies are more material.[8] But the intellect which defends the soul is one, being simple in its essence, and bears the mark of the indivisible monad, which death absolutely cannot touch in any way, for it cannot be sectioned or divided into parts.[13]

54.8. For "the one," that is, the first young man, who proposes the impassioned state of bodily life, says that "wine is the strongest,"[14] using the word "wine" to refer, in outline form, to all the deranged drunkenness of passions engrossed in pleasures, which causes one to go out of his mind, and debases the natural function of thinking. For "their wine is the wrath of dragons," it says, "and the incurable wrath of asps,"[15] calling the heat of carnal passions the "wine of dragons," and the tyrannical and arrogant contempt of obedience the "wine of asps."[16] For the asp, as they say, more than all the other creatures of the earth, closes its ears to charms, and in its arrogance tyrannizes the charmers.[17]

54.9. The "other," that is, the second young man, proposes that "the king is the strongest,"[18] giving the name of "king" to

12. Cf. 1 Esd 4.13–41.
13. The number two, or duality, is associated with corporeal bodies, which are composed of two basic elements, i.e., matter and form; cf. *Amb.* 10.106 (DOML 1:321).
14. 1 Esd 3.10.
15. Dt 32.33.
16. Cf. Evagrios, *Gnostic Chapters* 5.44: "If the 'anger of dragons is wine' [Dt 32.33], and if Nazirites [i.e., a biblical type of the ascetic or monk] abstain from wine, then the Nazirites have received the order to be without anger [cf. Nm 6.3]" (PO 28:195).
17. Cf. Ps 57.5–6; and Gregory Nazianzus, *Or.* 40.34: "Let the Word sound in you, or rather keep the one who has sounded in you; do not close your ears to the teaching and admonition of the Lord, as a snake to charms" (SC 358:276, lines 17–19).
18. 1 Esd 3.11.

every vain glory based on wealth, power, and other such superficialities. Such vainglory gives birth to ignorance, which is the dispersion of nature, since it makes all men ignorant of each other, and encourages them to fight with all for the sake of one thing, with each man desiring to be glorified by acquiring more power, wealth, and luxuries than anyone else. For it is by such things that men wish to be glorified when they are ignorant of the divine and enduring glory, and who take no thought for its power. These two young men are those who have, we might say, mired themselves in all the "slime of the depth"[19] of unnatural passions contained in their two proposals, and who make Darius the judge of their words—when, as I said, he is the prevailing law of nature—in the hope that he might incline toward their views.

54.10. But the "third" is the intellect presiding over virtue and knowledge, determined to free the soul from its evil slavery to the passions, and it says "women are strongest," and "truth triumphs over all."[20] By "women" he means the divinizing virtues, which constitute the love that unites us with God and with one another,[21] a love that raptures the soul away from all things subject to generation and decay, as well as from the intelligible essences that are above them, and entwines the soul with God Himself in a kind of erotic blending—to the extent that this is possible for human nature—and it mystically creates their pure and divine cohabitation. By "truth" he means the sole and unique Cause of beings, along with their governing principle, kingdom, power, and glory, from which and for which all things were made and are being made, and by which and through which they are all held together in existence, and for which those who love God expend all their effort and devote all their movement. To state the matter succinctly, through "women" he showed that the goal of the virtues is love, which is the unfailing pleasure and indivisible union of those who participate through their longing in what is good by nature. Through "truth"[9] he signaled the limit of all knowledge and

19. Ps 68.3.
20. 1 Esd 3.11–12.
21. Cf. Jn 13.34.

of all the things that can be known—and it is to this limit, as to the beginning and limit of all beings, that all natural movements are attracted by means of a certain general principle, for inasmuch as it is the truth, it triumphs over all things by its very nature, being the beginning and cause of beings, attracting to itself the movement of all things that have come into being.

54.11. Speaking in this manner to the law of nature, the philosophical intellect drives away all the deception of the wicked demons, persuading the thoughts and powers of the soul, held in bondage to the passions, to choose freedom[10] and to proclaim deliverance and release from the bonds of spiritual captivity to those confined in shadows, by which I mean attachment to objects of sense, so that ascending to Judea—which signifies virtue—they can build in Jerusalem, which signifies dispassion, the temple of the Lord, which is the knowledge capable of receiving wisdom.

54.12. Wise, and indeed exceedingly wise, is the great Zerubbabel, having received wisdom from God, through which he was able to counter each of the proposals put forward by the wicked spirits who struggled to defend the body in order to deceive and destroy the human race—and not simply to counter them but to triumph over them and destroy them, and by each of his own two proposals completely to obliterate each of the proposals of his opponents, and to liberate the soul from its evil slavery to the passions. For whereas the other speakers sought to honor the heat of carnal passions by invoking "wine," and to confirm the power of worldly glory by invoking the "king," Zerubbabel introduced the notion of boundless spiritual pleasure by invoking "women," and by championing the "truth" he pointed to that power which can never be shaken, and so persuaded his listeners to despise present goods and embrace those that are to come.

54.13. This, as it seems to me, is the honorable and wise meaning of the proposals, which were written for our instruction[22] and are not unworthy of the Spirit. But if someone is able to discover a loftier meaning of this passage, according to the capacity given to him to understand divine realities, there will

---

22. Cf. 1 Cor 10.11.

be no envy or resentment, for the grace of the Spirit is not of a nature to be diminished by the number of those who share in it (a situation that otherwise gives birth to the passion of envy), even if one has more grace and another less. For each person acquires the energy of the Spirit according to the measure of his manifest faith,[23] so that each person is a steward of his own grace.[11] Thus no one of good sense would envy another who is rich in grace, because the disposition that makes us capable of receiving the good things of God depends on ourselves.[24]

54.14. Let us now turn to another mystical contemplation, which presents us with the principal truth of the biblical text. The true and new Zerubbabel, who is announced figuratively through the old one, is our Lord and God Jesus Christ, who, in the confusion of our nature, was conceived, formed in the womb, was born, and became perfect man according to nature, so that by separating our nature from confusion, He might lead it back to Himself. For He did not become a captive together with us,[12] neither was He dragged away into the captivity of the passions, "for He committed no sin, neither was there any guile found in his mouth."[25] Instead, He was born among captives as if He were also a captive, and He was "reckoned among transgressors,"[26] "assuming the likeness of the flesh of sin[13] and con-

---

23. Cf. Rom 12.3.

24. Larchet (SC 554:206, n. 1) highlights three themes here: first, that grace is given "according to the measure" (i.e., κατὰ τὴν ἀναλογίαν) of the recipient's faith and disposition, and suggests that Maximos's emphasis on the personal, spiritual state of the recipient marks a shift away from the Dionysian sense of "analogy," which is determined by the hierarchical structure of beings (although there are limits to what humanity can receive, as Maximos regularly affirms); cf. Marius Portaru, "Gradual Participation according to St Maximus the Confessor," *SP* 68 (2013): 281–93; and Maximos Constas, "Maximus the Confessor, Dionysius the Areopagite, and the Transformation of Christian Neoplatonism," *Analogia* 1.2 (2017): 1–12, esp. 7–9. Second is the theme of "synergy" or cooperation of divine grace and human freedom, or between the divine activity/energy and the disposition of the human will. Third is the identification of the divine activity/energy with the grace given to human beings, indicating that Maximos does not restrict the notion of divine energy solely to the sense of "activity" or "operation."

25. 1 Pt 2.22; Is 53.9.

26. Mk 15.28; Is 53.12.

cerning sin."²⁷ He was in the "likeness of the flesh of sin," for whereas by nature He is impassible God, He deemed it worthy in His plan of salvation to become a naturally passible human being, without suffering any change in His divinity. And this was "concerning sin" inasmuch as He was led to death on account of our sins, and "for the sake of our sins He suffered, and on account of our sins He was wounded, and bruised on account of our iniquities, so that by His bruises we might be healed."²⁸ For "before our very eyes," Scripture says, "the Spirit who is Christ the Lord, was captured²⁹ in our corruption, of whom we had said, 'In his shadow we shall live among the nations.'"³⁰

54.15. He is the righteous Rising of dispersion that scatters our sins, about whom the Holy Spirit says, through the prophet, a righteous Rising will rise upon you, and, "Behold, a man, whose name is Orient, shall rise up from below—and he is the Sun of righteousness, and healing shall be in his wings."³¹ The phrase "from below"[14] discloses the ineffable mystery of the Incarnation of the Word, from which universal salvation has risen. The "wings" of the Sun of righteousness would be the two covenants, by which the Word flies within us and heals the wounds of our transgressions and grants us the perfect health of virtue. Through the Old Covenant, He brings about the destruction of evil, while through the New Covenant, He establishes the place of virtue. Or, again, the two wings are Providence and Judgment, by means of which He alights upon beings in a manner beyond knowledge, healing those who are willing by the principle of wisdom,[15] using forms of chastisement to treat those not easily moved to virtue, purifying the former of their defilement of flesh, and treating the defilements of soul found among the latter.³²

54.16. He is the one who brought back the true Israel from its captivity, not transferring the people from one land to an-

27. Rom 8.3.
28. Cf. Is 53.4–5.
29. The Greek verb συνελήφθη means to be captured or arrested, as well as being conceived in the womb.
30. Lam 4.20.
31. Zec 6.12; Mal 3.20.
32. On "providence and judgment," see below, Qu. 63.17.

other, as the old Zerubbabel did, but from earth to heaven, and from vice to virtue, and from ignorance "unto the knowledge of the truth" of God,[33] and from corruption to incorruption, and to immortality from death, and, to state the matter succinctly, from the visible world of perpetual flux and change to the stable and intelligible world, and from this life, which is fading away, to the one that never fades and abides forever. He is the true builder of the rational temple, which collapsed under the weight of our transgressions and was burnt by foreign fire, a fire which we kindled, running after the light and flame of our own fire, and, by this flame we not only made the intellective soul a slave to the "mind of flesh,"[34] but we also actively set aflame the material of the passions.[16]

54.17. He is the one who by wisdom persuaded and prevailed upon Darius the king, who signifies the law of nature—for in this passage it is not right to understand Darius as the devil, since he became the voluntary co-worker in the gift of gracious deliverance of the people, being persuaded that there is nothing more powerful or useful for the salvation of human nature than faith and good conscience. For faith possesses the principle of truth[17] and a good conscience, in which there is absolutely no transgression of the divine commandments, and which bears within itself the place of divine love, which is understood allegorically through the women.

54.18. He is the one who built within Himself, according to an ineffable and indivisible union, the "fallen tabernacle of David,"[35] by which I mean human nature corrupted on account of sin and condemned to death.

54.19. He is Zerubbabel, who gloriously raised up the fallen house of God, about which the Holy Spirit says: "and the glory of this final house shall be greater than the former,"[36] for the Word "communicated a second communion to nature, far more paradoxical than the first."[37] As much as He had previ-

33. 1 Tm 2.4.
34. Rom 8.7.
35. Am 9.11.
36. Hag 2.9.
37. A phrase from Gregory Nazianzus, *Or.* 38.13 (SC 358:134, lines 38–39), which is the focus of *Amb.* 36 (DOML 2:70–73).

ously given what was superior, to the same degree He later voluntarily received what was inferior, so that He might save the image, give immortal life to the flesh, obliterate the word of the serpent resounding throughout human nature,[38] and purify nature from evil, making it as it was in the beginning, and enriching the first creation by divinization. [18] And, just as in the beginning He brought it into being out of nothing, so too now His aim is to rescue and restore it from its fallen condition, preventing it from falling again by means of immutability,[39] and to realize for nature the entire design of God the Father, divinizing nature by the power of His Incarnation. For Scripture says that the "hands"[19] of the spiritual "Zerubbabel have established this house,"[40] the "house" being the human being; and that "his hands shall bring it to perfection,"[41] which refers to the first creation and the final recreation, which takes place within Him according to the ineffable union.

54.20. This is the true Zerubbabel, the redeemer of captives, who "holds in his hand a stone of tin,[42] which is adorned with the seven eyes of the Lord," and it is through these that God "looks upon all of the earth."[43] According to the literal account, Zerubbabel nowhere appears to hold in his hand a stone having "seven eyes"; neither were they the eyes of the Lord, nor were they "looking upon all the earth." Thus, since it is completely impossible to sustain such an interpretation on the level of the literal words, let us proceed to the inner meaning of what has been written.

54.21. Zerubbabel, as I have already said many times, is our Lord and God Jesus Christ. His "stone"[20] is faith in Him. And

---

38. An allusion to Eve's reception of the serpent's words and the Virgin Mary's conception of the Word "through hearing"; cf. Constas, *Proclus of Constantinople*, 273–90.

39. That is, immutability acquired through free will; cf. above, Qu. 42.

40. Zec 4.9.

41. Zec 4.10.

42. Or, "a plummet of tin." The CCSG editors give κασσιτήρινον, without citing any variants, but throughout late-antique Greek literature the word is attested more frequently as κασσιτέρινον. The mineral "cassiterite" or "tinstone" is the principal ore of tin.

43. Cf. Zec 4.10.

344   ST. MAXIMOS THE CONFESSOR

it is "in His hand" because faith in Christ is manifested by the practice of the commandments, for "faith without works is dead,"[44] just as "works are dead without faith."[45] The hand is obviously a symbol of practice.[46] By holding the stone in His hand, the Lord is teaching us that our faith in Him must be realized in actual practice, adorned with the seven eyes of the Lord, that is, the seven energies of the Holy Spirit.[47]

54.22. "And there will rest upon Him," it says, seven spirits, namely, the "spirit of wisdom, the spirit of comprehension, the spirit of knowledge, the spirit of true understanding,[48] the spirit of counsel, the spirit of might, the spirit of the fear of God."[49] The spirit of the fear of God[21] is abstention from committing evil deeds. The spirit of might is the voluntary effort and motion toward the actual keeping of the commandments. The spirit of counsel is the state of discernment, according to which we keep the divine commandments in a manner consistent with reason, distinguishing the greater from the worse.[50] The spirit of true understanding is the true knowledge of the modes of virtuous practice, and when these inform our practice we do not err with respect to the correct judgment of reason. The spirit of knowledge is the grasping of the intelligible principles contained in the commandments, according to which the modes of the virtues are constituted. The spirit of comprehension is the assent to the modes and principles of virtues—or, strictly speaking, their transformation—according to which there comes about a mixture[51] of our natural powers with the modes and principles of the commandments. The spirit of wisdom is the ascent to-

44. Jas 2.26.
45. Citing Gregory Nazianzus, *Or.* 40.45 (SC 358:306, lines 46–47).
46. Didymos, *Commentary on Zechariah* 1.330, makes the same connection between the "hand" and "practice" (SC 83:366, line 22); cf. above, Qu. 3.3.
47. Larchet (SC 554:212, n. 2) notes that, both here and in what follows, Maximos identifies the grace of the Holy Spirit with the "energy" of the Holy Spirit, using the word in the plural to designate the various forms according to which it is communicated to human beings.
48. Maximos has "true understanding" (ἐπιστήμη) instead of "piety" (εὐσέβεια), which latter is found in the Septuagint; cf. below, Qu. 63.6.
49. Cf. Is 11.2.
50. Cf. Heb 5.14.
51. On "mixture," see *Amb.* 10.38 (DOML 1:206–209).

ward and union with the Cause of the more spiritual principles found in the commandments, according to which, in a manner beyond knowledge, we are initiated (as much as is possible for human beings) into the simple principles of beings that are in God. From this, as if from a bubbling source of the heart, we offer to other men, in various ways, the truth found in complete and whole beings, beginning with those that are furthest from God, but which are near to us, to those which are first and closest to God, but remote from us, ascending step by step through all of them in sequence and order.

54.23. For it is by abstention[22] from evil, in the fear of God, that we advance in strength to the practice of the virtues. From the practice of the virtues we advance to the discernment of our voluntary deliberations. From discernment we advance to a settled state of virtues, that is, the true knowledge of the virtues. From the settled state of virtues we advance to the knowledge of the divine principles contained in the virtues themselves. From this knowledge we advance to the transformative state of the virtues themselves, by which I mean understanding; and from this to the simple and exact contemplation of the truth found in complete and whole beings. Being urged on by this contemplation, we will set forth a multitude of various pious principles concerning the truth as they emerge from our wise contemplation of sensible and intelligible essences. Ascending with these "eyes" of faith, that is, with these illuminations, we are gathered together towards the divine monad of wisdom,[23] and at the same time we gather together the division of the gifts (which were divided for our sake) by means of the partial ascents of the virtues, and lead the gifts back to their Source and Cause. With God's cooperation we omit none of the aforementioned steps, lest through even minor negligence we render our faith blind and devoid of eyes,[24] and thus be deprived of the illuminations of the Spirit which are given through actual deeds, and be justly punished for endless ages, for to the extent that it depended upon us, we blinded the divine eyes of faith which had opened within us according to the measure of our faith.

54.24. For anyone who abstains[25] from keeping the commandments gouges out the eyes of faith within himself, and is by all means condemned, for he no longer has God watching over him. And I think this is the reason why Scripture called faith a "stone of tin," for faith itself punishes those who do not adorn their faith by keeping the commandments, and it rewards those who preserve and keep it radiant by means of the energies of the Spirit. For the great Symeon says of the Lord, that: "He will be unto the fall and rising of many in Israel,"[52] namely, the fall of those who have no faith, but the rising of the faithful. For some say that tin is a compound of silver and lead. In this way, the element of lead symbolizes chastisement, punishment, and the weight of judgment, while "silver" is the figure of brightness, glory, and splendor. If this is so, it follows that faith, which is signified through the stone of tin,[26] also chastises, punishes, and condemns those who are untried in the faith inasmuch as they have abstained from the commandments. At the same time, the element of lead signifies the weakness of the flesh,[27] which is strengthened by the Word through the union, so that faith brightens again and glorifies and illumines and leads to divinization those who have proved themselves in it by keeping the commandments, inasmuch as faith contains, perhaps like silver, the divinity of the Word, which wholly flashes forth like lightning in the worthy, to the extent that this is possible.

54.25. Some have taken the "stone of tin" as a symbol of our Lord Jesus Christ, inasmuch as He is constituted from two natures, divinity and humanity.[53] If, however, someone wishes to contemplate faith in Christ, or Christ Himself, with a greater depth of knowledge,[54] he could say that faith in Christ and Christ Himself are "lead," inasmuch as He disciplines the soul, chastises the flesh, punishes the passions, and condemns demons. As "silver," He makes the mind radiant by means of the virtues, and glorifies it by knowledge, and by means of divinization makes it light, an image of the primal light. According to

52. Lk 2.34.
53. An argument made by Cyril of Alexandria, *Commentary on Zechariah* 2 (ed. P. E. Pusey, *S.P.N. Cyrilli archiepiscopi Alexandrini in XII prophetas*, vol. 2 [Oxford: Clarendon Press, 1868; repr. Brussels: Culture et civilisation, 1965], 341–42); cf. Didymos, *On the Trinity* 2 (PG 39:705AB), the authenticity of which remains under discussion.
54. I.e., γνωστικώτερον; cf. below, Qu. 63.18.

this same idea one should also understand the "fall" and the "rising" that come forth from Christ. This is because He brings about the fall of the flesh, that is, the fleshly mind,[55] and the passions, sins, and demons. At the same time, He is the resurrection of the intellect, that is, of the spiritual mind,[56] and of the natural powers, and the virtues, and of those thoughts that are constitutive of knowledge. To state the matter simply, the Word brings about, on the one hand, the fall of the whole "old man according to Adam,"[57] along with the letter of the law among those who are worthy, and, on the other, the resurrection of the "new man according to Christ,"[58] and of the spirit of the law.

54.26. And perhaps this is why Scripture likens to a stone of lead the faith of those who have tarnished[28] the virtue and knowledge that properly belong to faith, but who through repentance are able to brighten it once again by means of their ascetic practice and contemplation, and to receive anew the radiant brightness of life.[59]

Scholia

[1] The goal of practical virtue, they say, is the good, the attainment and completion of which comes about by divine activity. The rational part of the soul leads us to this completion, using its incensive and desiring powers according to nature, and it is in this completion that the beauty of the divine likeness is naturally manifested.[60] The goal of contemplative philosophy, they say, is the truth, which is uniform and indivisible knowledge of all the things around God. It is the pure intellect that leads us to such knowledge, after it has extinguished with-

---

55. Cf. Rom 8.6.
56. Cf. ibid.
57. Cf. Col 3.9; 1 Cor 15.45–49.
58. Cf. Col 3.10; 1 Cor 15.45–49.
59. A simplified version of this paragraph was included in the *Sayings of the Desert Fathers* 717: "Abba Maximos said: 'Just as tin that has become black shines again, so too believers, even if they are blackened by sinning, shine again when they repent. Perhaps this is why faith was compared to tin'" (trans. modified from John Wortley, *The Anonymous Sayings of the Desert Fathers* [Cambridge: Cambridge University Press, 2013], 569).
60. Cf. Gn 1.27.

in itself all judgments based on sense perception; and it is this knowledge that shows forth in unadulterated form the dignity of the divine image.[61]

[2] In the "women" he contemplated the virtues, the goal of which is love; "truth" he interpreted anagogically as knowledge without quantity. When the ruling law of nature comes to recognize their character—by which he means the character of love and knowledge—it casts out, as if it were wine, the pleasure of carnal passions, and, like a king, rejects the mad thirst for conceited glory that has conquered everyone without exception.

[3] A virtuous disposition, he says, constitutes the "face" of the contemplative intellect, inasmuch as it is turned heavenwards to the height of true understanding.

[4] This is another contemplation concerning this same phrase, according to which, he says, the "enrollment in the heavens" includes only those who have freely offered their whole selves, wishing to be enrolled and inscribed by the pen of the Spirit. For the Holy Spirit enrolls in the heavens those who wish to be so enrolled, not those who are forced to do so.

[5] No one can truly bless God, he says, unless he has sanctified his body by means of the virtues and illumined his soul by means of knowledge.

[6] Victory for the practical part of the soul, he says, is the conclusion of its struggles on behalf of divine things, and this is a pure and unmixed good. He also states that wisdom is the goal of the mystical visions grasped by the cognitive part of the soul, and this is simple and unqualified truth. We are led to these things when the intellect is purged of mental images arising from sense perception, and when reason has subordinated to itself the vital power of the soul. He says that the concurrence of victory and wisdom, that is, of goodness and truth, shows forth among those who attain it a single radiant glory of the unalloyed divine likeness.

[7] Fathers according to the spirit, he says, are constituted through their teaching, becoming voluntary fathers of voluntary sons, forming them according to God by means of their words and way of life. And sons according to the spirit, through

---

61. Cf. ibid.

their learning, become, by virtue of their free will, freely choosing sons of freely chosen fathers, intentionally being formed by the latter according to God by means of their words and way of life. For the grace of the Spirit makes both the birth of those who beget and those who are begotten a matter of the will's disposition, which is something that fathers according to flesh do not have, because they are involuntary fathers of involuntary sons, since the formation of those who beget and those who are begotten naturally is a work of nature and not of free choice.

[8] Here the "dyad" signifies matter and form, the concurrence of which is constituted by the genesis of a body and its dissolution, which naturally brings about its corruption. Thus beings arising from the concurrence of form and matter have an end that is naturally in contradiction to their beginning, inasmuch as corruption is the destruction of generation.

The "two powers," namely, desire and irascibility, assume the defense of generation and corruption. In and of itself, desire is disposed to maintain generation in existence, while the irascible or spirited power struggles to repel the dissolution caused by corruption. The wicked demons function as co-defenders of these powers, some of whom propose to the law of nature that desire (symbolized by the wine) should make the soul stand outside of divine realities, while others propose that the irascible power (imaged by the king) should rule despotically over material realities, wishing to persuade the soul to elect an impassioned way of life consistent with desire and anger.

The "monad," on the other hand, signifies the soul, which is simple according to its essence, as an image of the Tri-Hypostatic Monad, which according to its essence transcends nature. The co-defender of this monad, by which I mean the soul, is the intellect, inasmuch as the intellect is a single reality belonging to a single soul. Through the "truth" and the "women," the intellect demonstrates that faith in God and the love of God are more powerful than the law of nature, and persuades the law of nature to elect a form of sovereignty consistent with divine truth and love.

[9] It is by the transcendent privation of the many, he says, that the truth is of a nature to manifest itself as one and unique,

placing a veil over the soul's cognitive powers with respect to all that it can think or all that can be thought, since by its very existence the truth, which transcends all being, transcends all that thinks and is thought. By its infinite power it circumscribes the extremes of both the beginning and the end of beings, attracting toward itself the motion of all things. On some it bestows clear knowledge of the grace of which they have been deprived; to others it gives, through an ineffable perception obtained by participation, the manifest understanding of the goodness for which they longed.

[10] He understands the people in Babylon as an allegory of thoughts held in bondage to the slavery of the passions. Thus Darius is the law of nature; Zerubbabel is the mind engaged with knowledge; Judea is virtue; Jerusalem is the state of dispassion; the temple is knowledge receptive of wisdom; and the ascent from Babylon to Judea is the transposition of the mind through repentance from carnal to spiritual realities.

[11] He says that the cause of the distribution of divine goods is the measure[62] of each person's faith, for it is in proportion[63] to our faith[64] that we receive eagerness to practice the commandments. For whoever practices the commandments reveals the measure of his faith in proportion to his practice, and in proportion to his faith receives the due measure of grace. But whoever does not practice the commandments reveals by his lack of practice the measure of his lack of faith, and in proportion to his faithlessness the privation of grace. Thus the envious person acts badly in being jealous of the achievements of others, since the choice of being faithful and acting and receiving grace in proportion to his faith clearly depends on him, and not on anybody else.

[12] Here the contingent type is seen to accord well with the truth. For just as Zerubbabel was not a captive, but was born of those who at that time were captives in Babylon and became their deliverer, so too our Lord, being sinless, was reckoned as being from among us, within us, and as one from among us,

---

62. I.e., τὸ μέτρον.
63. I.e., κατὰ τὴν ἀναλογίαν.
64. Cf. Rom 12.6.

having voluntarily clothed Himself in the passible part of our nature, according to which He raised up our natural weakness toward the truth, freeing us from the power of corruption, and leading us from heaven to earth. By the power of His Incarnation he assumed in Himself the whole of our nature, lacking nothing, in an ineffable union; and by the call of grace, He granted solely to those who received this call with joy—as manifested in their works—the grace of recreation.

[13] The "flesh of sin" is flesh generated by male seed, and this is why it possesses by nature in equal measure the capacity for both sin and corruption, having sin as its beginning and corruption as the end of its proper existence. But the flesh that is in the "likeness of the flesh of sin"[65] is the flesh of the Lord, which was constituted without male seed. In terms of its nature it is corruptible, making Him "like" us, but in terms of its power it is naturally sinless, making Him "unlike" us.[66]

[14] He is saying that inasmuch as the principle of the Incarnation is second with respect to the absolute purity and sublime extremity of theology—for the latter refers to the essence of the extreme Word, and the second is what holds together the most extreme activity of providence—the Spirit called the incarnate Word the "dawn rising from below."[67] For the creation of the ages, and all that is contained in an age, are contained in the principle of the Incarnation, as well as the extension of the life of beings into infinity through grace that transcends the ages.

[15] The lover of beautiful things, he says, in accordance with Providence and by means of the principles of wisdom, voluntarily hastens toward the grace of divinization. The one who has no love for such things, on the other hand, by the just

65. Rom 8.3.
66. For Maximos, there can be no separation of a nature from its natural power or potential, any more than there can be a separation of nature from its natural motion or activity. The final clause of this scholion, then, should be taken as a reference to the power of Christ's divine nature, which of course is naturally sinless, and which makes him "unlike us." On the larger question of the transmission of sin and its relation to biological reproduction, cf. Jean-Claude Larchet, *Maxime le Confesseur, médiateur entre l'Orient et l'Occident* (Paris: Cerf, 1998), 77–112.
67. Cf. Zec 6.12.

judgment of God and by means of various modes of chastisement, is involuntarily driven away from evil. The lover of God is divinized through providence; the lover of matter, on the other hand, being chastened by divine judgment, is not permitted to enter into condemnation.

[16] The law of the flesh is a blameworthy fire within us. The light of this fire is the habitual movement of the passions in accordance with this blameworthy law, while the blameworthy flame is the active burning of the passions. Or, again, the blameworthy fire is evil, its blameworthy light being the state of evil, while the flame is its activity. It follows that the intellect must not be warmed by such a fire, nor be illumined by such a light, nor be set afire and burnt by its flame, for the light that brings pleasure to the senses is the deepest darkness for the intellect.

[17] Real faith is constitutive of truth, containing no falsehood, while a good conscience bears the power of love, containing not even the slightest transgression of God's commandments.

[18] The resurrection is the recreation of nature, surpassing the fashioning of nature in paradise; it does this in general through the universal immutability it confers on all beings, and in particular through the ineffable grace of divinization conferred on the saints.

[19] By "hands" Scripture is perhaps referring to the creative power of the spiritual Zerubbabel, according to which we were created for well-being, as well as to His power of restoration, according to which we receive the grace of eternal well-being. Or they refer to His beneficent grace, working within us for the practice of the virtues and the subsequent undispersed diffusion of knowledge that occurs in contemplation.

[20] Faith was called a "stone" on account of the firm, immutable, foundational, and completely immovable truth to which it corresponds, and which in no way yields to the uprisings of falsehood. This stone is "in the hand" because of faith's activity on the level of practice, and because it contains and holds together all the virtues. And the stone has "seven eyes" consistent with faith's powers of discernment and contemplation, and its ability to contain the whole, true knowledge of all

that exists within time; and because it is receptive of—as in the case of unmixed numbers—the pure and sevenfold activity of the all-holy Spirit.

[21] Here there are distinctions being made that demonstrate the characteristic property of each spiritual gift. What is characteristic of "fear" is refraining from evil; of "might" the performing of good deeds; of "counsel" the discernment of contraries; of "true understanding" the unadulterated recognition of one's obligations; of "knowledge" the active grasping of the divine principles contained in the virtues; of "comprehension" the thorough concordance of the soul with respect to its objects of knowledge; of "wisdom" inscrutable union with God, according to which the desire of those who are worthy becomes enjoyment, making the participant God by means of participation, and establishing him as a teacher of the divine blessedness, in his unceasing and discrete statements and interpretations offered to those who need them.

[22] Fear, he says, which should be the first among our good actions, was numbered last by Scripture, inasmuch as it is the "beginning of wisdom."[68] Taking this as our point of departure, we ascend to wisdom's goal, which is understanding, after which we draw near to God, having wisdom alone mediating between us and our union with Him. For it is not possible for a person to receive wisdom unless he first, through fear and the remaining gifts mediated by fear, has completely shaken off from himself the occluding fluids of ignorance and the dust of evil. This is why, in the order established by Scripture, wisdom is placed close to God, and fear close to us, so that in this way we might learn the definition and law of good order.

[23] Wisdom, he says, is a monad contemplated indivisibly in the various virtues that arise from it, and it is uniformly gathered together by means of the activities of all the virtues. Again, wisdom is shown to be a simple monad or unity when the virtues that come from it are restored to it. This happens when we—for whose sake wisdom produces this procession for the generation of each virtue—are gathered together through each virtue in an ascending manner toward wisdom.

---

68. Ps 110.10; Prv 1.7, 9.10.

[24] He is saying that whoever does not keep the divine commandments of the faith has a faith that is blind. For if the commandments of the Lord are light,[69] it is obvious that whoever does not keep the commandments is without the divine light, and bears the mere but not real name of faith.

[25] If, he says, Scripture called the energies of the Spirit the "eyes of the Lord," then the person who does not open those eyes by fulfilling the commandments does not have God looking down upon and watching over him. It stands to reason that God is not of a nature to look upon those on earth through any other eyes, inasmuch as the ray of divine vision is our illumination through the virtues.

[26] The "stone of tin," he says, which naturally possesses the properties of silver and lead, is characteristic of faith. For when it is not safeguarded it punishes, holding, like a weight of heavy lead, the accusation of those who did not safeguard it through the ages; but it glorifies those who treasured it and kept it safe, holding as diaphanous silver the advocacy of those who safeguarded it through the ages.

[27] No one who sins, he says, is able to invoke as an advocate for his sin the weakness of his flesh. This is because the union of the whole of human nature with God the Word fortified nature by freeing it from the curse, so that we have no excuse if our will remains attached to the passions. For the divinity of the Word, being ever present by grace to those who believe in Him, withers away the law of sin found in the flesh.

[28] In the same way, he says, that the "stone of tin" may again be brightened after it is tarnished, so too those who believe, even if they are tarnished by their sins, may again be made bright through repentance, and this may be the reason why faith was likened to the stone of tin.

69. Cf. Is 26.9.

QUESTION 55

"ALL THOSE OF Israel, from twelve years old and upward, besides children and women, were forty-three thousand three hundred and sixty; their menservants and handmaidens were seven thousand three hundred and seven; there were eight hundred and fifty-five musicians and chanters; there were four hundred and thirty-five camels, seven thousand seven hundred and thirty-six horses, eight hundred and forty-five mules, and five thousand twenty-five beasts under the yoke."[1] Please be so kind as to explain to me these great and sublime things concerning the return from exile, which were uttered by the Holy Spirit through the words of the prophets. I wish to know the meaning of this base and unsuitable[2] passage, which appears to be so unworthy of the Spirit, preoccupied as it is with the exact numbering of camels, horses, mules, and donkeys.

Response

55.2. To speak about these matters with precision belongs solely to those who, on account of their great purity of intellect, have received from God all the fullness of the grace of the Spirit that human beings are capable of receiving.[1] By means of this grace they cognitively traverse the ocean of mystical contemplations, beholding solely the inner principles of the words of Scripture stripped of their conventional figures. In general they say nothing concerning the figures by which the principles are symbolized, unless in their wisdom they should somewhere

---

1. Cf. 1 Esd 5.41–42.
2. Or "inopportune," i.e., ἀκαιρόγραφος, a word that is not otherwise attested; cf. below, Qu. 55.32 = ἄκαιρος. Eriugena paraphrases the word as *scripta simpliciter* (CCSG 7:480, line 9).

wish[2] to express them in a corporeal manner for the sake of those who, because of their intellectual immaturity, cannot see beyond the level of the senses. Their hope is that such persons, having first exercised themselves with sense-perceptible figures, might acquire a longing to advance to the archetypical principles beyond the senses. Yet for us to pursue loftier interpretations by means of conjecture, following our natural capacity of desire for the knowledge of divine realities, is by no means pointless, inasmuch as conjecture offers two benefits for those who possess genuine piety for the things of God.[3] Because those who approach divine realities conjecturally will either attain the truth of intelligible realities, and joyfully offer as a "sacrifice of praise"[4] their gratitude to God,[3] who grant-

---

3. "Conjecture" (στοχασμός) is a key term in the *Ambigua*, where Maximos professes to be speaking "conjecturally and not by way of proofs" (στοχαζόμενος καί οὐκ ἀποφαινόμενος) (*Amb*. 71.11 [DOML 2:328–29]); cf. *QThp*.: στοχαστικῶς ἀλλ' οὐκ ἀποφαντικῶς (75, line 35; a phrase repeated in *Amb*. 7.11; 10.105; and 19.3); *Ep*. 5: ζητητικῶς ἀλλ' οὐ δογματικῶς (PG 91:432C); *Amb*. 19.3: στοχαστικῶς εἰπεῖν (DOML 1:402; cf. *Amb*. 19.5; 21.2); *Amb*. 20.4: κατὰ στοχασμὸν νομίζω (DOML 1:414); and *Cap. theol*. 2.88: στοχαστικῶς ἐρεῖ τις (PG 90:1165D). Philo employs "conjecture" in his biblical exegesis, as for example in *On the Creation of the World* 72–73 (LCL 1:56), but there are closer parallels in Gregory of Nyssa, where the term and its cognates appear more than 70 times (but only twice in Gregory Nazianzus, and not at all in the *corpus Dionysiacum*). In the *Life of Moses* 2.173, Nyssa leaves the more "profound examination [of the celestial tabernacle] to those illumined by the Spirit," while he himself "will speak conjecturally (στοχαστικῶς)" (SC 1bis:218–20), which is also how Maximos uses the term (cf. below, Qu. 65.2); see Mariette Canévet, *Grégoire de Nysse et l'herméneutique biblique: Étude des rapports entre le langage et la connaissance de Dieu* (Paris: Études augustiniennes, 1983), 52–55. Given Maximos's theology of human seeking and questing, which is a process of inquiry driven by natural capacities implanted by God in the soul (cf. below, Qu. 59), "conjecture" is not simply logical deduction, inference, or speculation on the part of those lacking experience (although it may of course be invoked as a modesty topos). In classical Greek, στοχασμός also means to "divine the future" or simply "divination," and thus suggests a mode of contemplation relative to future or transcendent realities. Thus for Nyssa, *Commentary on the Song of Songs* 1 (GNO 6:37), the term is a function of his apophatic theology, which "conjectures about the incomprehensible." Maximos has argued throughout the *Responses*, as he does here, that only a search by an intellect free of the passions "will attain the truth of intelligible realities," generating a conjecture that will receive a response from the Spirit.

4. Ps 49.14; Heb 13.15.

QUESTION 55

ed them the knowledge of what they were seeking, or they will find that the meaning of the text has escaped them, and consequently revere the things of God even more greatly, realizing that divine realities transcend their capacity of comprehension.[5] Thus, I too, undertaking a conjectural examination of the passage before us, call upon God to help in the things that will be said, for I find that the power of my mind is in every way inferior to the sublimity of the enigmas of Scripture. And should I, on the one hand, succeed in my task, the success will belong entirely to God, who through my effort to comprehend will lead me to gratitude. If, on the other hand, it should happen that I fail in my attempt, the benefit of incomprehension will again be from God, who through His providence rightly hinders in advance[4] the conceit that is born from knowledge, and thus He will make my incomprehension an occasion for modesty.[6]

55.3. Approaching, then, as I said, the meaning of this text by way of conjecture, I begin with the things set forth in Scripture. In the preceding chapter, it is written of Zerubbabel that: "When the young man had gone forth, he lifted up his face to heaven toward Jerusalem, and blessed the king of heaven."[7] It is clear[5] that, after the presentation of the proposals to Darius the king, he "went forth" from the face of none other than the same Darius. As I have already said prior to embarking on this examination, Darius is the prevailing law of nature.[8] Understanding him like this is clearly consistent with the interpretation of his name, which means "generation," or "genealogy," or "one who figures in a genealogy," according to those with expertise in this language. Indeed the words "generation" and "genealogy" express the characteristic property of the natural law insofar as the human genus and all that figures in genealogies are subject to nature,[6] and a genealogy concerns the things around nature. Darius is therefore correctly taken as a

---

5. Cf. the parallel formulation in Basil, *Hexaemeron* 2.1 (SC 26bis:138–40).
6. A phrase indebted to Gregory Nazianzus, *Or.* 43.1 (SC 384:118, lines 24–29).
7. 1 Esd 4.58.
8. See above, Qu. 54.4.

symbol of the law of nature, for this law contains the genera and species that are subject to nature along with what is observed around nature, by which I mean time and place, for together with every created being one may observe the necessary conditions for its possibility of existence.[9]

55.4. Darius, then, as I said, is the law of nature. Zerubbabel, on the other hand, is the contemplative intellect that "went forth," as if from Darius, meaning from the law of nature, and transcended the splendid array of visible realities subject to time and place, and lifted up the face of its cognitive disposition for virtue toward heaven, that is, toward the height of intelligible essences, toward the intelligible Jerusalem which is in the heavens. By this I am referring to that Jerusalem whose "walls are painted upon the hands" of the Lord,[10] in which is the "dwelling place of all those that rejoice,"[11] and toward which the true return of the captives takes place, who are seeking, in the words of the Apostle, their "dwelling place in heaven."[12] [7] Such captives are those who, together with the great David, are able to say: "If I forget you, O Jerusalem, let my right hand be forgotten; may my tongue cleave to my larynx, if I do not remember you."[13] Perhaps this is to be taken in

---

9. The Greek phrase rendered here as "necessary conditions" (τῶν [ὧν] οὐκ ἄνευ) is the equivalent of the Latin *sine qua non*, indicating necessary actions or conditions without which other things cannot exist. Neoplatonic writers use the phrase to denote two or more objects or entities whose existences are mutually and qualitatively conditioned (if not necessarily mutually caused); cf. below, Qu. 64.3; and Qu. 65.23. The notion that "time and space" are among such necessary conditions, which also appears in *Amb.* 10.58; and ibid., 10.91 (DOML 1:242; 292), is attested in the *Anonymous Prolegomena to Platonic Philosophy* (ed. L. G. Westerink [Amsterdam: North-Holland, 1963], 16): "Time and place constitute the *sine qua non* for existence." The phrase was also used by Philo, *On the Decalogue* 31.1: "Those who study the doctrines of philosophy say that the categories in nature, as they are called, are ten only, that is, substance, quality, quantity, relation, activity, passivity, state, position, along with the necessary conditions for the possibility of their existence, namely, time and place" (LCL 7:20–21); cf. idem, *On Arithmetical Numbers*, ed. K. Staehle (Leipzig: Teubner, 1931), 99, lines 4–5.

10. Is 49.16.
11. Ps 86.7.
12. 2 Cor 5.2.
13. Ps 136.5–6.

the sense that the "right hand" signifies the spiritual practice of divine and praiseworthy things, while the "tongue cleaving to the larynx"[8] signifies the cognitive activity of reason, cleaving in ignorance to the "throat," in other words, closed by that passion in the vicinity of the throat, and remaining immovable in terms of its appetite for ineffable good things, and thus not able to "taste how good the Lord is."[14]

55.5. If, however, while hastening toward Jerusalem, Zerubbabel steps outside the principles of time and nature,[9] whether we understand him to be the contemplative intellect within us or the Creator Word who transcends us—who dwelt among us and became like us, and thus became man, so that He might, through His Incarnation, raise up to Himself those who exiled themselves from dispassion and life to the passions and death of the flesh—it is only natural that, as much as is lawful, he takes with himself[15] those who closely resemble him,[16] and leads them to the Jerusalem of the heavens, whose sublime extremity of virtue and knowledge Scripture symbolically diversified and likened to the various species and numbers in this passage. For every person who is righteous and loves God, when he returns to the Jerusalem which is above,[17] completes the spiritual principle of each species and each number mentioned in this passage, gathering them together into a single fulfillment of virtue and knowledge.

55.6. This can be seen quite clearly in the passage from Scripture that is under examination, which says: "All those of Israel, from twelve years old and upward, besides children and women, were forty-three thousand three hundred and sixty."[18] One cannot but admire here the precision of the words of the Spirit, which indicates that absolutely none of those numbered among Israel, who came forth from Babylon—by which I mean the confusion of this present age—were under twelve years old.

---

14. Cf. Ps 33.8.
15. Here both subjects are implied, i.e., Zerubbabel as a symbol of both the contemplative intellect and the transcendent Word of God.
16. Cf. Heb 2.14.
17. Cf. Gal 4.26.
18. 1 Esd 5.41.

Here the word of Scripture mystically affirms that only the person who is not subject to sensation and time—for this is what the number twelve signifies, being the sum of five on account of the senses, and seven on account of time—and who has broken off his soul's relation to them, only such a person, I say, steps outside of their confusion, hastening toward the city which is above, having, without counting women and children, the total number of forty-three thousand three hundred and sixty.

55.7. The "children"[10] may perhaps signify the thoughts of the natural and blameless passions that do not come under our control, while "women" may perhaps signify the mind's conceptions, or the natural appetites and desires that bring no accusation to those who possess them, insofar as they are necessary concomitants of natural appetite.[19] Ordinary food, for example, can quite naturally and apart from our own wishes produce pleasure, satisfying an outstanding need. So too does drink relieve the pangs of thirst; and sleep renews the strength exhausted through wakefulness, and so on with all our other natural passions, which are necessary for the maintenance of life, and which are used by the diligent in the acquisition of virtue.[20] Even if such "children" are not counted together with the men, they nonetheless go forth together with every intellect fleeing from the confusion of sin. This takes place so that the intellect does not, on their account, remain a captive slave of the blameworthy and unnatural passions, the control of which lies within our power, but that instead they should have no governing principle within them other than the movement of the natural passions. And they are not numbered together with the rest,[11] for it is not natural that the passions, which bind our

---

19. The natural and blameless passions are distinct from those passions that are contrary to nature and blameworthy, which are linked to human passivity and fallen human nature. Among the former, Maximos mentions the involuntary experience of hunger, thirst, and the need for sleep. The latter are constituted through the willful abuse of these passions, so that, for example, the natural and blameless need to eat degenerates into the unnatural and blameworthy vice of gluttony; cf. *Amb.* 4.4; ibid., 5.15 (DOML 1:25; 47); and above, Qu. 21.

20. On the "diligent" and the role of the passions in the life of virtue, see above, Qu. 1.3.

nature to this present life, should accompany us into immortal and eternal life.[21]

55.8. The "forty thousand"[22] is the tetrad of the general virtues, with which the intellect, having passed through nature and time, is restored to the blessed state of dispassion.[23] For a myriad[24] is recognized solely by the element of the monad,[12] and it is completely impossible for it to be signified through any other numerical letter or symbol, insofar as the myriad is identical with the monad on the level of its substrate—even if it admits of difference from it solely on the level of thought—for the end of the monad is the myriad, and the beginning of the myriad is the monad, or, to speak more strictly, the myriad is the monad in motion, and the myriad when motionless is the monad. In the same way, each of the general virtues has as its beginning and end the divine and ineffable Monad, by which I mean God, because each virtue is from God, having both its originating principle and final end in Him, and is identical with God, differing from Him only according to the rationale of thought, for it is clearly from God, and in God, and unto God that every virtue comes into being.[25]

---

21. Just as the passions did not exist (or were not operative) in paradise, neither will they be found in the future life, where the human person will no longer experience biological hunger, thirst, the need for sleep, or corporeal pleasure and pain, inasmuch as the enjoyment of the righteous and the sufferings of the damned will be spiritual in nature.

22. 1 Esd 5.41. Literally, the "four units of ten thousand."

23. Following Plato, *Republic* 4.427e and 428b–29a, the four ("cardinal") virtues are σοφία/φρόνησις (wisdom, prudence), ἀνδρεία (courage), σωφροσύνη (temperance), and δικαιοσύνη (justice); cf. Maximos, *Ep.* 5 (PG 91:421C); *Carit.* 2.79 (ed. Caresa-Gastaldo, 132); *Pyrr.* (PG 91:309C–312A); Evagrios, *Praktikos* 89 (SC 171:680–88); idem, *Gnostikos* 44 (SC 356:172–74); and *Amb.* 21 (DOML 1:431–35). These virtues are "general" or "generic" not because they are the source of other "species" of virtue, but in the sense that they are the condition for the acquisition of other virtues and constitute the foundation on which the latter are established.

24. I.e., a unit of ten thousand.

25. In *Amb.* 7.21 (DOML 1:103), Maximos states that Christ is the "essence of the virtues." The virtues, moreover, are not restricted to the sphere of voluntary activity, but they are an ontological reality proceeding from the divine itself. Such a conception of the virtues aligns them very closely with the divine

55.9. Or it could be that, in speaking of "forty thousand," Scripture is referring to the four stages of those who, in the breadth of their contemplation and knowledge, are advancing in the decad of the divine commandments. For instance, among beginners, after their initial flight from evil,[13] the first stage is the simple practice of the commandments, which completes the first decad, which is also the monad. The second stage is the comprehensive observance of all the commandments, realized through the actual observance of each commandment, producing both the decad and the century, which are brought to completion by the reciprocal activity of each commandment, for when the decad is multiplied by ten, it produces the century.[26] The third stage is the tenfold multiplication of the century according to the law of nature, for the law of nature is a multiple of ten, inasmuch as it is constituted by a unit of ten, by which I mean the three powers of the soul, the five senses, the activity of speech, and natural fecundity. To be sure, the law of nature uses the soul's power of reason in order to seek and search for the Cause and the good things that pertain to the Cause; it uses the power of desire to make us long for the things we are seeking; and it uses the incensive, spirited power for safeguarding and caring affectionately for those things. It uses the senses for the purpose of making distinctions, a process which is itself divisible by five, and from which true understanding naturally arises—for there are universal distinctions marking divisions between things that began in time and things that did not begin in time;[14] between what is intelligible and what is not intelligible; between what can be spoken and what cannot be spoken; between what can be done and what cannot be done; and between corruptible things and things that are incorruptible. It uses the power of speech to manifest outwardly what is inward, and it uses natural fecundity for the increase of the good things that are sought, desired, cared for, known, and expressed. In this manner the century, multiplied by ten according to the law

---

energies, communicated to human beings as the gift of grace of the Holy Spirit, who was the focus of the previous Question.

26. On the interconnections among the commandments, see above, Qu. 4 and Qu. 12.

QUESTION 55

of nature, becomes the myriad. The fourth stage is the ascent, moving through contemplation and knowledge of the natural law according to the above-mentioned divisions, toward the more primal principle of each commandment. It is in light of this ascent that the myriad is contemplated as gathered into itself, recognized by the elemental mark of the primal monad.

55.10. For the one who has generally kept the commandments, and who by the keeping of each particular commandment has comprehended all the rest, and who to this comprehension has immediately joined the distinction obtaining within the natural law, and who, again, has cognitively raised up this law toward the principle of each commandment, has gathered together and summed up the four thousand, for at every stage of his progress he is honored by the mystery of the monad, toward which the principle of the myriad is gathered together.

55.11. Or, again, the four myriads can be said to signify what are called the four general dispassions.[27] The first type of dispassion, which is found in beginners, is the complete abstention from the actual committing of evil things.[15] The second, which is found among those who have advanced to the rational pursuit of virtue, is the complete rejection of the mind's assent to all evil thoughts.[16] The third, found among those who behold the principles of visible realities through creation's outward forms, is the complete immovability of desire in relation to the passions.[17] The fourth type of dispassion is the complete purification of even the merest mental images of the passions, and this is found in those who, through knowledge and contemplation, have made the governing power of their soul a pure and transparent mirror of God.[18]

55.12. Thus, whoever has purified himself of the activity of the passions, and freed himself from assenting mentally to them, and who has brought to a halt the movement of his desire for them, and who has cleansed his intellect of the stain of even their mere mental representations, possesses the forty

---

27. Mirroring the "four general virtues," the "four general dispassions" appears to be a uniquely Maximian doctrine; on Evagrios's "two dispassions," see Antoine Guillaumont, *Évagre le Pontique, Traité Pratique ou Le Moine*, SC 170, 98–112.

thousand and thus goes forth from matter and material realities, hastening toward the divine and peaceful limit of intelligible realities. Let us, then, understand the "forty thousand" in this manner. As for the "three thousand,"[28] they signify the perfect, correct, and pious theological principle concerning the Holy and Consubstantial Trinity, according to which the Holy Tri-hypostatic Monad is praised and believed by us to be one God.[19]

55.13. The "three hundred"[29] would here seem to hint at the principle of Providence, not simply because the physical form of the letter[20] signifies the power from on high directed downward, which encompasses laterally the extremities on either side (which manifests Providence as ineffably binding together the universe), but also because it is honored with the figure of the cross, on which the great, and first, and hidden mystery of Providence was accomplished.[30] For the great mystery of the Incarnation of God is the ineffable mode of Providence, and it was perhaps by taking courage from this figure and from the name of Him who for our sakes was nailed upon it, that the great patriarch Abraham, together with the "three hundred and eighteen,"[31] which is the figure and name of Jesus, went forth and triumphed over the opposing powers, symbolized through the kings. Because even through the physical forms of the letters of the alphabet, Scripture often reveals its own proper purpose to those who have purified themselves for the sake of that purpose.[32]

28. 1 Esd 5.41.
29. Ibid.
30. As explained in the scholion, the alphabetical symbol for 300 is the Greek letter *tau*, which, like the English letter "t," has the form of an upright cross; cf. *Amb.* 32.2–3 (DOML 2:55–57), where Maximos further expands on the form of the cross as a figure of divine providence.
31. Gn 14.14.
32. On the symbolic forms of Greek letters, see Cordula Bandt, *Der Traktat "Vom Mysterium der Buchstaben." Kritischer Text mit Einführung, Übersetzung und Anmerkungen* (Berlin: de Gruyter, 2007); eadem, "The Alphabet as Henotikon: The Tract *On the Mystery of Letters* against the Background of the Origenist Controversies of the 4th and 6th Centuries," *Historia Religionum* 6 (2014): 45–57; and Guy G. Stroumsa, "The Mystery of the Greek Letters: A Byzantine Kabbalah?" *Historia Religionum* 6 (2014): 35–44.

55.14. If, on the other hand, someone wishes to search for the meaning of Scripture through its numbers, he will find that even these reveal the workings of Providence, for the work of Providence is not only to safeguard nature in all its fullness, according to Providence's own principle of being, but also to manifest nature as possessing fully the principle of well-being, acquired by means of grace. Thus if one adds the one hundred to the two hundred, he obtains three hundred, which signifies nature and grace. For they say that the number two hundred quite often signifies nature, which is composed of two elements, namely, matter and form, while matter is fourfold on account of the four elements, and form is fivefold on account of sense perception, which shapes material mass into form; and if you multiply forty by five, or fifty by four, you obtain two hundred. The number one hundred signifies perfect virtue,[21] since it possesses the decad of divine commandments multiplied by ten. When Abraham attained this virtue, he became the father of the great Isaac, and, though dead according to nature, he became the begetter of life and joy according to the spirit.[33] And if you were to add one hundred to the two hundred, you would obtain the number three hundred, which designates Providence, which maintains nature according to the principle of well-being.

55.15. The number sixty signifies the natural power to perform the commandments perfected by means of the principles of the virtues. For if the number six signifies the productive power of nature—inasmuch as it is a perfect number and consists of its own parts, which is why it is written that God created the world in six days[34]—and if the number ten designates the perfection of the virtues contained within the commandments, then the number sixty clearly points to the capacity of nature to receive the divine principles contained in the commandments.[22]

55.16. It follows that the forty thousand, together with the three thousand three hundred and sixty, designate, respectively, the perfect principle concerning virtue, the venerable mys-

33. Cf. Gn 21.1–5.
34. Gn 2.2.

tery of theology, the true purpose of divine providence, and the practical power of nature imbued with the virtues. And it is together with these that a person completely goes forth, having separated, by means of the Spirit, his intellect from the flesh, from sensation, and from the world, and, leaving behind their mutual mixing and confusion—as those of old left Babylon—he hastens toward the city which is above, with his intellect free of any attachment or relation to anything whatsoever.

55.17. "Their menservants and handmaidens were seven thousand three hundred and seven."[35] Concerning menservants and handmaidens, the law proclaims that Hebrew menservants and handmaidens must work for six years and be liberated in the seventh year.[36] The foreign menservants and handmaidens, however, are to be slaves for the duration of the age,[37] although "age," I think, means the fiftieth year, at which point they are to be set free. The Hebrew manservant and the Hebrew maidservant are to be understood as reason and discursive thinking, which are the servants of the practical philosopher for six years, until such time, that is, that they establish the idea of ethical propriety and discover the ways of virtue. For in relation to every intellect engaged in practice, reason and discursive thinking (just like a manservant and a maidservant) are placed in service, conceiving and realizing practices amenable to virtue, and having, as it were, all their power drawn up against the spirits of wickedness that oppose practical philosophy. Having completed the work of practical philosophy, hinted at by the six years of their service (for we said that the number six signifies practical philosophy), they are granted their freedom and thus advance to the spiritual contemplation of kindred principles contained in beings. And when reason and discursive thinking reach the seventh year,[23] that is, the settled habit of dispassion, the passions of the soul, being tamed and subdued by the great labor of reason and the discursive reasoning united to it, withdraw and retreat.

55.18. The foreign manservant and the foreign maidservant,

---

35. 1 Esd 5.41.
36. Cf. Dt 15.12.
37. Cf. Lv 25.44–46.

on the other hand, are anger and desire, which the contemplative intellect perpetually subjugates to the absolute rule of reason, so that they might, through courage and temperance, be of service in the life of virtue. They are not in any way granted their freedom until the law of nature is completely swallowed up by the law of the Spirit, just as the death of the wretched flesh will be swallowed up by life everlasting,[38] that is, not before the entire image of the unoriginate kingdom[24] is clearly revealed, mimetically manifesting in itself the entire form of the archetype. Upon reaching this state, I say, the contemplative intellect grants anger and desire their freedom.[25] It frees desire by transforming it into the unalloyed pleasure and undefiled bliss of divine love; it frees anger by translating it into a spiritual fervor, a fiery perpetual movement, and a right-minded madness. Indeed it was while he was in this state that the great ray of the pure light, the great apostle Paul, heard King Agrippa say: "Paul, you are mad!"[39] and, again, when describing himself to the Corinthians, he said: "If I am outside myself in ecstasy, it is for God, and if I am in my right mind, it is for you,"[40] clearly calling the godly and right-minded madness "ecstasy," inasmuch as it places the right-minded and ecstatic intellect outside of beings.[41]

55.19. I suppose the number of the menservants and maidservants signifies Providence as active within time and according to reason, together with the modes of dispassion.[26] In accordance with this Providence, the intellect engaged with practice, pressing upon both reason and discursive thinking, as if they were the Hebrew menservants and maidservants, defines the measure of their labor in the service of virtue, making them useful for contemplation, and—taking charge of anger and desire as foreign menservants and maidservants, as a master over slaves—guiding them, with an eye on the goal, to an

---

38. Cf. 1 Cor 15.54; 2 Cor 5.4.
39. Acts 26.24.
40. 2 Cor 5.13.
41. Cf. *Amb.* 7.10; ibid., 20.2 (DOML 1:87–89, 409–11); Gregory of Nyssa, *Homilies on the Song of Songs* 10 (GNO 6:309); and Sherwood, *Earlier Ambigua*, 124–54.

equal and honorable share in freedom.[27] It does this by transforming desire into an appetite delighting in divine realities, and anger into an unceasing force of the delighting appetite, by grace transforming foreign slaves into true Hebrews.[42]

55.20. "There were eight hundred and fifty-five musicians and chanters."[43] "Musicians" are those who, in their practice, by means of the modes of the virtues, vocalize the divine word, but without contemplation.[28] "Chanters," on the other hand, are those who, by means of the modes of the virtues, together with the cognitive enjoyment of contemplation, initiate others into the divine word, and delight their intelligible ears.[29] Their number designates the true understanding of eternal realities, to the extent that this is attainable by human beings. For the number eight hundred alludes to the principles of knowledge, and the number fifty to the future principles of virtues.[30] The number five represents the true understanding of knowledge and virtue, as was mentioned a moment ago when we considered this number.

55.21. "Four hundred and thirty-five camels."[44] The camels, going forth with the sons of Israel, being released with great freedom from their bitter captivity, are the different natural contemplations of visible realities. Not unlike camels, they have, in terms of sense perception, feet, that is, the impure surfaces of visible realities; in terms of intellect they have the camel's head, that is, the pure and loftier spiritual principles found within visible realities.

55.22. And perhaps it was concerning such camels that the great Isaiah, prophetically proclaiming in advance the glory of the intelligible Jerusalem, said: "The camels of Midian and Ephah shall cover you,"[45] meaning the spiritual contemplations of the natural passions.[31] For Midian means "secretion" or "bloody clay" or "human and maternal sweat," while Ephah means "possession of the back," which is contemplation elevated to a height beyond the passions pertaining to the flesh, and

42. Cf. above, Qu. 1.3.
43. 1 Esd 5.41.
44. 1 Esd 5.42.
45. Is 60.6.

the flesh is the "back" of the soul, as its "hind part." It is by these things, Scripture says, like walls around a holy city, that the spiritual portion of the peaceful and untroubled knowledge of mystical contemplations is covered.

55.23. This same number[46] designates the aforementioned power, which signifies rational motion in relation to nature and time.[32]

55.24. "Seven thousand seven hundred and thirty-six horses."[47] A "horse" is a person who maintains, throughout his life, all the vigor of his spirited capacity focused on the race for the virtues. For they say that horse bile is useful for common foot sores.[48] This is why, of all the tame animals that have been domesticated by man, the horse has been judged to be the most suited and most powerful for racing. And this is also why the great prophet Habakkuk, inspired by the Spirit, compared the holy apostles to horses, saying: "And you make your horses enter the sea, troubling all the waters."[49] He called the holy and blessed apostles "horses," because they carried the saving message of truth to nations, kings, and the whole world, which latter the prophet figuratively called a "sea." And he likened the nations to waters, which were stirred up and troubled by the great power of the word of the Spirit, and, by means of this salvific shock, the nations were moved from faithlessness to faith, and to knowledge from ignorance, and from vice to virtue.

55.25. And this is made clear by the very number of the horses,[33] which is a figure of the settled state of practical philosophy with respect to the virtues. For the number seven thousand

46. I.e., four hundred.

47. 1 Esd 5.42.

48. "Bile" (χολή) is linked to anger or wrath, and thus is naturally aligned with θυμός and the irrational, animal part of the soul; cf. *Amb.* 10.111; and *Amb.* 13.5 (DOML 1:327–29; 353–55). For the use of horse bile in the treatment of ulcers, see *Hippiatrica Cantabrigiensia,* chaps. 11.13, 69.3; *Hippiatrica, Additamenta Londinensia ad hippiatrica Cantabrigiensia,* section 23.1 (ed. Eugene Oder and Charles Hoppe, *Corpus Hippiatricorum Graecorum* II [Leipzig: Teubner, 1927; repr. 1971], 159). I am thankful to Stavros Lazaris of the Centre National de le Recherche Scientifique for helpful discussion on this passage, and for providing me with references to Galen on the use of animal bile in the treatment of ulcers.

49. Hab 3.15.

seven hundred signifies, in chronological terms, swift movement in the virtues, while the number thirty-six signifies practical activity of nature running in conjunction with the virtues.

55.26. "Eight hundred and forty-five mules."[50] According to the praiseworthy meaning,[51] a "mule" is a settled state of mind completely sterile of evil. Thus it was quite fitting and appropriate to the spirit of Scripture that the one whose lot it was to rule Israel was commanded to sit, not on a horse, but on a mule,[52] indicating clearly that the contemplative intellect must rule over the conceptual forms, objects of contemplation, and proper movements that exist within beings, and must have a settled state of mind barren of evil. In other words, such an intellect should absolutely neither conceive of evil nor give birth to it, and it is while seated upon such a state that it should move and be borne toward contemplation, so that, while engaged in the spiritual investigation of beings, it will not unwittingly fall into the hands of one of the wicked spirits that endeavor, through some sensible object, to corrupt the pure disposition of the heart.

55.27. At the same time, we know that the mule also has a blameworthy meaning in Scripture, as in the verse: "Be not like the horse and the mule, which have no understanding."[53] Here Scripture calls the state of a soul neighing for the pleasures of the passions a "horse," and it calls the state that neither conceives the good nor gives birth to it a "mule," equally forbidding both states to those who desire salvation, inasmuch as the former is productive of evil, and the latter is impotent with respect to virtue. Also taken in a blameworthy sense is the mule of Absalom, upon which he sat when he went forth seeking the death of his father.[54] Through these things the Spirit reveals that a person who is wounded by any kind of vainglory on account of virtue or knowledge vainly grows the hair of his

---

50. 1 Esd 5.42.
51. Cf. above, Qu. 38.2, on "praise- and blameworthy meanings" in Scripture.
52. Cf. 3 Kgs 1.33.
53. Ps 31.9.
54. 2 Kgs 18.9.

self-conceit in complicated and crossbred contrivances. Like a seemingly virile yet sterile mule, he makes a display of his moral conduct in order to deceive others. Hanging in midair by such hair, he thinks he will supplant the father who begot him through the word of his teaching, because in his arrogant tyranny he wants to usurp as his own the reputation of virtue and knowledge that his father had received as a gift from God. When, however, such a person, aiming to use reason to fight for truth, goes forth into the broad place[34] of natural contemplation in the spirit, his hair gets caught on the seething sensations found in the "thick boughs of the oak tree" growing in the field of material appearances. With his intellect now fatally entangled by his empty conceit, he is left "suspended between heaven and earth."[55] For the knowledge of the vainglorious man is not like heaven, which would draw him upward from the conceit that drags him downward; neither is his knowledge like the earth—by which I mean the humility that forms the foundation of ascetic practice—which would draw him downward from the conceit that draws him upward. And when he dies, he is mourned by the teacher who begot him,[56] for this man is compassionate and loves God, and thus he imitates God, who "does not desire the death of a sinner, but that he should turn and live."[57]

55.28. To consider this passage from another point of view, it seems to me that David himself clearly designates the practical intellect, whereas Absalom signifies the self-conceit that is born from the coupling of the practical intellect with sensation. For King Geshur's daughter signifies sensation, which David took to himself and thus begot Absalom.[58] Geshur, moreover, means "guidance of the wall." Here the word "wall" obviously means the body, while the "guidance" of the body is the law of the body, that is, sensation, from which Absalom is born, whose name means "father of supposed peace," which is clearly what self-conceit is. For if we suppose that we will make peace with

55. Ibid.
56. 2 Kgs 19.1.
57. Ezek 33.11.
58. 2 Kgs 3.3.

the passions, we are presumptuous and conceited. And when the great David saw such conceit rising up before him, he acted with knowledge, and, leaving the Tabernacle and Jerusalem and Judea, he fled beyond the Jordan to the land of Gilead,[59] which means the "migration of mourning," or the "migration of testimony" or "their revelation." He fled because he judged himself unworthy—on account of his uprising of conceit—of the holy Tabernacle, that is, of mystical theology. He likewise judged himself unworthy of Jerusalem, which is the peaceful and highest visionary knowledge of divine realities, and of Judea, which is the confession of the joy of the practical life. In this, David is a symbol of the intellect transferring[35] its own proper powers to a place of mourning, bringing with them the testimony of its conscience concerning what these powers had formerly done, along with the recollection of each of its faults according to their kind (for this is their "revelation"). To speak simply, he is a symbol of the mind's return to a moment before the advent of grace (for this is what it means to go "beyond the Jordan"), when the intellect was estranged from the grace of virtue and knowledge. And, by recognizing its own weakness, and having acquired humility as a powerful antidote to conceit—a humility it received through the awareness of what is proper to it—it finds itself in the state of beautiful and noble mourning, and puts to death the tyrant of conceit, and returns once again to its own proper glory, and rules over the land of Judah and Jerusalem, ruling as king over the holy Tabernacle of God, and offering Him pure and spotless worship.

55.29. But let us return to the number of mules that the Jews took with them when they were released from captivity, considering, according to our ability, the spiritual meaning contained within their number. Scripture says that there were "eight hundred and forty-five mules."[60] This number indicates the perfect dispassion of the intellect with respect to objects of sense and sensation, according to its permanent state of sterility in relation to evil, that is, a state that does not give birth to evil. For

---

59. Cf. 2 Kgs 15.13–17; 17.22. On Gilead, cf. *Exp. Ps.* 59 (CCSG 23:14, lines 201–209).

60. 1 Esd 5.42.

the number eight hundred[36] taken in its praiseworthy sense signifies the characteristic dispassion of the future age, while the number forty signifies objects of sense, and the number five signifies the senses.

55.30. "Five thousand twenty-five beasts under the yoke."[61] What comes "under the yoke" is the body that is yoked to the soul in order to bear the burdens of the practical life for the sake of virtue, that is, the permanent state of the body according to virtue. And it was perhaps on the backs of such beasts that the sons of the great Jacob transported the wheat from Egypt for nourishment in the Promised Land, enclosing within the "pouches" of their minds the spiritual knowledge gleaned from natural contemplation, like wheat taken from Egypt, bearing it upon their bodies through ascetic practice, and transporting it to the future life.[62] And the number of these beasts, being a wholly spherical number,[37] indicates the unvarying motion of the body's virtuous state in relation to ascetic practice, a motion which accords unchangeably with the principle of knowledge. For those who are wise in these matters say that the spherical motion alone is changeless, for of all the other motions of beings it alone possesses in all things an unparalleled evenness.[63]

55.31. Here, then, is my interpretation of the things found in this passage, according to my ability to understand and express them. If, however, someone should wish to say that these things also foreshadow the different grades of the faithful in the Church, that is, different dispositions, as we would say, he would not be mistaken. From this point of view, "men" are those who have reached, according to the measure of their desire, "the measure of the fullness of Christ,"[64] attaining virtue consonant with love through the spontaneous inclination of their free will. "Menservants" and "handmaidens" are those who, through fear

61. 1 Esd 5.42.
62. Cf. Gn 42.26–27, 44.1.
63. Alluding perhaps to the "circular motion" described by Dionysios, *DN*, 4.8–9; 9.9 (143–54; 213; 704D–705D, 916CD); cf. Maximos *Amb.* 7.6; and *Amb.* 10.9 (DOML 1:81; 163); yet Dionysios never uses the word "spherical" in any context, and thus the source seems closer to a passage in Proclus, *Theologica Platonica* 1.14 (ed. Saffrey and Westerink, 1.65, lines 4–13).
64. Eph 4.13.

of the threat of eternal punishments, take on the weight of practical philosophy. "Musicians" are those who correctly explain the reason for ascetic practice, and who heal the passions of others. "Chanters" are those who through contemplation bring to light the beauty of the knowledge of the divine words, and who disperse like gloom the ignorance of others. "Camels" are those who through reason tame what is crooked and make it suitable for virtue. "Horses" are those who run nobly along the course of a godly life. "Mules" are those who are mixed in their way of life, and who without harm display a philosophical ethos to the public. The "beasts under the yoke" are those who toil in the ascetic life and who through contemplation receive reason like a rider. If someone gathers all of these together, he will assemble the fullness of the holy Church, adorned by and through many beautiful forms of virtue.

55.32. It seems to me that our spiritual contemplation of this difficult passage has reached an end. If, however, there is someone rich in the grace of knowledge, who, like the great Samuel, spiritually beholds future realities, let him clearly reveal to us the meaning concealed within the veiled words of this passage, a meaning that flashes forth in the mind with the sublime light of the truth that is present in beings. And let him persuade those who are capable of learning that the Holy Spirit has written nothing that is unsuitable or to no purpose, even if we are unable to grasp it, for all things were written mystically and suitably for the sake of human salvation. The beginning and the end of this salvation is wisdom, which in the beginning produces fear,[65] but afterwards, when it is perfected, gives rise to longing.[38] Or rather, in the beginning, in Her economy for us, Wisdom manifests Herself for our sake as fear,[39] so that the lover of evil might cease, but later She appears in Her natural state for Her own sake as desire, so that She might fill with spiritual laughter those who have abandoned their companionship with all existing things in order to dwell with Her.[66]

55.33. I believe that it is about such men that the Spirit has written, such menservants and handmaids, such musicians

65. Cf. Prv 9.10.
66. Cf. Prv 3.13–17.

QUESTION 55 375

and chanters, such camels, such horses, such mules, and such beasts under the yoke—it is about these, I say, that the Holy Spirit knows how to write, not about those whom the senses of the body are by nature able to describe, but those whom the pure intellect receives to be shaped and figured by the writing pen of grace.[67]

Scholia

[1] The fullness of the Spirit's grace is the wisdom that, in terms of its potential, state, and activity, encompasses all the knowledge accessible to human beings who have been made perfect according to Christ. Through this wisdom, the intellect finds itself outside of sense-perceptible figures, and draws near to the inner principles of all that has come into being, and of all things that have been written, stripped of all their diversity. Such wisdom, gathering around itself the divine characters contained within these figures, configures them into a single, divinely suitable form. By means of this form, it receives, as much as possible, the indivisible knowledge of all beings in a uniform manner, through which the light of truth shines forth like lightning.

[2] When, he says, true men of knowledge teach the inner principles of the mysteries contained in the Scriptures, they make use of the literal figures as examples, adapting the spirit of the contemplation to the literal words for the sake of the spiritual elevation[68] of those being taught. Their aim is that the type be preserved by means of sense perception, and the inner principle by means of the intellect, because the human person is constituted of soul and body, with respect to which both intellect and sensation naturally subsist, being elements of one and the same human being.

[3] "Praise" is a word that expresses divine beauty. "Praising" is the relationship of the one who praises to what is praised, that is, the recounting of words expressive of divine majesty,

---

67. Cf. *Amb.* 7.24: "God neither knows sensory things by sensation, nor intelligible things by intellection (for it is not possible that He who is beyond all beings should know beings in a manner derived from beings)" (DOML 1:109).
68. I.e., ἀναγωγή.

through which the state of knowledge is of a nature to be constituted, transforming the one who praises into what he praises. The "sacrifice" of such praise is not only the perfect mortification of passions contrary to nature and their transposition with those according to nature, but also the complete drawing near to God of the one who praises.

[4] If in our ascetic practice, he says, knowledge is not curbed by the fear of God, then it produces conceit, inasmuch as the conceited man regards as his own the knowledge that has merely been lent to him, and he uses his borrowed knowledge to win praise for himself from others. When, however, our practice is augmented by desire for God, and we receive no knowledge of anything beyond the level of our practice, practice makes the practitioner modest, humbling him in the face of principles that transcend his ability to understand.

[5] Whoever, he says, through faith in God and love for Him, has conquered the irrational movements of the passions contrary to nature, finds himself outside the sphere of the natural law itself, and is wholly transferred to the realm of intelligible realities, and, together with himself, he releases from foreign slavery all that is kindred to his nature along with whatever is related to it.

[6] Everything that in any way is a substrate, or which can be predicated of a substrate, or which is in a substrate, is as a rule subject to nature, and it is from these principles that definitions are established for things susceptible of being defined. For any of the items that complete the different natures of beings are themselves of a nature to be included in the definitions for the precise meaning of what is signified, insofar as they subsist in the substrate and together with the substrate, and it is from these items and by means of them that the substrate comes into being, and they are not predicated of it externally. What pertains to nature are those conditions that are conceived of as being both anterior and posterior to that nature. This is both because all created beings came into existence relative to a "where" and a "when," and because simultaneously with their coming into existence we may observe together with them their universal position and motion, which very things are place and

time, by means of which nature exists relative to an outward position and in terms of its motion toward its principle of origin, but not according to its subsistence.[69] For nature is not created out of these conditions, but possesses externally and by means of these conditions the principle of its being and position. It follows that when we observe solely the principles of being associated with genera, species, and individuals, we grasp together with these items the constitutive differences of their essential principles. But when, on the other hand, we establish a genealogy, we necessarily grasp together with created beings a "where" and a "when," that is, the conditions of time and place, observing their principle of origin and position, without which absolutely no created being exists, because no created being is free from the circumscription of its principle of origin and place.

[7] Jerusalem and the heavenly dwelling place are the dispassionate state of virtue and the form of knowledge possessing no erroneous mental representation warring against it.

[8] The tongue, he says, is a symbol of the soul's cognitive activity, and the larynx is a token of the natural self-love for the body. Thus the one who in a blameworthy manner cleaves them together is not able to remember the peaceful settled state of virtue and knowledge, for by means of the confusion of the two he zealously takes pleasure in his bodily passions.

[9] Darius, he says, is taken to mean the law of nature containing both nature and time, for Darius as the law has authority to use all things that are according to nature or which pertain to nature. The intellect, then, which goes forth from the law of nature as if from Darius, finds itself beyond time and nature, not being hindered by any mental representations of things subject to nature and time, so that it might not, by bearing about the images of corruptible realities, become a temple of idols containing multiple forms of unclean passions for veneration instead of the one God.[70]

---

69. For an extended discussion of time and place, see *Amb.* 10.91–92 (DOML 1:291–93).

70. Cf. *The Anonymous Sayings of the Desert Fathers* 600: "Take careful thought, for there is an altar and a sanctuary and a virtual execrable idol in the soul.... For he who is a slave to fornication is an idol-worshiper, having

[10] In the menservants, who are not counted together with their masters, but who go forth with them, he contemplated the thoughts of passions that are not subject to our free will, the use of which (if not their existence) is nonetheless subject to our free will, for we are their masters. In the women, on the other hand, he contemplated the appetites that arise blamelessly from passions that are not subject to our free will, which the intellect takes with itself and leads to life in God, so that they do not become captives to the slavery of unnatural passions.

[11] Here he is speaking of the reason why Scripture did not count the children and the women together with the men.

[12] In the same way that the myriad is the end of a monad in motion, while the beginning of an unmoving myriad is the monad—for the beginning of every end is clearly its motionlessness, and the end of every beginning is the completion of its motion—so too, faith, being the natural beginning of the virtues, has as its end the completion of the good through the virtues; and that which by nature is good, as the end of the virtues, having faith as its beginning, is innately gathered up in faith. For faith is an innate good, and the good is actualized faith. God is by nature both faithful and good,[71] the former inasmuch as He is the primal good, and the latter inasmuch as He is the ultimate object of desire. These attributes are in every way identical with each other, and they cannot be divided from each other by any principle whatsoever, but only on the level of thought, on account of the motion of all things that take their beginning from God and attain their end in Him. Thus the myriad, as a figure of the ultimate object of desire, contains within itself the perfect desire of all that moves toward it. And the monad, as a symbol of the primal good, constitutes the perfect foundation of all that moves outward from it. It follows that the four myriads are the final perfect good that is shown forth analogously through the activity of each general virtue.

[13] The one who has fled from evil, he says, and who has

---

within himself the effigy of Aphrodite. Or again, he who is the slave of anger and wrath … has Ares within himself as a god" (trans. John Wortley [Cambridge: Cambridge University Press, 2013], 481–83).

71. Cf. Mt 19.17.

kept the decad of commandments simply by refraining from sin, and who has shown that the practice of any one commandment perfectly contains the other nine (for all are understood in each in the observance of one), has made the decad a century—for the perfect keeping of each commandment is the complete observance of all the rest—and, indeed, having acquired through true knowledge the perfect natural discernment of the commandments, he has made the century a miliad. And, finally, having drawn near in intellectual contemplation to the naked principles of these commandments, he made the miliad a myriad, so that from the expansion that unfolds through practice he gathers them together through contemplation into a unique monad. To state the matter simply, whoever has kept the commandments inviolate through his perfect flight from evil, and who has demonstrated the perfection of their practice, and has attained their most complete natural discernment, and who has reached the perfect end of their spiritual contemplation, has come to possess the four myriads, gathering them together in the perfect principle at each stage of his progress. For that which is perfect possesses inseparably the principles both of the beginning and of the end.

[14] There was a time, he says, when evil began to be, for it has its beginning in our movement contrary to nature. The good, however, has no beginning, for by its nature it exists before every age and time. The good, he says, is intelligible, and our intellect should be engaged with this alone. Evil, on the other hand, is not intelligible, and our intellect should never be engaged with it. The good, he says, can be spoken about, and this alone should be the object of our speech; but evil may not be spoken, and this alone must not be the object of our speech. He further says that the good comes into being—for whereas by nature it is unbegotten, by grace and on account of God's love for mankind it deigns to come into being for the divinization of all of us who do, speak, and think the good—and it is the good alone that should come into being, and not evil, which is the only thing that should not come into being. For evil, he says, is corruptible, because corruption is the nature of evil, which does not in any way whatsoever possess its own existence. The

good, on the other hand, is incorruptible, inasmuch as it exists eternally, and will never cease to be, and it guards all things in which it dwells.[72] It is, then, the good that we seek after by means of reason, long for by means of our desire, keep inviolate by means of our incensive power, distinguish in separation from what is contrary to it by means of sense perception informed by knowledge of its cause, and by speaking the good through our power of speech we manifest it to those who are ignorant of it, and by our power of spiritual fecundity we multiply it, or rather, to speak the truth, it is we who are multiplied by it.

[15] He calls the active movement of the body that has no contact with sin "first dispassion."

[16] He calls the soul's complete rejection of impassioned thoughts "second dispassion," which withers the movement of the passions of the first dispassion, since it no longer has impassioned thoughts to incite it to sinful activity.

[17] He calls the complete motionlessness of desire in relation to the passions "third dispassion," through which the second dispassion is naturally generated, for it is constituted by purity of thoughts.

[18] He calls the mind's complete setting aside of all sensory images "fourth dispassion," through which the third dispassion came into being, since the mind no longer possesses the mental images of sensory objects imprinting upon it the forms of the passions.

[19] The miliad is a monad having no need of perfection or completion, for it possesses the most complete principle of all the monads anterior to itself and those of which it is composed. This is why, when a monad is added together, it is productive again of a monad, but not a decad, because the monad receives the addition of the miliad, according to those who have accurately investigated the meaning of numbers. It is only natural, then, that the triad of miliads on the level of theology signifies the principle of the Trinity, and it is in possession of this principle, together with perfect virtue, that one "comes forth," having left behind the Babylon of the mind.

---

72. See above, Intro. 1.2.11–12.

[20] The letter *tau* is a figure of the cross, bearing within its form the outlines of the cross. The *iota*, as the initial letter of the name of Jesus, signifies the awesome Name. The *eta*, which is the second letter, points to the permanent ethos of virtue.[73] Mystically combining these figures into a number, the patriarch Abraham courageously came forth against the opposing powers, for he possessed "three hundred and eighteen household servants";[74] that is, through the three hundred he possessed the principle of theology which contains the universe; through the ten he possessed the ineffable mystery of the divine Incarnation of the Word; and through the eight he possessed the perfect mode of the permanent state of virtue. The word of Scripture called these things the members of his "household," for to the one who possesses them they are the progeny of the heart and divine by grace.

[21] The number one hundred is the multiplication by ten of the divine decad of commandments, for it is the perfect comprehension of all the decads, insofar as each one is actualized through the others. And the comprehension of all of them, which is actualized through each, is absolutely complete and whole virtue. Virtue that is perfect and complete is wisdom, and wisdom is the infallible knowledge of truth. Thus whoever has infallibly known the truth has become "one hundred" years old, as was the great Abraham,[75] and likewise understands his body to be mortified; that is, he sees life according to the senses departing into deadness, and gives birth in the spirit to "living joy," for this is what that name Isaac means.[76] Thus the mark of

---

73. See Larry Hurtado, "The Origin of the *Nomina Sacra:* A Proposal," *JBL* 117 (1998): 655–73, on the contracted form of the name of Jesus, the "first of the Christian *nomina sacra*," which, along with its numerical significance, is traced to the Jewish abbreviation of the name YHWH, which was not a scribal space-saving device but a form of reverence toward the divine name.

74. Gn 14.14. Genesis notes that Abraham actively "calculated" (ἠρίθμησε) the number in question (Gn 14.14); cf. Michel Aubineau, "Les 318 serviteurs d'Abraham (Gn 14, 14) et le nombre des Pères au concile de Nicée," *Revue d'histoire ecclésiastique* 61 (1966): 5–43.

75. Gn 21.5.

76. According to Philo, *On the Rules of Allegory* 3, 43, 87, the name Isaac means "the soul's joy" (ἡ τῆς ψυχῆς χαρά) (LCL 1:329, 359); cf. idem, *On the Change of Names* 131 (LCL 5:209).

providence is not only to preserve nature intact according to its own inner principle, but also to divinize the inclination of the will, through its complete reception of the qualities of the virtues, according to the wisdom that has been acquired; and when nature is contemplated with wisdom, the number three hundred is naturally completed.

[22] The number six perfectly discloses the being of beings; the number ten signifies the constitutive well-being of beings. By multiplying six by ten, or ten by six, one arrives at the sum of sixty, a number that discloses the actual condition of the well-being of being.

[23] When, he says, dispassion is reached, which is signified by the seventh year, both reason and discursive thinking return to the contemplation of realities that are kindred to themselves, being liberated from their service to the corporeal modes of the virtues.

[24] The image of the unoriginate kingdom is the intellect's immutable concentration on true knowledge and the incorruption of the senses in relation to virtue. This occurs when soul and body are mutually bound together through the spiritual transformation of the senses into intellect, which takes place solely by virtue of the divine law. According to this law, they possess the ever-moving, vital, and penetrating energy of reason, in which there is absolutely nothing unlike or opposed to the divine.

[25] Desire that has been actualized, they say, is pleasure, when, consistent with its definition, something good is actually present. Pleasure that has not been actualized is desire, when, consistent with its definition, the actual good is in the future. Anger is the movement of premeditated rage,[77] and rage is anger actualized.[78] Thus, whoever subjects these powers to reason will find that his desire is changed into pleasure through the undefiled union of his soul by grace with the divine, and his anger changed into an undefiled ardor protecting his pleasure in the divine, as well as a right-minded rage consistent with the

77. A free rendering of μανία, which also means "madness" and "inspired frenzy."

78. See the parallel discussion in *Amb.* 10.108–11 (DOML 1:325–29).

soul's power of attraction for the divine, which makes it stand completely outside the realm of beings.

But as long as the world lives within us, due to our soul's voluntary attachment to material things, we must not grant freedom to these powers, lest they couple with the sensible realities that are kindred to them, and wage war on the soul and take hold of it, like a prisoner of war taken captive by the passions, as in ancient times the Babylonians took Jerusalem.[79] For in speaking of an "age" during which the law commanded that foreigners be kept as slaves,[80] Scripture signifies the attachment of the soul's inclination to this world, that is, to this present life, subtly disclosing the spiritual meaning through the literal words of the text.

[26] The number seven thousand, which is found here in its praiseworthy sense, signifies this temporal, present life adorned by virtue and reason. For if the number one thousand signifies the written and the natural law, consistent with the meaning given to it in the analysis of the myriads—which was concerned with the life of those who love God, for whom both laws are mutually appropriate—it is obvious that the number seven thousand indicates the entire life in time of those who love God, protected by both of these laws. The number three hundred points to providential care for being according to nature and the well-being according to grace of those under divine care. The number seven signifies dispassion in one's way of life. Whoever, then, through his proper and natural powers, has, consistent with the will of Providence, preserved his own life in a state of impassibility, goes forth from the confusion of the passions together with "seven thousand three hundred and thirty-seven menservants and handmaidens."[81]

[27] By the "end" he means even the dispassion according to practice attained in this life, and the divinization according to grace in the life to come.

[28] He calls "musicians" those whose life of practice cries out and proclaims the intentions of God.[82]

79. Cf. 4 Kgs 25.4.
80. Cf. Lv 25.40–41.
81. 1 Esd 5.41.
82. On the plural sense of the divine "intentions" or "wills," cf. *Amb.* 7.24 (DOML 1:107–108).

[29] He says that "chanters" are those who not only carry out the divine intentions, but who also explain the mysteries contained in them to others.

[30] The number eight possesses both stability and motion. It possesses stability when it is contemplated in and of itself, for every even number is motionless, inasmuch as it has no center. It possesses motion when it is added to the number that precedes or follows it, for thus it generates an odd number, and every odd number is mobile in itself, given the equal distance of its extremes to the mean. Whatever the number eight produces among numbers below ten, the same is produced by the number eighty in numbers below one hundred, and likewise the number eight hundred in numbers ranged below one thousand. Thus, when contemplated by itself, the number eight possesses stability, since it circumscribes the motion of the odd number that precedes it, for the numbers seven, seventy, and seven hundred manifest the property of time. Inasmuch, then, as sense perception comprehends all that is subject to time and the process of becoming, it remains for the perfected intellect to receive the infallible knowledge of ages and intelligibles, that is, the true understanding[83] of these things, for "true understanding" is defined as infallible knowledge of the substrate.

The number fifty, which generates an odd-numbered monad when it is multiplied seven times with the heptad, signifies the limit of the production of the virtues among the worthy. For whoever has attained to that which is good by nature is no longer in motion regarding the production of the virtues, but has received stability within himself, for the monad is the beginning and end of every motion. The number five, on the other hand, signifies the true understanding of these matters, for it contains the principles of intelligible, rational, sensible, living, and existing beings, which only divine wisdom is naturally able to contain, a wisdom which is defined as the infallible understanding of the truth.

[31] When the "camels of Midian"[84] are interpreted as "secretion," they are, he says, understood as the true contempla-

---

83. I.e., ἐπιστήμη.
84. Is 60.6.

tions of things that come into being and eventually disappear. When interpreted as "bloody clay," they are understood as the principles of providence relative to this transient and unstable life. As "human and maternal sweat," they are the principles of divine judgment operative in this life, which are gathered together both by the thoughts of discursive reasoning and by the sensory imagination of visible realities, from which—I mean from thoughts and mental images—a true opinion of being is established, which is the fruit of sensory-based discursive reasoning. The words "human and maternal sweat" are to be understood as the thoughts of discursive reason and their mental images produced through labor, which nurses us like a mother.

"Camels of Ephah"[85] means the "possession of the back," for the "back" of the soul is the flesh, which exists for the sake of the soul. If, then, we make right use of our flesh, it will serve the soul in the formation of the virtues, and we will understand only those divine principles by which it was made. Together with these we will gather together, as if they were the camels of Midian, the principles of visible realities, and we will conceal our own Jerusalem, covering the soul all around with the divine contemplations of beings, making it invisible and unassailable by the passions.

[32] The number four hundred signifies the nature of the corporeal world, for it is comprised of four elements. The number thirty-five signifies the movement of the virtuous in time and according to reason, for when the number seven is multiplied by five, it produces the number thirty-five. Thus the number seven signifies temporal motion, while the number five signifies rational and true understanding. When one adds together four hundred with thirty and five, he manifests rational and true understanding, consistent with nature and time, of the saints who live within these conditions.

[33] The things numbered are in agreement with the numbers. The horse is swift on its course, for its feet possess an ever-moving and upward-bearing element. Time flies acutely in its movement and flows forward without interruption. The activity of the things numbered is indeed effective, being made

---

85. Ibid.

clear by the cyclical number, for when the number six is multiplied by itself six times, it gives birth to six times as much. Thus the word of the Spirit made clear the swift, acute, and effective state of virtue of the saints, who mystically disclosed these things through the horses and their number.

[34] Anyone, he says, who repeats words he has stolen, creates a false impression of himself, and, like Absalom,[86] deceives those who lack understanding, by defiling (as if they were women) the good and God-loving contemplations of his teacher in the hearing of the uninitiated—like the counsel of Ahithophel, which means "a brother who scatters ashes," that is, a brother who feigns to be a friend. Such a person, he says, is proven to be mad for worldly glory. And he falls at the hands of the children of David,[87] taking his place in battle, with all his impudence, on the higher plane of variegated natural contemplations. For he is shown forth as neither treading on the earth (since he had no stability of character or virtue), nor in any way drawing near to heaven (for he had in no way even touched the truly sublime height of knowledge). And he dies being struck in the heart by three arrows, by which I mean the recollection of his injustice to his teacher, his shame for his conceit concerning his knowledge that was no knowledge, and his anticipation of the inescapable judgment that will come upon him for these things. When he is exposed for such things, the man who loves empty glory dies as if he were struck by arrows. And his own death was preceded, as was only right, by the death by hanging of the evil counselor Ahithophel,[88] who taught children to rise up in revolt against their parents, and who saw his evil counsel come to naught. For he could no longer endure to live having cloaked himself in false friendship to David, since he was unable to show that the one mad with glory and possessed of false knowledge had the sovereign power of reason.

[35] The name Gilead, he says, interpreted as the "migration of mourning," signifies the laborious toil of repentance. As "migration of testimony," it signifies the voice of the conscience

---

86. 2 Kgs 16.21–33.
87. Cf. 2 Kgs 18.9–15.
88. 2 Kgs 17.23.

condemning sins. As "their revelation," it is a figure of the confession of sins according to their particular kinds. When an intellect, which had grown conceited owing to its pursuit of some perceived good, finds itself in this situation, it slays the conceit that it conceived through its coupling with foreign sensation, and returns again to Judea and Jerusalem, and to the Tabernacle, by which I mean to the confession and acknowledgment of God's mercies to it, and the complete dispassion of the virtues, and the peaceful spiritual contemplation of beings, and to mystical theology that is pitched upon them, like a divine tabernacle, in which are mystically veiled the beauties that are completely concealed from others.

[36] When contemplated in and of themselves, the numbers eight (which is one of the numbers in the decad), eighty (which is in the century), eight hundred (which is in the miliad), and eight thousand (which is in the myriad) are immobile with respect to abatement and intensification. When, therefore, these numbers are found in Scripture according to their praiseworthy sense, they symbolize perfect immobility in relation to the passions; that is, they symbolize the disappearance of the passions. This, moreover, is characteristic of the condition of the future age, in which the passions do not come into being. The number forty is an image of sensible realities, and the number five images the senses, under which falls, according to natural science, the sensible world. Thus it was only right that this number signifies the sterile state of evil and the perfect indifference of the saints to sensible objects relative to their five senses.

[37] He calls the number five "spherical," since it is cyclical and returns to itself after every combination with any odd number. For whenever the number five is multiplied five times by any odd number, you will find that the multiplication always ends in the number five. For example, $5 \times 3 = 15$, $5 \times 5 = 25$, $5 \times 7 = 35$, $5 \times 9 = 45$. Continuing thus into infinity, you will find five produced by each odd number multiplied by five. Likewise, if you multiply the number fifty, and five hundred, and five thousand, you will again find the number five restoring itself in the end, which is a property of circular and spherical motion. Quite rightly, then, did those who are wise in these

matters call the number five both spherical and circular, for it never goes completely outside of itself in its multiplication with so-called odd numbers. As such it signifies general scientific knowledge, which, in its ceaseless cognitive movement around all things, never goes outside of itself, and by the power of reason comprehends all things.

[38] Wisdom creates fear, delivering us from the passions through the expectation of punishment; but by accustoming the intellect to the acquisition of the virtues, it creates the desire for it to behold the blessed things of the age to come.

[39] To those who have no desire for it, wisdom is fear, because of the loss they suffer through their flight from it; but in those who love it, wisdom is a longing, a permanent state productive of spiritual delight.

QUESTION 56

AGAIN IT HAS been written in the second book of Esdras: "When the enemies of the tribe of Judah and Benjamin heard it, they came to find out what the sound of the trumpets meant. And they learned that those who had returned from the captivity were building the temple for the Lord God of Israel. So they approached Zerubbabel and Jeshua, and the chiefs of the families, and said to them: 'We will build together with you. For we, likewise, as you do, obey your Lord, and we have been sacrificing to Him ever since the days of Asbasareth, the king of the Assyrians, who brought us here.' Then Zerubbabel and Jeshua and the chief of the families of Israel said to them: 'It is not for us and you to build together a house unto the Lord God.'"[1] What do these things mean, and what especially is the nature of the envy by which they refused to build together with them, seeing that they worshiped the same God?

Response

56.2. The name Judah when translated means "confession,"[2] and the meaning of this word is twofold. The first meaning is gratitude for good things that have been given. The second is a response to evil deeds that have come under censure and accusation. In other words, "confession" includes both the grateful acknowledgment of divine benefactions on the part of the beneficiaries, and the acknowledgment of evil deeds on the part of those who committed them. Both of these activities are

---

1. 1 Esd 5.63–66.
2. See above, Qu. 52.6.

productive of humility.[1] This is because a person who is grateful for good things, as well as a person who is charged with accusations, are both equally humbled: the former because he judges himself unworthy of the gifts, the latter because he begs to receive forgiveness of his sins.

56.3. The name Benjamin, strictly translated from the Hebrew, means "mourning" or "lamentation of the mother," or "measure of the mother," or "son of the right hand," or "edification of the people."[3] It follows that everyone who confesses according to one or the other of the ways mentioned above, belongs to the tribe of Judah. And everyone who mourns for the sake of virtue,[2] or who, like a mother, has righteousness rightly measuring his life and words, or who, through his abundance of virtue and the outpouring of his teaching, becomes for many a way of salvation and edification, belongs to the tribe of Benjamin. It is people such as these that Scripture recognizes, who have received their freedom from the captivity of the passions, and who have departed from their attachment to things of sense, and who are able, in their state of dispassion, to build a house for the Lord. By "house" I mean an intellect that is built up from various virtues and principles in the course of ascetic practice and contemplation, forming a "dwelling place of God in the Spirit."[4]

56.4. The enemies of such people are the four nations that were relocated to the land of Israel under Asbasareth, the king of Assyria,[5] for he was the first to settle men from Babylon, Cuthah, Hamath, and Ava, in the land of Israel.[6] The Babylonians signify pride, and their name when translated means "confused mind."[3] The men of Cuthah signify vainglory, turning their minds from virtue to fruitless conceit, for when translated their name means "to stand outside."[4] The men of Hamath signify the vice of "pleasing men,"[7] for Hamath translated means "spectacle of visible things," and it is through this vice that the

---

3. Cf. Gn 35.18.
4. Eph 2.22.
5. 1 Esd 5.66.
6. 2 Kgs 17.24.
7. Cf. Eph 6.6; 1 Thes 2.4. This vice is noted by Thalassios, *Centuries* 4.30: "In fleeing from gluttony, guard yourself against pleasing men, making a display of the pallor of your face" (PG 91:1461B).

largest profits are distributed to those who superficially pursue virtue for the sake of men.[5] The men of Ava, finally, signify the deceit of hypocrisy, for their name in translation means "serpentine," and like the first serpent they banish from the place of virtue those who, like Adam, have been deceived by their craftiness and hypocritical friendship.[6] Asbasareth, who relocated these men to the land of Israel, means to "take captive from behind," which means "invisibly" or "secretly." He is clearly the devil, who does all things secretly with the aim of subjugating human nature, and he tightens the chains of each human being by means of his sins. He is the one who introduced into the land of Israel (I mean into the state of virtue and knowledge) the vices of pride, vainglory, the pleasing of men, and hypocrisy, yoking these vices to men of virtue and knowledge, so that he might nullify the labors of those who toil, sophistically diverting the goal of creatures to things other than their Cause.[7]

56.5. And it was perhaps knowing that these demons closely follow virtuous human beings that the divine Apostle prevailed upon the Corinthians, saying that he was not among them "as one using words of flattery"—like a hypocrite, for perhaps they were thinking this about him—"nor as one seeking glory from men," as if he were vainglorious.[8] But concerning pride he said nothing, for he possessed the obvious marks of humility, numberless persecutions, bodily sufferings, extreme poverty, and lack of skill in his speech, for "even if I am unskilled in speech," he says, "I am not unskilled in knowledge."[9]

56.6. "When they heard the sound of the trumpet, they came to find out what the sound meant. And they learned that those who had returned from the captivity were building the temple for the Lord God of Israel."[10] The "trumpets," the sound of which is heard by the unclean demons, are the words of virtue and knowledge.[8] The "sound" of these words are works of virtue and the stability of ethical conduct among those who returned from vice to virtue, and who have ascended from ignorance to the knowledge of God.

8. 1 Thes 2.5–6.
9. 2 Cor 11.6.
10. 1 Esd 5.63.

56.7. "So they approached Zerubbabel and Jeshua, and the chiefs of the families, and said to them: 'We will build together with you. For we likewise, as you do, obey your Lord, and we have been sacrificing to him.'"[11] Zerubbabel is the practical intellect, and Jeshua is the contemplative intellect.[9] The chiefs of the families are the powers of the soul, from which arise the modes of virtue and the principles of knowledge. It is these powers that the unclean demons of pride, vainglory, the pleasing of men, and hypocrisy approach and say: "We will build the house of the Lord together with you." For none of these wicked demons ever hinders the eagerness of a virtuous person. To the contrary, such demons deceptively minimize the deficiencies of one's virtues, and urge a person to increase his efforts, joining in eagerly with the work of the spiritual struggler, so that they might draw to themselves the whole of his mind, for when it has lost the balance of moderation it will be unaware that it is advancing in the wrong direction.[12] This is why those evil men said: "For we likewise, as you do, obey your Lord." For the demons do not hate temperance, neither do they loathe fasting, or the distribution of wealth, or hospitality, or chanting, or reading, or the higher lessons, or sleeping on the ground, or keeping vigil—or any of the things that are characteristic of a life lived according to God—as long as they can twist the motivation and aim of these activities toward themselves. For the ascetic will perhaps quickly recognize other kinds of demons, and easily avoid suffering harm from them. But of these demons—who seem to cooperate with us on the way of virtue, and who wish, as it were, to help us in building the house of the Lord—what intellect, even from among the most highly advanced, can recognize their presence without the help of the "active and living Word, who penetrates through all things, even unto the division[10] of soul and spirit"?[13] Who, in other words, can recognize their presence without the Word, who knows which activities or thoughts are from the soul (that is, the natural forms or movements of the virtues) and

---

11. 1 Esd 5.68–69.
12. These and the following remarks are largely in response to Thalassios's questions noted above, Intro., 1.2.9.
13. Cf. Heb 4.12.

which ones are spiritual (that is, those beyond nature, which are characteristic of God, and which are given to nature by grace)? Who, I ask, can know this without the Word, who knows thoroughly the fitting or unfitting convergence of the "joints and marrow,"[14] that is, the modes of virtue to their spiritual principles,[11] and who "judges the thoughts and intentions[12] of the heart,"[15] that is, the hidden relationships between our words and our inner depth, and their invisible causes within the soul? What can be hidden from the Word, from whom "no creation is hidden," that is, among us, who think we escape His notice, for "all things are open and laid bare,"[16] and not only things we have already done and thought, but also what we will do and think? For perhaps the words "no creation is hidden" refer to our future actions and thoughts, and not merely to something that has already taken place, and which is already quite plain even to us. For it is hardly necessary for me to argue that God knows in advance all the infinite ages that have formerly existed, and that exist now, and that will exist, and by His nature grasps in advance the knowledge of the genesis of all things—a knowledge which He possesses within Himself, which He has acquired not from created things, but from Himself, for He alone is the natural knowledge of beings[13] inasmuch as He is the Cause of beings. Moreover, He is knowledge itself, inasmuch as He possesses knowledge of Himself by nature and not on the basis of causality. And He is established upon this according to the principle of His transcendent infinity, which wholly and infinitely transcends all things.[14] This is because He is the creator of our own so-called knowledge, and He is absolutely unapproachable by any other kind of knowledge that we can express or even imagine.

56.8. Who, then, I ask, not having this Word dwelling within the depth of his heart, will be able to escape the hidden guile of the demonic hypocrisy aimed against us, and be able to stand wholly by himself without mingling with them, and build the house of the Lord after the manner of Zerubbabel

14. Heb 4.12.
15. Heb 4.13.
16. Heb 4.12.

and Jeshua and the chiefs of the tribes? For in response to the deceptive spirits of pride, vainglory, the pleasing of men, and hypocrisy, they cry out in a loud voice: "It is not for us and you to build together a house unto the Lord God; for we alone will build a house for the Lord of Israel."[17] They say this knowing that any intercourse with them will lead to the overthrow and destruction of the entire edifice, and will despoil the joy of the beauty of the divine offerings and adornments. For no one is able to build anything of beauty for the Lord if he has any of the above-mentioned demons accompanying him in his virtue. This is because such a person, as he moves along the path of virtue, does not have God as his goal, but rather his own passions, which arise from his virtue. Thus it was not out of envy that those from the captivity did not permit the men of Babylon, Cuthah, Hamath, and Ava, to join them in the task of building the house of the Lord, but because they recognized the deceitful friendship of demonic malice, which uses the good secretly to bring about death through sin.

56.9. To the wicked spirits who invisibly approach us with their false spiritual friendship, and who say: "Let us build together with you the house of your Lord," let us always say: "It is not for us and you to build together a house unto the Lord our God; for we alone will build a house to the Lord of Israel."[14] And we will do this alone, for having been freed from the spirits that wage war on those who are deficient in virtue, and having come out from among them, we have no wish to be roused by their empty extravagances, and so become entangled in them and suffer a fall even worse than the first time.[15] For then there was the hope of an easy return through the forgiveness of our weakness, while now there is no such hope for us, or at best our return would be difficult, for we will be hated on account of our pride and for having created a good we imagined to be greater than what is truly good. And we will not in fact build this house alone, for in our good works we have as our helpers the holy angels, or rather God Himself, who is revealed within us by means of our works of righteousness, and who builds us up, and makes us His holy temple, free from every passion.[18]

17. 1 Esd 5.68.
18. Cf. 1 Cor 3.16, 6.19; 1 Pt 2.5.

Scholia

[1] Every form of confession, he says, humbles the soul. One form teaches the soul that it has been justified by grace, and the other, through sorrow of conscience, teaches the soul that it is guilty of the charges brought against it.

[2] Whoever grieves over his first sins, and has right faith in God to grant him rebirth in righteousness, and whose life and word is an example of every virtue, has made himself a member of the spiritual tribe of Benjamin, showing that his birth according to God was the work of his free will, and not the fruit of natural necessity. For a "son of the right hand"[19] is the one who receives voluntarily, as a work of free will, his birth according to God.

[3] By "Babylonians" he means "pride," since pride is the mark of a confused mind. This is because the passion of pride is composed of two kinds of ignorance, which, when they come together, create a confused way of thinking. For the only one who is prideful is the one who is ignorant of both divine assistance and human weakness. From this it follows that pride is a privation of divine and human knowledge, because by the negation of the two true extremes a false positive is created.

[4] By the "men of Cuthah" he means vainglory, because vainglory is a standing apart from one's goal in God, and a turning to some other goal instead of God. For the vainglorious man is the one who pursues virtue not for the glory of God but for his own glory, and by his labors he procures the illusory praises of men.

[5] "Hamath" he calls "pleasing men." The man-pleaser is concerned only about his external conduct, along with the words of those who flatter him, so that he might attract to himself the gaze of some and the hearing of others, those, that is, who are pleased or impressed by what they see and hear, and who reduce virtue to a thing perceptible merely by the senses. This is why we say that the vice of pleasing men is the outward display of seemingly virtuous mannerisms and words that are held in honor by men.

---

19. Gn 35.18.

[6] The "men of Ava" he calls "hypocrisy." Hypocrisy is the pretense of friendship, or hatred concealed beneath an outward form of friendship, or enmity expressed as goodwill, or envy imitating the marks of love, or a sin-loving disposition, which arrests the attention of observers by projecting virtuous mannerisms, or a life adorned by counterfeit and not real virtue, or the affectation of righteousness maintained by the mere idea that it is real, or a mode of ethical philosophy that conceals the hidden lack of a virtuous disposition, or deception having the form of truth, a form which is cultivated by those who imitate the way of the serpent in their way of life.

[7] God is the cause of beings and of whatever truly good things exist in beings. Thus whoever undertakes labors for the sake of virtue and knowledge, but who does not expand his own incapacity for gratitude to the measure of the progress he has made by grace, does not escape the evil of pride. Moreover, whoever pursues the good for the sake of his own glory prefers himself to God, being pierced by the nail of empty glory. And he who performs or pursues virtue so that it might "be seen by men"[20] has placed human approbation far above the favor of God, falling sick with the passion of pleasing men. Whoever, with the aim of maliciously deceiving others, has colored his manner of life with the semblance of virtuous modesty, concealing the wicked disposition of his will by the superficial appearance of piety, has bought virtue at the price of hypocritical guile. Thus the intelligible Asbasareth diverted the goal of each one to things other than its cause.

[8] When the words of God, he says, are spoken in a merely verbal manner, they go unheard, because they lack the "sound" that can be given to them only by the actual practice of the speakers. When, on the other hand, they are spoken by those who keep the commandments, the demons are dissolved by their sound, and human beings are moved to build the heart's house of the Lord by their progress in works of righteousness.

[9] Here he takes Zerubbabel as a figure of the practical intellect, being more warlike, whereas Jeshua is taken as a figure

---

20. Mt 23.5.

of the theoretical intellect, being a priest and assigned to speak always directly to God.

[10] Here he calls the difference between the natural virtues (whose natural principles we possess) and the virtues of the Spirit (whose grace we receive as a gift) the "division of soul and spirit,"[21] for the clear separation of these things is made by the judgment of reason.

[11] "Marrow" is the divine principle, which nourishes divine thoughts within us, as if they were bones, and which in turn support the body of the virtues. A "joint" is a mode of ascetic practice, according to which the union of thoughts with divine principles naturally comes about and forms a single fulfillment of virtue.[22]

[12] "Thoughts and intentions," of which, he says, the Word is the judge, are the relations of the soul with divine principles and human thoughts, as well as the causes of these relations. For thoughts set in motion our power of recollection, the proper mark of which is relation, whereas an intention aims toward a limit, which characterizes a cause.

[13] If God, he says, is essential knowledge, and if the intellect is logically prior to all knowledge, which is naturally subject to the intellect, then it follows that God transcends all knowledge inasmuch as He infinitely transcends every intellect, to which all knowledge is naturally subject.

[14] The demons are those who wage war based on our deficiency of virtue, teaching fornication, drunkenness, avarice, envy, and the like. Those who wage war through extravagances are the ones that teach conceit, vainglory, pride, and the like, and who by means of things on the right secretly introduce things from the left.[23]

[15] The definition of virtue is the conscious union of human weakness with divine power. Thus, whoever restricts himself solely to the limits of the weakness of his nature, has not drawn near to the definition of virtue. For this reason he also sins, since he has not yet received the power that fortifies weak-

21. Heb 4.12.
22. Ibid.
23. Cf. above, Qu. 48.20.

ness. Moreover, the one who arrogantly puts forward his own weakness as power in the face of divine strength has heedlessly ignored the definition of virtue, and for this reason he sins but is unaware of it, for he reckons his sin to be virtue. To be sure, the one who restricts himself to the limits of his natural weakness is more worthy of forgiveness, since he passively suffers a fall from virtue due to his sluggishness, whereas the one who puts forward his weakness as power in the face of divine strength for the accomplishment of his duties, actively brings about his fall from virtue due to his arrogance.

QUESTION 57

"HE SUPPLICATION of a righteous man accomplishes much when it is rendered effective."[1] What is the meaning of "rendered effective"?[2]

Response

57.2. I know of two ways in which the "supplication of a righteous man" is "rendered effective." The first way is whenever the one praying combines his supplication to God with the keeping of the commandments, not allowing his supplication to fall from his tongue as mere words and the empty echo of speech, lest it remain inactive and insubstantial, but rather as active and living, being animated by the observance of the commandments. For the substance of prayer and supplication is quite clearly its fulfillment through the virtues, according to which the righteous man's prayer is strong and able to do all things, being rendered effective by the keeping of the

---

1. Jas 5.16.
2. Here the difficulty is the passive participle ἐνεργουμένη ("rendered effective"), which English translations of the New Testament generally render in the active voice: "the prayer of the righteous man can accomplish much *while it is operative, while it is working, in its working*," etc. Maximos's response is essentially that given by Origen, *Homilies on First Kings*, fr. 5: "Scripture demonstrates that even if a prophet and a righteous man pray on behalf of each other, his prayer is not heard unless the one he is praying for repents, because the 'supplication of a righteous man is rendered effective' [Jas 5.16] through the other man's repentance. Indeed, both need to work together: the prayer of the righteous man and the effort of the one repenting" (GCS 3:297, lines 10–15). Note that the whole of Maximos's response was excerpted in the *Catena on James* (ed. Antony Cramer, *Catenae graecorum patrum*, vol. 8 [Oxford: Oxford University Press, 1864; repr. Hildesheim: Olms, 1967], 37–38).

commandments. The second way is when the one who needs the prayer of the righteous man undertakes and performs the works of prayer, that is, when he corrects his former way of life and thereby gives strength to the supplication of the righteous man, fortifying it through his own upright manner of life.

57.3. For there is no benefit from the supplication of a righteous man when the one who needs it takes greater pleasure in his faults than in the virtues. For even the great Samuel, when he was grieving over the faults of Saul, was not able to propitiate God, since his grief found no corresponding self-correction in the one who had sinned. This is why God stopped the mindless grief of His servant and said: "How long will you grieve over Saul? I have weakened him so that he might not be a king in Israel."[3]

57.4. And, again, Jeremiah, who was most compassionate, was not heard when he prayed for the people of Judea, who were mad with demonic delusion, because his prayer lacked the strength of their repentance from their godless deception. This is why God, releasing him from praying in vain, said: "Do not pray for the people, and do not ask mercy for them; and do not approach me about them, for I will not listen to you."[4]

57.5. Thus it is great folly, not to say madness, for someone to seek salvation through the prayer of righteous men when he himself is disposed to indulge and delight in destructive behaviors, and to seek forgiveness for the very things he revels in, and which by his own choice defile him. To the contrary, someone who needs the prayer of a righteous man must be neither heedless nor inactive—if, that is, he is truly revolted by his wicked deeds—but should rather render that supplication effective and powerful by means of his own virtues, giving it wings so that it might reach Him who is able to grant forgiveness of sins.

57.6. Thus, whether the supplication is rendered effective by the righteous man who offers the prayer, or by the one who asks the righteous man to pray, "the prayer of a righteous man accomplishes much."[5] For when it is rendered effective by the

3. 1 Kgs 16.1.
4. Jer 7.16.
5. Jas 5.16.

righteous man, it gives him boldness of speech before Him who is able to grant the requests of the righteous. And when, on the other hand, it is rendered effective by the one who asks the righteous man to pray, it releases him from his former depravity, transforming his disposition toward virtue.

QUESTION 58

"N THIS[1] you rejoice, even though now for a little while it may be necessary for you to experience grief[2] in various trials."[3] How can someone who is grieved by trials be able to rejoice in what grieves him?[4]

Response

58.2. The word of truth recognizes grief to be twofold. One kind of grief takes place in relation to the soul, and occurs invisibly. The other kind takes place in relation to the senses, and is manifested visibly. The one seizes the whole depth of the soul, which is tormented by the scourging of the conscience; the other encompasses the whole of sensation, which, from its

---

1. As noted in the Introduction to this volume, Dumitru Stăniloae, *Filocalia. Sau culegere din scrierile Sfinților Părinții care arată cum se poate omul curăți, lumina și desăvârși*, vol. 4 (Sibiu: Tipografia Arhidiecezană, 1948), 19, n. 1, demonstrated that the acrostic and subsequent chapters of Thalassios's *Third Century* are a résumé of this Question; cf. Blowers, *Exegesis and Spiritual Pedagogy*, 35, n. 74. This of course indicates that the Thalassian *Centuries* were written after the reception of the *Responses*.

2. "Experience grief" renders the Greek participle λυπηθέντες, which is consistent with some English translations of 1 Pt 1.6, although others translate "grief" as "pain." When Maximos speaks of "pleasure and pain," however, the terms are ἡδονή and ὀδύνη (although in Qu. 1, ἡδονή is paired with λύπη). "Grief," as it affects the soul, is the passion of "sorrow," and this is Maximos's normal usage. Here, however, the word is used on the level of the bodily senses or with respect to the faculty of sensation, and at Qu. 58.10, Maximos states that λύπη and πόνος are the same thing.

3. 1 Pt 1.6.

4. Maximos's dialectic of pleasure and pain has roots in Stoic psychology, in which the pair ἡδονή and λύπη were two of the four basic human passions that were foreign to reason; cf. the note above, at Intro. 1.2.14.

QUESTION 58 403

natural outward diffusion, contracts under the weight of its sufferings. And each one marks a consummation: the former of sensory pleasure, and the latter of the soul's spiritual gladness.[5] [1] Or rather, the former is the logical outcome of our voluntary inclinations to indulge the passions of sensation, whereas the latter is the logical outcome of involuntary sufferings that befall us contrary to our inclination.[6] For it seems to me that grief is a state or condition deprived of pleasures, whereas the privation of pleasure signals the onslaught of pain. Pain, moreover, is clearly a deficiency or departure of a natural, habitual state, and the deficiency of such a state is a passion of the natural power underlying that state. A passion of a natural power underlying a state is the mode according to which natural activity is misused, and such misuse of natural activity is the movement of our natural power toward that which is unnatural and does not exist according to nature.

58.3. In the same way that the word of truth, as I said, recognizes "grief" to be twofold,[2] I also understand[7] the mode of "trials" to be twofold: one mode being in accordance with the inclination of the will, and the other being contrary to the inclination of the will; the former creating voluntary pleasures and the latter attracting involuntary pain. For "trials" in accordance with the inclination of the will constitute voluntary pleasures resulting from our free choice, whereas trials contrary to the inclination of the will obviously result in involuntary pains contrary to our free choice.[8] The former is the cause of grief

---

5. That is, spiritual gladness curtails the pleasures of the senses, just as sensual pleasures produce sorrow in the soul; for a similar division of the intellective and the sensible, cf. Diadochos of Photike, *Gnostic Chapters* 25, 55, and 78 (SC 5:96–97, 116, 135–36).

6. Whereas the passions that are indulged in voluntarily are sinful and produce sorrow in the soul, involuntary passions are sufferings and afflictions that distress the senses.

7. Some manuscripts here read ἐπίσταται, taking the "word of truth" as the subject; Eriugena has *intellegit* (CCSG 22:28, line 23), which translates ἐπίσταται, and indicates that the variant (if it is to be considered such) entered the tradition at an early stage.

8. "Trial" translates πειρασμός, which also means "temptation," and both words describe an involuntary experience of suffering or weakness, often leading to sin in an effort to assuage pain or escape temptation. But when, on

for the soul,[3] whereas the latter is the cause of grief for the senses.

58.4. This is why, I think, our Lord and God, when teaching His own disciples how to pray, instructs them to pray that the kind of trials that are in accordance with one's will might not come upon them, saying: "And lead us not into trials."[9] In other words, the Lord teaches His own disciples to pray not to be abandoned to the experience of those trials related to pleasures that are voluntary and freely chosen.[10] I think this is also why the great James,[4] who is called the brother of the Lord, when teaching those who struggle for the sake of the truth not to cower at the involuntary kind of trials, says: "Count it all joy, my brethren, when you fall into various trials,"[11] namely, into involuntary temptations that are contrary to the inclination of one's will and which cause pain. They both indicate this clearly: in the one place, the Lord by adding: "but deliver us from evil";[12] and the great James, in the passage we are now considering, when he says: "knowing that the testing of your faith produces patience; but let patience have its full effect, so that you may be perfect and complete, lacking in nothing."[13] In this passage, "perfect" indicates the one who through self-control fights against the voluntary trials and who through patience perseveres during involuntary trials; "complete" indicates the one who achieves ascetic practice with knowledge, and contemplation without neglecting the practice of asceticism.[14]

58.5. Because grief and pleasure are distinguished differently with respect to the soul and to physical sensation, the person who cultivates the pleasure of the soul while simultaneously accepting and enduring the grief of sensation is tested and be-

---

the other hand, one rejects the temptation of pleasure, he must accept in its place the temptation or trial of suffering experienced by the senses, which at the same time brings joy to the soul.

9. Mt 6.13; Lk 11.4.
10. Cf. *Or. Dom.* (CCSG 23:72–73).
11. Jas 1.2.
12. Mt 6.13; Lk 11.4.
13. Jas 1.3–4.
14. Contemplation does not presuppose or require inactivity; neither does it do away with the prior stage of practical activity.

comes perfect and complete.¹⁵ Such a person is "tested" by the experience of opposition arising from the sensory world.[5] He becomes "perfect" as one who fights unyieldingly against both sensory pleasure and grief through self-control and endurance. And he becomes "complete" as one who preserves unharmed, in the stability of their rational identity, the permanent states of mind that combat the sensory dispositions, which war against each other. By these permanent states I mean ascetic practice and contemplation, which are mutually supportive and connected, so that neither is able to be separated from the other, inasmuch as ascetic practice through its various expressions manifests the knowledge of contemplation, while contemplation manifests, no less than reason, virtue strengthened by the breast-plate of ascetic practice.¹⁶

58.6. Since our argument has demonstrated that both grief and pleasure are twofold—with the one relating to the soul, and the other to sensation—let us, to the best of our ability, examine more comprehensively their respective causes. Now, the mode of grief on the level of the soul is twofold, being on the one hand constituted by our own faults, and, on the other hand, by the faults of others. The cause[6] of this grief is clearly the sensory pleasures of either the one who is grieving or of those for whom he grieves. Strictly speaking,[7] there is almost no sin at all among mankind that does not have as the origin of its own generation the irrational attachment of the soul to sensation for the sake of pleasure. The manifest cause[8] of the soul's pleasure, on the other hand, is grief with respect to physical sensation experienced by the person who both takes pleasure and rejoices in his own virtues or those of others. Strictly speaking,[9] there is almost no virtue at all among mankind that does not have as the origin of its own generation the soul's reasoned aversion toward sensation.

58.7. Once the soul has, for the sake of virtue, acquired an aversion toward sensation, sensation necessarily will be in a state of pain, being separated from the soul's power to conceive

---

15. Jas 1.4.
16. Cf. Eph 6.14. On the unity of ascetic practice and contemplation, cf. *Amb.* 10.2–6 (DOML 2:150–59).

and contrive[10] pleasurable things according to the inclination of its will. To the contrary, through self-control it courageously drives away the uprising of its natural pleasures; and through patient endurance it remains completely unwavering at the assault of unnatural and involuntary pains. It does not abandon virtue's godly dignity and glory for the sake of fleeting and insubstantial pleasures; neither does it fall from the heights of the virtues during the onslaught of pain, nor does it take thought for the flesh when the senses experience suffering.

58.8. The cause of grief for sensation is the soul's total preoccupation with things that are according to nature. Conversely, it is the soul's unnatural activity that clearly causes sensory pleasure, which can have no principle of existence other than the soul's rejection of things according to nature.[11] For intellect and sensation possess natural activities that are mutually opposed, due to the extreme difference and otherness of the objects that come under their power of perception.[12] For what the intellect perceives are intelligible and incorporeal essences, and it is of a nature to perceive them according to their essences, whereas sensation perceives sensible and bodily natures, which it too perceives naturally.[17]

58.9. Now, it is impossible for the intellect to make the passage toward kindred intelligible realities without the contemplation and mediation of the sensible realities that are presented to it, for the simple reason that this passage cannot in any way be achieved without sensation, which is joined to intellect and which is naturally kindred to sensible objects.[18] Thus, as would be expected, if the intellect becomes ensnared by the

---

17. The opposition between intellect and sensation is due to the "extreme difference and otherness" of their respective objects, namely, intelligible, incorporeal essences, and sensible, corporeal natures.

18. As Maximos makes clear, intellect and sense perception do not function independently or in isolation from one another. The intellect cannot contemplate intelligible objects directly, but only through the mediation of sensible objects can it make its "passage" (διάβασις) to the *logoi* concealed within phenomena. An impassioned attachment to objects of sense, on the other hand, which seeks from them only the sensation of pleasure, fails to see and engage the deeper reality of the phenomenal world, so that what was to serve as a place of transition is mistaken for an end in itself.

surface appearances of visible realities—thinking that sensation, which is joined to it, is its natural activity[13]—then it falls away from realities that by nature are intelligible, and seizes "with both hands," as they say, corporeal realities contrary to nature. When the intellect thus acts contrary to reason, having been vanquished by sensation, it generates the soul's grief, inasmuch as the soul is tormented by the frequent scourging of conscience. At the same time, the intellect becomes the conspicuous creator of sensory pleasure, growing oily and fattened with ideas about how to pamper the flesh. If, however, the intellect cuts through the superficial appearances of visible realities at the very moment they present themselves to it, and if it should see the spiritual principles of beings free of their outward forms, then, on the one hand, it will have produced pleasure in the soul without being dominated by anything perceived by the senses, and, on the other hand, it will have brought about the grief of sensation by depriving it of all things perceptible by nature.[19] For wherever reason takes precedence and directs[14] sensation in the contemplation of visible realities, the flesh is deprived of every natural pleasure, since it does not have sensation running about ungoverned, released from the bonds of reason for the pursuit of its own pleasures.[20]

58.10. Thus, as I have said, because sensory pleasure introduces grief into the soul—that is, pain, for the two are the same—and because the pleasure of the soul is of a nature to cause grief—that is, pain—for sensation, it stands to reason that whoever desires the "life of hope, through the resurrection from the dead of our God and Savior Jesus Christ, unto an incorruptible, undefiled, and imperishable inheritance, stored up in heaven,"[21] experiences exultation and joy unspeakable

---

19. The contemplation of the *logoi* through creation is what brings true pleasure to the soul.

20. The two forms of pleasure, of the soul and of the senses, cannot exist together; no one can experience both at the same time. On the contrary, the pleasures of the soul correspond to the pains of the senses, and vice versa. The person must therefore choose, in any given moment, pleasure for the one and pain for the other.

21. Cf. 1 Pt 1.3–4.

in his soul,[22] which radiates continually with the hope of the good things to come. At the same time, he experiences grief with respect to his flesh and sensation; that is, he experiences the pain and sufferings that come about through various trials. For every virtue is closely accompanied by pleasure and pain: pain of the flesh, which is deprived of soothing and softer sensations, and pleasure of the soul, which luxuriates in spiritual principles that are completely free of sensory elements.

58.11. Thus it is fitting for the intellect, during this present life—which is how I understand the word "now"[23]—to experience grief with respect to the flesh, on account of all the pain it experiences through trials, but nonetheless always to rejoice in soul[15] and to delight on account of the hope of eternal good things, even if sensation has been worn down by struggles: "For the sufferings of this present time are not worthy to be compared with the glory which shall be revealed in us,"[24] according to the divine Apostle.

58.12. And so this is how, as it seems to me, it is possible for a person to rejoice in the very thing that grieves him. Grieving with respect to the flesh because of the pain experienced in the pursuit of virtue, he nonetheless rejoices in his soul with respect to the same virtue, beholding the beauty of the things to come as though already present. It is for the sake of these things, following the example of the great David, that he dies every day[25] through his voluntary dying to the flesh, being perpetually renewed through the spiritual rebirth of the soul.[26] He thus possesses a saving pleasure and a beneficial grief.[16] By grief we do not mean irrational grief, which afflicts the many, whose souls are tormented by the privation of passions or material objects, which contrary to nature make us rush impulsively[17] toward things to which we should not rush, and to avoid[18] things that we should not avoid. Rather, I mean the grief informed by reason, and approved by those wise in divine

22. Cf. 1 Pt 1.8.
23. 1 Pt 1.6.
24. Rom 8.18.
25. Cf. Ps 43.22; 1 Cor 15.31.
26. Cf. 2 Cor 4.16.

things, and which makes us aware of an evil that is present. For they say that grief is an evil that is present, being constituted in the soul when sensory pleasure dominates the discernment of reason; but that it subsists within sensation when the soul's progress toward virtue unfolds without hindrance.[27] To the extent that the unfolding of this progression confronts sensation with pain, to the very same degree it introduces pleasure and joy to the soul that is drawn toward God through enlightenment—which is connatural to it—of virtue and knowledge.

Scholia

[1] He says that grief of soul results from sensory pleasure (because it is from this that grief of soul is constituted), just as pleasure of soul results in the grief of the flesh, for the gladness of the soul is the chastisement of the flesh.

[2] He says grief is twofold, the one kind pertaining to sensation resulting from the privation of bodily pleasures, the other kind pertaining to the intellect resulting from the privation of things that are good for the soul. He also says that trials are twofold, one kind being voluntary, the other kind being involuntary, and that the voluntary trials are fathers of sensory bodily pleasure, begetting grief in the soul. For sin is the only thing that brings grief to the soul. On the other hand, he says that involuntary temptations, which are manifested in pain experienced contrary to the inclination of one's will, are fathers of spiritual pleasure and begetters of bodily grief with respect to sensation.

[3] He says that trials[28] that are in accordance with the inclination of one's will bring about grief in the soul, and clearly create sensory pleasure. On the other hand, trials contrary to the inclination of one's will constitute the pleasure of the soul and the grief of the flesh.

[4] On the one hand, the Lord, he says, teaches us to avoid voluntary trials, for they create pleasure for the flesh and grief for the soul. On the other hand, the great James exhorts us to

---

27. Compare the parallel discussion in *Amb.* 10.108–11 (DOML 2:324–29).
28. I.e., in the sense of "temptations."

rejoice in involuntary trials, for they negate the pleasure of the flesh and the grief of the soul.

[5] A person who has experienced the grief and pleasure of the flesh could be called "tested," in that he is well-experienced in the things that ease and hinder the flesh; "perfect" is the one who has overthrown the pleasure and suffering of the flesh by the power of reason; and "complete" is the one who has preserved unchanged the firm habit of ascetic practice and contemplation through the intensity of his longing for the divine.

[6] Every grief that arises in the soul, he says, has been preceded by the pleasure of the flesh.

[7] If it were not for the soul's impassioned attachment to sensation, he says, there would not exist any sin whatsoever.

[8] The one who tames the flesh by means of voluntary pain, he says, gladdens the soul spiritually.

[9] The genesis of true virtue, he says, is the voluntary estrangement of the soul from the flesh.

[10] He calls the intellective power of the soul conceptual and inventive. This power, when separated from its relation to sensation, leaves the flesh bereft of any provision for pleasure in relation to the will's inclination; neither does it tolerate the suffering of the flesh to be alleviated, when, in the orientation of its will's inclination, it devotes itself entirely to divine realities.

[11] The soul's rejection of natural things, he says, naturally becomes the beginning of sensory pleasure, for when the soul suffers pain for the sake of natural good things, it does not have the power that is able to discover the modes of sensory pleasure.

[12] Sensible things are subject to sensation, whereas intelligible things are subject to the intellect, and great indeed is the difference between intelligibles and sensibles.

[13] Once the intellect considers sensation to be one of its own natural powers, and becomes entangled with surface appearances, it conceives of the pleasures of the flesh, not being able to pass through[29] the nature of visible things, since it is

---

29. I.e., διαβῆναι (διάβασις), which is Maximos's signature term for the mind's passage to divine realities *through* and *by means of* the forms of the material world; cf. Blowers, *Exegesis and Spiritual Pedagogy*, 95–117.

encompassed and held back by its impassioned relation toward sensation.

[14] When reason rules within us, he says, the flesh, which has been enslaved to reason, will necessarily be chastened in the acquisition of virtue.

[15] The flesh belongs to the soul, but not the soul to the flesh. For the lesser belongs to the greater, he says, but not the greater to the lesser. And so, because of transgression, the flesh has become mixed up with the law of sin[30]—which is sensory pleasure—and the flesh has in turn been sentenced to death through pain and sufferings. For this reason, he who has conceived of the destruction of the law of sin and has understood that due to sin (and for its very destruction) death was later introduced—this person will always rejoice in his soul, which, through various pains, sees the law of sin receding from his own flesh, so that it can accept that blessed life in the Spirit which is to come. It is not possible otherwise to achieve that blessed life in the Spirit, that is, if in this present life the law of sin is not first emptied from the flesh, in terms of the will's relation to the law of sin, as if from a kind of vessel.

[16] Salvific pleasure is what he calls spiritual joy in the pursuit of virtue, and beneficial sorrow is what he calls the grief of the flesh for the sake of virtue.

[17] He who cleaves to passions and material things rushes toward that which he should not rush toward.

[18] He who does not accept the circumstances that bring about the privations of passions and material things avoids the things he should not avoid.

---

30. Cf. Rom 7.23.

QUESTION 59

"THE PROPHETS who prophesied concerning the grace that was to be yours researched[1] and investigated[2] this salvation; they inquired[3] as to what person or time the Spirit of Christ within them was revealing in advance when He testified to the sufferings of Christ and the glory that would follow."[4] If the blessed prophets were taught these things under the direct inspiration of the Holy Spirit and left them in writing for us to research and investigate, then what was the nature of the research and investigation undertaken by the prophets themselves, who had the words of the Holy Spirit ringing in their ears, and who wrote down what was revealed to them?[5]

Response

59.2. The ability to search and inquire into divine realities was implanted essentially within human nature by the Creator

---

1. I.e., ἐζεζήτησαν.
2. I.e., ἐζηρεύνησαν.
3. I.e., ἐρευνῶντες. Cf. *Disp. Biz.*: "And Maximus said: 'If, according to you, one ought not to inquire into (ἐρευνᾶν) the words of Scripture, we are rejecting all Scripture, both the old and the new. For I have heard David say: "Blessed are those who inquire into his testimonies" [Ps 118:34] ... But you want us to be similar to the Jews who with simple words, as you call them—that is, with the letter alone blocking their mind like rubbish—have lapsed from the truth, having a veil over their hearts so that they cannot understand the spirit which belongs, and is hidden, in the letter. About this spirit Paul says: "The letter kills, but the spirit gives life"'" (2 Cor 3.6) (translation modified from Allen and Neil, *Documents from Exile*, 93).
4. 1 Pt 1.10–11.
5. On this question, see the detailed analysis of Blowers, *Exegesis and Spiritual Pedagogy*, 221–28; on the notion of ζήτησις, see Thunberg, *Microcosm and Mediator*, 220–21.

at the very moment it was brought into being. Revelations of divine realities, on the other hand, are given to us according to grace through the intervening power of the Holy Spirit. From the beginning, however, the Evil One, through sin, bound these abilities to the nature of visible realities, so that there was "no one taking notice or searching for God,"[6] because all those with a share in human nature had their power of intellect and reason narrowed to the surface appearances of sensible objects, and had no conception of any reality beyond what could be perceived through the senses.[7] Thus it was only natural that the grace of the All-Holy Spirit should visit those who had not by their own inclination deliberately fallen into deception, and, releasing them from their attachments to material things, re-establish within them their inherent natural power.[8] Having recovered this power purified by grace, they first searched and inquired, after which they researched and investigated by means of the same grace, that is, of the Holy Spirit.

59.3. Thus we are not permitted to say that,[1] among the saints, it was grace alone that produced knowledge of divine mysteries without any contribution from the natural capacities of the saints to receive such knowledge. Otherwise, we would have to concede that the holy prophets did not understand the power of illumination bestowed upon them by the All-Holy Spirit—and, in that case, how would he have spoken truthfully who said: "The wise man shall understand the things that come forth from his mouth"?[9] And neither was it without the grace of the All-Holy Spirit, that is, by means of searching with their own natural capacity, that they acquired the true knowledge of beings, because in that case the visitation of the Holy Spirit to the saints would be shown to be superfluous, in no way cooperating with them in the manifestation of the truth—and how then would that word be true which says: "For every good giving and every perfect gift is from above, coming down from the Father of lights,"[10] and: "To each one is given the manifes-

---

6. Ps 13.2; 52.2.
7. Here Maximos extends and develops the argument of Qu. 58.
8. I.e., their natural power to search and inquire.
9. Prv 16.23.
10. Jas 1.17.

tation of the Spirit for the common good"?[11] "For," it says, "to one is given through the Spirit the utterance of wisdom, to another the utterance of knowledge according to the same Spirit, to another faith by the same Spirit, and to another gifts of healing,"[12] and the rest, after which is added: "The one and the same Spirit works all things, apportioning to each one individually as He wills."[13] And it is quite obvious that the Spirit "wills" what is good and expedient for each one,[2] fully assuring the dispassionate desire of those who seek after divine realities. For he who without passions seeks after divine realities will certainly receive what is sought, whereas he who asks bearing even a trace of the passions will fail to attain what is sought, inasmuch as he asks wrongly, for it says: "You ask and do not receive, because you ask wrongly."[14]

59.4. From this it follows that the grace of the Holy Spirit does not give wisdom to the saints without the intellect that receives it;[3] nor knowledge apart from the receptive power; nor faith without the full assurance of the intellect and reason concerning the future things that were hitherto hidden from all; nor gifts of healing without a natural love of mankind; nor any other of the remaining gifts apart from a state of mind and inner capacity receptive of each gift. Nor indeed does a human being acquire a single one of the things enumerated above by his natural power without the divine power that provides them.

59.5. And all the saints clearly demonstrate this when, after receiving revelations of divine realities, they seek to clarify the principles of what has been revealed.[15] When Abraham, for example, received the promise of inheriting the land that God had shown him, saying: "I am God who brought you out of the land of the Chaldeans, so as to give you this land to inherit,"[16] he was not satisfied simply to receive what he was searching for when he departed from the land of the Chaldeans, but he in-

---

11. 1 Cor 12.7.
12. 1 Cor 12.8–9.
13. 1 Cor 12.11.
14. Jas 4.3.
15. On this point, see above, Qu. 27.2–3.
16. Gn 15.7.

quired into it, desiring to learn also the manner of the inheritance, saying to God: "Lord God, how shall I know that I shall inherit it?"[17] And Moses, after he received the power to work signs and wonders, sought to learn both the modes and the principles according to which he might confirm the signs given to him.[18] "For He established among them," David says, "the principles of His signs and His wonders in the land of Ham."[19] Elsewhere David, referring to himself, crying out to God, said: "Unveil my eyes, and I will perceive wondrous things out of Your law,"[20] and: "Your law is a lamp for my feet, and a light to my paths."[21] And the great Daniel, the "man of desires"[22] for divine visions, for the sake of which he fasted for three entire weeks while researching their principles, heard an angel speaking to an angel, saying: "Make him understand the vision."[23] And the great prophet Zechariah, throughout the whole of his prophecy, in each of his visions, introduces the angel who speaks within him, who shows him the visions, and who teaches him the principles of the visions, saying: "The angel who speaks within me showed me," and: "the angel who speaks within me said to me," and: "I said to the angel who speaks within me, 'Lord, what are these things?'"[24]

59.6. From this it is clear that all the saints both received revelations from the Spirit and searched out their principles in order to unveil what had been revealed to them, and that the grace of the Holy Spirit in no way abolishes the power of nature. To the contrary: grace makes nature—which had been weakened by habits[25] contrary to nature—strong enough once again to function in ways according to nature, and it leads it upward to comprehension of divine realities. For it is the Holy Spirit within us who is searching out and inquiring into

17. Gn 15.8.
18. Cf. Ex 4.1.
19. Ps 104.27.
20. Ps 118.18.
21. Ps 118.105.
22. Dn 10.11.
23. Dn 8.16.
24. Zec 3.1, 14, 17; 2.3. Cf. below, Qu. 62–63.
25. Literally, "modes" (τρόποι).

the knowledge of beings, not for his own sake—for the Spirit is God and is far beyond all knowledge—but rather for the sake of us who are in need of this knowledge. To be sure, neither does the Word become flesh for Himself, but it is for us that he accomplishes the mystery through His Incarnation. And in the same way that the incarnate Word did not effect the natural things of the flesh without flesh animated by a rational soul and intellect, neither does the Holy Spirit effect knowledge of divine mysteries in the saints without their natural power to search and inquire after such knowledge.[26]

59.7. Thus whether the saints searched or researched, or whether they inquired or investigated, they possessed the grace of the Spirit, which was moving their intellective and rational power to search and inquire into the salvation of souls. Without the Spirit they contemplated absolutely nothing spiritual, for without the divine light the human intellect is not of a nature to perceive divine and intelligible realities. Just as it is not possible for the eye to perceive sensible objects without the light of the sun, neither can the human intellect, in the absence of spiritual light, ever receive a spiritual contemplation.[27] The former[28] naturally illumines the sense of sight for the perception of corporeal objects, while the latter[29] shines upon the intellect for the contemplation and comprehension of realities that transcend sense perception.

59.8. "The salvation of souls," properly speaking, "is the aim of faith."[30] The aim of faith is the true revelation of the object

---

26. In this analogy, Maximos is applying a Christological model to anthropology. In the same way that the incarnate Word of God does not operate directly through his human flesh apart from the intermediary of his human soul and intellect, neither does the Holy Spirit operate in the saints apart from their natural capacities and potentials. This would seem to be a logical extension of Maximos's understanding of *perichoresis;* cf. Thunberg, *Microcosm and Mediator,* 26–27.

27. Cf. Basil, *On the Holy Spirit* 16.38 (SC 17bis:382–84), where, in an extended metaphor, the Spirit is said to be the medium of spiritual vision.

28. A marginal note found in some manuscripts states that the referent here is: "Sensible light, obviously."

29. A marginal note found in some manuscripts states that the referent here is: "Spiritual light, obviously."

30. 1 Pt 1.9. Here begins a lengthy rhetorical "climax," i.e., an arrange-

of one's faith. The true revelation of the object of one's faith is the ineffable relation of mutual love with that object according to the measure of each one's faith. The relation of mutual love with the object of faith is the final return of the faithful to their own beginning. The final return of the faithful to their own beginning is the fulfillment of every desire. The fulfillment of desire is the ever-moving rest around the object of desire by those who desire it.[31] The ever-moving rest around the object of desire by those who desire it is the perpetual enjoyment of the object of desire unbroken by any interval.[32] Perpetual enjoyment of the object of desire unbroken by any interval is participation in divine realities that transcend nature. Participation in divine realities that transcend nature is the likeness[33] of the participants to the participable. The likeness of participants to the participable is the actualized identity of the participants with the participable, which they receive through the likeness. The actualized identity of participants with the participable received through the likeness is the divinization of those made worthy of it. Divinization, to state the matter briefly, is the compass and limit of all times and ages, and of everything that exists within them. The compass and limit of times and ages and of everything within them is the unity unbroken by any interval, among those who are being saved, of the true and proper

---

ment of clauses in succession in which the last important word of one clause is repeated as the first important word of the next, each clause in turn surpassing its predecessor in the importance of the thought. There are parallel examples elsewhere in Maximos's writings, although this is the most elaborate; cf. *Carit.* 1.2–3 (ed. Ceresa-Gastaldo, 50).

31. Following Gregory of Nyssa, *Life of Moses* 2.243 (SC 1bis:272), Maximos synthesizes movement with stability in the perfect, who continue to perfect themselves inasmuch as the infinity and beauty of God insure that their desire to know and love God will not simply never cease but will continue to grow and progress; cf. below, Qu. 65.23.

32. A criticism of the Origenist doctrine of "satiety"; cf. *Amb.* 7.27: "What could be more desirable to those who are worthy of it than divinization? ... This state has rightly been described as pleasure, passion, and joy ... as joy because it encounters nothing opposed to it, for they say that joy neither remembers former sorrows, nor fears the possibility of any future satiety" (DOML 1:115).

33. Cf. Gn 1.27.

beginning with the true and proper end.[4] The unity unbroken by any interval, among those being saved, of the true beginning with the true end, is the surpassing ecstasy[5] of those who by nature are essentially measured by a beginning and an end.³⁴ The ecstasy of those who by nature are circumscribed by a beginning and an end is the immediate and infinite activity of God, which is all-powerful and transcends all power, and which is infinitely active among those made worthy to pass beyond—in a superior sense—the things of nature. The immediate and infinite activity of God, which is infinitely active, and which is all-powerful and transcends all power, is the ineffable and beyond ineffable pleasure and joy of those who, in their union with God beyond all language and concepts, are the recipients of God's activities—a joy which is absolutely impossible for intellect, reason, thoughts, or words, or anything else in the nature of created beings to capture or express. For nature does not possess the principles of realities that transcend nature, just as it does not possess the laws of things that are contrary to nature. When I say "realities that transcend nature," I mean the divine and incomprehensible pleasure of God, which God inherently brings about by nature when He unites Himself according to grace to those who are worthy. When, on the other hand, I say "things that are contrary to nature," I mean the privation of grace producing unspeakable pain and suffering, which God is accustomed to bring about by nature when He unites Himself contrary to grace to those who are unworthy. For God, in a manner known only to Himself, by uniting Himself to all in accordance with the quality of the disposition that underlies each, imparts perception to each one, inasmuch as each one was formed by Himself for the reception of Him who at the end of the ages will be completely united to all.³⁵

---

34. Here, "ecstasy" freely renders the Greek word ἔκβασις, which means "departure, leaving behind, going out from, escape from," and, in Dionysios, "overflowing" (*DN* 4.23). This "departure" does not signify a neglect or repression of natural powers, but a surpassing of such powers on a higher level.

35. Present in and to creation as its "beginning," the presence of God does not preclude human activity. Being joined to creation through the Incarnation, on the other hand, and being ultimately joined to creation in the eschaton as its proper "end," God alone will be active in relation to the receptive

59.9. I think that when Peter, the summit of the apostles, spoke of the "salvation of souls" as the "aim of faith,"[36] he was perhaps referring to participation in realities that transcend nature. And that it was clearly "concerning this salvation"—through the Holy Spirit, of course—that the "prophets researched and investigated as to what person or time the Spirit of Christ within them was revealing when He testified to the sufferings of Christ and the glory that would follow."[37] From this it follows that those who spiritually research the salvation of souls, and who investigate the spiritual principles and modes of this salvation, are led to comprehend them by the Holy Spirit, who does not allow their natural power for investigating divine realities to remain immobile and inactive. Thus the Spirit teaches them first to seek to mortify the power of choice in relation to sin, and sin in relation to choice,[6] or vivify choice in relation to virtue, or virtue in relation to choice; and also to inquire into the modes through which choice is mortified in relation to sin, and sin in relation to choice, and likewise into the principles concerning the resurrection of choice in relation to virtue, and of virtue in relation to choice, for it is through these modes and principles that the mortification of sin in relation to choice comes about, or of choice in relation to sin. To be sure, the resurrection of virtue in relation to choice, or of choice in relation to virtue, comes about naturally, obviously when it is accompanied in this present age (which the verse in question calls "time") by the "sufferings" of nature "of Christ," that is, undertaken for Christ, which very sufferings the Holy Spirit "revealed" in advance to the prophets, so that they might "come to share connaturally[7] in the likeness of the death of Christ through the mortification of sin and through the actual resurrection of virtue."[38] For in truth it is necessary for the one who will be saved not only to mortify sin by means of choice, but also to mortify choice itself in relation to sin; and

---

passivity of created beings; cf. above, Qu. 22.7; and *Amb.* 7.12 (DOML 1:91, n. 16).

36. 1 Pt 1.9.
37. 1 Pt 1.10–11.
38. Cf. Rom 6.5.

not only to resurrect choice by means of virtue, but also virtue itself by means of choice, so that choice, if it is wholly dead[8] and separated from the whole death of sin, will not perceive it, and if it is wholly alive will perceive the whole of virtue in a union unbroken by any interval.

59.10. Perhaps having first searched and inquired into these things, the saints reached the level of practical philosophy through the Holy Spirit. After this, having become pure and free of every defilement, through the same Spirit they turned their soul's intellective eye toward the goal of beings, researching the resurrection of free choice and the incorruptibility of human nature, and investigating both the modes and principles of the divinely fitting immortality associated with that incorruptibility. For they were not still searching for the resurrection of free choice, which they had already received from the Holy Spirit through practical philosophy. Neither were they inquiring into the modes concerning it, which they had already attained through grace. Instead, they were researching the incorruptibility of nature, which they did not have; and they were investigating the principles of their divinization associated with that incorruptibility. And they pressed on toward this divinization, desiring the glory of Christ associated with it, in order that, just as they suffered together with Him in the present age—which, as I said, the passage in question calls "time"—so too they might be glorified with Him in the future age, becoming, in a manner transcending their nature, "heirs of God" by grace, and, through the economy of salvation, "joint heirs with Christ," who by the power of His Incarnation assumed the whole of human nature.[39] For Christ, being God and man by nature, is inherited by us as God in a manner transcending human nature by means of grace according to an ineffable participation; and for our sake, and in our own form as man, he makes our nature His own, and thereby inherits Himself jointly with us according to His inconceivable condescension. Mystically beholding this in advance through the Spirit, the saints were taught that the future glory, which would be manifested in Christ on account of virtue, must be preceded in the present

39. Cf. Rom 8.17.

by sufferings experienced for Christ for the sake of virtue, for it says: "They inquired as to what person or time the Spirit of Christ within them was revealing in advance when He testified to the sufferings of Christ and the glory that would follow."[40]

59.11. Moreover, they researched and investigated, not simply the incorruptibility of nature and the principles of divinization associated with that incorruptibility, but also the time according to which the testing through sufferings for the sake of divinization would come about—a testing that would make manifest both the disposition of those who truly longed for divinization and the feigned appearance of those who falsely believed they loved it. At the same time, they researched and investigated that other time, by which I mean the age or aeon, according to which divinization will be present in actuality to all, transforming all human beings unto the divine likeness, in a manner proportionate to each, to the extent that each one is receptive of it.[41] And it is perhaps this likeness to God that the passage under consideration called "glory," which comes about after labors undertaken for the sake of virtue. These, then, are the things that one should say in apology to someone who asks: "Why did Scripture here not say 'search' and 'inquire' but rather 'research' and 'investigate'?" thereby clearly setting forth the plain sense of Scripture.[42]

59.12. But I know of another interpretation that I heard from a certain wise man.[43] For when considering the more mystical principle of the beginning and the end, and of the process of searching and researching, this man used to say that searching was naturally oriented toward the beginning, while researching was oriented toward the end. For one naturally does not

---

40. 1 Pt 1.11.

41. See above, Qu. 22.

42. I.e., in response to the potential objection of those who would say that the passage speaks not of ζήτησις and ἔρευνα but rather of ἐκζήτησις and ἐξερεύνησις. The following paragraph offers a second explanation of the intensive ἐξ- prefix.

43. This may be a reference to the "wise elder" whom Maximos mentions 7 times in the *Ambigua to John*, although in that work he is normally referred to as the "wise elder" (*Amb.* 28.2; 29.2; 35.2); or as the "blessed elder" (*Amb.* 43.2; 66.2), and only once as simply a "wise man" (*Amb.* 27.5); cf. DOML 1:xix–xx.

research the beginning, nor search for the end, but rather searches for the beginning and researches the end. He further said that because man, at the very moment of his coming into being,[44] put his own beginning behind him through disobedience, he was unable to seek what lay behind him; and since the beginning delimits the motion of beings that owe their existence to it, the beginning is rightly called the end as well, in which, inasmuch as it is also the cause of motion, the course of beings in motion has its terminus. Therefore, when man researches his own end, he arrives at his beginning, which is naturally found within his end. Having abandoned the search for his beginning, he naturally undertakes the research of that beginning as an end. For man cannot escape the limits of his beginning, which encompass him on all sides and delineate his movement. But because he could not seek his beginning, which, as I said, lay behind him, he researched his end, which lay in front of him, so that, through the end, he might know the beginning that he abandoned, since he did not know the end through the beginning. And this is perhaps the mystery that the wise Solomon disclosed when he said: "What is that which has been? It is that which will be," and: "What is that which has been done? It is that which will be done."[45] It is as if Solomon was wisely indicating the beginning through the end. For after humanity's transgression, the end can no longer be indicated through the beginning, but only the beginning through the end. Nor does one seek the principles of the beginning, but rather researches those principles that lead beings in motion to their end.[46]

44. On the "simultaneity" of human creation and the fall, see Larchet, *Divinisation*, 187–94.
45. Eccl 1.9. For further discussion on this verse, see *Amb.* 71.5 (DOML 2:319–21).
46. Larchet (SC 569:72, n. 1) notes that this discussion of the beginning and the end is part of Maximos's larger critique of Origenism, citing Sherwood, "Ἀρχή καὶ τέλος." While Maximos agrees with Origen that "the end is like the beginning" (*On First Principles* 1.6.2 [SC 252:196, line 46]), he understands this formula very differently, since the end is no longer a mere re-establishment of a lost primal order (which, through the fall of Adam, is no longer accessible), and the entire trajectory is reframed in the context of divinization by grace, which presupposes a different cosmology and anthropology, in

59.13. If, however, someone should think that this interpretation is questionable, insofar as Scripture often uses the word "search" in such passages as: "Search for peace and pursue it,"[47] and: "Search first for the kingdom of God and His righteousness,"[48] he can confirm what I have said if he carefully examines the words themselves. For when the Word says: "Search for peace and pursue it," He was counseling us to pursue the beginning in the end. And the kingdom, which is the beginning, he ordered us to research with the righteousness that is the end of the kingdom. In other words, the kingdom of God is prior to all righteousness; indeed—to speak more strictly—it is rather righteousness itself, and toward it, as toward its end, is directed the motion of every human being diligently striving for virtue. For if righteousness is the equal distribution to each person according to his worthiness, and if the kingdom is legitimate governance, then it follows that righteousness is the same as the kingdom, through which, as if to an end, those who wish may easily make their way to the kingdom, as if to their beginning. This is because righteousness is the kingdom actualized, and the kingdom is righteousness confirmed through works. For to govern beings legitimately means to distribute to each one the things that correspond to its worthiness, and the distribution to each being of what corresponds to its worthiness is legitimate governance. Thus among those who are wise in the knowledge of divine realities, the verbal difference in no way upsets the intelligible evenness[49] of Holy Scripture.

59.14. If, on the other hand, someone wished to understand in a different way what it means to seek and inquire, and to research and investigate, he would find that seeking and research are movements of the intellect, and inquiry and investigation are movements of reason. For the intellect naturally seeks, while it is natural for the reason to investigate.[9] For seeking,

---

which motion is not the effect of a fall from a primal state of unity (the henad), but a positive force by means of which mankind realizes the potential established for it according to the divine plan; cf. *Amb.* 7.2–29 (DOML 1:77–119).

47. Ps 33.14.
48. Mt 6.33.
49. On the "evenness" (or "smoothness") of Scripture, see *Amb.* 21.3 (DOML 1:423).

if I may put it in terms of a definition, is a simple movement of the intellect with desire toward something known. Inquiry is a simple distinction made by reason generating a certain concept[50] about something known. Research is the cognitive movement of the intellect, based on true understanding, toward something known, marked by precisely this sort of desire. Investigation is the distinction made by reason in actuality about something known, marked by precisely this sort of concept. When we transpose these definitions into the sphere of divine realities, we say that seeking is the primary, simple, and affective movement of the intellect toward its own Cause. Inquiry is the primary and simple distinction of reason, generating a concept about its proper Cause. Furthermore, research is the cognitive movement of the mind, based on true understanding and marked by a burning desire, toward its proper Cause. Finally, investigation is the distinction of reason, actualized through the virtues, about its proper Cause, generating a wise and intelligent concept.

59.15. Therefore, the holy prophets, who "researched and investigated the salvation of souls,"[51] possessed an intellect whose motion and desire was set on fire by true understanding and knowledge and burning with desire for God; just as they possessed a reason able to bring about in actuality an intelligent and wise distinction about divine realities. Those who imitate them research the salvation of souls with knowledge and true understanding, and, investigating it with prudence and wisdom, attend to distinctions among divine works.

Scholia

[1] Divine grace, he says, does not bring about illuminations of knowledge if the natural potential to receive such illumination is not present; neither does that which receives this illumination bring about knowledge without the grace that provides it.

---

50. I.e., ἔννοια, which also carries the sense of a concept or notion as an "intention," and thus bears a distinctively moral character.
51. 1 Pt 1.10.

QUESTION 59 425

[2] Whoever asks without passion receives the gift to be able to realize the virtues in actual practice; and the one who seeks dispassionately finds the truth of beings through natural contemplation; and the one who knocks dispassionately on the door of knowledge enters without hindrance into the hidden grace of mystical theology.[52]

[3] The intellect is the instrument of wisdom, he says, while reason is the instrument of knowledge. The assurance for both is the instrument of faith that is constituted from both, and the natural love of humanity is the instrument of the gift of healings. Thus every divine gift has within us a suitable and natural instrument, as if it were a faculty, or state, or disposition, capable of receiving it. For example, whoever has purged his intellect of all images of sensible realities, receives wisdom; whoever has placed his reason in authority over his innate passions—by which I mean anger and desire—receives knowledge; whoever possesses an unshakeable assurance about God in both his intellect and reason, receives faith that is able to do all things;[53] while he who has attained to the natural love of mankind, after having completely eliminated self-love from himself, receives the gifts of healing.

[4] The principle of being naturally implies that God is the beginning; the principle of well-being naturally implies that God is the end toward which every human being voluntarily hastens, desiring to find rest in God. The unity of the two is the principle of eternal well-being, which comes about through grace, and which implies God, who is natural beyond every beginning and end, but who makes those who possess a beginning and an end by nature to be without beginning or end by grace.

[5] The transformation on the level of quality that is brought about by grace for the purpose of divinization is the ecstasy[54] for those beings circumscribed naturally by a beginning and an end.

[6] First, he says, one seeks to put to death sin in relation to

---

52. Cf. Mt 7.7.
53. Cf. Mt 17.20.
54. I.e., ἔκβασις.

free choice, and free choice in relation to sin, after which he inquires into how he must, and by what means, put to death each of the remaining ones by the others. And, again, after their perfect, mutual mortification, he seeks the life of free choice in relation to virtue, and the life of virtue in relation to free choice, and thus he inquires how he must, and by what means, create the life of the one in the other. Searching is thus, in the form of a definition, the appetite for something desired, while inquiry is a way to realize in practice the appetite in relation to what it desires.

[7] Whoever has put to death, he says, free choice in relation to sin, has "become united to the likeness of the death" of Christ;[55] and whoever has raised free choice from the dead by means of righteousness has become "united to Christ's resurrection."[56]

[8] Sin and free choice, he says, when they are mutually put to death in relation to each other, possess a double lack of perception between them. And righteousness and free choice possessing their life in each other possess a double perception.

[9] The intellect, he says, is moved solely by desire in a manner beyond knowledge, and seeks solely the Cause of beings. Reason, on the other hand, in making its varied rounds of creation, inquires into the true principles found among beings.

55. Rom 6.5.
56. Ibid.

QUESTION 60

S A PURE and spotless lamb, Christ was foreknown before the foundation of the world, and manifested at the end of time for our sake."[1] By whom was Christ "foreknown"?[2]

Response

60.2. In this passage of Scripture, the mystery of Christ is itself called "Christ," and the great Apostle clearly bears witness to this when he says that "the mystery hidden from the ages and the generations has now been manifested,"[3] identifying the "mystery of Christ" with "Christ" Himself. This mystery is obviously the ineffable and incomprehensible union according to hypostasis of divinity and humanity. This union brings humanity into perfect identity, in every way, with divinity, through the principle of the hypostasis, and from both humanity and divinity it completes the single composite hypostasis, without creating any diminishment due to the essential difference of the natures.[4] The result, as I said, is that the hypostasis of the

---

1. 1 Pt 1.20.
2. See the study of this Question by Pascal Müller, "La Question LX à Thalassios de Lybie. Lecture, questions, commentaire et themes connexes," License en sciences religieuses, Faculté de théologie Université de Fribourg, semester d'été 1997 (Fribourg: University of Fribourg, 1997).
3. Col 1.26.
4. The notion of Christ's "composite hypostasis" was formulated by Leontios of Jerusalem, *Against the Nestorians* (PG 86:1485D), in response to the Monophysite doctrine of a "composite nature." Maximos employs the formula in a number of his Christological letters; cf. *Ep.* 12 (PG 91:489C, 492C–493A); *Ep.* 13 (525D–529A); and *Ep.* 15 (556D); see also Nicholas Madden, "Composite Hypostasis in Maximus the Confessor," *SP* 27 (1993): 175–97; Bathrellos, *Byzantine Christ*, 99–116; and the extended discussion below, Qu. 62.3–5.

two is one, and their natural difference remained inviolate, and thus the quantity[5] of each of the united natures is preserved undiminished even after their union. For when and wherever things united suffer no change or alteration, the essential principle of each of them remains pure and unmixed. And insofar as the essential principle of each remained inviolate even after the union, the natures retained their integrity in every way, neither nature disowning anything properly its own because of the union.

60.3. For it was fitting that the Creator of the universe,[6] who by the economy of His Incarnation became according to nature[7] what He was not, should preserve without change both what He Himself was by nature and what He became in His Incarnation.[8] For it is not natural to contemplate any change in God, in whom we cannot conceive of absolutely any movement whatsoever, and it is because of movement that things in motion are subject to change.[9] This is the great and hidden mystery. This is the blessed end for which all things were brought into existence. This is the divine purpose conceived before the beginning of beings, and in defining it we would say that this mystery is the preconceived goal for the sake of which everything exists, but which itself exists on account of nothing,[10] and it was with a view to this end that God created the essences of beings.[11] This is, properly speaking, the limit and goal of God's

---

5. "Quantity" refers to *numerical* quantity, and thus the sense here is that the two natures were not reduced or confused into one nature; cf. *Amb.* 5.22 (DOML 1:52–53); and *Ep.* 21 (PG 91:473B–481A).

6. I.e., the pre-incarnate Logos.

7. I.e., by being conceived in the womb of the Virgin.

8. What the Creator "was by nature" was God; what He "became according to nature" and "in His Incarnation" was man.

9. A point argued at length in *Amb.* 7.2–14 (DOML 1:76–95).

10. Cf. *Amb.* 7.7: "The end is that for the sake of which all things exist; it, however, is for the sake of nothing" (DOML 1:82–83).

11. Here Maximos is suggesting that even if Adam had never fallen, the Word would have become incarnate. The mystery of the Incarnation was foreordained from all eternity, and both human and non-human creation were fashioned with this goal in mind; the fall of Adam altered the mode of salvation, but not its inner principle; cf. *Amb.* 7.37: "We were predestined before the ages to be in Him as the members of His body ... He showed us that this was

providence, and of the things under His providential care, since the recapitulation of the things created by God is God Himself. This is the mystery which circumscribes all the ages, and which reveals the grand plan of God,[12] a super-infinite plan infinitely pre-existing the ages an infinite number of times.[13] The essential Word of God became a messenger of this plan[14] when He became man, and, if I may rightly say so, revealed Himself as the innermost depth of the Father's goodness while also displaying in Himself the very goal for which creatures manifestly received the beginning of their existence.[15]

60.4. And this is because it is for the sake of Christ—that is, for the whole mystery of Christ—that all the ages and the beings existing within those ages received their beginning and end in Christ. For the union of the limit of the age and limitlessness,[1] of measure and immeasurability, of finitude and infinity, of Creator and creation, and of rest and motion, was conceived before the ages. This union has been manifested in Christ at the end of time, and through itself bestows the fulfillment of God's foreknowledge, so that creatures in motion by nature might find rest around that which is absolutely immovable by essence, departing completely from their movement toward themselves and each other, so that they might acquire, by experience, an active knowledge of Him in whom they were made worthy to find their stability, a knowledge which is unalterable and always the same, and which bestows upon them the enjoyment of the One they have come to know.

60.5. The word of Scripture recognizes that knowledge of divine realities is twofold.[2] On the one hand, there is relative knowledge based only on reasoning and concepts, and lacking the actual perception of what is known through experience, and it is this knowledge that we use to order our affairs in this present life. On the other hand, there is knowledge that

---

why we were created, and that this was God's good purpose which underwent no innovation in its essential principle, but rather was realized through the introduction of another, newer mode" (DOML 1:131).

12. Cf. Eph 1.10–11.
13. Cf. above, Qu. 56.7.
14. Cf. Is 9.5.
15. Cf. above, Qu. 22.7.

is true and properly so called, which is gained only by actual experience—without reasoning and concepts—and provides, by grace through participation, a whole perception of the One who is known. By this latter knowledge we attain, in the future rest, the supernatural divinization that is actualized unceasingly. They say, moreover, that relative knowledge based on reasoning and ideas can motivate[3] our desire for the participative knowledge acquired through active engagement. They also say that this active, experiential knowledge, which by participation furnishes the direct perception of what is known, negates the relative knowledge based on reasoning and ideas.[16]

60.6. For those who are wise say that it is impossible for reasoning about God to coexist with the direct experience of God,[4] or for concepts about God to coexist with the immediate perception of God. By "reasoning about God" I mean the use of the analogy of beings in the cognitive contemplation of God. By "perception" I mean the experience through participation in good things that transcend nature. By "concepts about God" I mean the simple and unitary knowledge of God derived from beings. And perhaps this kind of distinction can be recognized with respect to every other object of knowledge as well, if, that is, the direct experience of a thing brings an end to mere reasoning about it, and if the direct perception of a thing puts to rest our concepts about it. By "experience" I mean knowledge itself based on active engagement, which comes about after all reasoning. By "perception" I mean that very participation in the known object that manifests itself after all conceptualization. This may very well be what the great Apostle is secretly teaching when he says: "As for prophecies, they will pass away; as for tongues, they will cease; as for knowledge, it will disappear,"[17] for here he is clearly referring to that knowledge which is based on reason and ideas.

60.7. This mystery was foreknown by the Father, the Son, and the Holy Spirit before all the ages. It was known to the Fa-

---

16. On this passage, see the remarks of Pierre Miquel, "Πεῖρα: Contribution à l'étude du vocabulaire de l'expérience religieuse dans l'oeuvre de Maxime le Confesseur," *SP* 7 (1966): 355–61.

17. 1 Cor 13.8.

ther according to His good will, to the Son according to His role in carrying it out, and to the Holy Spirit according to His cooperation in it.[18] For there is one knowledge of the Father, the Son, and the Holy Spirit, because their essence and power are also one. The Father and the Holy Spirit were not ignorant of the Incarnation of the Son, because the whole Father is by essence in the whole Son, who Himself carried out the mystery of our salvation through His Incarnation. The Father Himself did not become incarnate, but in His good will approved the Incarnation of the Son. Moreover, the whole Holy Spirit exists by essence in the whole Son, but neither did He become incarnate but cooperated in the Son's ineffable Incarnation for our sake. Whether, then, one speaks of "Christ" or the "mystery of Christ," the Holy Trinity alone—Father, Son, and Holy Spirit—possessed the foreknowledge of it. And no one should wonder how Christ, being one of the Holy Trinity, was foreknown by the Trinity, knowing that Christ was foreknown not as God but as man. In other words, it was His Incarnation for humanity's sake in the economy of salvation that was foreknown. For that which exists eternally, and which came forth from what eternally transcends every cause and reason, could never be foreknown, because foreknowledge is of beings that have a beginning and cause of their existence.

60.8. Thus Christ was foreknown not as what He was in Himself by nature, but as what He manifested when, in the economy of salvation, He later became man on our behalf. For it was truly necessary that He who by nature is the Creator of the essences of beings should also become the very Author of the divinization by grace of creatures brought into existence, in order that the Giver of well-being might appear also as the gracious Giver of eternal well-being. Since, therefore, no being in absolutely any way at all knows what itself or any other being is in terms of its essence, it follows that no being by nature has foreknowledge of any future events. Only God, who transcends beings, and who knows what He Himself is in essence, foreknows the existence of all His creatures even before they

---

18. Cf. above, Qu. 2.2; and the parallel formulation in *Or. Dom.* (CCSG 23:30, lines 91–96).

are brought into existence. And in the future He will by grace confer on those beings the knowledge of what they themselves and other beings are in essence, and reveal the principles of their genesis that pre-exist uniformly in Him.

60.9. But the notion, put forward by certain people, that Christ was "foreknown before the foundation of the world" by those to whom He was later "manifested at the end of time," as if they existed with the foreknown Christ before the foundation of the world, introducing the essence of beings as co-eternal with God, we reject as inadmissible since such a view is alien to the truth.[19] For it is absolutely impossible for creatures to have come into being together with Christ as He is, just as it is impossible ever to be separated completely from Him, if of course the consummation of the ages will by nature take place in Him, along with the stability of all that is now in motion, a stability wherein no being will be subject to any change whatsoever.

60.10. The word of Scripture calls Christ "pure and without blemish," since in soul and body He was by nature absolutely free from the corruption of sin. For His soul did not bear the impurity of evil, nor His body the blemish of sin.

Scholia

[1] A limit[20] is the boundary[21] enclosing things that by nature are circumscribed. A measure is the universal circumscription of quantity and the end of eternal and temporal natures. A boundary is the circumscription of things that by virtue of their creation are bounded by both a beginning and an end. Creation is the subsistence of whatever has been brought into being *ex nihilo*. The union of these things according to hypostasis was conceived in advance, he says, according to Providence, so that they would be united to the One from whom they came into being, so that the being of beings would be preserved on the level of essence, as is natural, and also so that it might re-

---

19. A reference to the Origenist doctrine of the pre-existence of souls; cf. *Amb.* 7.2 (DOML 1:77).

20. I.e., ὅρος.

21. I.e., πέρας.

ceive by divine grace its subsistence, that is, its mode of existence, and become immutable by virtue of their union with God in which all things will be transformed.

[2] Knowledge, he says, is twofold. The first is based on reason and divine concepts, but has no sensible perception of these concepts according to any form. The second is according to active engagement and possesses, separately from reason or concepts, solely the enjoyment of true things according to their form.

[3] Because, he says, it is natural for reason to signify an object of knowledge through knowledge, it sets in motion the desire of those who are moved by it toward the enjoyment of what is signified.

[4] Prior to every experience, he says, there exists a principle of knowledge, for it is solely through experience that enjoyment naturally predominates.

QUESTION 61

"THE TIME HAS come for judgment to begin from the house of God. And if it begins from us, what will be the end of those who disobey the gospel of God? And 'if the righteous man is scarcely saved, where will the impious man and the sinner appear?'"[1] What is the meaning of the phrase: "The time has come for judgment to begin from the house of God," and: "'If the righteous man is scarcely saved'"?

Response

61.2. God, who fashioned human nature, did not create sensible pleasure or pain together with it,[1] but instead devised for this nature a certain capacity for intelligible pleasure, whereby human beings would be able to enjoy God ineffably. The first human being, however, at the same moment that he was brought into being,[2] surrendered this capacity—I mean the intellect's natural desire for God—to physical sensation, and in his initial impulse toward sensory objects, mediated through his senses, he came to know pleasure activated contrary to nature.[3] God, however, in His providential concern for our salvation,[2] attached pain to this pleasure, as a kind of power of chastisement, whereby the law of death was wisely planted in the nature of our bodies in order to limit the madness of the intellect in its desire to incline unnaturally toward sensory objects.[4]

---

1. 1 Pt 4.17–18, quoting Prv 11.31.
2. Cf. *Amb.* 42.7 (DOML 2:135); and above, Qu. 1.1; and Qu. 59.12.
3. Cf. above, Intro., 1.2.13–19, on the fall of Adam and its consequences.
4. Larchet (SC 569:96, n. 1) considers this to be one of the most important Questions in the whole collection, containing Maximos's essential thinking

61.3. Because of the pleasure contrary to reason that had intruded into human nature, pain according to reason entered in opposition to it through the many sufferings in which and from which death comes upon us. This pain brings about the expulsion of pleasure contrary to nature[3] but not its complete eradication, and it is through the latter that the grace of divine pleasure is naturally manifested in the intellect. This is because all pain, the cause of whose proper generation is a prior act of pleasure, is naturally—in view of its cause—a debt that must be paid in full by all who share in human nature. To be sure, such suffering invariably follows unnatural pleasure in all those for whom the law of pleasure, without prior cause, preceded their birth. Of course, when I say "without prior cause," I mean the pleasure that came about through the transgression, which obviously did not follow a prior experience of pain.

61.4. Thus after the transgression, all human beings possessed pleasure as something naturally antecedent to their proper birth, and absolutely no one was by nature free from an impassioned birth conditioned by pleasure. Experiencing pain and sufferings as if in payment of a natural debt, all human beings had to submit to death, which followed upon their sufferings. Consequently the way to freedom was barred for all who were subject to the tyranny of unrighteous pleasure[4] and just sufferings, and who because of these just sufferings were naturally subject to a most just death. In order to bring about the abolition of this most unrighteous pleasure and the truly just sufferings that follow from it—by which suffering man had been so mercilessly torn asunder, having the beginning of his birth in the corruption associated with pleasure, and the end of his life in the corruption associated with death—as well as the restoration of suffering human nature, it was necessary that an unjust and likewise uncaused suffering and death be devised: a death "unjust" in the sense that it by no means followed a

---

about the nature of the fall, its effects, the nature of salvation in Christ, the understanding of pleasure, pain, suffering, and death, and humanity's new spiritual birth through grace supplanting biological birth; cf. *Amb.* 42.1–6, 31–32 (DOML 2:123–33, 181–85); above, Qu. 21; and Larchet, *Maxime, Mediator*, 77–124.

life given to the passions, and "uncaused" in the sense that it was in no way preceded by pleasure. Such an unjust suffering and entirely unjust death—which occupies a middle position[5] between unrighteous pleasure and entirely just suffering and death—would be necessary to do away completely with the unrighteous beginning in pleasure as well as the consequent just end of human nature occurring in death. In this way the human race would again be freed of pleasure and pain, and human nature would recover its good inheritance unsullied by any indication of subjection to birth and corruption.

61.5. This is why the Word of God, who is perfect God by nature, became perfect man, being composed just like us by nature of an intellectual soul and a passible body, except without sin.[5] His birth in time from a woman was not preceded in any way by the pleasure derived from the transgression, but in His love for mankind He accepted the pain resulting from unrighteous pleasure, which is the end of nature, so that by suffering unjustly He might destroy the principle of birth that tyrannized nature because of unrighteous pleasure.[6] In the case of the Lord, this principle was not a debt requiring the payment of death, as was the case with other human beings, but rather His death was something opposed to and which surpassed that principle, so that through death He might obliterate the just end of nature, which did not have illegitimate desire as the cause of its existence, and which was justly punished by death.

61.6. For in truth it was necessary—necessary, I say—that the Lord, who according to His nature is wise and just and powerful, should not, in His wisdom, ignore the means of curing us; nor, in His justice, despotically save humanity when it had fallen under sin by the inclination of its own will; nor, in His omnipotence, falter in bringing the healing of humanity to completion. He therefore made manifest the principle of His wisdom through the mode by which He healed humanity, namely, by becoming man without undergoing any kind of change or alteration. He showed the equality of His justice in the magnitude of His condescension, when He willingly submitted to the condemnation of nature in its passibility, and he

5. Heb 4.15.

made that very possibility a weapon for the destruction of sin and death, which is the consequence of sin,[6] that is, for the destruction of pleasure and the pain which is its consequence. And He did this because the rule of sin and death had established themselves in our condition of passibility, along with the tyranny of sin associated with pleasure and the oppression associated with pain, for the rule of pleasure and pain over our nature subsists within our passibility. Wanting to escape the oppressive sensation of pain, we sought refuge in pleasure,[7] attempting to console our nature when it was hard-pressed with pain's torment. But in hastening to blunt the onslaught of pain by means of pleasure, we bound ourselves all the more to the "bond of indebtedness,"[7] inasmuch as we are unable to experience pleasure without pain and suffering.[8] But the Lord manifested the might of His transcendent power by establishing within human nature a birth—which He himself experienced—unchanged by the contrary realities of pleasure and pain.[8] For by giving our nature impassibility through His Passion, relief through His sufferings, and eternal life through His death, He restored our nature, renewing its capacities by means of what was negated in His own flesh, and through His own Incarnation granting it that grace which transcends nature, by which I mean divinization.

61.7. God, then, truly became man and gave our nature the new beginning of a second birth, which through pain ends in the pleasure of the life to come. For our forefather Adam,[9] having transgressed the divine commandment, introduced into our nature another beginning of birth—in contrast to the one that had preceded it—constituted by pleasure, yielding to pain, and ending in death. Following the counsel of the serpent,[10] he conceived of pleasure not as succeeding any prior suffering, but rather as terminating in suffering, and so he subjected, through this unrighteous origination in pleasure, all

6. Cf. Rom 6.23.
7. Cf. Col 2.14.
8. Cf. above, Intro. 1.2.14.
9. Cf. Rom 5.12.
10. Cf. Gn 3.1.

those who like him were born of the flesh, together with himself, to the just end of death through suffering. Conversely, our Lord, having become man, and having created for our nature a new beginning of birth through the Holy Spirit, and having accepted the death through suffering that was justly imposed on Adam, but which in Him was completely unjust—since it did not have as the principle of its beginning the unrighteous pleasure that arose from the disobedience of the forefather—destroyed both of these two extremes (I mean the beginning and the end) of human birth according to Adam, neither of which was brought into being by God. To all those who were mystically reborn of Him in the Spirit,[11] He granted freedom from liability to those extremes, since they no longer possessed the pleasure associated with birth that came from Adam,[9] but only the pain that, on account of Adam, remains active within them and produces death, not as a debt owed for sin, but according to the economy of salvation, as a natural condition that counteracts sin.[12] For when death does not have pleasure as a mother bringing it to birth—a pleasure which death by its very nature punishes—it obviously becomes the father of eternal life.[13] Just as Adam's life of pleasure is the mother of death and corruption, so too the death of the Lord, which came about for the sake of Adam, and which was free of the pleasure associated with Adam, is the progenitor of eternal life.

61.8. It seems to me, then, the word of Scripture has rightly distinguished between how, on the one hand, generation[14] from Adam accompanied by pleasure, in tyrannizing our nature, was providing food for the death[15] that arose in conse-

11. I.e., through baptism.
12. Among those who are born anew in the Spirit, death ceases to be a necessary consequence of sin, and instead becomes a providential means granting access to eternal life; cf. Larchet, SC 569:102, n. 1.
13. The Greek word for "pleasure" is a feminine noun, while the word for "death" is a masculine noun.
14. I.e., γένεσις. While this paragraph presents two distinct understandings of "generation" (i.e., human generation and birth), both of which Maximos applies to Christ, the two notions are not as rigorously distinguished as they are in *Amb.* 42.2–5 (DOML 2:123–131).
15. Cf. *Amb.* 10.60, where Adam, refusing the divine nourishment of the Word, "handed over all creation as food for death" (DOML 1:249).

quence of that pleasure; and how, on the other hand, the birth of the Lord in the flesh, which came about because of His love of mankind, eliminated both of these things, by which I mean the pleasure associated with Adam and the death that came about because of Adam, eradicating Adam's punishment along with his sin. That is, it was not possible for the Lord's generation as man—which was in no way touched by that beginning whose end was death—to be conquered in the end by corruption through death.[10] This is because, as I said, the word of Scripture has distinguished these things from one another, because for as long as our nature was being tyrannized solely by the characteristic marks of Adam in its beginning and end, by which I mean generation and corruption, it was "not the time for the judgment" enabling the complete condemnation of sin "to begin."[16] But when the Word of God appeared to us through the flesh and became perfect man but without sin,[17] and in the flesh of Adam willingly bore only the punishment of Adam's nature,[18] and when He "condemned sin in the flesh,"[19] innocently suffering as "righteous for the sake of the unrighteous,"[20] and converted the use of death, reworking it into the condemnation of sin but not of nature, then, I say, "it was the time for the judgment to begin," a judgment consistent with this conversion of death and leading to the condemnation of sin.

61.9. What I mean to say is this: In the beginning, sin enticed Adam and persuaded him to transgress the divine commandment, and through transgression sin gave subsistence to pleasure, and through pleasure sin affixed itself to the very foundations of our nature, condemning the whole of our nature to death, and through the human person it was pushing the nature of all created beings away from existence.[11] For this was what had been devised by the wicked devil, who is the sower of

16. 1 Pt 4.17.
17. Cf. Heb 4.15.
18. The Word assumed the nature of Adam with all the consequences of sin (i.e., natural passibility, corruptibility, and mortality), but without the presence of any sin in the assumed nature; see Larchet, *Maxime, Médiateur*, 97–104.
19. Rom 8.3.
20. 1 Pt 3.18.

sin and the father of evil, who through his own arrogance banished himself from the divine glory, and, in his envy both toward us and toward God, banished Adam from paradise, aiming to destroy the works of God and to break apart what God had brought together for the generation of life and existence. For the devil, who is utterly defiled, does not envy us because of the glory of God granted to us on account of our virtue, but he is envious of God Himself, because of the all-praised power that God exercises for the sake of our salvation.[12]

61.10. Therefore, death, which came about because of the transgression, was ruling powerfully over all of human nature, having as the basis of its rule the pleasure that set in motion the whole process of natural generation, which was the reason why death was imposed on our nature. But the Lord, when He became man without any unrighteous pleasure (because of which the just condemnation of death was imposed on our nature) preceding His birth in the flesh, and when He naturally willed to undergo death itself in the passibility of His human nature—obviously through the suffering of His Passion—He converted the use of death, so that henceforth in Him death would no longer be a condemnation of nature, but clearly only of sin.[21] That is, it was not possible for death to be the condemnation of nature in one whose birth was not based on pleasure, but rather to be the destruction of the sin of the forefather, through which the fear of death held sway over the whole of human nature.[22] For if, in Adam, death was the condemnation of his nature, inasmuch as it possesses the beginning of its own generation in pleasure, it stands to reason that, in Christ,

---

21. In Qu. 42, Maximos considered Christ's assumption of human passibility, which was assumed as a consequence of the fall, but without the sin associated with it or committed in any sinful acts. Blowers, *Cosmic Mystery*, 138, n. 8, rightly points to the "good use" (χρῆσις) of the human passions highlighted in Qu. 1, so that the argument here makes Christ's good use of death, which is the ultimate moment of human passivity (and its end), the key to human salvation.

22. In *Pyrr.* (PG 91:297B), Maximos speaks of Christ's "blameless" use of the fear of death, since Christ alone turns it into a "voluntary" fear that encourages the faithful in their own confrontation with death; cf. *Opusc.* 7 (PG 91:80D); and *Or. Dom.* (CCSG 23:34, lines 135–42).

death became the condemnation of sin, with the result that in Christ human nature has recovered a birth free of pleasure. Thus, just as in Adam, sin based on pleasure condemned our nature to corruption through death and signaled the "time" for our nature to be condemned to death because of its sin, so too in Christ, on the basis of His righteousness, human nature condemns sin through death and inaugurates the "time" for sin to be condemned to death because of righteousness, inasmuch as in Christ our nature has been completely stripped of birth through pleasure. For it was on account of this birth that death, like a debt owed by everyone, necessarily accompanied our condemnation, so that in Adam the very same death was the condemnation of human nature because of sin, whereas in Christ it is a condemnation of sin because of His righteousness. The one who suffers because of sin resulting in the condemnation of his nature justly endures death, whereas the one who does not suffer because of sin, but instead bestows His grace on human nature in the divine dispensation for the condemnation of sin, willingly submits to the death caused by sin in order to destroy sin.[23]

61.11. It follows, then, that because of Adam, who by his disobedience established the law of birth through pleasure and the condemnation of death that was consequently imposed on human nature, all those who received their being from Adam (according to this law of birth through pleasure) are necessarily subject—even if unwilling—to the death that is powerfully bound up with this birth and which serves to condemn our nature. Thus it was "time" for nature to be condemned because of sin, since the law of birth based on pleasure held nature in its power. In the same way, because of Christ—who completely removed from human nature the law of birth through pleasure, and who willingly took up the use of death (which on Adam's account had condemned human nature) solely for the purpose of condemning sin—it came about that all those who in the Spirit are willingly reborn of Christ "with the bath of regeneration"[24]

---

23. Maximos's entire argument here is largely a theological exegesis of Rom 5.12–21.
24. Ti 3.5.

are able by grace to put off their former birth from Adam based on pleasure. By keeping the gospel commandments they preserve the baptismal grace of sinlessness and the undiminished and undefiled power of mystical adoption in the Spirit.[25] It is not without reason, then, that those who are thus regenerated possess the use of death as an effective means for condemning sin, taking the "time" to "condemn sin in the flesh."[26] In a general sense,[13] according to nature and by means of grace, owing to the great mystery of the Incarnation, this is the time that began when the Word became flesh. In a particular sense, according to activity and by means of grace, it is the time that began with baptism, when each person received the grace of adoption. Thanks to this grace, which is rendered effective by their voluntary keeping of the commandments, they possess only their birth in the Spirit, and they endure many sufferings for the condemnation of sin, patiently awaiting the use of death when it comes upon them. For it is no longer because of sin that one who is baptized and who guards that baptism, which is reinforced by keeping God's commandments, spurns death as a debt owed for sin. Instead, the baptized acquires the use of death to condemn sin, which in turn mystically leads that person to divine and unending life. Such will ensue if indeed the saints, for the sake of truth and righteousness, have virtuously finished the course of this life with its many sufferings, liberating their nature within themselves from death as a condemnation of sin and, like Christ, the "captain of our salvation,"[27] transfigured death from a weapon to destroy human nature into a weapon to destroy sin. For if sin possesses death as a weapon to destroy human nature in those who, with Adam, keep sin active, how much more will human nature possess death as a weapon to destroy sin in those who realize righteousness through faith in Christ.

61.12. Thus beginning with the mystery of the Incarnation, when God in the flesh completely uprooted—in those who after Him are born in the Spirit—the birth of nature according to the law of pleasure, "the time" arrived, as I said, "for judg-

---

25. Cf. above, Qu. 6, on the gift of the Spirit in baptism.
26. Rom 8.3.
27. Heb 2.10.

ment to begin from the house of God,"[28] that is, for the condemnation of sin, which took the beginning of its condemnation from the sufferings of the faithful who knew the truth and who through baptism put aside birth according to pleasure. For Scripture calls them the "house of God," just as the most divine apostle Paul testifies, saying that: "Christ was faithful over God's house, and we are his house."[29] And Peter himself, the chief of the apostles, sets forth the same through the following words: "If we are to be judged first, then what will be the end of those who disobey the gospel of God?"[30] It is as if he were asking: If we, who are deemed worthy to become the "house of God" by grace through the Spirit, are obliged to demonstrate so great a patience amid suffering for the sake of righteousness and for the purpose of condemning sin; and if, while evildoers hold death in contempt, we, being virtuous, are obliged to embrace death eagerly, "then what will be the end of those who disobey the gospel of God?" In other words, what sort of end or judgment awaits those who have not only kept alive and active—both in soul and in body, both in will and in nature—the birth from Adam based on pleasure, but who embrace neither our God and Father, who appeals to them through His incarnate Son, nor the Mediator and Son Himself, who acts as ambassador for the Father, and who was Himself willingly sent, by the Father's counsel, to reconcile us to the Father, to die for our sake, so that in Himself He might glorify us, illuminate us with His beauty and His own divinity, precisely to the extent that, because of us, He submitted to being dishonored by our sufferings? This, it seems to me, is the "gospel of God," namely, that the incarnate Son is God's ambassador and advocate for humanity, and has earned reconciliation to the Father for those who yield to Him for the divinization[14] that is without origin.[31]

61.13. This is why the great apostle Peter inveighs against the disobedient when he asks: "And if the righteous man is scarcely

---

28. 1 Pt 4.17.
29. Heb 3.6.
30. 1 Pt 4.17.
31. On the phrase "divinization without origin," see the note below, at schol. 14.

saved, where will the impious man and the sinner appear?"[32] By "righteous man" he is most likely referring to a person who is faithful and who guards the grace bestowed in baptism; a person who, through many sufferings, has preserved inviolate his adoption through the Spirit. The "salvation" of which the Apostle speaks is the fullest grace of divinization that will be bestowed on the worthy, which will "scarcely" be attained even by one who completely and utterly adheres to all the things of God. The "impious man" and the "sinner," on the other hand, refer to the one who is alien to the grace of the gospel. He is "impious" because he has no faith in Christ, and a "sinner" because the ancient birth is alive and well in him in the corruption of the passions. Or perhaps Scripture called "impious" the one who is wholly bereft only of the knowledge of Christ, and "sinner" the one who has kept faith but, like me, transgresses the gospel commandments, which keep clean the tunic of incorruptibility given to us through holy baptism. Their placement—that of the impious and the sinner, I mean—is made known to those who exercise some measure of diligence in acquiring mystical knowledge. For the mention of "where" they will be clearly indicates a position that is not without a share in localized circumscription. And if indeed the place of the righteous man is diametrically opposed to this, he will not be anywhere at all in terms of a particular place, having by grace received God Himself as his place, as God has promised. For God is not "somewhere," but is unqualifiedly beyond all "where." In Him will be the sure foundation of all who are saved, according to the words: "Be to me a protecting God, and a strong place to save me."[33] Whosoever does not participate in the power of well-being in relation to God will be like a part of the body utterly bereft of the soul's vital energy.

61.14. Or, again, since the "place" of the saved will be God Himself, who is uncircumscribed, unlimited by time or space,

---

32. 1 Pt 4.18.

33. Ps 70.3. Cf. *Amb.* 7.18: "God is the 'place' for all those deemed worthy of such blessedness, just as it is written, 'Be Thou to me a protecting God, and a strong place to save me' [Ps 70.3]" (DOML 1:99); and *Amb.* 10.91–92 (DOML 1:291–95).

and infinite, "becoming all things to all"[34] in proportion to their righteousness, or rather granting Himself to each person according to the measure they have suffered knowingly for the sake of righteousness—just as the soul reveals itself as active in the parts of the body according to the capacity underlying each part, while maintaining in itself the existence of the parts, and sustains them in life—then, I ask, "where will the impious man and sinner appear?" For "where" will one, who is unable to receive the presence of God, actualized in the state of well-being, "appear" after having suffered separation from divine life, which transcends age, time, and place?

61.15. Thus, according to the first interpretation, by way of affirmation, the impious man and the sinner will be found in a place that is by no means free of a life without limits,[15] since he will not enjoy that life which fully escapes limitation and is beyond any location. According to the second interpretation, by way of negation, there is no "where" in which he might appear, since he does not enjoy God as sustaining his life unto well-being. In either case, "how"[16] will he exist when he does not have God as his very own location, the only sure foundation of well-being, which is God? Simply stated, if, only after much vexation, "the righteous man will be saved," what will happen or what will become of the person who in this present life has no interest in piety or virtue?

Scholia

[1] Pleasure and pain, he says, were not created together with the nature of the flesh. Instead, the transgression conceived both the former, resulting in the corruption of free choice, and the latter, resulting in the condemnation and dissolution of nature, so that pleasure would bring about the soul's voluntary death through sin, and so that pain, through dissolution, might bring about the destruction of the existing form of the flesh.

[2] By His providence, God gave nature involuntary pain and the death that results from it as punishment for voluntary pleasure.

34. 1 Cor 9.22.

[3] The thought of voluntary pains and the onslaught of involuntary ones, he says, removes the impulse of pleasure, bringing to a standstill its active motion, without, however, destroying its power, which exists within its nature as a law impinging on birth. For the philosophy which aims at virtue naturally brings about the dispassion of the will, but not of nature, according to which—that is, the dispassion of the will—the grace of divine pleasure comes about in the intellect.

[4] "Unrighteous pleasure" is what he calls the "law of sin"[35] that was mixed into nature at the time of the transgression.

[5] The pain and death of the Lord, he says, should be seen as a mean beneficial for the destruction of the extremes, inasmuch as His birth was free from pleasure, and the death of His divine flesh (which came about for our sake) was pure of the life of passions. According to this way of coming into being and of birth, He voluntarily endured death for our sakes, so that He might destroy our birth from pleasure, and our death from a life of passions, Himself appearing in the middle, leading us to another life, free of temporal beginning and end, which is not created by nature but rather by grace.

[6] It was, he says, absolutely impossible for nature, which had been subjected to voluntary pleasure and involuntary pain, to have returned again to the life it had from the beginning, had not the Creator become man, freely accepting the pain that came about as punishment for the pleasure freely chosen by nature, but which was not preceded by birth from pleasure, so that He might free nature from its condemned manner of birth, accepting a birth whose beginning was not in pleasure.

[7] How we further extend the natural chastisement of pain, endeavoring to assuage it through pleasure.

[8] The wisdom of God, he says, is revealed in the fact that He truly became man by nature; His righteousness, in the fact that in His birth he assumed the passivity of nature like unto us; and His omnipotence, in the fact that, by means of His sufferings and death, He created eternal life for human nature and a state of dispassion that will never be moved.

---

35. Rom 7.23.

QUESTION 61   447

[9] The Lord, having removed the pleasure that came about through the law of sin, in order to put aside birth according to the flesh for those who are born in Him by the grace of the Spirit, permits death—which had originally been imposed on them for the condemnation of nature—so that they might now receive the condemnation of death.

[10] After the transgression, he says, the beginning of human nature was conception from seed through pleasure, and birth through a flow of blood, while its end was death through corruption in pain. The Lord, however, not possessing such a beginning for His birth in the flesh, was not subjected by nature to its end, that is, to death.

[11] The devil, anticipating the destruction into non-being for the nature of things that came into being, struggled to show forth man as a transgressor of the divine commandment.

[12] The devil, being envious of both God and us, and having persuaded man by guile into thinking that God was envious of him,[36] prepared man to transgress the commandment. He envied God, and did not want His all-hymned power to be manifested in act by creating man; and he obviously envied man, and did not want him to share in the glory of God through a life of virtue.

[13] He says that the general condemnation of the law of nature, which came to prevail after the transgression, is the true Incarnation of God. The particular condemnation of this law is the rebirth of each person's will in Christ.

[14] "Divinization without origin" is what he calls the specific[37] enhypostatic illumination of the divinity, which has no origin, but appears as an incomprehensible manifestation in those who are worthy of it.[38]

36. I.e., man.
37. I.e., κατ' εἶδος, which later Byzantine writers would understand as referring to a visible manifestation of the uncreated light of God; cf. David Dishypatos, *To Nikolaos Kavasilas, Against Barlaam and Akindynos* (ed. Demetrios Tsamis [Thessaloniki, 1973], 72, lines 18–21).
38. Maximos's notion of "divinization without origin" (i.e., ἀγένητος θέωσις, which can also be translated as "uncreated divinization") attracted significant attention among late Byzantine theologians, who frequently cite this scholion, which speaks of an *enhypostatic* illumination in God. Though the

[15] Whoever, he says, does not take hold of pure divine life, in which there is absolutely no principle of limitation, will not be free of pain, because he will continually be limited and contained by created existence, and not ungenerated existence, which is free of all local position in place, motion, and time, and which cannot be comprehended and thus cannot be circumscribed.[39] For divine life is beyond comprehension, and even if it gives its own enjoyment to those who by grace will come to participate in it, it does not give them comprehension. Instead, it remains always incomprehensible, even if those who enjoy it participate in it, because inasmuch as it is unoriginate by nature, it is infinite.

[16] God, he says, according to a unique, infinitely powerful intention of His goodness, will contain all angels and human beings, both the good ones and the evil ones. Not all of them, however, will participate equally in God, who will indeed enter into all without distinction, but in a manner proportion-

---

scholion itself does not appear to have been written by Maximos, these later writers took both the text and the scholion as constituting a single statement; cf. Kallistos and Ignatios, *Method and Rule for those Practicing Hesychasm* (Φιλοκαλία [Athens: Aster, 1970], 4:262); and Kallistos the Patriarch, *On Prayer* (ibid., 337). Gregory Palamas, *Triads* 3.1.28, also cites the scholion, as do Gregory Akindynos, *Or.* 2.2 (CCSG 31:87); ibid., 2.38 (136, lines 11–12); David Dishypatos, *To Nikolaos Kavasilas* (ed. Tsamis, 72); and the anonymous compiler of an important Palamite florilegium; cf. Peter Van Deun, "Les citations de Maxime le Confesseur dans le florilège palamite de l'Atheniensis, Bibliothèque Nationale 2583," *Byzantion* 57 (1987): 127–57, esp. 147. Palamas argues that the divine light or energy is *enhypostatos* but not *authypostatos;* that is, it subsists naturally in the Trinity but in the saints by grace, being extended to them by the Spirit (without ever being separated from the Spirit), "since this," he says, "is the proper meaning of *enhypostaton*, namely, that something is contemplated not by itself and not in the essence but in the hypostasis" (ed. John Meyendorff [Louvain: Catholic University of Louvain, 1959], 610–11). Meyendorff's edition identifies the Maximian excerpt with 12 lines of Palamas's text, but states that "this is a passage from Maximos that we have not been able to identify" (610, n. 2). In fact, Palamas's quotation of the scholion occupies only the first 3 lines, while the remaining 9 are taken largely from Maximos, *Myst.* 20 (CCSG 69:47).

39. Created existence itself does not inflict pain on the human person, but rather the condition of being limited, a condition that may be overcome by means of a person's communion with God.

ate to each. On the one hand, those who in all things kept the disposition of their will in equilibrium with nature, making it actually receptive of the principles of nature, in accordance with the whole principle of eternal well-being, shall—owing to the receptivity of their will to the intention of God—participate in the whole of divine goodness, which will shine upon them just as it will upon angels. Those, on the other hand, who in all things did not maintain the disposition of their will in equilibrium with nature, and who in fact scattered the principles of nature in relation to the whole principle of well-being, shall—owing to the antipathy of their will to the intention of God—fall away from the whole of divine goodness, according to the manifest intimacy of their will with ill-being. This will be the reason for the separation between God and individuals such as these, for the disposition of their will lacks the principle of well-being vivified by actual works of virtue, for it is by this principle that divine life is of a nature to shine forth. On the day of judgment, then, the principle of nature will be the balance weighing the will of each one, revealing its movement toward either what is good or evil, for it is according to such movements that participation or lack of participation in divine life is of a nature to be actualized. For God, when He becomes present to all, will contain all according to the principles of being and eternal being, but according to the principle of eternal well-being, He will contain only, and in a special way, holy angels and holy human beings, leaving those who are not such as these to receive eternal ill-being as the fruit of the disposition of their will.

QUESTION 62

WHAT IS THE meaning of what the holy prophet Zechariah says: "And I lifted up my eyes, and I looked, and behold, a flying sickle, twenty cubits in length, and ten cubits in width, and he said to me: 'This is the curse that goes forth from over the face of the whole earth,'" and shortly after this: "And I will bring it forth, says the Lord Almighty, and it shall enter into the house of the thief, and into the house of him that swears falsely by my name; and it shall rest in the midst of his house, and shall consume it, and its wood and its stones"?[1] What is the sickle, and what is the meaning of its length and width? And why is it flying? And who is the thief, and the swearer of oaths, and what is his house, and its wood and the stones?

Response

62.2. God, who said: "I have multiplied visions, and by the hands of the prophets I have been represented in a likeness,"[2] established in advance, by means of symbols, various figurations of his wondrous arrival in the flesh for the salvation of human beings. Each of the prophets presented this arrival differently, that is, in the manner that each was able to comprehend it. To the great prophet Zechariah, God granted initiation into His own mysteries, and, presenting to the prophet's sight, as it were, an object enabling him to understand the power of His imminent manifestation in the flesh, He wisely fashioned a sickle for him to contemplate. In this way, He taught that the same God, who had mystically fashioned Himself through many and

---

1. Zec 5.1–3, 4.
2. Hos 12.10.

various figures in the visions of the prophets, would voluntarily and in truth submit Himself to be fashioned in human nature, and thus show by means of realities the truth that had formerly been announced through figures.

62.3. The sickle, then, is our Lord Jesus Christ, the only begotten Son and Word of God, who with respect to Himself is by nature simple, and exists, and will remain forever; with respect to me, however, He became composite according to hypostasis, in a manner that only He knows, through the assumption of flesh having soul and intellect.[3] And He did this without allowing the extreme hypostatic unity with the flesh to result in the confusion of a single nature, nor did He divide Himself into a duality of sons by the extreme difference according to nature.[4] By "extreme" I mean the absolutely indivisible character of the union according to hypostasis, and by the "extreme difference according to nature," I mean the absolutely unconfused and unaltered character of the hypostatic union. This is because the mystery of the divine Incarnation in absolutely no way entails that, because of the otherness of the natures of which it is constituted, there should also be a difference of hypostasis. The former[1] so that there would be no addition to the Trinity, the latter so that there would be nothing according to nature that would be connatural and consubstantial with the Divinity. For the Incarnation was the concurrence of two natures in one hypostasis, not in one nature, so that both the unity according to hypostasis would be shown to be constituted from the mutual concurrence of the two natures *and* that the difference of the natures, which came together in an unbreakable union, would be believed to remain, on the level of natural identity, outside of every change and confusion.

62.4. For if the concurrence of the natures resulted in the generation[2] of another nature, the mystery of our salvation

---

3. On Christ's "composite hypostasis," see above, Qu. 62.2.

4. That is, the "confusion" of the human and divine natures characteristic of Monophysite Christology, and the separation of the natures into a "duality of sons" characteristic of Nestorian Christology, both of which are excluded by the four adverbs of the Chalcedonian *Definition of Faith*, namely, "without confusion or change," and "without division or separation" (*ACO* 2, I, 2, 129–30).

would be completely unrecognizable, and we would have neither a "whence" or a "how" by which we might learn of God's gracious condescension to us.[5] Our salvation would have likewise been undermined if the flesh had been changed into the divine nature on account of its union with the divine, or if the divine nature was changed into the substance of the flesh, or if both had somehow been mixed together bringing another reality into being, different from each of them, and failing to preserve intact the essence of either of the two natures out of which the union is constituted. Because if either the flesh was changed into the nature of divinity, or if the nature of divinity was changed into flesh, or if the mode of union forcibly impelled the two natures toward one nature, I would have no knowledge of the mystery of the divine Incarnation, finding no natural difference in the mystery between flesh and divinity after the union. If, however, there exists in Christ after the union a difference according to nature of the flesh and the divinity (for divinity and flesh are never identical according to essence), then the union of the concurring elements in no way resulted in the generation of a single nature, but rather a single hypostasis, with respect to which we find no difference in Christ in any way whatsoever. For according to hypostasis, the Word is identical with His own flesh.[6] For if Christ[7] admits of any kind of difference, then it would not be possible for Him to be "one" in any way at all. But insofar as He absolutely admits of no difference, it is in every way pious to say that Christ is one.

62.5. Thus, because every difference, inasmuch as it *is* a difference, absolutely has as its foundation the quantity of the items that differ (for without quantity, difference would never exist; in addition to which, quantity does not exist without number), because of this, I say, we would do well to accept the number, but solely as an indication of the difference of the natures from which Christ *is* after the union, signifying that the natures are preserved without change after the union, but not dividing the union by the number of the things that came to-

---

5. Cf. *Amb.* 5.12 (DOML 1:43).
6. Which is to say that the Word of God truly became man.
7. I.e., the *hypostasis* of Christ.

gether in the concurrence unto one hypostasis. And we make this clarification with the understanding that, with respect to the principle of the hypostasis, we in no way introduce any kind of number, for of that in which absolutely no difference is observed, no quantity is predicated, and that which does not include quantity does not admit of a number indicative of difference. We therefore confess Christ to be compound according to hypostasis, the identity of which is in every way understood to be unique, but not compound according to nature, the difference of which is in every way understood to be not unique, so that we must both preserve the identity and uniqueness of the hypostasis and confess the difference of natures concurring in the one hypostasis. This is what the wondrous Zechariah beheld flying in the form of a sickle, for the Word of God cuts down every evil of ignorance.

62.6. "Twenty cubits in length, and ten cubits in width."[8] Christ, on the one hand, inasmuch as He is God and Word, is of a nature to be progressively widened by the mode of providence into "ten cubits," by which I mean the divine commandments unfolding in actual practice. For being widened into the decad of commandments—through which He established laws for things that should and should not be done—the Word of God encompassed the entire movement of the will's voluntary inclination among those who come under His providence.[9] On the other hand, inasmuch as the same Word became flesh and perfect man,[10] He is lengthened into "twenty cubits" for the composition of the elements pertaining to the senses in the formation of the body. For there are five senses and four elements, out of which and by whose concurrence human nature is constituted. For when five is multiplied by four, it obviously produces the number twenty. "Length" is what Scripture, in this instance, calls the mode of the economy of salvation, on account of the height of the mystery of the divine Incarnation, which transcends every nature. And the sickle is "flying" because it possesses nothing earthly, and because of its rapidity,

8. Zec 5.2.
9. Cf. above, Qu. 62.6; and *QD*. 142 (CCSG 10:101, lines 12–21).
10. Cf. Jn 1.14.

and its sharp and sudden motion, and, to state the matter succinctly, because of the "concision of the word,"[11] which incises the entire salvation of beings solely in the heart of those being saved, a salvation which is secured by faith[3] and a good conscience. For nothing is swifter than faith, and nothing is easier for someone to do than to confess with his mouth[12] the grace of Him in whom he believes. The one indicates the vital love of the believer for his Creator, the other his disposition toward his neighbor, which is pleasing to God. Love and a genuine disposition—that is, faith and a good conscience—are obviously the work of an invisible movement in the heart, which has absolutely no need of external matter in order to be born, for it says: "The Lord will create a concise word upon the earth."[13]

62.7. He is "the curse" that God the Father sent forth "upon the face of the whole earth,"[14] which in reality is the curse of the true curse.[15] The primal disobedience ushered in the curse through transgression, preventing the commandment from bearing fruits of righteousness, through which creation would have received the blessing. In response, He who by nature is the Blessing of God the Father placed Himself under the curse of Adam, becoming a curse upon the curse in order to oppose sin and cast down the disobedience that was increasing the growth of the fruits of unrighteousness, and at the same time to render creation barren of its growth in sin. For according to the divine Apostle, He who loosed my curse and "took away the sin

---

11. Is 10.23.
12. Cf. Rom 10.9.
13. Rom 9.28; Is 10.22–23.
14. Zec 5.3.
15. Cf. Theodoret, *Eranistes* 3: "As a 'curse' upon the accursed serpent, He fulfills the figure; and as 'sin' He shows forth the type of the sacrificial goat" (ed. Gerard H. Ettlinger, *Theodoret of Cyrus, Eranistes* [Oxford: Clarendon Press, 1975], 211, lines 4–5); and Leontios presbyter of Constantinople, *Homily on Palm Sunday* 2: "If Christ our Master was called a 'curse' [Gal 3.13] and 'sin' [2 Cor 5.21], He was not Himself defiled, but rather took our sins upon Himself. He took everything upon Himself not as one responsible and called to account, but as the mediator. Thus He took upon Himself the debt of Adam and paid it off, and wiped away the bond of our sins [Col 2.14] on the cross with the sponge of His philanthropy" (CCSG 17:93, lines 206–13).

of the world"[16] became for my sake a sin and a curse.[17] For I was subject to two curses: the one was the fruit of my own free will, that is, sin, through which the soul's fecundity for virtue fell to earth; the other was death,[4] to which nature was justly condemned on account of my free will, pushing nature by necessity, and apart from its own wishes, to that place where the movement of my own free choice had sown it by the inclination of my free will.[18]

62.8. Thus God, who gave existence to the generation of nature, voluntarily took upon Himself the curse to which nature had been condemned, by which I mean death. And the curse that was also living within me on account of my free choice for sin, He slew and put to death by His own death on the cross. Thus the curse and death of my sin became the curse of my God, which prevented the transgression from progressing and producing the fruits of unrighteousness, but instead, in accordance with the commandment and divine righteousness, became a blessing and life without end.

62.9. This "sickle," that is, our Lord and God Jesus Christ, cuts down the "thief and swearer of oaths" and "destroys his house, throwing down its wood and stones."[19] To be sure, the thief and swearer of oaths is the wicked devil. He is, on the one hand, a thief, since he stole paradise from Adam by means of deceit—even though Adam was the work and creation of God, and His precious possession—and he brought him to this place of hardships, and he defiled the image of the divine glory with the stains of many sins, seeking to make his own a treasure that did not belong to him, wickedly desiring goods that were not his, not so that he might watch over and protect them, but rather to "steal, sacrifice, and cast them into perdition."[20] [5] On the other hand, he is also a swearer of oaths, inasmuch as he is a liar and a cheat, for promising to give Adam the glory of divinity, he cast him down to the dishonorable and insulting con-

---

16. Jn 1.29.
17. Cf. 2 Cor 5.21; Gal 3.13.
18. On these two "curses," see above, Qu. 42.
19. Zec 5.4.
20. Cf. Jn 10.10.

dition of irrational animals,[21] and, to state the main problem, he made him even more dishonorable than animals, surpassing the animals by the hubris of his irrationality to the same degree that unnatural passions are more despicable in comparison with natural ones; and, estranging him from immortality, he defiled him by covering him with corruption.

62.10. The "house" of this "thief and swearer of oaths" is this present world of corruption and continual confusion, a world which the devil arrogated to himself by plundering Adam, whom he was in fact permitted to plunder for reasons known to God,[6] who has permitted him to plunder for as long as the cyclical course of time should endure. But the Word of God, dwelling in this world as if in a house, by means of His ineffable Incarnation, bound the devil and abolished his power,[22] and completely destroyed the "wood and the stones" of this world, utterly obliterating the wooden idols, the sacrificial altars, and the temples of the idols, through which the devil, who is the father of deception, as a kind of bizarre, polymorphic god, thought he would be worshiped by those he deceived, making their ignorance the basis for his own glory, since he is even more ignorant than those he deceived. For what is more mindless than to think that something exists when in fact it has no real existence?

62.11. It was this "house" of the thief and swearer of oaths, I mean in this world, in which the Redeemer of our souls and bodies, who loves mankind, dwelt by means of the flesh, and which He wholly destroyed[7] according to the previous mode of deception,[23] and which He wholly restored according to the principle of true knowledge. To state the matter simply, having expelled the thief from possessions that were not his, the same Lord once again through virtue became the ruler of His own things, building His Holy Church in magnificent fashion throughout the whole world.

---

21. Cf. Ps 48.13.
22. Cf. Mt 12.29.
23. According to a marginal note appearing in some manuscripts, this is a reference to the "divine deception," through which the Word, concealed behind a veil of flesh, was able to deceive and triumph over the devil; cf. above, Qu. 21.4.

62.12. Or perhaps the devil is a "thief" since even now he works through guile and deception to attract and transfer the desire of each and every human being to himself. And he is a "swearer of oaths," as well as a deceiver, since he persuades the more foolish to abandon the good things they have in hand; and for those under the power of his persuasion, he secretly creates pain for the pleasure they take in what only seems to be pleasing. The "house" of this thief and liar is the sin-loving disposition of every human heart, built up, as if from stones, from the heart's hardness and insensitivity to good and beautiful things. The wood of such houses is the incendiary memories of the unclean fires of the passions.

62.13. Or perhaps Scripture uses the word "wood" to speak figuratively about desire. For it is written of the wood, that is, of the tree of desire,[24] that contrary to nature it first corrupted the movement of desire, and this is why the soul is receptive of every passion just as combustible material is receptive of fire. The "stones," on the other hand, might perhaps be the hardness and insensitive movements of anger, which do not submit to the principle of virtue. All of these materials, along with the house in which they happen to be found, that is, the disposition of the heart, are wiped out and destroyed by the advent of God the Word. He does this first by expelling through faith the devil, who by means of deception had formerly dwelled in it. And with unbreakable bonds He bound the one who thought he was strong, despoiled his house,[25] and at the same time drove from the human heart that condition which aroused the passions and produced insensitivity toward good and beautiful things.

62.14. Or perhaps by "stones"[8] Scripture is referring to the soul's indifference to good things, having become insensitive to the virtues, and calls eagerness for vice "wood," since it is these materials that the Word completely drove out from the hearts of the faithful, "never ceasing to create peace and reconcile into one body" of virtue "those who were far off and those who were near," clearly "tearing down the middle wall of sepa-

---

24. Cf. Gn 3.2. In Greek, the words for "wood" and "tree" are the same (i.e., ξύλον).

25. Cf. Mk 3.27; Mt 12.29.

ration,"[26] by which I mean sin, and nullifying the "contract,"[27] which bound the inclination of the will to evil, and he subjected the "mind of the flesh" to the "law of the Spirit."[28] Scripture says "far off," I think, in reference to the movements of the soul according to sensation, which by their nature are "far off" and utterly foreign to the law of God. What is "near," on the other hand, are the soul's intellective activities. These are akin to and not far from the Word, and, after the abrogation of the law of the flesh, the Word conjoins[9] them, just as the virtues are conjoined, binding them one to another by the Spirit. For I believe that Scripture called the natural law of the body in its relation to the passions the "middle wall," while the attachment, according to the natural law, of the flesh to the passions (in other words to sin) it called "separation." For only the attachment of the law of nature—that is, of the passible part of human nature—to the dishonorable passions becomes a "separation" dividing the body from the soul, and reason from the virtues, obstructing, on the level of practice, the passage of the principle of the virtues to the flesh through the mediation of the soul.

62.15. But the Word in His advent conquered the law, that is, the passible element within human nature, and He abolished its attachment to passions contrary to nature. It is He who is "my Lord and my God,"[29] Christ Jesus, whom the prophet beheld as a "sickle, twenty cubits in length,"[10] because He contains all the activity of the senses in relation to objects of sense; and "ten cubits wide," because my God and Savior is determinative of every rational movement. For they say that numbering by nature belongs only to reason, while the limit and end of every number is the decad. Thus the Word of God not only contains the powers of sense perception, but also the activities of the intellect, inasmuch as He is the creator not only of corporeal but also of incorporeal realities. And He was called a "sickle" in the vision, not only because He "cuts away" evil from rational nature—an evil which He "did not plant"—and "gathers" nature

26. Eph 2.14–17.
27. Col 2.14.
28. Rom 8.7.
29. Jn 20.28.

"together," which He "did not scatter"[30]—but also because in His harvest He places those who are being saved within His divine storehouses. In addition to this,[11] He gently and without force grows together with the practical powers of the soul, just as He does with the activities of the virtues.

62.16. If, however, someone should think that the word of Scripture is speaking of two persons and two houses, the destruction of which is brought about by the sickle, inasmuch as it says: "And it shall enter the house of the thief, and into the house of him that swears falsely by my name,"[31] we should be of the opinion that, to the two general activities of the devil's deception (which contain all of his activities), Scripture gave the name of two persons, that is, two modes of activities; while it called "houses" the two general dispositions that define all other human dispositions to deception. For example, when through the guile of deception the devil plunders nature's innate knowledge of God, he arrogates it to himself, for he is a thief, and endeavors to transfer to himself the worship that belongs to God. He endeavors, in other words, to snatch the soul's intellective contemplation from the spiritual principles in creation, and to confine our intellective power solely to the superficial appearances of visible realities. When, on the other hand, he has begun to operate through our natural movements, he uses his sophistry to bend and pervert our practical powers to things contrary to nature. And when, through things believed to be good, he nails our desire to what is worse through the seductions of pleasure, he falsely swears an oath in the name of the Lord, leading the soul persuaded by him to things other than what was promised. And he is a thief[12] inasmuch as he steals for himself the knowledge of nature, having as his dwelling place the ignorant disposition of those whom he has deceived. And he is a swearer of oaths inasmuch as he persuades the practical powers of the soul to labor in vain for things contrary to nature, having as his dwelling place the sin-loving disposition of the will in those who condone him.

62.17. Thus the devil is a thief, as I said, perverting the

30. Mt 25.24.
31. Zec 5.4.

knowledge of nature; and a swearer of false oaths, distorting, on the level of practice, human nature's ability to realize the virtues. The dwelling of the thief is the disposition occupied by an error on the level of knowledge; the dwelling of the swearer of false oaths is the disposition imbued with the defilement of the dishonorable passions. When the saving Word of God in His love for mankind enters into these dwellings, He makes them a dwelling place of God through the Spirit, giving rise to the knowledge of truth instead of deception and ignorance, and to virtue and righteousness instead of vice and wickedness, through which He is of a nature to manifest Himself among the worthy. It follows, then, that instead of persons, the word of Scripture designated the modes of various evils of one and the same devil, and, instead of dwellings, the natural dispositions among those who are under the operation of these diabolical modes.

62.18. Again, a thief[13] is someone who, in order to deceive his listeners, appears to exercise himself in the divine words of Scripture, when in fact he does not know the power of these words through actual works, but thinks he will acquire glory through their mere pronunciation, and be reckoned as righteous simply because of words uttered by his tongue, seeking the praise of his audience.[32] To state the matter simply, a person whose life is not in harmony with his words, and whose disposition of soul is inconsistent with his knowledge, is a thief, for on the basis of good things that are not his own, he cannot have or appear with any moral beauty. To such a person the Word rightly says: "To the sinner, God said: 'Why do you speak of my commandments, and take up my covenant in your mouth?'"[33]

62.19. And again, a thief[14] is whoever, through superficial manners and behaviors, conceals the deeper, hidden evil of his soul, disguising his inward disposition behind a mask of gentility; and, just as the one who by pronouncing mere words of knowledge steals the minds of his listeners, so too, by his hypocritical manner and comportment, he steals[15] the perceptions

---

32. Cf. below, Qu. 65.5.
33. Ps 49.16.

of those who see him. To such a person it was likewise said: "Be ashamed, you who clothe yourself in strange garments,"[34] and: "On that day, the Lord will uncover their outward appearance."[35] To be sure, a day does not go by when, in the hidden workshop of the heart, I seem to hear God telling me these very same things, insofar as I am guilty of both.

62.20. And a swearer of oaths, that is, one who swears falsely in the name of the Lord, is he who promises God that he will live a virtuous life, but whose actions are in fact contrary to what he has promised, and who violates the terms of his promise to lead a pure life by his failure to practice the commandments, as is the case with myself. To state the matter succinctly, whoever has elected to live according to God, but who has not completely mortified himself in relation to this present life, is a liar and a swearer of false oaths. Having sworn an oath to God, that is, having promised to pursue the pure course of divine struggles, but not fulfilling these promises, he receives no praise whatsoever, for it says: "Everyone who swears by Him will be praised,"[36] everyone, that is, who has promised God to live a godly life, and who fulfilled the oaths of his good promises through the truth of his works of righteousness. And if there is no question that the one who fulfills his promises is praised, because he has sworn to God and kept his promises, it is obvious that the one who transgressed his own promises will receive censure and dishonor, because he swore an oath to God and he lied.

62.21. It is into the hearts, as if they were dwelling places, that is, into the dispositions of each person, that the "sickle" enters, by which I mean the Word of God the Father, for according to essence He is knowledge and virtue, and He completely destroys these dwelling places, and, by means of a transformation to what is superior, He obliterates completely the former condition of each heart, guiding each person to participation in the good in which he is deficient, making the thief of knowledge an unashamed worker of virtue, and the thief of feigned

34. Cf. Zep 1.8.
35. Is 3.17.
36. Ps 62.11.

morals an expert cultivator of the soul's hidden disposition, and the swearer of oaths a true keeper of his promises, confirming his promises by means of his deeds.

Scholia

[1] We do not affirm in Christ, he says, a difference of hypostases, since the Trinity remained a Trinity even when the Word of God became flesh, without this bringing about an addition of a fourth person to the Holy Trinity on account of the Incarnation. We do, however, affirm a difference of natures, and thus we do not subscribe to the view that the flesh is by nature consubstantial with the Word.

[2] Whoever does not acknowledge a difference of natures has no basis for confessing that the Word became flesh without change, for such a person fails to recognize that, even after the union, the nature of what was taken and assumed was preserved in the one hypostasis of the one God and Christ.

[3] Faith, based on hope, constitutes perfect love for God; a good conscience, based on the keeping of the commandments, is the cause of love for one's neighbor. This is because a good conscience does not have a broken commandment accusing it of transgression. Trust in these virtues is of a nature to be found only in the heart of those who desire true salvation.

[4] He says that because man had set his desire in motion toward the earth, it was to the earth that he was driven against his will by death.[37]

[5] "Stealing" is the wicked spoliation of nature by deceit. "Sacrifice" is that by which the devil sacrifices those who have been stolen by him; it is the slaughter of the free will that has chosen a godly life, and the utter destruction of even the memory of such a life. "Perdition" is the ignorance that befalls those who are sacrificed after the privation of the knowledge of God.[38] This is why the devil steals by snatching one's thoughts, namely, so that he might bring about the privation of a life of virtue and knowledge.

---

37. Cf. Gn 3.19.
38. Cf. Rom 9.22–23.

[6] Someone might say conjecturally that the devil is permitted to steal for the following reasons: so that human beings might know evil by experience; so that when the devil is exposed he will be hated all the more; so that by the experience of trials human beings' dispositions might all be made mutually manifest; and so that each person will naturally bear within himself either the good witness or the accusations of his own conscience. For God has no need of learning things from experience, since He possesses essentially the knowledge of all things, even before they are created.

[7] The destruction of the "house," that is, this world in its error, came about through the Incarnation.

[8] He offered this contemplation as fitting for those subject to the passions. Because the person who is sick with the disease of being completely immovable in relation to the good is clearly supple and mobile with respect to evil, since it is impossible to be immobile with respect to both.

[9] When the motion of sense perception is conjoined to the activity of the intellect, it creates virtue coupled with knowledge.

[10] Understood simply as the Word, he says, the Lord possesses twenty and ten cubits. He possesses twenty inasmuch as He is the maker of the corporeal world, and ten as the creator of the intelligible world.

[11] Reason grows together with the practical powers of the soul, just like the sickle in the hand of the harvester, cutting down the passions and gathering together the virtues.

[12] The devil is a thief, he says, because he creates ignorance; and as a swearer of false oaths he is the creator of evil, having, as if they were his dwelling places, the deceived mind of the person who is ignorant, and the sin-loving disposition of the person who is evil.

[13] This contemplation is beautiful and quite useful for us, who through love of empty glory have adulterated the glory of virtue and knowledge.

[14] A thief, he says, is also anyone who hypocritically puts forward virtue by a deceptive disguise of manners, as well as anyone who conceals his wicked mind.

[15] Anyone who, for the sake of his own glory, he says, hypocritically feigns knowledge through mere words, steals the mind of those who listen to him. And anyone who, for the sake of his own glory, feigns virtue through mere outward actions, steals the vision of those who behold him. And both of them deceive through their duplicity: the former deceives the mind of the soul of those who listen to him, and the latter the sense perception of the bodies of those who behold him.

QUESTION 63

GAIN, IN the same prophet it is written: "And he said to me: 'What do you see?' And I replied: 'I see, and behold: a lampstand all of gold, and on top of it the light, and seven lamps upon it, and seven funnels for the lamps, and two olive trees above it, one to the right of the lamp and one to the left.'"[1] What is the lampstand? And why is it gold? And what is the light on top of it? What are the seven lamps, and what are the seven funnels for the seven lamps? And what are the two olive trees? And why is one to the right of the light and the other to the left?[2]

Response

63.2. Using symbols to describe the multi-faceted radiance and brilliant magnificence of the Church, the Word varied the prophet's vision in the manner you see here, setting forth, it seems to me, the meaning of the new mystery contained in the vision. For the all-praised Church of God is a lampstand fashioned entirely of gold, pure and undefiled, unsullied, un-

---

1. Zec 4.2–3. Following the language of the biblical text and its parallels, Maximos employs a large number of Greek words for lighted oil lamps, lanterns, lights, and their various accouterments. While it did not prove possible in every instance to translate each word consistently, the choice for each rendering was determined by the particular context and intention of Maximos's interpretation.

2. Maximos's ecclesiological and Christological interpretation of this passage bears comparison with Cyril of Alexandria, *Commentary on Zechariah* 2 (ed. P. E. Pusey, *Sancti patris nostri Cyrilli Archiepiscopi Alexandrini in xii Prophetas*, vol. 2 [Oxford: Clarendon, 1868], 328–34); his anthropological and spiritual interpretation is closer to Didymos, *Commentary on Zechariah* 1.271–90 (SC 83:334–45).

alloyed, undiminished, and receptive of the true light. For they say that pure gold is not darkened when buried in the ground, nor destroyed by corrosive elements, nor diminished when completely submerged in fire, and that its natural activity and effects strengthen and renew the power of sight among those who gaze upon it.[3] Such is the all-glorious Church of God by nature, and through these things it is truly imaged, being analogous to the purest nature of gold. For the Church is unalloyed, having nothing at all in the mystery of theology according to faith that is tainted or foreign. She is pure, being glorious and shining with the brilliance of the virtues. She is undefiled, not being polluted by any stain of the passions. She is unsullied inasmuch as no evil spirit can touch her; neither is she blackened by material exigencies or harmed by any corrosion of wickedness. The Church admits of neither diminishment nor cessation, for she is not consumed in the furnace of periodic persecutions. And when she is tested by the successive outbreaks of heresies in word or life—that is, in faith or practice—she does not undergo the slightest slackening under the weight of tribulation. Thus, for the minds of those who piously understand her, the Church by grace is a source of strength. We see this when she calls out to the impious, presenting them with the light of true knowledge; and she preserves those who love to contemplate her mysteries, keeping the eye of their mind clear and unperturbed. She calls back those who have been beset by any kind of tempest, and by her consoling word she renews the mind that has suffered.

63.3. This, then, according to one interpretation of the text, is how we understand the lampstand beheld by the prophet. The light, which is on top of the lampstand, is the Father's "true light, which enlightens every man[1] who comes into the world,"[4] that is, our Lord Jesus Christ, who, by assuming our flesh from us, became and was called a "light." Indeed, the enhypostatic Wisdom and Word of God the Father by nature, who is proclaimed in the Church of God through pious faith and

---

3. The qualities of gold are put to similar metaphorical use by John Chrysostom, *Catechetical Instructions* 1.3 (PG 49:227).

4. Jn 1.9.

a virtuous way of life through the keeping of the commandments; who is "exalted among the nations";[5] and who brilliantly appears shining "to everyone in the house"[6]—by which I mean the world, as God the Word Himself says: "No one lights a lamp and places it under a bushel, but places it on the lampstand, and it gives light to everyone in the house"[7]—this same Word and Wisdom clearly calls Himself a "Lamp," because, being God by nature, He became flesh according to the dispensation of salvation. Thus, after the manner of a lamp, He who is light according to essence, was, through the intermediary of the soul, contained (but without circumscription) like fire around a wick within the earthen vessel of the flesh.[8] This, I think, is what the great David had in mind when he called the Lord a "lamp"—since He is both the Word of God the Father and the Natural Law—saying: "Your law is a lamp unto My feet, and a light for my paths,"[9] because He who is my Savior and my God dissolves the darkness of ignorance and evil, and is rightly called a "lamp" in Scripture, for a lamp is what dissolves the night, and "night" is what those who study words call darkness. Since He alone dissolves the gloom of ignorance and the darkness of evil, He became for all the "way of salvation"[10] through virtue and knowledge, conveying to the Father all those who, by keeping the divine commandments, are willing to, as it were, travel in Him, for He is the "Way of righteousness."[11]

63.4. Scripture likewise called the holy Church a "lampstand," upon which the Word of God shines forth through the Church's proclamation and illumines, by rays of truth, everyone in this world as though in a house, filling the minds of all with divine knowledge. The "bushel" is how Scripture, through a mode of symbolic fashioning,[12] refers to the synagogue of the Jews, that is, the corporeal worship prescribed by the law,

5. Cf. Is 2.2–3; Ezek 29.15.
6. Mt 5.15.
7. Ibid.
8. Cf. 2 Cor 4.7.
9. Ps 118.105.
10. Acts 16.17.
11. 2 Pt 2.21; cf. Jn 14.6.
12. On the notion of "symbolic fashioning," see above, Qu. 28.2.

which, on account of the grossness of its literal symbols,[13] completely failed to recognize the light of true knowledge contained in the inner meanings of the letter.[14] The Word in no way wishes to be kept under this bushel, but rather to be placed at the height of the majesty of the Church's beauty. Otherwise, when the Word is confined by the letter of the law, as by a bushel, it deprives everyone of the eternal light, offering no spiritual contemplation to those who endeavor to cast off sense perception as something deceitful and deceived and capable of grasping only the corruption of bodies sharing the same nature. And this is why, as I said, He wishes to be placed on the lampstand, that is, on the Church, by which I mean rational worship in spirit.[15] His aim is to enlighten all, teaching people throughout the world to live and conduct themselves solely according to reason, and to be concerned about the body only in order to cut off completely, through much effort, the soul's attachment to bodily things, and to give the soul absolutely no image of anything material. He urges them to make this task their eager pursuit, since reason has already begun to extinguish[2] sensation, which in the beginning pushed reason aside and embraced the irrationality of pleasure, like the snake that creeps on the ground. This is why the sentence of death was justly handed down, namely, to oppose sensation[3] and thereby prevent the devil's entry into the soul. For sensation is one according to genus but fivefold according to its forms, and it convinces the deluded soul, through the apprehending activity of each of these forms, to cherish what is sensual and similar to it in nature instead of God. Thus the person who wisely follows the way of reason before he is overtaken violently and involuntarily by death, condemns the flesh to death, completely separating the inclination of his will from sensation.[16]

13. Cf. above, Qu. 31.2.
14. On the difference between letter and spirit as corresponding to the differences between the Church and the synagogue, cf. above, Qu. 32.2; Qu. 52.4–5; and below, Qu. 65.3–5, 8–9.
15. Cf. Jn 4.24.
16. Death was introduced to halt the activity of the senses operating independently of reason; without the latter, the human person is separated from God, bound to the surface of visible phenomena, and falls prey to the

63.5. On the other hand, whoever adheres solely to the letter of Scripture has nothing but sensation ruling over his nature, and this reveals the attachment of his soul to the flesh. For the letter, when not understood spiritually, contains only what is sensory, which restricts the meaning of the text to its verbal utterance, and does not allow it to pass to the level of the intellect.[17] And if the letter engages sensation alone, then everyone who receives the letter literally, in a Jewish manner, lives according to the flesh. Moreover, such a person voluntarily dies the daily death of sin on account of sensation's vitality, because he is not able, by the Spirit, to put to death the deeds of the body in order to live the blessed life in the Spirit. This is why the Apostle says: "If you live according to the flesh, you will die, but if by the Spirit you put the deeds of the body to death, you will live."[18] Therefore, having lit the divine lamp—that is, the illuminating word of knowledge—through contemplation and action, let us not place it under the bushel, lest we be condemned for using the letter to circumscribe the power of its incomprehensible wisdom. Instead, let us place it on the lampstand—by which I mean the Church—in the height of true contemplation, burning with the light of divine dogmas for all to behold.

63.6. Using figures, the law quite likely proclaimed the Church in advance, prescribing that the lampstand should be made of closely pressed and finely worked gold;[19] the former because no portion of the Church is without a share in the power of the Word, and the latter because she is absolutely free of all material excess and every earthly thing. Astonished upon seeing this somewhat unusual lampstand, the great Zechariah observed that together with the light there were "also seven lamps upon it."[20] Here we must understand the seven lamps differently than the lamp in the Gospel, because things pronounced in

---

devil. To "extinguish the senses" and to "separate the will from sensation" is to put to death a purely bodily way of life and to resurrect and vivify the deadened intellect.

17. Cf. below, Qu. 65.5.
18. Rom 8.13.
19. Cf. Ex 25.31.
20. Zec 4.2.

the same way are not always understood in the same way.²¹ Instead, each of the things described is to be understood in relation to its underlying meaning, that is, in light of its place in Scripture, if, that is, we wish to speculate correctly concerning the aim of what has been written. My sense is that, in this passage, the Holy Scripture depicts as "lamps" the activities of the Holy Spirit, or rather the gifts of the Spirit. And it is natural for the Word to give these gifts to the Church, since He is the "head of the entire body,"²² "upon whom," Scripture says, "the Spirit of God shall rest, the spirit of wisdom and comprehension, the spirit of counsel and might, the spirit of knowledge and piety shall fill Him; the spirit of the fear of God."²³

63.7. If the head of the Church is Christ according to the principle²⁴ of His humanity, then the Church has received Him who, being God by nature, possesses the Spirit and the activities of the Spirit. For the Word, becoming man for me, also accomplishes the whole of salvation for me, giving to me in return, through my own things, those things that are proper to Him according to nature. He gives these things to me for whose sake He became man, and, taking on these things for me, He reveals that which is His. And as a friend of mankind He considers the grace given to me as His own, and He ascribes to me His power of those accomplishments proper to Him according to nature. And it is for my sake that He is now said to receive that which belongs to Him by nature in a manner without beginning and transcending reason. For just as the Holy Spirit by nature and according to essence exists of God the Father, so too by nature and according to essence is the Spirit of the Son, insofar as the Spirit proceeds essentially from the Father ineffably through the begotten Son, giving its own proper energies,

---

21. Cf. *Opusc.* 25: "Homonyms are often the cause of great confusion, leading the hearer to a meaning other than that intended by the word" (PG 91:273B).

22. Col 1.18.

23. Is 11.2–3. Cf. above, Qu. 29.2–3; and Qu. 54.22, where Maximos, who is probably citing these passages from memory, offers a slightly different list of the seven spirits.

24. I.e., ἐπίνοια; cf. above, Qu. 47.9.

like lamps, to the lampstand—that is, to the Church.[25] For in the manner of a lamp that dissolves the darkness, every energy of the Spirit is of a nature to expel and drive away the manifold manifestation[26] of sin. Thus wisdom destroys folly; comprehension takes away the lack of knowledge; counsel abolishes the lack of discernment; might casts off weakness; knowledge obliterates ignorance; piety banishes impiety and the depravity of its works; and fear drives away the callousness of contempt. For not only are the commandments light,[27] but the energies of the Spirit are also light.

63.8. The different ranks and ministries that complete the Church's beautiful arrangement, and which, through the Church, shine the light of salvation in every life, are also "lamps." For example, a wise teacher of divine and exalted dogmas and mysteries is a lamp, uncovering those things that previously eluded most people.[28] A person who listens with understanding and knowledge to the "wisdom spoken among the perfect"[29] is also a lamp, because he is an understanding listener preserving in himself the light of the truth of the things spoken.[30] Another person, who with counsel discerns the appropriate times for things, and chooses his words in a timely and

25. This passage, which speaks of the Holy Spirit's procession "through" (διά) the Son, figured prominently in debates over the western doctrine of the *Filioque*; see Alexander Alexakis, "The Greek Patristic Testimonia Presented at the Council of Florence in Support of the *Filioque* Reconsidered," *Revue des études byzantines* 58 (2000): 149–65; Jean Claude Larchet, *Saint Maxime le Confesseur, médiateur entre l'Orient et l'Occident* (Paris: Cerf, 1998), 62–64; and Edward Siecienski, *The Filioque: History of a Doctrinal Controversy* (Oxford: Oxford University Press, 2010), 73–86.

26. Literally, "genesis" or "coming into being" (γένεσις).

27. Cf. Prv 6.23.

28. Didymos, *Commentary on Zechariah* 1.289, states that orthodox teachers are "lights" in the Church (SC 83:344).

29. 1 Cor 2.6.

30. Teachers and those who listen to them with understanding participate in a dialogue of mutual illumination; cf. Basil of Caesarea, *Long Rules (Preface)*: "You have clearly manifested your desire to learn something of matters pertaining to salvation, while I am under obligation to proclaim the statutes of God" (PG 31:889A); and idem, *On the Holy Spirit* 1.1–2, where he places particular emphasis on the "understanding listener" for the correct apprehension of truth (SC 17bis:250–52).

suitable manner, not allowing them to become unsuitably confused—he too, as a "wonderful counselor,"[31] is a lamp. Whoever endures the assaults of involuntary temptations with an unshakeable mind, like the blessed Job and the noble martyrs, is a powerful lamp who maintains the light of salvation unquenched, which he does through the mode of courageous endurance, because he "has the Lord as his strength and his song."[32] A person who knows the machinations of the evil one and is not ignorant of the wiles of the invisible wars—he too, shining with the light of knowledge, is another lamp, saying, as is fitting, with the great Apostle: "We are not ignorant of his devices."[33] He who lives his life piously, according to the commandments and directed toward the virtues, is another lamp, being a pious person who in his pious ways confirms his piety. And yet another lamp is the person who, in expectation of the judgment and through abstinence, has walled off the entry of the passions into his soul. Through diligence concerning the fear of God, he has purified himself of the stains of his acquired passions, making his life splendid and brilliant by the casting-off of defilements that are contrary to nature.

63.9. The Holy Spirit brings about purification[4] for those who, through fear and piety and knowledge, have become worthy of the purity of the virtues. The Spirit bestows illumination concerning the genesis of beings and the principles of their existence to those who, through strength, will, and understanding, have become worthy of His light. The Spirit grants perfection through the most brilliant, simple, and complete wisdom to those who are worthy of divinization, and without any intermediary it completely leads them upward toward the Cause of beings—as much as this is possible for human beings—those, I mean, who are known only by the divine characteristics of goodness.[34] According to this goodness, they know themselves

31. Is 9.6.
32. Ps 42.2; Ex 4.2.
33. 2 Cor 2.11.
34. Cf. *Amb.* 7.11, where the divinized person will "no longer be able to wish to be known from his own qualities, but rather from the circumscriber [i.e., God], in the same way that air is thoroughly permeated by light" (DOML 1:89); and *Amb.* 10.43, where the divinized saints are "not characterized by the

by knowing God, and they know God by knowing themselves, there being no kind of intermediary separating them from God, for between wisdom and God there is no intermediary. They will, moreover, possess unchanging immutability, since they will have passed through all the intermediaries[5] (in which there was once a danger of erring with respect to knowledge); and in ineffable, unspeakable silence, and in a manner beyond knowledge that is unutterable and inconceivable, they will be led up by grace to that summit which is infinite and for all infinity is infinitely beyond all things an infinite number of times.[35]

63.10. "And seven funnels for the seven lamps above it."[36] The contemplative interpretation of the lamps, it seems to me, has now been put forward through two approaches. We may henceforth embark on the interpretation of the funnels. They say that this funnel is a kind of container in the form of a cup, in which people customarily put oil that is poured into the lamp for the maintenance and preservation of the light.[37] According to the anagogical interpretation, the funnels of the seven lamps are the habitual states and dispositions receptive of the different principles, modes, and behaviors that nurture and preserve the seven lamps, that is, the activities of the Spirit, among those in the Church who have received the distribution of spiritual gifts. Just as it is impossible for a lamp to be kept lit without oil, so too it is impossible for the light of the gifts of the Spirit to be kept lit without a stable habit, which nurtures good things by means of principles, modes, behaviors, thoughts, and proper reasoning. For every spiritual gift requires the proper habit, which unceas-

---

property of the things they abandoned, but are named from the magnificence of what they have assumed, for which and in which alone they exist and are known" (DOML 1:217).

35. Errors in knowledge are at the root of moral instability, and will arise for as long as human beings exist among, and make erroneous deductions from, created "intermediaries." When, on the other hand, human beings attain an unmediated relation to God, and the truth (which is God) is experienced directly to the extent that this is possible, there is no longer any possibility for error, for there is no longer anything standing between the created intellect and God; cf. above, Qu. 6.2; and *Amb.* 7.13 (DOML 1:93).

36. Zec 4.2.

37. On the funnels (ἐπαρυστρίδες), see Constas, *Proclus of Constantinople*, 189–90.

ingly pours upon it, like oil, spiritual substance, in order that it continue according to the habit kept by the one who accepts it. Thus the funnels of the seven lamps are the habits appropriate to the divine gifts of the holy Church, from which—as if from receptacles, according to the example of the wise virgins in the Gospel[38]—is poured the "oil of gladness"[39] by the wise and vigilant guardians of the good things handed down to us.[40]

63.11. "And two olive trees above it, one to the right of the light, and one to the left." The Word beautifully and most fittingly fashioned this vision so that it would converge evenly toward itself. For having mentioned the lampstand, the light, the lamps, and the funnels, He also introduced two olive trees. It was necessary, and it was truly necessary, that together with the light we also grasp the generative cause of the power that preserves the light, so that the light might not cease from the lampstand, being extinguished because of a lack of sustenance. For this very reason, the two olive trees of the golden lampstand—which is the holy, Catholic Church—are the two Testaments. From these, as if from olive trees pressed through pious seeking and inquiry, the power of intelligible meanings flows forth like olive oil, nourishing the light of the divine gifts. This power fills each person's habitual state in proportion to his proper capacity, and thus he watches over the unquenched light of grace that is proportionate to him, preserved, like oil, by the intelligible meanings derived from the Scriptures. Just as it is impossible to find genuine oil naturally and truly without the olive tree, and just as it is impossible to contain the oil without some kind of reservoir that is receptive of it, and just as the light of the lamp surely goes out if it is not supplied with oil, so too, without the holy Scriptures, there is truly no possibility for intelligible concepts or meanings suitable to God. Without a stable habit of mind, like a reservoir, receptive of intelligible meanings, divine meaning could never be sustained, and if the

---

38. Mt 25.4.
39. Ps 44.8.
40. Ps 44.8 figures prominently in the theology and ritual of baptism; cf. Basil, *On the Holy Spirit* 12.28 (SC 17bis:344); and Chrysostom, *Baptismal Instructions* 3.9 (SC 50:156).

light of knowledge in the gifts of the Spirit is not nourished by divine meanings, it will not be preserved unquenched among those who possess it.

63.12. Thus, rightly elevating the prophetic vision for spiritual contemplation, our interpretation likened the lampstand to the Church, and the light to the incarnate God, who put on our nature according to hypostasis and without change. The foregoing interpretation also likened the seven lamps to the Spirit's gifts—that is, activities—as the great Isaiah clearly foretold, and it likened the funnels to the habitual states that are receptive of the divine meanings of Scripture. These states belong to those who accept the divine gifts. Further, it likened the two olive trees to the two Testaments, from which the power of the divine meanings, when wisely cultivated, naturally emerges, and through which the light of the divine mysteries, when sustained, is preserved unquenched.

63.13. "And one," it says, "to the right of the light, and one to the left."[41] It seems to me that the prophet calls the more spiritual part of the Word "right," and the more bodily part "left." And if he indicates the more bodily part of the Word by the "left" and signifies the more spiritual part by the "right," I suppose that the olive tree to the left indicates the Old Testament, which points toward the more practical philosophy, while the olive tree on the right signifies the New Testament, which teaches a new mystery, and which creates a contemplative habit of mind in each of the faithful. The first offers modes of virtue, while the second offers spiritual principles of knowledge to those who philosophize concerning divine realities. The one, snatching us from the midst of visible things, raises the intellect toward that which is akin to it, insofar as it has been purified of every material imagination. The other purifies the intellect from all its passionate attachments to material things, and, with courageous force, as with the claw of a hammer, pulls out the nails that keep the inclination of the will fastened to the body. The Old Testament[6] raises up the body in relation to the soul, by means of the virtues, preventing the intellect from

---

41. Zec 4.3.

descending toward the body, while the New Testament raises the intellect toward God, giving it wings that soar on the flames of love. The former makes the body identical with the intellect according to their localized motion, while the latter makes the intellect identical with God by the acquisition of grace. This makes the likeness toward God so great that, through the intellect, as in the case of an image and its archetype, God—who, according to His nature does not become known to anyone in any way—becomes known. Let these things be understood, then, in the manner described above.

63.14. If, however, someone also wants to understand the meaning of these words as they apply to individual human beings, he will hardly be at a loss for beautiful and pious contemplations. For one can understand the soul of each person as a golden lampstand, since it is by nature intellective and rational, incorruptible and immortal; it is honored with the most regal power of self-determination, and bears the light of faith, that is, the Word made flesh, whom the soul steadfastly believes and truly worships. On top of this lampstand is placed the lamp of the Word, being lit with knowledge, in accordance with the teaching and admonition of God the Word Himself, who says: "No one lights a lamp and places it under a bushel, but on a lampstand, and it gives light to everyone in the house."[42] By "lamp" He is perhaps referring to the principle of knowledge pertaining to spiritual practice, that is, the "law of the spirit";[43] and by "bushel," the earthly "mind of the flesh,"[44] that is, the impassioned law of the body, under which we must not place the law of grace. Instead, we must place it upon the soul, the truly golden lampstand, so that it might shine with the lightning flashes of righteous works and wise thoughts to all in the house, meaning to all those in the Church, or in this world, and make those who see it imitators of the good, so that they might glorify—through works of virtue and not merely by the utterance of simple words—the Father[7] in heaven,[45] that is, God, who in the heights of the mystical contemplations of knowledge en-

42. Mt 5.15.
43. Rom 8.2.
44. Rom 8.6.
45. Cf. Mt 5.16.

genders, in those who are worthy, the magnificence of works of righteousness that shine forth according to virtue, "so that they may see your good works," as it says, "and glorify your Father in heaven."[46]

63.15. This is how, then, a person who rejoices in the intellectual contemplations of Holy Scripture will understand the lampstand seen in the vision as well as the light. As for the seven lamps, he will take them to be the distribution of the various gifts of the Spirit, which, in accordance with the interpretation given above, mystically shines and rests upon whoever becomes perfect according to Christ through virtue and knowledge. This is "because Scripture acknowledges as Christ whoever lives according to Christ,"[47] for such a person is distinguished by the same ways and words, as far as this is possible. If, that is, he too possesses wisdom and understanding, will and strength, and knowledge and piety and fear, through which, as if through spiritual eyes, God is said to look upon the whole earth of each person's heart:[48] "For there are seven eyes of the Lord," it says, "that watch from on high over all the earth."[49]

63.16. "And seven funnels for the lamps upon it." Funnels are the practical and contemplative habits of those who are worthy of the distribution of the divine gifts, from which, as though from reservoirs, they pour out, as if it were oil, the power of mystical conceptions, thus keeping unquenched the light of the gifts of the Spirit. By the two olive trees, one will understand, as I said a moment ago, the two Testaments: the Old Testament,[8] on the left of the light, which in the cognitive part of the soul (that is, the contemplative part) generates, like oil, the practical modes of virtues; and the New Testament, on the right, which in the passive part of the soul (that is, the practi-

---

46. Mt 5.16.
47. A quotation from Gregory Nazianzus, *Or.* 21.10 (SC 270:128, lines 4–5).
48. Cf. below, Qu. 63.19; and *Exp. Ps.* 59 (CCSG 23:9, lines 104–105). The phrase, the "earth of the heart," is most likely an influence from the writings attributed to Makarios of Egypt, where it is heavily attested; cf. *Or.* 31.6.3 (GCS 56:16, lines 5–9); and Marcus Plested, *The Macarian Legacy: The Place of Macarius-Symeon in the Eastern Christian Tradition* (Oxford: Oxford University Press, 2004), 239–42.
49. Zec 4.10.

cal part) generates through contemplation in an ever-flowing manner, like oil, the spiritual principle of knowledge. The aim is that, through both, the light of theology, like a light, together with the innate gifts of the Spirit, might be further strengthened, furnishing from the Old Testament the modes that honor knowledge through practice, and from the New Testament the principles that illumine the practice of the virtues through spiritual contemplation, so that, from both, a single beauty might be realized, namely, the mystery of our salvation, reckoning life as the proof[9] of the Word and the Word as the glory of life; and practice as actualized contemplation, and contemplation as practice being initiated into the mysteries. To state the matter briefly, it makes virtue the revelation of knowledge, and knowledge the preserving power of virtue. And through both, I mean virtue and knowledge, it shows one wisdom being established, in order for us to know that the two Testaments, according to grace, agree[10] with each other in all things unto the completion of one mystery, to a greater degree than the body and soul coincide with one another in the creation of one composite human being.

63.17. But if someone aspiring to intellectual contemplations chooses to call the two olive trees the two laws—I mean the natural and spiritual laws—he will not have departed from the truth. On the one hand, the natural law,[11] being to the left of the light, that is, to the left of the incarnate God the Word, will be understood as bringing to reason, through its connatural sense perception, the modes of virtue present in sensible things. On the other hand, intellective law, that is, the spiritual law, being to the right, through its connatural intellection, gathers the principles present in beings unto spiritual knowledge. Whenever these two laws have filled, as though through funnels, the various habits of spiritual gifts with practical and cognitive contemplations, we preserve unquenched the light of the truth.

63.18. When considered from the perspective of higher knowledge,[50] perhaps this passage of Scripture, through the two olive trees to the right and left of the light, is pointing to prov-

---

50. I.e., γνωστικώτερον; cf. above, Qu. 54.25.

idence and judgment.[51] In the midst of these stands—I mean in the midst of the holy Catholic Church, or in the soul of each holy person—as if upon a golden lampstand spreading the light of the truth to all, the Word, who as God contains all things and reveals the true and most general principles of providence and judgment that hold all beings together. It was according to these principles that the mystery of our salvation, foreordained before all the ages and accomplished in these latter times, was realized.[52] Thus we behold providence,[12] as if it were an olive tree standing to the right of the light, in the ineffable manner of the Word's hypostatic union with flesh rationally endowed with a soul, and we see this by faith alone. And to the left, in a manner beyond words, we recognize judgment in the mystery of the incarnate God's life-giving sufferings, which He underwent for our sake. Inasmuch as He is good, the former came about first according to His will,[13] for by nature He is the Savior of all. Inasmuch as He loves mankind, He consequently endured

---

51. "Providence" and "judgment" were signature Evagrian categories (cf. *Gnostikos* 48 [SC 356:186]) that Maximos radically transformed. For Evagrios, they designated key moments in the fall of rational beings from (and their restoration to) the divine *henad* (cf. *Amb.* 7.2 [DOML 1:77]), with "judgment" referring to the creation and diversity of the material world (as well as the banishment of rational beings into material bodies), and "providence" denoting the reversal of this sentence and the restitution of the fallen minds to their original unity. In *Amb.* 10.37 (DOML 1:207), Maximos redefined the terms to denote the differentiation of created beings in accordance with their *logoi*, as well as the activity that maintains this differentiation in the process of drawing such beings back to God. In addition, and as can be seen in this passage, Maximos also applied these cosmological categories to Christology (cf. above, Qu. 53.2; and Qu. 54.15). From this point of view, "providence" refers to the Incarnation and gift of divinization, which transcends creation, and "judgment" to the "life-giving passion" of the Word incarnate, which eradicates whatever is contrary to nature, and at the same time brings about the "restoration" (ἀποκατάστασις) of nature to its primal condition; cf. Thunberg, *Microcosm and Mediator*, 66–72; Luke Dysinger, "The *Logoi* of Providence and Judgment in the Exegetical Writings of Evagrius Ponticus," *SP* 37 (2001): 462–71; and Grigory Benevich, "Maximus Confessor's Teaching on God's Providence," in *The Architecture of the Cosmos. St Maximus the Confessor: New Perspectives*, ed. Antoine Lévy (Helsinki: Luther-Agricola-Society, 2015), 123–40, especially 130–37.

52. Cf. 1 Cor 2.7; 1 Pt 1.20.

the latter voluntarily and with forbearance, for by His nature He is the Redeemer of all—because God did not first become man in order to suffer, but rather to save man through His sufferings, because man had subjected himself to suffering when he transgressed the divine commandment, even though in the beginning he was impassible.

63.19. On the right, then, is the mystery, according to providence, of the Incarnation of the Word, which by grace brings about divinization in a manner transcending nature for those who are being saved.[53] This mystery was predetermined before the ages, and absolutely no principle of beings can approach it by nature. On the left is the mystery,[14] according to judgment, of the life-giving passion of the God who willed to suffer in the flesh. This mystery brings about the utter destruction of all the properties and movements contrary to nature that were introduced into nature through the primal disobedience. It also produces the perfect restoration of all the properties and movements that were previously in nature, according to which absolutely none of the principles of beings can ever be adulterated. From these, by which I mean providence and judgment, that is, from the Incarnation and the Passion, there came forth—because of the stability, purity, and incorruptibility of courageous virtue and immutability on the level of practice, and because of the clarity and brilliance of mystical contemplation and knowledge—there came forth, I say, like horse-drawn chariots racing "through the middle of two brass mountains,"[15] the holy "tetrad" of the Gospels.[54] It overtook and "traversed all the earth,"[55] healing the wound of Adam's transgression; and through faith, and through good conduct in life according to faith, it gave rest to the Spirit of God "in the land of the North,"[56] that is, among the Gentiles,[16] who were ruled by the gloom of ignorance and whose nature was tyrannized by the darkness of sin. Or, again, one may take them to

---

53. Cf. 2 Cor 2.15.
54. Cf. Zec 6.1.
55. Zec 6.7.
56. Cf. Zec 6.6.

be the power of the four general virtues,[57] which are equal in number to the holy Gospels,[58] overtaking the entire heart, like the earth, of each of the faithful, treating the wound inflicted on them by the "dishonorable passions,"[59] and "giving rest" to the Spirit of God[60]—which through works of righteousness shines "in the land of the North," that is, in the flesh—and manifests the "law of the Spirit."[61]

63.20. Or, again, one can understand the two olive trees as contemplation and ascetic practice. Of these, the providence relative to the Incarnation allows the principle of contemplation[17] to appear, while judgment relative to the Passion allows the mode of practice to be actualized, since what concerns the soul is on the right of the Word, while what concerns the body is on the left—the former calling the intellect toward kinship with God, the latter sanctifying sense perception by the Spirit and taking away the marks imprinted by the passions.

63.21. Or, again, one may understand the two olive trees as faith and a good conscience, in the midst of which stands the Word. With respect to faith He is adored correctly by the faithful, and with respect to good conscience He is worshiped devoutly through mutually well-pleasing relationships.

63.22. Or Scripture has likened the two olive trees to two peoples, that is, to the Gentiles and to the Jews, calling them "sons of fatness,"[62] interpreting the olive trees in terms of spiritual birth and the grace of adoption unto deification. In the midst of these stands the incarnate God, as upon a lampstand, that is, the one and only Catholic Church, reconciling the two

---

57. I.e., the virtues of prudence, justice, temperance, and courage, which are called "general" or "generic" because they are the states or conditions by which all the other virtues are acquired.

58. Both Irenaeos, *Against Heresies* 3.11.8 (SC 211:60–67), and Origen, *Commentary on the Gospel of John* 1.4.21 (SC 120:68), align the four elements with the four Gospels, as does Maximos; cf. above, Qu. 4.2; *Amb.* 21.5–6 (DOML 1:425–27); *Amb.* 66.3 (DOML 2:285); *Myst.* 5 (CCSG 69:27); and *QD.* 87 (CCSG 10:68).

59. Rom 1.26.
60. Zec 6.8.
61. Rom 8.2.
62. Zec 4.13.

peoples to Himself and to each other, and making them generative of the light according to virtue and knowledge.

63.23. But perhaps by the two olive trees Scripture is mystically alluding to the soul and the body: the soul because it is full, like the olive tree, with principles of true knowledge; and the body because it is bedecked with acts of virtue.

63.24. If, though, by the two olive trees, Scripture is intimating the two worlds—by which I mean the intelligible world and the sensible world—this would also be a good way to understand the text. Standing in between these is the Word, as God, mystically inscribing the intelligible world so that it appears[18] by means of figures in the sensible world, teaching the sensible world, by means of its inner principles, that it truly exists within the intelligible world.[63]

63.25. And if, by means of the olive trees, the vision represented the present life and the future one, this too would be a fitting mode of contemplation. In between these stands the Word, diverting men from the present life through virtue, and leading them up to the future life through knowledge. Perhaps it is with this understanding that the wondrous Habakkuk says: "You will be known in the midst of two living beings,"[64] for just as the great Zechariah calls them "brass mountains" and "olive trees," Habakkuk calls them "living beings," yet they both mean two worlds or ages. Or they are the lives that are akin to them; or the soul and the body; or ascetic practice and contemplation; or the habit of the good and its activity; or the law and the prophets; or all of the Old and New Testaments; or the two peoples, the Gentiles and the Jews; or the two laws, the natural and the spiritual; or faith and good conscience. In the midst of them all stands the Word, who in all things is hymned and glorified, guiding all things toward one agreement of the good, since He is the God of all, who created all things in order to become the indissoluble bond of their identity in the good, through their mutual union with one another.

---

63. The "perichoresis" of the sensible and the intelligible is a fundamental principle of Maximos's cosmology; see, for example, *Myst.* 2 (CCSG 69:16–17); and *QD.* 116 (CCSG 10:85).

64. Hab 3.2.

63.26. Perhaps in the vision, Scripture called both the Church and the soul a lamp, since both possess by nature the acquired, adventitious light of grace, inasmuch as the good, according to nature, belongs only to God; and it is from Him, according to participation, that all things that by nature are receptive of light and goodness are enlightened and made good.

63.27. Let these things, which my discourse has considered, suffice for the matters at hand, so as not to exceed the bounds of good measure. Now you, yourself, O righteous Father, with God's help, add even greater contemplations to these, and make glad my dim-sighted soul by the enduringly bright rays of your intellect.

Scholia

[1] Not every person coming into this world, he says, is completely illumined by the Word, for there are many who remain without illumination and without a share in the light of knowledge. Instead he clearly means every person coming by his own will into the world of virtues. This is because everyone who, by means of his own freely chosen birth, truly comes into this world of virtues, is completely illumined by the Word, and receives an immovable condition of virtue and the understanding of true knowledge.

[2] Here he understood the woman as sensation, and the serpent as pleasure, for both are diametrically opposed to reason.

[3] When sensation subjects the intellect to itself, it teaches polytheism, for with each sensation, owing to its enslavement to the passions, it reveres each sensory object as if it were divine.

[4] Fear, piety, and knowledge, he says, bring about practical philosophy. Strength, counsel, and understanding, on the other hand, firmly establish natural contemplation in the spirit, but divine wisdom alone bestows mystical theology.

[5] He calls the essence of sensible and intelligible realities "intermediaries," through which the human intellect is of a nature to be led toward God as the Cause of beings.

[6] The Old Testament, he says, being a symbol of ascetic practice and virtue, prepares the movements of the body to be in harmony with the intellect. The New Testament, on the oth-

er hand, being productive of contemplation and knowledge, illumines with divine characteristics the intellect that mystically adheres to it.

[7] God, he says, by grace is called and becomes Father of those who through virtue possess a pure and voluntary birth. Because of such a birth, the face, as it were, of their soul bears the features of God who bore them, which may be seen through their life of virtue.[65] These features, moreover, prepare those who behold them to glorify God through the transformation of their manner of life, offering to them for imitation their own life as an exceptional example of virtue. For God is not of a nature to be glorified by mere words alone, but rather by deeds of righteousness, which far more than words proclaim the magnificence of God.

[8] The Old Testament, he says, provides a person of knowledge with the modes of the virtues, while the New Testament gives true principles of knowledge to the person engaged in ascetic practice.

[9] Whoever, he says, has embodied his knowledge by means of practice, and ensouled his practice by means of knowledge, has found the precise mode of true divine action.[66] But whoever possesses either one of these in separation from the other has either made knowledge a mere mental phantom or his practice a soulless idol. For knowledge without practice in no way differs from fantasy, since it does not have practice providing it with a foundation in reality; and practice deprived of reason is no different from a soulless idol, since it does not have knowledge to give it a soul.

[10] In the same way that soul and body produce a human being through their composition, the concurrence of ascetic practice and contemplation constitute a single, cognitive knowledge; so too the Old and New Testaments together realize a single mystery.

[11] The natural law, on account of sense perception, is on

---

65. In *Amb.* 10.43 (DOML 1:215–17), God is said to give his own features to adopted human beings, and, recognizing his own likeness in them, readily grants their prayers.
66. I.e., θεουργία.

the left, leading reason to the modes of the virtues, and putting knowledge into operation. The spiritual law, on the other hand, on account of the intellect, is on the right, mingling the spiritual principles that exist in beings with sense perception, and filling practice with reason.

[12] Providence, he says, is manifested in the Word's union according to hypostasis with the flesh, while judgment is seen in the Word's accepting to suffer the Passion on our behalf. Through these, that is, union and passion, universal salvation is constituted.

[13] The Incarnation, he says, took place for the salvation of human nature, whereas the Passion took place for the redemption of those who because of sin were under the power of death.

[14] The mystery of the Incarnation, he says, expels those properties that are contrary to human nature, while at the same time reestablishing those that are according to nature.

[15] He took the "brass mountains" to mean providence and judgment, as well as Incarnation and Passion, from which arises the tetrad of the Gospels.

[16] He took the "land of the North" to be the Gentiles, who formerly dwelt in the deception of ignorance, as if it were a region of darkness, but who have now entered a region of light. This came about through knowledge of truth according to the grace of the holy tetrad of the Gospels, which are like four incorruptible elements, and thus, according to the inner and intellective man, they were refashioned through faith unto life eternal.

[17] The person engaged in contemplation, he says, manifests the principle of the Incarnation according to providence. The person engaged in ascetic practice, on the other hand, shows forth, in actuality, the mode of the Word's sufferings according to judgment.

[18] Whoever turns his intellect to the visible world contemplates the intelligible world. For using his power of imagination,[67] he imprints intelligible realities within sense perception, and, on the level of his intellect, he gives shape to the inner principles that he has beheld. In this way he brings the

---

67. I.e., φανταζόμενος.

structure of the intelligible world to bear, in a variety of forms, on sense perception, and brings the composition of the sensible world, in a complex manner, to bear on the intellect. Thus, on the one hand, he grasps with his intellect the sensible within the intelligible, having transposed sense perception to the intellect by means of the inner principles, and, on the other hand, he grasps the intelligible within the sensible, transposing, by means of the sensible figures and with true knowledge, the intellect to sense perception.

QUESTION 64

HAT IS THE meaning of the statement in the prophet Jonah concerning Nineveh, which says: "In which more than twelve myriads of men dwell, who do not know their right hand or their left"?[1] The literal sense provides no solution to the problem. For example, the text did not say "children," so that I might think it is speaking of infants, but rather it says "men." But what kind of man, being of sound mind, is unable to distinguish his right hand from his left? Tell me, then, who these "men" are, and what are the "right hand" and the "left hand" according to an anagogical interpretation?[2]

Response

64.2. None of the things written in Scripture—persons, places, times, or other things, whether these be animate or inanimate, sensible or intelligible—have their literal or contemplative meanings rendered always according to the same interpretive mode. This is why the person who endeavors to receive unerringly the divine knowledge of the Holy Scripture must allow for the differences of the events and sayings, and give each of the things enumerated an appropriate interpretation consistent with its place or time.[3] This is because the names of each

---

1. Jon 4.11.
2. For a general study of this Question, see Carl Laga, "Maximi Confessoris ad Thalassium Quaestio 64," in *After Chalcedon: Studies in Theology and Church History Offered to Professor Albert van Roey for his Seventieth Birthday*, Orientalia Lovaniensia Analecta 18, ed. Carl Laga, et al. (Leuven: Departement Oriëntalistiek, 1985), 203–15.
3. Cf. *Amb.* 37.5–9 (DOML 2:79–87), where Maximos enumerates ten such interpretive modes, building on the categories of place, time, genus, person, rank, and occupation.

of the things signified in Scripture, according to the possibilities inherent in the Hebrew language, in fact have multiple meanings, which is exactly what we find here in this passage.[4]

64.3. Thus according to different Hebrew pronunciations, the name Jonah is translated as "rest," "house of God," "healing from God," "the grace of God for them," the "pain of God,"[5] "dove," "flight from beauty," and "their laboring."[6] Jonah himself, moreover, is described as being present "in Joppa," "in the sea," "in the whale," "in Nineveh," and "under the gourd plant." Joppa, on the other hand, is translated as "watchtower of joy," "wondrous beauty," and "powerful joy." Surely, then, the prophet Jonah is a figure of Adam and our common nature, and also of Christ, of the gift of prophecy, and of the ungrateful Jewish people, who are annoyed by every good thing,[7] and resentful of those who receive divine gifts.

64.4. For example, Jonah presents us with the figure both of Adam and of our common nature when he flees from Joppa to the sea, which is why he is called "flight from beauty" according to the meaning of his name. Joppa is a figure of paradise, the true "watchtower of joy," and the true and truly named "powerful joy" and "wondrous beauty" on account of the riches of incorruptibility contained within it—whatever that paradise may have been, planted as it was by the hand of God, for, as Scripture says: "The Lord planted a garden in Eden, and placed there the man whom he had formed,"[8] and whatever may have been the trees that were there, in terms of either sight or mental contemplation, and the "Tree of Life, which was in the middle of the garden."[9] And whereas Adam received the command to eat from all these trees, he did not even touch them, for it says: "You may eat from every tree in the garden."[10]

---

4. Cf. above, Qu. 54.2.

5. The primary sense of the Greek word πόνος is "labor" or "toil," but Maximos's use of the word in this Question suggests that the secondary meaning of "physical pain" is the better rendering, without, however, excluding the sense of pain generated by hard work.

6. Cf. Lagarde, *Onomastica Sacra*, 170.

7. Cf. Acts 4.2.

8. Gn 2.8.

9. Gn 2.9.

10. Gn 2.16.

64.5. Again, Joppa also signifies virtue and knowledge as well as the wisdom associated with them. It signifies virtue when it is translated as "wondrous beauty," knowledge when it is taken as "watchtower of joy," and wisdom when it signifies "powerful joy." In relation to this wisdom, a man who is perfected receives ineffable joy, which is powerful and truly capable of maintaining him in a divine constitution according to God, if it is true that "Wisdom is a tree of life to all that lay hold of her," according to what is written, "and she is a secure help for all that rely on her, as on the Lord."[11] For we observe the nature of human beings perpetually fleeing from Joppa, like Adam from paradise on account of his disobedience, fleeing, that is, from the stable habit of virtue and knowledge and the wisdom associated with them. This is because the human mind is intensely fixated on evil things and is voluntarily dragged away to the sea, by which I mean the brine of sin, in the same way that our forefather Adam slipped and fell from paradise into this world. In this sea of sin, human nature preoccupies itself closely with the instability of material things, and thus it both bears and is borne about on the ever-shifting tides of deceit and confusion. Those who remain in this ocean of confusion gain nothing except to be dragged down into its depths and swallowed by the whale, with "water poured around them up to the soul, encompassed by the final abyss, with their heads submerged to the clefts of the mountains, and going down into the earth, whose bars are eternal barriers."[12] It should be obvious that this is the depth of the final, ultimate abyss, "a truly dark and gloomy land, the land of eternal darkness, where there is no light, nor can anyone see the life of mortals."[13]

64.6. The prophet Jonah, then, signifies Adam, that is, the common nature of human beings, and in himself he mystically figures our nature, which slipped away from the good things of God, as if from Joppa, and descended, as though into the sea, into the misery of this present life. Our nature, I say, which was submerged[14] in the chaotic and roaring ocean of material

11. Prv 3.18.
12. Cf. Jon 2.5–6.
13. Jb 10.21–22.
14. Here begins an extended rhetorical construction in which the fall of

attachments; which was swallowed by the whale, that intelligible and insatiable beast, the devil; and which was inundated by water on all sides, taking on, up to its very soul, the water of temptations to evil, so that human life was submerged in temptations; and which was encompassed by the final abyss, that is, imprisoned by the complete ignorance of the intellect, and overwhelmed by the great weight of evil pressing down on its power of reason. Our nature, whose head[1] was sunk into the clefts of the mountains, that is, whose primary principle concerning faith, which is the head, as it were, of the whole body of virtues, was locked away, as if in the clefts of dark mountains, by the designs of evil powers, and divided into multiple opinions and false imaginings—for Scripture called "clefts of mountains" the deceptive designs of the spirits of wickedness who lie somewhere in the depth of the final abyss of ignorance. Our nature, which descended into the earth,[2] whose bars were its eternal barriers, that is, carried off into a desert barren of all feeling for God, where its habit of mind was devoid of the vital movement of the virtues, and had absolutely no sense of goodness, and took no thought of the movement of its desire toward God. It was this nature, I say, upon which the darkness of ignorance and the indescribable depth of evil settled like an abyss,[3] and into which the mountains of deception sank their roots—I mean the "spirits of wickedness"[15]—and inasmuch as human nature was receptive to their deception and evil, it initially entered into these clefts. But later, nature itself became their very basis, on account of its most wicked disposition, possessing, like eternal bars,[4] innate attachments to material things, which do not permit the mind to be free from the darkness of ignorance, and so prevent it from beholding the light of true knowledge. It was perhaps just such an evil disposition, as I said a moment ago, that the great Job was alluding to when he spoke of the "dark and gloomy land, the land of eternal darkness."[16] It is "dark" because it is barren of all true knowledge

---

human "nature" (φύσις) is described through a series of twelve passive feminine participles (i.e., ἐξολισθήσασαν, κατενεχθεῖσαν, καταποντισθεῖσαν, καταποθεῖσαν, etc.).

15. Eph 6.12.
16. Jb 10.21.

and contemplation, and it is "gloomy" because it is deprived of all virtue and ascetic practice. And in this land, he says, "there is no light"[5] —that is, of knowledge and truth—"nor can one see the life of mortals,"[17] which clearly means the proper way of life for rational beings.

64.7. Perhaps the prophet Jonah found himself in these circumstances when, figuring within himself the passions of humanity (which humanity wretchedly inflicted upon itself), he made his own the things of our common nature, adapting most fittingly to himself, as a type of Adam, the meaning of his name, which means "flight from beauty." But when, on the other hand, he prefigures God, who for our sake came to us and became like us through flesh possessing soul and intellect, "save only without sin,"[18] he sketched out in advance the mystery of the economy of salvation and the sufferings associated with it. Thus he signifies the Word's descent from heaven into this world[6] by his passage from Joppa into the sea, and he points to the mystery of His death, burial, and resurrection by being swallowed by the whale and emerging from it intact after three days and nights.[19] This is why he is correctly and fittingly called by the name meaning "rest"[7] and "healing from God" and the "grace of God for them," and perhaps he is also fittingly called the "pain of God" on account of the voluntary Passion. For through his own dramatic experiences the prophet mystically sketched out in advance the one who is the true "Rest" of those who have been "wearied" by their sufferings,[20] the "Healing" of those who have been broken, and the "Grace" of the remission of sins, which is Christ Jesus, the true God. For our Lord and God Himself became man and entered into the ocean of our life, as if descending into the sea of this life from the heaven of Joppa, which translated means "contemplation of joy," as Scripture says: "He is the one who, for the joy that was set before Him, endured the cross, despising the shame."[21] He

---

17. Jb 10.21–22.
18. Heb 4.15.
19. Cf. Mt 12.40.
20. Cf. Mt 11.28.
21. Heb 12.2.

even willingly descended into the "heart of the earth,"[22] where the Evil One had swallowed us through death and was keeping us prisoners; and when He snatched us away through the resurrection, He led up the whole of our captive nature to heaven. And He is truly our rest, and our healing, and our grace. Rest, because through His brief life He abolished the law of our dire slavery to the flesh. Healing, because through His resurrection He healed us from the wound of death and corruption. Grace, because through faith He distributes adoption in the Spirit of God the Father,[23] and the grace of divinization to each who is worthy. For it was necessary, truly necessary, for the Light and Power of God[24] to enter into that land of darkness and eternal bars, so that, dispelling the darkness of ignorance (inasmuch as He is the Light of the Father), and breaking the bars of evil (inasmuch as He is the enhypostatic Power of God), He might free our nature, which the devil had cruelly bound in these conditions, giving it the inextinguishable light of true knowledge and the unshakeable power of the virtues.

64.8. When, however, the prophet mystically leaves Joppa, he figures in himself the grace of prophecy, a grace which departed, as it were, from the "Joppa" of the corporeal observance of the law (formerly thought to be glorious), and he conveyed the message of the Gospel to the Gentiles, so that the Jewish people, because of their unbelief, were left barren of the joy they once took in the law. At the same time, this grace prefigures the return of the church of the Gentiles, like Nineveh, to God, a return that takes place through many afflictions, dangers, adversities, sufferings, persecutions, and death. By leaving Joppa, the prophet signifies that the grace of prophecy separates itself from the observance of the law, and enters the sea of involuntary adversities, with its rising tide of persecutions, along with the struggles, sufferings, and dangers that result from them, therein to be swallowed by the whale of death, yet by no means being completely destroyed. For nothing from among anything that exists—neither "tribulation, nor distress, nor persecution,

---

22. Mt 12.40.
23. Cf. Eph 1.5.
24. Cf. Jn 8.12; 1 Cor 1.24.

nor famine, nor danger, nor sword"[25]—has the strength to impede the advance of the grace that was proclaimed to the Gentiles. To the contrary, through these very adversities grace was strengthened[26] and prevailed over all those who rose up against it. By means of suffering it triumphed all the more over those who agitated against it, and it returned our nature, which had been deceived, back to the living and true God, just as Jonah had done with Nineveh. Even if the Evil One seemed to conceal this grace through the onslaught of the persecutions—as the whale concealed the prophet—he was nevertheless incapable of constraining it permanently, being unable to weaken or otherwise alter the power producing the grace. Indeed, he succeeded only in making this grace shine all the more brightly in its disciples after their experience of adversities, and, as much as he did this, he undermined[8] his power by means of his own assaults. Moreover, he saw for himself that this grace was not only completely invincible, but also that the physical weakness of the saints, who proclaimed this grace to the Gentiles,[27] itself became a strength capable of destroying his power and utterly destroying "every proud obstacle to the knowledge of God,"[28] becoming all the more powerful spiritually when it seems to be overcome physically by his assaults.

64.9. Learning this very thing from the experience of his own suffering, Paul, the great trumpet of the truth, who lived "in the newness of the Spirit and not in the oldness of the letter,"[29] and who was a minister to the Gentiles of the prophetic grace in Christ, said: "We have this treasure in earthen vessels,"[30] calling the principle of grace a "treasure," and this passible body of ours an "earthen vessel." Or perhaps the word "vessel" refers to Paul's alleged lack of training in public speaking,[31] which nevertheless triumphed over all the wisdom of the world,[32] or which rather

25. Rom 8.35.
26. Cf. Col 2.7.
27. Cf. 2 Cor 12.9.
28. 2 Cor 10.5.
29. Rom 7.6.
30. 2 Cor 4.7.
31. Cf. 2 Cor 11.6; 1 Cor 2.1–5.
32. Cf. 1 Jn 5.4.

contained, as much as was possible, the wisdom of God, which is absolutely uncontainable by the world, and which filled the whole of the inhabited earth with its light of true knowledge, "so that," as he says, "it might be shown that the transcendent power belongs to God and not to us, for we are afflicted in every way, but not crushed; perplexed, but not driven to despair; persecuted, but not forsaken; downcast, but not destroyed. We always carry in the body the death of Jesus, so that the life of Jesus may also be manifested in our bodies. For as long as we live, we are constantly being consigned to death for Jesus's sake, so that the life of Jesus may be made manifest in our mortal flesh. So death is at work in us, but life is at work in you."[33] Thus those who are innocent but who voluntarily and patiently endure death in the midst of sufferings for the sake of truth[9] become heralds of the word of grace, actively bringing about spiritual life among the Gentiles according to the knowledge of the truth. And this is exactly what befell Jonah, who mystically prefigured this grace within himself, enduring dangers such as these so that he might turn the Ninevites from their deception to God, and this is why his name can also be fittingly translated as "gift of God" and "pain of God." To be sure, the grace of prophecy addressed to the nations is both a gift of God (and a truly beloved and philanthropic gift), and a divine and praiseworthy source of pain. A "gift," since it bestows the light of true knowledge on those who receive it, and offers them incorruptible life; and the "pain of God," since it convinces its ministers to adorn themselves with their own painful labors on behalf of the truth, and teaches those who are anxious about their life in the flesh to be enlarged more through sufferings than through comforts,[34] making the flesh's natural weakness in the face of suffering the foundation[10] of transcendent spiritual power.

64.10. It was thus through many trials that the word of grace passed to human nature, that is, to the church of the Gentiles, just as through many afflictions Jonah went to the great city of Nineveh. And grace persuaded the reigning law of nature[11] to rise up from its "throne," that is, from its former state of evil

---

33. 2 Cor 4.7–12.
34. Cf. Ps 4.1.

in relation to the senses; and to remove its "robe," by which I mean to set aside the arrogance of worldly glory evident in its comportment; and to clothe itself in "sackcloth," in other words, the mourning and the difficult and rough way of hardships, which is fitting to a life lived according to God; and to sit in "ashes," these being the "poverty of the spirit,"[35] in which sit all those who have been taught to live piously, and who possess the scourge of conscience tormenting them because of their sins.[36] And when the word of grace is proclaimed in this manner, it not only persuades the "king" to believe in God, but also the "men" of the city, those human beings, in other words, who constitute human nature, giving them the full assurance to confess and proclaim faithfully that the one God is Creator and Judge of the universe, preparing the complete rejection of their former evil deeds, and, "from the least to the greatest of them,"[37] to "put on sackcloth," which means eagerly to pursue hardships that mortify the passions. It is my sense that here, according to the anagogical interpretation,[38] the "least" and the "greatest" are those identified by Scripture as having committed lesser or greater evil.

64.11. "And the men of Nineveh," Scripture says, "believed God, and proclaimed a fast, and put on sackcloth, from the least to the greatest of them. And the word reached the king of Nineveh, and he arose from his throne, took off his robe, put on sackcloth, and sat on ashes. And the king and his nobles issued a proclamation and had it announced in Nineveh, saying, 'Let not men, cattle, oxen, or sheep taste or eat anything or drink any water.'"[39] The "king" of nature, as I said a moment ago, is the law of nature. His "captains" are the rational, irascible, and desiring powers of the soul.[40] The "men"[12] of his city, that is, of nature, according to one interpretation, are those who stumble in terms of reason, and who hold mistaken knowledge con-

---

35. Cf. Mt 5.3.
36. Cf. *Amb.* 12 (DOML 1:347).
37. Jon 3.5.
38. Cf. above, Intro. 1.2.3.
39. Jon 3.5–7.
40. Cf. above, Qu. 49, where a similar interpretation is put forward with respect to Hezekiah and his elders and captains.

cerning God and divine realities. The "cattle" are those who sin in terms of desire, and who bear burdens of pleasure along with their bodily sufferings. The "oxen" are those who exhaust the entire motion of their irascibility in acquiring earthly things, for they say that drinking the blood of the ox causes the one who drinks it to die immediately, and blood is obviously a symbol of irascibility.[41] The "sheep," they say—that is, from a blameworthy point of view[42]—are those who, devoid of intelligence, graze solely on the contemplation of visible things, as if it were grass, in order to satisfy their passions. For we implicitly understand that all the things found in this passage of Scripture are taken in a blameworthy sense until the moment the Word took hold of them and changed them for the better. This is why Scripture goes on to add the following: "Let no one eat anything or drink any water,"[43] impeding, in other words, the former constitutive causes of the passions among each of the things mentioned above. And having destroyed these causes, Scripture indicates the change for the better of those formerly dominated by evil behaviors when it further adds: "And the men and cattle were clothed in sackcloth, and cried out earnestly to God; and each one turned from his wicked way and from the iniquity in his hands."[44] As I have already pointed out, we should understand "men" here as referring to those who, through a mistaken judgment of reason, have become enslaved to passions of the soul; "cattle" as those who for the sake of pleasure abuse their irascible and desiring powers,[45] being

---

41. Like many ancient writers, Aristotle, *History of Animals* 3.19, believed that the blood of oxen coagulated quickly, and that drinking it produced a lethal choking effect in the stomach and throat (LCL 1:219). Maximos could have read something similar in Basil, *Hexaemeron* 5.4, where this belief is assumed to be general knowledge: "Just because the blood of the ox is poison for you, should this animal, whose strength we need for many things in life, not have been created?" (SC 26:292).

42. See above, Qu. 38.2.

43. Jon 3.7.

44. Jon 3.8.

45. *Carit.* 3.3: "It is by abusing the soul's powers that the vices of the desiring, irascible, and rational aspects of the soul arise within us" (ed. Ceresa-Gastaldo, 144).

attached to the passions of the body.[46] And we should understand all of them as having clothed themselves in the sackcloth of the "mortification of their members upon the earth,"[47] that is, every earthly law and way of thinking. And as "crying out earnestly," that is, with a loud voice, which means confessing, with boldness in the face of sin, their freedom from the licentiousness of their former sins, and departing, as if from a road, from their habitual behavior, and from the unrighteousness brought about by their deeds, as if by "hands."

64.12. Inasmuch, then, as Nineveh is understood as our common human nature, or as the church of the Gentiles, we see Jonah, who symbolizes the word of prophetic grace that is always preaching within it, and every day turning back to God those who are lost and wandering. If, on the other hand, we apply the understanding of Nineveh to the contemplation of each particular person, we would say that the great city is each and every soul, to which, in its transgression, the Word of God is sent, preaching repentance unto life.[48] We understand the "king" of this "city" to signify the intellect; the "captains" are its innate powers; "men" are its impassioned thoughts; "cattle" are its movements of desire associated with the body; "oxen" are its covetous movements of irascibility associated with material objects; and "sheep" are the movements of its senses apprehending sensible objects independently of the mind. The "king" is the intellect who rises from the throne, as it were, of the state created by its former ignorance, and it sets aside, as if it were a robe, its false opinion concerning beings, clothing itself instead with repentance, as if it were sackcloth, for its evil ways of thinking. And thus it sits in ashes, that is, the state of mind characterized by poverty of spirit, and it orders its "men, cattle, oxen, and sheep" to fast from the food of evil, and to

---

46. Larchet (SC 569:212, n. 2) contends that here Maximos has adopted a different classification of the passions than what was outlined in the work's Introduction. The distinction between "passions of the soul" and "passions of the body" is found in Ps.-John of Damascus, *On Virtues and Vices of the Soul and Body* (PG 95:88B), a work probably written around the beginning of the sixth century.

47. Col 3.5; cf. 2 Cor 4.10.

48. Cf. Jon 3.1–4.

refuse the drink of ignorance. This means to abstain from evil deeds and from the deluded contemplation of the senses; and to put on sackcloth, that is, the habit of mind that mortifies the passions contrary to nature, but which produces virtues and knowledge according to nature; and to cry out fervently to God, which obviously means to confess earnestly their former sins, and by their humility to propitiate Him who is able to grant forgiveness for their former ways. And to ask, moreover, for immutable power in their actualization of superior things, and in the guarding of their power of free choice, for God eagerly grants this to those who ask to receive it, and, as if from an "evil way," to impede their mind from returning to its former deception, and to cast off from the soul's practical powers the state of mind that conceives wickedness.

64.13. In this "great city"—which is the common nature of human beings and the church of the Gentiles, or the individual soul of each and every human being—which has been saved through the word of virtue and knowledge, that is, faith and a good conscience, there exist "more than twelve myriads of men who do not know their right hand or their left."[49] According to the principles of anagogical interpretation, my understanding is that, by the "twelve myriads," Scripture is referring to the principles of time and nature, in other words, the necessary conditions[13] without which one cannot comprehend the knowledge of visible creation.[50] For if the number twelve is constituted by adding five to seven, and if nature is fivefold according to the senses, while time is sevenfold,[51] it follows that the number twelve clearly points to nature and time. Scripture, moreover, emphasizes that there were "more than twelve myriads" of men, in order for us to know that, while this number is limited, it is also exceeded by those who, being far more numerous, constitute by themselves a quantity indefinitely transcending the number twelve.

---

49. Jon 4.11.
50. On the phrase, "necessary conditions," see above, Qu. 55.3.
51. On the sevenfold nature of time, cf. *Amb.* 56.2; 65.2; 67.3 (DOML 2:249; 277–79; 289); *Cap. theol.* 1.79 (PG 91:1112D); *QD.* 41 (CCSG 10:35, lines 20–22); and *Exp. Ps.* 59 (CCSG 23:5, lines 36–39).

64.14. Thus the all-praised Church of God—holding in her embrace those who[14] in their virtue and knowledge have gone beyond the principles of time and nature,[52] and have passed over to the magnificence of eternal and intelligible realities—has "more than twelve myriads of men who do not know their right hand or their left." For whoever through lawful virtue forgets the passion of the flesh on his "left," and who, because of his unerring knowledge, does not fall ill with swollen conceit over his accomplishments on his "right," becomes a man who "does not know his right hand," since he does not desire fleeting glory, "or his left hand," since he is not roused by the passions of the flesh. It seems, then, that Scripture called vainglory relative to supposed accomplishments the "right hand," and licentiousness relative to shameful passions the "left hand."[53]

64.15. Moreover, every soul made radiant by contemplations of intelligible realities has acquired "men who do not know their right hand or their left." For every soul, having withdrawn and contracted its discursive power from the contemplation of nature and time, possesses, like these men, natural thoughts that surpass the number twelve, because such thoughts no longer toil in relation to the principles of things subject to nature and time. To the contrary, they are concerned with the comprehension and true understanding of divine mysteries, and for this reason they "do not know their right hand or their left." This is because the rational knowledge of the virtues, that is, the true and active knowledge of the causes[15] of the virtues, is of a nature to produce complete ignorance of the excess and deficiency that are found, like right and left hands, on either side of the mean of the virtues.

64.16. For if by its nature there is absolutely nothing irrational in reason,[16] then clearly one who has been elevated to the rational principle of the virtues will by no means yield any place to the irrational.[54] For it is not possible to observe two

---

52. That is, through the gift of divinization; cf. *Amb.* 7.26 (DOML 1:111–13); *Amb.* 10.42–43 (DOML 1:213–17); *Amb.* 20.3 (DOML 1:411–13); and *Amb.* 30.2–3(DOML 2:37–39).
53. Cf. above, Qu. 48.20.
54. Here, the language of λόγος and παράλογος plays on human "rational-

opposite realities at one and the same time, nor to imagine that the one can simultaneously appear with the other. For if no rational principle of faith can be found in the lack of faith,[17] and if light by nature is not the cause of darkness, and if one cannot point to the devil and Christ at the same time, it is clear that absolutely nothing contrary to reason can coexist together with reason. And if nothing contrary to reason can possibly exist by any means together with reason, then the one who has been elevated to the rational principle of the virtues does not, as I said, acknowledge any place for things contrary to reason, because he knows only virtue,[18] and he knows it only as it is, not as it is thought to be. This is why he knows neither the "right hand" through excess, nor the "left hand" through deficiency, for in both of these things one may clearly see what is contrary to reason. For if reason is the limit[19] and measure of beings, then being moved contrary to that limit, and contrary to that measure, or again to move beyond that limit and beyond that measure, is equivalent to the absence of reason and is therefore irrational. For both alike cause those who move in this manner equally to fall away from that which really exists. The former[55] does this by persuading them that the movement of their course is unclear and without limits,[20] since the intellect's lack of measure does not possess God as its foreordained goal—and thus they are shaped more to the right than the right itself. The latter[56] does this by persuading them, contrary to their goal, to conduct the motion of their course solely in the direction of sense perception,[21] since the intellect's lack of vigor makes them think that their foreordained goal is to be confined within the realm of the senses. But the one who is ignorant of these things, having no experience of them, is the one who is united solely to the rational principle of virtue, to which he restricts the entire motion of his intellect's proper power, and for this

---

ity" and the "irrational," as well as the rational principle (*logos*) that is at once the metaphysical ground, determinative intelligible structure, and origin and goal of creatures in God. To be or move in conformity with the rational principle of a thing is to be in conformity with reason, nature, and the divine.

55. I.e., being moved beyond one's proper limit and measure.
56. I.e., being moved contrary to reason's limit and measure.

QUESTION 64   501

reason he is not able to think of anything either beyond reason or contrary to reason.

64.17. If, however, someone with the ambition desires to extend his intellect toward an even loftier meaning, he will of course understand the "right hand" as the rational principles of incorporeal beings, and the "left hand" as the rational principles of corporeal beings. To be sure, the intellect that has without qualification been extended to the Cause of beings[22] will be absolutely ignorant of these rational principles, contemplating no principle in the reality of God, who by essence transcends every principle as far as all causality is concerned. Such an intellect, being contracted toward God and away from all beings, knows none of the principles of the beings from which it has withdrawn, but beholds solely the One to whom it has drawn near by grace and in a manner beyond interpretation.

64.18. God takes thought for these "men" and those like them, and for their sakes He takes thought for the whole world of such men, who in truth do not know their blameworthy right hand or left hand—for virtually everything in Scripture may be taken in either a praiseworthy or a blameworthy way.[57] And this is true even if the envious Jewish people—those ungrateful, graceless misanthropes, who are hostile to all philanthropy, and who are thus pained by the salvation of mankind, and so dare to fight against the goodness of God—grind their teeth, renounce life, and make the salvation of the Gentiles in Christ a cause for mourning.[58] For in their mindlessness they

---

57. Cf. above, Qu. 38.2.

58. The vehemence of these and subsequent remarks goes well beyond the argument's rejection of a reductively "Jewish" literal reading of Scripture, and may reflect contemporary tensions between Christians and Jews in Byzantine North Africa; cf. Carl Laga, "Maximi Confessoris *ad Thalassium* Quaestio 64: Essai de lecture," *Orientalia Lovaniensia Analecta* 81 (1985): 203–15; expanded in idem, "Judaism and Jews in Maximus Confessor's Works: Theoretical Controversy and Practical Attitude," *Byzantinoslavica* 51 (1990): 177–88; Robert L. Wilken, "The Restoration of Israel in Biblical Prophecy: Christian and Jewish Responses in the Early Byzantine Period," in *To See Ourselves as Others See Us: Christians, Jews, "Others" in Late Antiquity*, ed. Jacob Neusner and Ernest S. Frerichs (Chico: Scholars Press, 1985), 443–71; Blowers, *Exegesis and Spiritual Pedagogy*, 6–7; Sarah Gador-Whyte, "Christian-Jewish Conflict in Light of Heraclius' Forced Conversions," in *Religious Conflict from Early Christianity to the Rise of Islam*, ed. Wen-

reckoned the "gourd plant" to be far superior to the salvation of the Gentiles, and so they mourned when they saw the gourd withered by the worm. I had said earlier that the great Jonah prefigured in his person the folly of the Jews, not that he himself suffered from any of the things associated with the Jews—away with the idea!—but rather, in his own person he refuted in advance the impiety for which the Jews fell away from their former glory, as if from a kind of Joppa.

64.19. This is why the Holy Spirit mystically bestowed upon him the sort of name he has, which can be interpreted in different ways in order to indicate the dispositions[59] of all those whom he prefigures. When, therefore, in himself he figuratively refutes in advance the madness of the Jews—who were pained by the salvation of the Gentiles, confused by the paradox of their calling, and, contrary to the will of God, blasphemously chose death and even preferred it over life because of the withering of the gourd plant—the name "Jonah" is interpreted as "their laboring," which the word of Scripture proclaims when it says: "And God saw their works"—clearly referring to the Ninevites—"that they turned from their evil ways; and God repented of the evil which He said He would do to them, and He did it not. And Jonah was deeply grieved, and was confounded, and said: 'Now, sovereign Lord, take my soul from me, for it is better for me to die than to live,'" and again: "And the Lord God commanded a worm the next morning, and it smote the gourd plant, and it withered away. And on the next day, at the rising of the sun, God summoned a wind of burning heat, and the sun smote the head of Jonah, and he fainted, and despaired of his life, and said: 'It is better for me to die than to live.'"[60]

64.20. Nineveh, then, is the church of the Gentiles, which re-

---

dy Mayer (Berlin: EVA, 2014), 201–14; and Paul Magdalino, "All Israel Will Be Saved? The Forced Baptism of the Jews and Imperial Ideology," in *Jews in Early Christian Law: Byzantium and the Latin West, 6th–11th Centuries*, ed. John Tolan, et al. (Turnhout: Brepols, 2014), 231–42; and above, Qu. 54.1.

59. In Qu. 28.2, Maximos stated that the language of Scripture is "fashioned" in relation to the "dispositions" of different readers. Here these "fashionings" are embodied in the narrative and activities of a particular biblical personage, including the different pronunciations of his name.

60. Jon 3.10; 4.1–3, 7–8.

ceived the word of grace, turned away from its former delusion of idol worship, and is now being saved and counted worthy of heavenly glory. The tent, which Jonah made for himself after he went forth from the city, represents the Jerusalem that is below,[61] as well as the "temple built there by human hands."[62] The gourd plant signifies the transient shadow of the corporeal observance of the law, which possesses nothing at all that is permanent or capable of enlightening the mind. The worm is our Lord and God Jesus Christ, since He says of Himself, through the prophet David: "I am a worm and not a man,"[63] who became and was truly called man on account of the seedless flesh He assumed. For in the same way that worms are born without copulation or any prior sexual mingling, so too the birth of the Lord in the flesh was not preceded by any prior mingling.[64] In addition, the Lord placed His flesh around the fishhook of His divinity as a lure to deceive the devil, so that the insatiable, intelligible dragon would swallow it (since by nature the flesh is easily overcome) and thus be caught on the fishhook of the divinity, and, by virtue of the holy flesh of the Word that He took from us, would vomit out the whole of human nature that he had already consumed. The Lord's aim was that, just as the devil had formerly swallowed human beings by luring them with the prospect of divinity, so too the devil himself might now be lured by the covering of humanity and subsequently vomit out his human prey, which had been deceived by the expectation of divinity, with the devil himself being deceived by his expectation of devouring humanity. Consequently, the transcendent nature of God's power would be manifested through the weakness of defeated human nature, conquering the strength of the one who conquered it, demonstrating that God would be

61. Cf. Gal 4.26.
62. Mk 14.58.
63. Ps 21.6.
64. Cf. Origen, *Homilies on Luke* 14.8: "Without male seed a new offspring began to grow. Hence the Savior says, '"I am a worm, and not a man" [Ps 22.6], for a man is normally born from a male and a female, but I was not born thus, but like the worm, which does not get seed from outside itself, but rather reproduces in itself and from itself, and produces offspring from its own body alone'" (SC 87:226–28).

shown forth as one who conquers[23] the devil all the more by using the covering of the flesh than the devil did by promising humanity the nature of the divinity.[65] This, then, is the worm that "smote the gourd plant and caused it to wither," by which I mean the one who abolished the observance of the law, as if it were but a shadow, and withered the prideful conceit that the Jews took in it.

64.21. "And on the next day at the rising of the sun."[66] "On the next day," because, after the figural enigmas of the law were left behind, along with the time ordained for their corporeal observance, the grace of the new mystery rose like the dawn, bringing to light a different day: a day bringing forth sublime knowledge and divine virtue, and divinizing those who take hold of it. For after this worm smote the gourd plant, this same sun [...].[67] Because the same one who is the "worm"[24] is also the "Sun of righteousness"[68]—the former, because He was born in the flesh without male seed, and because His conception was beyond all human comprehension; and the latter, because He went underground, as it were, for my sake, in the mystery of His death and burial, and because in Himself by nature He is Light eternal—and rising like the sun from the dead, "God summoned a scorching east wind, and the sun smote Jonah's head."[69] For after the rising of the "Sun of righteousness," that is, after the resurrection and ascension of the Lord, the scorching east wind that burns up temptations came and set itself against those Jews who remained unrepentant, and it smote them on their heads

---

65. Cf. Gn 3.5. The analogy of the divine "fishhook" and the "deception of the devil" is based on Gregory of Nyssa, *Catechetical Oration* 24, 26 (GNO 3.4:62, 65–66); cf. Maximos, *Cap.* 1.11: "By enticing the insatiable serpent with the bait of the flesh, He provoked him to open his mouth and swallow it. This flesh proved poison to him, destroying him utterly by the power of divinity within it; but to human nature it proved a remedy restoring it to its original grace" (PG 90:1181D–1184A); and Nicholas Constas, "The Last Temptation of Satan: Divine Deception in Greek Patristic Interpretations of the Passion Narrative," *HTR* 97 (2004): 139–63.

66. Jon 4.8.

67. There is a small lacuna in the text at this point; Blowers, *Cosmic Mystery*, 161, suggests "smote Jonah," or "smote the Jews."

68. Mal 3.20.

69. Jon 4.8.

with its righteous judgment, "turning," as it says, "their toil back onto their own heads,"[70] just as they anticipated when they invoked a vow against themselves, saying: "May His blood be upon us and our children."[71] For clearly after the resurrection and ascension of the Savior, the retribution of the Gentiles, like an exceedingly scorching east wind, fell upon them; and the glory and power of their entire nation, as if it were their head, was struck and overpowered by my Sun of righteousness, to which they closed the eyes of their minds, and for this reason failed to see the light of truth which shone upon them.

64.22. Or, again, the "wind of burning heat,"[25] which rose up against the Jews who disobeyed the word of grace, is divine abandonment. This wind hinders the rain of knowledge and the dew of prophecy, and dries up the natural spring of the heart's pious thoughts—which justly came upon them, inasmuch as their hands were covered with innocent blood, and they betrayed truth for a lie, and denied the Word of God, who, without undergoing any change, came in our form for the salvation of human beings. This is why they were handed over to the law of their own delusion, in which one cannot find, in any form whatsoever, a disposition watered by piety and the fear of God, but only the inclination of a will that is dry, barren, and marked by every evil passion. Arrogance alone is a mark of such a will, for it is an accursed passion consisting of two evils in combination: pride and vainglory.[26] Of these two, pride denies the Cause of virtue and nature, while vainglory adulterates nature and virtue itself, because the prideful person does nothing according to God, while nothing natural comes forth from a vainglorious person. The mixture of these two produces arrogance, which is contemptuous of God, and so it blasphemously calumniates His providence. Arrogance, moreover, is estranged from nature, and so it uses everything in nature in a manner contrary to nature, and destroys the beauty of nature by its abusive mode of behavior.

64.23. To state the matter briefly, because the Jewish people did not believe in Christ, their mind was permitted to be

70. Ps 7.16.
71. Mt 27.25.

bound by the arrogant demon of pride, and thus they came to despise God and man equally. They hold God inferior to carnal pleasure, which is why they reject worship in the Spirit;[72] and they consider those who by race are not descended in the flesh from Jacob to be utterly alienated from the Creator, which is why they consider murder perpetrated against us to be something pleasing to God.[73] Thanks to their vain foolishness, they seem to be ignorant of the fact that the body is not as capable of intimacy and kinship with God as a soul bearing the same seal of faith as other souls, and which has achieved identity with all men according to the disposition of its will toward the Good. On the basis of this identity, the law of the flesh[27] has been completely abolished, and the Word of God alone is brightly manifested through the Spirit, unifying the minds of all in the knowledge of the one God, and in one mutual love and harmony, a union in which no one is completely separated spiritually from anyone else, even if they are physically located at great distances from each other.

64.24. The "wind of burning heat," then, is arrogance, a passion which at once hates both God and man. It dries up the heart of unbelievers, withering pious thoughts about God and correct principles about nature, consistent with the image of burning heat. For they say that this wind arises from the mixing of easterly and southerly winds, and for this reason dries up moisture distributed across the earth. They also say that it is called Euroklydon and Typhonikon.[74] "Euroklydon," because it stirs up disturbances on all sides of both land and sea; and "Typhonikon," because it produces an arid darkness, which is exactly what arrogance does: it introduces a great disturbance into the soul and fills the mind with the darkness of ignorance. It was this "wind of burning heat" that God stirred up against them for their insolence to Christ, which is to say that God allowed this to come upon them because it suited the disposition of those possessed of such insolence, and so that their free choice with respect to God and humanity would be per-

---

72. Cf. Jn 4.24.
73. Cf. Jn 16.2.
74. Cf. Acts 27.14.

fectly clear to everyone. Thus, being utterly consumed by the darkness of ignorance, they voluntarily drove themselves to the fate of opposing God. And being left with nothing except to be troubled by the salvation and glory given to the Gentiles through faith, and anguished by the abrogation of their carnal laws, they say: "Now, Lord, take our lives from us, for it is better for us to die than to live,"[75] all on account of a withered gourd plant, by which I mean their ritual observance of the law in the shadows, which was abolished, and which was both created and destroyed at night,[28] since it was limited solely to the enigmas and figures of symbols, and so did not possess any intelligible light capable of illuminating the mind.

64.25. But let us, however, through the faith and righteousness that accompany it, spiritually embrace the spiritual Nineveh—by which I mean the church of the Gentiles, which is truly the "great city unto God," as it says in Scripture,[76] and which was saved by repentance through the "three days" allotted for its conversion—and let us strive to become citizens of this "great city unto God" through repentance and our transformation to what is superior. For the word of Scripture states explicitly, in these very words, that "Nineveh was a great city unto God."[77]

64.26. Where in Scripture does the Jew, who is concerned about the truth of the earthly city of Jerusalem, find these exact same words applied to Jerusalem? Absolutely nowhere, at least as far as I can tell, for having read through all of Holy Scripture many times over, I have never come across the phrase: "Jerusalem was a great city unto God." Who, then, would have such confidence in the power of his reason, and in the wealth of his ideas, as to think he could limit and measure the greatness of this city, which is and which is called "great unto God"? For me this would be an absolutely insurmountable difficulty. And I think it would likewise be impossible for any man of intelligence, who has even a slight sense of the majesty of God, and who is not unaware that God's judgments must necessarily be

---

75. Jon 4.3.
76. Jon 3.3.
77. Ibid.

analogous to God Himself. But how, we may still ask, did the capital of the Assyrians, where the confusion of error existed, where the empire of the madness of idolatry was established, and which was so far away from the so-called "holy land" promised to the corporeal Israel, come to be a "great city unto God"? How, indeed, unless God had seen in it the future greatness[29] of the faith of the church of the Gentiles, which God saw and accepted as being already present, and so deigned to dwell in what recently had been foreign to Him, in a city, I say, which once was most vile on account of its godlessness, but which God rendered divine and most precious by His word, so that now no word can define its greatness, and about which God through the prophet clearly said: "And Nineveh was a great city unto God." It was to this city that the prophetic word of grace was sent to preach its blessed destruction, saying: "Three days still,[78] and Nineveh will be destroyed."[79]

64.27. Having arrived at the passage which speaks of the three days designated for their repentance, I think I can set aside whatever else can be said by those who interpret the text anagogically, and instead, pursuing a single focus through precise examination, speak of that which, in being spoken, will perhaps not be found outside the truth. When I hear the prophet categorically proclaiming: "Three days still, and Nineveh will be destroyed," I take this to mean that the judgment against Nineveh is irrevocable, and, to speak more precisely, that this divine visitation will take place for the sake of Nineveh. For I understand that after the three days, which the prophet spent figuratively in the belly of the whale—and through which by anticipation he prefigured in himself the Lord's three-day burial and resurrection—the word of Scripture expected yet another three days,[30] in which the light of the truth and the true fulfillment of the mysteries announced in advance would be revealed, and in which the city would certainly be destroyed. These three days would no longer merely prefigure the future truth of the Savior's burial and resurrection, but instead would

---

78. Or, "Yet three days," in the sense of "three days longer" or "in another three days."

79. Jon 3.4.

clearly show this very same truth realized by the realities themselves, and the anticipatory prefiguration of this truth was of course the triad of days that Jonah was in the whale. For if every figuration is of an anticipated truth, and if, consistent with the figuration, Jonah remained for three days in the belly of the whale, it is obvious that this mystery, as a figure, would manifest the truth in a completely new way, which nonetheless follows the figure, namely, that the Lord spent three days and three nights in the heart of the earth, just as the voice of the Lord proclaims: "Just as Jonah was in the belly of the whale three days and three nights, so too the Son of Man will be three days and three nights in the heart of the earth."[80] For to say "three days still" tacitly indicates that three days have already passed; otherwise, the word "still" would not be placed here, which is to say that yet another three days would pass and then Nineveh would be destroyed. Thus it was not the figure that destroyed Nineveh according to the divine sentence, but rather the truth, about which Scripture says "three days still," as if the prophet were saying: "After the figure seen in me, another three days of a more mystical burial and a greater resurrection shall pass, and then Nineveh will be destroyed."

64.28. But someone might perhaps bring forward the following difficulty: How is God being truthful when He gives the order for the destruction of the city but then does not destroy it? To this person we respond by saying that God in truth both destroys and saves the same city: the former, by making it desist from its error; the latter, by bringing about its acquisition of true knowledge—or rather He destroys its error through the revitalization of its faith, and realizes its salvation by the death of that error. Now Nineveh translated means "parched blackness" and "smoothest beauty." In agreement with the meaning of this translation, the Lord, after His three-day burial and resurrection, destroyed the "parched blackness" of error that had accrued to human nature through the transgression, and renewed the "smoothest beauty" of that nature through the obedience of faith. And, again, through the resurrection, He showed forth the beauty of nature's incorruptibility to be ex-

---

80. Mt 12.40.

ceedingly smooth and in no way coarsened by anything material. What is being said here may also be suitably applied to our common human nature, to the holy Church, and to each individual soul, which through faith and a good conscience has set aside the "earthly image" of the old Adam, and clothed itself in the "image of the heavenly Adam."[81]

64.29. It has now been clearly demonstrated that the prophet Jonah can be contemplated in a variety of ways consistent with the meaning of his name, and that each particular interpretation of his name has been suitably adapted to the particular passage of Scripture in which it appears. For instance, when translated as "flight from beauty," his name signifies[31] Adam and our common nature. As "rest of God," "healing from God," and "pain of God," he signifies our Lord and God, consistent with the meaning of the interpretation given above. Announcing the grace of preaching through the riches of the Spirit that it contains, he is called a "dove," "gift of God," and "pain of God," on account of the many struggles of those who became the ministers of this true calling. Alluding to the folly of the Jews in regard to the truth, his name is interpreted as "their laboring," which is envy of good things acquired by others, and which gives birth to grief in those who succumb to it. This vice became natural for those Jews who embraced hatred of God and mankind, and for this reason they seek only one thing: the unrestrained destruction of human nature through bloodshed and murder.

64.30. But my discourse has run ahead of the argument, and we have neglected the contemplation of the "journey of three days," because the text says: "Nineveh was a great city unto God, of about a three-day journey."[82] If it seems good to you, let us now briefly fill in what is missing. One must take the three-day journey on the road as three different ways of life on the path to God, that is, the formation and training proper to each of the three general laws. By "general laws" I mean the natural law, the scriptural law, and the law of grace,[83] each of which is marked by

---

81. 1 Cor 15.49.
82. Jon 3.3.
83. Cf. above, Qu. 39; and below, Qu. 65.14, and Qu. 65, schol. 19.

a particular way of life and a course of action appropriate to it, inasmuch as the disposition eventuating from each one differs according to the will of those who follow it—for each law is of a nature to produce a different disposition in each of those who submit to it.

64.31. For example, the natural law,[32] whenever it does not have sensation dominating reason, convinces all human beings to embrace that which is of a shared nature and kinship—and it does this spontaneously, without requiring any teaching, for it has nature itself as a teacher to assist them in terms of what they need, and to encourage everyone to seek for others what each one considers desirable to be done to him by them. And this is what the Lord teaches when he says: "Whatever you desire for men to do to you, do likewise to them."[84] For among those upon whom nature bestows reason, it is only natural that they should also possess the same disposition. And those who possess the same disposition are of a nature obviously to share the same ethical conduct and way of life. And among those who share one and the same ethical conduct and way of life, it is obvious that they share one and the same bond of mutual affection according to the inclination of their wills, leading them all in unity of will toward the one principle of human nature, in which there is absolutely no division of nature such as we now see prevailing because of self-love.

64.32. The scriptural law,[33] on the other hand, customarily uses the fear of punishment to constrain the disordered impulses of those lacking in prudence, teaching them to look only to the equitable distribution of things, so that the rule of justice, confirmed over time, will be translated into nature, gently and gradually turning their fear into a disposition governed by a voluntary inclination of the will for the good. At the same time, it turns their customary behavior into a permanent state, purified through the forgetting of its former ways and giving birth to the love of others, by means of which the law naturally reaches its fulfillment, because all are harmoniously joined to each other in love. For the mutual bond of love among those who

---

84. Mt 7.12; Lk 6.31.

share a common nature is the "fulfillment of the law,"[85] which presents natural reason crowned by the desire for love, while the addition of desire makes the law of nature radiant. For the law of nature is natural reason undertaking various means to subdue sensation. The scriptural law, on the other hand—that is, the fulfillment of the scriptural law—is natural reason taking spiritual desire to itself as a helper in its mutual connection to what is naturally related to it. This is why it says: "You shall love your neighbor as yourself,"[86] and not: "You shall consider your neighbor as yourself," for the latter[34] indicates only the natural bond of sharing in being, whereas the former signifies the providence that leads toward well-being.

64.33. Finally, the law of grace immediately teaches those who follow it to imitate God Himself, who loved us so much more than Himself—if I may be permitted to speak in this way—and, not least, at a time when we were His enemies because of sin,[87] so that, even though He is beyond every essence and nature, He entered into our essence without undergoing change and in a manner transcending essence, and so became man, wishing to live among human beings. And He did not hesitate to make our condemnation His own condemnation, and to make us Gods by grace to the same degree that He undertook in His economy of salvation to become man by nature, so that we would learn not only to be close to each other naturally, and to love one another spiritually, as we love ourselves, but also to be concerned for others in a divine manner, that is, more than for ourselves. And the proof of this love for one another is to be ready to die voluntarily and virtuously for others, for as the Lord says: "There is no greater love than this, that a man lay down his life for his friends."[88]

64.34. Thus the law of nature, to speak concisely, is natural reason that has subdued the senses in order to remove irrationality, which is the cause of division among those united by nature. The scriptural law is natural reason that, after the

---

85. Rom 13.10.
86. Mt 22.39; cf. Lv 19.18.
87. Cf. Rom 5.10.
88. Jn 15.13.

removal of irrationality arising from the senses, has taken spiritual desire to itself to maintain its mutual connection to what is naturally related to it. Finally, the law of grace is reason that has been established beyond nature, and which refashions nature for divinization without changing it, and in this nature, as if in an image, it shows, in a manner beyond comprehension, the Archetype that transcends essence and nature and offers permanent dwelling in eternal well-being.[89]

64.35. If, then, the three laws are understood in this manner, it would seem to follow quite naturally that the great city of God—which is the Church, or the soul of each and every particular person—is in fact a three-day journey,[35] insofar as it is receptive of and embraces righteousness according to nature, law, and the Spirit. In these three laws, the entire beautiful arrangement of the Church is contained, encompassing its breadth of virtue, its width of knowledge, and the depth of the wisdom of its mystical theology.[90]

64.36. But let us not, like the Jewish people, be separated from this city in terms of our inner disposition, cherishing our bodies as Jonah cherished his tent, and attending to the fleeting pleasures of the body, as if to a gourd plant. Otherwise, the worm of our conscience will smite our disposition (deceived as it is by pleasure) and cause it to wither away; and, like a wind of burning heat, retribution will come in the form of involuntary sufferings for all of the evil things that we have done, and we will renounce life and be greatly vexed by the divine judgment. For each one of us who has been overtaken by the deception of material things, and whoever has taken delight in the pleasures of the body receives the word of God as something smiting his conscience like a worm, and devouring his attachment to pleasure like the root of the gourd plant. But with the perfect rising of the illumination of the teachings of the Spirit, the word of God withers the activity of sin; and through the memory of eternal punishments, like a wind of burning heat, it smites—as

---

89. "Reason" is not merely a natural power or capacity, but can function on a level beyond nature. Elevated by grace beyond nature, and without suffering any change in itself, reason beholds the "Archetype" that transcends essence.

90. Cf. Eph 3.18.

if it were a head—the origin of the evil passions in the provocations of the senses. And this happens so that we might come to learn the principles of providence and judgment,[36] which give priority to eternal things over what is transitory, the privation of which typically causes the human race to grieve.

64.37. In sum, if the word of Scripture presented us with a man grieving over his tent and a gourd plant—by which I mean his flesh and the pleasure of the flesh—and presented God caring for Nineveh, then it is obvious that, when compared to what seems precious to human beings, that which is beloved by God is far superior and far more precious than everything that exists, to say nothing of things that do not exist, and which only seem real because of an error in judgment, but which in fact have absolutely no principle of existence, being nothing more than a fantasy deceiving the mind, providing passion[91] with the empty appearance, but not the reality,[92] of things that have no being.

Scholia

[1] He calls the first principle concerning the monad a "head," since it is the beginning of every virtue; the "clefts of mountains" are the evil thoughts of the spirits of wickedness, which engulfed our intellect in the fall.

[2] "Earth" is what he calls the lowest habitual state of the soul, which has no perception of divine knowledge, or which makes no movement of any kind toward the life of virtue.

[3] "Abyss" is what he calls the ignorance covering the habit-

---

91. Or, perhaps here, simply "experience" (πάθος).

92. I.e., σχῆμα ("appearance") and ὑπόστασις ("reality"); cf. Gregory of Nyssa, *Refutation of the Confession of Faith of Eunomios* 54: "Their arguments are as weak as a spider's web, for just as the web has a form (σχῆμα) but lacks substance (ὑπόστασις)—since anyone touching it touches nothing solid or substantial (οὐδενὸς ὑφεστῶτος), insofar as the spider's threads dissolve at the touch of a finger—so too is their vain, insubstantial web of words" (GNO 2:334, lines 12–17); and John Chrysostom, *Homilies on Romans* 20.2: "The 'form (σχῆμα) of this world is passing away' [1 Cor 7.31], for it has nothing enduring or permanent about it, but everything is temporary; and whatever is thought to be great in this life, such as wealth, glory, or bodily health, is merely an appearance (σχῆμα), not the reality, an outward display and a mask, but not a substance (ὑπόστασις) that endures" (PG 60:597).

ual state of evil, over which, as if it were land, the oceans of evil rose up.

[4] He called "earth" the fixed habitual state of evil, and "eternal bars" the impassioned attachments to material things that sustain the worst habitual state.

[5] He calls true understanding a "shining light," while the manner of life fitting to rational beings he calls the "life of mortals," which is lacking in someone possessing a state of mind habituated to evil.

[6] Here he took the "sea" to mean this world, into which the Lord entered through the flesh.

[7] He calls the Lord "rest" inasmuch as He is the deliverance from toils undertaken for virtue; and "healing from God" inasmuch as He is the physician of the wound of death; "grace of God" inasmuch as He is redemption; and "pain of God" inasmuch as He takes on our sufferings.

[8] The patient endurance of the saints, he says, exhausts the wicked power that strikes against us.

[9] That the saints, by voluntarily enduring suffering and death in the body for the sake of truth, brought about life in the spirit among the Gentiles.

[10] The natural weakness of the saints, which the Lord showed to be superior to the pride of the devil, is the foundation for the surpassing power of God.

[11] The "king," he says, is the natural law; the "throne" is the impassioned habitual state of the senses; the "robe" is the covering of vainglory; the "sackcloth" is mourning prompted by repentance; the "ash" is humility.

[12] He calls "men" those who err in relation to reason; "cattle," those who err in relation to desire; "oxen," those who err in relation to anger; and "sheep," those who err in relation to the contemplation of visible things.

[13] The "necessary conditions" are time and place, without which no being can exist.

[14] Because the Church possesses the principles of virtue and knowledge, as does the soul of each and every person, and because these principles transcend time and nature, the Church possesses more than twelve myriads. This is because

the principle of virtue, which is of the left hand, does not know sin, whereas the principle of the soul's knowledge, which is of the right hand, does not know evil.

[15] God is the cause of the virtues. Actualized knowledge of God is when the habitual state of the one who knows God is transformed in the direction of the spirit.

[16] By means of the virtues, he says, the principle of nature elevates the person diligently engaged in ascetic practice to the level of the intellect. By means of contemplation, the intellect leads to wisdom the person who desires knowledge. Irrational passion, on the other hand, persuades whoever disregards the commandments to be dragged away toward sensation, the end of which is the attachment of the intellect to pleasure.

[17] By "unbelief" he means the denial of the commandments; by "faith" he means acceptance of the commandments; "darkness" is ignorance of the good; and "light" is the knowledge of the good. He called Christ the essence of these and their subsistence, and the devil their worst habitual state, which gives birth to all the vices.

[18] "Virtue" is what he calls the most dispassionate and fixed habitual state in relation to the good, on either side of which stands nothing, for it bears the characteristic mark of God, to whom nothing stands in opposition.

[19] If, as is natural, an inner principle determined the genesis of each being, no being is naturally superior or inferior to itself. From this it follows that the limit of beings is their desire for and knowledge of the Cause of beings, and their measure is their actual imitation (as much as this falls in their power) of the Cause.

[20] When, he says, the desire of beings in motion is carried beyond its limit and measure, it deprives the course of their movement of meaning, inasmuch as they do not arrive at their goal in God, in whom the desire of all that is moved comes to rest, receiving as their self-subsisting goal the enjoyment of God.

[21] When, he says, the desire of beings in motion is carried contrary to its limit and measure, it deprives the course of their movement of meaning, for instead of God they arrive at sense

perception, in which they will find only the non-subsisting enjoyment of impassioned pleasures.

[22] The intellect running back to God in ecstasy leaves behind equally the principles of corporeal and incorporeal realities, since it is not natural for anything sequent to God to be seen together with God.

[23] Far more did the Lord conquer the power of the tyrant by putting forward the weakness of His flesh than the devil conquered Adam by promising him the rank of divinity.

[24] The Lord is a "worm" because He was born in the flesh apart from seed. He is the "sun" because He set in the tomb, through which the Word as man went under the earth; and by His nature and essence He is Light and God.

[25] The "wind of burning heat" signifies not only trials but also abandonment by God, who takes away from the Jews the dispensation of divine gifts.

[26] It is the mark of pride, he says, for someone to deny that God is the begetter of virtue and nature, and it is the mark of vainglory to divide nature in such a way as to diminish it. Arrogance is begotten of both, being a compound state of evil, which voluntarily denies God and is ignorant of the equality that exists in nature.

[27] The soul's close spiritual kinship releases the attachment of free choice to the flesh, and through desire binds it fast to God.

[28] He calls the symbols of the law "night," under which the law is accomplished. If these symbols are not understood spiritually, it is not possible to find in them any illumination for the soul.

[29] By virtue of the great mystery of the divine economy of salvation, which cannot be comprehended by any human discourse, the Church was called "the great city unto God."

[30] Truth, he says, in terms of its essence, precedes figures, but according to their manifestation, figures are chronologically prior to the truth. Thus, because Jonah in himself described the truth in advance through figures, remaining in the belly of the whale for three days and three nights, he said, "three days still," referring to the three days of the Lord's burial and res-

urrection, after which came about the destruction of the error and ignorance of the Gentiles.

[31] This is a brief exposition of the interpretation of the name of Jonah, according to the sense relative to each of the personas and places applied to him.

[32] The work of the natural law, he says, is the relation of the will's inclination toward equality of honor among all people with all people.

[33] The scriptural law, he says, uses fear to hinder unrighteousness, and so accustoms one to righteousness. In time, however, custom produces a disposition that loves justice.

[34] To "consider" your neighbor as yourself is to be concerned merely with life as it relates to being, which is the basis of natural law. To "love" your neighbor as yourself, on the other hand, is to take forethought for your neighbor and his well-being in virtue, which the scriptural law commands. But to love your neighbor more than yourself is the characteristic mark only of the law of grace.

[35] The "journey of three days," he says, is the perfection of righteousness through the three laws accomplished by the one who keeps them.

[36] Whoever is hindered, he says, from impulses leading to bodily pleasure, learns the principles of providence, which forestall the matter that inflames the passions. Whoever accepts afflictions leading to bodily pain, on the other hand, is taught the principles of judgment, which purge him from his former impurities by means of involuntary pains.

QUESTION 65

IN THE second book of Kings, it is written that: "In the days of David, there was a famine for three successive years. And David sought the face of the Lord. And the Lord said: 'This injustice is on account of Saul and his house, because he put the Gibeonites to death.' Then David summoned the Gibeonites and said to them: 'What shall I do for you? How shall I make atonement so that you will bless the Lord's inheritance?' They answered the king: 'As for the man who killed us and persecuted us and planned to decimate us, we must utterly destroy him, so that he will have no place anywhere within the territory of Israel. Give us, then, seven men from among his sons so that we might expose them to the sun before the Lord on Mount Saul.' And the king took the two sons of Rizpah, the daughter of Aiah, the concubine of Saul, and the five sons of Saul's daughter Merab, whom she had borne to Adriel, and gave them into the hand of the Gibeonites, who exposed them to the sun on the mountain before the Lord, and all seven of them fell together in that same place. And they were put to death in the days of the harvest, at the beginning of the harvest of barley. And Rizpah the daughter of Aiah took sackcloth and spread it out for herself on a rock, until rain poured down on them from God. And they did everything commanded by the king. After these things, God hearkened to the cry of the earth."[1] Why, after the death of Saul, was justice demanded of David, when there was a famine prevailing over the land, so that he handed over seven men from the seed of Saul to be put to death by the Gibeonites? What is the meaning of these words, and how might we contemplate them spiritually?

1. 2 Kgs 21.1–6, 8, 10–14.

Response

65.2. The precise knowledge of the words of the Spirit is of a nature to be revealed only to those who are worthy of the Spirit, who on account of their great diligence in virtue have purified[1] their intellect from the grimy soot of the passions, making it like a clear and shining mirror, so that with a single glance they receive the knowledge of divine realities reflected within themselves like a face.[2] On the other hand, it seems to me that those whose life is marked by the stains of the passions are barely able, by means of various plausible conjectures,[3] to reach any conclusive proofs concerning divine knowledge, which of course does not enable them to presume that they can conceive and speak of such knowledge with any precision. And I myself am clearly aware, honorable father, that you yourself know divine things[2] directly, inasmuch as you have experienced them,[4] and on the basis of your experience you possess true understanding of them, whereas I know only how to speak about them, being unable to express them on the basis of any direct experience. Nevertheless, what falls within one's power is not to be rejected, and certainly not by you, who set me to the task of responding to your questions, placing me in the position of speaking about things that are beyond my capacities.

65.3. To begin, then, we can say that Saul, in this passage

---

2. Cf. above, Qu. 46.2.

3. I.e., στοχασμοί; cf. above, Qu. 55.2.

4. "Experienced" translates the Greek participle πάσχων, which means to have "suffered" something (such as receiving a divine revelation or divine grace) while being in a state of "passivity," i.e., to the extent that one's powers of sensation and intellection are inactive; cf. above, Qu. 22.7; *Amb.* 10.28 (DOML 1:191); *Amb.* 20.3 (DOML 1:413); *QThp.* (73, lines 6–7); and Dionysios, *DN* 2.9: "My teacher [i.e., Hierotheos] praised whatever he learned from sacred writers, whatever his own study of the Scriptures uncovered for him, or whatever was made known to him through that more divine inspiration, not only learning but also suffering divine things" (134, lines 1–2; 648B); and ibid., 3.2: "Being caught up in a state of ecstasy, he [i.e., Hierotheos] suffered communion with the things he was praising" (141, lines 12–13; 684A). See also Ysabel de Andia, "Παθὼν τὰ θεῖα," in *Platonism in Late Antiquity*, ed. Stephen Gersh and Charles Kannengiesser (Notre Dame: University of Notre Dame Press, 1992), 239–58; and Larchet, *Divinisation*, 540–45.

of Scripture,[3] signifies the written law, which rules over carnal Jews according to the power of the carnal commandment. In other words, he signifies the corporeal way of life or thinking that rules over those who are guided solely by the letter of the law. According to one interpretation, the name Saul means "Hades that is asked for," for by preferring a life enamored of pleasure to the virtuous life and kingdom in the Spirit of God, the Jewish people "asked for Hades," meaning that they wanted ignorance to rule over them instead of knowledge. This is because all those who have fallen away from divine love have the law of the flesh as their king, which rules over them through pleasure, and they are unable to keep even a single divine commandment, and in fact have no wish to do so.

65.4. According to another mode of interpretation, Saul means "given as a loan" or simply "loan." To those who received it, the written law was not given as their permanent possession and property, but rather as a tutor of the expected promise.[5] This is why, when God gave the kingdom to Saul, He did not, in the covenant He made with him, promise it to him forever. For every loan is given not to become the permanent possession of the one who receives it, but as an occasion for labor and toil in the acquisition of something else.

65.5. Saul's concubine, Rizpah, means the "course[6] of the mouth." The course of the mouth is the learning of the law that is limited solely to the pronouncing of words. The person who occupies himself solely with the corporeal observance of the law unlawfully cohabits with such learning, and from their union is born nothing that is pious or loves God. This is because the one who exercises himself with the corporeal learning of the law solely in terms of pronouncing its words[4] does not live lawfully with the word, that is, with the learning of the law.[7] This is why his offspring are miserable and cast out. For

---

5. Cf. Gal 3.24.
6. I.e., δρόμος, and thus "running," "rapid delivery," etc.
7. Cf. Origen, *Homilies on Luke* 5.1–2, who makes a similar criticism based on the "muteness" of Zechariah (Lk 1.22): "He compensated for the loss of his voice with signs, since there are deeds that are no different from empty signs because they lack words and reason. Consider the Jewish practices: They lack words and reason (*ratio et sermo*), and thus the Jews cannot give a reason for

from his illicit coupling with Rizpah, Saul became the father of Armoni and Mephibosheth, whose names mean "anathema on them" and "shame of their mouth" (because Armoni, according to one interpretation, means "anathema on them," and Mephibosheth means "shame of their mouth"). "Anathema on them" is the sinful corruption that occurs in the body due to the activity of the passions.[5] "Mephibosheth" is the unnatural movement of the intellect toward evil, that is, the intellect's capacity to recall and reflect on the vile things it has conceived, which is and is called the "shame of their mouth," the "mouth" here designating the intellect.

65.6. Alternately, "anathema on them"[6] signifies the place where nature is now subjected to the prevailing punishment, that is, this world, as the region of death and corruption, which came about on account of sin. It is into this place that the first man fell from paradise after he transgressed the divine commandment. And it is in this world, due to the will's attachment to the love of pleasure (that is, its passionate attachment to the world), that the learning of the law as the mere pronunciation of its words gives birth to one whose intellect does not make the passage to the divine beauty of the spirit contained within the letter of the law. The "shame of their mouth" is attention to thoughts inspired by love of the world and love of the body. For of anyone in whom the world is of a nature to be born from the pairing of the superficial physical configuration of the letter of the law with the attachment of the will[7] (by which I mean a disposition enamored of the world), it is only reasonable to expect that attention to the law that is enamored of the world and the body will also be born together with it.

65.7. Or, again, "anathema on them"[8] is the movement of the passions, which, being inclined to matter, is ugly and lacking in form. The "shame of their mouth" is the movement of the intellect that gives a form to the passions, and fashions

---

their practices. What happened to Zechariah is a type of what is fulfilled in the Jews even to this day. Their circumcision is like an empty sign. Passover and other feasts are empty signs rather than the truth" (SC 87:136–38). The editors of this text, which survives only in Jerome's Latin translation, note that *ratio et sermo* translate the single Greek word λόγος (ibid., 136, n. 1).

beautiful images that give pleasure to the senses. For no passion would ever arise without the intellect's conceptual capacity to fashion such forms.

65.8. It follows, then, that whoever limits the power of the divine promise to the letter of the law has made the learning of the law a concubine and not his lawful wife. Such learning necessarily gives birth to anathema and shame—not because of itself, but because of the person who receives it and couples with it in a corporeal manner. For whoever believes that God established sacrifices, feasts, Sabbaths, and new moons for the enjoyment and satisfaction of the body, will in every way become absolutely subject to the activity of the passions and to the shame of the defilement of the vile thoughts they produce. He will be subject to this corrupted world and preoccupied in his thoughts with love for the body and the matter and forms of the passions. That he is incapable of possessing anything precious apart from things subject to corruption is likely the reason why he wickedly begets Merab, who in turn bore five sons to Adriel.[8] Merab translated means "filling of the throat," which is gluttony.[9] For she alone, contrary to the commandment, and in a Jewish manner, was permitted to give birth to ways of misusing the senses by her marriage to Adriel, that is, the contemplative part of the soul. For Adriel translated means "divine power" or "strong help" or "powerful sight," which signifies the intellect as the image of God, in this case having been persuaded to cohabit with gluttony, which is the offspring of the law subordinated to the flesh, by which I mean the letter. For when the intellect has been convinced[9] that, according to the written law, carnal enjoyment has been prescribed by a divine commandment, it will cohabit with nothing else but gluttony, believing it to be divine and the offspring of the royal law, and from it he will bring forth various ways of misusing his bodily senses. Whenever the contemplative aspect of the soul,

---

8. Merab was the daughter of Saul.

9. Gluttony is one of the three "most general" passions, together with avarice and vainglory; cf. *Carit.* 3.56 (ed. Caresa-Gastaldo, 170); above, Intro. 1.2.14; *QD.* 2, 37, 80 (CCSG 10:3, 31, 61); and John Klimakos, *Ladder of Divine Ascent* 14 (PG 88:844C–872A).

according to the commandment in the written law, embraces carnal enjoyment as something divine and cohabits with it, it will subsequently misuse the senses in a manner contrary to nature, and will give no place for the manifestation of any activity according to nature.

65.9. Thus whoever exercises himself in learning the law in a corporeal manner[10] possesses knowledge of divine things as having a concubine and not a lawful wife, and from her he begets the "anathema" of the activity of the passions and the "shame" of the disgusting thoughts they produce. As offspring, he receives from Merab—the gluttonous daughter of the law— ways of misusing the senses, which habitually slay, like Gibeonites, the principles and thoughts found in the nature of beings, that is, those principles and thoughts that are according to nature. For the translation of Gibeonites is "mountainous" or "raised up," clearly indicating the loftier principles of natural contemplation, or those natural thoughts that depend on us. It is these, I say, that Saul kills, along with anyone else who is now another Saul according to his disposition, for, being deceived by grasping only the letter of the law, he does not fail to reject or falsify the principles of nature.[10] For no one who is attached solely to the corporeal observance of the law will ever be able to receive a natural principle or thought, for symbols are not identical with nature.[11] And if symbols are not identical with nature, then anyone who is fixated on the symbols[11] of the law as if they were prototypes, and who for this reason irrationally rejects natural principles, will never be able to see with any clarity the natural generation of beings.[12] Such a person does not realize that he must preserve those who were saved by Joshua,[13] for whose sake, and against the five kings that rose up against

---

10. Because mere sense perception by itself cannot apprehend the spiritual principles of nature, and will inevitably abuse and distort them.

11. According to Larchet (SC 569:264, n. 2), this means that these symbols have a value that is inferior to nature, because, owing to the difference of their *logoi*, they do not express the same spiritual essence.

12. That is, it is only by recognizing the *logoi* of beings that one is able to know their origin and goal, which is the Logos.

13. Cf. Jos 9.20. In Greek, the names "Joshua" and "Jesus" are the same.

them, he waged that terrible war,[14] in which heaven itself became his ally in the fight against those who rose up against the Gibeonites, raining down hail stones on them. And he made them bearers of wood and bearers of water for the holy Tabernacle,[15] that is, the holy Church, which was prefigured in the Tabernacle, the incarnate Word, Jesus, who put to death the impassioned behaviors and thoughts of the senses which had risen up against them. For Jesus, the Word of God, always preserves the principles of natural contemplation, making them the bearers of wood and water for the holy Tabernacle of His mysteries, inasmuch as [12] He is the provider of the material that sparks the light of divine knowledge and washes away the stain of the passions, and He is the impetus for the distribution of life in the Spirit. For without natural contemplation the power of the mysteries cannot by any means be maintained.

65.10. If, on the other hand, the Gibeonites signify that portion of the Gentiles which approached Joshua, the heir of the divine promises, and which, by being saved, was taught to become a bearer of wood and water, which means to bear on the shoulders of virtues,[16] by means of ascetic practice, the mystical and salvific principle concerning the cross and divine rebirth through water. In this way their practice provides the divine ark of faith with the wood, as it were, of the "mortification of the members on the earth,"[17] while their contemplation provides, as if it were water, the flowing streams of spiritual knowledge, neither of which is out of place or foreign to piety.

65.11. Whether, then, the Gibeonites prefigure the principles of natural contemplation, or the portion of the Gentiles saved through faith, they have as the enemy and adversary of their salvation the one who chooses to live, in a Jewish manner, solely according to the written law.[13] For anyone who "reckons his stomach to be God, and who boasts in his shame as if it were his glory,"[18] knows only how to embrace eagerly the dis-

---

14. Cf. Jos 10.3–14.
15. Cf. Jos 9.27.
16. On this imagery, see above, Qu. 3.3.
17. Col 3.5.
18. Cf. Phil 3.19.

honorable passions as if they were divine, and thus attends only to what is transitory, that is, to matter and form,[14] and to the misuse of the activity of his five senses—the former as the two children of Rizpah the concubine, and the latter as the five offspring of the disgraced daughter Merab. To be sure, when the senses are mixed with matter and form, it produces a passion, while at the same time it smites and kills the principles of nature. This is because the principle of nature[15] is never in any way manifested together with the passions, just as the passions cannot be conceived and born together with nature.¹⁹

65.12. Thus anyone who, like Saul, adheres solely to the letter of Scripture, will surely reject the principles of nature; he will not accept the mystical calling of the Gentiles proclaimed by the prophets, but will be concerned only with the enjoyment of the flesh, which he thinks is prescribed by the law. When such a corporeal disposition concerning the law dominates those who live solely in accordance with the flesh, the famine[16] of divine knowledge in the spirit is not immediately evident. For in truth a famine is the privation of good things known through experience, and a shortage and utter scarcity of the spiritual nourishment that sustains the soul. This being the case, how could someone consider as a famine, or reckon as a loss, the privation of good things that he himself has never known? Thus, for as long as Saul lives, there is no famine, for while the letter of the law is alive and ruling over those Jews whose thoughts incline toward material things, it is not possible for anyone to recognize the need for spiritual knowledge. But whenever the light of the grace of the Gospel shines forth, and when the all-hymned David—who is the law according to the Spirit—accedes to the royal understanding of spiritual realities after the death of Saul, that is, after the death of the letter (for David means "contempt,"²⁰ and "powerful in vision," the former re-

---

19. Contemplation of the *logoi* follows upon purification of the passions, since the passions are the very things that obscure the vision of the spiritual depth of nature, and were not originally part of human nature; cf. above, Qu. 1.2.

20. "Contempt" renders the Greek word ἐξουδένωσις, which can also be understood as "humiliation," or in its verbal form "setting to naught."

ferring to the Jews,[17] among whom the letter prevails over the spirit, and the latter to Christians, among whom the spirit conquered the letter), it is then, I say, that the famine of spiritual knowledge will become evident—in a general way among the faithful people of God, and in a particular way in the soul of each and every person—since they will have realized that the external, superficial garment of the letter had been preferred over mystical contemplation in the spirit, and that the soul[18] of Scripture, as it were, had been made inferior to its body.[21]

65.13. This is because the people of faith who know the truth, and the individual soul, are truly famished when they neglect the spiritual contemplation of grace, and find themselves enslaved through figures to the letter, which does not nourish the intellect with the brilliance of Scripture's inner meanings, but rather gluts the senses with impassioned images based on the corporeal figures of the scriptural symbols. This is why there is a great famine of divine knowledge that lasts for "three successive years,"[22] since everyone who does not accept the spiritual contemplation of Scripture also rejects the natural law, as the Jews do, and so is ignorant of the law of grace, which grants divinization to those who are guided toward it.

65.14. It follows, then, that the "famine of three years"[19] signifies the dearth of knowledge concerning the three laws in terms analogous to each—by which I mean the natural law, the scriptural law, and the law of grace—among those who take no thought for their spiritual contemplation. Because whoever rejects the contemplation of the natural principles of beings is absolutely incapable of arriving at the true understanding of Scripture; instead he clings solely to material symbols, and as

---

21. Cf. *Amb.* 10.29, 33: "The garments of the Word are a symbol of the words of Holy Scripture ... but we must necessarily take thought for the 'body' of Holy Scripture, by which I mean its inner meanings, which are far superior to its 'garments,' for is not 'the body more than clothing'? [Mt 6.25] Otherwise there may come a time when we are caught having nothing, failing to take hold of the Word, and so find ourselves like that Egyptian woman, who grasped only the garments of Joseph, completely failing to attain intercourse with the object of her desire [cf. Gn 39.12]" (DOML 1:193, 201); and the parallel passage in *Cap. theol.* 2.57 (PG 90:1157D).

22. 2 Kgs 21.1.

a result cannot arrive at any spiritually elevated meanings. As long as a merely historicizing exposition[20] of the Scriptures predominates, the reign of the mind absorbed in transitory and temporal things has not been toppled, and the children of the dead Saul continue to live, along with his offspring, which are seven in number, that is, the corporeal and transitory observance of the law. From such an observance, as explained above, an impassioned disposition is commonly born among lovers of the body, having as its helper the outward commandment found in the symbols. This is the reason why I think there was no famine in the days of Saul, that is, in the time of the corporeal observance of the law, when the dearth of spiritual knowledge remained undiagnosed, but rather was recognized in the time of the Gospel of grace. For should we, after the passing of the rule of the letter, during this latter time fail to receive the whole of Scripture spiritually, a famine will surely overtake us, and we will not enjoy the mystical and spiritual devotion which is fitting for Christians. When, however, we return to our senses, like David, and we "seek the face of the Lord,"[23] [21] we are clearly taught that the grace of knowledge had been taken away from us because we did not receive the principles of nature, by which we might have attained to mystical contemplation in spirit, but rather remained clinging to corporeal thoughts concerning the letter of the law.

65.15. "And David," it says, "sought the face of the Lord. And the Lord said: 'This injustice is on account of Saul and his house, because he put the Gibeonites to death.'"[24] "David" is every insightful intellect that sees according to Christ, ever "seeking the face of the Lord." The "face of the Lord" is the true contemplation and knowledge of divine realities according to virtue, and, in seeking this, one is taught the cause of its dearth and shortage. It is then that one receives the command to hand over to death the two sons of Saul, who were born of the concubine, and the five sons of his daughter Merab. Saul, as I have already said, means "Hades that is asked for," that is, "desired ignorance," and desired ignorance[22] is clearly the letter of the law, by which I

23. 2 Kgs 21.1.
24. Ibid.

mean the corporeal reign of the law's observance (which is precisely the corporeal character of the law), or an intellect that is attached corporeally, by means of the senses, solely to the material aspects of the letter. Rizpah, consistent with the interpretation of her name, means "course of the mouth," which is nothing other than the methodical learning of the law limited solely to its verbal pronunciation. For whoever is estranged from the spiritual contemplation of the law truly possesses a course of the mouth, but not of the mind. The "sons of Rizpah are Armoni and Mephibosheth."[25] Armoni means "anathema on them," which is the sinful corruption that occurs in the body due to the activity of the passions, or the place—that is, the world—in which punishment was imposed for the transgression, by which I mean our interior attachment to the world based on pleasure, or perhaps it is the movement of the mind inclined toward matter, which is ugly and lacking in form. Mephibosheth means "shame of their mouth," which is the unnatural movement of the intellect toward evil, that is, the intellect's inventive capacity to conceptualize passions. Or perhaps it signifies a rumination on thoughts inspired by love of the world and love of the body, or the motion of the intellect that gives a form to the passions, fashioning beautiful images pleasurable to the senses. These, in any case, are the sons that are naturally born through the learning of the law that is limited solely to verbal pronunciation, engendered by both the written law and the intellect that sits solely at the feet of the letter of the law.[26] Saul's daughter, Merab, according to the interpretation of her name, is the "filling of the throat," which points to the passion of gluttony. For the law, which limits its adherents to a literal understanding of its symbols, and the intellect which—because of its love for the life of the flesh—confines the law to figures reduced to their literal meaning, know only how to engender the delight of the body and a disposition that enjoys material things. The "five sons of Merab, the daughter of Saul,"[27]

---

25. 2 Kgs 21.8.
26. Cf. *Cap. theol.* 2.42 (PG 90:1144C). Maximos's language here is indebted to Basil, *On the Holy Spirit* 21.52 (SC 17bis:434, lines 43–49); and Gregory of Nyssa, *Against Eunomios* 3.1 (GNO 2:15, lines 35–36).
27. 2 Kgs 21.8.

are the impassioned ways of misusing the five senses, which she habitually bears by Adriel, that is, through the contemplative part of the soul, a disposition which, consistent with the law, is solely preoccupied with the body.

65.16. These two sons of Saul are matter and form,[23] and his five grandchildren are the five ways of misusing the five senses preoccupied with matter and form, by which I mean the impassioned and unnatural coupling of the senses with sensible things, that is, with whatever is subject to time and the flow of nature. After the death of Saul—that is, after the passing of the corporeal observance according to the letter of the law, and the passing away of ignorance—these sons and grandsons are handed over by the wondrous David to the Gibeonites to be put to death according to the divine oracle.[28] In other words, the spiritual law or the intellect, as a kind of David, by means of the loftier principles and thoughts grasped through natural contemplation, destroys and puts to death the most universal relation in the symbols of things governed by time and inclined toward sensation and the body. If, that is, the Gibeonites have attained the height of the mountain of Saul, which is the height of spiritual contemplation. For if someone, having first come to consider naturally[24] the incongruity[29] of the scriptural symbols in relation to divine and intellective realities, does not subsequently come to yearn in his intellect—leaving his senses completely outside the innermost shrine of divine realities—he

---

28. 2 Kgs 21.9.
29. Or "absurdity," i.e., ἀπέμφασις, a word which occurs frequently in Origen's exegetical writings; cf. Origen, *Against Celsus* 4.45, where Lot's wife turning into a "pillar of salt" (Gn 19.17) prompts Origen to "endeavor to soften down the incongruities (ἀπέμφασις) of the story" (SC 136:300, lines 15–16), which Henry Chadwick, *Origen, Contra Celsum* (Cambridge: Cambridge University Press, 1965), 220, translates as "discreditable features"; cf. Origen, *Philokalia* 11.2 (on Ezek 34.17–19): "As the Shepherd's sheep, let us never avoid feeding even on those parts of the Scriptures that are incongruous at first glance, as far as their literal meaning (τῷ ῥητῷ) is concerned, and are trampled on because of the literal wording (τῆς λέξεως)" (SC 302:380, lines 1–5); idem, *Commentary on John* 6.54.280 (SC 157:342, line 30); and Didymos, *Commentary on the Psalms*, where God's "wrath" is described as "incongruous" with the deity (ed. Ekkehard Mühlenberg, *Psalmenkommentare aus der Katenenüberlieferung*, vol. 1 [Berlin: De Gruyter, 1977], fr. 709, lines 16–19).

QUESTION 65   531

will be incapable of being released from the corporeal multiplicity of figures, and will not progress toward the beauty of divine realities, for in the midst of this multiplicity, and for as long as he endeavors to advance while being bound to the letter, his indigence resulting from the famine of knowledge will find no relief. Indeed, it is the "earth" of Scripture, that is, its corporeal element, which he has condemned himself to eat, according to the guile of the serpent[30] and not according to Christ—who is "heaven," that is, the spirit and soul of Scripture—failing to nourish himself on the heavenly and angelic bread, by which I mean the spiritual contemplation of the knowledge of the Scriptures in Christ, which God gives lavishly to those who love Him, just as it is written: "He gave them the bread of heaven, and man ate the bread of angels."[31]

65.17. It follows, then, that any merely sensual interpretation focused on the corporeal elements of Scripture, insofar as it quite obviously gives birth to the passions and to a disposition attached to temporal and fleeting things—that is, the impassioned activity of the senses in relation to sensible realities—must, like the children and offspring of Saul, be destroyed through natural contemplation, by elevating, as if on a mountain, the divine words of Scripture,[32] if, that is, we truly desire to be filled with divine grace. For if "this injustice is on account of Saul and his house," according to the divine oracle, "because he put the Gibeonites to death,"[33] it is clear that such injustice is equally perpetrated against the truth by the law, when it is understood solely according to the letter, and by the Jewish people, along with anyone who might imitate their way of thinking (since this is what Scripture means by the "house of Saul"). Both of these limit the power of the law's meaning to the letter, and do not accept natural contemplation for the manifestation

30. Cf. Gn 3.14; and above, Qu. 5.
31. Ps 77.24–25. Cf. *Amb.* 10.60: "If Adam had trusted God, and been nourished from the Tree of Life, [he would have eaten] the 'bread that came down from heaven and gave life to the world' [Jn 6.33], but instead he fell away from divine life" (DOML 1:249); and Origen, *On Prayer* 10–11 (GCS 2:370).
32. Or, "by means of the anagogical interpretation of the divine words of Scripture."
33. 2 Kgs 21.1.

of the knowledge mystically concealed in the letter, for natural contemplation is midway between figures and the truth, freeing those bound to the former and leading them to the latter. Those, on the other hand, who completely deny natural contemplation, place themselves outside of any initiation into divine realities. It is, therefore, this corporeal and transient interpretation of the law, subject to time and the flow of matter, that those who eagerly seek divine visions should put to death through natural contemplation on the mountain, as it were, of knowledge.

65.18. "Then David summoned," it says, "the Gibeonites and said to them: 'What shall I do for you? How shall I make atonement so that you will bless the Lord's inheritance?' They answered the king: 'As for the man who killed us and persecuted us and planned to decimate us, we must destroy him, so that he will have no place anywhere within the territory of Israel. Give us, then, seven men from among his sons so that we might expose them to the sun before the Lord on Mount Saul.' And the king took the two sons of Rizpah, the daughter of Aiah, the concubine of Saul, and the five sons of Saul's daughter Merab, whom she had borne to Adriel, and gave them into the hand of the Gibeonites, who exposed them to the sun on the mountain before the Lord, and all seven of them fell together in that same place. And they were put to death in the days of the harvest, at the beginning of the harvest of barley."[34]

65.19. Where in the literal account of Scripture do we read that the Gibeonites destroyed Saul, so that he "had no place anywhere within the territory of Israel," when his grandson Meribbaal, the son of Jonathan, was saved by King David, along with many other members of Saul's family, as it is reported in Chronicles?[35] And how, having taken seven of Saul's male descendants, could they have said about him: "We must destroy him, so that he will have no place anywhere within the territory of Israel," when Saul had died many years before this? Here, as it seems, something illogical has been mixed in with the literal account in order for us to search for the true meaning of what has been written. Accordingly, the corporeal understanding of

---

34. 2 Kgs 21.1–6, 8–9.
35. Cf. 1 Chr 8.33–34.

Scripture, which is Saul, is completely removed from all the territory of Israel by the person who—through the "Gibeonites," as it were, of ascetic practice and natural contemplation—puts to death the soul's hedonistic, body-loving attachment to unstable and flowing matter, which is engendered in the soul by the written law. And by means of natural contemplation, he slaughters, as if they were the children of Saul, the mind of the law that clings to the earth, and he does this on the mountainous height of knowledge, and he makes manifest before the Lord, through confession, the former corporeal interpretation of the law. This is how lovers of learning may understand the fact that they were "exposed to the sun before the Lord," and that "they exposed them to the sun on the mountain before the Lord," namely, that they brought to the light,[25] obviously through knowledge, the literal preconception of the law that was lost in error. For it is clear that everyone who has killed the corporeal understanding of the law also kills the letter of the law, and has "destroyed it, so that it has no place within the territory of Israel,"[36] that is, no place within any mystical mode or principle of spiritual contemplation.[26] For if Israel means "the intellect that sees God,"[37] it is clear that absolutely no corporeal element of the law exists in any mode of spiritual contemplation among those who prefer the spirit over the letter, if it is true, as Scripture says, that "God is spirit, and those who worship Him must worship in spirit and truth,"[38] but not in the letter, because "the letter kills, whereas the spirit gives life."[39] This is why that which by its nature kills must itself be killed by the life-creating Spirit, because it is absolutely impossible in actual practice for the corporeal and divine aspects of the law, that is, the letter and the spirit, to coexist mutually and simultaneously,[27] just as that which is able to destroy life is not of a nature to be in harmony with that which gives life.[40]

36. 2 Kgs 21.5.
37. Cf. above, Qu. 23.2.
38. Jn 4.24.
39. 2 Cor 3.6.
40. A formal parallel to the mutual exclusion of simultaneous experiences of intellective and sensory pleasure, discussed above in Qu. 58.

65.20. Thus, if we take this passage according to its literal sense, we will not find Scripture to be speaking truly. For where did the Gibeonites "destroy Saul, so that he had no place anywhere in the territory of Israel"? It is well known that, after these events, many of Saul's relatives were found among the people. When, however, we understand the passage according to contemplation, we will clearly find that, through the intermediary of natural contemplation, at the height of knowledge, the written law, that is, the corporeal institution of legal observances in symbols, completely vanishes. For where will fleshly circumcision be found when the law is understood spiritually? Where the Sabbaths and the feasts of the new moon? Where the celebrations of feasts? Where the tradition of sacrifices? Where the fallow years of the land, and the rest of the law in terms of its corporeal observances? For we know that, when we approach these things[28] from the point of view of nature, perfection is not found in the cutting away or reduction of the fullness given to nature by God (because a nature mutilated by human craft or contrivance adds nothing to the perfection given to it by God in terms of the principle of its creation); otherwise, we introduce human contrivance as mightier than God in the assurance of justice, and make the contrived diminishment of nature a completion of a supposed deficiency of justice in the work of creation. To the contrary, from the localized position of the circumcised part, we are taught to undertake voluntarily the circumcision of the impassioned disposition of the soul, since it is by such a disposition that the inclination of the will is trained to adapt itself to nature, correcting the impassioned law of its acquired mode of birth. This is because mystical circumcision is the complete removal of the intellect's impassioned relation to the mode of generation that was subsequently added to it. The Sabbath,[29] on the other hand, is the complete inactivity of the passions and the universal cessation of the intellect's movement around created realities, and the perfect passage toward the divine.[41] Anyone who, through vir-

---

41. See Maximos's symbolic interpretation of the Sabbath and circumcision in his *Cap. theol.* 1.36–41; 2.64–65 (PG 90:1097AD; 1152D–1153A); *Amb.* 65.2 (DOML 2:277–79); and *QD.* 10; 113 (CCSG 10:9; 83–84). Taken together,

QUESTION 65

tue and knowledge, has properly arrived at this moment must absolutely not call to mind any kind of matter, like wood,[42] that will incite the passions; neither should he in any way gather up the principles of nature, lest we propound, according to the Greeks, a God who is pleased by the passions or measured by the limits of nature, for God is proclaimed solely by perfect silence, and rendered present by surpassing and absolute unknowing.

65.21. We say that the new moons, moreover, are the different illuminations in the cycle of the days of virtue and knowledge, by means of which, racing through all the ages, we complete the "year that is acceptable to the Lord,"[43] adorned with "the crown of His goodness."[44] The crown of goodness is a faith that is pure, flowering, as if covered with precious stones, with lofty doctrines and spiritual principles and concepts, entwined around the head, as it were, of the intellect that loves God. Or better still: the crown of goodness is none other than the Word of God Himself, who, by the variety of the modes of providence and judgment, that is, by self-control[30] in voluntary sufferings and patient endurance in involuntary sufferings, renders the intellect, as if it were a head, more beautiful than itself by participation in the grace of divinization. As regards the feasts, the first is the symbol of practical philosophy, which provides passage to virtue for those who are bound in sin (as if in Egypt). The second is the figure of natural contemplation in the spirit, which offers to God a pious opinion about beings, as if it were the first fruits of the harvest. The third is the mystery of theology,[45] which is the habitual state of knowledge concerning all the

---

these texts understand the Sabbath to mean the cessation of sin; cessation of activities directed toward created realities; and the intellect's ascent to God, which stands in contrast to Evagrios, *Gnostic Chapters* 4.44: "The Sabbath is the rest of the rational soul which does not go beyond the boundaries of nature" (PO 28:155). While for the Confessor, the Sabbath symbolizes the intellect's passage beyond all created realities toward God, for Evagrios it is merely a recollection of nature within its own created limits.

42. Cf. Nm 15.32–34.
43. Is 61.2; Lk 4.19.
44. Ps 64.11. For further discussion of this biblical verse, see *Amb.* 46.4 (DOML 2:203–205).
45. Note the progression from symbol, to figure, to mystery.

spiritual principles that exist within creatures, and the absolute sinlessness given through grace according to the economy of salvation of the incarnate Word, along with the resulting perfect and immortal immutability in the Good, which, like festal trumpets, signals atonement and the building of tents.

65.22. Thus far, this is my understanding, according to one approach, of the honor given to these days in Scripture. For God's aim in commanding that honor be given to the Sabbath, and the new moons, and the feasts, was not so that human beings might honor days of the week—for thus[31] He would have taught us to "worship creation rather than the Creator,"[46] and, consistent with the law of the commandment, we would have thought the days of the week were venerable by nature and thus worthy of worship. To the contrary, through these days the Word symbolically disclosed that He Himself should be honored. For He is the Sabbath, inasmuch as He Himself is the rest for the soul's labors in the flesh, and the cessation of sufferings undertaken for righteousness. And He is the Pasch, inasmuch as He is the liberator of those who were bound within the bitter slavery of sin. And He is Pentecost,[32] inasmuch as He is the beginning, the end, and the principle of beings, in whom all things subsist by nature.[47] For if Pentecost comes about after the period of the sevenfold multiplication of the week, and if Pentecost is clearly the decad multiplied by five, then it should be obvious that the nature of beings, according to its own principle, is fivefold on account of the senses, from which it follows that after the natural passage through time and the ages, it will no longer admit of any limit, for it will have come to be in God, who by nature is One, and in whom there is absolutely no spatial or temporal interval.[48]

---

46. Rom 1.25.

47. For further discussion on the mystical meaning of Pentecost, see *Amb.* 65 (DOML 2:275–81); and Evagrios, *To Monks in Monasteries and Communities* 40, 42 (ed. Hugo Gressmann, *Nonnenspiegel und Mönchsspiegel des Euagrios Pontikos*, TU 39.4 [Leipzig: J. C. Hinrichs, 1913], 143–65, at 156).

48. The world of created beings and natures comprises a relative stability between two boundaries or limits (e.g., beginning and end, birth and death). Each creature must cross from one to the other, and spatial and temporal "intervals" insure that it remains in motion, is able to live but also to die, or to

65.23. Some people say that the Word is a decad, because in His providence He expanded by procession into the decad of commandments.[49] But when nature will be conjoined to the Word by grace, there will no longer be those necessary conditions[33] without which it could not exist,[50] because the changeable movement of things naturally subject to motion will cease. This is because the state which is definitively bounded—in which the movement of things subject to motion will, through change, naturally and necessarily come to rest—must receive its consummation in the presence of a state that is unbounded, in which it is natural for the movement of things in motion to cease. For any motion that has come to be within something that possesses a natural boundary or limit must certainly be changeable. But in that state in which there is no natural boundary or limit, it is equally certain that no changeable movement of any kind will be found among the things within it. If, then, the world is a place that is definitively bounded, and a state that is circumscribed, and if time is circumscribed motion,

---

be transformed when the final cessation of movement brings it to its ultimate boundary. In God, however, there is no boundary or limit; neither is God contained within two borders or encompassed by intervals, so that in him there is no movement, but only an internal, absolute stability. Reaching and transcending their final limit, created beings nonetheless do not acquire God's absolute freedom from intervals, but rather a synthesis of stability (or "rest") and motion, as Maximos notes below, Qu. 65.23; and above, Qu. 59.8. See also *Amb.* 15.7: "The beginning of every natural motion is the origin of the things that are moved, and the beginning of the origin of whatever has been originated is God, for He is the author of origination. The end of the natural motion of whatever has been originated is rest, which, after the passage beyond finite things, is produced completely by infinity, for in the absence of any spatial or temporal interval, every motion of whatever is naturally moved ceases, henceforth having nowhere, and no means whereby, and nothing to which it could be moved, since it has attained its goal and cause, which is God, who is Himself the limit of the infinite horizon that limits all motion. Thus the beginning and end of every origin and motion of beings is God, for it is from Him that they have come into being, and by Him that they are moved, and it is in Him that they will achieve rest. But every natural motion of beings logically presupposes their origin, just as every condition of rest logically presupposes natural motion" (DOML 1:369); and *Amb.* 15.10–11 (DOML 1:373–75).

49. Cf. above, Qu. 62.6.
50. On these "necessary conditions," see above, Qu. 55.3.

it follows that the movement of things living within it is subject to change. When, however, nature in actuality and thought will pass beyond place and time (in other words, beyond the necessary conditions without which it could not exist, that is, the limits of stasis and motion), then, without any intermediary, nature will be conjoined to providence, finding providence to be a principle that is naturally simple and stable, without any kind of circumscription, and thus absolutely without motion. This is why, as long as nature exists in this world being subject to chronological duration, its motion will always be changeable, on account of the world's definitively bounded state and the alternating character of the movement of time. When, however, it comes to be in God, having arrived at Him who by nature is a Monad, it will acquire an ever-moving stasis and a stable movement identical with itself,[51] which will move eternally around the same, unique, and sole God, which reason knows to be an immediate, permanent foundation around the First Cause, for those beings who were created by it.[52]

65.24. The mystery of Pentecost, then, is the immediate union of Providence with those beings under its providential care, which is the union of nature with the Word according to the design of providence, a union in which there is no imprint of time or becoming. The Word is also the "trumpet" heralding this feast,[34] for within us He resounds with divine and ineffable

---

51. Cf. above, Qu. 59.8; below, schol. 32; and *Amb.* 71.5 (DOML 2:319–21). The notion of an "ever-moving stasis" or "rest" is derived from Gregory of Nyssa, *Life of Moses* 2.243 (SC 1bis:272). For the philosophical background, see Paul C. Plass, "Moving Rest in Maximus the Confessor," *Classica et Mediaevalia* 35 (1984): 177–90; Stephen Gersh, *ΚΙΝΗΣΙΣ ΑΚΙΝΗΤΟΣ. A Study of Spiritual Motion in the Philosophy of Proclus* (Leiden: Brill, 1973); and Sotiris Mitralexis, "Ever-Moving Repose: The Notion of Time in the Philosophy of Maximus the Confessor" (PhD diss., Freie Universität, 2014).

52. This passage represents another version of Maximos's celebrated triad of genesis, kinesis, and stasis, which was his reconceptualization of the Origenist schema of stasis, kinesis, genesis, originally put forward in *Amb.* 7 (DOML 1:75–95); cf. Sherwood, *Earlier Ambigua*, 92–102. More generally, it signals Maximos's commitment to a larger eschatological vision of creation; cf. Maximos Constas, "Dionysios the Areopagite and Maximos the Confessor," in *The Oxford Handbook to Dionysios the Areopagite* (Oxford: Oxford University Press, forthcoming).

knowledge. He is also our "atonement," for, having become like us, He dismissed in Himself the charges against us, and by the gift of grace in the Spirit, He divinized our nature which had sinned. And He is the "Feast of Tents," for He is the fixity of our immutability in the Good according to a habitual state that imitates God, and the bond holding together our transformation unto immortality. Now, that God is delighted by the sacrifice of irrational animals[35] and with the sprinkling of their blood, and that He somehow recompenses and pays for such worship by forgiving sins is not something we believe if we approach Scripture from the point of view of nature, lest we unwittingly worship an impassioned God, for we will have made Him greatly and passionately desire things that, when we see human beings desire the same things in an impassioned way, we condemn them for their lack of temperance and self-control. Instead, we recognize not only the mortification of the passions—when we slay them "with the sword of the Spirit, which is the Word of God"[53]—as spiritual sacrifices,[36] but also the voluntary offering of the whole movement of our carnal existence, as if it were blood, along with a way of life in accordance with philosophy,[54] and indeed all of our natural powers, consecrated to God and consumed in the fire of the grace of the Spirit, rising up to divine rest.[55]

65.25. Thus when we look upon each of the symbols presented to us in Scripture, as if from the summit of a mountain, that is, from the height of mystical theology, we put to death—as if they were the seven men born from the children of Saul—the transitory and temporal transmission of the law, that is, the earthly mind concerned solely with the literal word of Scripture, so that "it has no place anywhere within the territory of

---

53. Eph 6.17.
54. I.e., the practical philosophy of asceticism.
55. The ultimate union of the human person and God is marked by the rest, repose, and cessation of all natural human powers and capacities, as the person is ecstatically drawn out of himself into the greater reality of God; cf. above, Qu. 22; Qu. 60; and *QD.* 73 (CCSG 10:55–56); *Amb.* 7.12–13; 10.28, 42–45 (DOML 1:89–93; 191, 213–21); *Cap. theol.* 1.54 (PG 90:1104AB); *Opusc.* 20 (PG 91:228B–229B); and Larchet, *Divinisation*, 527–33.

Israel,"[56] that is, within the mode of spiritual contemplation. For in truth such a mind,[37] by limiting the law solely to the flesh, brings to an end, drives away, and destroys the principles and thoughts that are according to nature. And it honors as divine the "dishonorable passions,"[57] which are the very things that thoughts according to nature, receiving permission from the "law of the spirit,"[58] kill and "put to death in that place at the beginning of the harvest of barley."[59] The "beginning of the harvest of barley" is the gathering of the virtues of practical philosophy[60] according to the measure of reason, during which it is natural to put to death whatever is terrestrial in Scripture, and to remove completely every earthly movement. For at the very same time that a person[38] advances in a reasonable manner to the philosophy of virtues,[61] he will in that same moment have naturally transferred the interpretation of Scripture to the Spirit, worshiping God in practice through his sublime contemplations "in the newness of the Spirit, and not in the oldness of the letter."[62] The latter, however, with its ignoble reception of the law according to sense perception pandering to the body, will only make him, as happened with the Jews, a cultivator of the passions and a worshiper of sin. For one must, through ascetic practice and thoughts according to nature, know how to handle the impassioned and corporeal understanding of the law, just as the word of Scripture itself teaches: "And the king took the two sons of Rizpah, the daughter of Aiah, the concubine of Saul, and the five sons of Saul's daughter Merab, whom she had borne to Adriel, and gave them into the hand of the Gibeonites."[63] The "hand" of the Gibeonites is the virtuous re-

---

56. 2 Kgs 21.5.
57. Rom 1.26.
58. Rom 8.2.
59. 2 Kgs 21.9.
60. I.e., the first stage of the spiritual life, which is the purification of the passions and the acquisition of the virtues.
61. I.e., to natural contemplation in the spirit, indicating that the spiritual interpretation of the Scriptures is "natural," since it conforms both to human nature and the nature of Scripture itself.
62. Rom 7.6.
63. 2 Kgs 21.8–9.

alization in practice of natural thoughts, and it is this hand that puts to death the sons of Rizpah, Armoni and Mephibosheth, that is, the activity of the passions, begotten from the corporeal learning of the law limited solely to its verbal pronunciation, and the unrestrained movement of lascivious thoughts. It also puts to death the five sons of Merab, who signify the five lascivious modes of the five senses, which are begotten from licentiousness derived from the unnatural use of the senses. These five are naturally put to death all at once, on the mountainous height of spiritual contemplation, "at the beginning of the barley harvest," which signifies the prelude of virtuous practice or of natural pious contemplation. And this is accomplished by every intellect that is lofty and elevated according to God, which simultaneously slays both the activity of the passions and the shameful movement of thoughts, in addition to which it also slays lascivious modes that abuse the activity of the senses.

65.26. "And all seven of them," it says, "fell together in that same place. And they were put to death in the days of the harvest, at the beginning of the harvest of barley. And Rizpah the daughter of Aiah took sackcloth and spread it out for herself on a rock, until rain poured down on them from God."[64] Rizpah, as I have said, when translated means "course of the mouth," which is the teaching of the law solely in terms of pronouncing its words. After the death of the passions born from her, and after the manifestation[39] on high of natural contemplation in the heart of those formerly beholden to her, she unfolds repentance, like sackcloth, on the rock[40] of the word[65] of faith in Christ. And through repentance she takes thought for the spiritual ordinances of Christ, and through memory holds before her eyes, day and night, as if they were her children, the former carnal way of life according to the law, until the waters of God fall from heaven, that is, until the divine knowledge of the Scriptures is sent down from the height of spiritual contemplation, which both extinguishes the passions and renews the virtues. For it is natural that the learning of the law, having by means of repentance advanced to Christ, who is the true and

---

64. 2 Kgs 21.9–10.
65. Or "principle."

solid rock,⁶⁶ will receive the divine rain of the spiritual knowledge of the Scriptures, according to the precept of David, that is, the intellect strong in vision, for it says: "And they did everything commanded by the king. After these things, God heard the cry of the earth."⁶⁷

65.27. For when the divine Scriptures are studied and learned according to the commandment of David the king (that is, according to the spiritual law or the intellect strong in vision), it is only natural that the sackcloth of repentance will be transferred through the practice of the virtues to the rock, which is Christ. When this is done, it calls out for the rain of divine knowledge; it cannot but ask God to hear the cry of the earth of its heart,⁶⁸ begging him to grant the divine rain of spiritual gifts, which will provide an abundance of the fruits of righteousness, and to end the former famine of ignorance of divine things, and to make the land overflow with spiritual goods, so that the soul might be filled with wheat, wine, and oil.⁶⁹ Wheat,[41] so that it might be supported by the principle of practical knowledge; wine, so that it might delight in the divine and renewing desire of voluntary, unifying ardor for God;⁷⁰ and oil, so that the face of its virtues—made gentle, smooth, transparent, and radiant—might shine by means of the mode and principle of dispassion.⁷¹

65.28. But let us also, as did the great David, remove Saul from the entire territory of Israel, that is, from the earthly and corporeal institution of the law, or the manner of Jewish observance, or the more corporeal and superficial understanding of the whole of Scripture based solely on the written word. Let us remove these things, I say, from every mode of our contemplative mystagogy, and let us draw near to the spiritual divinization of the realities grasped by the intellect. And let us acquire the Gibeonites, that is, the natural principles of beings—which were preserved inviolate by Jesus,⁷² the true inheritor of the di-

66. Cf. 1 Cor 10.4.
67. 2 Kgs 21.14.
68. See above, Qu. 63.15.
69. Ps 103.15.
70. Cf. 1 Cor 10.4.
71. Cf. Ps 103.15.
72. Cf. Jos 9.20.

vine promises—for it was because Saul killed them that God held back the rain of mystical knowledge. And so through these same Gibeonites, that is, through natural contemplation, let us put to death, as if they were the seven descendants of Saul, the impassioned, materialistic, and ephemeral interpretation of the law, which Rizpah naturally gives birth to, insofar as she is the "course of the mouth" (which is the corporeal learning of the law), and Merab too, whose name means "filling of the throat," that is, the delight of the belly. The former gave birth to Mephibosheth and Armoni (whose names mean "shame of the mouth" and "anathema on them," respectively), that is, the habitual state and activity of the passions. The latter, on the other hand, gave birth to five sons by Adriel, that is, by the contemplative part of the soul, from which arose the impassioned five modes that abuse our senses. By putting these to death through natural contemplation, we propitiate God's wrath, and we are conducted from the letter to the spirit, calling down the divine rain of knowledge and enjoying the fruits of righteousness that so richly arise from it. For when the letter of the law, like a kind of Saul, or the materialistic interpretation born of the letter among the earthly minded, like the children and offspring of Saul, are elevated by us through natural contemplation to the height of spiritual mystagogy, then every corporeal, superficial, and, strictly speaking, earthly understanding of the law is put to death. If, that is, together with God we too have hated Saul, "rejecting him from reigning in Israel,"[73] that is, if we have rejected the plainly carnal mode of Scripture, which is Judaism, preventing it from reigning over our intellective power and subjugating it to the slavery of the flesh.

65.29. For it is necessary that Saul, in other words the corporeal institution of the law, be hated and expelled from the kingdom, along with "Agag, king of the Amalekites,"[42] and the best of his "sheep, oxen, and vineyards,"[74] and the olive tree, by which I mean the things that incite and create anger and desire, and the causes of bodily delight. And he himself[75]

73. 1 Kgs 16.1.
74. 1 Kgs 15.8–9.
75. I.e., Agag.

must be brought alive[76] into the land of promise, which is to say that the calf, the earthly mind of the flesh,[77] must be brought to divine knowledge, by which I mean the heart. For Agag means "calf," perhaps the one which that foolish and unthinking Israel[43] fashioned in the wilderness and made into a god,[78] preferring the pleasure of their stomachs to divine worship. This is the calf that Moses and Samuel destroyed: the former, by grinding it into dust and scattering it under the water;[79] the latter, by slaying it with a spiritual sword; that is, by the living and active grace of holy baptism (for this is Moses), and obedience to God by keeping the commandments (for this is Samuel). For Moses means "scattered in the water,"[80] and Samuel means "obedience to God," which is true faith and a godly life.

65.30. Thus the grace of baptism is of a nature to destroy the power of sin, that is, the "mind of the flesh,"[81] and active obedience to the divine commandments puts it to death by the "sword of the Spirit,"[82] which is the word of divine knowledge in the spirit, crying out mystically to the passion of sin, as the great Samuel did to Agag: "As your sword has made women childless, so today will your own mother be childless among women."[83] Indeed, the passion of gluttony, with its smooth thoughts of pleasure, has, like a sword, rendered many virtues childless. It kills, for example, the seeds of chastity by intemperance; it destroys the equity of justice by greed; it divides the natural continuity of mutual love by self-love; and, to state the matter succinctly,[44] the passion of gluttony is destructive of all the offspring of virtue. And, as I said, this passion can be destroyed only by the grace of baptism and a way of life obedient to the commandments of God. This is why God repents of having anointed this law—taken liter-

---

76. 1 Kgs 15.8.
77. Rom 8.6.
78. Cf. Ex 32.4.
79. See above, Qu. 16.2, 6–7.
80. Cf. Ex 32.2–3.
81. Rom 8.6.
82. Eph 6.17.
83. 1 Kgs 15.33.

ally and productive of this passion—to reign as a king in Israel,[84] and so transfers the royal power to David, that is, to the spiritual law of the Gospel, or, in other words, to the son of Jesse, whose name means "work of God."[85]

65.31. The holy Gospel is the offspring of this work, for it is the work that God himself accomplished through the flesh, which will possess the kingdom for infinite ages; a kingdom in which we possess indestructible joy and exultation, as if it were the day of an endless, unwaning sun. For it says: "This is the day that the Lord has made: let us rejoice and be glad in it."[86] When it says "day," it means the grace of the Gospel, or the mystery that grants us this grace, in which all of us, according to the divine Apostle, "should, as if in the day, walk decently" in knowledge and truth.[87] For Christ is the Day of eternal light, in which all who believe in Him must live decently through the virtues. For Christ alone was born in the flesh without seed according to God's plan, and He innovated the laws established within nature,[88] which He "prepared before the face of all peoples; a light for revelation to the Gentiles, and the glory of the people of Israel."[89] For truly our Lord is the light of the Gentiles, for through true knowledge He opens the eyes of their minds, which had been covered by the darkness of ignorance; and He prepared Himself as a good example of a virtuous and divine way of life for the faithful people, becoming for them a model and prototype of the face of virtue. And by looking to Him as the "initiator of our salvation,"[90] and by imitating Him as much as lies within our power, we accomplish the virtues through practice. But God the Word is also the "glory of the people of Israel," for through mystical contemplation He brightens the intellect by means of the divine light of knowledge. Or perhaps by "peoples" Scripture is referring to those principles that are

84. Cf. 1 Kgs 15.35.
85. Or, "creation (ποίησις) of God."
86. Ps 117.24.
87. Rom 13.13.
88. For an extended discussion of the "innovation of nature" in the Incarnation, see *Amb.* 41 (DOML 2:102–21); cf. *Amb.* 5.6–7 (DOML 1:37–39).
89. Lk 2.31–32.
90. Heb 2.10.

according to nature, while their "face" is the true and infallible belief[91] concerning beings, the "preparation" for the knowledge of which is the Word Himself, since He is the creator of nature. The "Gentiles" are the passions contrary to nature, which He uncovers when they were hidden, granting the light of knowledge, and completely expelling them from nature. And the Word is the "glory of Israel," for He purges unnatural passions from the intellect, and adorns it with principles according to nature, and crowns it with the immutable diadem of divinization. For the true "glory of Israel" is the deliverance from passions contrary to nature, the establishment of principles according to nature, and the acquisition of good things that transcend nature.

65.32. The person who receives this spiritual David, even if he is envied by Saul, is not taken captive but, quite to the contrary, because of his great love of human beings (inasmuch as he has been delivered from the passions)—and even though he is "hated"[92]—he takes up the harp of the Spirit and heals his enemy, who was being tormented by a wicked spirit,[93] and restores him to his right mind, releasing him, as if from a wicked demon, from the evil convulsions of the earthly mind. For whoever out of envy hates and spreads malicious accusations about a person who struggles to live a life of virtue and who has distinguished himself by the abundance of his spiritual knowledge, is Saul, tormented by a wicked spirit, and cannot bear the honorable reputation of one who is his superior in virtue and knowledge,[94] and so rages against him all the more, since he cannot lay a hand on his benefactor. Quite often he will harshly persecute his most beloved Jonathan,[95] by which I mean the innate voice of the conscience, when it reproves his unjust hatred and when in its love of truth it recounts the good deeds of the man he hates,[96] as happened long ago with that

---

91. Playing on the "glory" (δόξα) of Israel and the "belief" or "notion" (δόξα) regarding beings.
92. Cf. 1 Kgs 16.14–23.
93. Cf. 1 Kgs 16.14.
94. Cf. 1 Kgs 18.8–9.
95. Cf. 1 Kgs 20.30–33.
96. 1 Kgs 19.4.

foolish Saul, to whom Samuel said: "You have done a foolish thing, for you have transgressed my commandment, which was commanded of you from God."[97]

65.33. Saul, as I said a moment ago, is the written law, or the Jewish people who live according to it. For inasmuch as they are mutually entangled in an earthly understanding, the Spirit of God—which is spiritual contemplation and knowledge—remains distant from both. In its place comes a wicked spirit, that is, a mind mired in material concerns, assailing those caught in the cycle of generation and corruption with successive disturbances and turmoil, tormenting them, as if with convulsions, through the instability of their thoughts. For the law, understood in an earthly way solely in relation to the letter, produces convulsions, being agitated by a thousand contradictions, and containing no agreement within itself. And the Judaizing intellect, reduced to near-madness by the unstable whirling about of material things, necessarily comes to possess an inner disposition that is equally unstable and changing. When, however, the David who by nature is the true musician, our Lord Jesus, charms both the law and the Jew through the spirit of cognitive contemplation, he makes what was earthly spiritual, and transforms faith into belief. For the law and the Jewish people, like Saul, are subject both to convulsions and to soundness of mind. The law suffers convulsions when, as I said, it is taken in an earthly way; and the Jew suffers convulsions whenever he wishes to worship God in an earthly way. But the law is sound when it is understood spiritually, and the Jew is likewise sound when he passes from corporeal observances to the spiritual worship of God.

65.34. It is worth noting that Saul kills those who are being saved by Jesus, because the letter is of a nature to kill those who acquire the spirit of Scripture. This is why God repents of anointing the literal law to rule as a king in Israel, inasmuch as the Jews received it in a carnal manner, and so instead He gives the power of the kingdom to the spirit, which is close to the letter but is a good that transcends the letter. "And I shall give," it says, "the kingdom to one who is close to you but better

97. 1 Kgs 13.13.

than you."[98] Just as David was close to Saul, so too was the spirit clearly bound to the letter of the law, but is of a nature to be manifested only after the death of the letter.[45]

65.35. Let us, then, implore the intelligible David[46] to strike the harp of spiritual contemplation and knowledge, and make it resound in our intellects, which are convulsed by material things, and expel the wicked spirit that diverts our senses toward material things, so that we might be able to understand the law spiritually, and find the mystical meaning buried within it, and make it our abiding possession and provision on our journey to eternal life. Otherwise, we will have but a symbolic law, loaned to us, as it were, in written letters,[47] and thus be deprived of the spiritual knowledge given by grace, and, like those who cannot see, we will be content with mere questions about divine realities, but all the while deprived of the true, direct, and brilliantly luminous vision of the mystical words of Scripture. For when translated into Greek, the name "Saul" conveys both of these meanings. In addition to what has already been said, his name means "given as a loan" and "question," which is exactly what the written law is. First, because it is not a possession that belongs to nature; neither is it in any way coextensive with natural existence. Second, because it sets us in motion toward true knowledge and original wisdom, for we do not believe that a mere question alone constitutes understanding of the archetype of the divine realities that we seek, but rather that it is only through the sensible symbols of the law, as if through a kind of question, that we hasten toward the understanding of the good things of God, so that we might cease being interested in asking questions (which very often contain the possibility of error), and come to be in the truth of the things we have been seeking, being transformed by the blessedness found within them, unchangeably manifested within us through participation, and making its own form the distinguishing mark of our life in Christ Jesus, our God and Savior, to whom be glory unto the ages. Amen.

---

98. 1 Kgs 15.28.

Scholia

[1] The intellect, having been thoroughly purified through the virtues, is of a nature to be taught the principles of the virtues, fashioning into its own face the knowledge that emerges from them, and which bears the characteristic mark of the divinity. For by itself every intellect is without any form or features that might characterize it, but rather possesses a form that has been assumed either from the spiritual knowledge constituted through the virtues, or from the ignorance that is an accompanying feature of the passions.

[2] Whoever receives as the form of his intellect the divine knowledge in the spirit that emerges from the virtues, is said to have suffered or experienced divine realities, for he did not acquire this knowledge naturally according to his mere existence, but rather by grace according to participation. But whoever does not receive such knowledge through grace, even if he says something pertaining to such knowledge, does not know, based on his own experience, the meaning or power of what he says, for mere learning does not bestow the actual condition of knowledge.

[3] Well did he say that in this passage Scripture is referring to Saul, since in other passages of Scripture Saul is understood in many different ways, each one naturally corresponding to the contemplation arising from the literal narrative.

[4] In the same way, he says, that someone who couples with a concubine has not entered into lawful marriage, so too whoever pursues the learning of the law in a corporeal manner has not entered into lawful marriage with it, and from it gives birth to adulterated teachings that corrupt life together with the flesh.

[5] Whoever receives the teaching of Scripture, he says, with a view toward the body, and from Scripture is taught to commit actual sin in practice, to think about sin in his mind, to pursue pleasures and intemperate couplings, and to envy, is taught from the letter of the law to loathe the whole of God's creation.

[6] This is a contemplation according to another approach, according to which the world is called "anathema," insofar as

it is a place of condemnation, which is borne by the penchant for passions of a person who in his intellect does not make the passage from the law to the spirit.

[7] Whatever we are disposed to be attached to, he says, is what we will also dwell on in our intellect.

[8] According to another contemplation, "anathema" is also the movement of the passions that does not contain an image. "Shame of the mouth" is the movement of the intellect that gives passion a perceptible form, and which through conceptualization provides the passion with suitable material.

[9] Whoever has been persuaded that corporeal pleasure according to the law is a divine commandment gladly takes gluttony as his wife and reckons her to be a gift from God. From such a union are born modes of abusive thought and conduct that defile the activity of the senses.

[10] This is a brief summary of what had been previously considered, showing that whoever understands the law in a corporeal manner makes his study of Scripture a concubine, giving birth to the habitual state of the passions and their activity. He cohabits with gluttony as if it were something divine, and generates modes of abusive thought and conduct that pollute the senses, leading to the destruction of the natural principles and seeds[99] present within beings.

[11] Whoever remains, he says, with the symbols of the law, is not able to see with his mind the nature of beings, or to acquire the principles that the Creator placed essentially within beings, owing to the difference of the symbols from the nature of beings.

[12] The principles of nature that "carry wood" become material for the knowledge of divine things; when they "carry water," they cleanse the passions and circulate vital spiritual energy.

[13] The one who submits himself solely to the letter of the law both rejects the principles of beings and despises the salvation of the Gentiles.

[14] On the level of contemplation, he says that Armoni and Mephibosheth are matter and form, while the five sons of Mer-

---

99. I.e., σπέρματα.

QUESTION 65   551

ab are the fivefold abuse of the senses. When they are all joined together, that is, when the senses are combined with matter and form for the union of the law with the flesh, then anyone who limits his intellect to the letter of the law will bring about carnal passion and destroy natural principles.

[15] According to the principle of existence, passion and nature can by no means mutually coexist.

[16] Whoever does not believe, he says, that Scripture is spiritual, does not perceive his lack of true knowledge.

[17] Whenever David, he says, is understood as the law, emphasizing the letter according to the Jews, his name is interpreted to mean "contempt" since he hands over the divine precepts to the flesh. According to Christians, however, placing emphasis on the spirit, his name means "strength of vision," on account of his intellective contemplation of knowledge.

[18] The spirit, he says, is the soul of Scripture, and the letter is its body.

[19] He calls the three years "three laws," namely, the written law, the natural law, and the law of grace, which are mutually connected.[100] Thus whoever apprehends the law in a corporeal manner does not nourish his soul by the virtues; and whoever does not apply himself to the principles of being does not honorably focus his intellect on the multiform wisdom of God; and whoever does not know the great mystery of grace does not rejoice in the hope of future divinization. From this it follows that deficiency in the spiritual contemplation of the written law will result in a lack of multiform wisdom in the understanding of the natural law, which will assuredly result in ignorance of divinization, which is a gift of grace according to the new mystery.

[20] Whoever does not understand the law spiritually—even if the law is dead to him insofar as he does not adhere to its

---

100. Here the scholiast has changed the order of the three laws from the order given in the text, placing the written law first, followed by the natural law. This would seem to correspond to the three stages of spiritual ascent: namely, the practice of the virtues (here understood as keeping the commandments of Scripture); the contemplation of nature; and divinization. Without fulfilling the commandments of Scripture, one cannot attain to the contemplation of the *logoi* in nature, or to union with the incarnate Logos.

corporeal observances, but nonetheless clings to base conceptions concerning the law—fosters the children and offspring of Saul, on account of whom he is tormented by the famine of ignorance.

[21] Just as the face is the distinguishing feature of each individual, so too does spiritual knowledge expressly distinguish the divine, and it is this knowledge which is sought by the person who is said to "seek the face of God."[101]

[22] Whoever fattens the flesh according to the letter of the law by means of bloody sacrifices possesses a "desired ignorance," receiving the commandment solely to indulge his pleasures.

[23] Whoever, he says, worships in a corporeal manner according to the law begets actual sin as if it were matter, and in a material manner gives shape to the form of his inner assent to sin by indulging the pleasures of his senses. But the one who receives the law spiritually puts to death, on the height of contemplation by means of natural thoughts, the activity of sin as if it were matter. At the same time, he also puts to death the assent to sin, which is its form, along with the modes that abuse the senses for the sake of pleasure, as if they were the sons and grandsons of the literal sense of the law alone.

[24] Without natural contemplation no one can recognize that the symbols of the law are incongruous with divine realities.

[25] He understands the phrase "exposure to the sun" to mean revealing—through contemplation on the height of spiritual knowledge—the letter of the law to be dead.

[26] He takes the "territory of Israel" to mean every principle and mode of spiritual contemplation, in which the corporeal transmission of the law has absolutely no place.

[27] The spirit, he says, is productive of life, while the letter is destructive of life. From this it follows that it is not possible for the letter and the spirit to operate in the same way, just as it is not possible for the source of life and the source of corruption to coexist.

[28] The prepuce, he says, is natural, and everything natural

---

101. Cf. Ps 104.4.

is the work of God's creation. If something is a work of God's creation, then it is also exceedingly good, according to the words that say: "And God saw all that He created, and behold it was exceedingly good."[102] The law, on the other hand, which commands that the prepuce be removed by circumcision as something unclean, introduces God as correcting his own work by means of artifice—but even to think of such a thing is the greatest impiety. Whoever, then, approaches the symbols of the law in a natural way, knows that God does not correct nature by means of artifice, but instead commands us to circumcise the passible part of the soul, which is subject to reason (which is indicated figuratively through the removal of part of the body), which knowledge is of a nature to set aside in practice through the courage of the will. For the priest who performs circumcision signifies knowledge that possesses, as if it were a knife, the courage of reason taking action against the passions. And thus when the spirit abounds, the corporeal transmission of the law is removed.

[29] This is a definition of the mystical legislation concerning the Sabbath, which sets forth that of which the Sabbath consists mystically; and the nature of its spiritual principle; and how it is the cessation of the passions; and the movement of the intellect around the nature of beings.

[30] Here he says that self-control is the work of providence, inasmuch as it purges the voluntary passions, while patient endurance is the accomplishment of judgment, inasmuch as it ranges itself against involuntary trials.

[31] Note how the law destroys those who understand it in a corporeal manner, persuading them to "worship the creature instead of the Creator,"[103] and to think that creatures by nature are worthy of veneration, being ignorant of the One who created them.

[32] In his teaching concerning the mystery of Pentecost, in which he mystically initiates one into the spiritual significance of the things disclosed through the feast, he called God "Pentecost." This is because the monad, remaining stable after the con-

---

102. Gn 1.31.
103. Rom 1.25.

centration[104] back into itself after seven hebdomads, constitutes a unit of fifty,[105] and, again, when by processions it returns to itself and becomes a decad multiplied by the pentad, it produces a unit of fifty, being the beginning and the end of the things that emerge from it—the beginning, as prior to all quantity, and the end, as transcending all quantity. In the same way, God, he said, who is analogous to the monad according to a figurative likeness, is also the beginning and the end of beings, and is their Principle, "in whom all things subsist."[106] He is the Beginning, because He is prior to all essence and motion, that is, time and nature. He is the End, because He transcends all essence and motion. And He is the Principle, because He is the providential cause of all things, as well as the Cohesion holding them together as a kind of underlying form, according to which each being has its abiding permanence in its own proper principle.

But when times and ages, to which, he says, the hebdomad is analogous, will reach their limit, God will then be absolutely and uniquely singular, apart from the intermediation of necessary conditions,[107] that is, places and times, holding together in Himself in a true union the existence of beings among those who are being saved, that is, created nature, which he likened to the pentad, not only because of the five senses to which nature is subject but also because of universal knowledge, which encompasses the whole of intellective and rational beings as well as those beings possessing sense, life, and existence in true knowledge.

Thus there will come a time when the nature of beings among those being saved will cease to rest in a place or move in time, because nature will transcend the things that came into being because of it (that is, time and place), on account of the true conjunction with God (for whom nature was created). For nature—having reckoned God Himself, according to the principle of providence, into a proper quality for itself by the decad

---

104. I.e., συνέλεξις; cf. Dionysios *DN* 4.14 (160, line 14; 713A); ibid., 4.9 (153, line 11; 705A).
105. I.e., Pentecost.
106. Col 1.17.
107. On this phrase, see above, Qu. 55.3.

of commandments, that is, the mark proper to divinization given by grace—will be liberated from the stasis of circumscription in place and from the change of motion in time, and will receive as an ever-moving rest the infinite enjoyment of divine realities, and, as a movement in repose, the insatiable appetite for them.

[33] That is, space and time, without which nothing in this world is born, or lives, or moves; wherefore the Greeks call them TA ΩN ANEY, "the things without which," that is, space and time.[108]

[34] In the seventh month, three feasts are celebrated, namely, the feast of the Trumpets, Atonement, and the Building of Tents. Of these, the trumpet is a figure of the law and the prophets and the knowledge they proclaim. Atonement is the symbol of the reconciliation of God to human beings through the Incarnation, because, having voluntarily assumed the condemnation of the one condemned, He abolished the enmity that had been established against him. The feast of the Tents, finally, is the prefiguration of the resurrection and the transformation of all toward immutability.

[35] The person who takes joy in mere blood sacrifices, he says, prepares those who sacrifice to be zealous for the passions, because he himself is filled with passions. For whoever offers genuine worship rejoices in what brings joy to what he worships.

[36] The Word, he says, recognizes as sacrifices the slaughter of the passions and the offering of our natural powers. Of these latter, the ram is a figure of reason, the ox is the symbol of anger, and the goat signifies desire.

[37] The earthly understanding of Scripture, dominating the soul, rejects the natural principles and casts them off completely by the misuse of its own natural powers.

[38] As soon as someone ceases, he says, receiving Scripture in a sensual way oriented toward the body, he naturally hastens in his intellect to the spirit, spiritually enacting those things

---

108. This scholion is found only in Eriugena's Latin translation (CCSG 22:320, lines 168–71); Laga and Steel believe it was written by Eriugena (CCSG 7:ci).

that, when done in a corporeal manner by the Jews, provoke the wrath of God.

[39] Exposure to the sun, he says, is the manifestation of what the passions suffer when they are defeated by the sublime thoughts of nature through sublime contemplation.

[40] The teaching of the law concerning the body, he says, seeing that the corporeal ideas concerning the law have died through repentance, adheres closely to the word of Christ, and receives like rain the heavenly illuminations of knowledge.

[41] He said that wheat is the support of the soul, since it represents practical knowledge. Wine gladdens the heart of man[109] since it produces ardent desire for God. Oil, he said, fills the face with gladness since it is characteristic of spiritual grace to brighten the intellect through dispassion.

[42] Amalek is gluttony, which is the king of the earthly mind. His oxen and sheep are the materials that nourish the passions; his vineyard is the rash movement of anger; his olive tree is the smoothness of pleasure that inflames desire. These are the things that a person who adheres to the corporeal law must transport to the land that is holy, that is, to the habitual state of divine piety, for which he will receive, as if in payment, a turning back to God.

[43] He called the Jewish people "foolish" for their disbelief in God, and "lacking in understanding" for their evil deeds, which means they are impious and sinful.

[44] The passion of gluttony, he says, is of a nature to kill the divine offspring of the virtues. But the passion itself is killed by the grace of faith and obedience to the divine commandments through the principle of knowledge.

[45] When someone kills the corporeal meaning in the letter of the law, he simultaneously receives its inner *logos* like a king reigning in the spirit.

[46] He took David to signify the Lord, the Gospel, the spiritual law, knowledge, contemplation, purposeful practice, and the new people, and, by means of many other modes of contemplation analogous to the passages, he adapted the contemplation to the underlying need of each.

---

109. Cf. Ps 103.15.

QUESTION 65

[47] The one who possesses the figures but not the archetypes of the mysteries has a question about, but not knowledge of, spiritual illumination. Such a person has taken out a loan at interest, namely, the experience of the sensible symbols of the law. His soul, however, suffers a famine of the spirit, and is blind with respect to the question that might have guided him to true knowledge.

INDICES

GENERAL INDEX

Abel, 159, 257, 264, 290, 291n34, 295
Abraham, 42, 157–58, 160, 190, 191n7, 194, 224, 239, 258, 265, 364, 365, 381, 414
Absalom, 370–71, 386
absurdity, 530n29
acrostic, 10–11, 402n1
activity, divine, 123, 150–53, 194, 196n6, 198, 199, 340n24, 347, 351, 375, 418, 458, 463
activity, human, 76n16, 82, 101n6, 153, 155, 179, 197, 220, 228, 233, 253, 284, 288–89, 294, 314, 329, 332, 334, 340n24, 352, 353, 361n25, 403, 407, 468, 524, 526
Adam, 8, 11, 22n59, 25n75, 28n85, 45, 83n39, 87n55, 94n2, 106–7, 143–46, 192, 224, 236, 241, 242n5, 243, 245, 249–51, 290, 295, 306n6, 308n10, 347, 391, 428n11, 437–43, 454, 455, 456, 480, 488, 489, 491, 510, 531n31
adoption, 108–10, 128–29, 159, 442, 444, 481, 492
Adriel, 519, 523, 530, 532, 540, 543
Aelian, 309n18, 310n20
Agag, 543–44
age, 70, 112, 114, 150–56, 179, 224, 225, 261, 328, 351, 359, 366, 373, 379, 383, 387, 419–21, 429, 445
Ahab, 250
Ahaz, 299, 301, 304
Ahithophel, 386
Aiah, 519, 532, 540, 541

allegory, 26n79, 47, 48, 50, 172, 223, 319, 342, 350
alphabet, 30, 364
altar, 215–16, 377n70, 456
Amalek, 556
Amalekites, 543
Ambigua to John, 7n15, 11, 13n36, 14, 32, 58, 70n6, 228
Ammonios, 44n139
Amnon, 159
Amoz, 297, 299, 301, 304
anagogy, 14n38, 45–47, 48–49, 50n158, 74, 88, 106, 163, 164n5, 223, 232, 292, 297n3, 325, 331, 348, 473, 487, 495, 498, 508, 531n32
analogy, 17, 18, 28, 29, 30, 31, 43n135, 48, 71n8, 179, 233, 340n24, 378, 416n26, 430, 466, 504n65, 508, 527, 554, 556
Anastasios (disciple of Maximos the Confessor), 56n177
Anastasios of Sinai, 7, 54, 219n6
angels, 30n94, 47, 88n57, 120–21, 134–36, 157, 160, 161, 162, 163, 168, 179, 249, 284, 290, 293, 29, 298, 301, 303, 314, 323, 329, 394, 415, 448, 449, 531
anger, 24, 26n79, 85, 94n1, 131, 133, 156, 186n23, 270n13, 302, 313, 327, 337n16, 349, 367–68, 369n48, 377n70, 382, 425, 457, 515, 543, 555, 556. *See also* irascibility *and* spiritedness
Antichrist, 49
Antony, St., 30

561

GENERAL INDEX

Aphrodite, 377n70
apophatic theology, 29, 36, 76n16, 166n17, 169, 356n3
aporia, 42–45
aptitude, 289n27, 294–95
Ararat, 287n23
Aristotle, 44, 82n35, 82n37, 152n19, 215n4, 244n7, 248n6, 276n33, 289n27, 496n41
Armenia, 287
Armoni, 522, 529, 541, 543, 550
Asaph, 281–82
Asbasareth, 389, 390, 391, 396
asceticism, ascetic practice, 5, 25, 26–27, 45, 46n144, 59, 73, 77, 95n4, 100, 101n6, 101n10, 107, 109, 132, 145n13, 162, 164, 166, 167, 169, 174, 180, 181, 185, 187, 188, 213, 220, 222, 227, 229, 253–54, 255, 258, 260, 304, 311, 314, 319–20, 322–24, 325, 328, 329, 331, 334, 335–36, 347, 371, 373–74, 376, 390, 392, 397, 404, 405, 410, 481, 482, 483, 484, 485, 491, 516, 525, 533, 539n54, 540
Ashpur, 285
Ashur, 283, 297, 301–2, 304
Assyria, 174, 287, 301, 389, 390, 508
Athanasios of Alexandria, 30n93, 191n12, 192n18, 245n8, 328n18
attributes, divine, 42, 70, 202, 378.
  See also properties
Ava, 390, 391, 394, 396

Babel, Tower of, 111, 249
Babylon, 172, 174, 175, 176, 177–78, 180, 284, 334n5, 350, 359, 366, 380, 390, 394
Balthasar, 178
baptism, 25, 41n30, 102, 108–10, 128, 145n13, 200–201, 259, 438, 442–44, 474n40, 544
Barsanouphios and John, 7
Baruch, 178n26
Basil of Caesarea, 7, 38n119, 53, 81n34, 88n57, 95n5, 97n4, 194n22, 318n6, 357n5, 416n27, 471n30, 474n40, 496n41, 529n26
beauty, 33, 69–70, 71, 72, 76, 86, 102, 117, 119, 141, 142, 164, 180, 188, 258, 260, 268, 282, 286, 292, 305, 327, 328, 329, 335, 347, 374, 375, 394, 408, 417n31, 443, 460, 468, 478, 488, 489, 491, 505, 509, 510, 522, 531
Benjamin, 389–90, 395
Bethany, 140
bile, 369
birth, 143–45, 148
blood, 135, 186, 212–14, 215–17, 230n4, 238, 447, 496, 505, 539, 555
bread, 45, 106–7, 230n4, 531

Cain, 159, 290–91, 295–96
calf, molten, 130–33, 544
camel, 355, 368, 374, 385
Cana, 230
Cappadocian *Philokalia*, 30n94, 43n134, 43n135, 192n16, 231n7, 530n29
Carmel, 267, 271, 272, 275, 276, 278
Carthage, 5, 8
Cause, God as, 28, 69, 71, 82–83, 85, 87, 92, 97n6, 98n8, 124, 125, 153, 156, 170, 171, 185, 188, 205, 227, 229, 233, 257, 258, 261, 265, 278, 289n27, 314, 320, 331, 338, 339, 345, 362, 391, 393, 396, 424, 426, 472, 483, 501, 516, 538, 554
chanters, 355, 368, 374, 375, 384
Christ, Jesus, 27n82, 100, 138, 152, 235, 242, 269, 272, 325, 326, 340, 343, 346, 362, 364, 381, 407, 451, 455, 458, 466, 491, 494, 503, 525, 547, 548
Christology, 3, 9, 17–18, 24, 49–50, 71n8, 88n57, 143–49, 150–51, 241–45, 416n26, 427–32, 436, 451–53, 479n51, 480, 536n48, 538
Church, 37, 39, 159, 186, 198, 246, 269, 273, 277, 326, 373, 374, 456,

GENERAL INDEX

465–83, 492, 494, 497, 498, 499, 502, 507, 508, 510, 513, 515, 517, 525
Clement of Alexandria, 157n6, 187n26, 204n2, 270n13, 310n20
clothing metaphors. *See* garments
confession, 268, 319, 372, 387, 389, 395, 533
Confessor, 3
conjecture, 356, 357, 463, 520
contemplation, 13–14, 25, 27, 34n108, 40, 44, 47, 59, 69, 74, 98, 100, 101, 104, 119n19, 123, 124, 131, 135, 136, 155, 165, 167, 174, 184, 185, 188, 189, 190, 202n4, 205, 217, 220, 221, 222, 225, 226, 229, 253, 254, 256, 257, 258, 263, 265, 268, 271, 272, 273, 276, 277, 278, 280, 283, 291, 297, 299, 300, 301, 302, 304, 307, 311, 314, 316, 318, 319, 320, 321, 322, 324, 325, 327, 328, 329, 331, 334, 335–36, 340, 345, 352, 355, 363, 366, 368–69, 374, 375, 379, 382, 385, 386, 387, 404–5, 406, 416, 450, 459, 468, 469, 476, 477–78, 480, 527, 528, 529, 531, 533, 541, 547
Cornelius, 182
corner, 267–69, 273–74, 277, 326
creation, 25, 26, 29–32, 33–34, 36, 83, 86, 87, 88, 90n66, 91, 93, 97–98, 105, 123–25, 126, 150, 183, 184, 185, 191, 194, 205, 233, 305–7, 310, 311, 313, 314, 316, 343, 351, 363, 393, 418n35, 432, 454, 459, 479n51, 498, 534, 536, 549, 553
curse, 74, 107, 140, 299, 354, 450, 454–55
Cuthah, 390, 394, 395
Cyril of Alexandria, 71n8, 157n6, 224n4, 271n17, 287n23, 346n53, 465n2

Darius, 335, 336, 338, 342, 350, 357, 358, 377
David, 42, 117, 157, 158, 159, 160, 177, 227, 290, 319, 326, 327, 328, 329–30, 331, 335, 342, 358, 371–72, 386, 408, 412n3, 415, 467, 503, 519, 528, 530, 532, 542, 546, 547, 548, 556
David Dishypatos, 447n37, 447n38
death, 18n52, 135, 136, 146, 147, 172, 200, 214, 219, 220, 222, 242, 243, 244, 245, 247, 251, 318, 322, 326, 337, 341, 342, 367, 370, 371, 386, 411, 419, 434, 435–43, 445, 446, 447, 455, 468, 485, 491, 492, 494, 502, 504, 519, 522
decad, 231, 288n26, 294, 295, 362, 365, 379, 380, 381, 387, 453, 458, 536, 537, 554, 555
deer, 309, 315
demons, 21–22, 24n73, 34n107, 49, 78–79, 81, 90, 92, 105, 120, 126, 145, 144–48, 168, 177, 179, 187, 223, 224, 225, 266, 269, 275, 279, 285, 288, 290, 300, 302, 304, 309, 313, 321, 322, 323, 325, 339, 346, 347, 349, 391–94, 396, 397, 400, 490, 506, 546
desire, 23–24, 44, 71, 82–83, 84, 89, 94, 95, 106, 110, 119, 131, 132, 133, 147, 148, 156, 166, 186, 194, 198, 227, 228, 236, 237, 266, 270n13, 281, 282, 292, 293, 301–2, 313, 320, 325, 327, 349, 353, 356, 360, 362, 363, 367–68, 373, 376, 378, 380, 382, 414, 417, 424, 425, 426, 430, 433, 434, 457, 459, 462, 490, 496, 497, 512, 516, 517, 543, 556
devil, 80, 149, 172–81, 239, 249–50, 251, 274, 286–87, 290, 293, 294, 301–3, 304, 323, 324, 327, 330, 342, 391, 439–40, 447, 455, 456, 457, 459, 460, 462, 463, 468, 490, 492, 500, 503–4, 515, 516, 517
diabasis, 32, 35, 46, 56n5, 74n5, 406n18, 410n29
Diadochos of Photiki, 81n34, 108n3, 403n5

Didymos the Blind, 223n3, 250n6, 344n46, 346n53, 465n2, 471n28, 530n29
Dionysios the Areopagite, 5, 31n96, 34n108, 35n112, 43n135, 46, 53, 55, 59n185, 69n2, 75n13, 77n23, 96n9, 113n3, 113n5, 120n1, 123n2, 127n3, 129n7, 143n3, 165n14, 167n18, 190n2, 213n7, 287n24, 305n3, 309n17, 312n27, 373n63, 520n4
divinization, 18, 29, 55n176, 57, 87n56, 109, 110, 114–15, 121, 128, 129, 142, 151–54, 155, 156, 206, 213, 214, 231, 234, 235, 236, 343, 346, 352, 379, 383, 417, 420, 421, 422n46, 425, 430, 431, 437, 443, 444, 447, 472, 480, 492, 499n52, 513, 527, 535, 542, 546, 551, 555
Doctrina patrum, 56n177, 227n7, 300n12
Dorotheos of Gaza, 178n25
dove, 310
dreams, 79
dyad, material, 194, 349

eagle, 309
ear, 132
earth, 45, 74, 76, 92, 106–7, 109, 172, 178, 231, 265, 270, 271, 298, 299, 302, 311, 328, 343, 371, 450, 454, 462, 477, 481, 489, 492, 514, 515, 531, 533
ecstasy, 278, 279, 367, 418, 517, 520n4
Egypt, 46n146, 111, 130, 134, 135, 176, 265, 373, 535
elements, 30, 105, 184, 481n58
Eliakim, 281
Eliaph, 159
Elias (philosopher), 215n4
Elijah, 33n106, 42n131
Elisha, 218, 221
enhypostaton, 447n38
enigma, 255–56
Enoch, 257

Enosh, 257, 264
Ephah, 368, 385
epinoia, 264n34
Epiphanios of Cyprus, 245n8, 250n6
Er, 159
Eriugena, 52n167, 54, 57, 58n180, 63n1, 91n69, 91n70, 92n71, 92n73, 110n10, 125n9, 142n10, 148n22, 149n23, 171n27, 171n30, 203n5, 217n11, 403n7
Esau, 159
Esdras, 333, 389
etymology, 50–51
Euroklydon, 506
Eusebios of Caesarea, 7, 271n17, 306n3
Evagrios, 10, 25n78, 26n79, 30, 37, 40n128, 59, 70n4, 95n5, 101n6, 107n9, 119n19, 133n14, 186n23, 202n4, 210n4, 223n3, 223n4, 283n10, 285n16, 321n14, 337n16, 361n23, 363n27, 534n41, 536n47
evil, 81–82, 85–86

faith, 101, 102, 108, 110, 112, 114, 126, 128, 135, 152, 155, 158, 159, 160, 164–67, 169, 170, 182, 183, 185, 197, 207–9, 210, 211, 215–16, 218, 221, 224, 234–35, 257, 258, 259, 272, 280, 281, 282, 292, 307, 308, 314, 315, 327, 336, 340, 342, 343–44, 345–46, 347, 349, 350, 352, 354, 376, 378, 414, 416, 417, 442, 444, 454, 462, 466, 479, 480, 481, 490, 492, 500, 507, 509, 516, 525, 547, 556
fall, 8, 21, 83, 94–95, 107, 224, 347, 428n11, 514
fantasy, 78–79, 130n5
fear, 88, 89, 94, 116–19, 134, 146, 147, 148, 272, 273, 344, 353, 373–74, 376, 388, 440, 470, 471, 472, 483, 511, 518
fig tree, 140–42
Filioque, 471n25
fishhook, 503

GENERAL INDEX 565

free choice, 108, 109, 127, 172, 173, 200, 201, 230n2, 241–44, 349, 403, 420, 426, 445, 455, 498, 506, 517
funnels, 465, 473–75, 477, 478

Galilee, 230
garments of skin, 94n2, 161n2
garments, symbolism of, 33–34, 36, 104–5, 122, 143, 527n21
gazelle, 309
Geshur, 371
Gibeonites, 519, 525
Gilead, 372
gnostic, 59, 76n15
gold, 465–66
Gomorrah, 158
grace, 16, 27, 28, 34, 42, 70, 81, 87, 91, 98, 101, 104, 108–10, 115, 120, 121, 128, 137, 138, 141, 151, 152, 153, 154, 155, 156, 159, 166, 170, 174, 175, 181, 182, 183, 196n6, 197, 198, 213, 218, 219, 221, 224, 226, 227, 229, 234, 235, 236, 240, 241, 246, 248, 259, 263, 277, 282, 317, 319, 321, 324, 331, 340, 344n47, 349, 350, 351, 352, 354, 355, 365, 372, 375, 379, 383, 393, 395, 412–26, 430, 431–32, 433, 435, 437, 441, 442, 443, 444, 446, 447, 470, 473, 474, 476, 480, 481, 488, 491, 492, 493–96, 505, 510, 512, 527, 531, 535, 537, 539, 544, 546, 549, 551, 555
grass, 106–7, 178, 179, 496
Gregory Akindynos, 447n38
Gregory Nazianzus, 7n15, 8n20, 10n26, 13n37, 31, 32n99, 53, 75n11, 81n34, 88n57, 96n7, 96n8, 101n9, 145n13, 158n9, 183n8, 187n27, 192n13, 196n4, 202n4, 276n33, 313n29, 317n4, 323n19, 337n17, 342n37, 344n45, 356n3, 357n6, 477n47
Gregory of Nyssa, 7n15, 23n65, 37, 38n119, 53, 84n44, 86n53, 94, 95n3, 97n4, 113n5, 135n7, 194n22, 215n4, 227n7, 251n10, 282n9, 310n19, 320n13, 328n18, 356n3, 367n41, 417n31, 504n65, 514n92, 529n26, 538n51
Gregory Palamas, 447n38
Gregory Thaumaturgus, 227n7
grief, 94, 95, 148, 402–11

Habakkuk, 369, 482
Hades, 112, 245n8, 521, 528
Hadot, Pierre, 20–21
Hamath, 390, 394, 395
Hamor, 291
Harran, 258
heart, 81n34, 93, 107, 127, 129, 135, 175, 188, 199, 202n4, 207, 208, 253, 259, 263, 271, 317, 318, 319, 321, 323, 345, 370, 381, 386, 393, 454, 457, 461, 462, 477, 481, 506, 541, 542, 544, 556
hebdomad, 554
heptad, 384
hermeneutics, biblical, 13–15, 23, 37–51, 77, 96, 104, 111, 116, 120, 134, 136, 190, 202, 450, 469, 487, 520
Herod, 161
Hesychast Controversy, 57
Hesychios of Sinai, 10n26, 145n13
Hezekiah, 40n128, 42, 280–92, 297–304, 305–6, 311–13, 317–24, 326, 329, 495n40
Hilkiah, 281
Hippolytus, 178n28
Holy Spirit, 33, 38n119, 39n123, 40n128, 43, 60, 70, 73, 74, 98, 99, 101, 102, 104, 108–10, 113–15, 122, 124, 125, 127–29, 140, 153, 169, 178, 183n8, 193–94, 196–99, 225, 235, 253, 260, 262, 270, 277, 298, 336, 339–40, 341, 342, 344, 345, 346, 348, 349, 351, 353, 354, 355, 359, 361n25, 366, 369, 370, 374–75, 386, 411, 412–26, 431, 438, 441–44, 447, 458, 460, 469–

Holy Spirit (*cont.*)
73, 475, 477–78, 480–81, 492, 493, 502, 506, 520, 533, 539, 540
Holy Trinity, 26n79, 37, 98, 113, 124, 125, 191, 193–94, 221, 222, 193–94, 232, 236, 283n10, 364, 380, 431, 447n38, 451, 462
homonym, 244n7, 470n21
horse, 369–70, 386, 480
house, 101–2, 121, 158, 258, 265, 268, 276, 342, 343, 389–94, 396, 443, 456, 457, 459, 463, 467, 476
hypostasis, 71, 82n36, 150, 154, 193, 195, 227, 243, 276, 312n27, 349, 364, 427, 432, 451, 452–53, 462, 475, 479, 485

Iamblichus, 82n35, 289n27
Iconoclasts, 53n168
idol, idolatry, 36, 49, 377, 456, 484, 503, 508
ignorance, 34n107, 76n16, 80, 83–85, 88, 89, 90, 91, 92, 93, 105, 111, 114, 132, 137, 140, 168, 182, 186n23, 188, 205, 210, 211, 220, 222, 230, 238, 250–51, 260, 275, 292, 293, 299, 302, 314, 320, 322, 335, 338, 353, 391, 395, 431, 453, 456, 459–60, 462, 467, 471, 490, 497, 499, 501, 506–7, 528, 530, 542, 549, 551
illumination, 101, 153, 226, 228, 232, 299, 303, 309, 315, 323, 324, 334, 345, 346, 348, 354, 413, 416, 424, 443, 467, 469, 472, 478, 483, 484, 507, 513, 535
illumination, enhypostatic, 57, 447
image of God, 40n125, 70, 95, 133, 193, 270n13, 299, 328, 329, 348, 455, 476, 523
immutability, 73n3, 87, 90, 235, 241n2, 242, 243, 343, 352, 433, 473, 480, 498, 536, 539, 555
impression, 46n146, 130n5, 187, 191n6, 255, 288
incongruity, 530

infinity, 38–39, 77, 151, 153n22, 154, 331, 351, 387, 393, 417n31, 429, 473, 536n48
insensitivity, 70n4
intellect, 16, 17, 22n62, 25n75, 26n79, 29n91, 41, 44n137, 48, 49, 47n152, 49, 69, 71–72, 73, 76, 80, 83, 85, 86, 87, 90n65, 91, 95, 100–103, 104, 109, 117, 123, 124, 128, 130–33, 134, 135, 137, 153, 156, 161, 164–71, 173, 176, 180, 184, 185, 187–88, 191, 192, 202, 204–5, 208–9, 211, 220–21, 226, 227, 232, 233, 234, 236, 247–48, 257, 261–62, 268, 272, 273–79, 280–94, 300, 302, 306, 307–12, 314, 315, 318–20, 321, 323, 325, 328–29, 331, 334–35, 337, 338, 339, 347, 348, 349, 352, 355, 358, 361, 366–67, 371–72, 375, 377, 379, 382, 387, 390, 392, 397, 406–10, 413, 414, 416, 420, 423–24, 425, 426, 434, 458, 463, 469, 475–76, 481, 483, 485–86, 497, 500–501, 516, 517, 522–23, 527, 528–29, 530, 533, 534, 535, 542, 545–46, 549, 551
iota, 381
irascibility, 132, 228, 282, 292, 293, 302, 304, 349, 495, 496–98. *See also* anger *and* spiritedness
Irenaeos, 194n22, 481n58
Isaac, 158, 239, 258, 381
Isaiah, 196–97, 299
Ishmael, 159
Israel, 130, 132, 133, 157, 355, 533
Issachar, 187

Jacob, 30n94, 157–60, 240, 258, 265, 291, 373, 506
Jairus, 238
Jeremiah, 290, 400
Jeroboam, 160
Jerusalem, 140, 174, 178, 182, 187, 196–97, 267, 269, 273, 280, 287, 291, 293, 303, 305, 306, 312,

GENERAL INDEX

317–24, 326, 328–29, 333, 335, 339, 350, 357–59, 368, 372, 377, 383, 385, 387, 503, 507
Jeshua, 389
Jesse, 196
Jewish manner (of interpretation), 272, 298, 303, 328, 412, 467, 469, 501n58, 521, 523, 525, 526–27, 531, 540, 542, 547, 551
Jews, 36, 141, 142, 182, 202–3, 215, 269, 299, 326, 327, 328, 333n2, 330, 372, 412, 467, 481, 482, 488, 492, 501–2, 504, 505–6, 510, 513, 517, 527, 547
Joah, 281–82
Job, 177
John, evangelist, 13, 32, 33n103, 100, 104, 108, 113, 114, 118
John Chrysostom, 230, 255n1, 474n40, 514n92
John Klimakos, 53, 523n9
John of Damascus, 18n52, 79n27, 275n31
John of Skythopolis, 59n185
John the Baptist, 259
Jonah, 51, 487–514
Joppa, 51, 186–88, 489, 491–92
Jordan, 372
Josephus, 49
Joshua, 524
Judah, 43n136, 172, 180, 272, 285, 305, 317–21, 323, 326, 328–29, 331, 372, 389–90
Judea, 40n128, 174, 319, 321, 322, 325, 339, 350, 372, 387, 400
judgment, 21, 58, 82, 132, 344, 348, 397, 496
judgment and providence, 30n94, 107, 213, 327, 341, 479–80, 485, 514, 535
Judgment, Day of, 120–21, 168, 449
judgment, divine, 27n83, 111, 117, 119, 175, 180, 229, 245, 258, 318, 322, 324, 346, 352, 385, 386, 434–49, 472, 480, 485, 507, 508, 513

law, Jewish, 33n106, 39, 100, 128, 129, 137, 138–39, 140–41, 142, 182–83, 184, 189, 204–5, 215, 224, 227, 229, 238–40, 298–99, 327–28, 330–31, 366, 383, 468, 469, 492, 503, 504, 507, 519–57
law, natural, 34, 138, 177–79, 181, 226, 227, 228, 229, 308–9, 314, 315, 332, 335, 336, 357, 363, 376, 383, 458, 467, 478, 485, 510, 511, 515, 518, 527, 551. *See also* nature, law of
law, of sin, 71, 144, 290, 291, 354, 411, 446, 447
Leontios of Byzantium, 71n8
Leontios, presbyter of Constantinople, 454n15
light, 32–33, 76, 101, 109, 113, 121, 153, 170, 191, 226–29, 268, 302, 309, 315, 319, 330, 342, 346, 352, 354, 367, 374, 375, 415, 416, 447n37, 466–79, 489, 490–91, 492, 494, 500, 504–5, 507, 525, 545–46
lion, 35n112, 190, 310, 315, 327
liturgy/worship, 16n45, 41, 86, 88, 126, 230n4, 306n6
logoi, 27, 30, 32, 76n15, 87n54, 87n56, 88n58, 97n6, 105n8, 123n3, 165n12, 177n24, 185n20, 204, 205–6, 212–14, 216n9, 234, 272n18, 406n18, 407n19, 479n51, 524n11, 526n19, 551n100, 556. *See also* principles
Logos–logoi, 27, 35n110, 59, 97n6, 120n5, 165n12, 192n18, 204–6, 206n11, 212–14, 226n2, 524n12
Lot, 191
love, 24n73, 26, 75, 89, 90, 91, 110, 113, 116–18, 142, 145, 147, 156, 168, 173, 197–98, 216, 218, 220, 232–34, 236, 243, 262, 272, 280–82, 292, 293, 307, 328, 335, 338, 342, 348, 349, 352, 367, 373, 376, 379, 383, 388, 414, 417, 425, 436, 439, 454, 460, 462, 466, 476, 506, 511–12, 518, 531, 546

Magi, 307
Makarios/Symeon, 86n53, 477n48
Manasseh, 159
mantle, 104–5
Mark the Monk, 7, 108n3
Maximos the Confessor: *Amb.*,
  6n10, 7n15, 13n36, 13n37, 14n39,
  16n42, 18n50, 18n51, 18n52,
  18n53, 21n58, 23n65, 24n69,
  24n71, 25n75, 25n76, 27n82,
  27n83, 28n85, 28n86, 29n89,
  29n91, 31n97, 31n98, 32n99,
  32n100, 33n103, 33n104, 33n106,
  34n107, 34n108, 35n110, 35n111,
  36n114, 39n123, 40n125, 41n130,
  42n131, 42n132, 49n157, 55n175,
  55n176, 56, 70n3, 73n3, 74n10,
  76n14, 79n26, 81n32, 86n48,
  86n51, 87n55, 87n56, 88n57,
  89n59, 90n61, 90n66, 91n68,
  92n72, 94n1, 94n2, 95n5, 98n7,
  98n8, 100n4, 101n6, 103n14,
  104n3, 104n6, 107n6, 108n6,
  113n3, 117n8, 119n19, 120n7,
  123n2, 124n5, 124n6, 130n6,
  132n12, 133n13, 143n6, 153n21,
  153n22, 154n25, 155n30, 157n6,
  158n7, 161n2, 164n10, 165n13,
  165n14, 171n28, 173n6, 174n10,
  174n13, 177n23, 179n32, 183n8,
  184n15, 186n21, 191n6, 193n19,
  196n6, 198n12, 199n15, 203n4,
  204n2, 212n6, 223n4, 226n2,
  228n10, 231n7, 232n13, 233n15,
  256n4, 259n14, 263n30, 264n34,
  268n6, 270n13, 270n14, 274n26,
  274n28, 278n39, 282n9, 287n24,
  298n5, 300n13, 304n21, 306n6,
  310n22, 313n29, 328n18, 329n20,
  337n13, 342n37, 344n51, 356n3,
  358n9, 360n19, 361n23, 361n25,
  364n30, 367n41, 369n48, 373n63,
  375n67, 377n69, 382n78, 384n82,
  405n16, 409n27, 417n32, 418n35,
  421n43, 422n45, 422n46, 423n49,
  428n5, 428n9, 428n10, 428n11,
  432n19, 434n2, 434n4, 438n14,
  438n15, 444n33, 452n5, 472n34,
  473n35, 479n51, 481n58, 484n65,
  487n3, 495n36, 498n51, 499n52,
  520n4, 527n21, 531n31, 534n41,
  535n44, 536n47, 536n48, 538n51,
  538n52, 539n55, 545n88; *Ascet.*,
  4n5, 145n13, 232n13, 268n6; *Cap.*,
  18n51, 49n157, 504n65; *Cap. theol.*,
  17n49, 23n63, 26n80, 29n89,
  32n100, 33n104, 40n125, 49n157,
  50n158, 101n6, 153n21, 161n2,
  171n29, 202n4, 356n3, 498n51,
  527n21, 529n26, 534n41, 539n55;
  Carit., 49n156, 81n34, 83n43,
  95n5, 118n13, 119n19, 133n14,
  186n23, 200n3, 232n13, 311n25,
  361n23, 416n30, 496n45, 523n9;
  Disp. Biz., 204n2, 412n3; *Ep.*,
  9n22, 9n23, 27n81, 85n45, 157n6,
  232n13, 356n3, 361n23, 427n4,
  428n5; *Exp. Ps. 59*, 101n6, 157n6,
  319n11, 372n59, 477n48, 498n51;
  Myst., 17n49, 48n153, 50n158,
  152n18, 184n12, 205n8, 447n38,
  481n58, 482n63; *Opusc.*, 4n6,
  9n21, 147n17, 241n2, 440n22,
  470n21, 539n55; *Or. Dom.*, 147n17,
  171n29, 207n5, 270n13, 272n21,
  404n10, 431n18, 440n22; *Pyrr.*,
  18n52, 25n74, 272n21, 287n82, 147n17,
  361n23, 440n22; *QD.*, 16n42,
  18n50, 29n89, 32n100, 46n145,
  46n146, 157n6, 161n2, 186n24,
  187n27, 190n1, 191n9, 191n12,
  230n1, 231n7, 235n22, 291n34,
  305n3, 453n9, 481n58, 482n63,
  498n51, 523n9, 534n41, 539n55;
  QThp., 74n10, 129n7, 204n2,
  208n9, 215n4, 272n21, 356n3,
  520n4; *Rel. mot.*, 174n13
mean, 233, 237, 275n31, 384, 446,
  499
Melchizedek, 42, 55n176
Mephibosheth, 522, 529
Merab, 519, 529

GENERAL INDEX

metaphors, biblical, 14
Midian, 368, 385
mimesis, 41–42
mirror, 255–56
mixture, 150n4, 344, 505
monad, 26n79, 56, 185, 189, 193n21, 205, 361, 278, 295, 337, 345, 349, 353, 361, 362–64, 378–79, 380, 384, 514, 538, 553–54
Moses, 29n91, 33n106, 41, 42, 46n146, 90n66, 130, 239n33, 134, 136, 158, 224, 544
motion, 34n108, 46, 56, 69, 82, 90n61, 124, 127, 128, 134, 135, 136, 148, 166, 170, 178, 179, 185, 189, 216, 227, 235, 237, 247, 248, 250, 315, 329, 344, 350, 351n66, 361, 369, 373, 376–77, 378, 380, 384, 385, 388, 422–23, 424, 428, 429, 432, 446, 448, 463, 476, 500, 516, 529, 536n48, 537–38, 548, 554, 555. *See also* movement
movement, 26n79, 28n85, 46–47, 82, 83, 95, 98, 99, 125, 168, 194, 221, 227, 236, 241n2, 257, 265, 275, 282–83, 293, 302, 309, 313, 315, 316, 325, 331, 338–39, 360, 363, 367, 370, 379, 382, 385, 386, 388, 392, 403, 417n31, 422, 423–24, 428, 429, 449, 453, 454, 455, 457–59, 480, 490, 497, 516, 522, 529, 534, 537–41, 550, 553. *See also* motion
musicians, 368, 374, 384
myriad, 363
mystical theology, 28–29, 47n152, 165, 167, 169, 372, 387, 425, 483, 513, 539

names, etymology of, 50–51, 487–88
natural contemplation, 8, 26m79, 27–28, 29, 80, 107, 119, 123n3, 131, 132, 161, 164, 166, 167, 169, 185, 212n6, 231, 258, 270, 274, 280–96, 312, 315, 328, 331, 368, 371, 373, 386, 425, 483, 524–25,

530–32, 533, 534, 535, 540n61, 541, 543, 552
nature, book of, 30–32, 34–35
nature, human, 102
nature, law of, 34, 127, 145, 177, 179, 194, 209, 237, 335n6, 337, 338, 339, 342, 348, 349, 350, 357–58, 362, 367, 377, 447, 458, 494, 495, 512. *See also* law, natural
Nebuchadnezzar, 172, 177, 178, 181
Neoplatonism, 30n92, 37, 82n35, 117n8, 289n27, 305n3, 358n9
Nicene Creed, 249
Nicomachus of Gerasa, 231n7
Niketas of Heracleia, 56n178
Nineveh, 51, 64, 487, 494, 495, 507–8
Noah, 239, 258
numbers, symbolism of, 15–16, 231, 288–90, 294–95, 355–66

Odysseus, 95n3
Onan, 159
Origen, 7n16, 17n48, 22n61, 23n65, 25n25, 30n94, 31n98, 33n105, 37, 38n119, 40n128, 43n134, 43n135, 44n138, 46, 47n151, 50, 79n28, 102n12, 121n9, 122n2, 172n4, 186n22, 188n33, 190n1, 190n4, 191n12, 192n16, 192n18, 204n3, 231n7, 240n15, 244n7, 254n4, 264n34, 268n6, 271n17, 273n22, 287n24, 298n5, 309n18, 310n20, 310n22, 399n2, 417n32, 422n46, 432n19, 481n58, 503n64, 521n7, 530n29, 538n52

Pasch, 103n14, 536
passibility, 18, 144–49, 219, 241–45, 436–37, 439n18, 440, 458
passions, 8, 11–12, 17–18, 21–25, 26n80, 38, 71, 74n7, 76, 77–81, 83–90, 92, 94–96, 105, 106–7, 109, 116, 122, 129, 130–33, 135, 136, 144n8, 145–46, 148, 149, 161, 172–73, 176, 186, 180, 227–28, 229, 238, 248, 258, 260, 261–62,

GENERAL INDEX

passions (cont.)
  263, 265, 270, 272n18, 274–75, 277–78, 280–96, 299, 301, 302–4, 306, 309, 311–13, 314, 320, 323, 324, 325, 327, 334–35, 337–40, 342, 346–47, 350, 352, 354, 359, 360n19, 361, 363, 366, 368, 370–74, 376, 377, 378, 380, 383, 387, 390, 394, 395, 403, 406n18, 414, 425, 436, 440n21, 444, 446, 456, 457–58, 466, 481, 483, 496, 497, 499, 505, 514, 516, 520, 522–23, 524, 526, 529, 534–35, 540, 541, 544, 546, 549, 550–56
passivity, 18, 82, 144n8, 152–53, 155, 358n9, 360n19, 440n21, 446, 520n4
Passover, 100, 102, 103n14
Paul, St., 112, 114, 137, 174, 176, 196–99, 207, 218–22, 367
pentad, 554
Pentecost, 101n9, 536, 538, 553–54
Peter, St., 100, 161, 182–88, 419
Pharaoh, 177
Philo, 50, 152n19, 157n6, 191n9, 191n12, 223n3, 231n7, 270n13, 275n31, 309n17, 328n18, 358n9, 381n76
Philokalia, 56
Photios of Constantinople, 5n7, 52n167
Physiologus, 223n3, 309n17
Plato, 31n95, 44n139, 287n24, 361n23
pleasure and pain, dialectic of, 23–24, 26, 78, 83–89, 92, 93, 106, 146–47, 173, 247, 261, 266, 361n21, 402–11, 434–49, 457
Plotinus, 48n154,
Porphyry, 223n4, 274n26
practical philosophy, 26, 100–101, 107, 117, 316, 319, 328, 366, 369, 374, 420, 475, 483, 535, 539n54, 540
prayer, 166, 170, 210–11, 300, 399–401, 404

principles (*logoi*), 27, 28n85, 30n94, 32, 34n107, 47, 48n153, 59, 70, 73, 80, 87, 91, 93, 97, 102, 105, 116, 123, 124n5, 130, 132, 136, 152, 153, 154, 156, 164, 165n13, 166, 167, 170, 184, 185, 188, 189, 211, 215, 216, 219, 220, 227, 232, 234, 236, 255, 269, 270, 273, 274, 277, 278, 283n10, 284n13, 291, 300, 305–16, 323, 327, 328, 329, 331, 344, 345, 351, 353, 355–56, 359, 363, 365, 366, 368, 375, 376, 377, 379, 384, 385, 390, 392, 393, 397, 407, 408, 414, 415, 418–22, 426, 432, 449, 459, 472, 473, 475, 478, 479, 480, 482, 485, 486, 498–99, 501, 506, 514, 517, 518, 524–28, 530, 535–36, 540, 542, 545, 546, 550, 551, 555
Proclus (philosopher), 43n135, 127n3, 129n7, 152n19, 289n27, 306n3, 312n27, 373n63
Procopius of Gaza, 309n18
properties, divine, 124, 193, 195, 235
providence, 37, 79, 121, 127, 341, 365, 479
providence and judgment. *See* judgment and providence
Ps.-Basil, 308n13
Ps.-Gregory of Nyssa, 245n8
Ps.-Iamblichus, 288n26
Ps.-John of Damascus, 497n46
Pythagoras, 15

quality, 59n185, 77, 82, 88, 92n73, 117, 170, 219, 235, 236, 310, 324, 358n9, 418, 425, 555
quantity, 82, 88, 92n73, 166, 170, 205, 348, 358n9, 428n5, 432, 452, 453, 498, 554
"Questions and Responses," literature of, 6–8

reason, 22n62, 24–25, 27, 35n110, 69–71, 73, 76, 80–81, 83, 90, 92, 95, 107, 122, 127, 130, 132, 133,

GENERAL INDEX

135–36, 153n22, 156, 165, 166, 168, 170, 180, 181, 186, 224, 228, 233, 236, 247, 282, 284, 286, 292, 293, 294, 302, 315, 316, 325, 330, 334, 348, 359, 362, 366–67, 371, 374, 380, 382, 383, 387, 388, 397, 407–9, 410, 411, 413, 414, 418, 423, 424, 425, 426, 435, 463, 468, 470, 478, 483, 484, 485, 490, 496, 499–501, 511, 512, 513n89, 515, 553, 555

revelation, 18n51, 74, 115, 182, 183, 232n9, 268, 372, 387, 416–17, 478, 545

Rhapsaces, 285

rhetoric, 70n6

right hand, 268, 358–59, 390, 395, 487, 498, 499, 500, 501, 516

Rizpah, 519, 521–22, 529

Ruben, 159

Sabbath, 28, 523, 534, 536

Sadducees, 223

saints, 34n108, 38n119, 42, 55, 96, 113, 124n6, 162, 219, 221, 222, 282, 328, 329, 336, 352, 385, 386, 387, 413, 414, 415–16, 420, 442, 472n34, 493, 515

Samaritan woman, 238

Samuel, 374, 400, 544

Satan, 174

Saul, 327, 519–22, 526, 546

Sayings of the Desert Fathers, 347n59, 377n70

scholia, 52–57, 72

scriptural contemplation, 27n83

scriptural mystagogy, 27n83

Scripture, intention of, 37–39

Scripture, literal sense of, 14, 36, 40, 48–49, 104, 136, 272, 283, 297n3, 298n5, 322, 323, 343, 375, 383, 468, 469, 487, 529, 430n29, 532, 533, 534, 539, 547, 549, 552

seed, 108–9

self-love, 83–85, 88, 89, 174n10, 233, 295, 377, 425, 511, 544

semicinctia, 218, 220

Sennacherib, 286

sensation, 23–25, 26–27, 44n137, 48n154, 58, 71, 74, 79, 80–86, 87n56, 90n66, 91, 93, 131, 133, 164, 167, 170, 183–84, 205, 208, 247–48, 274, 283–88, 291, 294–95, 302, 313, 318, 327, 330, 360, 371, 372, 375, 387, 402–11, 434, 437, 458, 468–69, 483, 511, 512, 516. *See also* sense perception

sense perception, 15, 23n63, 25n75, 28n85, 32, 34, 36, 43, 47, 58, 72, 73, 87n55, 90n65, 91, 105, 135, 162, 165n12, 179, 184–85, 202, 204, 211, 261–62, 284, 286, 288–89, 295, 302, 305, 334, 348, 350, 365, 368, 375, 380, 384, 406n18, 458, 463, 468, 478, 481, 485–86, 500, 524n10

serpent, 74, 96, 308, 309, 337

Seventh Ecumenical Council, 3

Shebnah, 281

Shechem, 291

Shephela, 267, 275

Shinar, 191

shoulder, 101, 253–54

sickle, 450–51

silence, 76, 88, 246

silver, 346

sin, 22n59, 49, 71, 78, 80, 92, 108–10, 118, 129, 130–31, 143–45, 148, 149, 151, 164, 177, 222, 235, 241–45, 259, 290–91, 317n2, 318, 340–42, 351, 354, 379, 380, 390, 405, 409, 410, 411, 413, 419–20, 425–26, 432, 436–37, 438–43, 445, 454–55, 458, 469, 485, 489, 491, 512, 522, 535, 544, 549, 552

Sisera, 177

Sixth Ecumenical Council, 4

Sodom, 111, 158

Solomon, 176, 422

spiritedness, 186, 282, 292, 349, 362, 369. *See also* anger *and* irascibility

spiritual contemplation, 14 44, 278, 318, 331, 366, 374, 379, 387, 416, 468, 475, 478, 527, 529, 530, 531, 533, 540, 541, 547, 548, 551, 552
spiritual progress, stages of, 25–29
Stoicism, 94n1, 95n5
substrate, 58n182, 289n27, 302, 322, 325, 361, 376, 384
symbol, 35–36, 40, 202, 204, 524, 527–28, 535, 539, 548, 550, 553
Symeon, 346

tau, 364n30, 381
Thalassios, 8–11, 390n7
Theodoret, 7, 172n4, 454n15
theological mystagogy, 28, 232
theological negation, 33, 47. See also apophatic theology
theology, 26n79, 28–29, 45, 47n152, 107, 117, 130, 132, 165, 167, 169, 185, 213, 214, 232, 351, 366, 372, 380, 381, 387, 425, 466, 478, 483, 513, 535, 539
Theophilos of Antioch, 223n4
time, 82, 102, 111, 141, 179, 265, 353, 358–61, 362, 367, 369, 377, 379, 383, 384, 385, 386, 419, 420, 421, 427, 434, 441–42, 444–45, 448, 487, 498, 499–500, 515, 530, 537–38, 554–55
Transfiguration, 32–37, 47
Tree of Knowledge, 86–88, 246–48
tropology, 50
tunic, 104, 122, 142
Tunis, 5
Typhonikon, 506
typology, 47, 50

universals, 97–99, 100, 144, 215n4, 226, 228, 232, 236, 238, 274, 278, 362, 376, 432, 530, 554
Uzziah, 43n136, 267, 272–73, 276

vice, 59, 85, 96, 78n24, 85, 122, 135, 162, 220, 230, 261, 288, 289, 294, 295, 342, 369, 390, 391, 395, 457, 460, 510
viper, 220
Virgin Mary, 29n91, 160, 234–35, 235n22
virtue, 25n74, 26, 27n82, 38, 59, 69, 77, 79–80, 91, 97–98, 104, 105, 122, 135, 136, 148, 156, 166, 168, 185, 201, 211, 213, 226, 227, 230, 232, 233, 236, 255, 261–62, 265, 266, 275n31, 294, 295, 301, 304, 306, 313, 315, 320, 323, 325, 342, 347, 361, 365, 373, 381, 382, 383, 386, 390–91, 392, 396–98, 405, 408, 419–20, 478, 482, 484, 489

water, 42n133, 77, 94n1, 100–102, 131–32
wilderness, 226, 257, 259
will, 108n5
wisdom, 26n80, 69, 117, 119, 121, 124, 125, 127, 128, 134, 135, 140, 154, 181, 205–6, 213, 227, 240, 246, 247–48, 301, 305, 306, 310, 312, 333, 335–36, 344–45, 348, 353, 361n23, 374, 375, 381–82, 384, 388, 414, 425, 436, 446, 466–67, 470–71, 489, 513, 548, 551
wise elder, 421n43
women, 239, 258, 265, 338–39, 342, 348, 349, 355, 359–60, 378, 386, 544
Word of God, 16, 17–18, 21, 29, 31, 40, 42, 77, 120; prayer to, 16, 268
worm, 503–4
wrath, 321

Zechariah, 273, 415, 450
Zerubbabel, 43n136, 333–34, 336, 340, 343, 350, 357, 389
Zion, 187
Zipporah, 135

INDEX OF HOLY SCRIPTURE

Note: MT = Masoretic Text

Old Testament

Genesis
1.1–25: 231
1.4: 228
1.5: 228
1.26: 21, 70, 95, 97, 133, 193, 194, 299
1.27: 229, 328, 329, 347, 417
1.31: 189, 553
1.31–2.2: 97
2.2: 365
2.8: 488
2.8–9: 93
2.9: 66, 246, 488
2.15–17: 239
2.16: 488
2.16–17: 83, 224
2.17: 86
3.1: 437
3.1–6: 22, 22
3.2–6: 83
3.2: 457
3.5: 250, 504
3.14: 74, 531
3.16–19: 239
3.17: 63, 106
3.17–19: 224
3.18: 106
3.19: 106, 107, 299, 462
3.21: 161
3.22: 66, 192, 249, 251
3.24: 178
4.4: 257, 264
4.8: 159, 290
4.15: 295, 296
4.26: 257, 264
5.19–24: 258
5.24: 265
7.21–23: 111
9.1–7: 224
9.8–17: 239
11.2: 191
11.2–4: 192
11.7: 65, 190, 194
11.8: 111
12.1: 258
14.14: 364, 381
15.7: 414
15.8: 415
17.1–14: 239
17.9–14: 224
18.1–2: 194
18.1–15: 191
19.1: 191
19.17: 530
19.24–26: 111
21: 159
21.1–5: 365
21.5: 381
22.1–2: 224
22.1–8: 258

22.15–18: 239
23–28: 258
26.2–6: 265
27.11–16: 258
27.28: 179
27.41: 159
30.18: 187
31.17–21: 259
34.2: 291
35.18: 390, 395
38.9: 159
38.11: 159
39.1–3: 177
39.12: 527
40.12: 226
42.26–27: 373
44.1: 373
47.28: 265
50.1–3: 265

Exodus
4.1: 415
4.2: 472
4.19–26: 134
4.22: 159, 160
4.24: 136
4.25: 135
12.29: 111
12.46: 212
14.27–29: 111
19.26: 64
20–21: 239

Exodus (*cont.*)
  20.1–17: 224
  20.11: 231
  25.31: 469
  27.9–19: 116
  32.2–3: 130, 544
  32.4: 64, 130, 544
  32.9: 130
  32.20: 130, 133
  32.24: 130

Leviticus
  7.24: 66, 253
  17.14: 186, 214
  19.18: 512
  25.40–41: 383
  25.44–46: 366
  26.23–24: 250

Numbers
  6.3: 337
  15.32–34: 535
  24.17: 334
  24.17–19: 223

Deuteronomy
  6.5: 199
  9.14: 158
  12.27: 66, 215
  15.12: 366
  18.15: 224
  24.16: 318
  28.14: 275
  32.33: 337

Joshua
  5.14–15: 88
  9.20: 524

Judges
  4–5: 177
  6.37–40: 179
  9.20: 542
  9.27: 525
  10.3–14: 525

1 Kings (LXX;
1 Samuel in MT)
  3.4–9: 181
  5.1–12: 177
  13.13: 547
  15.8: 544
  15.8–9: 543
  15.28: 548
  15.33: 544
  15.35: 545
  16.1: 400, 543
  16.12: 327
  16.14: 322, 546
  16.14–23: 546
  16.18: 322
  17.4: 327
  17.36: 327
  18.8–9: 546
  19.4: 546
  20.30–33: 546
  24.4–5: 327
  26.12: 327
  26.22: 327
  28.1–19: 322

2 Kings (LXX;
2 Samuel in MT)
  3.3: 371
  7.5: 9
  13: 159
  13.21: 221
  15.13–17: 372
  16.21–33: 386
  17.22: 372
  17.23: 386
  17.24: 390
  18.9: 370
  18.9–15: 386
  19.1: 371
  21.1: 527, 528, 531
  21.1–6: 519, 532
  21.1–14: 68
  21.5: 533, 540
  21.8: 519, 529
  21.8–9: 532, 540
  21.9: 530, 540

  21.9–10: 541
  21.10–14: 519
  21.14: 542

3 Kings (LXX; 1 Kings
in MT)
  1.33: 370
  2.35: 271
  11.23–25: 176
  18.21: 159
  22.15–23: 250

4 Kings (LXX; 2 Kings
in MT)
  3.21–27: 9
  4.32–35: 219
  13.21: 218
  18.1–2: 306
  18.18: 281
  18.26: 285
  18.36: 285
  19.1: 284
  19.35: 284, 288
  19.36: 287
  21: 159
  25.4: 383

1 Chronicles
  8.33–34: 532

2 Chronicles
  26.4–5: 267
  26.4–10: 67
  26.9: 267
  26.9–10: 267
  26.16–21: 276
  32.2–4: 67, 280
  32.4: 284
  32.20–21: 67, 297, 301
  32.21: 313
  32.23: 67, 305
  32.25: 67, 317
  32.25–26: 317
  32.33: 67, 326

INDEX OF HOLY SCRIPTURE

Job
  1.11–12: 177
  10.21: 490
  10.21–22: 489, 491

Psalms
  4.1: 494
  7.16: 505
  8.2: 172
  9.6: 159
  13.2: 413
  15.2: 307
  17.45: 159
  18.1: 123
  18.1–5: 313
  18.9: 118
  21.6: 327, 503
  22.6: 503
  31.9: 370
  33.8: 359
  33.9: 116
  33.10: 118
  33.14: 423
  38.2: 290
  41.4: 268
  42.2: 472
  43.22: 408
  44.5: 9
  44.8: 474
  45.2: 33
  48.10: 153
  48.12: 83, 330
  48.13: 456
  48.20: 83
  48.22: 330
  49.14: 356
  49.16: 460
  52.2: 413
  57.5–6: 337
  61.12: 319
  62.1: 230
  62.11: 461
  64.11: 535
  65.6: 40
  68.3: 338
  70.3: 444
  72.8–9: 186
  77.24–25: 531
  83.5: 264
  86.3: 335
  86.7: 358
  87.5: 245
  88.7: 118
  102.15: 107
  103.15: 271, 542, 556
  103.26: 145
  104.4: 552
  104.27: 415
  110.10: 353
  117.22: 269, 326
  117.24: 545
  118.18: 415
  118.34: 412
  118.35: 268
  118.105: 227, 228, 415, 467
  136.5–6: 358
  138.16: 30

Proverbs
  1.7: 278, 353
  3.13–17: 374
  3.16: 119
  3.18: 66, 246, 489
  6.4–5: 310
  6.23: 228, 471
  8.9: 134
  9.1: 121
  9.1–2: 213
  9.2: 216
  9.10: 353, 374
  11.31: 434
  16.23: 413
  27.6: 286

Ecclesiastes
  1.9: 422

Wisdom
  1.4: 127
  10.5: 192
  12.1: 64, 127
  13.7–8: 310

Isaiah
  1.4–6: 158
  2.2–3: 467
  3.17: 461
  5.5–6: 322
  6.10: 202
  9.5: 429
  9.6: 472
  10.22–23: 454
  10.23: 454
  11.1–3: 196
  11.2: 244
  11.2–3: 470
  26.9: 254
  26.10: 262
  26.19: 179
  34.4: 30
  35.5–6: 268
  40.3–5: 257
  40.5: 262
  40.7: 107
  49.16: 358
  53.2: 33
  53.4–5: 341
  53.9: 340
  53.12: 340
  60.6: 368, 385
  61.2: 535
  66.1: 300, 304

Jeremiah
  6.25: 290
  7.16: 400
  8.5: 158
  27.17: 174
  34.1: 172
  34.1–11: 65
  34.6: 172
  34.8: 172
  34.11: 172

INDEX OF HOLY SCRIPTURE

Lamentations
4.20: 341

Baruch
1.1–14: 178
1.11: 178

Ezekiel
1.16: 48, 184
18.20: 318
29.15: 467
33.11: 371
34.17–19: 530
39.18: 257, 264

Daniel
1.15: 34
4.22–23: 178
8.16: 415
10.11: 415

Hosea
6.4: 179
12.10: 450
14.6: 179

Joel
3.1: 262

Amos
9.11: 342

Jonah
2.5–6: 489
3.1–4: 497
3.3: 507, 510
3.4: 508
3.5: 495
3.5–7: 495
3.7: 496
3.8: 496
3.10: 502
4.1–3: 502
4.3: 507
4.7–8: 502
4.8: 504
4.11: 68, 487, 498

Habakkuk
2.15: 285
3.2: 482
3.3: 330
3.15: 369

Zephaniah
1.8: 461

Zechariah
2.3: 415
3.1: 415
3.3: 122
3.14: 415
3.17: 415
4.2: 469, 473
4.2–3: 68, 465
4.3: 475
4.9: 343
4.10: 343, 477
4.13: 481
5.1–4: 68, 450
5.2: 453
5.3: 454
5.4: 455, 459
6.1: 480
6.6: 480
6.7: 480
6.8: 481
6.12: 334, 341, 351

Malachi
3.20: 226, 324, 341, 504

New Testament

Matthew
2.11: 307
3.7: 258
3.8: 208
4.1–11: 145, 285
5.3: 495
5.8: 255, 263
5.13–14: 76
5.15: 467, 476
5.16: 476, 477
5.17: 298
6.13: 404
6.25: 527
6.33: 210, 423
7.7: 425

7.12: 511
7.14: 308
8.25: 220
9.20: 238
10.6: 308
10.10: 63, 104
10.16: 310
10.28: 117
11.28: 491
12.29: 456, 457
12.40: 491, 492, 509
12.45: 295
13.15: 202
13.45–46: 204
15.32: 66, 226

17.2: 32
17.20: 208, 425
19.17: 378
21.18: 140
21.18–21: 65, 140
21.19: 141
21.19–21: 142
21.22: 210, 211
21.42: 326
22.23–28: 66, 223
22.25–28: 238
22.29–30: 225
22.37–39: 199
22.39: 512
23.5: 396

INDEX OF HOLY SCRIPTURE

24.15: 49
25.4: 474
25.24: 459
25.35–36: 233, 236
27.25: 505
28.19: 182

Mark
1.12–13: 145
3.27: 457
5.22–35: 238
7.25–30: 238
7.32: 268
9.3: 32
9.23: 209
10.38: 65, 200
11.11: 140
11.12–14: 140
11.13: 141
11.23: 66, 207, 208
11.24: 66, 210
14.12–16: 100
14.58: 503
15.28: 340

Luke
1.22: 521
1.25–28: 160
1.32: 65
1.32–33: 157
1.55: 160
1.78: 334
2.31–32: 545
2.34: 346
3.4: 67, 257, 259
3.4–6: 257
3.6: 262
3.7: 258, 258, 265
4.1–13: 145
4.19: 535
6.31: 511
9.29: 32
11.4: 404
13.6–9: 140
13.11: 238
15.9: 282

17.21: 207
22.7–13: 63, 100
22.8: 100
22.10: 101
22.11: 101
24.49: 104

John
1.1: 33
1.9: 466
1.12: 110
1.14: 33, 140, 212, 453
1.29: 259, 455
2.3: 232
2.6: 66, 230, 231
2.7: 232, 233
2.8: 232, 233
2.9: 234
2.10: 231, 234
3.5: 109
3.5–6: 108
3.9: 108
3.27: 300
4.5–6: 240
4.5–15: 240
4.11: 240
4.14: 77
4.16–18: 66, 238
4.18: 239
4.23: 89
4.23–24: 140
4.24: 468, 506, 533
5.17: 63, 97, 98
5.39: 74
6.33: 531
6.53: 66, 212
8.12: 492
8.39: 42
10.9: 269
10.10: 455
10.11: 327
11.49–51: 223
12.43: 174
13.2: 22
13.34: 338

14.2: 117
14.6: 90, 467
14.9: 166
14.23: 117
14.30: 147
15.13: 512
16.2: 506
19.23: 34, 104
19.31–36: 66, 212
20.28: 458

Acts of the Apostles
2.1–4: 183
2.17: 262
4.2: 488
4.11: 269
10.1–29: 182
10.8: 186
10.11: 182, 184
10.11–12: 183
10.12: 184
10.13: 184
10.13–15: 184
10.15: 189
10.16: 185
10.19: 182
10.28: 182, 188
10.34: 188
10.44–45: 182
11.2: 182
11.3–18: 182
11.10: 188
11.12: 182, 207
12.10: 65, 161
14.22: 278
16.17: 467
17.24: 202
17.27: 204
19.12: 218
21.4: 196
21.5: 196
21.11: 197
21.13: 199
21.27–32: 197
26.24: 367
27.13–20: 220

Acts of the Apostles
(*cont.*)
  27.14: 506
  27.26: 220
  28.2–3: 220
  28.3: 220
  28.3–5: 218
  28.27: 202

Romans
  1.19–20: 73
  1.20: 64, 123, 124, 164
  1.20–21: 86, 310
  1.23–25: 83
  1.25: 64, 86, 126, 306, 536, 553
  1.26: 26, 107, 176, 311, 320, 481, 540
  2.4: 264
  2.12: 64, 138, 139
  2.12–16: 138
  2.13: 64, 137
  2.16: 138
  4.23–24: 215
  5.10: 512
  5.12: 144, 242, 437
  5.12–21: 441
  5.15–20: 242
  6.4: 41
  6.5: 419, 426
  6.23: 437
  7.6: 493, 540
  7.14: 137, 215
  7.22: 137
  7.23: 208, 411, 446
  7.25: 71, 290
  8.2: 274, 476, 481
  8.3: 341, 351, 439, 442
  8.6: 180, 208, 258, 293, 347, 476, 544, 544
  8.7: 290, 342, 458
  8.9: 129
  8.13: 469
  8.14–15: 128
  8.15: 108
  8.17: 420
  8.18: 408
  8.27: 295
  8.35: 90, 493
  8.39: 198
  9.6–7: 157, 161
  9.22–23: 462
  9.27: 157
  9.28: 454
  9.31: 141
  10.2: 211
  10.4: 137, 138
  10.9: 454
  10.12: 182
  11.5: 160
  11.35: 308
  12.3: 340
  12.6: 197, 272, 350
  13.8–9: 236
  13.10: 512
  13.13: 545
  15.4: 38
  15.8: 160

1 Corinthians
  1.24: 269, 492
  1.25: 92
  2.1–5: 493
  2.6: 117, 471
  2.6–8: 22
  2.7: 479
  2.9: 114, 314
  2.10: 74, 114
  2.16: 277
  3.16: 394
  4.7: 323
  5.1–5: 176
  5.5: 174, 293
  6.12: 210, 211
  6.19: 394
  7.31: 514
  8.1: 317
  9.22: 263, 264, 445
  9.27: 285
  10.4: 542
  10.11: 28, 65, 150, 151, 152, 154, 155, 202, 215, 323, 339
  10.18: 157
  11.1: 42, 73, 198
  11.3–5: 65, 163
  11.10: 163
  12.4: 196
  12.7: 414
  12.8–9: 414
  12.8–11: 197
  12.11: 414
  13.2: 255
  13.8: 115, 430
  13.9: 115
  13.10: 115
  13.11: 216
  13.12: 66, 115, 134, 255
  13.13: 280
  15.23: 117
  15.31: 408
  15.45–49: 347
  15.47–48: 285
  15.49: 303, 510
  15.53–54: 242
  15.54: 367

2 Corinthians
  2.11: 472
  2.15: 480
  2.16: 220, 222
  3.6: 14, 134, 205, 299, 412, 533
  3.18: 90, 91, 328
  4.7: 467, 493
  4.7–12: 494
  4.10: 112, 497
  4.16: 137, 408
  5.1: 102
  5.2: 335, 358
  5.4: 367
  5.7: 114, 199
  5.13: 367

INDEX OF HOLY SCRIPTURE

5.21: 66, 241, 454, 455
6.4: 176, 262
6.7: 275
6.11: 102
10.4: 281
10.5: 96, 261, 263, 300, 493
11.6: 391, 493
12.1: 114
12.9: 493

Galatians
1.12: 114
2.20: 112
3.4: 157
3.13: 454, 455
3.24: 521
3.28: 270
4.26: 359, 503
5.4: 137
5.25: 112
6.2: 226

Ephesians
1.5: 492
1.10–11: 429
1.11: 150, 151
1.19: 76
2.7: 65, 150, 151, 154, 155, 156
2.14–17: 458
2.22: 390
3.18: 513
4.3: 269, 320
4.6: 98
4.9: 151
4.10: 151
4.13: 373
4.22: 308
6.6: 390
6.11: 81
6.12: 22, 38, 187, 490
6.14: 405
6.17: 185, 539, 544

Philippians
1.11: 308
2.7: 236, 326
2.8: 245
2.9: 151
3.8: 198
3.13: 115
3.14: 114, 135, 262
3.19: 159, 272, 525
3.21: 277

Colossians
1.17: 554
1.18: 326, 470
1.26: 427
2.2: 77
2.3: 169
2.7: 493
2.12: 41
2.14: 146, 437, 454, 458
2.15: 65, 143, 146, 147
2.19: 269
2.22: 328
3.5: 101, 222, 497, 525
3.9: 347
3.9–10: 308
3.10: 347

1 Thessalonians
2.4: 390
2.5: 260
2.5–6: 391
2.6: 174
4.17: 299

2 Thessalonians
3.2: 210

1 Timothy
2.4: 342
6.16: 145

2 Timothy
2.5: 262, 275
3.2: 83
3.16: 42

Titus
3.5: 441

Hebrews
1.1: 191
2.10: 442, 545
2.14: 359
3.6: 443
4.10: 147
4.12: 392, 393, 397
4.13: 393
4.15: 143, 151, 155, 177, 436, 439, 491
4.16: 331
5.13: 216
5.14: 216, 344
9.11: 216
10.1: 128
10.22: 77
10.26: 210, 211
11.1: 169, 199, 207, 258, 314
11.12: 157
11.32: 264
12.2: 491
12.23: 355
13.15: 356

James
1.2: 404
1.3–4: 404
1.4: 405
1.17: 75, 300, 413
1.21: 132
2.26: 344
4.3: 414
5.16: 67, 399, 400

1 Peter
1.3–4: 407
1.6: 67, 402, 408

1 Peter (*cont.*)
  1.8: 408
  1.9: 416, 419
  1.10: 424
  1.10–11: 68, 412, 419
  1.11: 421
  1.13: 282
  1.20: 68, 427, 479
  1.24: 107
  2.5: 394
  2.7: 269
  2.9: 160
  2.22: 340
  3.18: 439
  4.6: 64, 111, 112
  4.17: 439, 443
  4.17–18: 68, 434
  4.18: 444

2 Peter
  1.4: 330
  1.9: 205
  1.19: 334
  2.21: 467

1 John
  1.5: 64, 113
  1.7: 113
  1.14: 212
  2.6: 230
  3.2: 64, 114, 115
  3.9: 64, 108
  4.18: 64, 116, 118
  5.4: 493

Jude
  6: 64, 120
  23: 64, 122

Revelation
  2.28: 334
  22.16: 334

INDEX OF GREEK WORDS

ἀγένητος θέωσις, 447n38
ἀγκραθῆναι, 150n4
αἴσθησις, 58
αἴτιον, 205n9
ἀκαιρόγραφος, 355n2
ἄκαιρος, 355n2
ἀμήχανον, 43n136
ἀναγωγή, 46, 375n68
ἀναισθησία, 70n4
ἀνακινεῖν, 127n3
ἀναλέγεται, 164n10
ἀναλλοιώτως, 150n5
ἀναλογία, 340n24, 350n63
ἀναμιμνήσκων, 281n6
ἀνατολή, 334n4
ἀνδρεία, 361n23
ἀνεπίγραφος, 53n168
ἀνήρ, 163n1, 270v13
ἀνοησία, 76n16
ἀντιρρητική, 285n16
ἀπέμφασις, 530n29
ἀπήχημα, 305n3
ἁπλούστεροι, 298n5
ἀποκατάστασις, 479n51
ἄπορα, 6
ἀπορίαι, 6
ἀποτίθεσθαι, 131n7
ἀποφαντικῶς, 250n6
ἄρρεν, 270n13
ἀρχή, 58-59, 120n1
ἀσάφεια, 44n139
ἀτρέπτως, 143n4
ἄυλον γνῶσιν, 119n19
αὐτόθεος, 192n18

αὐτολόγος, 192n18, 240n17
αὐτοματισμός, 223n4
αὐτοσοφία, 336n10
αὐτοφία, 169n23
ἀφαίρεσις, 165n14

βούλημα, 105n7
βούλησις, 230n2

γέγονεν, 242n6
γένεσις, 59, 143n6, 438n14
γέννησις, 143n6
γλιχόμενος, 56
γνώμη, 108n5
γνῶσις, 119n19, 211n13, 274n24
γνωστικός, 59m 76n15
γνωστικώτερον, 346n54, 478n50
γραφικὴ θεωρία, 27n83
γραφικὴ μυσταγωγία, 27n83
γράψαντος, 206n10
γρηγόρησις, 191n12
γυνή, 163n1

δαιμόνια, 78n24
διάβασις, 44n139, 74n5, 406n18, 410n29
διάγνωσις, 274n24
διαγνωστικός (νοῦς), 308n16

διάθεσις, 190n3
διάκρησις, 207n1
διαπλάττειν, 190n2
διασφιγχθεῖσα, 320n13
δι' ἐσόπτρου, 255n1
Διήγησις ψυχωφελής, 8n19
δικαιοσύνη, 361n23
δόξα, 546n91

εἴδη, 97n1
εἴδησις, 215n3
εἶδος, 114n3, 114n4, 213n8, 447n37
ἐκ, 249n2
ἔκβασις, 418n34, 425n54
ἐκθεωτική, 129n7
ἐκτιναγμός, 191n12
ἐκτύπωμα, 130n5
ἐλεγκτικῶς, 250n6
ἐνεργουμένη, 399n2
ἐνιδρύοντες, 328n19
ἔννοια, 424n50
ἔνυλον γνῶσιν, 119n19
ἐξεζήτησαν, 412n1, 421n42
ἐξηρεύνησαν, 412n2, 421n42
ἕξις, 59
ἐξουδένωσις, 526n20
ἐπαινετόν, 223n3
ἐπαρυστρίδες, 473n37
ἐπίγνωσις, 211n11, 211n13
ἐπιθυμία, 94n1

581

INDEX OF GREEK WORDS

ἐπίνοια, 264n34, 470n24
ἐπιστήμη, 58, 344n48, 384n83
ἐπιτηδειότης, 289n27
ἐπιτόμως, 272n21
ἐρευνῶντες, 412n3
ἔτυχεν, 223n1
εὐσέβεια, 344n48
ἐφίεται, 82n32

ζήτησις, 412n5
ζώνη, 218n1

ἡδονή, 94n1, 402n2, 402n4
ἠρίθμησε, 381n74

θεαρχικός, 143n3
θέλημα, 200n2
θέλησις, 108n5, 200n2
θεουργία, 484n66
θεωρία, 47
θέωσις, ἀγένητος, 57
θεωτική ἐνοίκησις, 129n7
θεωτική ἕξις, 129n7
θῆλυ, 270n13

ἱμάτια, 104n2, 104n6, ἰστέον, 54n170

καθ' ὑπεροχήν, 165n14
κακία, 59, 81n33, 261n19
κασσιτήρινον, 343n42
κατασκοπή, 187n26
κράσις, 150n4

λατρεία, 126n3
ληπτότερον, 213n10
λόγος, 35n110, 59, 70, 164n6, 234n19,
234n20, 499n54, 521n7
λύπη, 402n4

μανία, 382n77
μαρτυρία καταβάσεως, 287n23
μετέβαλεν, 230n4
μέτρον, 350n62
μνῆμα, 221n17
μνήμη, 221n17
μονή, 117n8, 329n20

νόημα, 212n5
νόμος, 238n3
νοῦς, 164n5, 204n2, 308n16

ξύλον, 457n24

ὀδύνη, 94n1
οἴησις, 317n4
οἰκία, 102n11
ὁμολογητής, 3n4
ὁμολογία, 192n14
ὅρος, 208n9
ὅρος, 432n20
οὐσίωσις, 242n2

πάθη, 78n24
πάθος, 144n8, 514n91
παράλογον, 43n136, 499n54
παράχρησις, 186n23
παρυπόστασις, 312n26
πάσχειν, 144n8, 152n19
πάσχων, 520n4
πάχος, 202n4
παχύνεται, 202n4
πειρασμός, 403n8
πέρας, 151n9, 432n21
περιφερής, 295n40
πίστις, 210n1
ποιεῖν, 152n19
ποίησις, 545n85
πολύθεον ἀθεῖαν, 192n13
πόνος, 488n5
προαίρεσις, 108n5, 200n2, 241n2
προαποκειμένη, 131n7
προβολή, 28n85
πρός τι, 248n6

σέβας, 126n2
σημειώσεις, 7n6
σημειωτέον, 54n170
σημικίνθια, 218n1
σιωπή, 88n57
σοφία, 361n23
σπέρματα, 550n99
σπουδαῖοι, 95n4
στέρησις, 165n14
στοιχεῖα, 30
στοχασμός, 356n3, 520n3
στοχαστικῶς, 356n3
συναπολήγων, 297n2
συνέλεξις, 554n104
συνελήφθη, 341n29
συνένευσις, 277n36
συνεπεκτείνεται, 215v4
συμφωνία, 192n14
σχῆμα, 514n92
σχόλια, 7n16, 52n166
σωφροσύνη, 361n23

ταὐτόν, 34n108
τετηρημένος, 120n4
τέχνη, 107n6
τρόπος, 415n25
τυπικῶς, 202n3
τυπούμενος, 48n153
τύφος, 141n6
τῶν οὐκ ἄνευ, 358n9

ὑπερέχουσα, 165n14
ὑποκειμένη διάθεσις, 190n3

INDEX OF GREEK WORDS 583

ὑπομνηματογράφος, 281n6
ὑπόστασις, 514n92

φαντασία, 130n5, 170n25, 485n67

φησί, 55n173
φορυτῷ, 204n2
φυσιούσης οἰήσεως, 317n4
φύσις, 60, 224n5, 238n3

χολή, 369n48
χρῆσις, 440n21
χρώς, 218n2

ψεκτόν, 223n3
ψυχή, 238n3, 381n76

RECENT VOLUMES IN THE FATHERS
OF THE CHURCH SERIES

EUSEBIUS OF CAESAREA, *Against Marcellus and On Ecclesiastical Theology*, translated by Kelley McCarthy Spoerl and Markus Vinzent, Volume 135 (2017)

TYCONIUS, *Exposition of the Apocalypse*, translated by Francis X. Gumerlock, with introduction and notes by David C. Robinson, Volume 134 (2017)

RUFINUS OF AQUILEIA, *History of the Church*, translated by Philip R. Amidon, SJ, Volume 133 (2016)

DIDYMUS THE BLIND, *Commentary on Genesis*, translated by Robert C. Hill, Volume 132 (2016)

ST. GREGORY OF NYSSA, *Anti-Apollinarian Writings*, translated by Robin Orton, Volume 131 (2015)

ST. EPHREM THE SYRIAN, *The Hymns on Faith*, translated by Jeffrey T. Wickes, Volume 130 (2015)

ST. CYRIL OF ALEXANDRIA, *Three Christological Treatises*, translated by Daniel King, Volume 129 (2014)

ST. EPIPHANIUS OF CYPRUS, *Ancoratus*, translated by Young Richard Kim, Volume 128 (2014)

ST. CYRIL OF ALEXANDRIA, *Festal Letters 13–30*, translated by Philip R. Amidon, SJ, and edited with notes by John J. O'Keefe, Volume 127 (2013)

FULGENTIUS OF RUSPE AND THE SCYTHIAN MONKS, *Correspondence on Christology and Grace*, translated by Rob Roy McGregor and Donald Fairbairn, Volume 126 (2013)

ST. HILARY OF POITIERS, *Commentary on Matthew*, translated by D. H. Williams, Volume 125 (2012)

ST. CYRIL OF ALEXANDRIA, *Commentary on the Twelve Prophets, Volume 3*, translated by †Robert C. Hill, Volume 124 (2012)

www.ingramcontent.com/pod-product-compliance
Lightning Source LLC
Chambersburg PA
CBHW020312010526
44107CB00054B/1812